Lecture Notes in Computer Scie

Commenced Publication in 1973
Founding and Former Series Editors:
Gerhard Goos, Juris Hartmanis, and Jan van Leeuwen

Jean M. Bacon   Brian F. Cooper (Eds.)

Middleware 2009

ACM/IFIP/USENIX
10th International Middleware Conference
Urbana, IL, USA, November 30 - December 4, 2009
Proceedings

 Springer

Volume Editors

Jean M. Bacon
Computer Laboratory, University of Cambridge
William Gates Building, JJ Thomson Avenue, Cambridge CB3 0FD, UK
E-mail: jmb25@cl.cam.ac.uk

Brian F. Cooper
Yahoo! Research
4401 Great America Parkway, Santa Clara, CA 95054, USA
E-mail: cooperb@yahoo-inc.com

Library of Congress Control Number: 2009938872

CR Subject Classification (1998): D.4, B.1, D.2, C.2, C.2.4, D.1, D.2.5

LNCS Sublibrary: SL 2 – Programming and Software Engineering

ISSN 0302-9743
ISBN 978-3-642-10444-2 Springer Berlin Heidelberg New York

springer.com

© Springer-Verlag Berlin Heidelberg 2009

Typesetting: Camera-ready by author, data conversion by Scientific Publishing Services, Chennai, India
Printed on acid-free paper   SPIN: 12791705   06/3180   5 4 3 2 1 0

Preface

This edition marks the tenth Middleware conference. The first conference was held in the Lake District of England in 1998, and its genesis reflected a growing realization that middleware systems were a unique breed of distributed system requiring their own rigorous research and evaluation. Distributed systems had been around for decades, and the Middleware conference itself resulted from the combination of three previous conferences. But the attempt to build common platforms for many different applications required a unique combination of high-level abstraction and low-level optimization, and presented challenges different from building a monolithic distributed system.

Since that first conference, the notion of what constitutes "middleware" has changed somewhat, and the focus of research papers has changed with it. The first edition focused heavily on distributed objects as a metaphor for building systems, including six papers with "CORBA" or "ORB" in the title. In following years, the conference broadened to cover publish/subscribe messaging, peer-to-peer systems, distributed databases, Web services, and automated management, among other topics. Innovative techniques and architectures surfaced in workshops, and expanded to become themes of the main conference, while changes in the industry and advances in other research areas helped to shape research agendas. This tenth edition includes papers on next-generation platforms (such as stream systems, pervasive systems and cloud systems), managing enterprise data centers, and platforms for building other platforms, among others. However, a common theme runs through all this diversity: the need to build reliable, scalable, secure platforms to serve as the key ingredient for distributed applications.

Again, this year, the program reflected a very strong set of contributions. In the research track, 21 papers were selected from 110 submissions. The conference's industrial track reflected the ongoing need for researchers and practitioners to work together to realize middleware systems in practice. In addition, the conference included a diverse workshop program, including a symposium for doctoral students.

We would like to thank everyone who contributed to the conference this year. The Program Committee worked hard to provide high-quality reviews, and the rest of the Organizing Committee put a great deal of effort into planning and holding the conference. The Steering Committee, and Chairs of previous conferences, provided valuable advice and a needed continuity from previous years. Finally, we would like to thank the authors who made the effort to write up and share their research results with the community.

September 2009

Brian Cooper
Jean Bacon

Organization

Middleware 2009 was organized under the joint sponsorship of the Association for Computing Machinery (ACM), the International Federation for Information Processing (IFIP) and USENIX.

Organizing Committee

Conference Chair	Roy H. Campbell (University of Illinois at Urbana-Champaign, USA)
Program Chairs	Jean Bacon (University of Cambridge Computer Laboratory, UK)
	Brian Cooper (Yahoo! Research, USA
Industrial Chair	Dejan Milojicic (HP Labs, USA
Publicity Chairs	Vibhore Kumar (IBM Research, USA)
	Riccardo Scandariato (Katholieke Universiteit Leuven, Belgium)
Local Arrangements Chair	Reza Ferivar (University of Illinois at Urbana-Champaign, USA)
Workshops Chair	Cecilia Mascolo (University of Cambridge, UK)
Tutorials Chair	Francois Taiani (Lancaster University, UK)
Doctoral Symposium Chair	Peter Triantafillou (University of Patras, Greece)

Steering Committee

Gordon Blair (Chair)	Lancaster University, UK
Jan De Meer	SmartSpaceLab, Germany
Peter Honeyman	University of Michigan, USA
Arno Jacobsen	University of Toronto, Canada
Elie Najm	ENST Paris, France
Maarten van Steen	Vrije Universiteit, The Netherlands
Shanika Karunasekera	University of Melbourne, Australia
Renato Cerqueira	PUC-Rio, Brazil
Nalini Venkatasubramanian	University of California, Irvine, USA
Wouter Joosen	KUL-DistriNet, Belgium
Valerie Issarny	INRIA, France

Program Committee

Gustavo Alonso	ETH Zurich, Switzerland
Yolande Berbers	KUL-DistriNet, Belgium
Gordon Blair	Lancaster University, UK
Roy Campbell	University of Illinois at Urbana Champaign, USA
Renato Cerqueira	PUC-Rio, Brazil
Lucy Cherkasova	HP Labs, USA
Paolo Costa	Microsoft Research, UK
Francis David	Microsoft, USA
Fred Douglis	Data Domain, USA
Frank Eliasson	University of Oslo, Norway
Markus Endler	PUC-Rio, Brazil
David Eyers	University of Cambridge, UK
Paulo Ferreira	INESC ID / Technical University of Lisbon, Portugal
Nikolaos Georgantas	INRIA, France
Paul Grace	Lancaster University, UK
Indranil Gupta	University of Illinois at Urbana Champaign, USA
Qi Han	Colorado School of Mines, USA
Gang Huang	Peking University, China
Valerie Issarny	INRIA, France
Hans-Arno Jacobsen	University of Toronto, Canada
Wouter Joosen	KUL-DistriNet, Belgium
Shanika Karunasekera	University of Melbourne, Australia
Himanshu Khurana	University of Illinois at Urbana Champaign, USA
Fabio Kon	University of Sao Paulo, Brazil
Vibhore Kumar	IBM Research, USA
Joe Loyall	BBN Technologies, USA
Cecilia Mascolo	University of Cambridge, UK
Elie Najm	ENST Paris, France
Gian Pietro Picco	University of Trento, Italy
Peter Pietzuch	Imperial College, UK
Antony Rowstron	Microsoft Research, UK
Riccardo Scandariato	KU Leuven, Belgium
Rick Schantz	BBN Technologies, USA
Karsten Schawn	Georgia Tech, USA
Francois Taiani	Lancaster University, UK
Kian-Lee Tan	National University of Singapore, Singapore
Sotirios Terzis	University of Strathclyde, UK
Eli Tilevich	Virginia Tech, USA

Scott Trent   IBM Tokyo, Japan
Peter Triantafillou   University of Patras, Greece
Akshat Verma   IBM Research, India
Jun Yang   Duke University, USA
Pin Zhou,   IBM Research, USA
Jan De Meer   SmartSpaceLab, Germany

Referees

Ioannis Aekaterinidis	Peter Honeyman	Reza Sherafat
Mourad Alia	Jeff Kephart	Pushpendra Singh
Marco Antonio Casanova	Patrick Lee	Thomas Springer
Juliana Aquino	Guoli Li	Amir Taherkordi
Michael Atighetchi	Sand Luz Correa	Naweed Tajuddin
Mikael Beauvois	Marcelo Malcher	Luis Veiga
Arquimedes Canedo	Bala Maniymaran	Junyi Xie
Alex Cheung	Vinod Muthusamy	Chunyang Ye
Lincoln David	Nikos Ntarmos	Young Yoon
Oleg Davidyuk	Valeria Quadros	Apostolos Zarras
Frederik De Keukelaere	Jan Rellermeyer	Charles Zhang
Lieven Desmet	Kurt Rohloff	
Amer Farroukh	Romain Rouvoy	
Marco Gerosa	Francoise Sailhan	

Sponsoring Institutions

BBN Technologies (www.bbn.com)
IBM (www.ibm.com)
USENIX (www.usenix.org)
Yahoo! (labs.yahoo.com)
Department of Computer Science, University of Illinois at Urbana-Champaign
(cs.illinois.edu)

Table of Contents

Communications I (Protocols)

Communications II (Optimization)

Service Component Composition/Adaptation

Monitoring

Pervasive

Stream Processing

Failure Resilience

Support for Testing

MANETKit: Supporting the Dynamic Deployment and Reconfiguration of Ad-Hoc Routing Protocols

Rajiv Ramdhany, Paul Grace, Geoff Coulson, and David Hutchison

Computing Department,
Lancaster University,
South Drive,
Lancaster, LA1 4WA, UK
{r.ramdhany,gracep,geoff,dh}@comp.lancs.ac.uk

Abstract. The innate dynamicity and complexity of mobile ad-hoc networks (MANETs) has resulted in numerous ad-hoc routing protocols being proposed. Furthermore, numerous variants and hybrids continue to be reported in the literature. This diversity appears to be inherent to the field—it seems unlikely that there will ever be a 'one-size-fits-all' solution to the ad-hoc routing problem. However, typical deployment environments for ad-hoc routing protocols still force the choice of a single fixed protocol; and the resultant compromise can easily lead to sub-optimal performance, depending on current operating conditions. In this paper we address this problem by exploring a framework approach to the construction and deployment of ad-hoc routing protocols. Our framework supports the simultaneous deployment of multiple protocols so that MANET nodes can switch protocols to optimise to current operating conditions. The framework also supports finer-grained dynamic reconfiguration in terms of protocol variation and hybridisation. We evaluate our framework by using it to construct and (simultaneously) deploy two popular ad-hoc routing protocols (DYMO and OLSR), and also to derive fine-grained variants of these. We measure the performance and resource overhead of these implementations compared to monolithic ones, and find the comparison to be favourable to our approach.

Keywords: Ad-hoc routing, protocol frameworks.

1 Introduction

Mobile ad-hoc networks (MANETs) employ routing protocols so that out-of-range nodes can communicate with each other via intermediate nodes. Unfortunately, it is hard to design *generically-applicable* routing protocols in the MANET environment. This is for two main reasons: First, MANETs are inherently characterised by *dynamic variations in network conditions*—for example in terms of network size, topology, density or mobility. Second, MANETs are subject to a *diverse and dynamic set of application requirements* in terms of quality of service (QoS) demands and traffic patterns (i.e. in terms of messaging, request-reply, multicast, publish-subscribe, streaming, etc.). In response to these two types of pressures—from both 'below' and

J.M. Bacon and B.F. Cooper (Eds.): Middleware 2009, LNCS 5896, pp. 1–20, 2009.

'above'—MANET researchers have been proposing an ever-proliferating range of routing protocols: e.g. AODV [23], DYMO [5], OLSR [8], ZRP [14], TORA [22] and GPSR [17] to name but a few. However, none of these proposals comes close to providing optimal routing under the full range of operating conditions encountered in MANET environments; and it is becoming ever clearer that the 'one-size-fits-all' ad-hoc routing protocol is an impossibility.

We therefore believe that future MANET systems will need to employ *multiple* ad-hoc routing protocols and to support switching between these as runtime conditions dictate. Our view is that this is best achieved through a *runtime framework based approach* in which different ad-hoc routing protocols can be dynamically deployed—both serially and simultaneously—depending on current operating conditions. In our view, such a framework should further employ a fine-grained compositional approach so that ad-hoc routing functionality can be built by composing fine-grained building blocks at runtime. Such an approach would support the creation of variants and hybrids of protocols at run-time so that we can adapt to changing runtime conditions in a finer-grained manner than switching protocols. Such an approach would also support the sharing of common functionality between protocols (thus reducing both development effort and resource overhead), and ease the task of deploying and porting newly-designed protocols and protocol updates.

In this paper we propose such a framework. The specific goals of the framework, which is called MANETKit, are:

1. To support the dynamic deployment of ad-hoc routing protocols, both serially and simultaneously, and also to support their fine-grained dynamic reconfiguration.
2. To do this while achieving comparable performance and resource overhead to equivalently-functioning monolithic implementations.
3. To further support protocol diversity by shortening the protocol development cycle and the time to port protocols to different operating systems.

This paper is an in-depth motivation, description and evaluation of MANETKit. The remainder of the paper is structured as follows. Section 2 makes the case for MANETKit in more detail, based on an analysis of the design space of ad-hoc routing protocols and a survey of existing protocol construction frameworks. Section 3 then provides brief background on the key technologies and concepts underpinning our framework, Section 4 presents the framework itself, and Section 5 illustrates its use by means of case study implementations of some popular ad-hoc routing protocols (OLSR and DYMO). Section 6 then provides an empirical evaluation against the three goals specified above, and Section 7 offers our conclusions.

2   Related Work

Ad-hoc Routing Protocols. The design space of ad-hoc routing protocols can be divided into three broad categories:

- *Proactive* (or table-driven) protocols (e.g. [8]) continuously evaluate routes from each node to all other nodes reachable from that node.
- *Reactive* (or on-demand) protocols (e.g. [5]), on the other hand, discover routes to destinations only when there is an immediate need for it.
- *Hybrid* protocols (e.g. [14]) combine aspects of both proactive and reactive types—e.g. by employing proactive routing within scoped domains and reactive routing across domains.

As mentioned in the introduction, the pressures that are driving the proliferation of ad-hoc routing protocols are coming from both 'below' and 'above'. From 'below', the biggest determining factor in which protocol is the most appropriate is the size of the network: generally, proactive protocols are better suited to smaller networks, reactive ones to larger networks, and hybrid protocols to networks that can structured hierarchically. But where the network *varies* in size (e.g. grows), an initial choice of protocol (e.g. proactive) can become sub-optimal. As another example, a reactive protocol will do well where pairs of interacting source-destination nodes (i.e. an influence from 'above') tend to be stable, while proactive protocols are typically better where interaction patterns are more dynamic (although only where the network is not too big). In addition, peer-to-peer services running over MANETs tend to prefer proactive protocols [3]; and applications requiring QoS differentiation can benefit from intelligent path selection as enabled by multipath routing algorithms like TORA [22] or Multipath DYMO [10]—although these carry overhead that is unnecessary for other applications (or application use-cases).

As well as proposing many new protocols in each of the above categories, researchers have since investigated numerous variations on already-existing protocols. For example, path accumulation [5], pre-emptive routing [12], multi-path routing [10], power-efficient routing [33], fish-eye routing [34], and numerous styles of flooding [8, 26, 1, 15] are examples of techniques that can be 'switched on' to improve a particular property of an underlying base protocol under certain operating conditions, but which may be counter-productive under other conditions. Flooding (which is typically used to propagate control information) is a particularly rich area in this respect. For example, Multipoint Relaying [8] is good at reducing control overhead in denser networks, whereas Hazy-Sighted Link State [26] provides better performance as the network grows in diameter. Various epidemic/ gossip algorithms (e.g. [1] [15]) can also be applied in this context.

The key conclusion is that *no single protocol or class of protocols is well suited to more than a subset of the operating conditions to be found in any given MANET environment at any given time.*

Protocol Frameworks. We are not alone in recognising the benefits of the framework approach for ad-hoc routing protocols: MANET researchers have recently developed a number of such frameworks, prominent among which are ASL [18] and PICA [4]. ASL, for example, enhances underlying system services and provides MANET-specific APIs such that routing protocols can be developed in user-space. PICA alternatively provides multi-platform functionality for threading, packet queue management, socket-event notifications to waiting threads, and network device listing, as well as minimising platform-related differences in socket APIs, and kernel route table manipulation. We have therefore found these useful inspiration for the design of analogous functionality in MANETKit. In addition, the popular Unik-olsrd [32] implementation of OLSR supports a plug-in framework which has been well used by researchers [33, 34]. However, unlike MANETKit, all of these frameworks offer purely design-time and implementation-time facilities; they do not address the *run-time configuration/ reconfiguration* support which we argue is key to the support of future MANET environments.

As well as MANET-specific frameworks, a range of more general protocol composition frameworks have been proposed. These fall mainly into two lineages: the x-kernel [30] to Cactus [2] lineage, and the Ensemble [27] to Appia [24] lineage. Unfortunately, all such frameworks are of limited relevance to our ad-hoc routing domain. This is for two main reasons. Firstly, general purpose frameworks do not address the resource scarcity inherent to MANET environments. Cactus, for example, is significantly more resource hungry than MANETKit: the C version of Cactus occupies 466KB empty, whereas MANETKit supporting two ad-hoc routing protocols occupies only 236.6KB (see Section 6.2). Secondly, they focus on traditional end-to-end protocols such as TCP/IP and do not support or emphasise routing-specific functionality such as that supported by, say, PICA (see above). In addition, they offer poor support for the fact that application execution and packet forwarding are inherently concurrent in ad-hoc routing protocol deployments: Appia supports only a single-threaded concurrency model, and Cactus, while it supports multi-threading, leaves concurrency control entirely up to the developer. Furthermore, Appia's strictly layered model is problematic in the ad-hoc routing protocol domain where cross layer optimisation is important.

3 Background Concepts Underpinning MANETKit

Before introducing MANETKit, this Section briefly covers essential background that underpins our framework. This mainly consists of the OpenCom software component model [9] and its associated notion of 'component frameworks' which we use as the basis of modularisation, composition and dynamic reconfiguration in MANETKit. We also introduce the 'CFS pattern' [31] that we use to structure the implementation of ad-hoc routing protocols.

OpenCom and Component Frameworks. OpenCom is a run-time component model that uses a small runtime kernel to support the dynamic loading, unloading, instantiation/destruction, composition/decomposition of lightweight programming language independent software components. Components have *interfaces* and *receptacles* that describe their points of interaction with other components. OpenCom also supports so-called *reflective meta-models* to facilitate the dynamic inspection and reconfiguration of component configurations. In particular, it employs (*i*) an *interface meta-model* to provide runtime information on the interfaces and receptacles supported by a component; and (*ii*) an *architecture meta-model* that offers a generic API through which the interconnections in a composed set of components can be inspected and reconfigured. *Component frameworks* [16] (hereafter, CFs) are domain tailored composite components that accept 'plug-in' components that modify or augment the CF's behaviour. Plug-ins are inserted and manipulated by means of an 'architecture' reflective meta-model that is exported by each CF. Crucially, CFs actively maintain their integrity to avoid 'illegal' configurations of plug-ins—attempts to insert and manipulate plug-ins are policed by sets of integrity rules registered with the CF. As CFs are themselves components, they can easily be nested: i.e. more complex CFs can be built by composing simpler ones; and they can be loaded and unloaded dynamically so that only functionality that is actually instantiated needs to be paid for. Full detail on OpenCom and CFs is available in the literature [9].

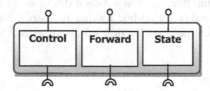

Fig. 1. MANETKit's Control-Forward-State (CFS) pattern (interfaces are shown as dots and receptacles as cups)

The Control-Forward-State Pattern. We have identified an architectural pattern called *Control-Forward-State* ('CFS' for short; see Fig. 1) that we have found useful in the structuring of protocol implementations in MANETKit. We first used the pattern in a different context in our GRIDKIT platform [31]. In the CFS pattern, the *Control* (C) element encapsulates the algorithm used to establish and maintain a virtual network topology (as often maintained by ad-hoc routing protocols); the *Forward* (F) element encapsulates a forwarding strategy over this topology; and the *State* (S) element gives access to protocol state (such as the neighbour list that embodies the virtual topology). The key benefit of the CFS pattern is that it naturally captures the typical elements of an ad-hoc routing protocol and thus allows the diversity such protocols to be treated in a consistent manner. Furthermore, when protocols are reconfigured it lets the C and F elements be replaced independently (e.g. maintaining the same overlay but changing the forwarding strategy, or vice versa). Additionally, the pattern naturally supports vertical stacking e.g. for piggybacking data on the packets of a lower CFS element. Such stacking can be at a finer-grained level than that of entire CFS units: for example, the C element of a higher level CFS unit may use (and therefore be stacked on) the F element of a lower level unit. Finally, because a CFS instance is a composition of components, it is naturally realised as a CF and thus benefits from the above-mentioned integrity maintenance machinery that is available to all CFs.

4 The Design of MANETKit

4.1 Overview

MANETKit is an OpenCom CF that supports the development, deployment and dynamic reconfiguration of ad-hoc routing protocols. It provides the developer with an extensible set of common ad-hoc routing protocol functionality (encapsulated in components), and tools to configure and reconfigure protocol graphs implemented as nested CFs. It builds heavily on OpenCom's support for the dynamic reconfiguration of component topologies (i.e. the architecture reflective meta-model), and on the support for nested composition and structural integrity provided by CFs (via integrity rules). In addition, thanks to OpenCom's inherent programming language independence, MANETKit supports the development of protocols in different programming languages.

The below presentation is structured by first describing and motivating, in Section 4.2, MANETKit's main CF types and its approach to protocol composition at two granularity levels: *coarse* and *fine*. Section 4.3 then discusses further built-in CFs that provide library-like functionality for ad-hoc routing protocols, Section 4.4 focuses on the important issue of concurrency, and Section 4.5 discusses MANETKit's approach to dynamic reconfiguration.

4.2   Protocol Composition

Our approach to protocol composition builds directly on the CFS architectural pattern outlined in Section 3. This naturally leads to a two-level composition model involving *coarse-grained* compositions of CFS units (i.e. protocol implementations); and *fine-grained* compositions of elements within CFS units. We now discuss these two levels.

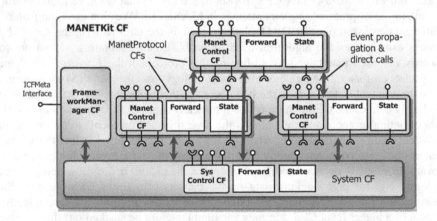

Fig. 2. Coarse-grained protocol composition in MANETKit

Coarse-grained Composition. At the coarse-grained level, MANETKit offers two key (sub)CFs: a so-called 'System CF' that encapsulates common system-related functions; and a generic 'ManetProtocol CF' that is instantiated and tailored for each ad-hoc routing protocol developed in MANETKit. As shown in Fig. 2, a MANETKit deployment running on a node typically comprises a number of composed ManetProtocol instances atop a single System instance. ManetProtocol instances may be placed at the same level or stacked on top of each other.

Communication between CFS units within a MANETKit deployment—e.g. the flow of packets or context information—is carried out using *events*[1]. The set of events supported in a given MANETKit deployment is based on an extensible polymorphic ontology. To leverage existing efforts in the direction of consolidation of ad-hoc routing protocols, we employ the increasingly-used PacketBB packet format [7] as the basis of our event structure.

Rather than being built explicitly, the organisation of a stacking topology of CFS units is derived automatically based on declarative statements of the types of event provided by and required by each CFS unit. More specifically, each unit defines a tuple: *<required-events, provided-events>* in which 'required-events' is the set of event types that the CF instance is interested in receiving, and 'provided-events' is the set it can generate. On the basis of these event tuples, the Framework Manager (see Fig. 2) automatically generates and maintains an appropriate set of receptacle-to-interface bindings between protocols such that, if an event *e* is in the *provided-event* set of protocol P, and the *required-event* set of protocol Q, the Framework Manager creates an OpenCom binding between interfaces/receptacles on P and Q to enable the passage of events of type e^2. Overall, the resulting loosely hierarchical organisation yields the following benefits:

- Changes in topology can be automatically updated when the event tuples on CFS units are changed at run-time (declarative automatic dynamic reconfiguration).
- The scheme naturally supports 'broadcast' event propagation (i.e. because multiple CF instances can 'require' an event of a single lower layer instance, or a lower layer instance can require an event of multiple higher-layer instances).
- It also naturally supports cross-layer interaction that omits layers, and minimises overhead where events need to pass directly between non-adjacent CF instances (avoids the need for strict layering).
- The inherent decoupling of protocols enables us to support different concurrency models without changing protocol implementations (see Section 4.4).

Finally, because it is an OpenCom CF, MANETKit can use the CF notion of integrity rules to sanity check the configuration defined by the provided-event / required-event mechanism. For example, we might use this mechanism to ensure that only one instance of a reactive routing protocol exists in a given MANETKit deployment.

Fine-grained Composition. At the fine-grained level, we structure the individual C, F and S elements of ManetProtocol instances in terms of component compositions (see Fig. 3). For the C element, we provide a generic sub-CF called *ManetControl* which encapsulates a number of areas of functionality (especially event management) that are

---

[1] As well as using events as discussed in this section, it is possible to make direct calls from one CFS unit to another. Such calls are typically used for 'out of band' purposes such as obtaining state from another's S element. Direct calls typically benefit from OpenCom's 'interface meta-model' to dynamically discover interfaces at runtime.

[2] This is a simplification. The design is slightly more complex—for example, to allow components to *exclusively* receive (require) a given event, meaning that other components would not receive the event even if it were in their required set. A mechanism to avoid loops is included for cases where a component provides and requires the same event type.

expected to be common across a range of ad-hoc routing protocols. For example, ManetControl's C component provides generic operations to initialise, start or stop a protocol's execution, maintains an Event Registry that supports the above-mentioned automatic event binding mechanism, and offers operations to push/pop events. The F and S areas are much more specific to individual protocol implementations; therefore there is less value in providing richly configurable sub-CFs in those areas.

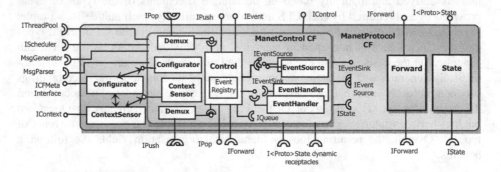

Fig. 3. Fine-grain protocol composition (i.e. within a ManetProtocol CF instance)

In general, each new ManetProtocol instance comes with default machinery and settings that can be modified or replaced depending on the developer's specific re-quirements. As at the coarse-grained level, subsequent tailoring of a new instance is a relatively safe process because the integrity rules (architectural constraints) built into all the generic CFs ensure that attempts to compose them do not violate per-CF structural invariants: for example, ManetControl rejects attempts to add more than one C element. Aside from this common functionality, the core logic of a routing protocol implementa-tion is embodied as a set of Event Source and Event Handler components within the ManetControl CF (Event Sources only emit events—typically driven by a timer—whereas Event Handlers process events, and may emit further events in response.) In general, interaction among these fine-grained components follows the same approach as interaction at the coarse-grained level: individual CFS elements and sub-elements com-municate both either via events or via direct calls.

4.3 Other Key Frameworks

We now briefly introduce two further key CFs supported by MANETKit. These are the above-mentioned *System CF*, a singleton CF that abstracts over low level systems oriented functionality; and the *Neighbour Detection CF*, which provides generic sup-port for network topology management. Aside from these, MANETKit provides a wide range of other utility components/CFs such as timers, threadpools, routing tables and queues.

The System CF. As we have seen, the System CF (see Fig. 4) is a base layer CFS unit on top of which ManetProtocol instances are stacked. Thanks to MANETKit's abstraction of inter-component communication, the System CF itself and ManetProtocol instances above it, need not be aware of the kernel-user boundary or whether the System CF itself is implemented as a kernel or a user-space module. The main role of the System CF is to facilitate portability by acting as a surrogate for OS-specific functionality such as thread management and routing environment initialisation. Its C component provides OS-independent operations to initialise the host's routing environment (e.g. IP forwarding, ICMP redirects) and provide access to system-oriented context information to inform dynamic reconfiguration. Its S component provides operations to manipulate the kernel routing table, and query/list network devices. Its F component provides send/receive primitives for the exchange of protocol messages that abstract over the use of multiple network technologies. Both the C and F elements provide and require events which higher-level ManetProtocol instances can specify in their event tuples. The raising and capturing of events is ultimately grounded in mechanisms such as network sockets, packet capture libraries (such as libpcap), and packet filters (like Netfilter in Linux or the NDIS intermediate driver in Windows).

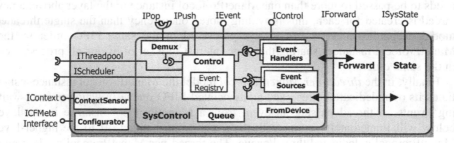

Fig. 4. The System CF

Neighbour Detection CF. This is a generally-useful ManetProtocol instance that maintains information on neighbouring nodes that are one or two hops away. Based on this information, it generates events to notify ManetProtocol instances about link breaks with lost neighbours for purposes of route invalidation. The information maintained by the CF is also useful as a means of optimising flooding approaches such as Multipoint Relaying. It is designed to be pluggable so that alternative mechanisms can be applied where appropriate (e.g. HELLO message based, or link layer feedback based). The CF additionally offers a useful means of disseminating information periodically to neighbours via piggybacking. For instance, AODV implementation might piggyback routing table entries so that neighbours can learn new routes.

4.4 Concurrency

MANETKit's concurrency provision is strictly orthogonal to the basic structure of the framework. This allows the use of alternative *concurrency models* within the framework, which in turn enables us easily to adapt the framework to different deployment environments. Regardless of which concurrency model is selected, the user-provided parts of a ManetProtocol instance can always be assumed to run as a single critical section. This has the beneficial effect that Event Handlers can always be assumed to run atomically.

In more detail, MANETKit supports the following concurrency models: single-threaded, thread-per-message or thread-per-ManetProtocol. Note that these designations apply only to the handling of events originating from 'below' the selected MANETKit instance (i.e. originating from the System CF): regardless of the concurrency model in use, it is always possible to use multiple threads to call MANETKit from above. In the *single-threaded* model, all ManetProtocol instances rely on a single thread hosted by the System CF. In cases where an event needs to be passed to more than one higher-layer ManetProtocol instance, the same thread is used to call each ManetProtocol instance in turn. Besides the obvious benefit of the absence of race conditions, this model potentially allows MANETKit to be applied in primitive low-resource environments such as sensor motes.

In the *thread-per-message* model (a slight variant of this, called the *thread-per-n-messages* model, is midway between single-threaded and thread-per-message) distinct threads are used to shepherd individual events up the protocol graph. Where an event needs to be passed to more than one ManetProtocol instance in the layer above, a new thread is created for each, thus providing more concurrency than the single threaded model. Regardless, events are always processed in the same FIFO order so that ManetProtocol instances sharing the same interest in a set of events all process them in the same order.

Finally, in the *thread-per-ManetProtocol* model the ManetProtocol instance instantiates its own dedicated thread and an associated FIFO queue in which to store waiting events. A thread passing an event from a ManetProtocol instance in the layer below will immediately return, with the event being handed off to the higher-layer ManetProtocol's dedicated thread/queue. The thread-per-ManetProtocol model represents an intermediate point in terms of protocol throughput and resource overhead between the single-threaded model (low resource overhead and low protocol throughput) and the thread-per-message model (high resource overhead and high protocol throughput).

To select either of the single-threaded or thread-per-message model it is only necessary to ask the System CF to use one or other model, and the selected model is applied throughout the MANETKit instance. The thread-per-ManetProtocol model, on the other hand, can be selected on a per-ManetProtocol instance basis, and will function the same regardless of whether the System CF uses one or more threads.

4.5 Reconfiguration Management

The focus of MANETKit is on *enabling* the dynamic reconfiguration of ad-hoc routing protocols. A fully comprehensive dynamic reconfiguration solution for ad-hoc routing protocols would involve a closed-loop control system that comprises: (i) context monitoring, (ii) decision making (based, e.g., on feeding context information to event-condition-action rules), and (iii) reconfiguration enactment. MANETKit provides the first and last of these elements (as described next) but leaves the decision making to higher-level software. For example, a complete reconfigurable system could be built by combining MANETKit with the decision-making machinery proposed in [13].

Context Monitoring. The System CF provides a range of event types relating to context information such as link quality, signal strength, signal-to-noise ratio, available bandwidth, CPU utilisation, memory consumption and battery levels.. In addition, individual ManetProtocol instances can choose to provide protocol-specific context events. For example, our DYMO implementation provides events relating to packet loss, and the number of route discoveries initiated per unit time. MANETKit also provides a 'concentrator' for context events in the Framework Manager CF (see Fig. 2). This acts as a façade for higher-level software and also hides the fact that some low level context information might be obtained by polling rather than by waiting for events.

Reconfiguration enactment. We support two complementary methods of reconfiguration enactment. The first is by updating the <*required-events, provided-events*> tuples of ManetProtocol instances. This enables protocol configurations to be rewired in a very straightforward, declarative, manner, although only at the coarse granularity level. The second method is more general and supports the fine granularity level: it follows the standard OpenCom approach of manipulating component compositions— i.e. by adding/removing/ replacing components and/or the bindings between them. This is carried out through standard OpenCom and CF facilities—especially the architecture reflective model outlined in Section 3. This method of reconfiguration enactment is considerably simplified by the fact that ManetProtocol instances are critical sections which only a single thread can enter at a time (see above), thus avoiding the possibility of race conditions between a reconfiguration thread and a protocol processing thread. By ensuring that any current processing of protocol events is completed before reconfiguration operations are run and further event-shepherding threads are blocked, the critical section enables the ManetProtocol instance to be in a stable state in which reconfiguration changes can be safely made. To date our experience has been that the integrity of almost all reconfiguration operations can be ensured with this critical section mechanism alone. For very complex reconfigurations (e.g. involving transactional changes across multiple ManetProtocol instances), we can fall back on OpenCom's general-purpose 'quiescence' mechanism as described in [25].

The other commonly-cited problematic issue in dynamic reconfiguration is state management. We have found that the CFS pattern is of considerable help here as it encourages designers to factor out the state from their protocol designs and put it into distinct S components. Given this, if it is required to replace one ManetProtocol instance with another while maintaining state it is often enough simply to carry over an S component from the old ManetProtocol instance to the new one.

5   Implementation Case Studies

To evaluate MANETKit, we have used the framework to implement a number of popular ad-hoc routing protocols. In the first instance, as a proof of concept, we used an initial Java-based implementation of MANETKit [35] to build the well-known AODV protocol. Thereafter, to investigate the feasibility of the framework in more memory-constrained devices, we developed a C version of MANETKit (based on the C version of OpenCom) and used this to implement RFC-complaint versions of the popular OLSR and DYMO protocols. In the remainder of this Section, we describe these implementations. In doing so, we illustrate how MANETKit makes it straightforward to develop and deploy ad-hoc routing protocols, and also how variants of protocols can easily to created via dynamic reconfiguration when current operating conditions call for them.

5.1 OLSR

MANETKit's OLSR implementation is built using two separate ManetProtocol instances: one for OLSR proper and the other for an underlying implementation of Multipoint Relaying (MPR) [8] that is used by OLSR. MPR is responsible for link sensing and relay selection; and maintains state in its S component to underpin these. The OLSR ManetProtocol itself uses topology information garnered by MPR and uses the latter's forwarding services to flood topology information.

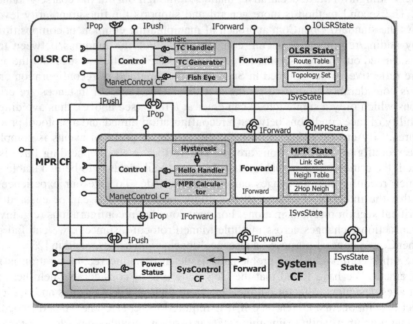

Fig. 5. The composition of OLSR in MANETKit; hatched boxes represent protocol-specific components (the rest are reusable generic components)

We have found that MANETKit simplifies the process of writing protocols such as OLSR. This is first manifested in the separation of concerns enabled by software components in general and the CFS pattern in particular. At a finer granularity than the OLSR/MPR split we have already seen, reifying protocol state into a distinct S component clarifies thinking about protocol design (as well as easing dynamic reconfiguration), and the ManetProtocol CF's plug-in Event Handlers naturally correspond to the way designers think about protocols. It is also useful to be able to call on MANETKit's range of generic tools such as routing table templates and timers (e.g. the latter are needed to drive the OLSR Event Source components that periodically diffuse link state information across the network).

Having written the elements of the protocol, installing it in a running MANETKit deployment mainly involves defining the *<required-events, provided-events>* event tuples of each ManetProtocol instance. The OLSR instance provides a TC_OUT event (this corresponds to an outgoing OLSR 'Topology Change' message); and it requires TC_IN, NHOOD_CHANGE (which notifies a change in the underlying network neighbourhood) and MPR_CHANGE (which notifies a change in relay selection). The latter two event types are provided by the MPR instance. The MPR instance also provides and requires, respectively, HELLO_OUT and HELLO_IN events used for neighbour detection. Finally, the MPR instance requires POWER_STATUS events. These are context events that report the node's current battery levels; they are used to dynamically determine the willingness of a node acting as a relay to forward messages on behalf of its neighbours, this 'willingness' metric being factored into the relay selection process.

Protocol installation also typically entails reconfiguring some existing MANETKit CFs and if necessary, loading additional components to satisfy specific requirements. In the OLSR case, the System CF is instructed to load a 'NetworkDriver' component that requires and provides HELLO_OUT/TC_OUT and HELLO_IN/TC_IN respectively, and a 'PowerStatus' component that generates POWER_STATUS events. Fig. 5 illustrates the final protocol composition for our OLSR implementation; only the major inter-layer bindings are shown in the figure for the sake of clarity.

Protocol Variations. It is straightforward to dynamically reconfigure our OLSR implementation to better suit new operating conditions it may encounter. We describe here two such variations: power-aware routing and fish-eye routing. The *power-aware routing* variant is based on the algorithm described in [33], and aims to maximise the lifetime of a route between selected source-sink pairs within the MANET. It operates by trying to find and maintain the route between such a pair that has the least energy consumption of all possible routes. It is interesting to consider this as an OLSR variation because it is only beneficial when an application requires this particular QoS emphasis (i.e. long lifetime connectivity between particular node pairs). If there is no such requirement, or the requirement goes away because the application no longer needs it, the variation becomes a hindrance (and therefore should be removed) because it incurs significantly more overhead than standard OLSR routing. To implement and deploy the power-aware routing variation, the MPR ManetProtocol's Hello Event Handler and MPR Calculator components (see Fig. 5) are replaced by power-aware versions (the new Hello Handler determines link costs in terms of transmission power; and this is then used by the new MPR Calculator to determine relay selection). In addition, a new 'ResidualPower' component is plugged into the OLSR CF to determine the node's residual battery level and to disseminate this to other nodes in the network via MPR's flooding service. Both adding and removing the variant behaviour is straightforward and incurs only a small number of operations on the OLSR CF's architecture reflective meta-model.

The purpose of the *fish-eye routing* variant [34] is to aid scalability when networks grow large, albeit at the cost of sub-optimal routing to distant nodes. It basically works by refreshing topology information more frequently for nearby nodes than for distant nodes. This variant is straightforwardly implemented as a component that modifies TC_OUT events according to the fish eye strategy outlined above (in fact it works by modifying the TTL and timing of OLSR Topology Change messages). The component is specified to both require and provide TC_OUT events; and so all that is required to insert it into the protocol graph is to request re-evaluation of the automatic event-tuple-based binding process. This automatically results in the component being interposed in the path of TC_OUT events passing between the OSLR and MPR CFs.

5.2 DYMO

The MANETKit configuration for DYMO consists of one new ManetProtocol instance atop the System CF. It also uses the Neighbour Detection CF that was discussed in Section 4.3. The three CF instances are configured using *<required-events, provided-events>* tuples is a similar manner to that already described for OLSR. For example, in order to be kept abreast of network neighbourhood changes, the DYMO instance requires a NHOOD_CHANGE event from the Neighbour Detection instance for route invalidation upon link breaks.

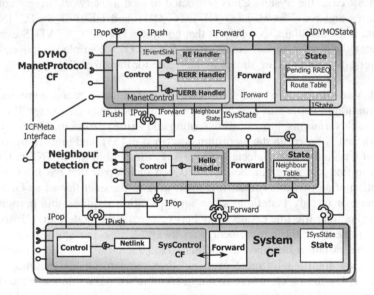

Fig. 6. The composition of DYMO in MANETKit; hatched boxes represent protocol-specific components (the rest are reusable generic components)

As a reactive protocol, DYMO requires additional machinery to ensure that route discoveries are triggered, and route lifetime updates are performed correctly. To achieve this, DYMO additionally requires the deployment of a 'NetLink' component in the System CF that is responsible for packet filtering. In implementation, this component encapsulates the loading of a kernel module that employs Linux Netfilter hooks to examine, hold, drop, etc. packets. It provides NO_ROUTE, ROUTE_UPDATE and SEND_ROUTE_ERR events which are used by the DYMO

ManetProtocol instance for the purposes of (respectively): route discovery (i.e. when no route is found for an outgoing data packet), extending existing route lifetimes, and initiating route invalidations. On successful route discovery, the DYMO ManetProtocol instance sends a ROUTE_FOUND event to the Netlink component to trigger the re-injection of buffered packets into the network.

Protocol Variations. The variations we describe for DYMO are optimised flooding and multi-path DYMO. In the *optimised flooding* variant, DYMO, like OLSR, uses Multipoint Relaying as a flooding optimisation. As with OLSR, this curbs the overhead associated with broadcasting control messages when a network topology is dense, although at the expense of maintaining additional state. To apply this variation, the Neighbour Detection CF is simply replaced with the MPR ManetProtocol instance discussed in the previous Section. If a co-existing OLSR ManetProtocol instance is already deployed in the framework, then the MPR CF is directly shareable between the reactive and proactive protocols, thus leading to a leaner deployment.

The goal of the *multi-path DYMO* variant is to reduce the overhead of frequent flooding for route discovery, although at the expense of additional route discovery latency. It works by computing multiple link-disjoint paths within a single route discovery attempt, based on the algorithm described in [10]—with the notable difference that our implementation is real rather than merely simulator based. To configure multi-path DYMO, three components need be replaced (please refer to Fig. 6). Firstly, the S component is replaced with a new version that accommodates the new formats of protocol messages and routing table entries (a path list now exists for each route). Secondly, the RE (Routing Element) Event Handler is replaced with a new version that contains the logic to compute link-disjoint paths. Atomic execution of this Handler (as guaranteed by MANETKit) is essential since duplicate route requests are no longer systematically discarded but rather processed to find alternative paths. Lastly, the RERR Event Handler is replaced with a new version that handles route error events/ messages differently. For instance, on receiving a SEND_ROUTE_ERROR event, the new Handler only sends a route error message when an alternative path is not available; otherwise, it installs the new path in the OS's kernel routing table.

6 Evaluation

Section 5 has illustrated the feasibility of supporting the dynamic deployment of multiple ad-hoc routing protocols in MANETKit, and also of supporting their fine-grained dynamic reconfiguration—i.e. the satisfaction of the first of the three goals set out in the introduction has already been demonstrated. In this Section, we evaluate the remaining two goals: i.e. Goal 2: to compare favourably with equivalent monolithic implementations of ad-hoc routing protocols in terms of *performance* (Section 6.1) and *resource overhead* (Section 6.2); and Goal 3: to shorten the protocol development cycle and time to port protocols (Section 6.3).

All measurements in this Section are based our C/Linux implementation of MANETKit and use the OLSR and DYMO implementations described above. These were deployed on a testbed consisted of an 802.11b/g ad-hoc network of 5 nodes (3.2 GHz CPU with 2 GB of RAM) running Ubuntu 7.10, with an Ethernet backplane for testbed management. The 5 nodes are arranged in a linear topology: we used a combination of MAC-level filtering and the MobiEmu emulator [28] to emulate the required multi-hop connectivity. We used *Unik-olsrd* [32] as a comparator for our OLSR implementation, and *DYMOUM v0.3* [29] for our DYMO implementation. These were chosen because they are the two most popular public domain implementations of these protocols. For comparability we configured our MANETKit implementations with the single threaded concurrency model and with identical configuration parameters to the comparator implementations (e.g. identical HELLO and Topology Change intervals, and route hold times).

6.1 Performance

Our metrics for performance are (i) *Time to Process Message*—i.e. the time taken to process a protocol message from receipt to completion within an MANETKit deployment (for OLSR this is a Topology Change message; and for DYMO it is a RREQ message); and (ii) *Route Establishment Delay*—i.e. the time taken to establish a route in our testbed environment (for OLSR this is the time taken for a newly-arrived node arriving at one end of the existing linear network topology to compute a fully-populated routing table; and for DYMO it is the time taken to perform a route discovery operation under similar circumstances). The former metric is a 'micro' level indicator of the overhead of MANETKit's componentisation of the protocol processing path, while the latter is a 'macro' measure of control plane performance.

Table 1. Comparative Performance of MANETKit Protocols

	Unik-olsrd	MKit-OLSR	*DYMOUM-0.3*	MKit-DYMO
Time to Process Message (ms)	*0.045*	0.096	*0.135*	0.122
Route Establishment Delay (ms)	*995*	1026	*37*	27.3

Referring to Table 1, we can see that on the *Time to Process Message* metric, the measurements are very small in absolute terms and, as such, probably insignificant in practice. The *Route Establishment Delay* metric puts them in perspective, and shows that comparable real-world performance levels are attained by the MANETKit implementations: MANETKit-OLSR is 3% slower than Unik-olrsd in establishing a route in our experimental set-up, whereas MANETKit-DYMO is actually 35% faster than DYMOUM-0.3. (Overall, our implementation of OLSR is slower on both metrics than the comparator, but our implementation of DYMO is faster on both.) We can conclude that that MANETKit achieves broadly comparable performance to typical monolithic implementations.

6.2 Resource Overhead

To assess the relative resource overhead of the MANETKit-implemented protocols we again compared these implementations with their monolithic counterparts—this time in terms of the memory footprints incurred. Memory footprint is the most direct measure of MANETKit's applicability for resource-constrained mobile nodes.

As can be deduced from in Table 2, MANETKit-OLSR incurs an 31% memory overhead over its monolithic competitor, and MANETKit-DYMO incurs an 48% overhead. These overheads are not surprising and are mainly due, of course, to the (necessary) inclusion of the generic MANETKit machinery and the OpenCom run-time (the latter occupies 22KB)[3]. However, as soon as we accept the premise that it is important to be able to deploy multiple ad-hoc routing protocols, as argued in this paper, we can see the benefits of MANETKit: the footprint of deploying the two protocols together in MANETKit is 8% *smaller* than the sum of the two monolithic protocol implementations; and the difference will clearly become more significant still as more protocols (plus variants) are added and the fixed MANETKit/ OpenCom overheads are further amortised. The key conclusion is that the overhead/flexibility trade-off is already in MANETKit's favour with only two protocols deployed.

Table 2. Comparative Resource Overhead of MANETKit Protocols

	Unik-olsrd	MKit-OLSR	DYMOUM-0.3	MKit-DYMO	Unik-olsrd + DYMOUM-0.3	MKit OLSR+ MKit-DYMO
Memory Footprint (KB)	136.3	179.0	120.4	178.1	256.7	236.6

6.3 Time Taken to Develop and Port Protocols

We now evaluate the extent to which the MANETKit approach can minimise the time needed to develop and port protocols. We do this in an indirect manner—specifically, by measuring the degree of code reuse achieved across the MANETKit implementations of OLSR and DYMO.

Table 3. Reused generic components in MANET protocol compositions

	Lines of Code	OLSR	DYMO
System CF Forward	1276	X	X
System CF State	702	X	X
Netlink (+ Kernel Module)	734		X
Queue	60	X	X
Threadpool	591	X	X
Timer	228	X	X
PacketGenerator	950	X	X
PacketParser	795	X	X
RouteTable	1046	X	X
ManetControl CF	827	X	X
NeighbourDetection CF	1684		X
MPRCalculator	745	X	
MPRState	3876[4]	X	
Configurator	405	X	X
Reused Generic Components	-	12	12
Protocol-specific Components	-	4	5

---

[3] Once a desired configuration has been achieved (which possibly includes multiple protocols) it is possible to unload the OpenCom kernel to free up memory space. The overheads would drop in such a case to 15% for OLSR and 30% for DYMO.

[4] The reason that this component is so large is that there are several different types of table involved for the various types of data stored. There remains significant scope for optimising this figure by coalescing table handling routines.

Table 3 gives a coarse-grained indication of the degree of code reuse by listing the generic components used in the implementation of these protocols (we also show the size of each component in terms of lines of code). In both cases, the generic components outnumber the specific ones (shown at the bottom of Table 3) by a factor of at least 2. This is especially significant because OLSR and DYMO are considered to be very different protocols.

Fig. 7 takes a finer-grained perspective by showing the number of lines of code in the generic, as well as the protocol-specific, components used by each protocol. The proportion contributed by the reusable components to each protocol's codebase is 57% for OLSR and 66% for DYMO, indicating a substantial saving in developer effort. Overall we can see that the structure of MANETKit fosters a significant degree of code reuse across protocols. Based on these measures and our knowledge of other ad hoc routing protocols we fully expect to see similar levels of reuse when we add further protocols to the framework.

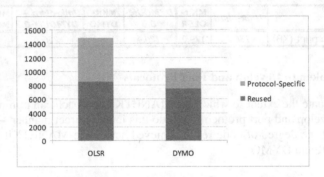

Fig. 7. The proportion of reusable code in each protocol

7   Conclusions and Future Work

This paper has proposed a run-time component framework for the implementation, deployment and dynamic reconfiguration of ad-hoc routing protocols. It is motivated by the fact that the range of operating conditions under which ad-hoc routing protocols must operate is so diverse and dynamic that it is infeasible for a single protocol to be optimal under all such conditions. MANETKit therefore supports the serial and simultaneous deployment of multiple protocols, plus the generation of protocol variants and hybrids via fine-grained dynamic reconfiguration. It uses the 'CFS' pattern and <*required-events, provided-events*> tuples to allow protocols to be easily stacked or composed in a variety of ways and to be straightforwardly dynamically reconfigured. Another novel feature of MANETKit is its use of pluggable concurrency models, which enables it to be used in a variety of deployment environments with varying performance/resource trade-offs. MANETKit also helps protocol developers in the traditional way by providing a rich set of tools specifically tailored to the ad-hoc routing environment, and by isolating developers from OS specificities (including whether protocols are implemented in kernel or user space). And it also enables researchers to experiment with protocol optimisation techniques.

We have evaluated MANETKit by showing how it can be used to straightforwardly build and dynamically deploy two major ad-hoc routing protocols (i.e. OLSR and DYMO) and how these deployments can be variegated in a number of ways to suit different operating conditions. Furthermore, our empirical evaluation shows that MANETKit meets our stated goals by achieving comparable performance to monolithic implementations of the same protocols, achieving smaller resource overheads when more than one protocol is implemented in comparison to the monolithic approach, and also achieving significant code reuse across protocols (the latter being a strong indicator that the MANETKit approach should generally shorten protocol development and porting time).

In the future, our immediate plans are to integrate MANETKit into a wider dynamic reconfiguration environment by incorporating policy-driven decision making. This will be based on existing work [13], and will also include coordinated distributed dynamic reconfiguration as well as merely per-node reconfiguration. We also plan to further explore reconfiguration strategies in real-world application scenarios, to further investigate the hybridisation of protocols, and to generally gain more experience of implementing protocols in the MANETKit environment.

A version of the MANETKit software is available for download from http://www.comp.lancs.ac.uk/~ramdhany/.

References

1. Bani-Yassein, M., Ould-Khaoua, M.: Applications of probabilistic flooding in MANETs. International Journal of Ubiquitous Computing and Communication (January 2007)
2. Bhatti, N.T., Schlichting, R.D.: A system for constructing configurable high-level protocols. SIGCOMM Comput. Commun. Rev. 25(4) (October 1995)
3. Borgia, E., Conti, M., Delmastro, F.: Experimental comparison of routing and middleware solutions for mobile ad-hoc networks: legacy vs cross-layer approach. In: E-WIND 2005 (2005)
4. Calafate, C.M.T., Manzoni, P.: A multi-platform programming interface for protocol development. In: 11th Euromicro Conference on Parallel, Distributed and Network-Based Processing (2003)
5. Chakeres, I., Perkins, C.: Dynamic MANET on-demand (DYMO) routing, draft-ietf-manet-dymo-11, IETF's MANET WG (November 2007)
6. Chiang, C.: Routing in clustered multihop, mobile wireless networks with fading channel. In: IEEE SICON 1997 (October 1997)
7. Clausen, T., Dearlove, C., Jacquet, P.: Generalized MANET message format, draft-ietf-manet-packetbb-07 internet draft (2007)
8. Clausen, T., Dearlove, C.: Optimized link state routing protocol, v2, draft-ietf-manet-olsrv2-03.txt
9. Coulson, G., Blair, G., Grace, P., Taiani, F., Joolia, A., Lee, K., Ueyama, J., Sivaharan, T.: A generic component model for building systems software. ACM Trans. Comput. Syst. 26(1) (February 2008)
10. Galvez, J.J., Ruiz, P.M.: Design and performance evaluation of multipath extensions for the DYMO protocol. In: 32nd IEEE Conference on Local Computer Networks, October 15 (2007)
11. Garlan, D., Monroe, R., Wile, D.: Acme: an architecture description interchange language. In: Conference of the Centre for Advanced Studies on Collaborative Research, Toronto, Ontario, Canada (November 1997)
12. Goff, T., Abu-Ghazaleh, N.B., Phatak, D.S., Kahvecioglu, R.: Preemptive routing in ad-hoc networks. In: MobiCom 2001 (2001)

13. Grace, P., Coulson, G., Blair, G.S., Porter, B.: A distributed architecture meta-model for self-managed middleware. In: ARM 2006 (2006)
14. Haas, Z.J., Pearlman, M.R., Samar, P.: The zone routing protocol (ZRP) for ad-hoc networks, Internet Draft, draft-ietf-manet-zone-zrp-04.txt (July 2002)
15. Haas, Z.J., Halpern, J.Y., Li, L.: Gossip-based ad-hoc routing. In: INFOCOM 2002 (2002)
16. Joolia, A., Batista, T., Coulson, G., Gomes, A.T.: Mapping ADL specifications to a reconfigurable runtime component platform. In: WICSA 2005 (2005)
17. Karp, B., Kung, H.T.: Greedy perimeter stateless routing for wireless networks. In: Proc. 6th Annual ACM/IEEE International Conference on Mobile Computing and Networking, MobiCom 2000 (2000)
18. Kawadia, V., Zhang, Y., Gupta, B.: System services for ad-hoc routing: architecture, implementation and experiences. In: MobiSys 2003 (2003)
19. Kon, F.: Automatic configuration of component-based distributed systems. PhD Thesis. University of Illinois at Urbana-Champaign (May 2000)
20. Kuladinithi, K.: University of Bremen Java-AODV implementation,
    http://www.aodv.org
21. Marina, M.K., Das, S.R.: On-demand multipath distance vector routing in ad-hoc networks. In: Proc. International Conference for Network Procotols (2001)
22. Park, V.D., Corson, M.S.: A highly adaptive distributed routing algorithm for mobile wireless networks. In: INFOCOM 1997 (1997)
23. Perkins, C., Royer, E.: Ad-hoc on demand distance vector routing, Internet Draft rfc3561 (2003)
24. Pinto, A.: Appia: A flexible protocol kernel supporting multiple coordinated channels. In: ICDCS. IEEE, Los Alamitos (2001)
25. Pissias, P., Coulson, G.: Framework for quiescence management in support of reconfigurable multi-threaded component-based systems. IET Software 2(4), 348–361 (2008)
26. Santiváñez, C.A., Ramanathan, R., Stavrakakis, I.: Making link-state routing scale for ad-hoc networks. In: Proc. 2nd ACM international Symposium on Mobile Ad-Hoc Networking (October 2001)
27. van Renesse, R., Birman, K., Hayden, M., Vaysburd, A., Karr, D.: Building adaptive systems using Ensemble. Technical Report. UMI Order Number: TR97-1638, Cornell University (1997)
28. Zhang, Y.: An integrated environment for testing mobile ad-doc networks. In: MobiHoc 2002 (2002)
29. Implementation of the dymo routing protocol dymoum-0.3,
    http://masimum.inf.um.es/?Software:DYMOUM
30. Hutchinson, N.C., Peterson, L.L.: The X-Kernel: An Architecture for Implementing Network Protocols. IEEE Trans. Softw. Eng. 17(1) (January 1991)
31. Grace, P., Coulson, G., Blair, G., Mathy, L., Yeung, W.K., Cai, W., Duce, D., Cooper, C.: GRIDKIT: Pluggable Overlay Networks for Grid Computing. In: Meersman, R., Tari, Z. (eds.) OTM 2004. LNCS, vol. 3291, pp. 1463–1481. Springer, Heidelberg (2004)
32. Implementation of the OLSR routing protocol, Unik-olsrd website:
    http://www.olsr.org/
33. Mahfoudh, S., Minet, P.: An energy efficient routing based on OLSR in wireless ad hoc and sensor networks. In: Proc. 22nd International Conference on Advanced Information Networking and Applications – Workshops (2008)
34. Gerla, M., Hong, X., Pei, G., Fisheye State Routing Protocol (FSR) for Ad Hoc Networks. IETF MANET Working Group Internet Draft (2002)
35. Ramdhany, R., Coulson, G.: ManetKit: A Framework for MANET Routing Protocols. In: Proc. 5th Workshop on Wireless Ad hoc and Sensor Networks (WWASN 2008), workshop attached to the International Conference on Distributed Computing Systems (ICDCS), Beijing, China (June 2008)

Automatic Generation of Network Protocol Gateways

Yérom-David Bromberg[1], Laurent Réveillère[1], Julia L. Lawall[2],
and Gilles Muller[3]

[1] University of Bordeaux, France
[2] University of Copenhagen, Denmark
[3] Ecole des Mines de Nantes / INRIA-Regal, France

Abstract. The emergence of networked devices in the home has made
it possible to develop applications that control a variety of household
functions. However, current devices communicate via a multitude of incompatible protocols, and thus gateways are needed to translate between
them. Gateway construction, however, requires an intimate knowledge
of the relevant protocols and a substantial understanding of low-level
network programming, which can be a challenge for many application
programmers.

This paper presents a generative approach to gateway construction,
z2z, based on a domain-specific language for describing protocol behaviors, message structures, and the gateway logic. Z2z includes a compiler
that checks essential correctness properties and produces efficient code.
We have used z2z to develop a number of gateways, including SIP to
RTSP, SLP to UPnP, and SMTP to SMTP via HTTP, involving a range
of issues common to protocols used in the home. Our evaluation of these
gateways shows that z2z enables communication between incompatible
devices without increasing the overall resource usage or response time.

1 Introduction

The "home of tomorrow" is almost here, with a plethora of networked devices
embedded in appliances, such as telephones, televisions, thermostats, and lamps,
making it possible to develop applications that control many basic household
functions. Unfortunately, however, the different functionalities of these various
appliances, as well as market factors, mean that the code embedded in these
devices communicates via a multitude of incompatible protocols: SIP for telephones, RTSP for televisions, X2D for thermostats, and X10 for lamps. This
range of protocols drastically limits interoperability, and thus the practical benefit of home automation.

To provide interoperability, one solution would be to modify the code, to take
new protocols into account. However, the code in devices is often proprietary,
preventing any modification of the processing of protocol messages. Even if the
source code is available, it may not be possible to install a new implementation
into the device. Therefore, gateways have been used to translate between the
various kinds of protocols that are used in existing appliances.

J.M. Bacon and B.F. Cooper (Eds.): Middleware 2009, LNCS 5896, pp. 21–41, 2009.
© IFIP International Federation for Information Processing 2009

Developing a gateway, however, is challenging, requiring not only knowledge of the protocols involved, but also a substantial understanding of low-level network programming. Furthermore, there can be significant mismatches between the expressiveness of various protocols: some are binary while others are text-based, some send messages in unicast while other use multicast, some are synchronous while others are asynchronous, and a single request in one protocol may correspond to a series of requests and responses in another. Mixing this complex translation logic, which may for example involve hand coding of callback functions or continuations in the case of asynchronous responses, with equally complex networking code makes implementing a gateway by hand laborious and error prone. Enterprise Service Buses [1] have been proposed to reduce this burden by making it possible to translate messages to and from a single fixed intermediary protocol. Nevertheless, the translation logic must still be implemented by hand. Because each pair of protocols may exhibit widely differing properties, the gateway code is often not easily reusable.

This paper. We propose a generative language-based approach, z2z, to simplify gateway construction. Z2z is supported by a runtime system that hides low-level details from the gateway programmer, and a compiler that checks essential correctness properties and produces efficient code. Our contributions are:

- We propose a new approach to gateway development. Our approach relies on the use of a domain-specific language (DSL) for describing protocol behaviors, message structures, and the gateway logic.
- The DSL relies on advanced compilation strategies to hide complex issues from the gateway developer such as asynchronous message responses and the management of dynamically-allocated memory, while remaining in a low-overhead C-based framework.
- We have implemented a compiler that checks essential correctness properties and automatically produces an efficient implementation of a gateway.
- We have implemented a runtime system that addresses a range of protocol requirements, such as unicast vs. multicast transmission, association of responses to previous requests, and management of sessions.
- We show the applicability of z2z by using it to automatically generate a number of gateways: between SIP and RTSP, between SLP and UPnP, and between SMTP and SMTP via HTTP. On a 200 MHz ARM9 processor, the generated gateways have a runtime memory footprint of less than 260KB, and with essentially no runtime overhead as compared to native service access.

The rest of this paper is organized as follows. Section 2 presents the range of issues that arise in implementing a gateway, as illustrated by a variety of case studies. Section 3 describes the z2z gateway architecture and introduces a DSL for describing protocol behaviors, message structures, and the gateway logic. Section 4 describes the compiler and runtime system that support this language. Section 5 demonstrates the efficiency and scalability of z2z gateways. Section 6 discusses related work. Finally, Section 7 concludes and presents future work.

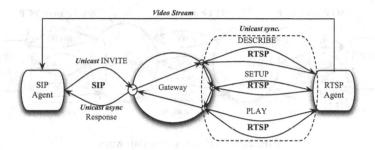

Fig. 1. SIP to RTSP gateway

2   Issues in Developing Gateways

A gateway must take into account the different degrees of expressiveness of the source and target protocols and the range of communication methods that they use. These issues are challenging to take into account individually, requiring substantial expertise in network programming, and the need to address both of them at once makes gateway development especially difficult. We illustrate these points using examples that involve a wide range of protocols.

Mismatched protocol expressiveness. The types of messages provided by a protocol are determined by the kinds of exchanges that are relevant to the targeted application domain. Thus, different protocols may provide message types that express information at different granularities. To account for such mismatches, a gateway must potentially translate a single request from the source device into multiple requests for the target device, or save information in a response from the target device for use in constructing multiple responses for the source device.

The SIP/RTSP gateway shown in Fig. 1 illustrates the case where the requests accepted by the target device are finer grained than the requests generated by the source device. This gateway has been used in the SIP-based building-automation test infrastructure at the University of Bordeaux. It allows a SIP based telephony client to be used to receive images from an Axis IP-camera.[1] This camera is a closed system that accepts only RTSP for negotiating the parameters of the video session. Once the communication is established, the gateway is no longer involved, and the video is streamed directly from the camera to the SIP client using RTP [2]. Because SIP and RTSP were introduced for different application domains, there are significant differences in the means they provide for establishing a connection. Thus, as shown in Fig. 1, for a single SIP INVITE message, the gateway must extract and rearrange the information available into multiple RTSP messages.

The SMTP/HTTP and HTTP/STMP gateways shown in Fig. 2 illustrate the case where information must be saved from a target response for use in constructing multiple responses for the source device. These gateways are used in

---

[1] Axis: http://www.axis.com/products/

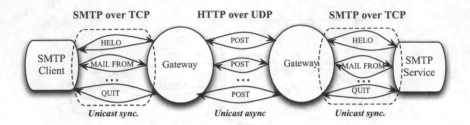

Fig. 2. HTTP tunneling gateways

a tunneling application that enables SMTP messages to be exchanged between two end-points over HTTP, as is useful when the port used by SMTP is closed somewhere between the source and the destination. The first gateway encapsulates an SMTP request into an HTTP message and sends it asynchronously using UDP to the second gateway, which extracts relevant information to generate the corresponding SMTP request. The response is sent back similarly.

Because all SMTP messages have to flow within the same TCP stream, the HTTP/SMTP gateway needs to know which TCP connection to use when an HTTP request is received. To address this issue, the gateway generates a unique identifier when opening the TCP connection with the destination SMTP server and includes this identifier within the HTTP response. The first gateway then includes this identifier in all subsequent HTTP requests, enabling the second gateway to retrieve the connection to use. To implement this, the first gateway needs to manage a state within a session to store the identifier returned in the first response in order to be able to find it for the subsequent requests.

Heterogeneous communication methods. Protocols differ significantly in how they interact with the network. Requests may be multicast or unicast, responses may be synchronous or asynchronous, and network communication may be managed using a range of transport protocols, most commonly TCP or UDP.

The gateway between SLP and UPnP shown in Fig. 3 involves a variety of these communication methods. Such a gateway may be used in a service discovery environment that provides mechanisms for dynamically discovering available services in a network. For example, a washing machine may search for a loudspeaker service and use it to play a sound once the washing is complete. In this scenario, the washing machine includes a SLP (Service Location Protocol) user agent and the speaker uses a UPnP (Universal Plug and Play) service agent to advertise its location and audio characteristics. UPnP is a wrapper for SSDP [3] and HTTP [4], which are used at different stages of the service discovery process.

From a multicast SLP SrvRQST service discovery request, the SLP/UPnP gateway extracts appropriate information, such as the service type, and sends a multicast SSDP SEARCH request. If a service is found, the UPnP service agent asynchronously returns a unicast SSDP response containing the URL of the service description to the gateway. Then, the gateway extracts the URL and sends a unicast HTTP GET request to it to retrieve the service description as

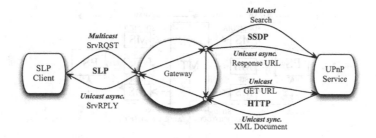

Fig. 3. SLP to UPnP gateway

an XML document. Finally, the gateway extracts information from the XML document and creates an SLP `SrvRPLY` response, which it returns to the SLP client. This gateway must manage both multicast and unicast requests, and synchronous and asynchronous responses. Mixing the translation logic with these underlying protocol details complicates the development of the gateway code.

3 Specifying a Gateway Using Z2z

As illustrated in Section 2, a gateway receives a single request from the source device, translates it into one or a series of requests for one or more target devices, and then returns a response to the source device. It may additionally need to save some state when the source protocol has a notion of session that is different from that used by the target protocol, or when the interaction with the target device(s) produces some information that is needed by subsequent source requests.

Our case studies show that there are two main challenges to developing such a gateway: (1) manipulating messages and maintaining session state, to deal with the problem of mismatched protocol expressiveness, and (2) managing the interaction with the network, to deal with the problem of heterogeneous communication methods. In z2z, these are addressed through the combination of a DSL that allows the gateway developer to describe the translation between two or more protocols in a high-level way, and a runtime system that provides network interaction and data management facilities specific to the domain of gateway development. We describe the DSL in this section, and present the architecture of the runtime system in the next section.

3.1 Overview of the z2z Language

To create a gateway, the developer must provide three kinds of information: 1) how each protocol interacts with the network, 2) how messages are structured, and 3) the translation logic. To allow each kind of information to be expressed in a simple way, z2z provides a specific kind of module for each of them: protocol specification (PS) modules for defining the characteristics of protocols, message specification (MS) modules for describing the structure of protocol messages,

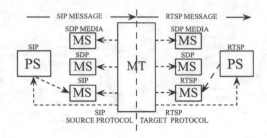

Fig. 4. The structure of a z2z gateway specification (arrows represent dependencies)

and a message translation (MT) module for defining how to translate messages between protocols. These modules are implemented using the z2z DSL, which hides the complexities of network programming and allows specifying the relevant operations in a clear and easily verifiable way.

As illustrated in Section 2, a gateway may involve any number of protocols. Thus, a gateway specification may contain multiple protocol specification modules and message specification modules, according to the number of protocols and message types involved. A gateway specification always contains a single message translation module. Fig. 4 shows the architecture of the SIP/RTSP gateway in terms of its use of these modules. We now present these modules in more detail, using this gateway as an example.

3.2   Protocol Specification Module

The protocol specification module defines the properties of a protocol that a gateway should use when sending or receiving requests or responses. As illustrated in Fig. 5 for the SIP protocol, this module declares the following information.

Attributes. Protocols vary in their interaction with the network, in terms of the transport protocol used, whether requests are sent by unicast or by multicast, and whether responses are received synchronously or asynchronously. The **attributes** block of the protocol specification module indicates which combination is desired. Based on this information, the runtime system provides appropriate services. For example, SIP relies on UDP (**transport** attribute, line 2), sends requests in unicast (**mode** attribute, line 2), and receives responses asynchronously. If the transmission mode is asynchronous, the protocol specification must also include a **flow** block (line 9) describing how to match requests to responses.

Request. The entry point of a gateway is the reception of a request. On receiving a request, the gateway dispatches it to the appropriate handler in the message translation module. The **request** block (lines 3-6) of the protocol specification module declares how to map messages to handlers. For each kind of request

```
1    protocol sip {
2      attributes { transport = udp/5060; mode = async/unicast; }
3      request req {
4        response invite when req.method == "INVITE";
5        response bye when req.method == "BYE";
6        void ack      when req.method == "ACK"; }
7      sending request req { ... }
8      sending response resp (request req) { resp.cseq = req.cseq; resp.callid = req.callid; ... }
9      flow = { callid, cseq }
10     session_flow = { callid } }
```

Fig. 5. The PS module for the SIP protocol

that should be handled by the gateway, the **request** block indicates the name
of the handler (**invite**, **bye**, and **ack**, for SIP), whether the request should be
acknowledged by a response (**response** if a response is allowed and **void** if no
response is needed), and a predicate, typically defined in terms of the fields of
the request, indicating whether a request should be sent to the given handler.

Sending. A protocol typically defines certain basic information that all messages
must contain. Rather than requiring the developer to specify this information
in each handler, this information is specified in a **sending** block for each of
requests and responses. The **sending** block for requests is parameterized by only
the request, while the **sending** block for responses is parameterized by both the
corresponding request and the response, allowing elements of the response to be
initialized according to information stored in the request. For example, the SIP
sending block for responses copies the **cseq** and **callid** fields from the request
to the response (line 8). The protocol specification module may declare local
variables in which to accumulate information over the treatment of all messages.

Flow and session_flow. When a target protocol sends responses asynchronously,
an incoming response must be associated with a previous request, to restart the
associated handler. The **flow** block (line 9), specifies the message elements that
determine this association. In SIP, a request and its matching response have the
same sequence number (**cseq**) and call id (**callid**). A **session_flow** block (line
10) similarly specifies how to recognize messages associated with a session.

The information in the protocol specification module impacts operations that
are typically scattered throughout the gateway. In providing the protocol specification module as a language abstraction, we have identified the elements of the
protocol definition that are relevant to gateway construction and collected them
into one easily understandable unit. Furthermore, creating a protocol specification module is lightweight, involving primarily selecting properties rather than
implementing their support, making it easy to incorporate many different kinds
of protocols into a single gateway, as illustrated by the SLP/UPnP gateway
described in Section 2.

3.3   Message Specification Module

A network message is organized as a sequence of text lines, or of bits, for a binary protocol, containing both fixed elements and elements specific to a given message. A gateway must extract relevant elements from the received request and use them to create one or more requests according to the target protocol(s). Similarly, it must extract relevant elements from the received responses and ultimately create a response according to the source protocol. Extracting values from a message represented as a sequence of text or binary characters is unwieldy, and creating messages is even more complex, because the element values may become available at different times, making it difficult to predict the message size and layout.

In z2z, the message specification module contains a description of the messages that can be received and created by a gateway. Based on this description, the z2z compiler generates code for accessing message elements and inserting message elements into a created message. There is one message specification module per protocol relevant to the gateway, including both the source and target protocols, as represented by the protocol specification modules, and one per any higher level message type that can be embedded in the requests and responses. For example, the SIP/RTSP camera gateway uses not only SIP and RTSP message specification modules but also message specification modules for SDP Media and SDP, which are not associated with protocol specification modules.

A message specification module provides a *message view* describing the relevant elements of incoming messages and *templates* for creating new messages. The set of elements is typically specific to the purpose of the gateway, not generic to the protocol, and thus the message specification module is separate from the protocol specification module. We illustrate the declarations of the message view and the templates in the SIP message specification module used in our camera gateway.

Message view. A message view describes the information derived from received messages that is useful to the gateway. It thus represents the interface between the gateway and the message parser. Z2z does not itself provide facilities for creating message parsers, but instead makes it possible to plug in one of the many existing network message parsers[2] or to construct one by hand or using a parser generator targeting network protocols, such as Zebu [5].

Because SIP is the source protocol of the camera gateway, its message view describes the information contained in a SIP request. An excerpt of the declaration of this view is shown in Fig. 6a. It consists of a sequence of field declarations, analogous to the declaration of a C-language structure. A field declaration indicates whether the field is mandatory or optional, whether it is public or private, its type, and its name. A field is mandatory if the protocol RFC specifies that it is always present, and optional otherwise. A field is public if it can be read by

---

[2] oSIP: http://www.gnu.org/software/osip
  Sofia-SIP: http://opensource.nokia.com/projects/sofia-sip/
  Livemedia: http://www.livemediacast.net/about/library.cfm

```
 1  read {
 2      mandatory private int cseq;
 3      mandatory private fragment callid;
 4      mandatory private fragment via;
 5      mandatory private fragment to;
 6      mandatory private fragment from;
 7      mandatory private fragment method;
 8
 9      optional private fragment to_tag;
10      optional private int cseqsss;
11
12      mandatory public fragment uri, body;
13      mandatory public fragment from_host;
14  }
```
a) View of SIP requests

```
 1  response template Invite_ok {
 2      magic = "foo";
 3      newline = "\r\n";
 4      private fragment from, to, callid, via, contact;
 5      private int cseq, content_length;
 6      public fragment body, to_tag;
 7  --foo
 8  SIP/2.0 200 OK
 9  Via: <%via%>
10  [...]
11  Content−Length: <%content_length%>
12
13  <%body%>
14  --foo }
```
b) Template for an INVITE method success response

Fig. 6. SIP message specification for the camera gateway

the gateway logic, and private if it can only be read by the protocol specification. The type of a field is either integer, fragment, or a list of one of these types. A field of type fragment is represented as a string, but the gateway logic can cause it to be parsed as a message of another protocol, such as SDP or SDP Media, in our example.

Templates. Z2z maintains messages to be created as a pair of a template view and a template. The template language is adapted from that of Repleo [6]. A message is created in the message translation module by making a new copy of the template view, and initializing its fields, in any order. At a send or return operation in the message translation module, the template representing the message is flushed, filling its holes with the corresponding values from the view.

Because SIP is the source protocol of our camera gateway, its templates describe the information needed to create SIP responses. Typically, there are multiple response templates for each method, with one template for each relevant success and failure condition. Fig. 6b shows the template for a response indicating the success of an INVITE request.

A template declaration has three parts: the structural declarations (lines 2-3), the template view (lines 4-6), and the template text (lines 7-14). The structural declarations indicate a string, **magic**, marking the start and end of the template text, and the line separator, **newline**, specified by the protocol RFC. The template view is analogous to the message view, except that the keywords **mandatory** and **optional** are omitted, as all fields are mandatory to create a message. The private fields are filled in by the **sending** block of the protocol specification. The public fields are filled in by the message translation module. Finally, the template text has the form of a message as specified by the protocol RFC, with holes delimited by **<%** and **%>**. These holes refer to the fields of the template view, and are instantiated with the values of these fields when the template is flushed. Binary templates, as needed for SLP messages in our service discovery gateway (Section 2), can be defined, using the keyword **binary**.

```
 1  fragment session_id = "";                      32  if ((rtsp_m.type == sip_m.type) &&
 2                                                  33       (rtsp_m.profile == sip_m.profile)) {
 3  sip response invite (sip request s) {           34  // Found something compatible
 4    rtsp response rr;                             35  if (empty(rtsp_m.control))
 5    sip response sr, failed;                      36    return failed;
 6    sdp_media message rtsp_m, sip_m, media_resp;  37  // Specify the transport mechanism
 7    sdp message sdp_rtsp, sdp_sip, sdp_resp;      38  rr = send(Setup(uri=rtsp_m.control,
 8    fragment list inv_medias, rtsp_medias;        39                   destination=s.from_host,
 9                                                  40                   port1=sip_m.port,
10    // Create error response                      41                   port2=sip_m.port+1));
11    failed=Invite_failure(code=400,to_tag=random()); 42  if (empty(rr.sessionId) ||
12                                                  43       empty(rr.code) || rr.code > 299)
13    sdp_rtsp = (sdp message)(s.body);             44    return failed;
14    inv_medias = (fragment list)(sdp_rtsp.medias); 45  session_start();
15                                                  46  session_id = rr.sessionId;
16    // Notify that something is happening          47  // Tell the server to start sending data
17    preturn Invite_provisional(body = "",         48  rr = send(Play(resource = s.uri_uname,
18                  to_tag = random());             49                 sessionId = session_id));
19                                                  50  if (empty(rr.code) || rr.code > 299) {
20    // Retrieve the description of a media object  51    session_end(); return failed; }
21    rr = send(Describe(resource = s.uri_uname));  52  media_resp = Media(type = sip_m.type,
22    if (empty(rr.body)) return failed;            53                     profile = sip_m.profile);
23    sdp_sip = (sdp message)(rr.body);             54  if (empty(rr.server_port))
24    rtsp_medias = (fragment list)(sdp_sip.medias); 55    media_resp.port = 0;
25                                                  56  else media_resp.port = rr.server_port;
26    // See whether a compatible video format exists 57  sdp_resp = Sdp_media(header=
27    foreach (fragment rtsp_m_ = rtsp_medias) {    58      sdp_rtsp.header,media=media_resp);
28      rtsp_m = (sdp_media message)rtsp_m_;        59  return Invite_ok(body = sdp_resp,
29      if (rtsp_m.type == "video") {               60                   to_tag = random());
30        foreach (fragment sip_m_ = inv_medias) {  61  }}}}
31          sip_m = (sdp_media message)sip_m_;      62  return failed; }
```

Fig. 7. The INVITE handler of the message translation module for the camera gateway

3.4 Message Translation Module

The message translation module expresses the message translation logic, which is the heart of the gateway. This module consists of a set of handlers, one for each kind of relevant incoming request, as indicated by the protocol specification module. Handlers are written using a C-like notation augmented with domain-specific operators for manipulating and constructing messages, for sending requests and returning responses, and for session management. Fig. 7 shows the invite handler for the camera gateway.

Manipulating message data. A handler is parameterized by a view of the corresponding request. The information in the view can be extracted using the standard structure field access notation (line 13). If a view element is designated as being optional in the message specification module, it must be tested using empty to determine whether its value is available before it is used (line 22). A view element of type fragment can be cast to a message type, using the usual type cast notation. In line 23, for example, the body of the request is cast to an SDP message, which is then manipulated according to its view (line 24).

A handler creates a message by invoking the name of the corresponding template (line 17). Keyword arguments can be used to initialize the various fields (lines 17-18) or the fields can be filled in incrementally (lines 54-56). A created message is maintained as a view during the execution of the handler and flushed to a network message at the point of a send or return operation.

Sending requests and returning responses. A request is sent using the operator **send**, as illustrated in line 38. If the protocol specification module for the corresponding target protocol indicates that a response is expected, then execution pauses until a response is received, and the response is the result of the **send** operation. If the protocol specification indicates that no response is expected, **send** returns immediately. There is no need for the developer to break the handler up into a collection of callback functions to receive asynchronous responses, as is required in most other languages used for gateway programming. Instead, the difference between synchronous and asynchronous responses is handled by the z2z compiler, as described in Section 4. This strategy makes it easy to handle the case where the gateway must translate a single request from the source device into multiple requests for the target device, requiring multiple **send** operations.

If the protocol specification module indicates a return type for a handler, then the handler may return a response. This is done using **return** (line 59), which takes as argument a message and terminates execution of the handler. A provisional response, as is needed in SIP to notify the source device that a message is being treated, can be returned using **preturn** (line 17). This operator asynchronously returns the specified message, and handler execution continues.

Session management. A session is a state that is maintained over a series of messages. If the protocol specification module for the source protocol declares how messages should be mapped to sessions (**session_flow**), then the message translation module may declare variables associated with a session outside of any handler. The camera gateway, for example, declares the session variable **session_id** in line 1. The message translation module initiates a session using **session_start()** (line 45). Once the session has started any modification made to these variables persists across requests within the session, until the session is ended using **session_end()**. At this point, all session memory is freed. The SMTP/HTTP/SMTP gateways described in Section 2 similarly use sessions to maintain the TCP connection identifier across multiple requests.

4 Implementation

Our implementation of the z2z gateway generator comprises a compiler for the z2z language and a runtime system. From the z2z specification of a gateway, the z2z compiler generates C code that can then be compiled using a standard C compiler and linked with the runtime system. The generated code is portable enough to run on devices ranging from desktop computers to constrained devices such as PDAs or home appliances. The runtime system defines various utility functions and amounts to about 7500 lines of C code. The z2z compiler is around 10500 of OCaml code. Note that the compiler can be used offline to produce the gateway code and therefore is not required to be present on the gateway device. We first describe the verifications performed by the compiler, then present the main challenges in code generation, and finally present the runtime system.

4.1   Verifications

The z2z compiler performs consistency checks and dataflow analyses to detect erroneous specifications and to ensure the generation of safe gateway code.

Consistency checks. As was shown in Fig. 4, there are various dependencies between the modules making up a z2z gateway. The z2z compiler performs a number of consistency checks to ensure that the information declared in one module is used elsewhere according to its declaration. The main inter-module dependencies are derived from the **request** and **sending** blocks of the protocol specification and the types and visibilities of the elements of the message views. The **request** block associated with the source protocol declares how to dispatch incoming requests to the appropriate handlers and whether a response is expected from these handlers. The z2z compiler checks that the message translation module defines a handler for each kind of message that should be handled by the gateway and that each handler has an appropriate return type. The **sending** block of a protocol specification module initializes some fields for all requests or responses sent using that protocol. The compiler checks that every template view defined in the corresponding message specification module includes all of these fields. Finally, the message specification module indicates for each field of a view the type of value that the field can contain and whether the field can be accessed by the message translation module (**public**) or only by the protocol specification module (**private**). The z2z compiler checks that the fields are only used in the allowed module and that every access or update has the declared type.

Dataflow analyses. The z2z compiler performs a dataflow analysis within the message translation module to ensure that values are well-defined when they are used. The principal issues are in the use of optional message fields, session variables, and created messages. A message specification module may declare some message fields as **optional**, indicating that they may be uninitialized. The z2z compiler enforces that any reference to such a field is preceded by an **empty** check. Session variables cannot be used before a **session_start** operation or after a **session_end** operation. The z2z compiler checks that references to these variables do not occur outside these boundaries. Finally, the z2z compiler checks that all public fields of a template are initialized before the template is passed to **send** and that all execution paths through the **sending** block of the corresponding protocol specification module initialize all **private** fields.

4.2   Code Generation

The main challenges in generating code from a z2z specification are the implementation of the **send** operation, the implementation of the variables used by the message translation module, and the implementation of memory management.

The **send** *operation.* The handlers of a z2z message translation module are specified as sequential functions, with **send** having the syntax of a function call that may return a value. If the target protocol returns responses synchronously, the z2z compiler does indeed implement **send** as an ordinary function call. If the target protocol returns responses asynchronously, however, this treatment is not sufficient. In this case, the implementation of **send** does not return a value, but must instead receive as an argument information about the rest of the handler so that the handler can be restarted when a response becomes available. The standard solution is to decompose the code into a collection of callback functions, which are tedious, error-prone, and unintuitive to write by hand. Fortunately, it has been observed that such callback functions amount to *continuations*, which can be created systematically [7]. The z2z compiler thus splits each handler at the point of each **send** to create a collection of functions, of which the first represents the entry point of the handler and the rest represent some continuation.

Fig. 8 illustrates the splitting of a handler performed by the z2z compiler when the target protocol of a **send** returns responses asynchronously. This code contains three **send** operations, one on line s1 and the others in each of the if branches (lines s2 and s3). The continuation function for the **send** on line s1 contains the code in the region labeled (2). The continuation function for the **send** on line s2 contains the code in region (3) and the one for the **send** on line s3 contains the code in region (4). As shown, the latter two continuation functions explicitly contain only the code within the corresponding if branch. The execution of the handler must, however, continue to the code following the if statement, which is in the continuation of both **send** operations. To reduce the code size, the z2z compiler fac-

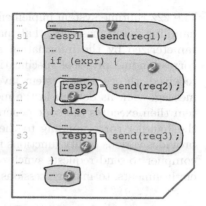

Fig. 8. Code slicing for continuations

torizes the code after the if statement into a separate continuation function, labeled (5), which is invoked by both (3) and (4) after executing the if branch code [8].

Variables. Splitting a handler into a set of disjoint continuation functions in the asynchronous case complicates the implementation of the handler's local variables when these variables are used across **send**s and thus by multiple continuations. The z2z compiler identifies handler variables whose values must be maintained across asynchronous **send**s, and implements them as elements of an environment structure that such a **send** passes to the runtime system. The runtime system stores this environment, and passes it back to the stored continuation function when the corresponding response is received.

Session variables are similarly always implemented in an environment structure, as by design they must be maintained across multiple invocations of the message translation module. Between handler invocations, the runtime system stores this environment with the other information about the session.

Dynamic memory management. Template constructors dynamically allocate memory, analogous to Java's **new** operation. This memory may be referenced from arbitrary local and session variables of the message translation module, and must be freed when no longer useful. Had we translated z2z into a garbage collected language such as Java, then we could rely on the garbage collector to free this memory. We have, however, used C, to avoid the overhead of including a fully-featured runtime system such as the JVM. To avoid the risk of dangling pointers, the z2z compiler generates code to manage reference counts [9]. An alternative, for future work, is to use a garbage collector for C code [10].

4.3 Runtime System

The z2z runtime system implements a network server capable of simultaneously handling many messages, that may rely on various protocols. The server is parameterized by the information specific to each protocol, as provided in the corresponding protocol specification module (Section 3.2). When a message is received, the runtime system invokes the corresponding parser to construct a message view as defined in the message specification module. The runtime system then executes the code generated from the message translation module for the handler corresponding to the incoming request. The runtime system also provides various utility functions that are used by the code generated by the z2z compiler to send requests synchronously or asynchronously, to save and restore environments, to manage sessions, and to perform various other operations.

Receiving network messages. The z2z runtime system is designed to efficiently juggle many incoming requests simultaneously. It is multithreaded, based on the use of a single main thread and a pool of worker threads. The main thread detects an incoming connection, and then assigns the processing of this connection to an available worker thread. The pool of worker threads avoids the high overhead that would be entailed by spawning a new thread per connection, and thus contributes to the overall efficiency of the approach. It furthermore avoids the mutex contention that would be incurred by the use of global shared variables. The z2z developer does not need to be aware of these details.

TCP poses further challenges. In this case, a stream of messages arrives within a single connection. Depending on the protocol, substantial computation may be required to isolate the individual messages within a stream. To avoid dropping messages, the main thread assigns two worker threads to a TCP connection. One, the *producer*, receives data from the incoming TCP stream and separates it into messages, while the other, the *consumer*, applies the gateway logic. These threads communicate via shared memory. When the producer has extracted a message from the incoming stream, it sends a signal to the consumer, which then reads the message in the shared memory and processes it. On completion, it sends a signal to the producer. This approach allows the main thread to multiplex I/O on a set of server sockets to provide gateway service to multiple devices.

Network protocol gateways furthermore must manage multiple concurrent connections between many devices. This adds significantly to the complexity of the gateway implementation. For example, to communicate with a device that uses SMTP, multiple requests must be sent inside the same TCP connection, while for a RTSP device each request requires the creation of a new TCP connection. The z2z runtime system hides these details from the gateway developer. As illustrated by the HTTP/SMTP example, the runtime system must keep open the TCP connection used to send SMTP requests even if incoming requests are responded to asynchronously. However, in this case, subsequent incoming requests are not related to each other and the runtime system needs to know which TCP connection to use. To address this issue, the runtime system maintains a table of current active TCP connections and provides references to them, so that they can be retrieved later. The runtime system can also seamlessly switch from IPv4 to IPv6, send messages in unicast or multicast, and use UDP or one or many TCP connections, as specified by attributes in the protocol specification module, without requiring any additional programming from the gateway developer.

Processing a message. When a thread is assigned the processing of a message, it executes the message parser of the corresponding protocol to construct a message view, as described in Section 3.3. Then, it calls the `dispatch` function, generated by the z2z compiler from the PS module, to select the handler to execute. If a handler sends requests asynchronously, the runtime system explicitly suspends the control flow and saves the current continuation, handler state, and session state in a global shared memory. The local memory allocated for the current thread is freed and the thread returns to the main pool. When a response is received by the main thread, the runtime system assigns its processing to an available worker thread, restores the corresponding states and continuation, and execution of the handler continues.

5   Evaluation

To assess our approach, we have implemented the SIP/RTSP, SLP/UPnP, SMTP/HTTP and HTTP/SMTP gateways described in the case studies of Section 2. In the latter case, although our experiments use HTTP over UDP or TCP for the encapsulation, it is possible to use other protocols such as SIP over UDP. We have implemented our gateways on a Single Board Computer (SBC) to represent the kind of limited but inexpensive or energy-efficient devices that are found in PDAs, mobile devices and home appliances. We use a Eukréa CPUAT91 card,[3] based on a 200 MHz ARM9 processor. The SBC has 32MB of SDRAM, 8MB of flash memory, an Ethernet controller, and runs a minimal Linux 2.6.20 kernel. For the SIP/RTSP experiment, we use the open-source Linphone videophone client[4] and an Axis RTSP camera. For the SLP/UPnP experiment, we

---

[3] Eukréa. http://www.eukrea.com/
[4] Linphone: http://www.linphone.org/

		Input specification (lines of z2z code)			Parser wrapper (lines of C code)	Z2z gateway (size in KB)		
		PS	MS	MT	Parser or wrapper	Generated modules	Runtime system	Total
SIP/RTSP		SIP	24	118		168			
		RTSP	20	104	102	210	72	80	152
		SDP	-	12		52			
		SDP_media	-	15		83			
SLP/UPnP		SLP	12	21		166			
		SSDP	6	31	5	223	44	80	124
		HTTP	9	43		178			
SMTP/HTTP	UDP	SMTP	10	23	83	96	40		120
		HTTP	9	92		103			
	TCP alive	SMTP	10	23	71	96	36	80	116
		HTTP	9	64		105			
	TCP non-alive	SMTP	10	23	83	96	36		
		HTTP	9	92		114			
HTTP/SMTP	UDP	HTTP	9	43	69	160	32		112
		SMTP	10	23		44			
	TCP alive	HTTP	9	43	63	488	36	80	116
		SMTP	10	23		34			
	TCP non-alive	HTTP	9	43	75	190	32		112
		SMTP	10	23		44			

Fig. 9. The size of the input specifications and the generated gateway

use a handcrafted SLP client based on the INDISS framework [11] and a UPnP service provided by CyberLink.[5] For the SMTP/HTTP/SMTP experiment, we use the multi-threaded SMTP test client and server distributed with Postfix [12] to stress the generated gateways.

Fig. 9 shows the size of the various specifications that must be provided to generate each gateway. A protocol specification module is independent of the targeted gateway and thus can be shared by all gateways relevant to the protocol. The message translation module for the SLP/UPnP gateway is particularly simple, being only 5 lines of code. Indeed, the complete z2z specification for this gateway is less than 100 lines of code. As described in Section 3.3, the message specification module must provide a parser for incoming messages. For our experiments, we have implemented simple parsers for each message type, amounting to at most 488 lines of C code. Each of the generated gateways does not exceed, in the worst case, 150KB of compiled C code, including 80KB for the runtime system.

Fig. 10 shows the response time for the SIP/RTSP, SLP/UPnP, and SMTP/-HTTP/SMTP gateways, as well as the native protocol communication costs. In each case, at the client side we measure the time from sending an initial request to receiving a successful response. These experiments were performed using the loopback interface to remove network latency. As illustrated in Fig. 10(a), the z2z implementation of the SIP/RTSP gateway does not introduce any overhead as compared to an ideal case of zero-cost message translation, since its response time is less than the sum of the response times for SIP and RTSP separately. The response time for the SLP/UPnP gateway is a little more than that of SLP and UPnP separately. The cost of the z2z gateway is due in part to the polling done by the main thread in the case of asynchronous responses, as described in Section 4.3. This strategy introduces some time overhead, but reduces memory requirements. The response time for UPnP, furthermore, depends heavily on the

---

[5] CyberLink: http://www.cybergarage.org/net/upnp/java/

Native service access

	SIP↔SIP	RTSP↔RTSP
Time	351	701

	SLP↔SLP	UPnP↔UPnP
Time	2	58

Z2z

	SIP/RTSP	SLP/UPnP
Time	986	78

(a)

Native service access - SMTP/SMTP

Nb client	Mail size (KB)	Nb Mail	Time
1	1	1	10
1	10	1	10
1	10	10	15
10	10	10	15

Z2z - SMTP/HTTP/SMTP

	Nb client	Mail size (KB)	Nb Mail	Time	increase factor
UDP	1	1	1	50	5
	1	10	1	65	6.5
	1	10	10	645	43
	10	10	10	146	9.7
TCP alive	1	1	1	48	4.8
	1	10	1	50	5
	1	10	10	410	27.3
	10	10	10	98	6.5
TCP non-alive	1	1	1	53	5.3
	1	10	1	53	5.3
	1	10	10	400	26.6
	10	10	10	111	7.4

(b)

Fig. 10. Native service access vs. z2z (ms)

stack that is used. If we use a Siemens stack[6] rather than the CyberLink stack, the native UPnP time rises to 593ms, substantially higher than the gateway cost.

Fig. 10(b) shows the performance of the gateways generated in order to tunnel SMTP traffic into HTTP. We consider three types of tunnel according to the nature of transport layer protocol being used to exchange either asynchronously (i.e. UDP or $TCP_{non\text{-}alive}$) or synchronously (i.e. TCP_{alive}) messages between the two tunnel end-points. When sending one e-mail, with a size from 1KB up to 10 KB, passing through a HTTP tunnel roughly increases the native response time by a factor of 5 whatever the tunnel considered. This overhead comes primarily from the mailing process. According to the SMTP RFC5321, sending an e-mail involves sending at least 5 SMTP commands and acknowledgements, of at most 512 bytes each, and splitting the mail content in order to send chunks of at most 998 bytes. Commands, acknowledgements, and data chunks are packets that need to be encapsulated into the HTTP protocol and de-encapsulated on both sides of the HTTP tunnel. Increasing the number of packets being encapsulated at tunnel end-points inherently increases the response time. Our experimental results show that sending a sequence of 10 emails increases the response times at most by 43 as compared to a native implementation in the worst case. However, when the mail is sent in parallel (10 clients), response times only increase by a factor of at most 10. The latter result highlights the efficiency of the parallelism provided by our generated gateways. Furthermore, note that the SMTP test server simply throws away without processing the messages received from network, whereas the tunnel end-points must process them, therefore increasing the response time. The native response time obtained with a real deployed SMTP server such as Postfix [12] may be up to 18x slower than the SMTP test server, which is much closer to the response times obtained via the generated gateways.

Finally, Fig. 11 shows the amount of dynamic memory used during the lifetime of each of our generated gateways. The memory footprint is directly related to

---

[6] Siemens UPnP: http://www.plug-n-play-technologies.com/

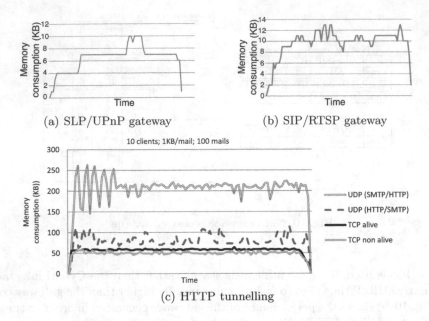

(a) SLP/UPnP gateway   (b) SIP/RTSP gateway

(c) HTTP tunnelling

Fig. 11. Dynamic memory consumption (KB)

the network input/output traffic. When idle, the memory consumption is low and does not exceed 2KB for the considered gateways. At peak time, both the SIP/-RTSP and SLP/UPnP gateways consume at most 14KB, as shown in Figs. 11(a) and 11(b). Comparatively, the SMTP/HTTP/SMTP gateways based on TCP use only at most 60KB to process 100 1KB mails sent by 10 simultaneous clients. However, the memory consumption of the UDP-based gateway may reach up to 159KB-260KB as shown in Fig. 11(c). This overhead is inherent in the use of UDP, as a dedicated 1500 byte buffer is allocated for each incoming UDP packet. TCP, on the other hand, enables reading variable-size messages into a stream.

6   Related Work

Other approaches to interoperability. The middlewares ReMMoC [13], RUNES [14], MUSDAC [15], and BASE [16] for use in networked devices allow the device code to be developed independently of the underlying protocol. Plug-ins then select the most appropriate communication protocol according to the context. Many applications, however, have not been developed using such middleware systems and cannot be modified because their source code is not available.

Bridges provide interoperability without code modification. Direct bridges, such as RMI-IIOP[7] and IIOP-.NET,[8] provide interoperability between two fixed

---

[7] RMI-IIOP:http://java.sun.com/products/rmi-iiop/
[8] IIOP-.NET: http://iiop-net.sourceforge.net/index.html

protocols. A direct bridge must thus be developed separately for every pair of protocols between which interaction is needed. The diversity of protocols that are used in a networked home implies that this is a substantial development task. Indirect bridges such as Enterprise Service Buses (ESBs) [1], translate messages to and from a single fixed intermediary protocol. This approach reduces the development effort, but may limit expressiveness, as some aspects of the relevant protocols may not be compatible with the chosen intermediary protocol. INDISS [11] and NEMESYS [17] also use a single intermediary protocol, but one that is specific to the protocols between which interoperability is desired. Still, none of these approaches addresses the problem of implementing the bridge, which requires a thorough knowledge of the protocols involved and low-level network programming. This makes it difficult to quickly integrate devices that use an unsupported protocol into a home environment.

Z2z can be used in the context of either direct or indirect bridges. Our approach targets the weak point of both: the difficulty of bridge development. We propose a high-level interface definition language that abstracts away from network details, makes relevant protocol properties explicit, provides static verification at the specification level, and automatically generates low-level code.

Compilation. Z2z uses a number of advanced compilation techniques to be able to provide a high-level notation while still generating safe and efficient code. Krishnamurthi *et al.* [7] pioneered the use of continuations to overcome the asynchrony common in web programming. Our implementation of continuations in C code is based on that presented by Friedman *et al.* [18]. Our dataflow analysis uses standard techniques [19], adapted to the operations of the z2z DSL. Finally, reference counting has long been used to replace garbage collection [9].

7   Conclusion and Future Work

In this paper, we have presented a generative language-based approach, z2z to simplify gateway construction, a problem that has not been considered by previous frameworks for gateway development. Z2z is supported by a runtime system that hides low-level networking intricacies and a compiler that checks essential correctness properties and produces efficient code. We have used z2z to automatically generate gateways between SIP and RTSP, between SLP and UPnP, and between SMTP and SMTP via HTTP. The gateway specifications are 100-400 lines of z2z code while the generated gateways are at most 150KB of compiled C code and run with a runtime memory footprint of less than 260KB, with essentially no runtime overhead.

We are currently extending the z2z approach to generate code that can be deployed on existing middleware systems such as ReMMoC [13]. We are also exploring the extension of z2z to enable dynamic adaptation of gateway code according to context information. Following our approach, there are a number of other application areas to explore in the future, including Web services and network supervision. These new application areas should enable us to further refine our language, compiler and runtime system. Finally, we are considering how z2z can efficiently handle failures within the participants of an interaction. To address this issue, we are defining language extensions to specify failure recovery policies and runtime primitives to support these new features.

Availability. Source code: http://www.labri.fr/perso/reveille/projects/z2z/

References

1. Chappell, D.: Enterprise Service Bus. O'Reilly, Sebastopol (2004)
2. Perkins, C.: RTP - Audio and Video for the Internet. Addison-Wesley, Reading (2003)
3. Goland, Y.Y., Cai, T., Leach, P., Gu, Y.: Simple service discovery protocol/1.0: Operating without an arbiter (October 1999),
   http://quimby.gnus.org/internet-drafts/draft-cai-ssdp-v1-03.txt
4. Fielding, R., Gettys, J., Mogul, J., Frystyk, H., Masinter, L., Leach, P., Berners-Lee, T.: Hypertext Transfer Protocol – HTTP/1.1. RFC 2616 (Draft Standard) (June 1999) Updated by RFC 2817
5. Burgy, L., Réveillère, L., Lawall, J.L., Muller, G.: A language-based approach for improving the robustness of network application protocol implementations. In: 26th IEEE International Symposium on Reliable Distributed Systems, Beijing, October 2007, pp. 149–158 (2007)
6. Arnoldus, J., Bijpost, J., van den Brand, M.: Repleo: a syntax-safe template engine. In: GPCE 2007: Proceedings of the 6th international conference on Generative programming and component engineering, pp. 25–32. ACM, New York (2007)
7. Krishnamurthi, S., Hopkins, P.W., McCarthy, J., Graunke, P.T., Pettyjohn, G., Felleisen, M.: Implementation and use of the PLT Scheme web server. Higher-Order and Symbolic Computation 20(4), 431–460 (2007)
8. Steele Jr., G.L.: Lambda, the ultimate declarative. AI Memo 379, Artificial Intelligence Laboratory, Massachusetts Institute of Technology, Cambridge, Massachusetts (November 1976)
9. Cohen, J.: Garbage collection of linked data structures. ACM Computing Surveys 13(3), 341–367 (1981)
10. Boehm, H., Weiser, M.: Garbage collection in an uncooperative environment. Software Practice & Experience 18(9), 807–820 (1988)
11. Bromberg, Y.D., Issarny, V.: INDISS: Interoperable discovery system for networked services. In: Alonso, G. (ed.) Middleware 2005. LNCS, vol. 3790, pp. 164–183. Springer, Heidelberg (2005)
12. Hildebrandt, R., Koetter, P.: The book of Postfix: state-of-the-art message transport. NO-STARCH (2005), http://www.postfix.org/
13. Grace, P., Blair, G.S., Samuel, S.: A reflective framework for discovery and interaction in heterogeneous mobile environments. SIGMOBILE Mob. Comput. Commun. Rev. 9(1), 2–14 (2005)
14. Costa, P., Coulson, G., Mascolo, C., Mottola, L., Picco, G.P., Zachariadis, S.: Reconfigurable component-based middleware for networked embedded systems. International Journal of Wireless Information Networks 14(2), 149–162 (2007)
15. Raverdy, P.G., Issarny, V., Chibout, R., de La Chapelle, A.: A multi-protocol approach to service discovery and access in pervasive environments. In: The 3rd Annual International Conference on Mobile and Ubiquitous Systems: Networks and Services, San Jose, CA, USA, July 2006, pp. 1–9 (2006)

16. Becker, C., Schiele, G., Gubbels, H., Rothermel, K.: Base: A micro-broker-based middleware for pervasive computing. In: PERCOM 2003: Proceedings of the First IEEE International Conference on Pervasive Computing and Communications, Washington, DC, USA, p. 443. IEEE Computer Society, Los Alamitos (2003)
17. Bromberg, Y.D.: Solutions to middleware heterogeneity in open networked environment. Phd Thesis, INRIA/UVSQ (2006)
18. Friedman, D.P., Wand, M., Haynes, C.T.: Essentials of Programming Languages. MIT Press, Cambridge (1992)
19. Appel, A.: Modern Compiler Implementation in ML. Cambridge University Press, Cambridge (1998)

Heterogeneous Gossip

Davide Frey[2], Rachid Guerraoui[1], Anne-Marie Kermarrec[2], Boris Koldehofe[3], Martin Mogensen[4], Maxime Monod[1,*], and Vivien Quéma[5]

[1] Ecole Polytechnique Fédérale de Lausanne
[2] INRIA Rennes-Bretagne Atlantique
[3] University of Stuttgart
[4] University of Aarhus
[5] CNRS

Abstract. Gossip-based information dissemination protocols are considered easy to deploy, scalable and resilient to network dynamics. Load-balancing is inherent in these protocols as the dissemination work is evenly spread among all nodes. Yet, large-scale distributed systems are usually heterogeneous with respect to network capabilities such as bandwidth. In practice, a blind load-balancing strategy might significantly hamper the performance of the gossip dissemination.

This paper presents HEAP, *HEterogeneity-Aware gossip Protocol*, where nodes dynamically adapt their contribution to the gossip dissemination according to their bandwidth capabilities. Using a continuous, itself gossip-based, approximation of relative bandwidth capabilities, HEAP dynamically leverages the most capable nodes by increasing their fanout, while decreasing by the same proportion that of less capable nodes. HEAP preserves the simple and proactive (churn adaptation) nature of gossip, while significantly improving its effectiveness. We extensively evaluate HEAP in the context of a video streaming application on a testbed of 270 PlanetLab nodes. Our results show that HEAP significantly improves the quality of the streaming over standard homogeneous gossip protocols, especially when the stream rate is close to the average available bandwidth.

1 Introduction

Gossip protocols are especially appealing in the context of large-scale dynamic systems. Initially introduced for maintaining replicated database systems [6], they are particularly useful for effective dissemination [1].

In the context of decentralized live streaming, for instance, gossip protocols [3,18,19] constitute an interesting alternative to classical mesh-based techniques for large-scale dynamic systems. While efficient under steady state, mesh-based solutions require sophisticated and sometimes expensive repair schemes to maintain possibly several dissemination paths in case of churn [17]. In the streaming

---

* Maxime Monod has been partially funded by the Swiss National Science Foundation with grant 20021-113825.

J.M. Bacon and B.F. Cooper (Eds.): Middleware 2009, LNCS 5896, pp. 42–61, 2009.

context, churn might be caused by failures, overloads, leaves and joins (e.g., users switching TV channels).

In a gossip protocol, each node periodically forwards every packet identifier it received to a subset of nodes picked uniformly at random. The size of this subset is called the *fanout*. Nodes subsequently request the packet whenever necessary. As no particular structure needs to be maintained, there is no need for a recovery protocol in case of churn, which is considered the norm rather than the exception. Robustness stems from the *proactive* and *random* selection of communication partners. This proactiveness is a major difference with respect to mesh-based techniques, relying on a rather static neighborhood, which *react* to churn by having every node select new neighbors after noticing malfunctions [17, 35]. In a sense, gossip-based protocols build extreme forms of mesh-based overlay networks with a continuously changing set of neighbors, and an ultimate splitting procedure where each packet is potentially disseminated through continuously changing dissemination paths, as opposed to explicit substream creation leading to multi-trees [4, 17, 35].

Gossip in action. Consider a stream of 600 kbps produced by a single source and intended to be disseminated to 270 PlanetLab nodes in a decentralized manner. Our preliminary experiments revealed the difficulty of disseminating through a static tree without any reconstruction even among 30 nodes. The static nature of the tree exacerbates the loss rate of UDP packets particularly in the presence of heavily loaded nodes, which may see their upload capabilities change by 20% from one experiment to the other. One might consider sophisticated reactive mechanisms to cope with the network dynamics but these are particularly challenging in highly dynamic environments.

Instead, we could obtain a good quality stream using a simple gossip protocol over all 270 PlanetLab nodes. Figure 1 reports on our experiments (which we

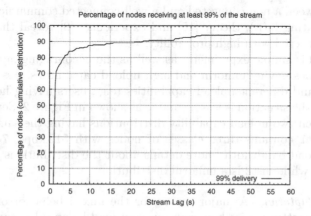

Fig. 1. Without constraining upload capabilities, a gossip with fanout 7 provides a stream of high quality and low lag to a large number of PlanetLab nodes

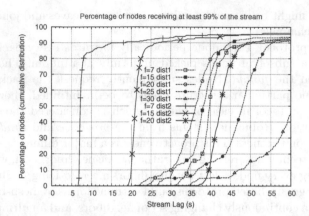

Fig. 2. When constraining the upload capability in a heterogeneous manner (with an average upload capability of 691kbps – dist1), the stream lag of all nodes significantly deteriorates. Adjusting the fanout (e.g., between 15 and 20) slightly improves the stream lag but a blind fanout increase (e.g., if it goes over 25) degrades performance. Moreover, the good fanout range in this case (fanouts of 15, 20 in dist1) reveals bad with a different distribution (uniform distribution - dist2) having the same average upload capability. With dist2, a fanout of 7 is optimal and much more effective than fanouts of 15 and 20.

detail later in the paper) by conveying a high *average delivery ratio* (the number of stream packets received over the total number of stream packets produced), and a low *stream lag* (the difference between the time the stream is produced at the source and the time it is viewed): 50% of the nodes receive 99% of the stream with a stream lag of 1.3 s, 75% of the nodes receive the same amount after 2.4 s and 90% after 21 s. The fanout considered here is 7. In a system of size n, and assuming a uniformly random peer selection, a fanout of $\ln(n)$ is the theoretical threshold between a non-connected and a well-connected communication graph. By overestimating $\ln(n)$, theory [15] and experiences [9] reveal that the graph gets fully connected with high probability.

However, this simple experiment, as well as the encouraging ones of [19,18], rely on all nodes having uniform and high upload capabilities. Assuming nodes with limited and different upload capabilities (e.g., users having heterogeneous bandwidths), the situation is less favorable as shown in Figure 2. Several fanouts are tested given two upload capability distributions having the same average of 691 kbps. Dist1 contains three classes of nodes with 512 kbps, 768 kbps, and 3 Mbps of upload bandwidth (more details about the distributions are provided in Section 3), while dist2 is a uniform distribution.

A case for adaptation. A major reason for the mixed behavior of gossip in a heterogeneous setting is its homogeneous and load-balanced nature. All nodes are supposed to disseminate the same number of messages for they rely on the same fanout and dissemination period. However, this uniform distribution of load ignores the intrinsic heterogeneous nature of large-scale distributed systems where nodes may exhibit significant differences in their capabilities. Interestingly, and as conveyed by our experiments (and pointed out in [7]), a gossip protocol does indeed adapt to heterogeneity to a certain extent. Nodes with high bandwidth gossip rapidly, get thus pulled more often and can indeed sustain the overload to a certain extent. Nevertheless, as the bandwidth distribution gets tighter (closer to the stream rate) and more skewed (rich nodes get richer whereas poor nodes get poorer), there is a limit on the adaptation that traditional homogeneous gossip can achieve.

Heterogeneous gossip. Echoing [2, 7, 17, 27, 29, 30], we recognize the need to account for the heterogeneity between peers in order to achieve a more effective dissemination. This poses important technical challenges in the context of a gossip-based streaming application. First, an effective dissemination protocol needs to dynamically track and reflect the changes of available bandwidth over time. Second, the robustness of gossip protocols heavily relies on the proactive and uniform random selection of target peers: biasing this selection could impact the average quality of dissemination and the robustness to churn. Finally, gossip is simple and thus easy to deploy and maintain; sophisticated extensions that account for heterogeneity could improve the quality of the stream, but they would render the protocol more complex and thus less appealing.

We propose a new gossip protocol, called *HEAP* (*HEterogeneity-Aware Gossip Protocol*), whose simple design follows from two observations. First, mathematical results on epidemics and empirical evaluations of gossip protocols convey the fact that the robustness of the dissemination is ensured as long as the *average* of all fanouts is in the order of $\ln(n)$ [15] (assuming the source has at least a fanout of 1). This is crucial because the fanout is an obvious knob to adapt the contribution of a node and account for heterogeneity. A node with an increased

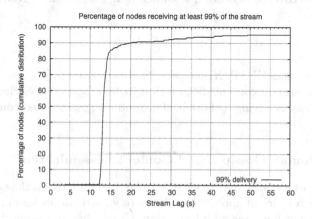

Fig. 3. With the same constrained distribution (dist1), HEAP significantly improves performance over a homogeneous gossip

(resp. decreased) fanout will send more (resp. less) information about the packets it can provide and in turn will be pulled more (resp. less) often. Second, using gossip dissemination, one can implement an aggregation protocol [13, 28] to continuously provide every node with a pretty accurate approximation of its relative bandwidth capability. Using such a protocol, HEAP dynamically leverages the most capable nodes by increasing their fanouts, while decreasing by the same proportion those of less capable nodes. HEAP preserves the simplicity and proactive (churn adaptation) nature of traditional (homogeneous) gossip, while significantly improving its effectiveness.

Applying HEAP in the PlanetLab context of Figure 2, i.e., assuming a heterogeneous bandwidth distribution exemplifying users using ADSL, we significantly improve streaming delay and quality (Figure 3). With an average fanout of 7, 50% of nodes receive 99% of the stream with 13.3 s lag, 75% with 14.1 s, and 90% with 19.5 s. More generally, we report on an exhaustive evaluation which shows that, when compared to a standard gossip, HEAP: *(i)* better matches the contributions of nodes to their bandwidth capabilities; *(ii)* enables a better usage of the overall bandwidth thus significantly improving the stream quality of all nodes and; *(iii)* significantly improves the resilience to churn.

Summary of contributions. We present HEAP, an information dissemination protocol that preserves the simplicity of standard gossip protocols, while significantly outperforming them with respect to the efficiency of streaming and resilience to churn. We also report on a full implementation of a P2P video streaming application using a proactive gossip protocol over a 270 PlanetLab node testbed with constrained and heterogeneous bandwidth distribution.

Roadmap. The rest of the paper is organized as follows. Section 2 gives some background on gossip-based content dissemination protocols and describes HEAP in detail. We report on the results of our experiments on PlanetLab in Section 3. Related work is covered in Section 4. Concluding remarks are given in Section 5.

2   HEAP

This section presents HEAP, *HEterogeneity-Aware Gossip Protocol*, a gossip protocol for collaborative content distribution in heterogeneous environments. We start this section by giving a short background on gossip-based content dissemination.

2.1   Background: Gossip-Based Content Dissemination

Consider a set of n nodes, and an event e to be disseminated in the system: e typically contains a series of application blocks (e.g., stream packets in a streaming application), as well as control information. Gossip-based content dissemination generally follows a three-phase push-request-push protocol as depicted in Algorithm 1. The use of a three-phase mechanism is essential when dealing with high payloads in that it guarantees that a packet may never be delivered more than once to the same node, thus causing the average data rate induced by the protocol to be less than or equal to the stream rate.

The protocol operates as follows. Each node periodically contacts a fixed number, f (fanout), of nodes chosen according to the selectNodes() function and proposes a set of event identifiers (ids) to them with a [PROPOSE] message (line 5 for the broadcaster and 6 for other nodes). A node receiving such a message pulls the content it has not yet retrieved by sending a [REQUEST] to the proposing peer. The peer being pulled sends back the actual content (the payload) in a [SERVE] message that contains the requested events. This procedure is then iterated according to an infect-and-die model [8]. Each node proposes each event id, exactly once, to f other peers, thus avoiding the need to deal with time-to-live.

Algorithm 1. Standard gossip protocol

Initialization:
1: $\bar{f} := \ln(n) + c$ {$\bar{f}$ *is the average fanout*}
2: eToPropose := eDelivered := eRequested := $\varnothing$
3: **start**(GossipTimer(gossipPeriod))

Phase 1 – Push event ids

procedure publish(e) **is**
4:    deliverEvent(e)
5:    gossip({$e.id$})

upon (GossipTimer mod gossipPeriod) = 0 **do**
6:    gossip(eToPropose)
7:    eToPropose := $\varnothing$ {*Infect and die*}

Phase 2 – Request events

upon receive [PROPOSE, eProposed] **do**
8:    wantedEvents := $\varnothing$
9:    **for all** $e.id \in$ eProposed **do**
10:       **if** ($e.id \notin$ eRequested) **then**
11:          wantedEvents := wantedEvents $\cup$ $e.id$
12:    eRequested := eRequested $\cup$ wantedEvents
13:    **reply** [REQUEST, wantedEvents]

Phase 3 – Push payload

upon receive [REQUEST, wantedEvents] **do**
14:    askedEvents := $\varnothing$
15:    **for all** $e.id \in$ wantedEvents **do**
16:       askedEvents := askedEvents $\cup$ event($e.id$)
17:    **reply** [SERVE, askedEvents]

upon receive [SERVE, events] **do**
18:    **for all** $e \in$ events **do**
19:       **if** ($e \notin$ eDelivered) **then**
20:          eToPropose := eToPropose $\cup$ $e.id$
21:          eDelivered := eDelivered $\cup$ e
22:          **deliver**(e)

Miscellaneous

function selectNodes(f) **returns** set of nodes **is**
23: **return** f uniformly random nodes

procedure gossip(event ids) **is**
24: commPartners := selectNodes(getFanout())
25: **for all** p $\in$ commPartners **do**
26:    **send**(p) [PROPOSE, event ids]

function getFanout() **returns** Integer **is**
27: **return** the fanout of gossip dissemination

As discussed in the introduction, standard gossip-based content dissemination works very well in unconstrained or otherwise homogeneous network environments, in which the load-balancing features of gossip provide the greatest benefit. Nevertheless, it becomes inefficient in constrained [9] and heterogeneous scenarios. In these, the standard homogeneous gossip described in Algorithm 1 stabilizes at a state in which low-capability nodes saturate their bandwidth, while high-capability ones are underutilized. This results in congested queues and increases the transmission delays introduced by low-capability nodes, impacting the overall performance experienced by all the nodes in the system.

2.2 Adapting Contribution

Algorithm 2. HEAP protocol details

Initialization:
1: capabilities := ∅
2: b := own available bandwidth
3: STDGOSSIP.**Initialization**
4: **start**(AggregationTimer(aggPeriod))

Fanout Adaptation

function getFanout() **returns** Integer **is**
5: **return** $b/\bar{b} \cdot \bar{f}$

Retransmission

upon receive [PROPOSE, eProposed] **do**
6: STDGOSSIP.**receive** [PROPOSE, eProposed]
7: **start**(RetTimer(retPeriod, eProposed))

upon receive [SERVE, events] **do**
8: STDGOSSIP.**receive** [SERVE, events]
9: **cancel**(RetTimer(retPeriod, events))

upon (RetTimer mod retPeriod) = 0 **do**
10: **receive** [PROPOSE, eProposed]

Aggregation Protocol

upon (AggregationTimer mod aggPeriod) = 0 **do**
11: commPartners := selectNodes($\bar{f}$)
12: **for all** p ∈ commPartners **do**
13:     fresh = 10 freshest values from capabilities
14:     **send**(p) [AGGREGATION, fresh]

upon receive [AGGREGATION, otherCap] **do**
15: merge otherCap into capabilities
16: update $\bar{b}$ using capabilities

HEAP addresses the limitations of standard gossip by preventing congestion at low-capability nodes through the adaptation of each node's workload. Consider two nodes A and B with upload capabilities b_A and b_B. HEAP adapts the contribution of each node to its capability and thus causes the upload rate resulting from node A's [SERVE] messages to be b_A/b_B times as large as that of node B.

Key to HEAP's adaptation mechanism is the fact that, in a non-congested setting, each [PROPOSE] message has roughly the same probability, p, to be accepted (thereby generating a subsequent [SERVE] message) regardless of the bandwidth capability of its sender[1]. HEAP exploits this fact to dynamically adapt the gossip fanouts of nodes so that their contribution to the stream delivery remains proportional to their available bandwidth. Specifically, because the average number of proposals accepted in each gossip round can be computed as $p \cdot f$, f being the fanout of the proposing node, we can derive that the fanout f_A of node A should be b_A/b_B times the fanout of node B.

$$f_A = \frac{b_A}{b_B} \cdot f_B \tag{1}$$

Preserving reliable dissemination. Interestingly, Equation (1) shows that determining the ratios between the fanouts of nodes is enough to predict their average contribution as the three phases of Algorithm 1 guarantee that the average upload rate[2] over all nodes is less than or equal to the stream rate. However, simply setting the fanouts of nodes to arbitrary values that satisfy Equation 1 may lead to undesired consequences. On the one hand, a low average fanout may hamper the ability of a gossip dissemination to reach all nodes. On the other hand, a large average fanout may unnecessarily increase the overhead resulting from the dissemination of [PROPOSE] messages.

HEAP strives to avoid these two extremes by relying on theoretical results showing that the reliability of gossip dissemination is actually preserved as long

---

[1] In reality, proposals from low-capability nodes incur in higher transmission delays and thus have a slightly lower probability of acceptance, but this effect is negligible when dealing with small [PROPOSE] messages in a non-congested setting.
[2] Not counting the overhead of [PROPOSE] and other messages.

as a fanout value of $\overline{f} = \ln(n) + c$, n being the size of the network, is ensured *on average* [15], regardless of the actual fanout distribution across nodes. To achieve this, HEAP exploits a simple gossip-based aggregation protocol (see Algorithm 2) which provides an estimate of the average upload capability $\overline{b}$ of network nodes. A similar protocol can be used to continuously approximate the size of the system [13], but, for simplicity, we consider here that the initial fanout is computed knowing the system size in advance. The aggregation protocol works by having each node periodically gossip its own capability and the freshest received capabilities. We assume a node's capability is either *(i)* a maximal capability given by the user at the application level (as the maximal outgoing bandwidth the user wants to give to the streaming application) or *(ii)* computed, when joining, by a simple heuristic to discover the nodes upload capability, e.g., starting with a very low-capability while trying to upload as much as possible in order to reach its maximal capability as proposed in [34]. Each node aggregates the received values and computes an estimate of the overall average capability. Based on this estimate, each node, p_i, regulates its fanout, f_{p_i}, according to the ratio between its own and the average capability, i.e., $f_{p_i} = \overline{f} \cdot b_{p_i}/\overline{b}$.

3   Evaluation

We report in this section on our evaluation of HEAP in the context of a video streaming application on a testbed of ~270 PlanetLab nodes. This includes a head-to-head comparison with a standard gossip protocol. In short, we show that, when compared to a standard gossip protocol: *(i)* HEAP adapts the actual load of each node to its bandwidth capability (Section 3.3), *(ii)* HEAP consistently improves the streaming quality of all nodes (Section 3.4), *(iii)* HEAP improves the stream lag from 40% to 60% over standard gossip (Section 3.5), *(iv)* HEAP resists to extreme churn situations where standard gossip collapses (Section 3.6). Before diving into describing these results in more details, we first describe our experimental setup.

3.1   Experimental Setup

Video streaming application. We generate stream packets of 1316 bytes at a stream rate of 551 kbps on average. Every *window* is composed of 9 *FEC-coded packets* and 101 buffered stream packets resulting in an effective rate of 600 kbps.

Gossiping parameters. The gossiping period of each node is set to 200 ms, which leads to grouping an average of 11.26 packet ids per [PROPOSE]. The fanout is set to 7 for all nodes in the standard gossip protocol, while in HEAP, the average fanout is 7 across all nodes. The aggregation protocol gossips the 10 freshest local capabilities every 200 ms, costing around 1 KB/s and is thus completely marginal compared to the stream rate.

Message retransmission and bandwidth throttling. Given the random nature of its gossip-based dissemination process, HEAP does not attempt to establish stable TCP connections, but rather combines UDP datagrams with a retransmission mechanism. To further reduce message losses, HEAP also exploits a bandwidth throttling mechanism. This guarantees that nodes never attempt to send bursts of data that exceed their available bandwidth. Excess packets resulting from bursts are queued at the application level, and sent as soon as there is enough available bandwidth. To guarantee a fair comparison in our evaluation, we also integrated both retransmission and bandwidth throttling into the standard gossip protocol.

PlanetLab and network capabilities. PlanetLab nodes, located mostly in research and educational institutions, benefit from high bandwidth capabilities. As such, PlanetLab is not representative of a typical collaborative peer-to-peer system [26], in which most nodes would be sitting behind ADSL connection, with an asymmetric bandwidth and limited upload/download capabilities. We thus artificially limit the upload capability of nodes so that they match the bandwidth usually available for home users. We focus on upload as it is a well-known fact that download capabilities are much higher than upload ones. As we rely on UDP, we implemented, at the application level, an upload rate limiter that queues packets which are about to cross the bandwidth limit. In practice, nodes never exceed their given upload capability, but some nodes (between 5% and 7%), contribute way less than their capability, because of high CPU load and/or high bandwidth demand by other PlanetLab experiments. In other words, the average used capability of nodes is always less than or equal to their given upload limit.

We consider three different distributions of upload capabilities, depicted in Table 1 and inspired from the distributions used in [35]. The *capability supply ratio* (CSR, as defined in [35]) is the ratio of the average upload bandwidth over the stream rate. We only consider settings in which the global available bandwidth is enough to sustain the stream rate. Yet the lower the capability ratio, the closer we stand to that limit. The ms-691 distribution was referred to as dist1 in Section 1.

Table 1. The reference distributions ref-691 and ref-724, and the more skewed distribution ms-691

Name	CSR	Average	Fraction of nodes		
			2 Mbps	768 kbps	256 kbps
ref-691	1.15	691 kbps	0.1	0.5	0.4
ref-724	1.20	724 kbps	0.15	0.39	0.46
Name	CSR	Average	3 Mbps	1 Mbps	512 kbps
ms-691	1.15	691 kbps	0.05	0.1	0.85

Each distribution is split into three classes of nodes. The skewness of an upload distribution is characterized by the various percentages of each class of nodes: in the most skewed distribution we consider (ms-691), most nodes are in the *poorest* category and only 15% of nodes have an upload capability higher than the stream rate.

3.2   Evaluation Metrics

In the following, we first show that HEAP adapts the contribution of nodes according to their upload capability, and then we show that HEAP provides users with a good stream. We consider two metrics. The first is the *stream lag* and is defined as the difference between the time the stream was published by the source and the time it is actually delivered to the player on the nodes.[3] The second is the *stream quality*, which represents the percentage of the stream that is viewable. A FEC-encoded window is *jittered* as soon as it does not contain enough packets (i.e., at least 101) to be fully decoded. A X% jittered stream therefore means that X% of all the windows were jittered. Note that a jittered window does not mean that the window is entirely lost. Because we use systematic coding, a node may still receive 100 out of the 101 original stream packets, resulting in a 99% delivery ratio in a given window. We therefore also assess the quality of the jittered windows by giving the average delivery ratio in all jittered windows.

3.3   Adaptation to Heterogeneous Upload Capabilities

We considered all three configurations. In ref-691, ref-724 and ms-691, resp. 60%, 54% and 15% of the nodes have an available bandwidth higher than the one required on average for the stream rate. As we observed similar results in ref-691 and ref-724, we only report on ref-691 in Figure 4a. Results on ms-691 are reported on Figure 4b.

Figure 4a depicts the breakdown of the contributions among the three classes of nodes. For example, the striped bar for standard gossip means that nodes having an upload capability of 768 kbps use 97.17 % of their available bandwidth. It is interesting to observe that nodes contribute somewhat proportionally to their upload capabilities even in standard gossip. This is because of the correlation between upload capability and latency: packet ids sent by high-capability nodes are received before those sent by lower-capability ones. Consequently, the former are requested first and serve the stream to more nodes than the latter. In addition, nodes with low capabilities are overloaded faster and therefore naturally serve fewer nodes (either because they are slower or because they are subject to more packet drops) Yet, despite this natural self-adaptation, we observe that high-capability nodes are underutilized in standard gossip. To the contrary, HEAP homogeneously balances the load on all nodes by correctly adapting their

---

[3] A different and complementary notion, *startup delay*, is the time a node takes to buffer the received packets until they are sent to the video player. Note that in a gossip protocol like HEAP the startup delay of all nodes is similar because of the unstructured and dynamic nature of gossip.

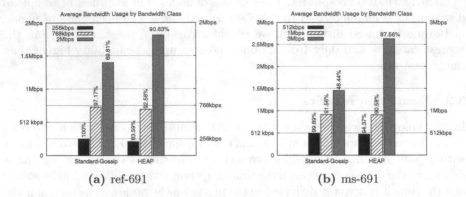

(a) ref-691   (b) ms-691

Fig. 4. Bandwidth consumption

gossip fanout: all nodes approximately consume 90% of their bandwidth. This highlights how the bandwidth consumption of standard gossip and HEAP on Figure 4a are caused by opposite reasons: congestion of low-capability nodes in standard gossip and fanout adaptation, which prevents congestion, in HEAP.

Figure 4b conveys the limits of the self-adaptation properties of standard gossip with an upload distribution in which only 15% of the nodes have an upload capability higher than the stream rate (ms-691). We observe that with standard gossip, the 5% nodes with high capabilities only use 48.44% of their bandwidth because their limited fanout does not allow them to serve more nodes. In HEAP, on the other hand, the 5% high-capability nodes can serve with up to 87.56% of their bandwidth, lowering the congestion of the low-capability nodes and providing much better performance than standard gossip in terms of quality as we show in next section.

3.4   Stream Quality

Our next experiment compares the percentages of jitter-free windows received by nodes in the three considered scenarios. Results are depicted in Figures 5, 6a and 6b. For instance, the black bar in Figure 5 for standard gossip indicates that nodes with low capabilities in ref-691 have only 18% of the windows that are not jittered (considering packets received with a stream lag of up to 10 s.). The same figure also shows that HEAP significantly improves this value, with low-capability nodes receiving more than 90% of jitter-free windows. This reflects the fact that HEAP allows high-capability nodes to assist low-capability ones. Results in Figure 6a are even more dramatic: high-capability nodes receive less than 33% of jitter-free windows in standard gossip, whereas all nodes receive more than 95% of jitter-free windows with HEAP.

Figure 6b clearly conveys the collaborative nature of HEAP when the global available bandwidth is higher (ref-724). The whole system benefits from the fact that nodes contribute according to their upload capability. For instance, the

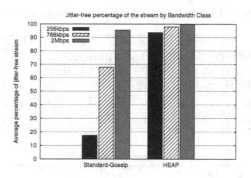

Fig. 5. Stream Quality (ref-691)

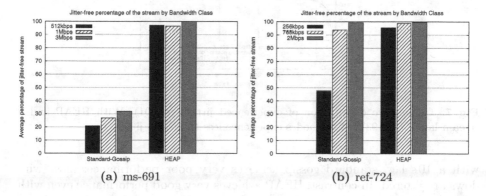

(a) ms-691   (b) ref-724

Fig. 6. Stream quality by capability class

number of jitter-free windows that low-capability nodes obtain increases from 47% for standard gossip to 93% for HEAP. These results are complemented by Table 2, which presents the average delivery ratio in the jittered windows for both protocols, for each class of nodes in the three considered distributions. Again, results show that HEAP is able to provide good performance to nodes regardless of their capability classes. It should be noted, however, that the table provides results only for the windows that are jittered, which are a lot more in standard gossip than in HEAP. This explains the seemingly bad performance of HEAP in a few cases such as for high-bandwidth nodes in ref-724.

Figure 7 conveys the cumulative distribution of the nodes that view the stream as a function of the percentage of jitter. For instance, the point $(x = 0.1, y = 85)$ on the HEAP - 10 s lag curve indicates that 85% of the nodes experience a jitter that is less than or equal to 10%. Note that in this figure, we do not differentiate between capability classes. We consider standard gossip and HEAP in two settings: offline and with 10 s lag. We present offline results in order to show that, with standard gossip, nodes eventually receive the stream. However,

Table 2. Average delivery rates in windows that cannot be fully decoded

	Standard gossip			HEAP		
upload capability	256 kbps	768 kbps	2 Mbps	256 kbps	768 kbps	2 Mbps
ref-691	63.4%	87.1%	89.3%	80.4%	77.1%	89.8%
ref-724	75.6%	88.6%	89.6%	87.9%	87.7%	64.4%
upload capability	512 kbps	1 Mbps	3 Mbps	512 kbps	1 Mbps	3 Mbps
ms-691	42.8%	56.5%	64.5%	83.7%	80.7%	90.9%

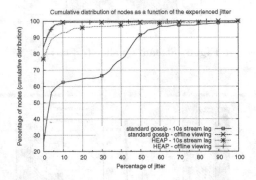

Fig. 7. Cumulative distribution of experienced jitter (ref-691). With HEAP and a stream lag of 10 s, 93% of the nodes experience less than 10% jitter.

with a 10 s lag, standard gossip achieves very poor performance: most windows are jittered. In contrast, HEAP achieves very good performance even with a 10 s lag.

3.5   Stream Lag

Next, we compare the stream lag required by HEAP and standard gossip to obtain a non-jittered stream. We report the results for ref-691 and ms-691 on Figures 8a and 8b, respectively. In both cases, HEAP drastically reduces the stream lag for all capability classes. Moreover, as shown in Figure 8b, the positive effect of HEAP significantly increases with the skewness of the distribution.

Figures 9a and 9b depict the cumulative distribution of nodes viewing the stream as a function of the stream lag, without distinguishing capability classes. We compare standard gossip and HEAP in two configurations: without jitter and with less than 1% of jitter. Sporadically, some PlanetLab nodes seem temporarily frozen, due to high CPU load and/or suffer excessive network problems explaining why neither protocol is able to deliver the stream to 100% of the nodes.[4] Still, both plots show that HEAP consistently outperforms standard gossip. For instance, in ref-691, HEAP requires 12 s to deliver the stream to 80% of the nodes without jitter, whereas standard gossip requires 26.6 s.

---

[4] Note that when running simulations without messages loss, 100% of the nodes received the full stream.

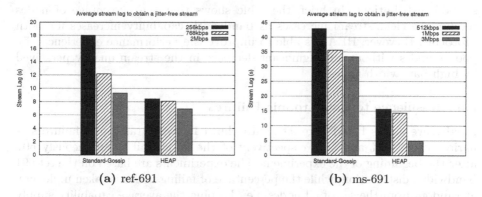

Fig. 8. Stream lag by capability class

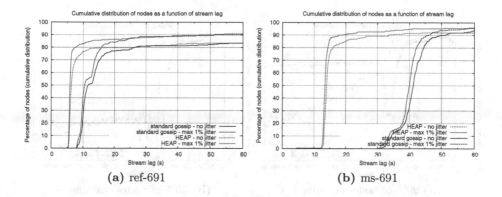

Fig. 9. Cumulative distribution of stream lag values

Table 3. Percentage of nodes receiving a jitter-free stream by capability class

	Standard gossip			HEAP		
bandwidth	256 kbps	768 kbps	2 Mbps	256 kbps	768 kbps	2 Mbps
ref-691 (10 s lag)	0	29.80	86.67	65.93	79.61	96.55
ref-724 (10 s lag)	0	07.52	97.73	61.95	74.34	93.02
bandwidth	512 kbps	1 Mbps	3 Mbps	512 kbps	1 Mbps	3 Mbps
ms-691 (20 s lag)	0	0	0	84.58	89.66	85.71

Table 3 complements these results by showing the percentage of nodes that can view a jitter-free stream for each bandwidth class and for the three described distributions. In brief, the table shows that the percentage of nodes receiving a clear stream increases as bandwidth capability increases for both protocols. However, HEAP is able to improve the performance experienced by poorer nodes without any significant decrease in the stream quality perceived by high-bandwidth nodes.

3.6   Resilience to Catastrophic Failures

Finally, we assess HEAP's resilience to churn in two catastrophic-failure scenarios where 20% and 50% respectively of the nodes fail simultaneously 60 s after the beginning of the experiment. The experiments are based on the ref-691 bandwidth distribution, while the percentage of failing nodes is taken uniformly at random from the set of all nodes, i.e., keeping the average capability supply ratio unchanged. In addition, we configure the system so that surviving nodes learn about the failure an average of 10 s after it happened.

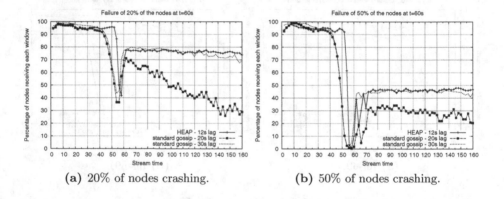

(a) 20% of nodes crashing.   (b) 50% of nodes crashing.

Fig. 10. Resilience in the presence of catastrophic failures

Figure 10a depicts, for each encoded window in the stream, the percentage of nodes that are able to decode it completely, i.e., without any jitter. The plot highlights once more the significant improvements provided by HEAP over standard gossip-based content dissemination. The solid line showing HEAP with a 12 s lag shows that the percentage of nodes decoding each window is always close to 100% (or to the 80% of nodes remaining after the failure) except for the stream packets generated immediately before the failure. The reason for the temporary drop in performance is that the failure of a node causes the disappearance of all the packets that it has delivered but not yet forwarded. Clearly, windows generated after the failure are instead correctly decoded by almost all remaining nodes. The plot also shows two additional lines depicting the significantly worse performance achieved by standard gossip-based dissemination.

The number of nodes receiving the stream with a 20 s lag in standard gossip is, in fact, much lower than that of those receiving it with only 12 s of lag in HEAP. Only after 30 s of lag is standard gossip able to reach a performance that is comparable to that of HEAP after 12 s. The figure also highlights that the number of packets lost during the failure is higher in standard gossip than in HEAP (the width of the drop is larger). The reason is that in standard gossip upload queues tend to grow larger than in HEAP. Thus packets that are lost as a result of nodes that crash span a longer time interval in standard gossip than they do in HEAP. Finally, the continuous decrease in the 20 s-lag line for standard gossip shows that the delay experienced by packets in standard gossip increases as time elapses: this is a clear symptom of congestion that is instead not present in HEAP.

Figure 10b provides similar information for a scenario in which 50% of the nodes fail simultaneously. HEAP is still able to provide the stream to the remaining nodes with a lag of less than 12 s. Conversely, standard gossip achieves mediocre performance after as many as 20 s of lag.

4 Related Work

When contrasting HEAP with related work, we distinguish two classes of content-dissemination protocols: *(i)* proactive protocols that continuously change the dissemination topology, namely gossip-based dissemination schemes, and *(ii)* reactive protocols which only change the dissemination topology (possibly in a random manner) in case of malfunctions (e.g., churn). This latter set includes tree and mesh-based protocols.

4.1 Proactive Protocols

Several proactive protocols have incorporated some adaptation features, but none does so by dynamically adapting the fanout of the nodes according to their relative (bandwidth) capabilities. The protocol of [10] aims at increasing the reliability of a spanning tree, by having each node in the tree dynamically adapt its number of children using global knowledge about the reliability of nodes and network links.

In Smart Gossip [16], nodes of a wireless network may decide not to gossip depending on the number of nodes in their surrounding. In CREW [7], a three-phase gossip protocol (similar to that of Section 2.1) is used to disseminate large content in the context of file sharing. Nodes locally decide, when their bandwidth is exhausted, to stop offering data.

In Gravitational Gossip [14], the fanin of nodes (i.e., the number of times a node is chosen as a gossip target) may be adjusted based on the quality of reception they expect. This is achieved by biasing the node selection such that some nodes have a higher probability to be selected for gossip than others. The technique is however static and focuses on the incoming traffic that nodes receive. Because of the three-phase nature of HEAP, nodes have a payload fanin of 1.

4.2   Reactive Protocols

Some tree- and mesh-based protocols do have nodes dynamically adapt their neighborhood sets. However, such adaptation is only achieved after churn or malfunctions, and as such it is not proactive as in HEAP, or in any gossip dissemination protocol.

Multi-tree schemes such as Splitstream [4] and Chunkyspread [29] split streams over diverse paths to enhance their reliability. This comes for free in gossip protocols where the neighbors of a node continuously change. In a sense, a gossip dissemination protocol dynamically provides different dissemination paths for each stream packet, providing the ultimate splitting scheme. Chunkyspread accounts for heterogeneity using the SwapLinks protocol [30]. Each node contributes in proportion to its capacity and/or willingness to collaborate. This is reflected by heterogeneous numbers of children across the nodes in the tree.

The approaches of [2, 27] propose a set of heuristics that account for bandwidth heterogeneity (and node uptimes) in tree-based multicast protocols. This leads to significant improvements in bandwidth usage. These protocols aggregate global information about the implication of nodes across trees, by exchanging messages along tree branches, in a way that relates to our capability aggregation protocol.

Mesh-based systems [5,17,20,22,23,24,35] are appealing alternatives to tree-based ones. They are similar to gossip in the sense that their topology is unstructured. Some of those, namely the latest version of Coolstreaming [17] and GridMedia [35] dynamically build multi-trees on top of the unstructured overlay when nodes perceive they are stably served by their neighbors. Typically, every node has a *view* of its neighbors, from which it picks new partners if it observes malfunctions. In the extreme case, a node has to seek for more or different communication partners if none of its neighbors is operating properly. Not surprisingly, it was shown in [17,20] that increasing the view size has a very positive effect on the streaming quality and is more robust in case of churn. Gossip protocols like HEAP are extreme cases of these phenomena because the views they rely on keep continuously changing.

Finally, [31] addresses the problem of building an optimized mesh in terms of network proximity and latency, in the presence of *guarded* peers, i.e., peers that are behind a NAT or firewall. This work led to mixing application level multicast with IP multicast whenever possible [34]. The core of this research is now commercially used in [33] but little is known on the dissemination protocol. At the time the prototype was used for research, some nodes were fed by super peers deployed on PlanetLab and it is reasonable to think that those super peers are now replaced by dedicated servers in the commercial product. It is for instance known that the dissemination protocol of PPLive [25] substantially relies on a set of super peers and thus does not represent a purely decentralized solution [12].

5   Concluding Remarks

This paper presents HEAP, a new gossip protocol which adapts the dissemination load of the nodes to account for their heterogeneity. HEAP preserves the simplicity and proactive (churn adaptation) nature of traditional homogeneous gossip, while significantly improving its effectiveness. Experimental results with a video streaming application on PlanetLab convey the improvement of HEAP over a standard homogeneous gossip protocol with respect to stream quality, bandwidth usage and resilience to churn. When the stream rate is close to the average available bandwidth, the improvement is even more significant.

A natural way to further improve the quality of gossiping is to bias the neighbor selection towards rich nodes in the early steps of dissemination. Our early experiments reveal that this can be beneficial at the first step of the dissemination (i.e., from the source) but reveals not trivial if performed in later steps.

We considered bandwidth as the main heterogeneity factor, as it is indeed crucial in the context of streaming. Other factors might reveal important in other applications (e.g., node interests, available CPU). We believe HEAP could easily be adapted to such factors by modifying the underlying aggregation protocol accordingly. Also, we considered the choice of the fanout as the way to adjust the load of the nodes. One might also explore the dynamic adaptation of the gossip targets, the frequency of the dissemination or the memory size devoted to the dissemination.

There are some limitations to adaptation and these provide interesting research tracks to pursue. While adapting to heterogeneity, a natural behavior is to elevate certain wealthy nodes to the rank of temporary superpeers, which could potentially have an impact in case of failures. Moreover, an attacker targeting highly capable nodes could degrade the overall performance of the protocol. Likewise, the very fact that nodes advertise their capabilities may trigger freeriding vocations, where nodes would pretend to be poor in order not to contribute to the dissemination. We are working towards a freerider-tracking protocol for gossip in order to detect and punish freeriding behaviors [11].

Finally, since gossip targets are periodically changing and because sent messages are very small, it is quite natural to transfer them via UDP. Nevertheless, doing so can have a negative impact on other applications competing for bandwidth. In other words, our protocol is not TCP-friendly as it might simply take priority over other applications, similar to most commercial voice-over-IP protocols. Making protocols using multiple incoming streams TCP-friendly was quite difficult [21, 32] assuming the serving nodes were static. Doing the same for ever changing neighbors such as in a gossip is therefore a problem on its own and needs further research.

Acknowledgements

The authors would like to thank Ken Birman, Pascal Felber, Ali Ghodsi and Dahlia Malkhi for useful comments.

References

1. Birman, K., Hayden, M., Ozkasap, O., Xiao, Z., Budiu, M., Minsky, Y.: Bimodal Multicast. TOCS 17(2), 41–88 (1999)
2. Bishop, M., Rao, S., Sripanidulchai, K.: Considering Priority in Overlay Multicast Protocols under Heterogeneous Environments. In: Proc. of INFOCOM (2006)
3. Bonald, T., Massoulié, L., Mathieu, F., Perino, D., Twigg, A.: Epidemic Live Streaming: Optimal Performance Trade-Offs. In: Proc. of SIGMETRICS (2008)
4. Castro, M., Druschel, P., Kermarrec, A.-M., Nandi, A., Rowstron, A., Singh, A.: SplitStream: High-Bandwidth Multicast in Cooperative Environments. In: Proc. of SOSP (2003)
5. Chu, Y.-H., Rao, S., Zhang, H.: A Case for End System Multicast. JSAC 20(8), 1456–1471 (2000)
6. Demers, A., Greene, D., Hauser, C., Irish, W., Larson, J., Shenker, S., Sturgis, H., Swinehart, D., Terry, D.: Epidemic Algorithms for Replicated Database Maintenance. In: Proc. of PODC (1987)
7. Deshpande, M., Xing, B., Lazardis, I., Hore, B., Venkatasubramanian, N., Mehrotra, S.: CREW: A Gossip-based Flash-Dissemination System. In: Proc. of ICDCS (2006)
8. Eugster, P., Guerraoui, R., Handurukande, S., Kermarrec, A.-M., Kouznetsov, P.: Lightweight Probabilistic Broadcast. TOCS 21(4), 341–374 (2003)
9. Frey, D., Guerraoui, R., Kermarrec, A.-M., Monod, M., Quéma, V.: Stretching Gossip with Live Streaming. In: Proc. of DSN (2009)
10. Garbinato, B., Pedone, F., Schmidt, R.: An Adaptive Algorithm for Efficient Message Diffusion in Unreliable Environments. In: Proc. of DSN (2004)
11. Guerraoui, R., Huguenin, K., Kermarrec, A.-M., Monod, M.: On Tracking Freeriders in Gossip Protocols. In: Proc. of P2P (2009)
12. Hei, X., Liang, C., Liang, J., Liu, Y., Ross, K.: A Measurement Study of a Large-Scale P2P IPTV System. TMM 9(8), 1672–1687 (2007)
13. Jelasity, M., Montresor, A., Babaoglu, O.: Gossip-Based Aggregation in Large Dynamic Networks. TOCS 23(3), 219–252 (2005)
14. Jenkins, K., Hopkinson, K., Birman, K.: A Gossip Protocol for Subgroup Multicast. In: Proc. of ICDCS Workshops (2001)
15. Kermarrec, A.-M., Massoulié, L., Ganesh, A.: Probabilistic Reliable Dissemination in Large-Scale Systems. TPDS 14(3), 248–258 (2003)
16. Kyasanur, P., Choudhury, R.R., Gupta, I.: Smart Gossip: An Adaptive Gossip-based Broadcasting Service for Sensor Networks. In: Proc. of MASS (2006)
17. Li, B., Qu, Y., Keung, Y., Xie, S., Lin, C., Liu, J., Zhang, X.: Inside the New Coolstreaming: Principles, Measurements and Performance Implications. In: Proc. of INFOCOM (2008)
18. Li, H., Clement, A., Marchetti, M., Kapritsos, M., Robinson, L., Alvisi, L., Dahlin, M.: FlightPath: Obedience vs Choice in Cooperative Services. In: Proc. of OSDI (2008)

19. Li, H., Clement, A., Wong, E., Napper, J., Roy, I., Alvisi, L., Dahlin, M.: BAR Gossip. In: Proc. of OSDI (2006)
20. Liang, C., Guo, Y., Liu, Y.: Is Random Scheduling Sufficient in P2P Video Streaming? In: Proc. of ICDCS (2008)
21. Ma, L., Ooi, W.: Congestion Control in Distributed Media Streaming. In: Proc. of INFOCOM (2007)
22. Magharei, N., Rejaie, R.: PRIME: Peer-to-Peer Receiver-drIven MEsh-based Streaming. In: Proc. of INFOCOM (2007)
23. Pai, V., Kumar, K., Tamilmani, K., Sambamurthy, V., Mohr, A.: Chainsaw: Eliminating Trees from Overlay Multicast. In: Castro, M., van Renesse, R. (eds.) IPTPS 2005. LNCS, vol. 3640, pp. 127–140. Springer, Heidelberg (2005)
24. Picconi, F., Massoulié, L.: Is There a Future for Mesh-Based live Video Streaming? In: Proc. of P2P (2008)
25. PPLive, http://www.pplive.com
26. Spring, N., Peterson, L., Bavier, A., Pai, V.: Using Planetlab for Network Research: Myths, Realities, and Best Practices. OSR 40(1), 17–24 (2006)
27. Sung, Y.-W., Bishop, M., Rao, S.: Enabling Contribution Awareness in an Overlay Broadcasting System. CCR 36(4), 411–422 (2006)
28. van Renesse, R., Birman, K., Vogels, W.: Astrolabe: A Robust and Scalable Technology for Distributed System Monitoring, Management, and Data Mining. TOCS 21(2), 164–206 (2003)
29. Venkataraman, V., Yoshida, K., Francis, P.: Chunkyspread: Heterogeneous Unstructured Tree-Based Peer to Peer Multicast. In: Proc. of ICNP (2006)
30. Vishnumurthy, V., Francis, P.: On Heterogeneous Overlay Construction and Random Node Selection in Unstructured P2P Networks. In: Proc. of INFOCOM (2006)
31. Wang, W., Jin, C., Jamin, S.: Network Overlay Construction under Limited End-to-End Reachability. In: Proc. of INFOCOM (2005)
32. Widmer, J., Handley, M.: Extending Equation-based Congestion Control to Multicast Applications. In: Proc. of SIGCOMM (2001)
33. Zattoo, http://www.zattoo.com
34. Zhang, B., Wang, W., Jamin, S., Massey, D., Zhang, L.: Universal IP multicast delivery. Computer Networks 50(6), 781–806 (2006)
35. Zhang, M., Zhang, Q., Sun, L., Yang, S.: Understanding the Power of Pull-Based Streaming Protocol: Can We Do Better? JSAC 25(9), 1678–1694 (2007)

CCD: Efficient Customized Content Dissemination in Distributed Publish/Subscribe

Hojjat Jafarpour, Bijit Hore, Sharad Mehrotra,
and Nalini Venkatasubramanian

Dept. of Computer Science, Univ. of California at Irvine
{hjafarpo,bhore,sharad,nalini}@ics.uci.edu

Abstract. In this paper, we propose a new content-based publish/ subscribe (pub/sub) framework that enables a pub/sub system to accommodate richer content formats including multimedia publications with image and video content. The pub/sub system besides being responsible for matching and routing the published content, is also responsible for converting the content into the suitable (target) format for each subscriber. Content conversion is achieved through a set of content adaptation operators (e.g., image transcoder, document translator, etc.) at different nodes in the overlay network. We study algorithms for placement of such operators in the pub/sub broker overlay in order to minimize the communication and computation resource consumption. Our experimental results show that careful placement of these operators in pub/sub overlay network can lead to significant cost reduction.

Keywords: Publish/Subscribe, Operator placement, Content dissemination.

1 Introduction

Publish/Subscribe (pub/sub) systems provide a selective dissemination scheme that delivers published content only to the receivers that have specified interest in it [1, 3, 5]. To provide scalability, pub/sub systems are implemented as a set of broker servers forming an overlay network. Clients connect to one of these brokers and publish or subscribe through that broker. When a broker receives a subscription from one of its clients, it acts on behalf of the client and forwards the subscription to others in the overlay network. Similarly, when a broker receives content from one of its clients, it forwards the content through the overlay network to the brokers that have clients with matching subscriptions. These brokers then deliver the content to the interested clients connected to them.

In this paper, we consider the problem of customized delivery in which clients, in addition to specifying their interest also specify the format in which they wish the data to be delivered. The broker network, in addition to matching and disseminating the data to clients also customizes the data to the formats requested by the clients. As the published content becomes richer in format, considering content customization within the pub/sub system can significantly reduce resource consumption. Such content customizations have become more attractive due to recent technological advances that has led to significant diversification

J.M. Bacon and B.F. Cooper (Eds.): Middleware 2009, LNCS 5896, pp. 62–82, 2009.

of how users access information. Emerging mobile and personal devices, for instance, introduce specific requirements on the format in which content is delivered to the user. Consider a distributed video dissemination application over Twitter[2] where users can publish video content that must be delivered to their followers (subscribers). Followers may subscribe to such a channel using a variety of devices and prefer the content to be customized according to their needs. Additionally, device characteristics such as screen resolution, available network bandwidth etc., may also form the basis for required customization. Another example of such customized content dissemination system is dissemination of GIS maps annotated with situational information in responding to natural or man made disasters. In this case, receivers may require content to be customized according to their location or language.

Simply extending the existing pub/sub architectures by forcing the subscribers or publishers to customize content may result in significant inefficiencies and suboptimal use of available resources in the system. Therefore, there is a need for novel approaches for customized dissemination of content through efficient use of available resources in a distributed networked system. The key issue in customized content dissemination using distributed pub/sub framework is where in the broker network should the customization be performed for each published content? An immediate thought is to perform requested customizations at the sender broker prior to delivery. Such approach could result in significant network cost. Consider a simple broker network in Figure 1 where node A publishes a high resolution video in 'mpeg4' format and nodes G, H and I have subscribers that requested this content in 'avi', 'flv' and '3gp' formats, respectively. By performing customizations in the sender broker, A, the same content is transmitted in three different formats through $<A, B>$ and $<B, D>$ links which results in increased network cost. The alternate might be to defer customizations to the receiver brokers or broker D. Consider another case where J, K and L have subscribers with hand held devices that requested the video in '3gp' format. If the customizations are deferred to receiver brokers, conversion from 'mpeg4' to '3gp' is done three times, once in each receiving broker which results in higher consumption of computation resource in brokers. This also increases the communication cost by transmitting larger size video in 'mpeg4' format while it could be transmitted in '3gp' format that has smaller size.

The resulting communication and computation costs can be reduced by intelligently embedding customization operators in the pub/sub overlay network. For instance, the increased network cost in the first scenario could be prevented if the published video is sent to broker D in the original format and the customization operators are performed in this broker. Also by performing the conversion once at broker A or C, computation cost can be reduced significantly in the second scenario.

The above example shows merit of placement of operators in the network. In this paper, we explore this problem systematically and develop algorithms for efficient placement of operators. We model published content and required customization operators as a graph structure called *Content Adaptation Graph (CAG)*. Then, we propose an optimal operator placement algorithm for small CAGs. The proposed algorithm performs the required operators in broker overlay such that the resulting communication and computation cost is minimized. For the larger CAGs, we show that the problem is NP-hard and propose a greedy heuristics-based iterative algorithm that significantly reduces customized dissemination cost compared to the cases where customizations are done either in the sender broker or in the subscriber brokers. Our extensive experiments show that the proposed algorithms considerably reduce bandwidth consumption and total customization cost in variety of scenarios.

The overall contributions of this paper are:

- We formally define the customized content dissemination, CCD, problem in a distributed pub/sub systems (Section 2). We also show that CCD with minimum cost is NP-hard when the number of requested formats is large.
- For small number of requested formats where enumeration of format sets is feasible, we propose an optimal operator placement algorithm in pub/sub broker network that minimizes the customization and dissemination cost (Section 4).
- For large number of requested formats we propose a greedy heuristics-based algorithm (Section 5).
- We present results of our extensive evaluation of the proposed techniques that show the considerable benefit of using them (Section 6).

We finally present related work in Section 7 followed by conclusions in Section 8.

2   Customized Content Dissemination

DHT-based Pub/Sub systems: Our CCD system architecture is based on a DHT-based pub/sub system [10, 11]. It consists of a set of content brokers that are connected through a structured overlay network. Each client connects to one of the brokers and communicates with the system through this broker. Often in DHT-based pub/sub, content space is partitioned among the brokers. Each broker maintains subscriptions for its partition of content space and is responsible for matching them with publications falling in its partition. In fact, each broker is the *Rendezvous Point (RP)* for the publication and subscriptions corresponding to its partition. When a broker receives a subscription from its client, it first finds the broker(s) responsible for partition(s) that the subscription falls in and forwards it to them. Similarly, when a broker receives a published content from its client, it finds the corresponding RP broker and forwards the content to the RP. The content is matched with the subscriptions at the RP and the list of brokers with matched subscriptions is created. Then the RP disseminates the content to all of these brokers through a dissemination tree constructed using the DHT-based routing scheme in the broker overlay network. Finally, every broker (with at least one client having a matching subscription) receive the content and transfer it to the respective clients. Since a broker acts as a proxy for all clients that connect to it, we can assume that it is the the subscriber or publisher and therefore simply concentrate on the broker overlay network. Various DHT-based routing techniques have been proposed in the literature [7, 8] that can be used for routing content from RP to the matching brokers. In this paper we use the *Tapestry* routing scheme [7], however, we can easily generalize our approach to other DHT-based routing schemes. In this paper we assume that given a set of subscribers (receivers), a broker can construct the dissemination tree as in Tapestry which then remains fixed for this particular instance of the dissemination event. For more details on dissemination tree construction we refer the interested reader to [9]. We choose the DHT-based pub/sub on Tapestry for a variety of reasons, two important ones being (i) In DHT-based pub/sub systems, for a given publication, a single broker (RP) has complete information about all brokers with matching subscriptions as well as formats in which content is to be delivered to them. (ii) Tapestry enables brokers to estimate the dissemination path for content, which is used to estimate the dissemination tree. Note that the estimated dissemination tree may not be same as the actual dissemination tree. An alternative for using the estimated dissemination tree is to discover the actual dissemination tree using a *tree discovery message* that is initiated at the RP and sent to all subscribing brokers. The leaf brokers in the dissemination tree then resend the message to the RP. Each message keeps information about the route from the RP to the leaf brokers which is then used by the RP to construct the exact dissemination tree for the given publication. In this paper we use tree discovery messages for constructing dissemination trees for publications. Figure 1 depicts a sample dissemination tree.

2.1   Content Adaptation Graph

We assume every client has a profile describing receiving-device characteristic (e.g., screen size and resolution) and connection characteristics (e.g., connection type and bandwidth). The client profile is registered at its broker and is used to determine the format(s) in which content needs to be delivered. Each subscription of the client along with its profile is forwarded to the corresponding RP which uses this information for optimal routing computation.

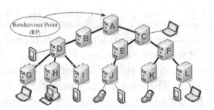

Fig. 1. Sample dissemination tree

Similar to the conventional DHT-based pub/sub systems, the published content is forwarded to the corresponding RP. However, after detecting the brokers with matching subscriptions, the published content must be customized and disseminated according to the profiles of the matched subscriptions. For simplicity, let us assume that the computational resources at the brokers and transmission links between them (represented by edges in the dissemination tree) are identical, i.e., their characteristics such as bandwidth, delay, CPU speed etc. are same in every part of the tree[1]. Now, if the set of required formats is $F = \{F_0, ..., F_{m-1}\}$, for content $\mathbb{C}$ and format $F_i \in F$, we can associate a transmission-cost $\mathcal{T}_{F_i}(\mathbb{C})$ for each link. Let $O_{(i,j)}$ denote the operator that converts content format from F_i to F_j and its associated

---

[1] We have also considered the general case where brokers and links are not identical, however, due to space constraint we do not present it in this paper.

conversion cost by $\mathcal{C}_{O_{(i,j)}}(\mathbb{C})$. This represents the computation cost of performing this operator at any broker[2]. Note that it may not always be feasible to convert content from any given format F_i into another format F_j. For example, it might not be possible to convert a low resolution image into a higher resolution one. Alternatively, the system might not support particular conversions even if it were possible, e.g., converting video in 'avi' format into 'flv'. In such cases we assume $O_{(i,j)}$ to be undefined.

We use a directed, weighted graph structure to represent the required formats for a published content and the relationship between these formats. We will call this the *Content Adaptation Graph (CAG)*. The vertices in CAG correspond to the various content formats and the directed edges between two vertices represents the operator that converts content from the source format to the sink format directly. The associated *conversion cost* is

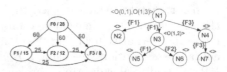

Fig. 2. A sample CAG and dissemination plan

represented by the weight of the edge. Similarly, a weight associated with each node of the CAG represents the per-unit *transmission cost* in that format. Figure 2 illustrates a CAG involving four formats of an 'mpeg4' video content with different frame sizes and bit-rates. In this CAG we represent the transmission cost in Megabytes (MB) and the conversion cost in seconds.

2.2   Cost-Based Customized Dissemination

Consider the problem of customized dissemination of content $\mathbb{C}$ in format F_0 from RP to a set of brokers $R = \{R_1, .., R_r\}$ ($R \subseteq N$). Let F^{R_j} be the set of formats required at broker R_j. Let $\mathbb{T}$ denote the dissemination tree constructed according to the Tapestry framework where $N = \{N_1, .., N_n\}$ be the set of nodes and E be the set of edges in this tree. We denote the rendezvous node RP by N_1.

For a given dissemination tree $\mathbb{T}$, a *customized content dissemination plan* or *CCD plan* is an annotated tree $\mathbb{P}$ (with the same set of nodes and edges as $\mathbb{T}$) where each node and edge is annotated by the customization operators performed at the node and the formats in which the content is transmitted along the link respectively. Figure 2 shows a sample plan where the published content is delivered in format F_1 to brokers N_2 and N_5, in format F_2 to broker N_6 and in format F_3 to broker N_7. A subtree in the customization plan is called a *subplan*.

A customization plan provides the following information for each node, N_i, and link $< N_i, N_j >$ in the dissemination tree.

- O_{N_i}: the operators that are performed at N_i. E.g., in the plan depicted in Figure 2, $O_{N_1} = \{O_{(0,1)}, O_{(1,3)}\}$ that convert format F_0 to format F_1 and format F_1 to format F_3, respectively.
- $F_{in}^{N_i}$: the set of content formats that are received at N_i (from its parent). E.g., $F_{in}^{N_2} = \{F_1\}$ in Figure 2.

---

[2] In general we will assume these costs to represent the per-unit costs.

- $F_{out}^{N_i}$: the set of content formats that are required in N_i or are being sent by N_i to its children. E.g., $F_{out}^{N_3} = \{F_1, F_2\}$ in Figure 2.
- $F_{<N_i,N_j>}$: the set of formats that content is transmitted over $< N_i, N_j >$. E.g., $F_{<N_1,N_2>} = \{F_1\}$.

In every customization plan the content to be disseminated is available at the root node (RP) of the dissemination tree in its original published format. In a *valid* plan at every node N_i the input format set is identical to the set of formats that N_i receives from its parent. The input format for each operation $O_{(m,n)}$ performed at node is either forwarded by its parent or is generated at the node as a result of other operations. Likewise, the formats in which content is forwarded by N_i to its children are either received from its parent or generated in situ as a result of an executed operation. Finally, in a valid plan for every link $< N_i, N_j >$ the formats transmitted over it needs to pre-exist at its source i.e., $F_{<N_i,N_j>} \subseteq F_{out}^{N_i}$.

Cost Model: The conversion cost of a plan is the sum of costs of carrying out the operators specified for each of its nodes and transmission cost is the sum of costs of transmitting the content in the specified formats over all the links in the dissemination tree. Our model is similar to the one used in [18, 20] for in-network stream processing and cache replacement. We denote the conversion cost of a plan $\mathbb{P}$ by $\varphi_{\mathbb{P}}$ and the transmission cost by $\tau_{\mathbb{P}}$.

The *total cost* of the plan $\mathbb{P}$ for content $\mathbb{C}$ is denoted by $\Theta_{\mathbb{P}}(c)$, as a function of its conversion and transmission costs. In general one can use an additive formula such as:

$$\Theta_{\mathbb{P}}(\mathbb{C}) = \alpha\tau_{\mathbb{P}} + \beta\varphi_{\mathbb{P}} \text{ , where } \varphi_{\mathbb{P}} \text{ and } \tau_{\mathbb{P}} \text{ are normalized values, } \alpha, \beta \geq 0$$

The parameters α and β in the above cost function provide flexibility to customize the total cost function based on the system characteristics. For instance, if processing resources in a system are limited and expensive, the total cost function can reflect this by giving more weight to computing cost. Based on the above discussion, the computation cost of the plan depicted in Figure 2 is 110 and the communication cost of this plan is 73. Assuming $\alpha, \beta = 1$, the total cost of this plan will be 183. Therefore, the optimization problem can be stated as follows:

Customized Content Dissemination (CCD) Problem: Given a dissemination task find a valid customization plan with minimum total cost.

Theorem 1. CCD problem is NP-hard.

Proof. We show that the CCD problem is NP-hard when there is only one broker in the system. Clearly, if the problem is NP-hard for one broker, it remains NP-hard for $n(> 1)$ brokers too. We show that the NP-hard problem of computing the *"Minimum directed Steiner Tree"* can be reduced to an instance of the CCD problem. The minimum directed Steiner tree problem is the following: Given a directed graph $G = (V, E)$ with edge-weights, a set of terminals (vertices) $S \subseteq V$, and a root vertex r, find a minimum weight connected tree rooted at r, such that all vertices in S are included in the tree [12]. It is easy to see that any instance of the directed Steiner tree problem is equivalent to the degenerate CCD problem where there is only one broker in the network, the content adaptation graph CAG is set to be the same as G, the vertices's in S correspond to the set of formats (corresponding to a set of nodes in the CAG) in which content is required, and r is the original format of content. Since the CCD problem is NP-hard for the case of one broker, it remains NP-hard in the general case as well.   □

3 Multilayer Graph Representation of CCD

An interesting observation is that CCD problem can be formulated as a minimum directed Steiner tree problem in a *multilayer graph* constructed from the given CAG and dissemination tree. In fact this observation was made in [13] for multicasting problem. A multilayer graph for CCD problem is constructed by combining the dissemination tree and the content adaptation graph (CAG) as follows:

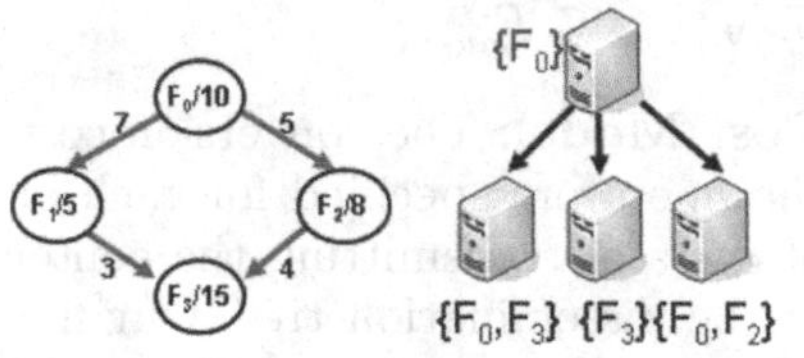

Fig. 3. A sample subtree and a CAG

Generate m replicas of the dissemination tree, each representing a layer corresponding to a format in the CAG (m is the number of formats in the CAG). The restriction being that within each layer, data can be transmitted along the edges in the format corresponding to that layer only. We denote the multilayer graph by $\mathcal{G}_{\mathcal{ML}} = (\mathcal{V}, \mathcal{E})$ such that $\mathcal{V} = V_d \times V_c$ where V_c is the set of vertices in CAG and V_d is the set of nodes in the dissemination tree. Each vertex in $\mathcal{V}$ is therefore associated with exactly one pair of nodes - where the first member of the pair is a node in the dissemination tree and the other corresponds to a format in the CAG. For a vertex v in a multilayer graph the corresponding format in the CAG is referred by $v.format$ and the corresponding node in the dissemination tree by $v.node$. The edge set of $\mathcal{G}_{\mathcal{ML}}$ comprises the following two kinds of edges - edges that connect two nodes in the same layer (called *transmission edges*) and edges that connect nodes across layers (called *conversion edges*. There is a directed transmission edge in every layer corresponding to a link in the original dissemination tree. Similarly, there is a directed conversion edge joining the vertices corresponding to the same (physical) node across layers L_i and L_j if and only if there is an edge from format F_i to F_j in the CAG. The weight of a transmission edge in layer L_i is equal to the transmission cost of its corresponding format, i.e., F_i. Similarly, the weight of a conversion edge between two layers L_i and L_j is the same as the conversion cost from format F_i to F_j in the CAG. As discussed in Section 2.2, we will assume that the transmission cost and conversion cost are measured in the same unit and have been normalized, i.e., one unit of transmission cost is same as one unit of conversion cost.

Now, it is easy to see that any valid plan for the CCD problem can be represented as a tree in the corresponding multilayer graph. In fact, the minimum cost plan for a CCD problem corresponds to the minimum cost directed Steiner tree in $\mathcal{G}_{\mathcal{ML}}$. For each format F_k that is assigned to a link between N_i and N_j in the optimum plan, the transmission edge between corresponding nodes for N_i and N_j in the layer associated to F_k is also included in the minimum cost Steiner tree. For each operator $O_{(s,w)}$ assigned to node N_i in the optimum plan, the conversion edge between corresponding nodes for N_i between the layers associated with F_s and F_w is included in the minimum cost Steiner tree. Finally, one can see that cost of the optimal CCD plan is the same as the total weight of the edges in the minimum Steiner tree in the multilayer graph.

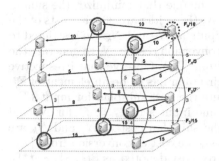

Fig. 4. Multi layer graph for Figure 3

As an example consider the CAG and dissemination tree depicted in Figure 3. Figure 4 depicts the associated multilayer graph for the given CAG and dissemination tree. The source for the Steiner tree in the multilayer graph is the corresponding node for the dissemination tree's root in the layer associated with the initial format. The set of terminals for the Steiner tree consists of the corresponding nodes for subscriber brokers in their layers associated with their requested formats. Therefore, in the next two sections we develop two CCD algorithms that generate CCD plans with a small cost. In fact our first algorithm is designed to find the optimum CCD plan and can be used when the number of formats in CAG is small (less than 5). The second algorithm is meant for large CAGs (more than 5 nodes) and uses heuristics to generate low cost plans.

4   Optimal CCD Algorithm

In this section we describe an algorithm for finding minimum cost dissemination plan when the CAG contains small number of formats (less than 5). In many situations we may be able to categorize the devices into a small set of classes where determining an optimum dissemination plan is possible. For instance, in an image dissemination system , e.g., "PC with high speed connection", "PC with dial-up connection", "Mobile device with Wi-Fi connection" and "Mobile device with GSM connection". An important advantage of this algorithm over the multilayer graph based approach is that it scales linearly with the dissemination tree size and can therefore be used for efficiently computing the optimal plan for large dissemination trees when the CAG is small.

Let us describe the main idea behind the optimal algorithm using an example. Consider a broker N_i that receives content in formats specified in the set $F_{in}^{N_i}$ from its parent (as shown in Figure 5). Let N_i have two children N_j and N_k. Let us assume that for every child node the minimum-cost dissemination plan for the subtree rooted at the node is known in advance for each possible input format set (recall, the sub-plan cost includes the transmission cost along the incoming edge at the node). Now, if the number of formats in the CAG is m, there are potentially 2^m distinct input sets for each child. Given the costs of these 2^m optimal sub-plans for each child of N_i (shown as arrays in the figure), let us see how to find the minimum cost plan for the subtree rooted at N_i parameterized on its input $F_{in}^{N_i}$. Take the simple case when $F_{in}^{N_i}$ is a singleton set $\{F_2\}$ from the CAG shown in Figure 2. To compute the minimum cost for this specific input, we generate all the formats that can be potentially generated from $\{F_2\}$ (based on the CAG) and note the corresponding conversion costs. For our example CAG, let the format sets generated from $\{F_2\}$ at N_i be denoted by $\mathbb{F}_i^* = \{\{F_2\}, \{F_3\}, \{F_2, F_3\}\}$. Of course, in the worst case $|\mathbb{F}_i^*| = 2^m$. Now, given the input $\{F_2\}$ at N_i, the best plan is the one that minimizes the sum of transmission cost of content in format F_2 to N_i (from its parent), the costs of the least expensive plans at N_j and N_k when inputs at N_j and N_k are restricted to be an element of $\mathbb{F}_i^*$ and the corresponding conversion cost at N_i to generate the union of the two input sets for N_j and N_k from $\{F_2\}$. Observe that irrespective of what formats are sent to N_j and N_k, their union has to be an element of $\mathbb{F}_i^*$. We use this observation to efficiently compute the best sub-plan for input $\{F_2\}$ at N_i as follows: For each $f_i^* \in \mathbb{F}_i^*$, determine input sets $f_j^* \subseteq f_i^*$ for N_j and $f_k^* \subseteq f_i^*$ for N_k independently such that the sub-plan cost at N_j and N_k are minimized. Add to the sum of these two costs, the cost of conversion from $\{F_2\}$ to f_i^* (i.e., the Minimum directed Steiner tree cost denoted as $\mathbb{S}(\{F_2\} \rightsquigarrow f_i^*)$). When there are k children this operation can be completed in $O(k.2^m)$ time if m is small and the array at each node is sorted in increasing order of sub-plan costs. We simply need to determine the minimum total cost over f_i^* (i.e., best element in $\mathbb{F}_i^*$). Since $|\mathbb{F}_i^*|$ is at most 2^m, we can determine the best plan for any given input at N_i ($\{F_2\}$ in this case) in $O(k.2^{2m})$. Further, since there are 2^m distinct inputs possible, we can fill the array at N_i in $O(k.2^{3m})$ time in the worst case.

Given the optimal substructure characteristic of this problem, we can give a dynamic programming based algorithm that computes the minimum cost plan for the CCD problem. Algorithm 1 shows the steps required for one broker N_i in the dissemination tree for a specified input format set $F_{in}^{N_i}$. The algorithm needs the input format set along with the dissemination subtree rooted at N_i and the list of arrays consisting

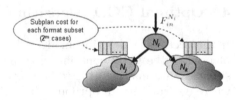

Fig. 5. Optimal CCD for a node

of the best plans at its children nodes ($ChildSubPlans_{N_i}[]$). As mentioned, the algorithm assumes that the minimum cost plan for all input format sets are available for every child of N_i. We then initialize the empty plan $\mathbb{P}$ with infinite cost (Lines 4-5). Now, for each possible output format set at N_i the algorithm first finds the conversion cost using a directed Steiner tree algorithm [12] in line (8). Note that the minimum conversion cost can be computed efficiently since the CAG is assumed to be small. Then it computes the least expensive plan as illustrated in the example above (Lines 9-13). If the newly computed plan

---

Algorithm 1. OptimalCCD

1: **INPUT:** $F_{in}^{N_i}$ (Set of input formats), $\mathbb{T}_{N_i}$(Dissemination subtree rooted at N_i),
   $ChildSubPlans_{N_i}$()(List of best child subplans)
2: **OUTPUT:** $\mathbb{P}_i$: Least cost subplan at N_i for input $F_{in}^{N_i}$;
3:
4: $\mathbb{P} \leftarrow$ Empty plan;
5: $\Theta_{\mathbb{P}} \leftarrow \infty$;
6: **for all** $F_{sub} \in PowerSet(F)$ **do**
7:   $\mathbb{P}_{temp} \leftarrow$ Operators performed in N_i;
8:   $\Theta_{\mathbb{P}_{temp}} \leftarrow \alpha\mathbb{S}(\mathbf{F_{in}^{N_i}} \rightsquigarrow \mathbf{F_{sub}})$; // $\mathbb{S}(F_{in}^{N_i} \rightsquigarrow F_{sub})$:the minimum cost of converting content
     from a set of available formats, F_{in} into set of output formats, F_{out}
9:   **for all** $N_j \in$ Children(N_i) **do**
10:    $\mathbb{P}_{N_j} \leftarrow$ MIN$\{ChildSubplans_{N_i}(N_j)\}$ s. t. $F_{in}^{N_j} \subseteq F_{sub}$;
11:    Add $\mathbb{P}_{N_j}$ to $\mathbb{P}_{temp}$;
12:    $\Theta_{\mathbb{P}_{temp}} + =$ **TotalCost**($\mathbb{P}_{\mathbf{N_j}}$); // $TotalCost(\mathbb{P})$: the total cost of the plan
13:   **end for**
14:   **if** $\Theta_{\mathbb{P}} > \Theta_{\mathbb{P}_{temp}}$ **then**
15:    $\mathbb{P} \leftarrow \mathbb{P}_{temp}$;
16:    $\Theta_{\mathbb{P}} \leftarrow \Theta_{\mathbb{P}_{temp}}$;
17:   **end if**
18: **end for**
19: $\Theta_{\mathbb{P}} + = (1 - \alpha) \sum_{F_k \in F_{in}^{N_i}} T_{F_k}(\mathbb{C})$;
20: return $\mathbb{P}$;

---

had smaller cost than the previous plans, the algorithm updates the minimum
plan and its cost (Lines 14-17). Finally, the computed minimum plan's cost is
updated by the transmission cost of the input format set and is returned as the
minimum cost plan.

To find the minimum cost plan for a given dissemination tree, we call the
OptimalCCD algorithm in the RP broker with $F_{in}^{RP} = \{F_0\}$. After running the
algorithm, the minimum cost plan is available and the system uses it to detect
which operators must be executed in each broker and which content formats
must be transmitted over each link. Each node in the dissemination tree receives
the content formats along with the portion of plan corresponding to the subtree
rooted at that node. It then investigates the received plan and performs the
operators that are assigned to it in the plan and forwards the content in the formats indicated in the plan to each of its children along with their corresponding
parts of the dissemination plan.

Theorem 2. The complexity of the optimal CCD algorithm is $O(nk_{avg}2^{3m}\mathbb{S})$,
where n is the number of nodes in the dissemination tree, m is the number of
formats in the CAG, k_{avg} is the average number of children a node has and $\mathbb{S}$
is the complexity of computing the minimum cost directed Steiner tree in the
CAG .

Proof. The algorithm is recursively called for each node and there are n nodes in
all. Now, if we denote the average number of children of a node in the dissemination tree by k_{avg} and the maximum cost paid for an instance of the "Minimum
Steiner Tree" problem at any node by $\mathbb{S}$ (which is assumed to be almost linear due to the small value of m), then from the analysis done in the example

above (Figure 5), we can show that the worst case complexity of Algorithm 1 is $O(nk_{avg}2^{3m}\mathbb{S})$.   □

During implementation, the optimal CCD algorithm can be sped up by reducing the number of format sets to be considered in the output set of a node. If we cannot derive a particular format set from the input format set, there is no need to compute those sub-plans. However, in the worst case where CAG is a fully connected directed graph the algorithm may need to consider all 2^m subsets of formats.

5 CCD Problem for Large CAGs

In this section we present an iterative algorithm for CCD problems with large CAGs. Given an initial CCD plan, the algorithm iteratively selects a node in the dissemination tree and refines the local plan at the node to reduce the cost of the solution. The refining process may include the following two actions: (i) changing the conversion operators at this node and its children; (ii) changing the set of formats in which content is transmitted to each one of its children. The modified plan always has a cost lower than the previous one and acts as an input for the next iteration. The iterative CCD algorithms is shown below (Algorithm 2). We show through extensive experimentation (in Section 6) that these heuristics work very well in practice. In fact, in Section 6 we show empirically that the final plan costs are within a small factor of the minimum possible cost by establishing a theoretical lower bound to the cost of a CCD plan.

Algorithm 2. Iterative CCD algorithm for large CAG

1: **INPUT:** $\mathbb{P}$: The initial plan, $\mathcal{K}$: Number of iterations ;
2: **OUTPUT:** $\mathbb{P}$: The refined plan;
3:
4: **for all** $j = 0$ to $\mathcal{K}$ **do**
5:     N_i = SelectNode($\mathbb{P}$)
6:     RefinePlan($\mathbb{P}, N_i$)
7: **end for**
8: return $\mathbb{P}$;

The algorithm starts with an initial plan, then greedily selects a node using the *SelectNode* function call and applies the *RefinePlan* procedure to generate a better plan. In general, one may use a variety of criteria for termination, such as the magnitude of change in cost over successive iterations, number of iterations, time bound etc. In this paper, we just iterate for a fixed $\mathcal{K}$ times which is provided by the user as an input parameter. Next, we present details about the initialization, node selection and plan refinement steps of our iterative algorithm.

Step 1: Initial Plan Selection. We can initiate the above algorithm using any valid plan. In this paper, we seed the algorithm using either one of the three following strategies. We call the first plans the *All-in-root* plan and the second one *All-in-leaves* plan. Both of these algorithms avoid in-network placement of customization operators and perform all the required operators either at the dissemination tree's root or at the leaves. The *All-in-root* CCD algorithm generates all the required formats in the dissemination tree by performing the necessary operators in the root (RP). Then, the generated content in various formats are forwarded towards the leaves based on their requests. On the other hand, the *All-in-leaves* CCD algorithm forwards the published content to all leaves and all of the nodes with matching subscription convert the content into the formats requested by its clients from the original format. We refer to the third initial plan as the *Single-format* plan. In this plan content is transmitted over a link exactly in one format, the one with the smallest transmission cost.

Step 2: Node Selection for Plan Refinement. We considered several strategies for node selection. The first strategy is to select the nodes of the tree randomly in every iteration. We will refer to this as the RANDOM scheme. While the random scheme is the most obvious, a smarter approach would be to base the selection on some estimation of the potential cost-reduction one can achieve by *refining* a given scheme. We use a greedy heuristic that selects the next node (i.e., dissemination plan) based on the difference between the current cost of a sub-plan and the estimated *lower bound* to the minimum achievable cost for the sub-plan. The *SelectNode* function returns the node N_i^* from the set of all nodes N_i in the tree such that the *slack* in the total cost paid in the local region of N_i is maximized. The *slack = (total conversion cost paid in the local region of N_i - the lower bound of the total conversion cost in the local region of N_i) + (total transmission cost in the local region of N_i - lower bound to the total transmission cost in the local region of N_i).* We will refer to this as the SLACK scheme from here onwards. Since our cost model consists of content transmission and content conversion costs, to find a lower bound for a plan we need a lower bound for each of these components in the total cost. We describe how the lower bounds are computed next.

Transmission-cost lower bound: We define a lower bound for transmission cost for each link in the dissemination tree and define the lower bound for the tree as the sum of the lower bounds for each one of its links. Consider a link $< N_i, N_j >$ in the dissemination tree where N_j is a leaf node. The content formats transmitted over this link depend on the formats requested by the clients attached to N_j. Consider the case where content is requested only in F_k by the clients at N_j. Since the transmission costs are proportional to the "size" of the content format, the minimum transmission cost for the link is at least as much as the size of the smallest format in the CAG that we can convert into F_k. In other words, the minimum transmission cost along $< N_i, N_j >$ corresponds to the transmission cost for the format with the smallest size, say F_k^{min} such that there is a path from F_k^{min} to F_k in the CAG. In general, if the content is required in more than one format at a node, say $\{F_{k_1}^{min}, \ldots, F_{k_l}^{min}\}$ we can compute the corresponding smallest formats and take the transmission cost of the largest of these as the lower bound for the link. This lower bound applies to edges between internal nodes of the dissemination tree as well. The set of formats requested at any internal node N_t is simply taken to be the union of formats requested at any client of a node in the subtree rooted at N_t. Below, we describe how one can quickly determine such a format for any link in the dissemination tree.

We maintain a sorted array of all the formats in the CAG in ascending order of their transmission costs. This is a one time operation which takes $O(mlog(m))$ time at most. Then, for a given target format F_k we go down the array and select the smallest format such that there is a path from this format to F_k in the CAG (this could very well be F_k itself). The transmission cost of this format is chosen as the lower bound for F_k. When the content is required in multiple formats in the subtree rooted at the child node of the link, we determine the lower bound for each format separately and set the largest of these as the lower bound for the link. The lower bound to the transmission cost of the whole tree (subtree) is simply the sum of the lower bounds for every link in the tree(subtree). We will denote this by $T_{low}(t)$ for a subtree t or simply by T_{low} for the whole tree.

Conversion cost lower bound: Computing the lower bound for the total conversion cost is straightforward. The minimum conversion cost that needs to be paid for a plan is the cost of converting the original format into all the requested formats in the tree at least once. This is simply the cost of minimum directed Steiner tree of the CAG where the set of terminals is the set of all requested formats. We will denote this global lower bound to the conversion cost by C_{low}. Note, in contrast to the transmission cost which is a positive number for every link in the dissemination tree, the lower bound for conversion cost is zero for each node because there is always a valid plan in which no operation is performed at a given node. As a result the lower bound for conversion cost of any node is 0.

Algorithm 3. RefinePlan

1: **INPUT:** $\mathbb{P}$: The initial plan, N_i: Selected node ;
2:
3:   $\mathcal{G}_{\mathcal{ML}}(\mathcal{V}, \mathcal{E})$ = createMLGraph(N_i);
4:   $Source \leftarrow \phi$; //Set of source vertices;
5:   $Terminal \leftarrow \phi$; // Set of terminal vertices;
6: **for** every $v \in \mathcal{V}$ **do**
7:     **if** $v.node = N_i$ AND $v.format \in F_{in}^{N_i}$ **then**
8:         $Source = Source \cup \{v\}$;
9:     **end if**
10:    **if** $N_j \in Children(N_i)$ AND $v.node = N_j$ AND $v.format \in F_{out}^{N_j}$ **then**
11:        $Terminal = Terminal \cup \{v\}$;
12:    **end if**
13: **end for**
14: SteinerTree = MinSteiner($\mathcal{G}_{\mathcal{ML}}, Source, Terminal$);
15: **if** SteinerTree.cost < SubPlanCost($\mathbb{P},N_i$) **then**
16:     Update($\mathbb{P}$);
17: **end if**

Step 3: Plan Refinement Using Multilayer Graph. The *RefinePlan* procedure takes as input a valid plan and a node N_i and updates the plan to a new one with smaller cost by modifying conversion operations and transmissions in the local region of N_i. Algorithm 3 shows the steps of *RefinePlan* procedure. In line 3 it creates the multilayer graph corresponding to the local region of N_i. In other words, it creates the multilayer graph corresponding to the "stump" of the sub-plan underneath N_i involving N_i and its children only. Therefore, the refinement step focuses on the conversion operation performed at one of these nodes and the transmission formats along the links between N_i and its children in the current plan. Next, the source and terminal nodes for the minimum cost Steiner tree computation in the multilayer graph must be determined. Any vertex with N_i as its associated node and one of the input formats in $F_{in}^{N_i}$ is added to the set of source vertices for the Steiner tree. Similarly any vertex in the multilayer graph that corresponds to one of N_i's children and an output format of the child in the current plan is added to the set of terminals for the Steiner tree. Lines 6-13 show the steps of forming these source and terminal sets. Once these sets have been determined, we use an approximation algorithm for Steiner tree computation [12] as shown in line 14. Finally, if the total cost of the computed Steiner tree is strictly smaller than the cost before refinement the plan is updated to the reflect the new operations and transmissions in the dissemination tree as described below (lines 15-17).

The Update($\mathbb{P}$) process does the following: For each transmission edge in the Steiner tree, the format associated to the layer is added to the set of formats that are transmitted through the link between N_i and the corresponding child. Similarly, for each conversion edge in the Steiner tree the corresponding operator in the CAG is added to the list of operators that are performed at the associated node in the current plan. Note that the input format set for N_i and the output format sets for N_i's children remain unchanged after the call to *RefinePlan* procedure. Since we use approximate Steiner tree algorithm, the Steiner tree may result in the higher cost plan where in this case no action is taken. It is easy to see that the refined plan remains a valid plan after performing an update.

Note that since we construct a multilayer graph for a node and its children only, the size of the graph is significantly smaller than the multilayer graph for all of the dissemination tree. Assume the maximum number of children for a node in a network with 1000 brokers is 10 and there are 10 formats in the CAG and all formats are requested in every child. The multilayer graph in this case has 150 vertices. The complexity of the Steiner tree algorithm for $\mathcal{K}$ iteration is $O(160^2 \times 150^4 \times \mathcal{K})$ which is significantly less than $O(10000^2 \times 3500^4)$ which was the complexity of the example in Section 3.

6 Experimental Evaluation

6.1 System Setup

To evaluate our algorithms we developed a message level, event-based simulator on top of Tapestry routing scheme. We implemented our algorithms and customization operators in Java. Since the focus of this paper is content dissemination among brokers, we performed our simulations only for the broker overlay. There are 1024 brokers in the overlay network. We use the *matching ratio* as our main parameter, which is the fraction of the brokers that have matching subscriptions for a published content. As argued in [4], studying the behavior of our algorithms over the range of matching ratios enables us to interpret the results for both Zipf and uniform distribution of publications and subscriptions over the content space. For instance, the behavior of the algorithms for Zipf distribution in which a small portion of the event space is very popular while the majority of the event space has only few subscribers can be shown by the behavior of the algorithm for very high and very low matching ratios. For each matching ratio, the reported results are averages taken for 100 runs. We also use tree discovery message to detect the dissemination tree and the node and link costs. We account for the computation cost of performing our algorithms and the communication overhead of tree discovery message. Based on our prototyping, the average execution time of the algorithms was about 100ms and we set the probe message size to be 0.1 KB. Publishers and subscribers in the broker overlay are selected randomly for each run. Similarly, the requested formats by a subscriber are sampled uniformly at random from the set of all formats. Each broker has subscriptions for at most $\frac{1}{4}$ of the available formats in the CAG. The default value for α and β is set to 1 in the cost function indicating that the normalized communication and computation cost units have equal weight.

6.2   Dissemination Scenarios

For our experimental study we used variety of small and large CAGs, however, because of space limitation in this section we present our results for two CAGs representing two dissemination scenarios. The first CAG is a small one that is used to evaluate our optimal CCD algorithm while the second one is a large CAG that is used to evaluate the heuristic based CCD algorithm.

Annotated Map Dissemination: For the first scenario, we considered customized dissemination of annotated maps to subscribers in the context of emergency. For instance, in case of wild fire an annotated map depicting shelters for evacuees and open roadways in a specific geographic region might need to be disseminated to the local population.

The published content in this scenario is an annotated map along with brief text description about each annotated item. Our system provides content in four different formats. The original format of the annotated map is PDF (F0). Depending on their preference and device, receivers can request the content in JPG image format (F1), text format (F2) or voice format which is text to speech conversion of the first annotated item(F3). For PDF to JPG and Text

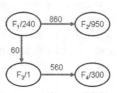

Fig. 6. Sample content and CAG for Annotated Map scenario

customizations we used PDFBox package (http://www.pdfbox.org/) and for Text to Voice conversion we used FreeTTS package (http://freetts.sourceforge.net/). Figure 6 depicts the corresponding CAG where the costs were computed based on our extensive prototyping.

Customized Video Dissemination: In the second scenario we consider dissemination of video content in variety of formats. In this scenario the CAG has 16 formats. The original content is in high quality 'mpeg4' format. The CAG contains four nodes in 'mpeg4' format that differ in frame size and bit rate. Also there are four nodes in CAG for each of 'avi', 'flv' and '3gp' formats. Similarly, each of these nodes represent specific frame size and bit rate for the video content. We also measure the content adaptation costs in the CAG based on extensive prototyping of possible transcoding between the available formats in the CAG. The costs of nodes in this CAG are in the range of [0,30]. For video transcoding we used *FFmpeg* which is a complete, cross-platform solution to record, convert and stream audio and video and includes libavcodec - a leading audio/video codec library[3]. The edge costs in this CAG are in the range of [0,60]. Because of very complex representation of this CAG (16 vertices and 210 edges) we only represent the CAG with 24 edges out of 210 edges in Figure 8.

6.3   Experiments

Based on the described system setup and the CAGs we present set of experiments that aim to evaluate the following:

- The effect of using optimal and heuristic CCD algorithms in reduction of content dissemination cost.
- The quality of the heuristic CCD algorithm results.
- The effect of different parameters.
- The effect of the relationship between communication and computation costs on the algorithm.

We use the small CAG from the annotated map scenario in the first two experiments to evaluate the benefit of using CCD algorithms and quality of the heuristic CCD algorithm compared to the optimal one. In the rest of experiments we use the large CAG of the video dissemination scenario to evaluate different factors that are involved in the heuristic CCD algorithm.

Effect of CCD algorithms on cost: In this experiment we evaluate the effect of using the proposed CCD algorithms in reducing the dissemination cost. We compare our CCD algorithms with two alternative approaches, *All-In-Leaevs* (AIL) and *All-In-Root* (AIR). Figure 7 represents the percentage of savings in the dissemination cost in our CCD algorithms compared to the AIL and AIR approaches for different α and β ratios. The first graph depicts the results for the optimal CCD algorithm and the small CAG and the second one shows the results for the heuristic CCD algorithm and the large CAG. As it can be seen in both cases using CCD algorithms result in reduction of dissemination cost, however, the amount of saving may significantly vary for AIL and AIR approaches as α and β change. The amount of cost reduction depends on several factors including the communication and computation costs in the CAG, the number of different requested formats in brokers and the relationship between communication and computation costs in the system. An interesting fact shown in the graphs is that the CCD algorithms result in much higher savings as compared to the AIL approach when $\frac{\alpha}{\beta} = 0.1$. In contrast, when $\frac{\alpha}{\beta} = 10$ the AIR approach performs much worse than the CCD algorithms. The reason is when $\frac{\alpha}{\beta} = 0.1$ computation cost unit is much higher than communication cost unit and since AIL performs operators in leaves, an operator may be performed several times which results in higher total cost. In such cases as expected the difference between CCD plans

---

[3] For information on FFmpeg please refer to "http://www.ffmpeg.org/"

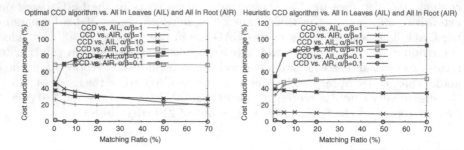

Fig. 7. Cost reduction percentage in Optimal and Heuristic CCD algorithms compared to AIL and AIR for different α and β values

and AIR is not very significant because the computation cost is minimized in AIR. On the other hand, when $\frac{\alpha}{\beta} = 10$ the generated plans by CCD algorithms are closer to AIL because communication cost is higher whereas AIR results in higher communication cost because of redundant transmission of the same content in different formats over some links. In general, these results show that regardless of CAG and requested formats in brokers, using our CCD algorithms always results in reduction of dissemination cost compared to at least one of the AIL or AIR approaches.

Quality of CCD heuristic: In this experiment we evaluate the effectiveness of the heuristic CCD algorithm in finding a dissemination plan. We compare the cost of the plan resulting from the heuristic CCD algorithm with the cost of the optimal dissemination plan that has the minimum cost. Since finding the minimum cost plan when the CAG is large is NP-hard we use our small CAG in this experiment. The minimum cost plan in this experiment is computed using our optimal CCD algorithm. Figure 9 depicts the percentage of cost difference between the minimum cost plan and the plan resulting from the heuristic CCD algorithm for 1000 iterations. The cost difference after a few iterations sharply falls to around 1% for all matching ratios. This shows that the proposed heuristic CCD produces dissemination plans significantly close to the minimum dissemination plans. Also this plan is achieved with very small number of iterations in the heuristic CCD algorithm.

In the previous experiments we showed that the CCD algorithms reduce the dissemination cost and the heuristic CCD algorithm results in close to optimal dissemination plans. In the rest of the experiments in this section we present the effect of different parameters on the effectiveness of the heuristic CCD algorithm.

Initial plan selection: In this experiment we compare three different dissemination plans, All In Root (AIR), All In Leaves (AIL) and Single format (SF). An important factor that affects the final plan cost is the relationship between communication and computation costs in the system. If the communication resources in a system are more expensive than computation resources, the initial plan that is used for the heuristic CCD algorithm may be different than when the computation resources are costlier than the communication resources. Figure 10 plots the costs of three initial dissemination plans for different matching

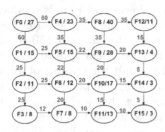

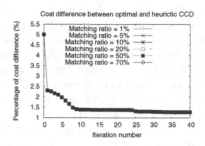

Cost difference between optimal and heurictic CCD

Fig. 8. Video dissemination CAG with sub-set of edges

Fig. 9. Goodness of the heuristic CCD algorithm compared to the optimal algorithm

rations in three different scenarios. As it is seen when the computation resources have more importance in the system ($\frac{\alpha}{\beta} = 0.1$), the AIR initial plan has smallest cost for all matching ratios. This is clear because of AIR plans have minimum computation cost. On the other hand, if the communication resources are more expensive, AIR plan results in more consumption of communication resources and therefore results in larger dissemination cost. Therefore, AIR s the worst initial plan when $\frac{\alpha}{\beta} = 10$. As it is seen in this case SF is a better initial plan to consider.

Note that these results are for specific CAG and subscription distribution among brokers. We have similar results for different CAGs and subscription distributions where single format or All In Root may result in better initial plan. Therefore, we conclude that to find a better initial plan, the heuristic CCD algorithm computes all possible initial CCD plans and selects the one with the smallest cost as the initial plan for refining the plan using iterations.

Next step selection: In this experiment we evaluate the random and slack based selection techniques. Figure 11 depicts the percentage of cost improvement compared to the cost of initial plan for 500 iterations and three matching ratios,

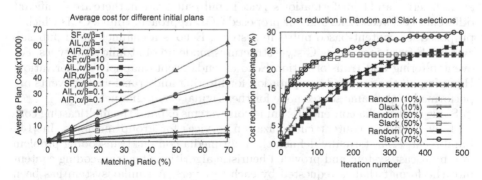

Fig. 10. Initial plan comparison for different α and β values

Fig. 11. Next node selection effect on cost reduction rate

10%, 50% and 70%. As it is seen for all matching ratios the rate in which the slack based techniques refines the dissemination plan to lower cost plan is significantly faster than the random technique. For instance, in 70% matching ratio the slack based technique results in 25% reduction in cost after around 150 iterations while it takes more than 500 iteration for the random technique to achieve the same percentage in cost reduction. Therefore, if we limit the number of iterations that the heuristic CCD algorithm performs for refining the plan, the slack based technique is superior to the random one. Another fact that is shown in the figure is that regardless of the next step selection technique, both random and slack based heuristic CCD algorithms converge to the same final dissemination plan after sufficient number of iterations. This means if there are enough resources available for a large number of iterations, both techniques achieve the same final refined dissemination plan.

7 Related Work

Most of the existing pub/sub systems have concentrated on providing efficient dissemination service for simple publication formats such as numerical or text content [1, 3, 5]. Shah *et al.* studied filter placement in content-based pub/sub network [15]. The objective of this approach is to minimize the total network bandwidth utilization resulting from dissemination of published content. However, their system does not consider the overhead resulting from filter operations in the cost function and only consider single filtering operation type. The content format also is not customized and published content is delivered in the same format to all receivers.

Diao *et al.* proposed ONYX, a customized XML dissemination framework that provides scalability and expressiveness [16]. ONYX provides incremental message transformation by using early projection and early restructuring of content. However, since content transformation operations are XML filtering and restructuring operations, ONYX does not consider overhead of transformation and only aims to minimize content transmission overhead.

The Echo pub/sub system is a high performance event delivery middleware designed for grid environments with large scale event rates [19]. While Echo provides event filtering and transformation service in pub/sub system, there are significant differences between Echo and our proposed CCD approach. Unlike CCD which is proposed for content-based pub/sub systems, Echo is a channel-based pub/sub system. Event types define C-style structures made up of atomic data types. For event filtering and transformation Echo extends event channels via derivation. However, all the required computation for filtering and transforming events are performed in the same source node for the original event channel.

Some multimedia content dissemination systems expand the multicasting concept by providing content customization services for group members. In [14], Lambrecht, *et al.* formally defined the multimedia content transcoding problem in a multicast system and provided heuristic algorithms for transcoding content into the format that is requested by each receivers. A similar system has been proposed in [13] where the multicast tree is mapped into a multilevel graph and an approximate Steiner tree algorithm to find efficient content transcoding in the network. However, unlike our proposed system, both of the systems assume that the multicast group is a fixed and predefined group. Also these systems only consider dissemination of multimedia content in the same file format which is a subset of the problem we consider here.

Content customization has been subject to extensive research in multimedia community. Nahrstedt *et al.* proposed *Hourglass*[17], a multimedia content customization and dissemination framework. Hourglass composes requested content formats from specified sources by efficiently placing composition services in the network and disseminates composed format to receivers in their requested formats. However, Hourglass assumes each adaptation service is performed only once in the system and also content dissemination is done using multiple dissemination trees: one for each content format. Both of these assumptions significantly simplify the customized content dissemination problem.

8   Conclusions and Future Work

We have introduced customized content dissemination system where content is only delivered to receivers that have requested it and in their desired format. We proposed operator placement algorithms on top of a DHT-based pub/sub framework in order to customize content format such that dissemination cost, which we defined as a linear function of customization (computing) and transmission (communication) costs, is minimized. We formally defined the problem and showed that it is NP-hard. We proposed two approaches to generate an efficient operator placement plan. Our first algorithm, the optimal CCD, finds the minimum cost CCD plan when the number of requested formats in the system is small. For the scenarios with large number of required formats we proposed an iterative heuristic algorithm that considerably reduces the CCD cost compared to performing customizations in the dissemination tree root or in the receiver brokers. We also showed the benefit of using our algorithms through extensive experiments. We have extended our proposed algorithms to take into account the heterogeneity of brokers and links along with the effect of concurrent publications in computing dissemination plans. However, due to the space limitation we did not present these extensions along with the corresponding experimental results in this paper.

In the heuristic CCD algorithm we used a multilayer graph for a subtree of depth one in the dissemination tree. As part of our future work we are investigating the trade-off in choosing subtrees with higher depth and complexity of the minimum directed Steiner tree computation. We are also working on a heuristic algorithm based on our Optimal CCD algorithm to generate a more effective initial plan for our heuristic CCD algorithm when the CAG is large. We are also investigating other cost models including dissemination time and the ways that the CCD algorithms can be adapted for such cost models.

References

1. Castelli, S., Costa, P., Picco, G.P.: HyperCBR: Large-Scale Content-Based Routing in a Multidimensional Space. In: IEEE INFOCOM 2008 (2008)
2. http://www.twitter.com

3. Aekaterinidis, I., Triantafillou, P.: PastryStrings: A Comprehensive Content-Based Publish/Subscribe DHT Network. In: IEEE ICDCS 2006 (2006)
4. Cao, F., Pal Singh, J.: MEDYM: Match-Early with Dynamic Multicast for Content-Based Publish-Subscribe Networks. In: Alonso, G. (ed.) Middleware 2005. LNCS, vol. 3790, pp. 292–313. Springer, Heidelberg (2005)
5. Li, G., Muthusamy, V., Jacobsen, H.A.: Adaptive Content-Based Routing in General Overlay Topologies. In: Issarny, V., Schantz, R. (eds.) Middleware 2008. LNCS, vol. 5346, pp. 1–21. Springer, Heidelberg (2008)
6. Tam, D., Azimi, R., Jacobsen, H.A.: Building Content-Based Publish/Subscribe Systems with Distributed Hash Tables. In: Aberer, K., Koubarakis, M., Kalogeraki, V. (eds.) VLDB 2003. LNCS, vol. 2944, pp. 138–152. Springer, Heidelberg (2004)
7. Zhao, B.Y., Huang, L., Stribling, J., Rhea, S.C., Joseph, A.D., Kubiatowicz, J.: Tapestry: A Resilient Global-scale Overlay for Service Deployment. IEEE Journal on Selected Areas in Communications 22(1) (2004)
8. Rowstron, A., Druschel, P.: Pastry: Scalable, distributed object location and routing for large-scale peer-to-peer systems. In: Guerraoui, R. (ed.) Middleware 2001. LNCS, vol. 2218, p. 329. Springer, Heidelberg (2001)
9. Zhuang, S.Q., Zhao, B.Y., Joseph, A.D., Katz, R.H., Kubiatowicz, J.: Bayeux: An Architecture for Scalable and Fault-tolerant Wide-Area Data Dissemination. In: Proceedings of ACM NOSSDAV 2001 (2001)
10. Baldoni, R., Marchetti, C., Virgillito, A., Vitenberg, R.: Content-Based Publish-Subscribe over Structured Overlay Networks. In: IEEE ICDCS 2005 (2005)
11. Gupta, A., Sahin, O., Agrawal, D., El Abbadi, A.: Meghdoot: Content-Based Publish/Subscribe over P2P Networks. In: Jacobsen, H.-A. (ed.) Middleware 2004. LNCS, vol. 3231, pp. 254–273. Springer, Heidelberg (2004)
12. Charikar, M., Chekuri, C., Cheung, T., Dai, Z., Goel, A., Guha, S., Li, M.: Approximation algorithms for directed steiner problems. In: ACM-SIAM symposium on Discrete algorithms (1998)
13. Henig, A., Raz, D.: Efficient management of transcoding and multicasting multimedia streams. In: 9th IFIP/IEEE International Symposium on Integrated Network Management (2005)
14. Lambrecht, T., Duysburgh, B., Wauters, T., De TurckBart Dhoedt, F., Demeester, P.: Optimizing multimedia transcoding multicast trees. Computer Networks 50(1, 16), 29–45 (2006)
15. Shah, R., Ramzan, Z., Jain, R., Dendukuri, R., Anjum, F.: Efficient Dissemination of Personalized Information Using Content-Based Multicast. IEEE Trans. Mob. Comput. 3(4), 394–408 (2004)
16. Diao, Y., Rizvi, S., Franklin, M.J.: Towards an Internet-Scale XML Dissemination Service. In: VLDB Conference (August 2004)
17. Nahrstedt, K., Yu, B., Liang, J., Cui, Y.: Hourglass Content and Service Composition Framework for Pervasive Environments. In: Elsevier Pervasive and Mobile Computing (2005)
18. Chang, C.-Y., Chen, M.-S.: On Exploring Aggregate Effect for Efficient Cache Replacement in Transcoding Proxies. IEEE Trans. on Parallel and Dist. Sys. 14(7) (2003)
19. Eisenhauer, G., Schwan, K., Bustamante, F.E.: Publish-Subscribe for High-Performance Computing. IEEE Internet Computing 10(1), 40–47 (2006)
20. Srivastava, U., Munagala, K., Widom, J.: Operator placement for in-network stream query processing. In: ACM PODS 2005 (2005)
21. Zhu, Y., Ammar, M.: Algorithms for assigning substrate network resources to virtual network components. In: IEEE INFOCOM 2006 (2006)

Calling the Cloud: Enabling Mobile Phones as Interfaces to Cloud Applications

Ioana Giurgiu, Oriana Riva, Dejan Juric, Ivan Krivulev, and Gustavo Alonso

Systems Group, Department of Computer Science, ETH Zurich
8092 Zurich, Switzerland
{igiurgiu,oriva,alonso}@inf.ethz.ch

Abstract. Mobile phones are set to become the universal interface to online services and cloud computing applications. However, using them for this purpose today is limited to two configurations: applications either run on the phone or run on the server and are remotely accessed by the phone. These two options do not allow for a customized and flexible service interaction, limiting the possibilities for performance optimization as well. In this paper we present a middleware platform that can automatically distribute different layers of an application between the phone and the server, and optimize a variety of objective functions (latency, data transferred, cost, etc.). Our approach builds on existing technology for distributed module management and does not require new infrastructures. In the paper we discuss how to model applications as a consumption graph, and how to process it with a number of novel algorithms to find the optimal distribution of the application modules. The application is then dynamically deployed on the phone in an efficient and transparent manner. We have tested and validated our approach with extensive experiments and with two different applications. The results indicate that the techniques we propose can significantly optimize the performance of cloud applications when used from mobile phones.

Keywords: Mobile phones, cloud applications, OSGi, performance.

1 Introduction

Mobile phones are set to become a main entry point and interface to the growing number of cloud computing services and online infrastructures. They are also increasingly perceived as the most convenient access point for a variety of situations: from payments to ticket purchase, from carrying boarding passes to hotel check in, from browsing a shop catalog to activating a coffee machine.

Today, the implementation of such scenarios is limited by the lack of flexibility in deploying mobile phone applications. They either run entirely on the server, typically incurring large data transfer costs, high latencies, and less than optimal user interfaces; or they run entirely on the phone, thereby imposing many limitations on what can be achieved due to the constraints of mobile phone hardware, as well as placing an undue burden on the end users who need to install, update,

J.M. Bacon and B.F. Cooper (Eds.): Middleware 2009, LNCS 5896, pp. 83–102, 2009.
© IFIP International Federation for Information Processing 2009

and manage such applications. In this paper we explore how to deploy such applications in a more optimal way by dynamically and automatically determining which application modules should be deployed on the phone and which left on the server to achieve a particular performance target (low latency, minimization of data transfer, fast response time, etc.). Having such a possibility creates a wealth of opportunities to improve performance and the user experience from mobile phones, turning them into an open, universal interface to the cloud.

To optimally partition an application between a mobile phone and a server, we approach the problem in two steps. First, we abstract an application's behaviour as a data flow graph of several inter-connected software modules. Modules encapsulate small functional units supplied by the application developer. Each module provides a set of services, and modules are connected through the corresponding service dependencies. Through an offline application profiling, modules and service dependencies are characterized in terms of their resource consumption (data exchange, memory cost, code size), thus providing the knowledge base for the optimization process. Given this graph, in the second step, a partitioning algorithm finds the optimal cut that maximizes (or minimizes) a given objective function. The objective function expresses a user's goal such as to minimize the interaction latency or the data traffic. Moreover, the optimization also takes into account a mobile phone's resource constraints such as memory and network resources available.

We propose two types of partitioning algorithms: ALL and K-step. We look at the problem both as a static and dynamic optimization. In the first case, the best partitioning is computed offline by considering different types of mobile phones and network conditions. In the second case, the partitioning is computed on-the-fly, when a phone connects to the server and specifies its resources and requirements. ALL fits the first scenario, while K-step the second one.

Our approach does not require new infrastructures as it uses existing software for module management such as R-OSGi [1] and a deployment tool like AlfredO [2], that can support the actual distributed deployment of an application between a phone and a server.

This paper makes the following contributions. First, we model the partitioning problem and the algorithms that can solve it. Second, we show the effectiveness of this approach with two prototype applications. Third, we present a comprehensive evaluation involving realistic application scenarios of mobile phones. Our measurements show that the system can quickly identify the optimal partition given various phone constraints, and provide an improvement of tens of seconds compared to the case in which the phone hosts the entire application or leaves all the service logic on the server.

The rest of the paper is organized as follows. The next section gives an overview of the AlfredO platform we use. Section 2.2 describes how application profiling is used to produce an application's consumption graph, while Section 3 presents the partitioning algorithms. Section 4 evaluates our approach and Section 5 describes an application using it. We then conclude and discuss limitations and open problems of your approach as well as related work.

2   Flexible Module Deployment

This section starts by providing background on AlfredO and then describes how application profiling is used to generate a consumption graph.

2.1   AlfredO Overview

We use AlfredO [2] to carry out the physical distribution of an application's modules between a mobile phone and a server. AlfredO is based on OSGi [3], which has been traditionally used to decompose and loosely couple Java applications into software modules. In the OSGi terminology, software modules are called *bundles*, and bundles typically communicate through *services*, which are ordinary Java classes with a service interface.

Given an OSGi-based application with a presentation tier, a logic tier, and a data tier, where each tier consists of several OSGi bundles, AlfredO allows developers to decompose and distribute the presentation and logic tiers between the client and server side, while always keeping the data tier on the server.

In a typical example of interaction, the minimal requirement for interacting with a certain application is to acquire the presentation tier. Once AlfredO has built the presentation tier, the logic tier's services can be invoked. This happens by either redirecting invocations to remote services provided by the server side or by acquiring and running some parts of the logic tier locally.

Figure 1 shows an example of client-server interaction. Both devices run OSGi with the R-OSGi [1] bundle installed, which enables remote service execution across OSGi platforms. The AlfredO system consists of three bundles: *AlfredO-Client* and *Renderer* on the client, and *AlfredOCore* on the server.

Upon explicit discovery (e.g., using a service discovery protocol such as SLP [4] provided by R-OSGi) or by direct connection to a known address (e.g., the remote server periodically broadcasts invitations), the connection is established and the client requests a selected application. Using one of the available partitioning algorithms (described in the next section), AlfredOCore computes the optimal deployment for such an application, and then returns to AlfredOClient

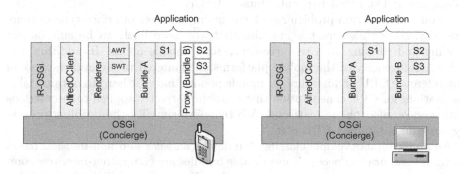

Fig. 1. AlfredO architecture

the application's descriptor (also explained later) and the list of services to be fetched. The application's descriptor is used by the Renderer to generate the corresponding AWT or SWT user interface, while AlfredOClient fetches the specified services via R-OSGi.

In the general case, a server provides bundles offering services. If a client wants to use a server's service, the server provides the client with the service interface of such a service. Then the R-OSGi framework residing on the client side generates from the service interface a *local proxy*. The local proxy delegates service calls of the client to the remote server and each proxy is registered with the local R-OSGi service registry as an implementation of the particular service. If it happens that the service interface references types provided by the original service module and these are located on the server side, the corresponding classes are also transmitted and injected into the proxy module.

Alternatively, rather than invoking a remotely executing service, a client can decide to fetch it. In the example in the figure, if the client wants to acquire S1, the corresponding bundle A is transferred to the client side and plugged into the OSGi platform. When the client receives the service interface of S1, it is also provided with a list of the associated service's dependencies. Let us assume that S1 depends on S2, and S2 depends on S3, which are both offered by another bundle B. The client can either acquire only S1 and create a local proxy for S2 and S3, or it can also acquire S2 and S3.

2.2 Application Profiling

The first step in optimizing an application's deployment is to characterize the behaviour of such an application through a resource consumption graph. We assume applications to be built using the OSGi module system, but the same method could be extended to work with applications modularized in other ways.

We instrument every bundle composing the application to measure the consumed memory, the data traffic generated both in input and output, and its code size. We then execute the instrumented application on one or multiple phone platforms and collect on a debug channel the amount of consumed resources. Each bundle's cost represents how much a phone has to pay if it wants to acquire and run that particular bundle locally.

In our optimization problem, we focus mainly on user interface type of functionality, since these are the modules that are more likely to be suitable for moving and running on a resource-constrained mobile phone. In addition, the large heterogeneity of the mobile platforms encountered today and the lack of one reference CPU architecture for mobile phones makes it hard to obtain stable estimations for CPU consumption that could be correctly applied to interactions with non-profiled phone platforms. We therefore simplify the profiling process by omitting a bundle's CPU cost.

An application developer classifies bundles as *movable* and *non-movable* based on their computation needs. Non-movable bundles are computing-intensive components that are bound to always execute on the server side. This simplification has so far proven sufficient for the interactive applications we have considered and that AlfredO primarily targets, since the most critical factor in the overall performance is usually the amount of transferred data.

The profiling output is then used to generate the application descriptor. A snippet of the descriptor used in the example of Figure 1 is the following:

```
<tier>
  <requires>
    <service name="S3" data="350"/>
  </requires>
  <provides>
    <service name="S2"/>
  </provides>
  <memory>155</memory>
  <code>30</code>
  <type>movable</type>
</tier>
```

This descriptor specifies that service S2 requires S3 for its execution (i.e., S2 depends on S3) and the total amount of data that needs to acquire from S1 and return to S3 is 350 bytes. Other requirements include the memory cost of S2 when executed on the phone, and the size of the bundle to which it is associated.

2.3   Consumption Graph

The output of the profiling process is used to represent the application as a directed acyclic graph $G = \{B, E\}$, where every vertex in B is a bundle B_i and every edge e_{ij} in E is a service dependency between B_i and B_j. Each bundle B_i is characterized by five parameters:

- *type*: movable or non-movable bundle,
- $memory_i$: the memory consumption of B_i on a mobile device platform,
- $code\_size_i$: the size of the compiled code of B_i,
- in_{ji}: the amount of data that B_i takes in input from B_j,
- out_{ij}: the amount of data that B_i sends in output to B_j.

Figure 2 shows an example of a graph consisting of 6 bundles. We call this an application's *consumption graph*. Notice that although our implementation currently considers these five parameters, the model is generic enough to be easily extended with more variables.

In this work we make the simplifying assumption that every bundle exposes only one service, i.e., *bundle:service* mapping is 1:1. This implies that a bundle can be interconnected to multiple bundles, but always through the same service interface. As ongoing work, we are relaxing this assumption by differentiating among the type and number of service dependencies.

The graphs we consider for optimization are not extremely large because, first, we focus on the presentation layer, and, second, modularity is not at the class or object level, but at the functional level. Therefore, we expect applications to have in most cases a few tens of modules.

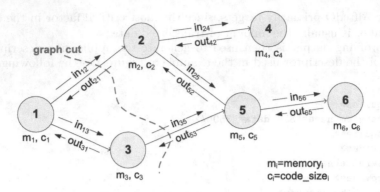

Fig. 2. Example of application's consumption graph

3 Partitioning Algorithms

In this section, we describe the AlfredO's algorithms used to optimize an application's distribution between a phone and a server. The server is assumed to have infinite resources, while a client is characterized by several resource constraints. We start by describing how the optimization problem is defined and which assumptions are made, and then present the partitioning algorithms.

3.1 Optimization Problem

The partitioning problem seeks to find a cut in the consumption graph such that some modules of the application execute on the client side and the remaining ones on the server side. The optimal cut maximizes or minimizes an *objective function O* and satisfies a phone's resource constraints. The objective function expresses the general goal of a partition. This may be, for instance, minimize the end-to-end interaction time between a phone and a server, minimize the amount of exchanged data, or complete the execution in less than a predefined time.

A phone's constraints include $memory_{MAX}$, the maximum memory available for all potentially acquired bundles, and $code\_size_{MAX}$, the maximum amount of bytes of compiled code a phone can afford to transfer from the server.

Let us consider an application consisting of n bundles of type movable, denoted as $B = \{B_1, ..., B_n\}$. A configuration C_c is defined as a tuple of partitions from the initial set of bundles, $< B_{client}, B_{server} >$, where $B_{client} = \{B_a | a \in [1, ..., k]\}$ and $B_{server} = \{B_b | b \in [1, ..., s]\}$ with $B_{server} \cap B_{client} = \phi$ and $B_{server} \bigcup B_{client} = B$.

An example of objective function that we will use to evaluate our approach minimizes the interaction latency between a phone and a server, while taking into account the overhead of acquiring and installing the necessary bundles. This can be modelled in the following way:

$$\min O_{C_c} = \min(\sum_{i=1}^{t<k} \sum_{j=1}^{w} \frac{(in_{ij} + out_{ji}) * f_{ij}}{\alpha} + \sum_{i=1}^{k} \frac{code\_size_i}{\beta} + \sum_{i=1}^{w<s} proxy\_cost_i)$$

The first part in the function models the cost due to the application's data exchange when k bundles run on the mobile phone and t bundles out of these have dependency relationships with w bundles residing on the server side. As we consider only movable bundles with a very low computation cost, this mainly consists of communication cost. The parameter α approximates the capacity of the communication link between the client and server achievable in real settings and also takes into account the overhead imposed by the device platform to set up the communication. Depending on the type of interaction a user may invoke a certain module multiple times. This is modelled through the f_{ij} parameter which specifies how many times the communication between i and j occurs.

The second part models the cost to fetch, install, and start the k bundles on the mobile phone. The parameter β takes into account the capacity of the communication link as well as the installation overhead. The third part represents the cost for building the local proxies necessary to interact with the w remote bundles. Notice that the f parameters appears only in the first member as having one or multiple interactions solely affects the amount of data sent back and forth between the mobile device and the server, while the cost of shipping the code and building local proxies remains the same.

Given the objective function and the consumption graph we want to find the optimal partition. Although many tools exist for graph partitioning, they do not prove to be suitable for our problem. Tools like METIS [5] are designed specifically for partitioning large scientific codes for parallel simulation. Moreover, they apply heuristic solutions in order to create a fixed number of balanced graph partitions, thus fixing predefined seeds and not allowing for flexibility. Other tools like Zoltan [6] represent an application as a graph, where data objects are vertices and pairwise data dependencies are edges. The graph partitioning problem is then to partition the vertices into equal-weighted parts, while minimizing the weight of edges with endpoints in different parts. This approach does not allow for unlimited and unspecified capacity for the server partition, and expects a single weight on each edge and each vertex. This constraint limits the applicability of the method, since it cannot support heterogeneity of different platforms.

Another option is to consider traditional task scheduling algorithms. However, the main drawback of task scheduling is that it does not fit a non-deterministic data flow model, since it assumes that all tasks are executed exactly once. Therefore, it does not fit scenarios where a user may interact with an application several times and spontaneously.

We therefore propose an alternative approach with two novel algorithms.

3.2 Pre-processing

Before running the actual algorithms, we pre-process the consumption graph to reduce the search space, but without eliminating optimal solutions. For large graphs, this step is essential to reduce the graph size and therefore the number of possible configurations, thus improving the algorithm's performance. The idea is to identify bundles that yield a very high cost and therefore cannot be moved to the client or bundles that exchange a lot of data, and therefore should always execute on the same device.

Given a consumption graph $G = \{B, E\}$, if the cost of an edge $e_{ij} \in E$ is such that $in_{ij} + out_{ji} > data_{MAX}$, then Bi and Bj are merged into one bundle B_i: all input and output edges are updated accordingly, and the cost of the new bundle B_i is given by the sum of the relative costs of the old B_i and B_j.

3.3   ALL Algorithm

After the pre-processing step, two classes of algorithms can be applied to find the optimal cut. The reason for having two different algorithms is that the optimization problem can be looked as a static problem, where the optimal partitioning for several types of mobile devices is pre-computed offline or as a dynamic problem where the partition must be calculated on-the-fly, once a mobile connects and communicates its resources. In this work, we consider both options and we propose ALL for offline optimization and K-step for online optimization.

The ALL algorithm always guarantees to find the optimal cut. It operates in three steps. First, it generates all "valid" configurations. Given B, we define $C = \{C_c | c \in [1, ..., m]\}$ the set of all valid configurations, where m is the total number of configurations obtained by traversing the consumption graph in an adapted topological order that combines both breadth-first and depth-first algorithms. A valid configuration is such that if bundle B_p and B_q belong to B_{client}, if B_p and B_q are not connected through a direct edge e_{pq}, then all bundles on the possible paths between B_p and B_q also belong to B_{client}.

Second, for all valid C_c configurations with k being the number of bundles to be fetched, installed, and run on the phone, it chooses the ones that satisfy the phone's constraints:

1. $\sum_{i=1}^{k} memory_i \leq memory_{MAX}$;
2. $\sum_{i=1}^{k} code\_size_i \leq code\_size_{MAX}$;

Third, the algorithm evaluates the objective function for each valid configuration and chooses the one providing its maximum (or minimum) value.

3.4   K-Step Algorithm

While the ALL algorithm inspects all possible configurations and identifies the "global" optimal cut, the K-step algorithm evaluates a reduced set of configurations and finds a "local" optimum. The K-step algorithm is therefore by design faster than the ALL algorithm, but can be less accurate.

Instead of generating all configurations and then choosing the best ones, this algorithm computes the best configuration at every step and on-the-fly. At the beginning, K-step adds to the current configuration the entry node of the graph and computes the current value for the objective function. Then, at each step, it adds K new nodes to the current configuration, only if these new nodes provide a configuration with an objective value larger (the goal is maximize O) or smaller (the goal is minimize O) than the current one and if the phone's constraints are still respected. Depending on K, the algorithm can add one single node (K=1) or a subgraph of size K (K>1) computed by combining depth-first and breadth-first.

More specifically, at each step the algorithm maintains a queue containing all nodes in the graph (not yet acquired) within a distance of K hops from all nodes present in the current configuration. The algorithm generates all possible configurations with the nodes in the queue and the nodes already added to the current configuration. It then evaluates the objective function for each new possible configuration. If any of the new configurations provides an objective value better than the current one, then a new local optimum has been found. However, the K nodes enabling such a configuration are added only if their resource demands respect the phone's constraints. If the constraints are violated, the algorithm will evaluate them for the second best new configuration and so forth until a better configuration respecting the phone's constraints is found. If none of the new configurations provide a better objective value, while satisfying the phone constraints, the algorithm stops and returns the current configuration. Otherwise, if a configuration is found, the new K nodes are added to the current configuration and removed from the queue. The queue will be updated and the evaluation continues. The algorithm ends when the queue is empty or when the objective value cannot be improved any further.

4   Evaluation

To evaluate our approach we have explored two directions. First, we have built from scratch a prototype application and used it to test our algorithms under various resource and network constraints. This application is specifically designed to allow several configurations and stress the operation of the algorithms. Second, we have taken an existing application for home interior design and modified it to support our approach. In this section we focus on the experiments with the first application, while the second use case is presented in the next section.

In all results presented in the following the client runs on a Nokia N810 Internet tablet and the server on a regular laptop computer (Intel Core 2 Duo T7800 at 2.60 GHz). N810 handhelds, released in November 2007, run Linux 2.6.21, have a 400 MHz OMAP 2420 processor, 128 MB of RAM, and 2 GB of flash memory built in. N810 devices were connected to the laptop either through IEEE 802.11b in ad hoc mode or through Bluetooth.

4.1   Application Bundles and Service Dependencies

The prototype application we built implements some of the Image composition functions of the interior design application described in the next session. This is a very interactive application exhibiting a good mixture of light and heavy processing components. Using it a user can upload an image of his/her house and a photo of a furniture item, position the furniture item on top of the house plan, set several properties such as object focus, rotation, color, and dimension, and then invoke specialized image processing libraries for image composition.

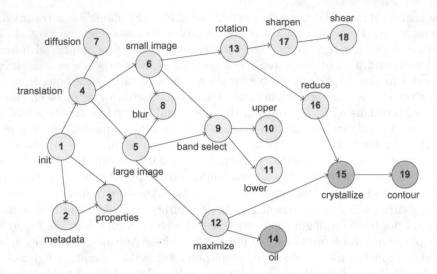

Fig. 3. Application graph

This application was built using the OSGi module system. The entire application consists of bundles with varying requirements in terms of processing and communication resources. The service dependencies between bundles generate the graph configuration shown in Figure 3, where we can identify two flows of bundles that process the small image (the furniture item in this case) and the large image (the house image) separately, and then merge through bundle 15 and 19. The heavy computation bundles, namely 14, 15 and 19, are marked as non-movable by the developer (in dark gray in the figure).

In the following experiments, we consider the objective function described in Section 3.3. The goal is to minimize the end-to-end interaction time observed by the client, including the time necessary to acquire and install the necessary code at the beginning of the interaction.

4.2   Startup Process

We start by analyzing the startup time of some selected configurations. We measure the time necessary to fetch, install, and start the necessary bundles to be run locally as well as to generate the R-OSGi proxies necessary for invoking services of remote bundles. The results are shown in Table 1.

The fetching time obviously increases with the number and size of the bundles acquired. The installation time is typically of 1–1.5 seconds per bundle. The proxy generation time depends on how many service dependencies exist with remote bundles. For example, in the first case, init has 3 dependencies: translation, properties, and metadata. Although the fetching and installation overhead can be even 30 seconds, as in the last case when 15 bundles are acquired, our algorithms opt for these kinds of configuration only when the performance gain is high enough. For smaller configurations, such as the first few

Table 1. Startup time (average and [standard deviation]) with Bluetooth

Configuration	Fetch & Install size (bytes)	Fetch & Install time (ms)	Proxy generation num	Proxy generation time (ms)	Total time (ms)
1	13940	4776 [180]	3	1044 [339]	5820
1–4	38907	9512 [100]	3	852 [66]	10364
1–5,12,14	98226	15006 [214]	5	1367 [196]	16373
1–4,6,13,16–18	82212	18650 [299]	4	1511 [176]	20161
1–6,9,12,13,16–18	109616	22666 [376]	8	2165 [221]	24831
1–6,8–13,16–18	135454	30413 [2180]	4	660 [93]	31073

cases, the overhead is comparable to the startup time of other common applications on mobile phones (e.g., text editor, web browser, etc.).

Once the interaction with an application ends, all the modules that have been fetched on the mobile device are erased such to free the phone's memory. This guarantees to consume resources only during the interaction.

4.3 Interaction Time

To assess the effectiveness of our algorithms in identifying the configuration that minimizes the given objective function, we first run some grounding experiments where we quantify the cost and performance of each valid configuration of the application's bundles. The performance is in this case the overall interaction time as observed by the user. The cost is the extra price in terms of fetched bundle code and allocated memory a client has to pay to run some bundles locally.

Figure 4(a) shows the interaction time both with WiFi and Bluetooth, and Figure 4(b) the resource consumption in terms of size of shipped code and memory consumed on the tablet. The pair of images submitted to the application is $< 100kB, 30kB >$. As the number of configurations for the given application's graph is more than 100, we report results for 25 random configurations.

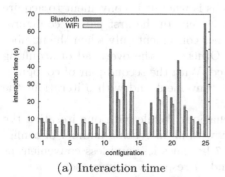

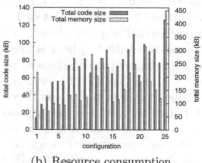

(a) Interaction time   (b) Resource consumption

Fig. 4. Overall interaction time (a) and resource consumption (b)

These experiments allow us to draw two important conclusions. First, there is no clear correlation between the interaction latency observed by the end-user and the number and size of bundles acquired by the client. There are cases in which acquiring more code does increase the interaction latency of more than 10 seconds (for example, passing from configuration 20 to 21) and others in which the opposite occurs (for example, passing from configuration 11 to 10). Second, there is a large variation in performance with even 60 seconds of difference from one configuration to the other. This indicates that there is potential to use the proposed algorithms to select the best configuration.

4.4   Multiple Service Invocations

The space of improvement is much larger than that shown by the previous results. Indeed, in running those experiments the test was configured for a "minimal number of iterations" (i.e., one invocation of every service). However, in reality this rarely occurs. For example, in setting the position, dimension, or rotation of a furniture item a user may need multiple iterations and will rarely get the properties set in a satisfying manner at the first attempt. Moreover, a user will typically place more than one furniture item in the same room thus invoking the same operations multiple items.

In these tests we investigate the impact of the number of iterations on the overall time. To this purpose we select 7 example configurations. In Figure 5 we plot the results obtained with the same images of before. The overall time includes the overhead for acquiring and installing the remote bundles and building the local proxies, and the actual interaction time measured using WiFi. The overhead installation time is 8.5 seconds for the $B_{client} = \{1, 2, 3\}$, 12 seconds for $B_{client} = \{1, 2, 3, 4\}$, and 16–18 seconds for all other configurations.

As the number of iterations increases different configurations may provide better or worse performance. In the graph in Figure 5(a), we compare the performance of the configuration $B_{client} = \{1, 2, 3\}$ with $B_{client} = \{1, 2, 3, 4\}$ when the number of invocation of bundle 4 increases, and of $B_{client} = \{1, 2, 3, 4, 5\}$ with $B_{client} = \{1, 2, 3, 4, 5, 12\}$ when the number of invocations of bundle 12 increases. The question in both comparisons is when it is convenient to acquire an additional bundle such as 4 or 12 respectively. In the first pair of configurations we see that acquiring bundle 4 becomes convenient only when the number of interactions with bundle 4 is above 2. Otherwise, the overhead of acquiring bundle 4 is higher than the benefit provided. With the second pair of configurations, acquiring bundle 12 is always more convenient and with 6 iterations the performance gain is more than 14 seconds.

In Figure 5(b), we see the opposite behaviour. While with one iteration the performance of all configuration is similar, with an increasing number of configurations the acquisition of bundle 16 or 17 becomes less and less convenient as the number of invocations of bundle 16 and 17 respectively increases.

The number of iterations of certain operations is therefore a key factor in deciding on the best configuration. This parameter can be estimated by averaging

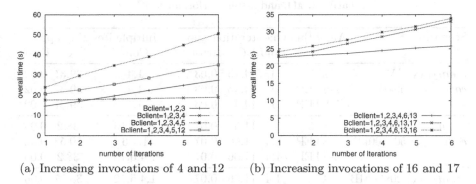

(a) Increasing invocations of 4 and 12   (b) Increasing invocations of 16 and 17

Fig. 5. Overall time with multiple service invocations with WiFi

over the behaviour of a few user interactions and it is strongly application-dependent. For example, a user interacting with a vending machine will more likely invoke the operations only once, unless in case of errors. Instead, in an application as the one considered that includes a visualization of the properties set, it is more likely to expect multiple iterations of the same function. These results clearly show that even light operations, such as bundle 4 that simply positions an image on top of another, can provide a high performance gain if performed locally (with 6 iterations, more than 12 seconds).

4.5   Algorithm Performance

The last set of tests quantifies the performance of the two proposed algorithms, ALL and K-step. We consider several user scenarios, with varying mem_{MAX} and $code_{MAX}$ constraints and two different consumption graphs. Table 2 presents the results obtained.

In the first consumption graph ("one iteration app"), every bundle is invoked exactly once. Therefore, we expect few components to be acquired on the client side, since the fetching overhead is in most cases higher than the performance gain. As expected, ALL provides in all scenarios the optimal solution. As the optimal solution always correspond to an early cut in the graph, the 1-step and 3-step algorithms also find the best solution.

The second consumption graph ("multiple iteration app") models the situation in which a user invokes an application's functions (i.e., bundles) multiple times. In this case, acquiring some bundles locally allows for a larger improvement of the performance. In most cases the optimal solution is to acquire 5 or more bundles, except in the first case where the phone's constraints do not allow for large acquisitions. The results of the three algorithms vary quite a lot, with 3-step outperforming 1-step in all cases.

Although the performance of ALL and K-step with an increasing K is typically the best, there exists a trade-off between processing time and accuracy of the solution. We explore this by measuring the processing time of ALL, 1-step,

Table 2. ALL and K-step performance

Scenario	Algorithm	One iteration app			Multiple iteration app		
		Conf	O	Error	Conf	O	Error
mem_{MAX}: 1MB	ALL	1	14.45	0.03	1,4	39.37	0.02
$code_{MAX}$: 50kB	1-STEP	1	14.45	0.03	1,4	39.37	0.02
	3-STEP	1	14.45	0.03	1,4	39.37	0.02
mem_{MAX}: 10MB	ALL	1,4	11.66	0.07	1,4,6,13	38.2	0.05
$code_{MAX}$: 50–100kB	1-STEP	1,4	11.66	0.07	1,4,6	50.53	0.32
	3-STEP	1,4	11.66	0.07	1,4,6,13	38.2	0.05
mem_{MAX}: 20–30MB	ALL	1,4	11.66	0.07	1,4,5,12	38.07	0.06
$code_{MAX}$: 50kB	1-STEP	1,4	11.66	0.07	1,4,5,6	47.72	0.32
	3-STEP	1,4	11.66	0.07	1,4,5,12	38.07	0.06
mem_{MAX}: 20–30MB	ALL	1,4	11.66	0.07	1,4–6,12,13,16	37.76	0.06
$code_{MAX}$: 100kB	1-STEP	1,4	11.66	0.07	1,4–6,13,16–18	49.78	0.24
	3-STEP	1,4	11.66	0.07	1,4–6,12,13,16–18	45.51	0.14

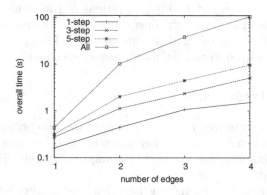

Fig. 6. Processing time for ALL, 1-step, 3-step and 5-step

3-step, and 5-step with an application graph consisting of 50 bundles and a varying number of bundle dependencies. Results are shown in Figure 6.

The processing time of all algorithms increases as the average number of edges from each node in the graph increases. This happens because a larger number of graph cuts become possible. The 5-step algorithm can be even 10 times faster than ALL and 1-step even 100 times faster.

We can conclude that while ALL suits an offline optimization, the K-step algorithm fits better dynamic scenarios where the decision has to be made on-the-fly. While 1-step can easily incur in a wrong local optimum, 3-step or 5-step provide a limited error.

5   Use Case

In addition to building the image composition application and assess the algorithms performance, we also took an existing application and applied AlfredO to it. This experience helped us to quantify the effort necessary to use AlfredO with real-world applications and to better identify the limitations of our approach. To this purpose, we used the open source Sweet Home 3D [7] application. This is a quite popular application for home interior design, which allows users to browse furniture items, place them in a 2D plan of their house, and visualize a 3D preview of it.

To run this application on a mobile phone several problems need to be considered. First, the application is too computational intensive to run on a phone platform. Second, its user interface uses Java Swing components, not supported by standard Java implementations available on phone platforms (i.e., Java ME CDC or CLDC). Third, considering the user interface of the application, the limited screen size of the phone would not allow for a good user experience.

To solve these problems, one possible solution would be to re-implement the entire application and customize it to the phone platform's characteristics. Instead, AlfredO solves these problems in a much faster way and provides a more extensible approach capable of integrating future extensions of the application.

We applied AlfredO by first modularizing the application and running it on the OSGi platform. As the application was originally designed according to the Model-View-Controller design pattern, this allowed us to quickly identify its main functional components. The current modularization accounts for 13 bundles. However, we are currently working on further decomposing some of the identified bundles to provide even more flexibility. A second modification we made was providing other alternative user interfaces implemented using the Java AWT library, which is supported by existing phone platforms. We currently support three different user interfaces with an increasing level of complexity. Also, having three rather than one user interface provides more flexibility and customization.

In the application's graph this translates in having different entry points to the same application. The appropriate entry point is selected by taking into account additional properties of the phone client such as screen size, color resolution, etc. Once the entry point is selected our algorithms are applied to determine the best graph cut and the corresponding configuration.

At a high-level, three classes of configurations can be supported. The simplest case is when the phone client acts only as a mouse controller of the remote application. The output returned to the mobile phone consists of a screenshot of the application display. This kind of interaction reuses the MouseController concepts we presented in [2].

A second possibility shown in Figure 7(b) is when the phone acquires the user interface necessary to select furniture items and specify their width and position (as x,y coordinates) locally. On the server side, items are placed accordingly in the 2D plan and the 3D preview is generated. A final option shown in Figure 7(c) is when the phone supports item selection and also placement in the 2D plan.

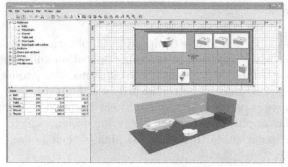

(a) SweetHome 3D server

(b) Catalog list and item placement on a N810

(c) Catalog list, item placement and map preview on N810

Fig. 7. Sweet Home 3D application running on a server (a) and on Nokia N810 handhelds (b and c)

Within each of these three types of configuration, different distributions of the application components are possible depending on the algorithm's decision. The overhead introduced by our modularization approach was found to be negligible compared to the original application.

6   Limitations and Open Problems

The experiment of using AlfredO with an existing application helped us to define better its scope of applicability and limitations.

In many applications, the user interface and the service logic are tightly coupled in complex relationships. This means that a modularization at the level of service logic requires changes at the user interface too. As we saw with Sweet Home 3D, we modularized the application into several bundles and identified three high-level functionalities, such as catalog selection and item placement, 2D plan operations, and 3D rendering and visualization. In order to support these functions alone or all together, we needed to provide different user interfaces: one that displays a list of furniture items and a table with the item properties, one that adds to the first interface a 2D plan, and one that adds a further image panel for 3D functions. On the other hand, we saw how with a much simpler application, such as the one for image composition that we built, one user interface was enough to allow high flexibility at the service level.

Our experience has shown that AlfredO can work well with both types of application. Obviously, more complex applications require to be modularized, but the effort has proven to be reasonable. In the case of Sweet Home 3D, a Master student, with no knowledge of the application and OSGi, took less than two months to modularize it and build the three user interfaces described in Section 5. Thereby, we expect that for simpler applications, less than a month would be enough to make them run on AfredO. Furthermore, the advantage of AlfredO is that it builds on existing technology for distributed module management, based on the OSGi standard. OSGi is maintained by the OSGi Alliance with many major players of the software industry, such as IBM, Oracle, and SAP, and also device vendors, such as Nokia, Ericsson, Motorola. Moreover, OSGi has been used in several applications including Eclipse IDE [8] and we expect that in the future more and more developers will be acquainted with it.

Finally, our algorithms require profiling of the resource consumption of an application's bundles and their inter-communication. We instrumented our applications manually, however there are tools available or under study for automatic profiling of applications. Some are discussed in the related work section.

7   Related Work

There is a considerable amount of reseach on how to automatically partition and distribute applications based on resource profiling. One of the very early work in this context was the Interconnected Processor System (ICOPS) [9]. ICOPS used scenario-based profiling to collect statistics about resource requirements. Static data such as procedure inter-connections and dynamic statistics about resource usage were then combined to find the best assignment of procedures to processors. ICOPS was the first system using a minimum cut algorithm to select the best distribution. On the other hand, ICOPS considered very small programs of seven modules and only three of these could be moved between the client and server. A more recent work in this context is Coign [10]. Coign assumes applications to be built using components conforming Microsoft's COM. It builds a graph model of an application's inter-component communication by scenario-based profiling. The application is then partitioned to minimize execution delay due to network communication. Several other works exist such as [11].

Our techniques share with these systems the idea of building a graph model of the application and applying a graph-cutting algorithm to partition it. However, we differ from them in several aspects. We do not focus on building a tool for application resource profiling, but rather on dynamically optimizing the interaction with an application given the constraints of the current execution environment. On the other hand, these or similar tools could be integrated in AlfredO to automatically characterize the resource requirements of an application's modules or even partition a non-modularized application. This would allow to extend AlfredO to non-OSGi applications.

A second important difference is the concept of "distribution" itself. The algorithms we propose do not target distributing an application on a cluster of machines or a cloud infrastructure, but rather installing all or parts of it in order to use on a mobile phone. The decision is intrinsically client-driven. In this sense, AlfredO is closer to a web browser that provides access to Internet services and requires the user to install plugins.

Finally, AlfredO is designed to work in heterogeneous and dynamic contexts. Clients exhibit large variability in terms of device platforms, local resources, type of network communication, etc. This heterogeneity needs to be captured by the optimization problem and hidden to the end user.

Related work is also in the context of other non-phone specific distributed systems. For example, in the context of sensor networks systems like Wishbone [12], Tenet [13], VanGo [14], in the context of mobile ad hoc networks with SpatialViews [15], and in the context of cluster computing with Abacus [16]. All these systems are not applicable to our problem space for different reasons. For instance, Wishbone partitions programs to run on multiple and heterogeneous devices in a sensor network. Wishbone is primarily concerned with high-rate data processing applications, aims at statically minimizing a combination of network bandwidth and CPU load, and is used at compile time. Abacus dynamically partitions applications and filesystem functionality over a cluster of resources. It primarily targets data-intensive applications and attempts to optimize the placement of mobile objects, by using a fixed objective function that combines variations in network topology, application cache access pattern, application data reduction, contention over shared data and dynamic competition for resources by concurrent applications. Our techniques target less computational- and data-intensive applications and provide support for multiple objective functions.

The vision of pervasive computing [17], as the creation of physical environments saturated with a variety of computing and communication capabilities, is also relevant to our work. The solutions proposed in that context allow devices to interact with the surrounding environment by either statically preconfiguring the devices and the environment with the necessary software [18], or by moving around the necessary software through techniques such as mobile agents [19,20]. The first approach can work only in static environments or to support applications that are accessed on a very frequent basis. The second approach is more flexible, but it is not used in practice due to security issues.

We address the problem in a different manner. To use an application on a mobile phone, today a user has two options: *1)* install the application locally or *2)* if this is available in the Internet, access it through a web browser. We propose a new model where the phone is seen as an application controller. The minimal configuration sees a phone that acquires only a user interface, thus achieving high security. For more advanced and optimized interactions, some parts of the application can be installed. The acquisition of an application occurs in a more controlled manner and with clearly identified boundaries dependent on the resource constraints of the mobile device and the type of network communication.

8   Conclusions

We have presented our approach to automatically and dynamically distributing several components of an application between a mobile and a serve in order to optimize different objective functions such as interaction time, communication cost, memory consumption, etc. Compared to the current state-of-the-art in building applications on mobile phones, our approach enables an efficient deployment of several types of applications on mobile phones thus allowing these resource-constrained platforms to achieve better performance with a controlled overhead. Our optimization has focused so far only on the client side and has assumed the server's resources to be infinite. As future work, we are investigating how to extend our application's model to include also CPU consumption and include into the optimization problem also how the server side can be distributed over a cloud infrastructure with heterogeneous resources.

Acknowledgments

The work presented in this paper was supported by the Microsoft Innovation Cluster for Embedded Software (ICES) and the ETH Fellowship Program. We thank Jan Rellermeyer for his advise and help during the development of AlfredO on top of R-OSGi.

References

1. Rellermeyer, J.S., Alonso, G., Roscoe, T.: R-OSGi: Distributed applications through software modularization. In: Cerqueira, R., Campbell, R.H. (eds.) Middleware 2007. LNCS, vol. 4834, pp. 1–20. Springer, Heidelberg (2007)
2. Rellermeyer, J.S., Riva, O., Alonso, G.: AlfredO: An Architecture for Flexible Interaction with Electronic Devices. In: Issarny, V., Schantz, R. (eds.) Middleware 2008. LNCS, vol. 5346, pp. 22–41. Springer, Heidelberg (2008)
3. OSGi Alliance: OSGi Service Platform, Core Specification Release 4, Version 4.1, Draft (2007)
4. Guttman, E., Perkins, C., Veizades, J.: Service Location Protocol, Version 2. RFC 2608, Internet Engineering Task Force, IETF (1999), http://www.ietf.org/rfc/rfc2608.txt
5. Karypis, G., Kumar, V.: A fast and high quality multilevel scheme for partitioning irregular graphs. SIAM J. Sci. Comput. 20(1), 359–392 (1998)
6. Boman, E., et al.: Zoltan: Parallel partitioning, load balancing and data-management services user's guide. Sandia National Laboratories (2007)
7. Sweet Home 3D: (2009), http://www.sweethome3d.eu/
8. Eclipse Foundation: Eclipse (2001), http://www.eclipse.org
9. Stabler, G.: A system for interconnected processing. PhD thesis, Providence, RI, USA (1975)
10. Hunt, G., Scott, M.: The coign automatic distributed partitioning system. In: Proceedings of the 3rd symposium on Operating systems design and implementation (OSDI 1999), pp. 187–200. USENIX Association (1999)

11. Hamlin, J., Foley, J.: Configurable applications for graphics employing satellites (cages). In: Proceedings of the 2nd annual conference on Computer graphics and interactive techniques (SIGGRAPH 1975), pp. 9–19. ACM, New York (1975)
12. Newton, R., Toledo, S., Girod, L., Balakrishnan, H., Madden, S.: Wishbone: Profile-based Partitioning for Sensornet Applications. In: Proceedings of the 5th Symposium on Networked Systems Design and Implementation (NSDI 2009), pp. 395–408 (2009)
13. Gnawali, O., Jang, K.Y., Paek, J., Vieira, M., Govindan, R., Greenstein, B., Joki, A., Estrin, D., Kohler, E.: The Tenet architecture for tiered sensor networks. In: Proceedings of the 4th international conference on Embedded networked sensor systems (SenSys 2006), pp. 153–166. ACM, New York (2006)
14. Greenstein, B., Mar, C., Pesterev, A., Farshchi, S., Kohler, E., Judy, J., Estrin, D.: Capturing high-frequency phenomena using a bandwidth-limited sensor network. In: Proceedings of the 4th international conference on Embedded networked sensor systems (SenSys 2006), pp. 279–292. ACM, New York (2006)
15. Ni, Y., Kremer, U., Stere, A., Iftode, L.: Programming ad-hoc networks of mobile and resource-constrained devices. In: Proceedings of the 2005 ACM SIGPLAN conference on Programming language design and implementation (PLDI 2005), pp. 249–260. ACM, New York (2005)
16. Amiri, K., Petrou, D., Ganger, G., Gibson, G.: Dynamic Function Placement for Data-intensive Cluster Computing. In: Proceedings of the 18th USENIX annual technical conference (USENIX 2000), pp. 307–322 (2000)
17. Weiser, M.: The Computer for the Twenty-First Century. Scientific American 265(3), 94–104 (1991)
18. Want, R., Pering, T., Danneels, G., Kumar, M., Sundar, M., Light, J.: The personal server: Changing the way we think about ubiquitous computing. In: Borriello, G., Holmquist, L.E. (eds.) UbiComp 2002. LNCS, vol. 2498, pp. 194–209. Springer, Heidelberg (2002)
19. Fuggetta, A., Picco, G.P., Vigna, G.: Understanding code mobility. IEEE Transactions on Software Engineering 24(5), 342–361 (1998)
20. Kindberg, T., Barton, J., Morgan, J., Becker, G., Caswell, D., Debaty, P., Gopal, G., Frid, M., Krishnan, V., Morris, H., Schettino, J., Serra, B., Spasojevic, M.: People, places, things: Web presence for the real world. In: Proceedings of the 3rd IEEE Workshop on Mobile Computing Systems and Applications (WMCSA 2000), p. 19 (2000)

Efficient Locally Trackable Deduplication in Replicated Systems*

João Barreto and Paulo Ferreira

Distributed Systems Group - INESC-ID/Technical University of Lisbon
{joao.barreto,paulo.ferreira}@inesc-id.pt

Abstract. We propose a novel technique for distributed data deduplication in distributed storage systems. We combine version tracking
with high-precision, local similarity detection techniques. When compared with the prominent techniques of delta encoding and compare-
by-hash, our solution borrows most advantages that distinguish each
such alternative. A thorough experimental evaluation, comparing a full-
fledged implementation of our technique against popular systems based
on delta encoding and compare-by-hash, confirms gains in performance
and transferred volumes for a wide range of real workloads and scenarios.

Keywords: Data deduplication, data replication, distributed file systems, compare-by-hash, delta encoding.

1 Introduction

Many interesting and useful systems require transferring large sets of data across
a network. Examples include network file systems, content delivery networks,
software distribution mirroring systems, distributed backup systems, cooperative groupware systems, and many other state-based replicated systems [1].
Unfortunately, bandwidth remains a scarce, and/or costly in battery and price,
resource for most networks [2], including the Internet and mobile networks.

Much recent work has proposed data deduplication techniques [3,4] for efficient transfer across the network, which may be combined with conventional
techniques such as data compression [5] or caching [6]. Consider two distributed
sites, a sender, S, and receiver, R. At some moment, each one locally stores a
set of versions (of some objects, not necessarily the same set of objects at both
sites), which we denote V_S and V_R, respectively. If S wishes to send some of its
local versions, T (where $T \subseteq V_S$), to R, some data chunks in T can be identical
to chunks in V_R. Data deduplication exploits such content redundancy as follows:
when S determines that a chunk of data in some version in T is redundant, S
avoids uploading the chunk and simply tells R where in V_R R can immediately
obtain the redundant chunk.

The key challenge of data deduplication is in detecting which data is redundant across the versions to send and the versions the receiver site holds. The

* Funded by FCT grant PTDC/EIA/66589/2006.

J.M. Bacon and B.F. Cooper (Eds.): Middleware 2009, LNCS 5896, pp. 103–122, 2009.
© IFIP International Federation for Information Processing 2009

difficulty of the problem greatly depends on the forms of chunk redundancy each approach tries to detect and exploit. We distinguish two such forms.

A first one arises from cases where newer versions borrow data chunks from older version(s) (of the same object, or of another object) that were locally available when the new versions were created. More precisely, consider some new version, v, created at S, that S wishes to send to R. If v shares a chunk with some older local version, v_{old} in V_S, and R also happens to hold v_{old} (in V_R), we say there exists *locally trackable redundancy*. In fact, in such conditions, if S (by some means) learns that v_{old} is common to both sites, S is able to detect the redundant chunk by merely comparing local versions (v and v_{old}).

Otherwise, we have *locally untrackable* redundancy. For instance, this is the case where two users, one at S and another at R, copy new identical data chunks from some common external source (e.g. a web page) and write it to new versions, v_S and v_R, that each user creates at her site, respectively. If S then decides to send v_S to R, clearly there exist redundant chunks in v_S that S can avoid transferring. However, in order to detect them, we must inevitably compare data chunks that are distributed across the two sites.

The prominent approach of *compare-by-hash*[1] [3,4,7,8,9,10] tries to detect both forms of redundancy by exchanging cryptographic hash values of the chunks to transfer, and comparing them with the hash values of the receiver's contents. Compare-by-hash complicates the data transfer protocol with additional round-trips (i), exchanged meta-data (ii) and hash look-ups (iii). These may not always compensate for the gains in transferred data volume; namely, if redundancy is low or none, or when, aiming for higher precision, one uses finer-granularity chunks [8,4,9]. Moreover, any known technique for improving the precision and efficiency of compare-by-hash [8,10] increases at least one of items (i) to (iii).

Earlier alternatives to compare-by-hash narrow the problem down to detecting locally trackable redundancy only. The most relevant example of *locally trackable deduplication* is delta-encoding [11,12,13,14,15]. Recent deduplication literature often regards such techniques as second-class citizens, leaving them out of the state-of-the-art that is considered when experimentally evaluating new deduplication solutions [3,4,7,8,9,10]. In part, two factors explain this. Firs, the inherent inability to exploit locally untrackable redundancy. Second, in the case of delta-encoding, the fact that, for some version, it can only detect redundancy with at most one other version (rather than across any set of versions, as in compare-by-hash) and the time-consuming algorithms involved [14].

This paper revisits locally trackable redundancy, proposing a novel combination of previous techniques. For a wide set of usage scenarios, we unify the advantages of both compare-by-hash and earlier locally trackable deduplication approaches. The key insight to our work is that detecting locally trackable redundancy exclusively is a much simpler problem, hence solvable with very efficient algorithms, than aiming for both forms of redundancy. It is easy to see that the problem now reduces to two main steps: (I) to determine the set of object versions that the sender and receiver site store in common; and (II) to determine

---

[1] We use the expression *compare-by-hash* for coherence with related literature, although it can have different meanings in other domains. By *compare-by-hash*, we mean *chunk-based deduplication through distributed hash exchange and comparison*.

which chunks of the versions to send are (locally trackable) redundant with such a common version set.

Since the versions that one must compare for redundancy detection (step II) now happen to exist locally at the sender site, we can now solve such a hard problem with local algorithms (instead of distributed algorithms that exchange large meta-data volumes over the network, such as hash values with compare-by-hash). No longer being constrained by network bandwidth, one can now: (i) perform a much more exhaustive analysis, thus detecting more locally trackable redundancy; (ii) and asynchronously pre-compute most of the algorithm ahead of transfer time. Furthermore, the network protocol is now a very simple one, (iii) with low meta-data overhead and (iv) incurring no additional round-trips: the receiver site simply needs to piggy-back some version tracking information in the request sent to the sender site (so that the latter performs step I).

For step I, we use very compact version tracking structures, called *knowledge vectors*. Most importantly, for step II, our approach can employ any local deduplication algorithm (e.g., [16,17,18]) for detecting locally trackable redundancy across *any* object and *any* version, with high precision and time efficiency. This is a significant distinction with regard to delta-encoding.

We have implemented our technique in the context of a novel distributed archival file system, called redFS. Using a full-fledged prototype of redFS for Linux, we have evaluated both single-writer/multiple-reader and multiple-writer usage scenarios based on real workloads, representative of a wide range of document types. By comparing redFS with popular state-of-the-art tools that rely on delta-encoding and compare-by-hash, we have confirmed our advantages over both approaches. Namely:

- redFS consistently transfers less (or, in few exceptions, comparable) bytes of data and meta-data than all evaluated solutions, obtaining reductions of up to 67% over relevant systems from both compare-by-hash and delta encoding approaches, namely LBFS [4], rsync [3] and svn [11].
- redFS transfers files considerably faster than all evaluated alternatives (or, exceptionally, comparable to the best alternative), accomplishing performance gains of more than 42% relatively to rsync, LBFS and svn, for networks of 11 Mbps and below. Except for svn, such gains even increase if we consider that file transfer starts after the local pre-computation steps of the redundancy algorithm have already completed. Furthermore, such speedups hold even for real workloads with relevant sources of locally untrackable redundancy, and assume reasonable log-space requirements.

The rest of the paper is organized as follows. Section 2 describes the system model. Section 3 then introduces our data deduplication protocol. Section 4 proposes two techniques that address the issue of efficient log storage. Section 5 describes the implementation of our protocol in redFS. Section 6 evaluates our solution, while Section 7 addresses related work. Finally, Section 8 draws conclusions.

2   System Model

We assume a replicated system where a number of distributed sites (denoted S, R, ...) can replicate a number of logical objects (such as files or databases). As we explain next, we impose little restrictions on the replication protocol, hence making our solution widely applicable. Each site has a pre-assigned, well-known unique identifier. For simplicity of presentation, and without loss of generality, we assume all sites are trusted, as well as communication.

When a local applications writes to a local replica, it creates a new value of the object, called a *version*. Replicas maintain a finite *version logs*, with their latest version histories. The oldest logged versions may be pruned at anytime.

To simplify presentation, we assume that no write contention exists, hence no version conflicts exist. Nevertheless, our solution can be transparently combined with commitment protocols [1] to handle concurrent/conflicting versions.

We divide the object space into disjoint sets of objects, called *r-units*. We assume the individual r-unit to be the minimum replication grain in the underlying system; possibly, a r-unit may comprise a single file. Each site may replicate any arbitrary set of r-units. A site replicating a r-unit maintains replicas for all objects of that r-unit. As we explain later, larger r-units allow sites to maintain, exchange and analyze less bytes and perform faster data deduplication; while smaller r-units enable finer granularity in the choice of which objects to replicate. The problem of optimal partitioning of the object space into r-units is out of the scope of this paper. For simplicity of presentation, and again without loss of generality, the set of sites replicating each r-unit is assumed to be static.

Each logged version is identified by the identifier of the site where the version was created (denoted $v.creator$) and a sequence number (denoted $v.sn$). Hence, even if two objects happen to be created at different sites with the same textual name, their actual identifier ($\langle v.creator, v.sn \rangle$) is unique. For a given r-unit, the sequence number monotonically increases among the versions created by site $v.s$ at any object belonging to that r-unit. For example, given r-unit $u = \{a, b\}$, if site S creates a new version of object a, then another version of object b, the first version will be identified by $\langle S, 1 \rangle$, the second one by $\langle S, 2 \rangle$, and so on.

According to some arbitrary replication protocol, sites replicating common r-units exchange new versions to bring each other up-to-date. Without loss of generality, such a step occurs in unidirectional pair-wise synchronization sessions, in which a sender site, S, sends a set of versions, $\mathcal{T}$, to a receiver site, R.

3   Data Deduplication Protocol

We now describe the data deduplication protocol, which complements the underlying log-based replication protocol. Our solution may be seen as a combination of a space-efficient version tracking and local similarity detection algorithms.

We follow such a structure in the following sections. Recall from Section 1 that the generic approach to locally trackable deduplication consists of 2 steps: (I) to determine the set of object versions that the sender and receiver site store in common; and (II) to determine which chunks of the versions to send are (locally trackable) redundant with such a common version set. We describe our novel solution to each such step in Sections 3.1 and 3.2, respectively. Section 3.3 then combines the two steps in a complete deduplication protocol.

3.1 Step I: Version Tracking

Given a pair of sites, S and R, that are about to synchronize, the goal of Step I is to make S infer the the set of common versions both sites currently share. We denote such a set as $\mathcal{C}$. One naive solution would be to maintain and exchange lists of version identifiers for each r-unit they replicate. Of course, the inherent space requirements, as well as network transfer and look-up times, would easily become prohibitive for systems with reasonably large object/version sets.

Instead, we rely on a pair of vectors, each with one counter per site replicating the r-unit, which we call *knowledge vectors*. Each site, S, maintains, along with each r-unit, u, that S replicates, two knowledge vectors, denoted $K_S^i(u)$ and $K_S^f(u)$. From $K_S^i(u)$ and $K_S^f(u)$, we can infer that S currently stores any version, v, of any object in u such that $K_S^i(u) \leq v.sn \leq K_S^f(u)$.

Such a pair of vectors can only represent a version set in which every version created by the same site i (for all i) have sequence numbers that can be ordered consecutively without any gap. When, for each r-unit a site replicates, the set of versions it stores satisfies the previous condition, knowledge vectors constitute a very space- and time-efficient representation. To simplify presentation, for the moment we assume that sites receive and prune versions in sequential number order, with no gaps. Under this assumption, we can precisely represent a site's version set by pairs of knowledge vectors, one for each r-unit the site replicates.

This assumption is not artificial, as most log-based replication protocols systems either ensure it (e.g. Bayou [19]), or may easily be adapted to accomplish it (e.g. Coda [20]). More generally, it is trivial to show that any system that guarantees the widely-considered *prefix property* [19] satisfies such an assumption. Section 4 then addresses cases where version gaps can occur.

Given some site, S, and a r-unit that site replicates, S maintains $K_S^i(u)$ and $K_S^f(u)$ as follows. Both vectors start as zero vectors. As S accepts a new write request, creating a new version v, it updates its vectors to reflect the new version: i.e. $K_S^f(u)[S] \leftarrow v.c$ (and, if $K_S^i(u)[S] = 0$, then $K_S^i(u)[S] \leftarrow v.c$). Furthermore, if S deletes a given version, v, it sets $K_S^i(u)[S] \leftarrow v.c + 1$ (recall that, for now, we assume that version deletions occurs in sequential number order). Besides versions that the local site creates and deletes, S's version set will also evolve as S receives a new version, v, from some remote site. In this case, S sets $K_S^f(u)[S] \leftarrow v.c$ (again, assuming the ordered propagation with no gaps).

When the receiver site, R, sends a first message requesting for synchronization to start from a sender site, S, R *piggy-backs* the knowledge vectors of each r-unit that R replicates. Thus, imposing no extra round-trips on the underlying synchronization protocol, S can infer which versions are common to both sites.

While such knowledge vectors tell S which versions R held *right before* synchronization started, at some point *during* synchronization R will already have received other versions (during the current synchronization session from S). Evidently, set $\mathcal{C}$ also includes the latter versions. In order to keep track of them, S maintains, for each r-unit, u, involved in the current (ongoing) synchronization session, a pair of knowledge vectors, denoted knowledge vectors $t_i(u)$ and $t_f(u)$. Both vectors start null (when synchronization starts) and grow to represent each version (of the corresponding r-unit) that S sends.

From the copy S has received of R's knowledge vectors, as well from $t_i(u)$ and $t_f(u)$ (for each r-unit involved in the synchronization session), S can easily determine whether a given version that S stores, v_S, is also stored at R (i.e. whether $v_S \in \mathcal{C}$) by testing if any of the following conditions hold:

$$K_R^i(v_S.runit)[v_S.creator] \leq v_S.sn \leq K_R^f(v_S.runit)[v_S.creator]$$
$$\text{or}$$
$$t_i(v_S.runit)[v_S.creator] \leq v_S.sn \leq t_f(v_S.runit)[v_S.creator].$$

Hence, we can determine whether $v_S \in \mathcal{C}$ in constant time, with few operations. The first condition means R already stored v_S before synchronization started, while the second one means that R has received v_S in the meantime.

3.2   Step II: Local Chunk Redundancy Detection

Given a set of versions to transfer, $\mathcal{T}$, from site S and R, and a set of common versions between S and R, $\mathcal{C}$, Step II determines which chunks of $\mathcal{T}$ are redundant across $\mathcal{C}$. We solve step II very efficiently by observing that most of it needs not be computed synchronously while the synchronization session is taking place.

We divide step II into 2 sub-steps. A first sub-step is the most computationally intensive. It detects redundancy across *every* version that S stores, writing its findings to *redundancy vertices* and per-version *redundancy vertex reference lists,* both maintained locally. This sub-step is independent of any synchronization session. Hence, it can be computed ahead of synchronization time as a background thread that updates the local redundancy vertices when S is idle.

When synchronization starts, only the second sub-step needs to run: determining, for the ongoing session, which chunks of $\mathcal{T}$ are redundant across $\mathcal{C}$. This sub-step takes advantage of the pre-computed data structures, being able to return a result by a simple query to such data structures.

The next sections describe each sub-step in detail.

Pre-Computing Chunk Redundancy Data Structures. Conceptually, we divide the contents of all the versions a site stores into disjoint contiguous portions, called *chunks.* We determine locally trackable redundancy relationships among the entire set of chunks a site stores by running some (local) redundancy detection algorithm. If such an algorithm finds that two chunks have identical contents, we designate them as *redundant across the set of versions.* A chunk with no redundant chunks is called *literal.*

In a typical configuration, the redundancy detection algorithm runs as a low-priority thread, which starts from time to time. At each run, it analyzes the set of local versions that, relatively to the last run of the algorithm, are new, comparing their chunks with the chunks of the remaining versions.

The resulting redundancy relationships are maintained in local data structures called *redundancy vertices.* Each redundancy vertex either represents a literal chunk or a set of redundant chunks (sharing identical contents). A redundancy vertex is simply a list of *[version identifier, byte offset, chunk size]* tuples, each pointing to the effective contents of a chunk within the local versions.

As we explain later, redundancy vertices should ideally reside in main memory, for the sake of synchronization performance. However, for sufficiently large data repositories, that may not be possible due to the fine chunk granularity our solution is designed for (e.g., 128 bytes). For example, in a file system with an average chunk size of 128 bytes, supporting up to 4G file versions, each up to 1 TB, would require 9-byte chunk pointers at redundancy vertices (one pointer per stored chunk). Thus, redundancy vertices would introduce a space overhead of 7%; e.g., 60 GB of version contents would imply 4-GB of redundancy vertices. If such space requirements exceed the available primary memory, we can store the redundancy vertices in secondary memory and maintain the elements that are more likely to be consulted in upcoming synchronization sessions in a cache in main memory (for instance, using a *least-recently-used* substitution policy). A detailed evaluation of this option is left for future work.

Any version that the redundancy detection algorithm has already analyzed has each of its chunks referenced by exactly one redundancy vertex. Along with each such version, the redundancy detection algorithm stores an ordered list of references to the redundancy vertices corresponding to each chunk in the version.

Our contribution is not tied to any particular redundancy detection algorithm, and we can transparently use any algorithm that works for local deduplication. Namely, approaches such as the fixed-size sliding block method of rsync [3], diff-encoding [14], similarity-based deduplication [18], among others [16].

Nevertheless, to better illustrate our solution, and without loss of generality, we hereafter consider one of such possible alternatives: a local variant of LBFS's distributed algorithm [4]. This algorithm is able to detect redundancy spanning across any versions, possibly from distinct objects or r-units.

Very succinctly, the algorithm works as follows. We maintain a *chunk hash table*, whose entries comprise a pointer to a redundancy vertex and the hash value of contents of the corresponding chunk(s). For each new version (either locally created or received from a remote site), we divide it into chunks (using LBFS's sliding window fingerprinting scheme [4]) and look their hash values up in the chunk hash table. If we find a match, then there exists at least one other identical chunk. In this case, we add a pointer to the new chunk to the existing redundancy vertex. Otherwise, the new chunk is literal, thus we create a new single-chunk redundancy vertex pointing to the chunk, and add a new entry to the chunk hash table (referencing the redundancy vertex and the chunk's hash value). Once we finish processing each version, we trivially construct the corresponding redundancy vertex reference list and store it along with the version.

Similarly to the previous discussion concerning redundancy vertices, maintaining an in-main-memory chunk hash table that covers every local fine-grained chunk can be impossible. Solving this problem is out of the scope of this paper. Possible directions include storing the chunk hash table in secondary memory and a cache in main memory, or resorting to similarity-based schemes [18].

Determining Redundant Chunks Across $\mathcal{T}$ and $\mathcal{C}$. Using the previously maintained data structures (redundancy vertices and redundancy vertex reference lists) as input, the actual step of determining which chunks to transfer are actually redundant across both sites is reduced to simple queries to such information.

More precisely, for each version v that site S is about to transfer (i.e. $v \in T$), we iterate over its redundancy vertex reference list and, for each reference, we (1) read the corresponding redundancy vertex; and (2) iterate over the redundancy vertex's chunk pointer list until we find the first chunk of a version $v_r \in C$ (using the expression from Section 3.1). If the latter chunk is found, we can just send a reference to where, among the versions R stores, R can obtain the redundant chunk. More precisely, the following *remote chunk reference* is sufficient to univocally identify such a location: *[$v_r.id$, offset, chunk size]*.

Since we consider fine-grained chunks, it is frequent to find consecutive remote chunk references to contiguous (and consecutive) chunks in some version in C. We optimize these cases by coalescing the consecutive remote chunk references into a single reference to a larger chunk comprising all the consecutive smaller chunks. This simple optimization has the crucial importance of dissociating the local redundancy detection granularity from the effective remote chunk reference volume that we send over the network.

As it is shown elsewhere [21], reference coalescing ensures that, by decreasing the average chunk size, either: (i) we transfer the same remote chunk reference volume (if no additional redundancy is detected); or (ii) the increase in remote chunk reference volume is compensated by the decrease in transferred data volume (if smaller chunks unveil more redundancy).

The algorithm above implies $O(d)$ verifications for membership in C using the condition from Section 3.1, where d is the average cardinality of each set of redundant chunks in a redundancy vertex. In contrast, LBFS's approach requires look-ups to the receiver site's chunk hash table that involve $O(log(n))$ hash comparisons, where n is the total number of local chunks. As, for most workloads, $d << log n$, the local computation phase of our protocol is substantially faster than the one of LBFS (an observation we confirm in Section 6).

3.3   Putting It All Together

After running the previous steps, site S can finally transfer each version $v \in T$ to R. The actual transfer of each such version involves sending three components. Firstly, v's identifier and size. Secondly, an array of remote chunk references to redundant chunks. We send remote chunk references in the order by which the corresponding chunks appear in v. Finally, we send the contents of every literal chunk of v, again in their order of appearance within the version.

Upon reception of the above components, R starts reconstructing v by copying the redundant contents from the locations (among R's versions) that the remote chunk references point to. The gaps are then filled with the literal contents that R has received.

4   Log Storage and Maintenance

The effectiveness of our data deduplication solution depends on the ability of each site to maintain long-term version logs. To substantially increase log efficiency, we can resort to two compression schemes.

A first scheme is called *redundancy compression*. The principle behind redundancy compression is the same as in local deduplication solutions [17]: whenever two or more versions share a common chunk, we store the chunk only once and suppress the redundant copies. We achieve this by storing only the first chunk referenced at each redundancy vertex. If there are additional chunks at that redundancy vertex, we set an *absent* flag at the redundancy vertex reference list of the versions such chunks belong to. This flag means that, to read the chunk's contents, we must follow the first chunk pointer in the redundancy vertex.

When redundancy compression is insufficient, we inevitably need to erase both the redundant and literal chunks of one or more versions, thus losing their contents. Still, we can retains the version's redundancy vertex reference list, which constitutes a *footprint* of the redundancy relationships of the erased version with other versions. The footprints of versions that have been erased at the sender site can still be (artificially) considered when determining the set of common versions, $\mathcal{C}$, during synchronization. In fact, if S determines that some version, v, for which S only holds its footprint (since it has already discarded its contents) is (fully) stored at the receiver site, R, then S considers v to be in $\mathcal{C}$. Hence, if S determines that some chunk to transfer is redundant with v (which S can determine by simply inspecting v's footprint), then S can exploit such redundancy and send a remote chunk reference to version v that R stores. Notice that the fact that S has already erased the contents of v is irrelevant as long as R still stores them. Incorporating footprints into the protocol described so far is straightforward; for space limitations, we describe it elsewhere [21].

Eventually, completely erasing both contents and footprint of a version will also occur, once space limitations impose it. In this case, care has to be taken in order to update the knowledge vectors of the r-unit in which the object being pruned is included. More precisely, such vectors need to be changed in order to reflect the smaller version set of the local site.

However, the completely erased version can cause a gap in the version set that was previously denoted by the knowledge vectors. For instance, if $K_S^i(u)[S] = 1$ and $K_S^f(u)[S] = 10$ and the user decides to delete version $\langle S, 3 \rangle$. In this case, we can no longer use the knowledge vectors to represent the version set. Instead, we set such vectors to represent a the *subset with highest identifiers* that has no gaps. Recalling the previous example, we would set $K_S^i(u)[S] \leftarrow 4$. The choice for the subset with the highest identifiers follows the heuristic that since versions with higher identifiers are probably most recent, then they are more likely to be synchronized to other sites. Therefore, it is more valuable for our deduplication solution to keep track of such versions than those with lower identifiers.

Similarly to complete erasure of a version, gaps can also happen when a site receives new versions from a remote site. In this case, the same solution is taken.

5   Implementation

We have instantiated our solution in a full-fledged distributed archival file system, called redFS.[2] redFS supports distributed collaboration through file

---

[2] Source code available at: http://www.gsd.inesc-id.pt/~jpbarreto/redFS.zip

sharing. Applications can create shared files and directories, and read from/write to them in an optimistic fashion. redFS implements on-close version creation [22].

redFS runs on top of the FUSE [23] kernel module, version 2.6.3, in Linux. For synchronization, redFS runs a variant of Bayou's update propagation protocol [19], complemented with our data deduplication scheme. We use SUN RPC over UDP/IP, resorting to TCP/IP sockets to transfer literal contents.

The unit of storage is what we call a *segment*. Each segment has a unique version identifier and is stored as an individual file in a native file system. Every directory and file version has its data stored in a segment.

For directories, we adopt a similar solution as in the Elephant file system [22]. A directory is stored in a single segment, identified by the directory version, and comprising a directory entry for each object in the directory. Changes to the directory (e.g., objects added, removed, or attributes changed) result in appending a new entry to the directory segment and setting an `active flag` (see [22]) of the previous entry corresponding to the affected object to false.

Each directory references a set of files/directories by storing the corresponding *file identifiers*. A file identifier of a given file/directory consists of the version identifier of the initial version of the file/directory. To open a file we need to map the file identifier to the identifier of its current version. redFS maintains a version information table, indexed by file identifier, which contains, for each file: version identifier, size, compression mode (*plain, redundancy* or *footprint-only*), and the segment identifier of the file log (if any), among other flags. If a file has only a single version, it has no log segment. This is an important optimization since many files of a file system are never changed. Otherwise, the log consists of a list of version information entries, similar to the ones in the version information table, providing access to archived versions.

A similarity detector thread runs asynchronously, and an explicit shell command starts each run. Currently, we maintain redundancy vertices and the chunk hash table exclusively in main-memory. Redundancy vertex reference lists are stored at the head of the corresponding versions.

6   Evaluation

Assuming a synchronization session from site S to site R, which transfers a set of versions, T, an efficient deduplication approach should minimize the following metrics:

1. *Transferred volume*, the amount of bytes (including both data and metadata) transferred across the network in order to transfer T;
2. *Full transfer time*, the time it takes for S to, immediately after obtaining T, transfer the versions in T to R.
3. *Foreground transfer time*, the time it takes for S to transfer T to R, assuming S has already had, in background, the opportunity to perform some local pre-computation phase.
4. *Space Requirements*, the amount of memory that both sites need to maintain.

We now evaluate redFS under different workloads and network settings, both in single-writer and multiple-writer scenarios. We compare redFS with relevant alternatives employing compare-by-hash and delta-encoding, and plain file transfer. Our evaluation tries to answer 2 questions. Firstly: *how does redFS compare to its alternatives in terms of transferred volume, full transfer time and foreground transfer time, assuming unbounded space resources?* Secondly: *how does redFS's efficiency degrade as the available (bounded) space resources decrease?*

For space limitations, the following sections discuss the most relevant results only. An exhaustive evaluation can be found in [21].

6.1   Experimental Setting

The experiments consider two sites replicating files from real workloads. As new versions are produced at either one or both sites, they synchronize their local replicas. To simplify our analysis, we start by assuming that both sites replicate a common r-unit only and have unbounded logs. Later in the section, we lift these restrictions, and extend our analysis to multiple r-units and bounded logs.

A first site, S, runs Ubuntu 6.06 (kernel version 2.6.15) on a Pentium 4 3GHz processor with 1GB of RAM. The second site, R, runs Debian 4.0 (kernel version 2.6.18) on an Athlon 64 processor 3200+ with 2 GB of RAM. All experiments were run during periods of negligible load from other processes running at each machine (approximately $< 1\%$ CPU usage by other applications). A 100 Mbps full-duplex Fast Ethernet LAN interconnected both sites. For more complete results, we use a class based queue (CBQ) to emulate relevant network technologies, namely IEEE 802.11g (54 Mbps) and 802.11b (11 Mbps) wireless LANs, Bluetooth 2.0 personal area networks (3 Mbps). Performance measurements were taken with the `time` command of Linux, with millisecond precision. The presented results are averages of 3 executions of the each experiment.

We evaluate a representative set of solutions, covering all relevant actual approaches for network traffic deduplication:

- *redFS* with different expected chunk sizes (128 bytes, 2 KB, 8 KB).[3]
- Solutions based on compare-by-hash, namely: *lbfs*, our implementation of LBFS's original protocol [4], in the same modes as for redFS (we do not directly evaluate LBFS because no public stand-alone implementation of the original solution was available); *rsync* [3], version 2.6.3 of the popular compare-by-hash Linux tool, using the default fixed chunk size, 700 bytes; and *TAPER*, using the published results [8] (no prototype nor full source code was publicly available).
- *svn* [3], version 1.4.6 of the popular distributed version control system, which relies on delta encoding for committing versions to the server, using its most efficient server (*svnserve*).
- Finally, as a base reference, we also evaluate *plain* remote file transfer.

The results presented herein were obtained with data compression [5] disabled. Not considering data compression simplifies our analysis, as it excludes any measurement noise caused by different data compression algorithms and options used

---

[3] The choice of chunk sizes is driven by the observations that: (i) lower chunk sizes than 128 bytes do not compensate the meta-data overhead of remote chunk references, and (ii) higher chunk sizes than 8 KB yielded no advantage.

by each evaluated system.[4] The exception is *svn*, in which data compression is hard-coded. For a fair comparison, we present measurements for a hypothetical variant of *svn* with no data compression, extrapolated by *svn*'s performance relatively to the one of *rsync* with compression on.

We replay replica updates with workloads taken from real world collaborative situations, ranging from more than 100 MB up to more than 500 MB, and from more than 850 files up to more than 42,000 files.

Single-Writer, Multiple-Reader Scenarios. A first group of workloads consists of workloads that relevant compare-by-hash work uses as their evaluation basis; namely, LBFS's [4] and TAPER's [8] original papers consider either such workloads or very similar ones. These workloads reflect a single-writer, multiple-reader scenario. It is easy to see that, by definition, all redundancy in this scenarios is locally trackable (assuming sufficiently large version logs).

Site S acts as a writer that sequentially produces two sets of versions in the r-unit. Site R is a reader, which synchronizes after each version set is ready.

We test workloads of different categories in such a scenario:

Software development sources. These workloads are representative of collaborative code development scenarios. They include, for different real-world open-source projects, two consecutive versions of their source code releases. We have selected the source trees of recent versions of the gcc compiler (versions 3.3.1 and 3.4.1), the emacs editor (20.1 and 20.7), and the Linux kernel (2.4.22 and 2.4.26). Hereafter we call such workloads gcc, emacs and linux-source, respectively. Nearly all redundancy in these workloads ($> 95\%$) is found between pairs of files with the same name (each from each version). The choice of projects and versions is the same as adopted for the evaluation of TAPER [8]; this allows us to compare our results with theirs.

Operating system executable binaries. One workload, usrbin, considers binary files, which have very different characteristics when compared to the previous text-based files (namely, in data compressibility and cross-file and cross-version redundancy). It includes the full contents of the /usr/bin directory trees of typical installations of the Ubuntu 6.06 32-bit and 7.10 64-bit Linux distributions, which include most of the executable code binaries that are bundled with a Linux installation. All redundancy is between files with the same name.

Multiple-Writer Scenarios. A second group of workloads consider multiple-writer scenarios, where actual concurrency (hence, locally untrackable redundancy) can finally occur. In this case, two writer sites, start with a common initial version set. Each writer site then independently modifies its local replicas. Finally, both sites synchronize their divergent replicas.

We consider two workloads, obtained from real collaborative document editing scenarios. Both result from real data from two undergraduate courses of Technical University Lisbon. Their data spans across a full semester.

A first workload, called course-docs, consists of snapshots of two CVS repositories shared by lecturers of each course to keep pedagogical material (e.g. tutorials, lecture slides, code examples and project specifications) and

---

[4] We confirm in [21] that enabling data compression yields equivalent conclusions.

private documents (e.g. individual student evaluation notes and management documents).

The initial version of the workload includes the contents of both repositories at the beginning of the semester. The type of files varies significantly, ranging from text files such as Java code files or html files, to binary files such as pdf documents, Java libraries, Microsoft Word documents and Microsoft Excel worksheets. Significant data was copied across different files: only 30% redundancy is found between versions with identical file names. Both courses were tightly coordinated, as their students are partially evaluated based on a large code project that is common to both courses. Consequently, lecturers of both courses carried an eminently collaboratively activity, involving regular meetings. Inevitably, both repositories had regular locally untrackable interactions, such as frequent email exchanges, and weekly meetings.

A second workload, student-projects, captures the collaborative work among students of both courses. Teams of 9 students were given the assignment of developing a code project in Java, which they were demanded to develop on a CVS repository. To ease their coding effort, they were provided with a bundle of auxiliary Java libraries and illustrative code examples. Most teams relied on this bundle as a basis from which they started developing their final project.

The project lasted for 3 months. The initial version set is a snapshot of the initial library/code bundle that was made available to every student. We then randomly selected two final projects from the CVS repositories, which constitute a divergent version set at each site. The snapshots consist mainly of binary Java libraries, Java code files, as well as Microsoft Word and pdf documents. Again, this workload had sources of locally untrackable redundancy; e.g. code examples that the students incorporated into their project were provided to both teams through the courses' web sites, hence locally untrackable.

6.2   Results

This section is organized as follows. We start by focusing on transferred volume, full and foreground transfer times. We start by considering the single-writer, multiple-reader scenario, where no locally untrackable redundancy can arise, and assuming infinite logs. We then depart to the expectedly more challenging multiple-writer scenario, where locally untrackable does occur. Finally, we analyze space requirements associated with finite logs of increasing depths.

Single-Write, Multiple Reader Scenarios. In a first experiment, we ran all workloads of the single-writer case, plus single-writer variants of course-docs and student-projects (considering only one of the two divergent versions).

On average over *all* workloads, the volume that redFS transfers across the network during synchronization is substantially lower than *rsync* and *lbfs* (on average over all workloads, both *rsync* and *lbfs-128* transfer 35% more bytes than *redFS-128*). TAPER's intricate solution transfers comparable volume to redFS (TAPER transfers 0.29% less on average).

With respect to delta encoding tools, since *svn* does not output transferred volumes, we evaluate the *xdelta* [24] local delta-encoding tool for such a measurement. redFS is, in general, more efficient (9% lower volume on average over all workloads). However, for workloads with a sufficiently stable directory/file tree and where in-object redundancy dominates cross-object redundancy (which is the case of the gcc workload), delta encoding can substantially outperform redFS. Hence, an interesting direction for future improvement is to complement redFS's similarity detection and reference encoding with a variant based on delta encoding. Such a hybrid approach is clearly compatible with our solution.

Figure 1 illustrates transferred volumes for a workload where most redundancy is across consecutive versions of the same file (gcc), and for a workload where cross-file redundancy is significant (course-docs).

Figure 1 includes *redFS-128 NCL*, a variant where we disable reference coalescing. It illustrates how crucial the optimization is to redFS when using fine-grained chunks. Coalescing references allows redFS-128 to send 8x and 14x less remote chunk references in gcc and course-docs, respectively. Overall, *redFS-128 NCL* entails 18% and 11% overheads in transferred volume, respectively.

More important than transferred volume is to analyze the actual performance of redFS relatively the other solutions, namely in terms of their full and foreground transfer times. Figure 2 presents such measurements for three very distinct workloads: emacs, a highly-redundant workload (more than 54% redundant chunks), where most redundancy occurs between consecutive versions of the same file; usrbin, a workload exhibiting less than 30% redundant chunks; and course-docs, with relatively high cross-file redundancy.

In the case of redFS, we depict the full and foreground transfer times with 128 bytes expected chunk size (resp. labeled redFS-128-fullsynch and redFS-128), as such variant exhibited best performance among the others. Regarding *svn* and *rsync*, we can only obtain their full transfer time, as their implementations only consider a full synchronization option (resp. svn-fullsynch and rsync-fullsynch). Just for curiosity, we also depict *svn*'s original full transfer time, with data compression on. Regarding our implementation of lbfs, for presentation simplicity, we depict its foreground transfer times only, and consider the highest performance variant, lbfs-8KB. Finally, in the case of plain transfer, its full and foreground times are, by definition, the same.

Perhaps the strongest conclusion from this analysis is that, considering all workloads, redFS-128's average full transfer times are lower than the same

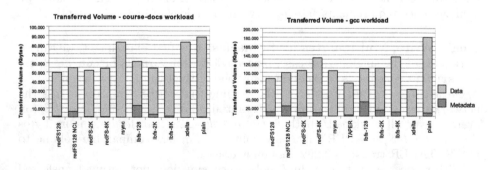

Fig. 1. Transferred data volumes for course-docs and gcc workloads

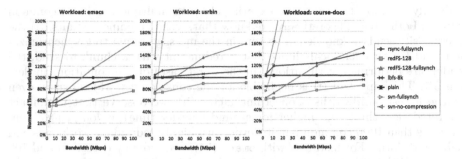

Fig. 2. Transfer times for different workloads, for varying bandwidths

measurement of *every* other evaluated solution (with data compression off), for bandwidths of 11 Mbps and below. Furthermore, this conclusion is true for workloads with very distinct characteristics, which Figure 2 shows. As we consider higher bandwidths, however, the time penalty of redFS-128's local chunk detection algorithm becomes increasingly decisive.

However, as Section 3.2 discusses, our technique is mainly intended to have the local chunk detection phase running in background. In typical cases, when the user initiates synchronization with another site, such a background algorithm will already have completed and, therefore, the only delay that the user will notice is the foreground transfer time – therefore, the most important metric.

Relatively to lbfs-8KB, redFS-128's foreground transfer time is consistently lower (from 5% with 100 Mbps to 34% lower with 3 Mbps). This is easily explained by lbfs's exchange of hash values across the network, as well by its lower precision in detecting redundancy (as analyzed previously). Naturally, the impact of such drawbacks become more dominant as bandwidth drops.

Unfortunately, we cannot precisely compare redFS's foreground transfer time with *rsync*'s. However, the portion of *rsync*'s algorithm that one can precompute is significantly smaller than in the case of redFS (most notably, *rsync* must exchange hash values of the versions to transfer in foreground). Hence, we can safely infer that, for the workloads where redFS's full transfer time is lower than *rsync*'s, redFS's foreground transfer times will also outperform *rsync*'s.

Since TAPER's source code is not fully available, we could not consider it in the present performance analysis. Nevertheless, our observations are that (i) the data volumes transferred by redFS and TAPER are comparable, as well as that (ii) redFS's single-round-trip protocol is expectedly lighter than TAPER's intricate 3-round-trip protocol. These strongly suggest that redFS would be faster than TAPER in the evaluated workloads.

Moreover, concerning *svn*'s delta-encoding solution, clearly its local delta encoding delays dominate *svn*'s full transfer times. Nevertheless, for the specific workloads in which delta encoding yielded lower transferred volumes, we expect *svn* to have lower foreground transfer times than redFS.

It is worth noting that, with the low redundancy usrbin workload, redFS-128 was the only solution to achieve an actual speed-up in foreground transfer time, an evidence of redFS's low protocol overhead.

Finally, we repeated the same experiments with multiple r-units in common between both sites. Theoretically, we know that, with r common r-units, (i) the receiver site sends r knowledge vectors in the message requesting synchronization; and (ii) for each local chunk that is redundant with a chunk to send, the sender site performs r verifications (in the worst case) of the conditions in Section 3.1. The impact of (i) is negligible for the considered workload sizes, even for the lowest bandwidths. Concerning factor (ii), we observe that its impact is limited (less than 10% higher foreground transfer time) as long as we consider less than 1000 common r-units, even with highly redundant workloads and high bandwidths. For instance, with emacs (54% redundancy detected) and 100 Mbps, *redFS-128*'s foreground transfer time drops linearly as the number of common r-units grows, reaching the 10% degradation limit at 2000 r-units.

Multiple-Writer Scenarios. In contrast to the previous single-write scenarios, multiple-writer scenarios, such as those arising from replicated systems supporting distributed collaborative work, incur locally untrackable redundancy. In order to assert whether redFS is still advantageous in such scenarios, we need to quantify locally untrackable redundancy. For that, we consider the two concurrent workloads, course-docs and student-projects.

The methodology for quantifying locally untrackable redundancy is to measure how much data volume *redFS-128* would be able to detect as (locally trackable) redundant, versus the data volume that *lbfs-128* would detect as redundant (both locally trackable and untrackable), and then to subtract both values.

Perhaps surprisingly, the redundancy that results from locally untrackable data exchanges during several months is almost insignificant when compared to locally trackable redundancy. In the course-docs workload, *lbfs-128* detects just 1,01% more (locally untrackable) redundant contents than redFS. The student-projects workload exhibits more locally untrackable redundancy, but still at relatively insignificant levels: *lbfs-128* detects 4,37% more redundant data.

Our results confirm that locally untrackable redundancy does occur in concurrent scenarios. But, most importantly, they show that locally trackable redundancy strongly dominates locally untrackable redundancy. Hence, the advantages of redFS over other state-of-the-art alternatives that the previous sections exposed are also effective in an important class of multi-writer scenarios.

We then evaluated redFS, *rsync* and lbfs when synchronizing sites holding the concurrent versions of course-docs and student-projects. The results confirm that the low values of locally untrackable redundancy have, as expected, a low impact on the effective transferred volume (data+metadata) and performance.

Space Requirements of Version Logs. Since redFS can only detect redundancy across the versions to send ($\mathcal{T}$) and the common version set ($\mathcal{C}$), the larger such an intersection is, the more redundancy redFS will be able to exploit. An assumption made so far is that the version logs at each synchronizing site could stretch arbitrarily. In practice, however, available log space is bounded. Hence, our ability to efficiently log versions determines how deep can the logged history at each replica be. The deeper the logged history, the higher the probability of larger $\mathcal{C}$ sets during synchronization with other sites.

To evaluate the impact of bounded log space on redFS's efficiency, we now consider multi-version variants of `course-docs` and `student-projects`.[5] For both workloads, we have obtained an exhaustive version set, comprising daily snapshots of the corresponding CVS repositories. Each version sequence spans across the whole duration of each workload: 168 days in `course-docs`, and 74 days in `student-projects`. Each version in the sequence exclusively includes the files whose contents have been modified relatively to the previous day's version.

For each workload, we assume that replica S has created every daily version of the workload, from day 0 to the last day, d, but may have already pruned the m oldest versions; hence, R stores every version from day $d - m$ to day d. In turn, replica R wishes to synchronize its stale replicas from S, as the last time S did that was in day d'. For simplicity, we assume R has enough space to log every version from day 0 to day d'.

When S and R synchronize, if $m > d'$, both replicas will share no common version (i.e., C is empty). Hence, in this case, S will detect no redundancy at all between the versions to send to R and the contents that R already stores.

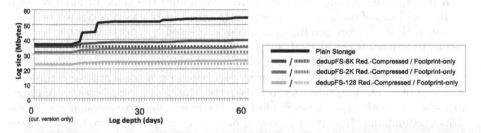

Fig. 3. Space requirements of version log for multi-version `student-projects` workload

Of course, S can only ensure sufficiently deep logs if their space requirements are below the available log space. Hence, we need to evaluate what are the space log requirements at S for increasingly deep logs. We have studied such requirements in both `course-docs` and `student-projects` workloads, considering the different schemes for log storage that Section 4 addresses: plain storage, redundancy compression and footprints, with different expected chunk sizes. Figure 3 presents such results for the latter workload.

A first observation is that, even with plain log storage, space cost grows only moderately with log depth. With `course-docs` (resp. `student-projects`), the space cost associated with a plain log is of additional 16.3% (resp. 16.3%) disk space than the most recent version, which requires 102 MB (resp. 37 MB), per logged month of update activity. Furthermore, more efficient log storage schemes are still able to substantially reduce such a space overhead. For both workloads, using redundancy compression, redFS can maintain the entire version history of 3 and 6 months, respectively, at the average cost of 4% space overhead per logged month of update activity. Finally, footprints offer almost negligible overhead, dropping to levels below 0.7% space overhead per logged month.

---

[5] Daily snapshots were not available for the other workloads.

7 Related Work

Significant work has addressed the exploitation of duplicate contents for improved storage and network dissemination of state-based updates. The main focus of our work is on the latter. We can divide most existing solutions to it into three main categories: delta-encoding, cooperating caches and compare-by-hash.

Systems such as SVN [11], Porcupine [12], BitKeeper [13], XDFS [14] and Git [15] use *delta-encoding* (or *diff-encoding*) to represent successive file versions. Starting from a base version of a file, they encode successive versions by a compact set of value-based deltas to the value of the preceding version. Systems that use delta encoding for distributed file transfer need to maintain some version tracking state at the communicating sites, similarly to our approach.

Our approach extends delta-encoding, improving the potential efficiency gains of the latter. Whereas delta-encoding is limited to locally untrackable redundancy between pairs of consecutive versions of the same file, we are able to exploit any cross-version and cross-object locally trackable redundancy.

A different technique [25] relies on a pair of cooperating caches maintained by a pair of sites. At any moment, both caches hold the same ordered set of n fixed-size blocks of data, which correspond to the last blocks propagated between the sites. Hence, before sending a new block, the sender checks whether its local cache already holds the block. If so, the site sends a token identifying the position of the block within the cache, instead of the block's contents.

Our approach shares the same principle, based on a conservative estimation of a common version/value set between the communicating sites. From such an estimate, both approaches exploit locally trackable cross-version and cross-object redundancy. Nevertheless, our approach scales gracefully to large numbers of sites and is able to cover a practically unlimited common version set; whereas cooperating caches need one cache per site and limit the common version set by cache size. Furthermore, cooperating caches cannot detect situations of transitive redundancy, whereas we can; i.e. when site A knows that it shares some chunk, c, with site B, and site B knows that it shares c with a third site, C, neither A nor C infer that both share c when they synchronize.

Finally, recent work [3,4,7,26,27] has followed the compare-by-hash approach for distributed data deduplication. They either divide values into contiguous (non-overlapping) variable-sized chunks, using content-based chunk division algorithms [4], or fixed-size chunks [3]. Compare-by-hash is able to detect both locally trackable and untrackable redundancy. Nevertheless, compare-by-hash has the important shortcomings discussed in Section 1.

Some work has proposed intricate variations of the technique for higher efficiency. The TAPER replicated system [8] optimizes bandwidth efficiency of compare-by-hash with a four-phase protocol, each of which works on a finer similarity granularity. Each phase works on the value portions that, after the preceding phase, remain labeled as non-redundant. A first phase detects larger-granularity redundant chunks (whole file and whole directories), using a hash tree; the Jumbo Store [10] distributed utility service employs a similar principle in a multi-phase protocol. A second phase runs the base compare-by-hash technique with content-based chunks. A third phase identifies pairs of very similar replicas (at each site) and employs rsync's technique upon each pair. Finally, a fourth phase employs delta-encoding to the remaining data.

8 Conclusions

We propose a novel technique for distributed locally trackable data deduplication. When compared with the prominent solutions for the distributed data deduplication problem, namely delta encoding and compare-by-hash, our solution borrows most advantages that distinguish each such alternative.

The results presented herein, obtained from real workloads, complement previous evidence [28] that contradicts a common conviction that, to some extent, is subjacent to most literature proposing compare-by-hash [4,7,8,10,9]. More precisely, our results show that, for the very workloads that the latter works consider and evaluate, there does exist a solution based exclusively on locally trackable deduplication that outperforms compare-by-hash. Perhaps more surprisingly, we show that even in scenarios with clear sources of locally untrackable redundancy, the impact of locally untrackable redundancy can be negligible. Consequently, our solution still outperforms compare-by-hash in such cases.

While it is easy to devise multiple-writer scenarios where locally untrackable redundancy prevails (e.g. two remote users that frequently copy identical data from a common external source, such a web site or an email server, to their local replicas of a object that both share), our work identifies important scenarios where it is advantageous to opt for locally trackable deduplication (which includes approaches such as delta-encoding, cooperative caching and ours) instead of compare-by-hash. More precisely, these include single-writer multiple-reader scenarios as long as sufficient disk space for logs is available, hence all redundancy is locally trackable. The same holds in multiple-writer scenarios where locally untrackable redundancy is negligible; our experience with workloads from real collaborative work scenarios suggests that this is often the case.

Acknowledgements

We would like to thank the anonymous reviewers, Lucy Cherkasova (our shepherd), Diogo Paulo and João Paiva for their helpful comments on previous versions of this paper.

References

1. Saito, Y., Shapiro, M.: Optimistic replication. ACM Computing Surveys 37(1), 42–81 (2005)
2. Dahlin, M., Chandra, B., Gao, L., Nayate, A.: End-to-end wan service availability. IEEE/ACM Transactions on Networking 11(2), 300–313 (2003)
3. Trigdell, A., Mackerras, P.: The rsync algorithm. Technical report, Australian National University (1998)
4. Muthitacharoen, A., Chen, B., Mazieres, D.: A low-bandwidth network file system. In: 8th ACM Symposium on Operating Systems Principles (SOSP), pp. 174–187 (2001)

5. Lelewer, D., Hirschberg, D.: Data compression. ACM Computing Surveys 19(3), 261–296 (1987)
6. Levy, E., Silberschatz, A.: Distributed file systems: Concepts and examples. ACM Computing Surveys 22(4), 321–374 (1990)
7. Cox, L., Noble, B.: Pastiche: Making backup cheap and easy. In: 5th Symposium on Operating Systems Design and Implementation, pp. 285–298. ACM, New York (2002)
8. Jain, N., Dahlin, M., Tewari, R.: Taper: Tiered approach for eliminating redundancy in replica sychronization. In: 4th USENIX FAST, p. 21 (2005)
9. Bobbarjung, D., Jagannathan, S., Dubnicki, C.: Improving duplicate elimination in storage systems. ACM Transactions on Storage 2(4), 424–448 (2006)
10. Eshghi, K., Lillibridge, M., Wilcock, L., Belrose, G., Hawkes, R.: Jumbo store: providing efficient incremental upload and versioning for a utility rendering service. In: 5th USENIX conference on File and Storage Technologies (FAST), p. 22 (2007)
11. Pilato, C., Fitzpatrick, B., Collins-Sussman, B.F.: Version Control with Subversion. O'Reilly, Sebastopol (2004)
12. Saito, Y., Bershad, B.N., Levy, H.M.: Manageability, availability, and performance in porcupine: a highly scalable, cluster-based mail service. ACM Trans. Comput. Syst. 18(3), 298 (2000)
13. Henson, V., Garzik, J.: Bitkeeper for kernel developers (2002), http://infohost.nmt.edu/~val/ols/bk.ps.gz
14. MacDonald, J.: File system support for delta compression. Masters thesis, University of California at Berkeley (2000)
15. Lynn, B.: Git magic (2009), http://www-cs-students.stanford.edu/~blynn/gitmagic/
16. Policroniades, C., Pratt, I.: Alternatives for detecting redundancy in storage systems data. In: USENIX Annual Technical Conference (2004)
17. Quinlan, S., Dorward, S.: Venti: A new approach to archival data storage. In: 1st USENIX Conference on File and Storage Technologies (FAST), p. 7 (2002)
18. Aronovich, L., Asher, R., Bachmat, E., Bitner, H., Hirsch, M., Klein, S.T.: The design of a similarity based deduplication system. In: ACM SYSTOR, pp. 1–14 (2009)
19. Petersen, K., Spreitzer, M., Terry, D., Theimer, M., Demers, A.: Flexible update propagation for weakly consistent replication. In: ACM SOSP, pp. 288–301 (1997)
20. Kistler, J.J., Satyanarayanan, M.: Disconnected operation in the coda file system. SIGOPS Oper. Syst. Rev. 25(5), 213–225 (1991)
21. Barreto, J.: Optimistic Replication in Weakly Connected Resource-Constrained Environments. PhD thesis, IST, Technical University Lisbon (2008)
22. Santry, D., Feeley, M., Hutchinson, N., Veitch, A., Carton, R., Ofir, J.: Deciding when to forget in the elephant file system. In: ACM SOSP, pp. 110–123 (1999)
23. Szeredi, M.: FUSE: Filesystem in Userspace (2008), http://sourceforge.net/projects/avf
24. MacDonald, J.: xdelta, http://code.google.com/p/xdelta/
25. Spring, N.T., Wetherall, D.: A protocol-independent technique for eliminating redundant network traffic. SIGCOMM Comput. Comm. Rev. 30(4), 87–95 (2000)
26. Tolia, N., Kozuch, M., Satyanarayanan, M., Karp, B., Perrig, A., Bressoud, T.: Opportunistic use of content addressable storage for distributed file systems. In: USENIX Annual Technical Conference, pp. 127–140 (2003)
27. Annapureddy, S., Freedman, M.J., Mazières, D.: Shark: scaling file servers via cooperative caching. In: USENIX Symp. Net. Sys. Design & Impl., pp. 129–142 (2005)
28. Henson, V.: An analysis of compare-by-hash. In: USENIX Workshop on Hot Topics in Operating Systems (2003)

QoS-Aware Service Composition
in Dynamic Service Oriented Environments

Nebil Ben Mabrouk, Sandrine Beauche, Elena Kuznetsova,
Nikolaos Georgantas, and Valérie Issarny

INRIA Paris-Rocquencourt, France
{nebil.benmabrouk,sandrine.beauche,elena.kuznetsova}@inria.fr,
{nikolaos.georgantas,valerie.issarny}@inria.fr

Abstract. QoS-aware service composition is a key requirement in Service Oriented Computing (SOC) since it enables fulfilling complex user tasks while meeting Quality of Service (QoS) constraints. A challenging issue towards this purpose is the selection of the best set of services to compose, meeting global QoS constraints imposed by the user, which is known to be a NP-hard problem. This challenge becomes even more relevant when it is considered in the context of dynamic service environments. Indeed, two specific issues arise. First, required tasks are fulfilled on the fly, thus the time available for services' selection and composition is limited. Second, service compositions have to be adaptive so that they can cope with changing conditions of the environment. In this paper, we present an efficient service selection algorithm that provides the appropriate ground for QoS-aware composition in dynamic service environments. Our algorithm is formed as a guided heuristic. The paper also presents a set of experiments conducted to evaluate the efficiency of our algorithm, which shows its timeliness and optimality.

1 Introduction

Service Oriented Computing (SOC) and its underlying technologies such as Web Services have emerged as a powerful concept for building software systems [1]. An interesting feature of SOC is that it provides a flexible framework for reusing and composing existing software services in order to build value-added service compositions able to fulfill complex tasks required by users. A key requirement in services' composition is to enable these tasks while meeting Quality of Service (QoS) constraints set by users.

QoS-aware service composition underpins this purpose since it allows for composing services able to fulfill user required tasks while meeting QoS constraints. Assuming the availability of multiple resources in service environments, a large number of services can be found for realizing every sub-task part of a complex task. A specific issue emerges to this regard, which is about selecting the best set of services (i.e., in terms of QoS) to participate in the composition, meeting user's global QoS requirements.

J.M. Bacon and B.F. Cooper (Eds.): Middleware 2009, LNCS 5896, pp. 123–142, 2009.
© IFIP International Federation for Information Processing 2009

QoS-aware composition becomes even more challenging when it is considered in the context of dynamic service environments characterized with changing conditions. The dynamics of service environments bring about two specific problems in service selection. First, as dynamic environments call for fulfilling user requests on the fly (i.e., at run-time) and as services' availability cannot be known a priori, service selection and composition must be performed at runtime. Hence, the execution time of service selection algorithms is heavily constrained, whereas the computational complexity of the problem is NP-hard. The second issue is about the fluctuation of QoS conditions due to the dynamics of such environments. This problem arises for example when one or more services that make part of a service composition are no longer available or their QoS decreases (e.g., due to network disconnection or weak network connectivity) during the execution of the composition. Thus, a service selected to participate in a composition based on its QoS may no longer provide the same QoS when the time comes to be actually invoked. The overall question asked to this regard is: how to cope with the dynamics of service environments during the selection, the composition and the execution of services?

In this paper, we present a service selection algorithm that copes with the above issues. Our algorithm is designed in the context of the SemEUsE research project[1], which targets semantic QoS-aware middleware for dynamic service oriented environments. The middleware architecture presented in SemEUsE is centered on *dynamic binding* [2,3] of services, i.e., binding one out of multiple possible services just-in-time before its invocation according to its QoS measured at runtime (hereafter referred to as *runtime QoS*). Our selection algorithm underpins this purpose since it selects multiple services for every sub-task part of a complex task required by users, based on their nominal QoS (hereafter referred to as *advertised QoS*). Our algorithm consists in a guided heuristic. Our choice of a heuristic-based approach addresses the two issues stated above for dynamic environments. First, since the time available for service selection is limited, brute-force-like algorithms are inappropriate for such purpose, as they target determining the optimal composition, which is NP-hard. Second, finding the optimal composition may prove useless in the end since, due to dynamics, there is no guarantee that the selected composition will be possible at runtime or that its runtime QoS will not decrease with respect to the advertised one. To this regard, our algorithm aims at determining a set of near-optimal service compositions, i.e., compositions that: (i) respect global QoS constraints imposed by the user on the whole composition, and (ii) maximize a QoS utility function. At runtime, if a specific service composition is no longer possible or its QoS decreases, an alternative composition will be executed. To give a concrete example where our approach can be applied, we present the following scenario.

Motivating Scenario. An important use case where our solution can take place is the management of medical visits in large hospitals. Traditionally the management of medical visits in hospitals is static with predetermined

---

[1] SemEUsE project: http://www.semeuse.org

allocation of visits to doctors. Nevertheless, the availability of doctors can change with respect to some conditions. For instance, one or more doctors may be absent or they may be overloaded with new visits (e.g., due to some emergency cases unforeseen during the scheduling of visits). Human-based re-scheduling of medical visits is a time-consuming process entailing negotiations with doctors with respect to their specialties and agreements on the number of additional visits to be taken in charge.

A second issue concerns the process (i.e., the different activities) entailed by medical visits. Related to this, patients need to move between different points in the hospital in order to fulfill their visits. Ordinarily, they have to register, to pay for the visit, to meet the doctor and then to go to the pharmacy for buying medicines, which is a long and hard process especially for patients.

To avoid such complicated situations and to prevent patients unnecessarily moving between different points, hospitals need to manage their medical visits as a single request by composing the aforementioned activities in a unique process. Moreover, they need to dynamically handle these processes in order to cope with changing conditions in the hospital.

The SOC paradigm offers a flexible framework for managing the medical visits by reusing and composing existing software services of the hospital. Medical visits will be thus formed as processes (e.g., BPEL processes) underpinned by Web Services (e.g., registration, payment, doctor's service, chemist's service).

Let us consider a scenario where patients use the terminals available in the waiting room of the hospital to submit their medical visit requests. Using our solution, the hospital software system will be able to discover, select and compose the medical visit services (e.g., registration, payment, doctor's service, chemist's service) on-the-fly with respect to their QoS. Our solution considers common QoS features (e.g., response time) and domain-specific QoS features (e.g., doctors' specialties). Additionally, if the doctor's availability changes in-between, the hospital system will be able to dynamically update the composition by affecting the visit to another available doctor having the same specialty.

The remainder of this paper is structured as follows. In Section 2, we give an overview of related work. In Section 3, we present our service composition approach and we define the QoS model and the composition model underpinning this approach. In Section 4, we give the details of our selection algorithm, and we conduct a set of experiments to evaluate its timeliness and optimality in Section 5. Finally, in Section 6, we conclude with a summary of our contributions and the future perspectives of this work.

2   Related Work

Several selection algorithms have been proposed to select service compositions with different composition structures and various QoS constraints. A taxonomy of these solutions may be produced based on their objectives and the way they proceed. According to this, a first class of approaches aim at determining the optimal service composition (i.e., composition with the highest QoS utility) using brute-force-like algorithms (e.g., Global Planning [4], BBLP, MCSP, WS-IP [5]). These solutions have high computational cost and they can not provide a solution in a satisfying amount of time, thus they are inappropriate to be used in the context of dynamic service environments.

To cope with this issue, other approaches propose heuristic-based solutions (e.g., WS-HEU and WFlow [5], Genetic algorithm [8,9,6,7,10,11,12]) aiming to find near-optimal compositions, i.e., compositions that respect global QoS constraints and maximize a QoS utility function. Yu et al. [5] present two heuristics, WS-HEU and WFlow, for the service selection problem. WS-HEU is specific heuristic applied to sequential workflows (i.e., workflows structured as a sequence of activities), whereas WFlow is designed for general workflow structures (i.e., sequential, conditional, parallel). The main idea of WFLow is to decompose workflows into multiple execution routes. WFlow considers a parameter ξ_i for every route indicating its probability to be executed. Therefore, it focuses on the route with the highest probability, whereas in our approach we aim at giving feasible service compositions regardless of the way the workflow will be executed.

Other approaches [8,9,6,7,10,11,12] present heuristics based on a genetic algorithm. The application of such algorithm to the service selection problem presents two main drawbacks: first, the order in which service candidates are checked is randomly chosen (e.g., Crossing [6]), whereas in our approach we aim at checking services in an ordered way to optimize the timeliness and the optimality of our algorithm. Second, as the genetic algorithm can run endlessly, the users have to define a constant number of iterations fixed *a priori*. However, fixing a high number of iterations does not give any guarantee about the quality of the result. Therefore, the genetic algorithm is deemed non useful for our purpose (i.e., selecting near-optimal compositions).

More recently, Alrifai et al. [13] presented a novel approach that combines local and global optimization techniques. This approach starts from the global level and resolves the selection problem at the local level. It proceeds by decomposing global QoS constraints (i.e., imposed by the user on the whole composition) into a set of local constraints (i.e., for individual sub-tasks, part of the composition). To do so, it uses MILP (mixed integer linear programming) techniques to find the best decomposition of QoS constraints. The main drawback of this approach is that it represents a greedy selection method, since it selects services at the local level and does not ensure that the global QoS constraints are respected.

3   Composition Approach Overview

Our approach starts from the assumption that the user (e.g., the patient in our scenario) uses a Graphical User Interface (e.g., terminals available in the waiting room of the hospital) to submit his/her request (e.g., medical visit). The interface guides the user to express his request in terms of functional and QoS requirements, and then it formulates these requirements as a machine-understandable specification.

User functional requirements are formulated as an abstract task (hereafter referred to as *abstract service composition*) brought about by the composition of a set of abstract sub-tasks (hereafter referred to as *activities*) (e.g., registration, payment, doctor's service, chemist's service). These activities are described with abstract information (i.e., function, I/O description). Abstract service compositions are later transformed into *concrete service compositions* by assigning a concrete service to every activity in the composition. Considering the multiple resources available in service environments, it is common that several concrete services are found for every activity; we refer to these services as *service candidates* of the considered activity.

Concerning user QoS requirements, they are formulated as a set of constraints (hereafter referred to as *global QoS constraints*) on the whole composition. These constraints cover several QoS attributes specified by the user. Further details about QoS attributes are given in Section 3.1, where we present the QoS model underpinning our approach.

Once user requirements are specified, we proceed by automatically building executable service compositions with respect to user requirements and the dynamics of the service environment. Building executable compositions consists of: (i) discovering, (ii) selecting, and (iii) composing services on-the-fly (i.e., at runtime).

Concerning services' discovery, we adopt a semantic-based approach introduced by Ben Mokhtar et al. [14,15]. This approach uses domain-specific and QoS ontologies to match user functional and QoS requirements to services available in the environment. The matching is based on an efficient semantic reasoning performed at runtime. For every activity in the composition, the discovery phase gives the set of service candidates able to fulfill the activity (i.e., functional aspect) and to respect user QoS requirements. Services' discovery uses advertised QoS of services to perform a preliminary filtering ensuring that individual service candidates respect user QoS requirements.

Refining the first filtering, the selection phase ensures user QoS requirements at the global level (i.e., for the whole composition) based on the advertised QoS of services. That is, it selects a set of service candidates for each abstract activity that, when composed together, meet global QoS constraints. To achieve this, we introduce a heuristic algorithm based on clustering techniques, notably K-Means [16]. Clustering techniques, applied to our purpose, allow for grouping services with respect to their QoS into a set of clusters, to which we refer as *QoS levels*. Further, we use the resulting QoS levels to determine the utility of service candidates regarding our objective, i.e., selecting near-optimal compositions. More specifically, our heuristic algorithm deals with the service selection problem in two phases: (1) a local classification phase, which aims at determining the utilities of service candidates using clustering; this phase is performed for every activity in the composition; (2) a global selection phase which uses the obtained utilities to guide the selection of near-optimal compositions.

Once the global selection is fulfilled, the composition phase uses the selected services to define an executable service composition, by replacing every abstract activity in the composition with a 'dynamic binding' activity that takes as input the set of selected candidate services for this activity. At runtime, a unique service is selected and enacted among the provided ones with respect to its runtime QoS.

3.1   QoS Model

We consider a generic QoS model based on our previous work [17], in which we introduced a semantic QoS model formulated as a set of ontologies for QoS specification in dynamic service environments. This model allows for specifying cross-domain QoS attributes like response time, availability, reliability, throughput as well as domain-specific QoS attributes, e.g., medical visit price with respect to our scenario. Our model provides a detailed taxonomy of QoS which is flexible and easily extendible. Herein, we introduce an extension that concerns a particular classification of QoS attributes needed for our composition approach. QoS attributes can be divided into two groups: quantitative attributes (e.g., response time, availability, reliability, throughput) and qualitative attributes (e.g., security, privacy of medical information in our scenario). The former attributes are quantitatively measured using metrics, whereas the latter attributes can not be measured, they are rather evaluated in a boolean manner (i.e., they are either satisfied or not). For the sake of simplicity and without loss of generality, in this work we will consider only quantitative QoS attributes, since qualitative attributes can be represented as quantitative attributes determined by boolean metrics (i.e., 0 and 1).

Quantitative QoS attributes are in turn divided into two classes: negative attributes (e.g., response time, medical visit price) and positive attributes (e.g., availability, reliability, throughput). The first class of attributes has a negative effect on QoS, (i.e., the higher their values, the lower the QoS), hence they need to be minimized. On the contrary, positive QoS attributes need to be maximized, since they increase the overall QoS (i.e., the higher their values, the higher the QoS).

On the other hand, QoS attributes' values are determined in two ways: During the selection of services, these values are given by service providers (e.g., based on previous executions of services or using users' feedback). As already stated, we refer to these values as *advertised QoS*, which is specified in services' descriptions. At runtime, QoS values are provided by a monitoring component to enable further dynamic evaluation of services. As already stated, we refer to these values as *runtime QoS*.

3.2   Composition Model

Our algorithm aims at determining a set of near-optimal compositions. Such purpose requires evaluating the QoS of possible service compositions with respect to their structure and the way QoS is aggregated. That is, the evaluation of QoS depends on the structuring elements used to build the composition, to which we refer as *composition patterns*, and also QoS aggregation formulas associated with each pattern. Next, we describe the composition patterns on which our approach is based and we give the aggregation formulas associated with QoS attributes and composition patterns.

Composition Patterns. We consider a set of patterns commonly used by composition approaches [4,5], which cover most of the structures specified by composition languages (such as BPEL) [18,19]:

- Sequence: sequential execution of activities
- AND: parallel execution of activities
- XOR: conditional execution of activities
- Loop: iterative execution of activities

Computing the QoS of Composite Services. For every activity in the abstract service composition, we represent the QoS of a single candidate service S_i by using a vector $QoS_{S_i} = \langle q_{i,1}, ..., q_{i,n} \rangle$, where n represents the number of QoS attributes required by the user and $q_{i,j}$ represents the value of the QoS attribute j ($1 \le j \le n$). The QoS of a service composition is evaluated based on the QoS vectors of its constituent services while taking into account the composition patterns. Regarding QoS associated with AND and XOR, we adopt a pessimistic approach that considers worst-case QoS values. That is, to determine the values of the QoS attributes of a service composition, we consider the worst QoS values of all the possible executions of the composition. For instance, to determine the response time of parallel activities (i.e., AND), we consider the activity with the longest response time. Concerning the particular case of iterative activities (i.e., structured as a loop), we adopt a history-based estimation that considers the maximum number of loops (i.e., pessimistic approach). This number is determined from previous executions of the activity. In Table 1, we show examples of QoS computation with respect to QoS attributes and composition patterns. These examples can be classified as cross-domain QoS attributes (e.g., *response time, reliability, availability, throughput*) and domain-specific QoS attributes (e.g., *medical visit price*), but also as negative attributes

Table 1. QoS computation examples: $rt_i, re_i, av_i, th_i, p_i$ represent respectively, response time, reliability, availability, throughput and the medical visit price of services candidates structured with respect the composition patterns, whereas RT, RE, AV, TH, P represent the aggregated values of response time, reliability, availability, throughput and the medical visit price, respectively

QoS attributes	Composition Patterns			
	Sequence	AND	XOR	Loop
Response time (RT)	$\sum_{i=1}^{n} rt_i$	$max(rt_i)$	$max(rt_i)$	$rt \times k$
Reliability (RE)	$\prod_{i=1}^{n} re_i$	$\prod_{i=1}^{n} re_i$	$min(re_i)$	re^k
Availability (AV)	$\prod_{i=1}^{n} av_i$	$\prod_{i=1}^{n} av_i$	$min(av_i)$	av^k
Throughput (TH)	$min(th_i)$	$min(th_i)$	$min(th_i)$	th
Medical visit price (P)	$\sum_{i=1}^{n} p_i$	$\sum_{i=1}^{n} p_i$	$max(p_i)$	$p \times k$

(e.g., *response time, medical visit price*) and positive attributes (e.g., *reliability, availability, throughput*). Let us consider for example, the QoS computation of the medical visit price. Concerning the Sequence and AND patterns, the price is the sum of p_i values associated with the involved services (e.g., meeting doctors, buying medicines). For the XOR pattern (e.g., meeting two doctors with different specialties in an exclusive manner decided based on pre-diagnosis) the price is the maximum among p_i values of the involved services. Finally, for the iterative pattern (i.e., loop), the aggregated price is the value p of the repeated service multiplied by the number of loops k.

Notations. To state the problem that we are addressing in a formal way, we use the following notations:

- $AC = \{A_1, ..., A_x\}$ is an abstract service composition with x activities.
- $CC = \{S_1, ..., S_x\}$ is a concrete service composition with x service candidates, every service candidate S_i is bound to an abstract activity A_i $(1 \leq i \leq x)$.
- $U = \{U_1, ..., U_n\}$ is a set of global QoS constraints imposed by the user on n QoS attributes.
- QoS of a service candidate S_i is represented as a vector $QoS_{S_i} = \langle q_{i,1}, ..., q_{i,n} \rangle$ where $q_{i,j}$ is the advertised value of QoS attribute j $(1 \leq j \leq n)$.
- QoS of a concrete service composition CC is represented as a vector $QoS_{CC} = \langle Q_1, ..., Q_n \rangle$ where Q_j is the aggregated value of QoS attribute j $(1 \leq j \leq n)$.
- Each service candidate S_i has an associated utility function f_i.
- Each concrete service composition CC has an associated utility function $\mathcal{F}$.

4   Service Selection Algorithm

In the literature, service selection algorithms fall under two general approaches: (i) local [4] and (ii) global selection [5]. The former proceeds by selecting the best services (in terms of QoS) for every abstract activity individually. This approach has a low computational cost but it does not guarantee meeting global QoS constraints imposed by the user. For instance, regarding our scenario, this approach proceeds by selecting services offering the best trade-off between the required QoS attributes (e.g., response time, availability, reliability, throughput and medical visit price) for every activity apart. Thus, it cannot handle, for example, the global response time of the whole composition.

Conversely, global selection ensures meeting global QoS constraints since it selects the optimal service composition, i.e, a composition which respects global QoS constraints and has the highest QoS. This approach considers all possible compositions of services and selects the optimal one.

Nevertheless, the computational cost of global selection is NP-hard. To meet global QoS constraints in a timely manner, we present a heuristic algorithm that combines local and global selection techniques. Starting from the assumption that service candidates (for every activity in the abstract process) are already given by the semantic discovery phase, our algorithm proceeds through the following phases:

1. **Scaling phase,** which is a pre-processing phase aiming to normalize QoS values associated with negative and positive QoS attributes;
2. **Local classification,** which aims at classifying candidate services (for every activity in the abstract process) according to different QoS levels; this classification is further used to determine the utilities of every service candidate regarding our purpose;
3. **Global selection,** which aims at using the obtained utilities to guide the selection of near-optimal compositions.

4.1   Scaling Phase

As already mentioned, QoS attributes can be either negative or positive, thus some QoS values need to be minimized whereas other values have to be maximized. To cope with this issue, the scaling phase normalizes every QoS attribute value by transforming it into a value between 0 and 1 with respect to the formulas below [4].

$$\text{Negative attributes}: \quad q'_{i,j} = \begin{cases} \frac{q_j^{max}-q_{i,j}}{q_j^{max}-q_j^{min}} & \text{if} \quad q_j^{max}-q_j^{min} \neq 0 \\ 1 & \text{else} \end{cases} \quad (1)$$

$$\text{Positive attributes}: \quad q'_{i,j} = \begin{cases} \frac{q_{i,j}-q_j^{min}}{q_j^{max}-q_j^{min}} & \text{if} \quad q_j^{max}-q_j^{min} \neq 0 \\ 1 & \text{else} \end{cases} \quad (2)$$

where $q'_{i,j}$ denotes the normalized value of QoS attribute j associated with service candidate S_i. It is computed using the current value $q_{i,j}$ and also q_j^{max} and q_j^{min}, which refer respectively to the maximum and minimum values of QoS attribute j among all service candidates.

The same formulas are also used to normalize the aggregated QoS values of concrete service compositions. Each composition CC is represented by a vector $QoS_{CC} = \langle Q_1, ..., Q_n \rangle$ with n QoS attributes. The normalization produces a QoS vector $QoS_{CC} = \langle Q'_1, ..., Q'_n \rangle$. The values of Q'_j $(1 \leq j \leq n)$ are computed based on the current value Q_j, and also Q_j^{max} and Q_j^{min}, which refer respectively to the maximum and minimum values of Q_j among all concrete service compositions.

4.2   Local Classification

Local classification is performed locally for every activity in the abstract service composition. It aims at classifying service candidates associated with a given activity into multiple QoS levels (i.e., clusters) with respect to their QoS. Each level contains the set of service candidates having roughly the same QoS. This classification is further used to determine the relative importance of service candidates regarding our objective (i.e., selecting near-optimal compositions). To do so, we use clustering techniques, notably the K-means [16] algorithm.

Classification Overview. K-means provides a simple and efficient way to classify a set of data points into a fixed number of clusters. These data points are characterized by their N-dimensional coordinates $\langle x_1, x_2, .., x_n \rangle$. The main idea of K-means is to define a centroid $c = \langle x_{c,1}, x_{c,2}, .., x_{c,n} \rangle$ for every cluster and to associate each data point $dp_i = \langle x_{i,1}, x_{i,2}, .., x_{i,n} \rangle$ to the appropriate cluster by computing the shortest N-dimensional Euclidian distance D between the data point and each centroid:

$$D_{(c,dp_i)} = \sqrt{\sum_{j=1}^{n}(x_{c,j} - x_{i,j})^2} \qquad (3)$$

Further, the values of centroids are updated by computing the average of their associated data points. The clustering iterates by alternating these two steps (i.e., updating centroids, clustering data points) continuously until reaching a fixpoint (i.e., centroids' values do not change any more). The result of K-means will be the set of final clusters and their associated data points. It is worth noting that K-means has a polynomial computational cost in function of the number of iterations [20].

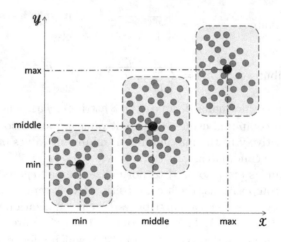

Fig. 1. Example of K-means with 2 dimensions (x, y) and 3 clusters: *min, middle* and *max*

In our context, we use K-means to group service candidates of every activity in the abstract service composition into multiple QoS levels. QoS levels are thus represented as clusters and service candidates are considered as data points determined by the QoS vectors $QoS_{S_i} = \langle q_{i,1}, ..., q_{i,n} \rangle$.

QoS Levels Computation. To cluster service candidates, we need first to determine the initial values of QoS levels (i.e., centroids). For this matter, we define m QoS levels (i.e., QL_l, $(1 \leq l \leq m)$), where m is a constant number fixed a priori (Fig. 2). The value of m differs from an activity to another and it is supposed to be given by domain experts with respect to the *service density*[17] of the considered activity. For instance, in our medical visit scenario, the number of QoS levels related to the doctors' activity is fixed by the hospital system administrator with respect to the number of doctors in the hospital. Once the number of QoS levels is fixed, the value of each level is determined by dividing the range of the n QoS attributes (fixed by the global QoS constraints) into m equal quality ranges qr with respect to the following formula:

$$qr^l_j = q^{min}_j + \frac{l-1}{m-1} * (q^{max}_j - q^{min}_j) \qquad 1 \leq l \leq m \qquad (4)$$

where qr^l_j denotes the quality range l of QoS attribute j with $(1 \leq j \leq n)$, whereas q^{max}_j and q^{min}_j refer to the maximum and minimum values of the attribute j, respectively. The initial value of each QoS level is then:
$QL_l = \langle qr^l_1, ..., qr^l_n \rangle$ with $1 \leq l \leq m$.

Once the initial values of QoS levels are determined, we perform the clustering of service candidates, and then we obtain the final set of QoS levels which is used to determine the utility of service candidates.

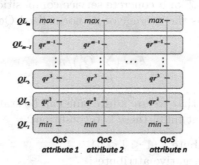

Fig. 2. Computation of Quality Levels

Service Utility Computation. The objective of our algorithm is selecting near-optimal compositions, but also obtaining a number of near-optimal compositions as large as possible. Indeed, the larger the number of selected compositions is, the larger is the choice of services allowed during dynamic binding. Additionally, providing a large number of compositions helps preventing the *starvation* problem during dynamic binding of services. This problem arises when, e.g., a few number of services are selected for dynamic binding but none of them is available at runtime.

For this matter, we consider a utility function f_i which characterizes the relative importance of a service candidate S_i regarding the objective above. The utility f_i is calculated based on two parameters: (i) QoS of S_i and, (ii) the number of services in the QoS level to which S_i belongs. The first parameter is interpreted as follows: the higher QoS of S_i, the higher its ability to be part of feasible compositions. Concerning the second parameter, it represents the importance of the QoS level QL_l to which S_i belongs, i.e., if the number of service candidates associated with QL_l is large, this means that using QL_l would eventually lead to finding more feasible compositions. Therefore, f_i is computed as follows:

$$f_i = (r/t) * qos_i \quad where \quad qos_i = (\sum_{j=1}^{n} q'_{i,j})/n \tag{5}$$

where r is the number of services in the QoS level QL_l to which S_i pertains, t is the total number of service candidates for the activity, and qos_i is the QoS utility of service S_i. It is computed as the average of the normalized QoS attributes' values $q'_{i,j}$. As the values (r/t) and qos_i are comprised between 0 and 1 (i.e., since $r \leq t$ and $0 \leq q_{i,j} \leq 1$, respectively), the value of f_i is also comprised between 0 and 1.

4.3   Global Selection

Global selection aims at selecting near optimal compositions, i.e., compositions that (i) respect global QoS constraints and (ii) maximize the utility function $\mathcal{F}$. The utility function $\mathcal{F}$ of a concrete service composition CC with $QoS_{CC} = \langle Q'_1, ..., Q'_n \rangle$ is defined as the average of its normalized QoS values Q'_j:

$$\mathcal{F} = (\sum_{j=1}^{n} Q'_j)/n \tag{6}$$

Therefore, the problem that we are addressing can be stated as finding concrete service compositions that fulfill these two conditions:

1. For every QoS attribute j ($1 \leq j \leq n$),
   - $Q_j \leq U_j$ for negative attributes;
   - $Q_j \geq U_j$ for positive attributes;
2. The QoS utility $\mathcal{F}$ is maximized.

Heuristic Overview. The goal of our heuristic is to use the utilities f_i resulting from the local classification phase to select near-optimal compositions without considering all possible combinations of services. Towards this purpose, we fix a utility threshold $\mathcal{T}$ that allows for considering only service candidates with a utility value $f_i \geq \mathcal{T}$, thus enabling to focus on the most eligible services (i.e., services with the highest f_i values).

The choice of the threshold $\mathcal{T}$ is of great importance in our algorithm since it allows for tuning the trade-off between the number of resulting compositions and the timeliness of the algorithm. Indeed, if $\mathcal{T}$ increases, the number of considered services possibly decreases and consequently so will the number of compositions to check. Hence, the execution time of the algorithm decreases, but the number of resulting near-optimal compositions decreases as well. Conversely, if $\mathcal{T}$ decreases, the number of services to consider possibly increases and hence, the number of obtained compositions possibly increases, too. However, the execution time of the algorithm increases as well.

The latter point leads to another important result, which is about the application of our algorithm. Indeed, tuning $\mathcal{T}$ makes our algorithm generic and flexible, so that it can be applied to multiple dynamic service environments according to their characteristics, particularly their *service density* [17] and also time constraints in such environments. For instance, if a service environment has a high service density, the system can tune $\mathcal{T}$ so that the algorithm will be more selective and give a satisfying number of service compositions. By the same, if the execution time in dynamic service environments is heavily constrained (e.g., highly dynamic environments), the system can also tune $\mathcal{T}$ to make the algorithm check a limited number of service compositions, thus enabling to respect timeliness constraints of such environments.

Pruning the Search Tree. Our algorithm proceeds by exploring a combinatorial search tree built from candidate services according to the following rules:

- Every service candidate S_i having $f_i \geq \mathcal{T}$ is a node in the search tree;
- If there is a link (i.e., control flow) from activity A_x to activity A_y in the abstract service composition, then the candidate services of A_x will be the child nodes of every service candidate in A_y;
- Child nodes (i.e., services associated with an activity A_i) are sorted from left to right according to their utility values f_i. Services with higher values of f_i are on the left and those with lower values are on the right.
- Add a virtual root node to all the nodes without incoming links.

Once the search tree is built, our heuristic algorithm ensures that its constituent service compositions meet user QoS requirements. Towards this purpose, it first generates a global QoS aggregation formula (i.e., for the whole composition) for every QoS attribute by exploring the structure of the composition. Then it uses the generated formulas to compute the aggregated QoS value of each attribute and the QoS utility of service compositions. The algorithm further checks the feasibility of these compositions by setting the global QoS constraints given by the user as upper bounds for the aggregated QoS values. The above step in performed along with the following optimizations aiming to prune the search tree of our algorithm.

- **Pruning using incremental computation.** As our algorithm traverses down the search tree from the root node to the leaf nodes, the aggregated QoS values increase along with the traversal of the tree. Consequently, if the aggregated QoS values calculated at any non-leaf node in the traversal of the tree, does not respect QoS constraints, then all the sub-tree under the non-leaf node will be pruned. This optimization is useful when we deal with long running processes having a large number of activities.

- **Pruning using utility values approximation.** This idea concerns an approximation rather than an exact optimization. It utilizes the fact that our algorithm explores the search tree in an ordered way, i.e., it checks services with higher f_i values first. Therefore, if a service candidate S_i does not lead to any feasible composition, all its following nodes (i.e., service candidates of the same activity but with lower f_i values) will be not considered for the rest of the computation, which reduces the number of services to check. This approximation is convenient when we have a large number of candidate services per activity.

Our algorithm uses the above optimizations together, along with an additional improvement allowing to enhance the timeliness of the algorithm. Indeed, to reduce the time needed for computing the aggregated QoS values of service compositions, we ensure that only one service candidate changes when the algorithm switches from a composition to another. That is, the difference between two consecutive compositions CC_v and CC_w is that a service candidate S_i in the first composition will be replaced by a service S_j in the second one. Thus, instead of computing the whole aggregated QoS values of CC_w, the algorithm updates the aggregated QoS values of CC_v with respect to QoS_{S_i} and QoS_{S_j}.

Finally, our algorithm produces as output the set of near-optimal compositions ranked according to their utilities $\mathcal{F}$. The obtained compositions are then used for the generation of an executable service composition underpinning dynamic binding of services.

5 Experimental Evaluation

5.1 Experimental Setup

We conducted a set of experiments to evaluate the quality of our algorithm. These experiments were conducted on a Dell machine with two AMD Athlon 1.80GHz processors and 1.8 GB RAM. The machine is running under Windows XP operating system and Java 1.6. In these experiments, we focus on two metrics:

- **Execution time.** This metric measures the response time of our algorithm with respect to the size of the problem in terms of the number of activities and the number of services per activity. In these experiments, we measure separately the execution time of local classification and global selection.
- **Optimality.** This metric measures how close the utility of the best composition given by our algorithm to the utility of the optimal composition given by the brute-force algorithm. The optimality metric is then given by the following formula:

$$Optimality = \mathcal{F}/\mathcal{F}_{opt} \tag{7}$$

where $\mathcal{F}$ is the utility of the best composition given by our heuristic algorithm and $\mathcal{F}_{opt}$ is the utility of the optimal composition given by the brute force algorithm.

In our experiments, we use the data given by previous studies about Web Services' QoS [21,22]. In these studies, the authors provide a set of QoS metrics (i.e., response time, throughput, availability, validation accuracy, cost) related to current email validation Web services (Table 2). We use these metrics as a sample input data for our algorithm. Nevertheless, the number of Web services considered in these studies is too limited compared to the number of services that we need to assess the scalability of our algorithm. To this regard, we developed a *Data Generator* that randomly generates input data for our algorithm between the minimmum and maximum values of the QoS metrics given in Table 2. Further, we developed a *Process Generator* that randomly generates abstract

Table 2. QoS metrics for email validation Web Services

Service Provider	Response Time (ms)	Throughput (req./min)	Availability (%)	Validation Accuracy (%)	Cost (cents/invoke)
XMLLogic	720	6.00	85	87	1.2
XWebservices	1100	1.74	81	79	1
StrikeIron	912	10.00	96	94	7
CDYNE	910	11.00	90	91	2
Webservicex	1232	4.00	87	83	0
ServiceObjects	391	9.00	99	90	5

processes to use as input for experimenting with our algorithm. The Process Generator takes as arguments the number of activities and the number of candidate services per activity, and it yields as output a process by structuring the activities with respect to randomly chosen composition patterns. The Process Generator uses the Data Generator to provide the QoS values associated with service candidates of each activity in the process.

For the purpose of these experiments, we vary the number of activities and the number of services per activity between 10 and 50. Concerning the number of QoS constraints, it is comprised between 2 and 5 constraints. Finally, for the sake of precision we execute each experiment 20 times and we calculate the mean value of the obtained results.

Once data input is generated, we need to fix the values of the following parameters before launching the experiments:

- We set the values of global constraints given by the user to the mean value m of every QoS attribute aggregated with respect to the structure of the generated process composition.
- We use the method of computing QoS levels described in Section 3.2 to cluster service candidates according to 3 clusters: *Min, Middle* and *Max.*
- Concerning the computation of the utility threshold $\mathcal{T}$, we fix it to $(m + \sigma)$ where m and σ denote respectively, the mean value and standard deviation of f_i utilities of all service candidates. As we have a large number of service

candidates, we assume that the values of f_i are normally distributed. According to this, the *central limit theorem*[23] states that the value $(m + \sigma)$ allows for discarding approximately 74% of service candidates.

5.2   Experimental Results

During the experiments, we aimed to compare the execution time of our algorithm to the execution time of a brute-force algorithm that we developed for the purpose of these experiments. Nevertheless, the latter algorithm takes a long time to execute (i.e., several hours) for a number of activities more than 20. Hence, we are not going to present the execution time of both algorithms, we will rather present the measurements obtained for our algorithm.

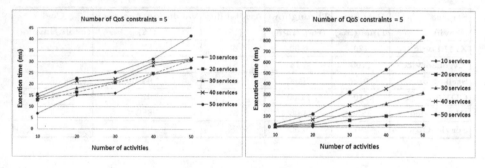

Fig. 3. Execution time of the local classification phase (for a fixed number of QoS constraints)

Fig. 4. Execution time of the global selection phase (for a fixed number of QoS constraints)

Figures 3 and 4 show the execution time of local classification and global selection, respectively. These measurements are obtained by fixing the number of QoS constraints to 5 and varying the number of activities and the number of service candidates per activity between 10 and 50. The obtained measurements show that the execution time of our algorithm increases along with the number of activities and the number of services per activity, which is an expected result. Conversely, in Figures 5 and 6, we measure the execution time of our algorithm while fixing the number of service candidates per activity to 50, and varying the number of activities between 10 and 50 and the number of QoS constraints between 2 and 5. These figures show that the execution time of our algorithm also increases along with the number of activities and the number of QoS constraints.

Additionally, it is worth noting that the execution time of the local classification phase is approximately negligible compared to the execution time of the global selection phase (i.e., 45ms $\ll$ 0.8s), which is an expected result given that K-Means is a simple algorithm with a polynomial computational cost[20]. Overall, in almost all cases our algorithm is executed in a reasonable amount of

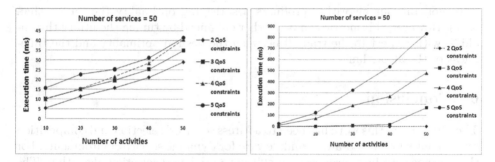

Fig. 5. Execution time of the local classification phase (for a fixed number of services)

Fig. 6. Execution time of the global selection phase (for a fixed number of services)

time (i.e., less than 0.9s) if we compare it, e.g., to the response time of the email validation Web services described in Table 2.

Concerning the optimality of our algorithm, we measure it while fixing the number of QoS constraints to 5, and varying the number of activities and the number of services per activity between 10 and 50. Figure 7 shows that the optimality of our algorithm increases along with the number of activities and the number of services per activity. This means that, when it deals a large number of compositions, our algorithm finds more feasible compositions that may provide a better utility. This is explained by the fact that the utility of the best composition increases along with the probability to find services with QoS values close to the optimal QoS (i.e., near-optimal QoS values). As the service candidates are randomly generated, this probability increases along with the number of generated services and also with the number of activities, thus increasing the utility of the overall composition.

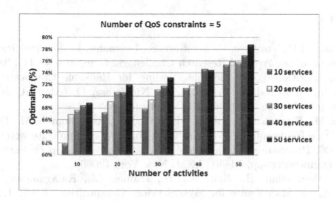

Fig. 7. Optimality of our algorithm

In general, our algorithm produces a satisfying optimality (i.e., more than 62%). However, this metric can be further enhanced by tuning the utility threshold T with respect to the trad-off between the desired optimality and the timeliness of the algorithm.

6   Conclusion

The objective of this work has been to address services' selection and composition in the context of a QoS-aware middleware for dynamic service environments. For this purpose, we have proposed an efficient QoS-based selection algorithm. The importance of our algorithm is three-fold. First, it introduces a novel approach based on clustering techniques. Applying such techniques for services' selection brings new ideas in this research area. Second, by producing not a single but multiple service compositions satisfying the QoS constraints, our algorithm underpins the concept of dynamic binding of services, which allows for coping with changing conditions in dynamic environements. Third and most importantly, our algorithm shows a satisfying efficiency in terms of timeliness and optimality, which makes it appropriate for on-the-fly service composition in dynamic service environments.

The presented work makes part of our ongoing research addressing QoS-aware middleware for pervasive environments. Our next steps concern further inverstigating clustering techniques for improving our heuristic algorithm, and considering in our QoS model network-level QoS and middleware-based QoS enhancement for service compositions.

Acknowledgement

This research is partially supported by the SemEUsE project[2] funded by the french National Research Agency (ANR).

References

1. Papazoglou, M.P., Traverso, P., Dustdar, S., Leymann, F.: Service-Oriented Computing: State of the Art and Research Challenges. Computer 40(11), 38–45 (2007)
2. Pautasso, C., Alonso, G.: Flexible Binding for Reusable Composition of Web Services. In: Gschwind, T., Aßmann, U., Nierstrasz, O. (eds.) SC 2005. LNCS, vol. 3628, pp. 151–166. Springer, Heidelberg (2005)
3. Di Penta, M., Esposito, R., Villani, M.L., Codato, R., Colombo, M., Di Nitto, E.: WS Binder: a framework to enable dynamic binding of composite web services. In: SOSE 2006: Proceedings of the 2006 international workshop on Service-oriented software engineering, pp. 74–80. ACM, New York (2006)
4. Zeng, L., Benatallah, B., Ngu, A.H.H., Dumas, M., Kalagnanam, J., Chang, H.: QoS-Aware Middleware for Web Services Composition. IEEE Trans. Softw. Eng. 30(5), 311–327 (2004)

---

[2] SemEUsE project: http://www.semeuse.org

5. Yu, T., Zhang, Y., Lin, K.-J.: Efficient Algorithms for Web Services Selection with End-to-End QoS Constraints. ACM Trans. Web 1(1), 6 (2007)
6. Jaeger, M.C., Mühl, G.: QoS-based Selection of Services: The Implementation of a Genetic Algorithm. In: Braun, T., Carle, G., Stiller, B. (eds.) Kommunikation in Verteilten Systemen (KiVS 2007) Industriebeträge, Kurzbeiträge und Workshops, Bern, Switzerland, March 2007, pp. 350–359. VDE Verlag, Berlin und Offenbach (2007)
7. Kobti, Z., Zhiyang, W.: An Adaptive Approach for QoS-Aware Web Service Composition Using Cultural Algorithms. In: Orgun, M.A., Thornton, J. (eds.) AI 2007. LNCS (LNAI), vol. 4830, pp. 140–149. Springer, Heidelberg (2007)
8. Canfora, G., Di Penta, M., Esposito, R., Villani, M.L.: An approach for qos-aware service composition based on genetic algorithms. In: GECCO 2005: Proceedings of the 2005 conference on Genetic and evolutionary computation, pp. 1069–1075. ACM, New York (2005)
9. Zhang, C., Su, S., Chen, J.: A Novel Genetic Algorithm for QoS-Aware Web Services Selection. In: Lee, J., Shim, J., Lee, S.-g., Bussler, C.J., Shim, S. (eds.) DEECS 2006. LNCS, vol. 4055, pp. 224–235. Springer, Heidelberg (2006)
10. Cao, L., Li, M., Cao, J.: Using genetic algorithm to implement cost-driven web service selection. Multiagent Grid Syst. 3(1), 9–17 (2007)
11. Gao, C., Cai, M., Chen, H.: QoS-aware Service Composition Based on Tree-Coded Genetic Algorithm. In: COMPSAC 2007: Proceedings of the 31st Annual International Computer Software and Applications Conference, Washington, DC, USA, pp. 361–367. IEEE Computer Society, Los Alamitos (2007)
12. Vanrompay, Y., Rigole, P., Berbers, Y.: Genetic algorithm-based optimization of service composition and deployment. In: SIPE 2008: Proceedings of the 3rd international workshop on Services integration in pervasive environments, pp. 13–18. ACM, New York (2008)
13. Alrifai, M., Risse, T., Dolog, P., Nejdl, W.: A Scalable Approach for QoS-based Web Service Selection. In: 1st International Workshop on Quality-of-Service Concerns in Service Oriented Architectures (QoSCSOA 2008) in conjunction with ICSOC 2008, Sydney (December 2008)
14. Mokhtar, S.B., Kaul, A., Georgantas, N., Issarny, V.: Efficient semantic service discovery in pervasive computing environments. In: van Steen, M., Henning, M. (eds.) Middleware 2006. LNCS, vol. 4290, pp. 240–259. Springer, Heidelberg (2006)
15. Mokhtar, S.B., Preuveneers, D., Georgantas, N., Issarny, V., Berbers, Y.: EASY: Efficient semAntic Service discoverY in pervasive computing environments with QoS and context support. J. Syst. Softw. 81(5), 785–808 (2008)
16. Lloyd, S.P.: Least squares quantization in PCM. Unpublished memorandum, Bell Laboratories (1957)
17. Mabrouk, N.B., Georgantas, N., Issarny, V.: A Semantic End-to-End QoS Model for Dynamic Service Oriented Environments. In: Principles of Engineering Service Oriented Systems (PESOS 2009), held in conjunction with the International Conference on Software Engineering, ICSE 2009 (2009)
18. Moscato, F., Mazzocca, N., Vittorini, V., Di Lorenzo, G., Mosca, P., Magaldi, M.: Workflow Pattern Analysis in Web Services Orchestration: The BPEL4WS Example. In: Yang, L.T., Rana, O.F., Di Martino, B., Dongarra, J. (eds.) HPCC 2005. LNCS, vol. 3726, pp. 395–400. Springer, Heidelberg (2005)

19. Wohed, P., van der Aalst, W.M.P., Dumas, M., ter Hofstede, A.H.M.: Pattern Based Analysis of BPEL4WS. In: Song, I.-Y., Liddle, S.W., Ling, T.-W., Scheuermann, P. (eds.) ER 2003. LNCS, vol. 2813, pp. 200–215. Springer, Heidelberg (2003)
20. Arthur, D., Vassilvitskii, S.: On the Worst Case Complexity of the k-means Method. Technical Report 2005-34, Stanford InfoLab (2005)
21. Al-Masri, E., Mahmoud, Q.H.: QoS-based Discovery and Ranking of Web Services, August 2007, pp. 529–534 (2007)
22. Al-Masri, E., Mahmoud, Q.H.: Discovering the Best Web Service. In: WWW 2007: Proceedings of the 16th international conference on World Wide Web, pp. 1257–1258. ACM, New York (2007)
23. Hogben, L., Greenbaum, A., Brualdi, R., Mathias, R.: Handbook of Linear Algebra. Chapman & Hall, Boca Raton (2007)

Self-adapting Service Level in Java Enterprise Edition

Jérémy Philippe[1], Noël De Palma[1,2], Fabienne Boyer[1], and Olivier Gruber[3]

[1] INRIA Rhône-Alpes, France
[2] Grenoble Institute of Technology
[3] University of Grenoble I
Firstname.Lastname@inria.fr

Abstract. Application servers are subject to varying workloads, which suggests an autonomic management to maintain optimal performance. We propose to integrate in the component-based programming model often used in current application servers the concept of *service level adaptation*, allowing some components to dynamically degrade or upgrade their level of service. Our goal is to be able, under heavy workloads, to trade a lower service level of the most resource-intensive components for a stable performance of the server as a whole. Upgrading or degrading components is autonomously performed through runtime profiling, which is used to estimate the application's hot spots and target adaptations. In addition to finding the best adaptations, this performance profile allows our system to characterize the effects of past adaptations; in particular given the current workload, it is possible to estimate if a service level upgrade might result in an overload. As a result, by stabilizing the server at peak performance via component adaptations, we are able to drastically improve both overall latency and throughput. For instance, on both the RUBiS[1] and TPC-W benchmarks[2], we are able to maintain peak performance in heavy load scenarios, far exceeding the initial capacity of the system.

Keywords: Quality of service, service-level degradation, control loop, performance profile, self-adaptation.

1 Introduction

Autonomic management is increasingly important, especially regarding adaptive behaviors in the presence of varying workloads. Application servers openly available on the Internet are especially subject to such workloads and offer the incentive to design and evaluate adaptive behaviors. Some of our previous work has studied autonomic optimization exploiting load balancing in clusters [1]. This work focuses on exploiting application-level adaptations that are naturally present in Internet applications.

---

[1] http://rubis.objectweb.org/
[2] http://www.tpc.org/tpcw/

J.M. Bacon and B.F. Cooper (Eds.): Middleware 2009, LNCS 5896, pp. 143–162, 2009.
© IFIP International Federation for Information Processing 2009

Indeed, it is our experience that components of Internet applications often contain the opportunity for behavioral adaptations. A common example of such adaptations can be found in the context of multimedia streaming servers, where the resolution and encoding of the content can be adapted to control the demand in CPU and network bandwidth [2]. Limiting the size and precision of search results is also a well-known and efficient adaptation of Internet applications. Sorting is always an expensive operation on large results, which may be avoided or approximated in some cases. Transactions are also a classical source of overheads that can be mitigated through smaller transactions, less consistency, or playing with the granularity of locks.

In our approach, we request component designers to explicit possible behavioral adaptations, in the form of alternative (and generally degraded) service levels. Each component can be individually moved up or down that sequence, raising or lowering the level of the provided service. At lower levels, a component generally uses less resources to provide its service. Explicit levels of service offer autonomic managers the opportunity to adapt the overall resource usage of an application, trading a lower service level of individual components for an improved quality of service of the application as a whole (i.e. better latency and peak throughput). We use a dynamic approach in which an autonomic manager decides to degrade or upgrade service levels at runtime, based on workload fluctuations.

The decision to apply or unapply an adaptation is fully autonomic. We only request that component designers express service levels. We felt important that we do not require them to measure or estimate the resource usage of these service levels. Indeed, such estimates are not only difficult to make accurately for an individual component but are almost impossible to make when considering all possible architectures and combinations of service levels for other components. To estimate resource usage, we rely on a traditional profiling technique based on request sampling, that we tailor to our component-oriented architecture. In particular, we abstract the traditional call stack into a more abstract *component stack* that provides an execution pattern in the sampled system. For each such execution pattern, we can estimate its intrinsic cost per resource. Using this intrinsic cost, we can calibrate the gains of adaptations per component stack and per resource. Through such gains, we learn about past effects of adaptations, helping us to optimize future adaptation decisions.

The challenge of this approach is to obtain *adaptation gains* that are workload independent. Indeed, gains are estimated on past workloads and used to predict effects of adaptation on future workloads. Using our knowledge of the architecture, we estimate our adaptation gains at the fine-grain level of component stacks, achieving enough workload independence. Our experiments show that effectively, our autonomic manager accurately estimates the effects of adaptations and efficiently corrects both overload and underload situations, even in the presence of varying workloads.

We prototyped our autonomic adaptation system in the context of Internet application servers based on the Java EE model (Java Enterprise Edition). This prototype is an extension of the open-source JOnAS middleware. The modifications are minimal and incur no significant overhead. In particular, our continuous 10Hz sampling incurs no measurable overhead in both RUBiS and TPC-W benchmarks. Our sampling rate is enough to compute component stack costs with good precision and thereby measure reliable adaptation gains. Our experiments show that our system consistently improves the overall performance of JEE applications under heavy workloads, both reducing latency and increasing throughput. Our experiments also show that our system is not prone to oscillations and adapts quickly to changing workloads.

The rest of this paper is organized as follows. In Section 2, we present the design of our autonomic adaptation system based on techniques from control theory. In Section 3, we details our sampling techniques and how we approach workload-independent gains. In Section 4, we present a simple example illustrating our performance metric and simple adaptive behaviors. In Section 5, we discuss the adaptive behavior obtained on the RUBiS and TPC-W benchmarks. In Section 6, we discuss related work. In Section 7, we conclude.

2 Autonomic Adaptation

Our autonomic adaptation system uses techniques from control theory, which has become a common practice in autonomic systems [3][4][5]. The configuration of our control loop is composed of two thresholds defined for each resource. The overload threshold is the usage ceiling above which the controller looks for a service degradation to lower the usage of the overloaded resource. The underload threshold is the usage floor upon which the controller *may* consider a service upgrade.

Our adaption system follows the simple state machine depicted in Figure 1. The adaptation system has a regulation mode and a calibration mode. In regulation mode, the control loop monitors the load of each resource. It reacts to overload situations by selecting the most efficient adaptation that is not yet applied and applies it. It reacts to underload situations by selecting amongst already applied adaptations which one is the most effective to unapply. After each regulation, the adaptation system steps into calibration mode for a fixed calibration period. During this calibration period, further regulations are inhibited.

In calibration mode, the autonomic adaptation system measures the impacts on resource usage of the adaptation it just applied. The calibration period has been experimentally fixed to 10 seconds, which is neither too short nor too long. Too short, we would not be able to accurately estimate the effects of a regulation on resource usage. Too long, changes in workloads could interfere with our estimate. Moreover, a long calibration delay hinders regulation since regulations are inhibited during calibration. Calibration will be detailed in Section 3.

Regarding regulation, one of the main challenges is stability, which we address using an asymmetrical selection of adaptations. In the overload case, the control loop looks for an adaptation δ to apply with a high effect on resource usage (noted $\Delta_\delta U_R$) and a low degradation on the level of service, noted w_δ. This

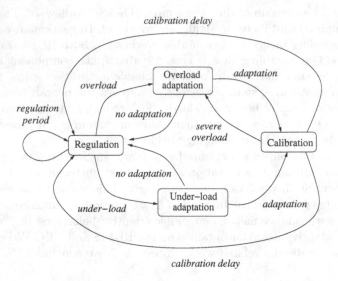

Fig. 1. Autonomic Adaptation Design

w_δ is provided by component designers who annotate their adaptations with their relative impact on the quality of service of their component. The $\Delta_\delta U_R$ is automatically estimated by our system, which is detailled later on. This overload goal is captured by the following definition where $E(\delta^+)$ is the efficiency of applying the adaptation δ:

$$E(\delta^+) = \frac{\Delta_\delta U_R}{w_\delta}$$

In the underload case, the control loop looks for an adaptation to unapply with a low effect on resource usage and a high improvement of the level of service. This goal is captured by the following definition where $E(\delta^-)$ is the efficiency of unapplying the adaptation δ.

$$E(\delta^-) = \frac{w_\delta}{\Delta_\delta U_R}$$

It is important to point out that these definitions imply, through $\Delta_\delta U_R$, a mean to estimate the effects of adaptation δ on resource usage. Also, estimating impact on resource usage is important to make sure that an adaptation targeting a particular resource will not overload another resource (in the case of adaptations intended to find a trade-off between several resources). To estimate $\Delta_\delta U_R$, we define characteristics called *adaptation gains*, which are evaluated based on the observed effects of the past regulations that used adaptation δ.

3   Adaptation Gains

The gain of an adaptation captures the effects on resource usage of that adaptation. We estimate the gain of an adaptation when it is applied under a certain workload but we want to predict the effects of applying or unapplying that same adaptation at some later time under a potentially unrelated workload.

The challenge is therefore to characterize the gain in a way that is as much workload independent as possible. We compute the gain when we calibrate by measuring the usage delta of a resource R which results from applying adaptation δ:

$$\Delta_\delta U_R = U_R^+ - U_R^-$$

U_R^+ is the usage of resource R sampled and averaged during the calibration delay, after adaptation δ is applied. U_R^- is the usage of resource R sampled and averaged right before adaptation δ is applied.

A simple approach to modeling the gain of adaptation δ on resource R could be to define the gain $G_\delta(R)$ as follows:

$$G_\delta(R) = \frac{U_R^+}{U_R^-}$$

However, this simple approach does not adequately isolate the effects of the adaptation δ. This gain captures the usage delta of the resource R due not only to tasks executing within the adapted component but also due to tasks whose executions are never touching the adapted component. Changes of workload, unrelated to the adaptated component, happening during calibration, could affect our gain estimate. In particular, the more the adapted component is involved in the workload, the higher the impact on resource usage. A better approach is to focus our gain estimation solely on tasks whose executions involve the adapted component.

We therefore need to separately account resource usage depending on the components involved in the tasks, which we achieve through a profiling technique called statistical sampling [6][7]. The traditional approach periodically captures the call stacks of active threads in a system. In our approach, we extract *component stacks* from call stacks as depicted in figure 2. In this example, we have a simple assembly of components in the architecture: a component A connected to two components B and C. We show the call stack of one active task, making function calls in component A and B. The corresponding component stack, noted $A - B$, abstracts away from the individual stack frames, providing an execution pattern (or signature) for the currently executing tasks from an architectural point of view.

Once we have component stacks, we can link them to resources as follows. Typically, we start by modelling the processor as a *CPU resource* and I/O subsystems as *I/O resources*. In a sample, we relate each component stack appearing in that sample with one and only one resource. Given the component stack of an active task, we associate that component stack with an I/O resource R if

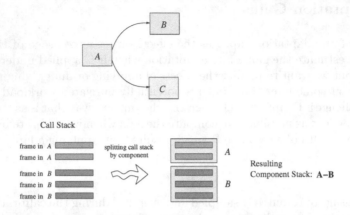

Fig. 2. From call stacks to component stacks

the corresponding task is explicitely waiting for I/O on that resource R when sampled. Otherwise, the component stack is associated with the CPU resource.

Once component stacks are associated with resources, we define for each sample the *hit rate* of a component stack. The hit rate of a component stack S, noted $H(S)$, is the percentage of component stacks S in the sample that are associated with the same resource R. Once we have the hit rate of component stacks, we compute for each sample the usage of the associated resource R by a given component stack S, which defined as follows:

$$U_R(S) = H(S).U_R$$

U_R is the overall usage of the resource R given by the operating system at the time of the sample. Having the resource usage per component stacks offers a better gain estimate, defined as follows:

$$G_R^\delta(S) = \frac{U_R^+(S)}{U_R^-(S)}$$

In practice, we experienced too much volatility when considering a single sample. In our empirical tests, we have found that averaging the samples over a fixed window (simple moving average) yields good results. Even using averaged $U_R(S)$, the previous gain is not workload independent enough. We certainly made progress since we focus our estimation on gains per component stacks on a resource R. However, this gain is still sensitive to the actual execution count of each component stack, which may vary from one workload to another.

To illustrate this variability, we assume that we have an adaptation δ that improves by 50% the CPU usage. With a constant workload, applying this adaptation would produce an estimated gain close to 0.5 for all stacks using the adapted component. Other stacks would see a gain close to one. However, a varying workload would affect these gain estimates. Indeed, if we assume that we have many

Metric	Name	Definition	Unit
$H(S)$	Hit ratio	Proportion of tasks with stack S in the profiling samples	None
$U_R(S)$	Resource usage	Proportion of time the resource R is used by a task with stack S	None
$W(S)$	Execution rate	Frequency at which tasks call the stack S	Hertz
$C_R(S)$	Cost	Usage duration of resource R each time the stack S is called by a task	Seconds

Fig. 3. Metrics used to define and measure adaptation gains

queued requests when we regulate (a common case in an overload situation), the idle CPU time that our regulation just freed is likely to be used to process some of the pending requests, right during our calibration. If these processed requests trigger the pattern S, $H(S)$ will increase since we have more executions of the stack S. This may yield a $G_R^\delta(CPU)$ that could be much higher than 0.5, i.e. the adaptation appears less efficient than it actually is. To remove this variability, we need to measure the execution rate of component stacks and introduce the *cost* of a stack S on a resource R, noted $C_R(S)$ and defined as follows:

$$C_R(S) = \frac{U_R(S)}{W(S)}$$

$W(S)$ captures the execution rate (or workload) of the component stack S, computed during each sample. $W(S)$ is obtained by counting the number of times a task enters a component with stack S. Using the cost rather than the resource usage of stacks, we can measure a gain that remains fine grain at the level of a single execution pattern and that becomes fairly independent of workload changes. Thus, the final definition of our gain is as follows:

$$G_R^\delta(S) = \frac{C_R^+(S)}{C_R^-(S)}$$

$C_R^+(S)$ is the cost of the stack S estimated right after we apply the adaptation δ. $C_R^-(S)$ is the cost of the stack S right before we apply the adaptation δ.

Using the measured gains $G_R^\delta(S)$ of adaptations that we applied in the past, we can make a good estimation of the future effects of these adaptations even if the workload changes. Through runtime sampling, we know the complete performance profile of the managed system: all resource usages ($\forall R, U_R$), the active stacks, their hit rate ($H(S)$), and their costs per resource ($C_R(S)$). Figure 3 summarizes these metrics and their meaning.

Using the current performance profile, our control loop can estimate the variation ($\Delta_\delta U_R$) on resource usage of applying or unapplying a given adaptation δ as the sum over all stacks in the current profile of the effects on the usage of the resource R:

$$\Delta_\delta U_R = \sum_{\forall S}(U_R^+(S) - U_R^-(S))$$

Since we have:

$$C_R(S) = \frac{U_R(S)}{W(S)}$$

We then have:

$$\Delta_\delta U_R = \sum_{\forall S}(C_R^+(S).W(S) - C_R^-(S).W(S))$$

We can express in this formula $C_R^+(S)$ with both $C_R^-(S)$ and $G_R^\delta(S)$. However, we have to consider the overload and underload case separately. In the case of an overloaded resource R, we expresss $C_R^+(S)$ as follows:

$$C_R^+(S) = G_R^\delta(S).C_R^-(S)$$

We therefore have:

$$\Delta_\delta U_R = \sum_{\forall S}(G_R^\delta(S) - 1).C_R^-(S).W(S) \tag{1}$$

In the case of underloaded resource R, we estimate $C_R^+(S)$ differently from $C_R^-(S)$ and $G_R^\delta(S)$:

$$C_R^+(S) = \frac{C_R^-(S)}{G_R^\delta(S)}$$

We therefore have:

$$\Delta_\delta U_R = \sum_{\forall S} \frac{(1 - G_R^\delta(S))}{G_\delta(S)}.C_R^-(S).W(S) \tag{2}$$

Using formula (1) or (2), our system can estimate accurately the effects of applying or unapplying the adaptation δ in the current workload. The estimate is accurate because the metrics are obtained at the fine granularity of individual stacks and we only sum the estimated effects for the relevant stacks. The relevant stacks are the very stacks identified in the last performance profile, which characterizes the current workload.

4   Example

Figure 4 represents a simple architecture with a resource R and three components A, B, and C. The table represents a possible performance profile for this system, showing our metrics $H(S)$, $U_R(S)$, $W(S)$ and $C_R(S)$. In this performance profile, the usage of resource R, $U_R(S)$, is 80%. The performance profile also shows the active component stacks associated with R: stack $A - B$ and stack $A - C$.

A performance profile allows to observe *how* a system uses its resources. For instance, the resource usage metric $U_R(S)$ shows that stack $A - B$ causes the same usage of R as stack $A - C$. Furthermore, the execution rate and cost $W(S)$ and $C_R(S)$ show that the cost of $A - B$ is lower than the cost of $A - C$ since both stacks cause equal resource usage, while $A - B$ receives an higher workload.

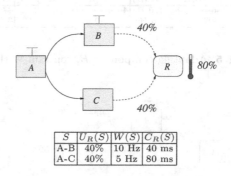

S	$U_R(S)$	$W(S)$	$C_R(S)$
A-B	40%	10 Hz	40 ms
A-C	40%	5 Hz	80 ms

Fig. 4. Example of a performance profile

Based on this performance profile, we now illustrate the results of several possible adaptations. Suppose that if we degrade component B, the degradation produces the effects described in the performance profile shown in figure 5. We see that the service degradation mechanism provided by B lowers the cost of stack $A - B$ from 40ms down to 20ms, but has no effect on the cost of stack $A - C$. This illustrates that adapting a component usually does not impact the stacks that are not involved with the adapted component.

Instead of degrading B, suppose that if we degrade the service level of A, this produces the effects described in figure 6. We see that the service degradation mechanism provided by A lowers the cost of stack $A - C$ from 80ms down to 40ms, but has no effect on the cost of stack $A - B$. This illustrates that adapting a component does not always impact all component stacks equally, i.e. an adaptation can affect only some of the tasks involving the adapted component.

Notice that we have no variation of workload in the above example. However, consider the case shown in figure 7, which depicts the effects of the same adaptation on component A but as the execution rate increases because of request queueing. We see that if our gain estimates were based on resource usage only, the adaptation gains would be incorrectly estimated. By using the cost metric, these estimations are protected from workload fluctuations.

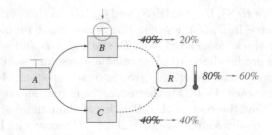

Fig. 5. Adapting component B, constant workload

S	$U_R(S)$	$W(S)$	$C_R(S)$	$G_R^{\delta A}(S)$	$G_R^{\delta B}(S)$
$A-B$	~~40%~~ → 20%	10 Hz	~~40 ms~~ → 20 ms	??	~~??~~ → 0.5
$A-C$	~~40%~~ → 40%	5 Hz	80 ms	??	~~??~~ → 1.0

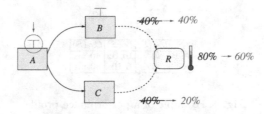

Fig. 6. Adapting component A, constant workload

S	$U_R(S)$	$W(S)$	$C_R(S)$	$G_R^{\delta A}(S)$	$G_R^{\delta B}(S)$
$A-B$	~~40%~~ → 40%	10 Hz	40 ms	~~??~~ → 1.0	0.5
$A-C$	~~40%~~ → 20%	5 Hz	~~80 ms~~ → 40 ms	~~??~~ → 0.5	1.0

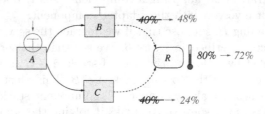

Fig. 7. Adapting component A, changing workload

S	$U_R(S)$	$W(S)$	$C_R(S)$	$G_R^{\delta A}(S)$	$G_R^{\delta B}(S)$
$A-B$	~~40%~~ → 48%	~~10 Hz~~ → 12 Hz	40 ms	1.0	0.5
$A-C$	~~40%~~ → 24%	~~5 Hz~~ → 6 Hz	~~80 ms~~ → 40 ms	0.5	1.0

5   Evaluation

5.1   Implementation Requirements

We have prototyped our autonomic adaptation system in the context of multi-tier Java EE application servers, which are based around a presentation tier (Servlets/JSP), a business logic tier (Enterprise Java Beans – EJBs) and a database tier. To enable adaptation capabilities, we have slightly extended the Java EE model to allow EJB components to provide alternative runtime modes. These alternative modes correspond to degraded or improved service levels, which can be enabled or disabled dynamically, either by the application server (programmatically) or by a human administrator (interactively). This dynamic configuration is currently done through the JMX API (Java Management Extensions).

Otherwise, we rely on the standard Java EE concepts of components and dependencies: capturing Servlets, EJBs and databases as components with explicit dependencies in the architecture. However, recall that our approach also requires that physical resources are made explicit in the model, to be able to link component stacks with resources. We currently do this at a relatively coarse grain through the application server's knowledge of the physical machine(s) used by each tier. For instance, a component stack that corresponds to an EJB component will be associated to the machine (or set of machines) running the EJB tier.

Then, to profile the application, we extend the application server in order to capture component stacks and count their execution rates. To achieve this, we associate each request with a *profiling context* that contains its current stack and we intercept component calls to update the stacks and execution counts. To make sure that the stack has a global scope, this context must be propagated both through local component calls (using a thread-local variable) and through remote component calls (using serialization mechanisms). Most often, such context propagation facilities are already present in Java EE application servers, for security and transaction management.

Once this low-level instrumentation is provided, our autonomic management extension is essentially composed of two services. A *profiling service* periodically samples the component stacks of all ongoing requests to produce the metric $H(S)$, and monitors their execution rates to produce the metric $W(S)$. Then, by monitoring resource usage, it produces the per-stack resource usage and cost metrics, $U_R(S)$ and $C_R(S)$. Secondly, an *adaptation service* implements our autonomic manager, by dynamically reacting to overload and underload conditions, using the profiling service to select optimal adaptations and estimate adaptation gains.

5.2   Software Environment

Our prototype is an extension of the JOnAS application server. Software versions are as follows: Java v1.5, JOnAS v4.8, MySQL v5.0 and Fedora Core 6 Linux. Our test machines have the following specifications: Intel Core Duo 1.66 GHz, 2 GB memory, Gigabit Ethernet network. In our experiments, three machines are dedicated to the application (one machine per tier) and one machine is dedicated to load injection (except when running the two benchmarks together, in which case two machines are used to isolate the load injectors).

Our performance evaluation is based on the RUBiS and TPC-W benchmarks. RUBiS simulates an online auction application [8]. Load injection in RUBiS is configured by a transition matrix, and two specific matrices are generally used to produce either a read-only workload or a read-write workload. Regarding TPC-W, we have used the implementation from Rice University, which is based on Servlets only. Since our prototype is based on adaptable EJB components, we have modified this implementation, wrapping the JDBC calls with session beans. An interesting side-effect of this modification is to produce a finer-grained component-oriented description. Load injection in TPC-W is also configured by transition matrices. The TPC-W specification defines a read-only matrix (browsing mix), a write-20% matrix (shopping mix), and a write-50% matrix (ordering mix).

5.3   Profiling Overhead

Our first experiment shows that the overhead of our profiling mechanism is negligible in the context of these benchmarks. We begin by noting that profiling overhead is mostly dependent on the following two factors:

- Interception of component calls, proportional to throughput.
- Request sampling, proportional to sampling frequency.

To measure the profiling overhead, we first checked that there is no performance difference between the baseline system (running the benchmarks in an unmodified environment) and the instrumented system when profiling is used with a very low sampling frequency (e.g. 0.1 Hz). Then, we measured the benchmark's peak performance for increasing sampling frequencies, since this parameter is crucial in controlling both the profiling precision and its overhead. As figure 8 shows in the case of the RUBiS benchmark, we have not been able to detect a significant overhead, even for high sampling frequencies. In practice, we observed that a frequency as low as 1 Hz provides a reasonable precision for the purpose of adaptation (although the following experiments were done with a 10 Hz frequency to improve precision). As a side knowledge, this figure also shows that the CPU of the database tier is the bottleneck in RUBiS. TPC-W yields the same results as RUBiS (i.e. no overhead and the database is the benchmark's bottleneck).

5.4   RUBiS Benchmark

In all experiments, calibration delay is set to 10 seconds and sampling frequency is set to 10 Hz. We first present the results of profiling RUBiS for a typical stationary workload: 256 emulated clients and a read-write mix, with 900 seconds of runtime. All metrics (hit rates, resource usage, workload and cost) were averaged over the entire experiment. We only show the performance profiles for the

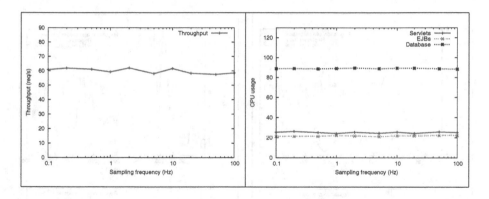

Fig. 8. RUBiS Performance vs. Sampling Frequency

database CPU, since we already established that this resource is the bottleneck and the only one triggering adaptations. The database is about 180 MB for a little over forty thousands items and one hundred thousands customer records. The four most database intensive stacks (i.e. those with the highest hit rate) were:

Stack	H(S)	W(S)	C(S)
SearchByCategory.Category	64.1 %	6.60 Hz	55.8 ms
SearchByRegion.Category	30.4 %	2.22 Hz	78.4 ms
AboutMe.User	0.95 %	11.4 Hz	0.49 ms
SearchByRegion.Item	0.83 %	16.7 Hz	0.29 ms

These results show that only two component stacks are responsible for most of the CPU usage on the database tier. These stacks—SearchByCategory.Category and SearchByRegion.Category, are associated to the search for auctioned items. Consequently, we have implemented two adaptations, both based on deactivating sorting—a costly operation on the database side, especially with large tables. One adaptation is on the SearchByCategory component and the other is on the SearchByRegion component. Our results show that the adaptation on SearchByCategory.Category is significantly more effective than the one on SearchByRegion.Category. This is because the former generally involves sorting more items than the later; the straightforward consequence of a less selective filter.

To evaluate our dynamic adaptation, we configure a workload that far exceeds the normal benchmark capacity (about 650 clients): 1024 emulated clients and a read-write mix, with 60 seconds of ramping up and 300 seconds of runtime. We are targeting an agressive goal in terms of CPU usage: overload threshold of 90% and underload threshold of 80%. The rationale is to show that we can target a high and narrow window of CPU usage, one that is sufficiently high for reaching and staying at peak performance but consistently avoiding the trap of thrashing. Only an automatic approach, with an accurate prediction, can attempt this; most systems have to be more conservative regarding their CPU usage target.

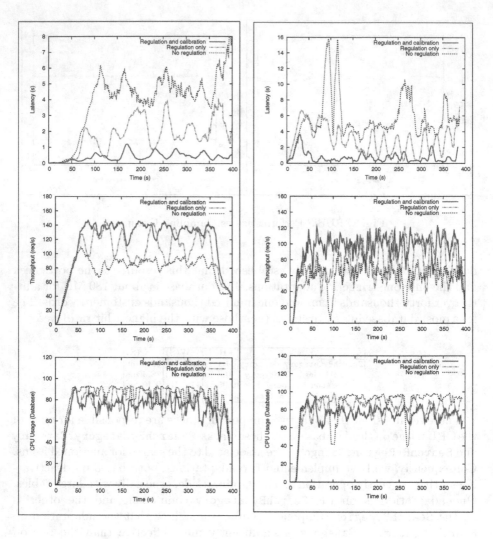

Fig. 9. RUBiS Performance   **Fig. 10.** TPC-W Performance

Figure 9 shows our results for RUBiS. We can see that our system maintains the database CPU around 80%, dividing latency by ten and improving throughput in the order of 75%. We can see that without regulations, the database CPU is consistently thrashing at about 95%, which explains the large latency and the poor throughput. With regulations but without calibration, we observe harmful oscillations since our system cancels adaptations as soon as the resource usage crosses the underload threshold. These oscillations are especially visible on latency and throughput where the performance with regulation but without calibration oscillates between the performance without regulation at all and the performance with regulation and calibration.

5.5   TPC-W Benchmark

We present the results of profiling TPC-W for stationary workload of 256 clients
and a shopping mix. Like RUBiS, our experiments show that the bottleneck
is the database CPU. The database is about 1.1GB, with an extra 2.6GB for
images (stored as static files). The database contains about 28.8 millions clients
and 10,000 books. The four most sampled stacks were:

Stack	H(S)	W(S)	C(S)
execute_search.author_search	39.0 %	1.98 Hz	119.2 ms
best_sellers	28 % %	1.73 Hz	97.5 ms
execute_search.title_search	18.4 %	2.03 Hz	54.9 ms
buy_confirm	2.5 %	2.25 Hz	6.75 ms

These results show that three component stacks are almost equally responsible
for most of the CPU usage on the database tier. These stacks—execute_search.
author_search, best_sellers, and execute_search.title_search—are associated to the search for books, by authors, by title, or by best sellers. Consequently, we have implemented three adaptations, one for each stack. For the
stacks execute_search.author_search and execute_search. title_search,
the adaptation limits searching by looking for an exact match on titles or authors,
avoiding costly substring matching. For the stack best_sellers, the adaptation
looks for recent sellers as opposed to best sellers.

Like for our RUBiS experiments, we evaluate dynamic adaptation with a
workload that exceeds the normal benchmark capacity (about 500 clients): 768
emulated clients and a shopping mix, with 60 seconds of ramping up and 300
seconds of runtime. We fixed the same agressive goal in terms of CPU usage,
for the same reasons. Figure 10 shows our results for TPC-W. We can see that
without regulations, the database tier is consistently thrashing with a CPU at
about 95%, which explains the large latency and the poor throughput. We can
also notice two sharp drop in CPU usage at time 100 and 260 seconds, that are
totally avoided with our adaptive approach.

The CPU usage patterns and improvements are entirely consistent across the
two benchmarks. With regulations but without calibration, our system is unable
to predict the effects of applying or unapplying adaptations, which produces
harmful oscillations. These oscillations are again quite visible on latency and
throughput. With calibration, our system maintains the database CPU around
80%, dividing latency by ten and improving throughput in the order of 60%.
Moreover, our system maintains a much more stable level of quality of service.
Notice how much smoother the regulated latency and throughput are compared
to the unregulated ones at 100, 250, and 350 seconds in the experiments. This
is also visible in the much more stable CPU usage when regulated.

5.6   Combining TPC-W and RUBiS

To evaluate our system under non-stationary workloads, we combined both
benchmarks as follows. We started TPC-W first and we started RUBiS about

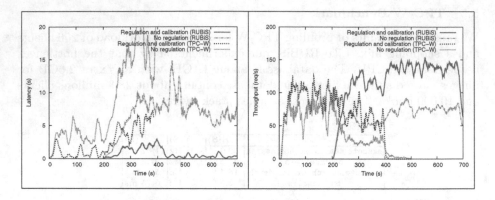

Fig. 11. TPC-W and RUBiS Combined

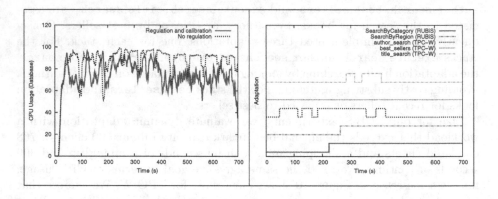

Fig. 12. CPU Usage and Adaptation Details

200 seconds later. The two benchmarks therefore overlaps for about 200 seconds. During the final period of 300 seconds, we only have RUBiS. The latency and throughput results are depicted in Figure 11.

As expected, the first period shows very similar results to TPC-W alone. During the overlap period, the system is heavily overloaded. Without regulation, latency increases sharply and throughput drops significantly, for both benchmarks. With regulation, our system preserves as much overall quality of service as possible—it divides latency by 4 and almost doubles throughput. Furthermore, it is important to notice that our autonomic management reacts quickly to workload changes. Indeed, there is no visible period of instability as the workload changes, that is, when RUBiS starts at 200 seconds in the experiement and when TPC-W stops at 400 seconds in the experiment.

Figure 12 shows when adaptions are applied and unapplied during this experiment, combined with the CPU usage of the database tier. Up to about 300 seconds in the experiment, all available adaptations but one are dynamically and incrementally applied. Notice some oscillations happen. These oscillations are however few and sparse since we only have four of them in total, over 700 seconds, even though we consider applying or unapplying adaptations every 5 seconds. This means our prediction works, avoiding the vast majority of oscillations. This is confirmed by the fact that, although the CPU usage is often just below our 80% threshold, our autonomic manager maintains the adaptations, accurately predicting the CPU overload situation that would result if any adaptation would be unapplied.

Our approach mostly avoids oscillations, but large variations in resource usage may temporarily trick our prediction. Notice that no oscillation happens during the last period where RUBiS runs alone; this is because RUBiS has a more stable workload than TPC-W. Indeed, we noticed throughout our experiments a relatively higher instability in CPU usage for TPC-W, which we explain by the fact that TPC-W queries are more complex on a larger working set. While temporary low CPU usage may trigger a mistake, such mistakes are corrected quite rapidly. Furthermore, we argue that such mistakes induce an acceptable volatility in latency and throughput, most of the time within 20%. In particular, notice that this volatility never resulted in our experiments in the regulated quality of service dropping below the unregulated quality of service.

6   Related Work

6.1   Service-Level Adaptation

Service-level adaptation provides an efficient mechanism to regulate resource consumption and avoid overload. However, it has been reserved in the past to specific types of systems, where adaptations are well-known and can be characterized in advance. For example, service adaptation has been used in the context of multimedia streaming servers, where increasing compression will save network bandwidth at the expense of content quality [2]. Another example resides in the context of security systems, where simpler encryption algorithms might require less processing while being less secure [9]. Similar examples can be found in the context of static web servers or distributed monitoring [10][11][12].

Our work contributes to service adaptation in the context of general distributed systems, where adaptations often cannot be characterized in advance. The key point of our approach is the dynamic construction of a performance profile, based on a component-based representation of the system.

6.2   Performance Profiles

Performance profiles are used to locate and analyze the bottlenecks of a computing system [13]. A typical method to build performance profiles consists in tracking execution to find the code involved in each task, combined with resource usage measurements to find the most resource-intensive tasks.

Complex distributed systems make it difficult to use OS-level techniques because not only tasks often involve non-obvious sub-tasks but resources are also accessed through intermediate abstraction layers. One solution is to introduce new OS abstractions, but this is a complex and non-generic solution [14][15].

At the other end of the spectrum, another approach is to use statistical regression techniques to measure correlation between workload and resource usage [16][17]. This requires no instrumentation but only works if workload is highly variable (non-stationary). Furthermore, the system must be observed during a significant period to compute the regression with reasonable accuracy, which makes it inapplicable in the context of our work since our adaptation model requires the ability to observe the immediate effects of applied adaptations.

Our approach is an intermediate solution, based on the work of Chanda *et al.* [18][19]. First, a context is attached to each task and is propagated through the distributed system. This context contains the current path of the task through the distributed system. Then, statistical sampling is used to indirectly measure resource usage, and requires no intrusive OS-level instrumentation [20].

However, the contributions of Chanda *et al.* stop at computing performance profiles—using profiles for optimization purposes is left to a developer or an administrator. Our approach goes farther by considering an autonomic approach that leverages the knowledge of the component architecture of the observed system. Using component stacks, we can estimate gains and make useful predictions of component-level adaptations that can be used by a closed-loop control [21][22].

7   Conclusion

In this article, we have presented a novel approach to automatically regulate resource consumption in Internet application servers, such as Java EE servers, which often use a component-based programming model. Our proposition is to integrate the concept of service level adaptation to allow for automatically lowering the service level of individual components in order to preserve the overall performance in high-workload situations. By focusing adaptations on costly execution patterns, our approach optimizes service level while ensuring that resource usage does not exceed a predefined threshold.

The heart of our approach is a performance profile, which is used to estimate the effects of component adaptations. The challenge was to characterize these effects in a workload independent way so that the observation of past adaptation attempts could be reused to predict the effects of future adaptations, even if the workload is completely different. Combining runtime sampling and the knowledge of the component architecture, we designed the concept of adaptation gains at the granularity of component stacks. Our experiments show that our gains are workload independent enough so that our predictions are accurate and support our decision making to apply or unapply adaptations. The potentially harmful phenomenon of oscillations is kept to a minimum and results in no substantial instability in latency or throughput. Also, even when oscillations occur, the performance of the regulated system is always much higher than that of the baseline system.

References

1. Taton, C., Palma, N.D., Hagimont, D., Bouchenak, S., Philippe, J.: Self-Optimization of Clustered Message-Oriented Middleware. In: The 9th International Symposium on Distributed Objects, Middleware, and Applications (DOA), Vilamoura, Portugal (November 2007)
2. Layaida, O., Hagimont, D.: Designing Self-adaptive Multimedia Applications Through Hierarchical Reconfiguration. In: Kutvonen, L., Alonistioti, N. (eds.) DAIS 2005. LNCS, vol. 3543, pp. 95–107. Springer, Heidelberg (2005)
3. Diao, Y., Neha, G., Hellerstein, J.L., Parekh, S., Tilbury, D.M.: Using MIMO Feedback Control to Enforce Policies for Interrelated Metrics with Application to the Apache Web Server. In: Proceedings of the IEEE/IFIP Network Operations and Management Symposium (NOMS), Florence, Italy (April 2002)
4. Abdelzaher, T.F., Shin, K.G., Bhatti, N.: Performance Guarantees for Web Server End-Systems: A Control-Theoretical Approach. IEEE Transactions on Parallel and Distributed Systems (TPDS) 13(1), 80–96 (2002)
5. Kihl, M., Robertsson, A., Andersson, M., Wittenmark, B.: Control-Theoretic Analysis of Admission Control Mechanisms for Web Server Systems. World Wide Web Journal 11(1), 93–116 (2008)
6. Graham, S.L., Kessler, P.B., Mckusick, M.K.: gprof: a Call Graph Execution Profiler. ACM SIGPLAN Notices 17(6), 120–126 (1982)
7. Liang, S., Viswanathan, D.: Comprenhensive Profiling Support in the Java Virtual Machine. In: Proceedings of the USENIX Conference on Object-Oriented Technologies and Systems (COOTS), San Diego, California, USA (May 1999)
8. Cecchet, E., Marguerite, J., Zwaenepoel, W.: Performance and Scalability of EJB Applications. In: Proceedings of the Symposium on Object-Oriented Programming, Systems, Languages and Applications (OOPSLA), Seattle, Washington, USA (November 2002)
9. Wright, C.P., Martino, M.C., Zadok, E.: NCryptfs: A Secure and Convenient Cryptographic File System. In: Proceedings of the USENIX Annual Technical Conference, San Antonio, Texas, USA (June 2003)
10. Abdelzaher, T.F., Bhatti, N.: Web Content Adaptation to Improve Server Overload Behavior. In: Proceedings of the World Wide Web Conference (WWW), Toronto, Canada (May 1999)
11. Elnozahy, M., Kistler, M., Rajamony, R.: Energy Conservation Policies for Web Servers. In: Proceedings of the USENIX Symposium on Internet Technologies and Systems (USITS), Seattle, Washington, USA (March 2003)
12. Sadler, C.M., Martonosi, M.: Data Compression Algorithms for Energy-Constrained Devices in Delay Tolerant Networks. In: Proceedings of the ACM Conference on Embedded Networked Sensor Systems (SenSys), Boulder, Colorado, USA (October 2006)
13. Menascé, D.A., Dowdy, L.W., Almeida, V.A.: Performance by Design: Computer Capacity Planning By Example. Prentice Hall, Englewood Cliffs (2004)
14. Banga, G., Druschel, P., Mogul, J.C.: Resource Containers: A New Facility for Resource Management in Server Systems. In: Proceedings of the Symposium on Operating Systems Design and Implementation (OSDI), New Orleans, Louisiana, USA (February 1999)
15. Blanquer, J., Bruno, J., Gabber, E., McShea, M., Özden, B., Silberschatz, A., Singh, A.: Resource Management for QoS in Eclipse/BSD. In: Proceedings of the FreeBSD Conference, Berkeley, California, USA (October 1999)

16. Stewart, C., Kelly, T., Zhang, A.: Exploiting Nonstationarity for Performance Prediction. In: Proceedings of the EuroSys Conference, Lisbon, Portugal (March 2007)
17. Zhang, Q., Cherkasova, L., Mathews, G., Greene, W., Smirni, E.: R-Capriccio: A Capacity Planning and Anomaly Detection Tool for Enterprise Services with Live Workloads. In: Cerqueira, R., Campbell, R.H. (eds.) Middleware 2007. LNCS, vol. 4834, pp. 244–265. Springer, Heidelberg (2007)
18. Chanda, A., Elmeleegy, K., Cox, A.L., Zwaenepoel, W.: Causeway: Operating System Support for Controlling and Analyzing the Execution of Multi-tier Applications. In: Alonso, G. (ed.) Middleware 2005. LNCS, vol. 3790, pp. 42–59. Springer, Heidelberg (2005)
19. Chanda, A., Cox, A.L., Zwaenepoel, W.: Whodunit: Transactional Profiling for Multi-Tier Applications. In: Proceedings of the EuroSys Conference, Lisbon, Portugal (March 2007)
20. Froyd, N., Mellor-Crummey, J., Fowler, R.: Low-Overhead Call Path Profiling of Unmodified, Optimized Code. In: Proceedings of the ACM International Conference on Supercomputing, Cambridge, Massachusetts, USA (June 2005)
21. Kephart, J.O., Chess, D.M.: The Vision of Autonomic Computing. IEEE Transactions on Computers 36(1), 41–50 (2003)
22. Sicard, S., Boyer, F., de Palma, N.: Using Components for Architecture-Based Management: The Self-Repair Case. In: Proceedings of the International Conference on Software Engineering (ICSE), Leipzig, Germany (May 2008)

A Cost-Sensitive Adaptation Engine for Server Consolidation of Multitier Applications

Gueyoung Jung[1], Kaustubh R. Joshi[2], Matti A. Hiltunen[2],
Richard D. Schlichting[2], and Calton Pu[1]

[1] College of Computing, Georgia Institute of Technology, Atlanta, GA, USA
{gueyoung.jung,calton}@cc.gatech.edu
[2] AT&T Labs Research, 180 Park Ave, Florham Park, NJ, USA
{kaustubh,hiltunen,rick}@research.att.com

Abstract. Virtualization-based server consolidation requires runtime resource reconfiguration to ensure adequate application isolation and performance, especially for multitier services that have dynamic, rapidly changing workloads and responsiveness requirements. While virtualization makes reconfiguration easy, indiscriminate use of adaptations such as VM replication, VM migration, and capacity controls has performance implications. This paper demonstrates that ignoring these costs can have significant impacts on the ability to satisfy response-time-based SLAs, and proposes a solution in the form of a cost-sensitive adaptation engine that weighs the potential benefits of runtime reconfiguration decisions against their costs. Extensive experimental results based on live workload traces show that the technique is able to maximize SLA fulfillment under typical time-of-day workload variations as well as flash crowds, and that it exhibits significantly improved transient behavior compared to approaches that do not account for adaptation costs.

1 Introduction

Cloud computing services built around virtualization-based server consolidation are revolutionizing the computing landscape by making unprecedented levels of compute power cheaply available to millions of users. Today, platforms such as Amazon's EC2, AT&T's Synaptic Hosting, Google's App Engine, and Salesforce's Force.com host a variety of distributed applications including multitier enterprise services such as email, CRM, and e-commerce portals. The sharing of resources by such applications owned by multiple customers raises new resource allocation challenges such as ensuring responsiveness under dynamically changing workloads and isolating them from demand fluctuations in co-located virtual machines (VMs). However, despite the well-documented importance of responsiveness to end users [1, 2, 3], cloud services today typically only address availability guarantees and not response-time-based service level agreements (SLAs).

Virtualization techniques such as CPU capacity enforcement and VM migration have been proposed as ways to maintain performance [4, 5, 6, 7, 8, 9]. However, there is little work that considers the impact of the reconfiguration actions themselves on application performance except in very limited contexts. For

J.M. Bacon and B.F. Cooper (Eds.): Middleware 2009, LNCS 5896, pp. 163–183, 2009.
© IFIP International Federation for Information Processing 2009

Table 1. End-to-End Response Time (ms) during VM Migration

Before	Apache	% Chg.	Tomcat	% Chg.	MySQL	% Chg.
102.92	141.62	37.60	315.83	206.89	320.93	211.83

example, while [10] shows that live migration of VMs can be performed with a few milliseconds of downtime and minimal performance degradation, the results are limited only to web servers. This can be very different for other commonly used types of servers. For example, Table 1 shows the impact of VM migration of servers from different J2EE-based tiers on the end-to-end mean response time of RUBiS [11], a widely used multitier benchmark, computed over 3 minute intervals. Futhermore, because of interference due to shared I/O, such migrations also impact the performance of other applications whose VMs run on the same physical hosts (see Section 4). Cheaper actions such as CPU tuning can sometimes be used to achieve the same goals, however. These results indicate that the careful use of adaptations is critical to ensure that the benefits of runtime reconfiguration are not overshadowed by their costs.

This paper tackles the problem of optimizing resource allocation in consolidated server environments by proposing a runtime *adaptation engine* that automatically reconfigures multitier applications running in virtualized data centers while considering adaptation costs and satisfying response-time-based SLAs even under rapidly changing workloads. The problem is challenging—the costs and benefits of reconfigurations are influenced not just by the software component targeted, but also by the reconfiguration action chosen, the application structure, its workload, the original configuration, and the application's SLAs.

To address these challenges, we present a methodology that uses automatic offline experimentation to construct cost models that quantify the degradation in application performance due to reconfiguration actions. Using previously developed queuing models for predicting the benefits of a new configuration [8], we show how the cost models allow an analysis of cost-benefit tradeoffs to direct the online selection of reconfiguration actions. Then, we develop a best-first graph search algorithm based on the models to choose optimal sequences of actions. Finally, experimental results using RUBiS under different workloads derived from real Internet traces show that our cost-sensitive approach can significantly reduce SLA violations, and provide higher utility as compared to both static and dynamic-reconfiguration-based approaches that ignore adaptation costs.

2   Architecture

We consider a consolidated server environment with a pool of physical resources H and a set of multitier applications S. We focus only on a single resource pool in this paper—a cluster of identical physical servers (hosts). Each application s is comprised of a set N_s of component tiers (e.g., web server, database), and for each tier n, a replication level is provided by reps(n). Each replica n_k executes

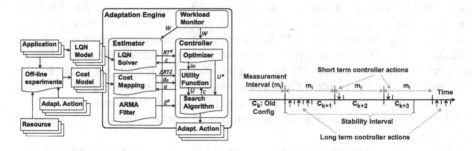

Fig. 1. Architecture   **Fig. 2.** Control Timeline

in its own Xen VM [12] on some physical host, and is allocated a fractional share of the host's CPU, denoted by $cap(n_k)$, that is enforced by Xen's credit-based scheduler. Therefore, system *configurations* consist of: (a) the replication degree of each tier of each application, (b) the name of the physical machine that hosts each replica VM, and c) the fractional CPU capacity allocated to the replica.

Each application is also associated with a set of transaction types T_s (e.g., home, login, search, browse, buy) through which users access its services. Each transaction type t generates a unique call graph through some subset of the application tiers. For example, a search request from the user may involve the web-server making a call to the application server, which makes two calls to the database. The workload for each application is then defined as a vector of the mean request rate for each transaction type, and the workload for the entire system as the vector of workloads for each application.

We associate each application with an SLA that specifies the expected service level in the form of a target mean response time for each transaction, and the rewards and penalties for meeting or missing the target response time, as computed over a pre-specified *measurement interval*. The rewards and penalties can vary according to the application workload, thus giving rise to a step-wise *utility function* that maps mean response time and workload to a utility value that reflects the revenue gained (or lost) during the measurement interval. Using other SLA metrics does not fundamentally alter our approach.

To decide when and how to reconfigure, the adaptation engine estimates the cost and the potential benefit of each adaptation in terms of changes in the utility. Since the utility is a function of the mean end-to-end response time, the *cost of adaptation* for a given adaptation depends on its duration and impact on the applications' response times. On the other hand, the *benefit of adaptation* depends on the change in applications' response times and how long the system remains in the new configuration.

The adaptation engine manages the shared host pool by performing various *adaptation actions* such as CPU capacity tuning, VM live-migration, and component replication. As shown in Figure 1, it consists of a workload monitor, estimator, and controller. The workload monitor tracks the workload at the ingress of the system as a set of transaction request rates for each hosted application.

The estimator consists of an LQN solver, a cost mapping, and an ARMA filter. The LQN solver uses layered queuing models [13] described in Section 3 to estimate the mean response time RT^s for each application given a workload W and configuration c. The cost mapping uses cost models to estimate the duration d_a and performance impact ΔRT_a^s of a given adaptation a. Both types of models are constructed using the results of an off-line model parametrization phase. Finally, the ARMA (auto-regressive moving average) filter provides a prediction of the *stability interval* E^p that denotes the duration for which the current workload will remain stable.

The controller invokes the estimator to obtain response time and cost estimates for an action's execution, which it uses to iteratively explore candidate actions. Using a search algorithm and the utility function, the controller chooses the set of actions that maximizes the overall utility. The search is guided by the upper bound on the utility U^* calculated using a previously-developed offline optimization algorithm [8] that provides the configuration that optimizes utility for a given workload without considering reconfiguration cost.

To balance the cost accrued over the duration of an adaptation with the benefits accrued between its completion and the next adaptation, the algorithm uses a parameter, called the *control window*, that indicates the time to the next adaptation. Adaptations occur only because of controller invocations. If the controller is invoked periodically, the control window is set to the fixed inter-invocation interval. If the controller is invoked on demand when the workload changes, the control window is set to the stability interval prediction E^p provided by the ARMA filter. An adaptation is only chosen if it increases utility by the end of the control window. Therefore, a short control window produces a conservative controller that will typically only choose cheap adaptation actions, while a longer control window allows the controller to choose more expensive adaptations.

Multiple controllers, each with different control windows can be used in an hierarchical fashion to produce a multi-level control scheme operating at different time-scales, and with different levels of aggressiveness. Our implementation of the adaptation engine uses a two-level hierarchical controller to achieve a balance between rapid but cheap response to short term fluctuations and more disruptive responses to long term workload changes (Figure 2). The *short term* controller is invoked periodically once every measurement interval, while the *long term* controller is executed on-demand when the workload has changed more than a specified threshold since the last long term controller invocation. To avoid multiple controller executions in parallel, the timer tracking the short term controller's execution is suspended while the long term controller is active.

3   Technical Approach

In this paper, we consider five adaptation actions: increase/decrease a VM's CPU allocation by a fixed amount, addition/removal of the VM containing an application tier's replica, and finally, migration of a replica from one host to another. Replica addition is implemented cheaply by migrating a dormant VM from a pool of VMs to the target host and activating it by allocating CPU capacity. A replica is removed simply by migrating it back to the standby pool. Some actions also require additional coordination in other tiers, e.g., changing the replication degree of the application server tier requires updating the front-end web servers with new membership.

Models. Our approach for cost estimation is based on approximate models that are constructed using off-line experimental measurements at different representative workloads using the following process. For each application s, workload w, and adaptation action a, we set up the target application along with a background application s' such that all replicas from both applications are allocated equal CPU capacity (40% in our experiments). Then, we run multiple experiments, each with a random placement of all the replica VMs from both applications across all the physical hosts. During each experiment, we subject both the target and background application to the workload w, and after a warm-up period of 1 minute, measure the end-to-end response times of the two applications $RT^s(w)$ and $RT^{s'}(w)$. Then, we execute the adaptation action a, and measure the duration of the action as $d_a^s(w)$, and the end-to-end response times of each application during adaptation as $RT_a^s(w)$ and $RT_a^{s'}(w)$. If none of application s's VMs are colocated with the VM impacted by a, no background application measurements are made. We use these measurements to calculate a delta response time for the target and the background applications, or $\Delta RT_a^s = RT_a^s - RT^s$ and $\Delta RT_a^{s'} = RT_a^{s'} - RT^{s'}$. These deltas along with the action duration are averaged across all the random configurations, and their values are encoded in a cost table indexed by the workload.

When the optimizer requires an estimate of adaptation costs at runtime, it measures the current workload w and looks up the cost table entry with the closest workload w'. To determine the impact of the adaptation a on its target application s, it measures the current response time of the application as RT^s and estimates the new response time during adaptation as $RT_a^s(w) = RT^s(w) + \Delta RT_a^s(w')$. For each application s' whose components are hosted on the same machine targeted by a, it calculates the new response times as $RT_a^{s'}(w) = RT^{s'}(w) + \Delta RT_a^{s'}(w')$. Although this technique does not capture fine-grained variations due to the difference between configurations or workloads, we show in Section 4 that the estimates are sufficiently accurate for making good decisions.

To estimate the potential benefits of a reconfiguration action, we use previously developed layered queuing network models. Given a system configuration and workload, the models compute the expected mean response time of each application. A high-level diagram of the model for a single three-tier application is shown in Figure 3. Software components (e.g., tier replicas) are modeled as FCFS queues, while hardware resources (e.g., hosts, CPU, and disk) are modeled as processor sharing (PS) queues. Interactions between tiers that result from an incoming transaction are modeled as synchronous calls in the queuing network. We account for the I/O overhead imposed by the Xen Dom-0 hypervisor, known to have significant impact (e.g., [14]), via a per-network-interaction VM monitor

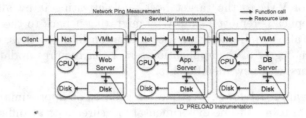

Fig. 3. Layered queueing network model

(VMM) delay. Although this effect impacts all VMs on the host, we model it on a per-VM basis to reduce the time to solve the model. Section 4 shows that the models provide sufficient accuracy despite this approximation.

The parameters for the models, i.e., the call graph for each transaction and the per-transaction service times at the CPU, network, disk, I/O queues at the various tiers are measured in an off-line measurement phase. In this phase, each application is deployed both with and without virtualization and instrumented at different points using system call interception and JVM instrumentation. It is then subjected to test transactions, one request at a time, and measurements of the counts and delays between incoming and outgoing messages are used to parameterize the LQNS model. The models are then solved at runtime using the LQNS analytical solver [13]. More details can be found in [8].

Estimating Stability Intervals. The *stability interval* for an application s at time t is the period of time for which its workload remains within a band of $\pm b$ of the measured workload W_t^s at time t. This band $[W_t^s - b, W_t^s + b]$ is called the *workload band* B_t^s. When an application's workload exceeds the workload band, the controller must evaluate the system for potential SLA misses. When the workload falls below the band, the controller must check if other applications might benefit from the resources that could be freed up. Both cases can entail reconfiguration. Thus the duration of stability intervals impacts the choice of actions. If the workload keeps on changing rapidly, reconfiguration actions such as live-migration and replication become too expensive because their costs may not be recouped before the workload changes again. However, if the stability interval is long, even expensive adaptations are worth considering. Therefore, good predictions of the stability interval can benefit adaptation action selection.

At each measurement interval i, the estimator checks if the current workload W_i^s is within the current workload band B_j^s. If one or more application workloads are not within their band, the estimator calculates a new stability interval prediction E_{j+1}^p and updates the bands based on the current application workloads. To predict the stability intervals, we employ an autoregressive moving averages (ARMA) model of the type commonly used for time-series analysis, e.g. [15]. The filter uses a combination of the last measured stability interval E_j^m and an average of the k previously measured stability intervals to predict the next stability interval using the Equation: $E_{j+1}^p = (1-\beta) \cdot E_j^m + \beta \cdot 1/k \sum_{i=1}^k E_{j-i}^m$. Here, the factor β determines how much the estimator weighs the current measurement against past historical measurements. It is calculated using an adaptive filter as described in [16] to quickly respond to large changes in the stability interval while remaining robust against small variations. To calculate β, the estimator first calculates the error ε_j between the current stability interval measurement E_j^m and the prediction E_j^p using both current measurements and the previous k error values as $\varepsilon_j = (1 - \gamma) \cdot |E_j^p - E_j^m| + \gamma \cdot 1/k \sum_{i=1}^{k} \varepsilon_{j-i}$. Then, $\beta = 1 - \varepsilon_j / \max_{i=0...k} \varepsilon_{j-i}$. This technique dynamically gives more weight to the current stability interval measurement by generating a low value for β when the estimated stability interval at time i is close to the measured value. Otherwise, it increases β to emphasize past history. We use a history window k of 3, and set the parameter γ to 0.5 to give equal weight to the current and historical error estimates.

Balancing Cost and Benefit. To convert the predicted response times to utility values, the controller first calculates the instantaneous rate at which an application accrues utility either during normal operation in a configuration c, or during the execution of an adaptation action a. To do so, it uses the SLA to get the per-application workload dependent target response times TRT^s, the per-application workload dependent reward of $R^s(W_i^s)$ that is awarded every measurement interval of length M if the target response time is met, and a penalty of $P^s(W_i^s)$ imposed if the target is not met. Therefore, if the predicted response time is RT^s, the rate u^s at which utility is accrued by application s is given by:

$$u^s = \mathbf{1}[RT^s \leq TRT^s] \cdot R^s(W_i^s)/M - \mathbf{1}[RT^s > TRT^s] \cdot P^s(W_i^s)/M \quad (1)$$

In this equation, $\mathbf{1}[\ldots]$ is an *indicator function* that returns 1 if its argument is true, and 0 otherwise. During normal operation in a configuration c, the predicted response time RT_c^s is provided by the queuing models. The cost due to adaptation action a is estimated as $RT_{c,a}^s = RT_c^s + \Delta RT_a^s$. Substituting these values instead of RT^s in Equation 1 yields u_c^s and $u_{c,a}^s$, the utility accrual rate during normal execution in configuration c, and during execution of adaptation action a starting from a configuration c, respectively.

The controller then uses the control window as an estimate of how long the system will remain in a new configuration after adaptation. The control window is statically set to the controller inter-invocation time for periodic controllers and dynamically set to the stability interval for on-demand controllers. Consider the controller at the end of measurement interval i with current configuration c_i, control window CW, and evaluating an adaptation sequence A_i represented as a series of actions $a^1, a^2, \ldots a^n$. Let $d^1, d^2, \ldots, d^n$ be the length of each adaptation action, and let $c^1, c^2, \ldots, c^n$ be intermediate configurations generated by applying the actions starting from the initial configuration c_i. Let c^0 be the initial configuration c_i and c^n be the final configuration c_{i+1}. Then, the utility is:

$$U = \sum_{a^k \in A_i} (d_{a^k} \sum_{s \in S} u_{c^{k-1}, a^k}^s) + (CW - \sum_{a^k \in A_i} d_{a^k}) \cdot \sum_{s \in S} u_{c_{i+1}}^s = U_a + U_c \quad (2)$$

The first term U_a of the equation sums up the utility accrued by each application during each action in the adaptation sequence over a period equal to its action

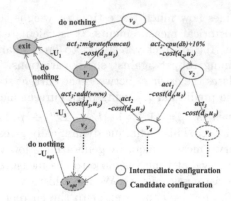

Fig. 4. Adaptation action search graph

length, and second term U_c sums the utility of the resulting configuration c_{i+1} over the remainder of the control interval.

Search Algorithm. The goal of the search algorithm is to find a configuration (and the corresponding adaptation actions) for which the utility U is maximized. Configurations must satisfy the following allocation constraints: (a) for each application, only one replica from each tier can be assigned to a host, (b) the sum of CPU allocations on a host can be at most 1, and (c) the number of VMs per host is restricted to fit the available memory on the host.

Starting from a current configuration, a new configuration at each step is built by applying exactly one adaptation action as shown in Figure 4. The vertices represent system configurations, and the edges represent adaptation actions. We frame the problem as a shortest path problem that minimizes the negative of the utility, i.e., maximizes the actual utility. Therefore, each edge has a weight corresponding to the negative of the utility obtained while the action is being executed (i.e., $-d_a \sum_{s \in S} u^s_{c,a}$). If multiple action sequences lead to the same configuration, the vertices are combined. Configurations can be either intermediate or candidate configurations as represented by the white and gray circles in the figure, respectively. A candidate configuration satisfies the allocation constraints, while an intermediate configuration does not, e.g., it may assign more CPU capacity to VMs than is available, requiring a subsequent "Reduce CPU" action to yield a candidate configuration. Neither type of configuration is allowed to have individual replicas with CPU capacity greater than one.

Only candidate configurations have a `do nothing` action that leads the goal state, labeled as `exit` in the figure. The weight for the `do nothing` action in a configuration c is the negative of the revenue obtained by staying in c until the end of the prediction interval (i.e. $-U_c$), assuming that the best known path is used to get to c. Then, the shortest path starting from the initial configuration to the `exit` state computes the best U, and represents the adaptation actions needed to achieve optimal revenue. Intermediate configurations do not have `do nothing` actions, and thus their utility is not defined.

Input: c_i: current config., W_i: predicted workload, CW: control window length
Output: $\mathcal{A}_{opt}^i$ - the optimized adaptation action sequence
$(c^*, u^*) \leftarrow \texttt{UtilityUpperBound}\ (W_i)$
if $c^* = c_i$ **then return** $[a_{null}]$ (do nothing)
$v^0.(a_{opt}, c, U_a, U, D) \leftarrow (\phi, c_i, 0, u^*, 0); \mathcal{V} \leftarrow \{v^0\}$
while *forever* **do**
    $v \leftarrow \text{argmax}_{v' \in \mathcal{V}} v'.U$
    if $v.a_{opt}[\text{last}] = a_{null}$ **then return** $v.a_{opt}$
    foreach $a \in \mathcal{A} \cup a_{null}$ **do**
        $v^n \leftarrow v, v^n.a_{opt} \leftarrow v.a_{opt} + a$
        if $a = a_{null}$ **then**
        | $u_c \leftarrow \texttt{LQNS}\ (W_i, v^n.c); v^n.U \leftarrow (CW - v^n.D) \cdot u_c + v^n.U_a$
        else
        | $v^n.c \leftarrow \texttt{NewConfig}\ (v^n.c, a); (d_a, u_a) \leftarrow \texttt{Cost}\ (v^n.c, a, W_i)$
        | $v^n.U_a \leftarrow v^n.U_a + d_a \cdot u_a; v^n.D \leftarrow v^n.D + d_a;$
        | $v^n.U \leftarrow (CW - v^n.D) \cdot u^* + v^n.U_a$
    if $\exists v' \in \mathcal{V}$ s.t. $v'.c = v^n.c$ **then**
    | **if** $v'.U > v^n.U$ **then** $v' \leftarrow v^n$
    else
    | $\mathcal{V} \leftarrow \mathcal{V} \cup v^n$

Algorithm 1. Optimal adaptation search

Although the problem reduces to a weighted shortest path problem, it is not possible to fully explore the extremely large configuration space. To tackle this challenge without sacrificing optimality, we adopt an A* best-first graph search approach as described in [17]. The approach requires a "cost-to-go" heuristic to be associated with each vertex of the graph. The cost-to-go heuristic estimates the shortest distance from the vertex to the goal state (in our case, the exit vertex). It then explores the vertex for which the estimated cost to get to the goal (i.e., the sum of the cost to get to the vertex and the cost-to-go) is the lowest. In order for the result to be optimal, the A* algorithm requires the heuristic to be "permissible" in that it underestimates the cost-to-go.

As the cost-to-go heuristic, we use the utility u^* of the optimal configuration c^* that is produced by our previous work in [8] using bin-packing and gradient-search techniques. This utility value represents the highest rate at which utility can be generated for the given workload and hardware resources. However, it does not take into account any costs that might be involved to change to that configuration, and thus overestimates the utility that can practically be obtained in any given situation. Therefore, the utility U calculated by using u^* instead of $\sum_{o \in \mathcal{E}} u_{o_{i+1}}^s$ in Equation 2 is guaranteed to overestimate the true reward-to-go (i.e., underestimate cost-to-go), and thus forms a permissible heuristic.

The resulting search algorithm is shown in Algorithm 1. After using the UtilityUpperBound function to compute the cost-to-go heuristic u^* for the initial configuration v^0, it begins the search. In each iteration, the open vertex with the highest value of U is explored further. New open vertices are created by applying each allowed adaptation action to the current vertex and updating $v.a_{opt}$, the optimal list of actions to get to v. When applying the do nothing action, the algorithm invokes the LQNS solver to estimate the response times of the current configuration and computes the utility. Otherwise, it invokes NewConfig to produce a new configuration and uses the cost model to compute both the adaptation cost U_a and the overall utility U as explained above. The algorithm terminates when $a.null$, i.e., "do nothing", is the action chosen.

Reducing the Search Space. The running time of the algorithm depends on the number of configurations explored by the search. The algorithm avoids lengthy sequences of expensive actions due to the optimal utility bound. However, to prevent it from getting stuck exploring long sequences of cheap actions such as CPU allocation changes, we have implemented several techniques to significantly reduce the number of states generated without affecting the quality of the adaptations produced. The first is *depth limiting* (DL), which limits the search of paths to those of no more than n adaptation actions and effectively makes the search space finite. In our experiments, we chose $n = 7$ as the largest value that ensured that the controller always produced a decision within 30 seconds. The second is *partial order reduction* (PO), which addresses the issue that CPU tuning actions can interleave in many ways to produce the same results, but require different intermediate states, e.g., WS+10%, WS+10%, DB-10% and DB-10%, WS+10%, WS+10%. To prevent multiple interleavings without affecting the actual candidate configurations, we consider all CPU increases and decreases in a strict canonical order of components. The final technique is *action elimination* (AE), which eliminates known poor action choices, for example, disabling add replica actions when the workload for an application has diminished.

Table 2. State Space Reduction

Technique	States	Time (sec)	Technique	States	Time (sec)
Naive	83497	3180	DL+PO	599	210
DL	19387	1420	DL+PO+AE	62	18

Table 2 shows the magnitude of reductions that are achievable with these techniques using an experiment in which 10 VMs across two applications were being optimized. Adding more replicas to an application does not affect the size of the state-space. However, adding more applications does. While these results indicate that the search algorithm can be made fast enough to be used in an on-line manner while still retaining a high quality of adaptation for deployments of small to moderate size (Section 4), scalability is potentially a problem for large deployments. We are addressing this limitation in ongoing work using a combination of both better engineering and better algorithms.

4   Experimental Results

The experimental results are divided into three parts. In the first part, we describe the testbed and workloads used, and then present the measurements used

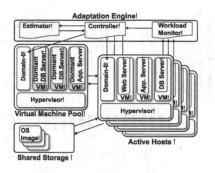
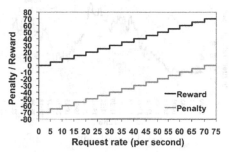

Fig. 5. Test-bed architecture   **Fig. 6.** SLA-based utility function

in the adaptation cost models. In the second part, we evaluate the accuracy of the individual controller components: the LQNS performance models, the cost models, and the ARMA-based workload stability predictor. Finally, in the third part, we evaluate our approach holistically in terms of the quality of the adaptation decisions the controller produces and their impact on application SLAs.

4.1 Model Calibration and Testbed

Testbed. Our target system is a three-tier version of the RUBiS application [11]. The application consists of Apache web servers, Tomcat application servers, and MySQL database servers running on a Linux-2.6 guest OS using the Xen 3.2 [12] virtualization platform. The hosts are commodity Pentium-4 1.8GHz machines with 1GB of memory running on a single 100Mbps Ethernet segment. Each VM is allocated 256MB of memory, with a limit of up to 3 VMs per host. The Xen Dom-0 hypervisor is allocated the remaining 256MB. The total CPU capacity of all VMs on a host is capped to 80% to ensure enough resources for the hypervisor even under loaded conditions. Figure 5 illustrates our experimental test-bed. Four machines are used to host our test applications, while two are used as client emulators to generate workloads (not shown). One machine is dedicated to hosting dormant VMs used in server replication, and another one is used as a storage server for VM disk images. Finally, we run the adaptation engine on a separate machine with 4 Intel Xeon 3.00 GHz processors and 4 GB RAM. For MySQL replication, all tables are copied and synchronized between replicas. The Tomcat servers are configured to send queries to the MySQL replicas in a round-robin manner. We deploy two applications RUBiS 1 and RUBiS-2 in a default configuration that evenly allocates resources among all components except for the database servers, which are allocated an additional 20% CPU to avoid bottlenecks. The rewards and penalties for the applications are as specified in Figure 6 for meeting or missing a target mean response time of 84 ms in every measurement interval, respectively. The target response time was derived experimentally as the mean response time across all transactions of a single RUBiS

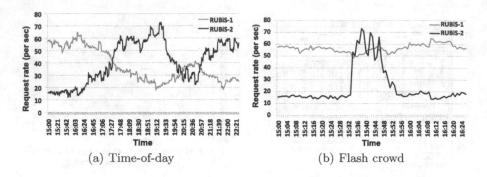

(a) Time-of-day   (b) Flash crowd

Fig. 7. Workloads

application running in isolation in the initial configuration driven by a constant workload equal to half of the design workload range of 5 to 80 requests/sec.

Workload Scenarios. During experiments, we drive the target applications using two workloads, a time-of-day workload and a flash crowd workload. The time-of-day workload was generated based on the Web traces from the 1998 World Cup site [18] and the traffic traces of an HP customer's Internet Web server system [19]. We have chosen a typical day's traffic from each of these traces and then scaled them to the range of request rates that our experimental setup can handle. Specifically, we scaled both the World Cup requests rates of 150 to 1200 requests/sec and the HP traffic of 2 to 4.5 requests/sec to a range of 5 to 80 requests/sec. Since our workload is controlled by adjusting the number of simulated clients, we created a mapping from the desired request rates to the number of simulated RUBiS clients. Figure 7(a) shows these scaled workloads for the two RUBiS applications from 15:00 to 22:30, where RUBiS-1 uses the scaled World Cup workload profile and RUBiS-2 uses the scaled HP workload profile. The flash crowd workload shown in Figure 7(b) uses the first 90 minutes of the time-of-day workloads, but has an additional load of over 50 requests per second added to RUBiS-2 around 15:30 for a short interval.

Adaptation Costs. To measure adaptation costs, we deployed both applications and used the methodology described in Section 3. One application was the "target application" for the action, while the other was the "shared application" that was co-located with the target application, but was not reconfigured. We measured the adaptation length d_a and response time impact ΔRT_a^s for all adaptation actions and combinations of workloads ranging from 100 to 500 users for both the target and shared application. For example, Figures 8(a) and 8(b) show ΔRT_a^s and d_a for the target application when subjected to actions affecting the MySQL server and when the workload for both applications is increased equally. As is seen, ΔRT for adding and removing MySQL replicas increases as workloads increase, but the adaptation durations are not greatly affected. The costs of CPU reallocation are very small in terms of both ΔRT and d_a.

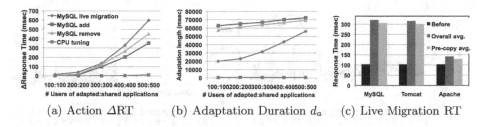

(a) Action ΔRT   (b) Adaptation Duration d_a (c) Live Migration RT

Fig. 8. Costs for various adaptation actions

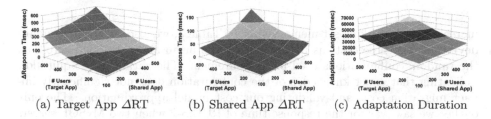

(a) Target App ΔRT   (b) Shared App ΔRT   (c) Adaptation Duration

Fig. 9. Costs for MySQL live-migration

The most interesting results were those for live migration, which has been proposed in the literature as a cheap technique for VM adaptation (e.g., [10]). However, we see that live-migration can have a significant impact on a multi-tier application's end-to-end responsiveness both in magnitude and in duration. For each of the three server types, Figure 8(c) shows the mean end-to-end response time for RUBiS measured before migration of that server, over the entire migration duration, and during the "pre-copy" phase of migration. This figure shows that although live-migration is relatively cheap for the Apache server, it is very expensive for both the Tomcat and MySQL servers. Moreover, most of this overhead incurs during the pre-copy phase. During this phase, dirty pages are iteratively copied to the target machine at a slow pace while the VM is running. In the subsequent stop-and-copy phase, the VM is stopped and the remaining few dirty pages are copied rapidly. Claims that VM migration is "cheap" often focus on the short (we measured it to be as low as 60msec) stop-and-copy phase when the VM is unavailable. However, it is the much longer pre-copy phase with times averaging 35 sec for Apache, 40 sec for MySQL, and 55 sec for the Tomcat server that contributes the most to end-to-end performance costs.

Migration also affects the response time of other VMs running on the same host. Figures 9(a) and 9(b) show the ΔRT for the target and shared applications, respectively during MySQL migration. While increases in the shared application's number of users (i.e., workload) impact the target application's response time, the target application migration has an even more significant impact on the shared application, especially at high workloads. Figure 9(c) shows how the adaptation duration increases with the target workload due to an

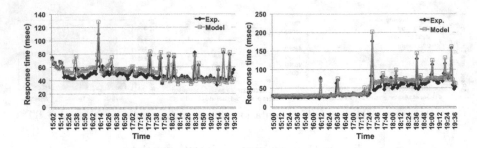

Fig. 10. Prediction accuracy for both applications under time-of-day workload

increase in the working set memory size. In Table 3, we also show the standard deviations for these costs as percentages of the mean and calculated across all the random configurations used for measurement. The variances are quite low indicating that exact knowledge of the configuration does not significantly impact migration cost, and validating our cost model approximations. The only outlier we saw was for the response time of RUBiS-2 when two MySQL servers were co-located under high load.

Table 3. Variance of Adaptation Costs for MySQL Migration

Workload	Action Length	RUBiS-1 ΔRT	RUBiS-2 ΔRT
100:500	2.34%	2.95%	14.52%
300:500	7.45%	10.53%	17.14%
500:500	8.14%	6.79%	101.80%

4.2   Model Prediction Accuracy

We evaluate the accuracy of the LQN models and the cost models in a single experiment by using the first 220 minutes from the time-of-day workloads. Specifically, at each controller execution point and for each application, we recorded the response time predicted by the models (RT^s) for the next control interval and then compared it against the actual measured response time over the same time period. This comparison includes both the predictions of adaptation cost and performance. Figure 10 shows the results for each application. Despite the simplifications made in our cost models, the average estimation error is quite good at around 15%, with the predictions being more conservative than reality.

Second, we evaluated the accuracy of our stability interval estimation. To do this, the ARMA filter is first trained using 30 minutes of the respective workloads. As shown in Figure 11(a), the filter is executed 68 times during the time-of-day experiment and provides effective estimates. The absolute prediction error against the measured interval length is around 15% for the time-of-day workloads. Meanwhile, the flash crowd workload causes an increase in the estimation

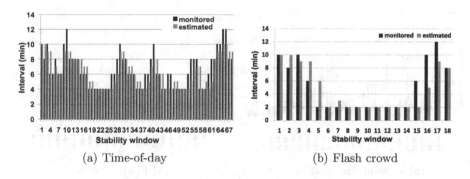

(a) Time-of-day   (b) Flash crowd

Fig. 11. Stability interval prediction error for different workloads

error of the ARMA filter due to the short and high unexpected bursts. The results are presented in Figure 11(b). The error reaches approximately 23% because the filter over-estimates the length until the 5th stability interval when the flash crowd appears. However, the estimation quickly converges on the lower length and matches the monitored length of the stability interval until the 14th interval, when the flash crowd goes away and the filter starts to under-estimate the length. Even under such relatively high prediction errors, we show below that our cost-sensitive strategy works well.

4.3 Controller Evaluation

We evaluate our Cost-Sensitive (CS) strategy under both time-of-day workload and flash crowd scenarios by comparing its response time and utility against the following strategies: *Cost Oblivious* (CO) reconfigures the system to the optimal configuration whenever the workload changes, and uses the optimal configurations generated using our previous work [8]. *1-Hour* reconfigures the system to the optimal configuration periodically at the rate of once per hour; this strategy reflects the common policy of using large consolidation windows to minimize adaptation costs. *No Adaptation* (NA) maintains the default configuration throughout the experiment. Finally, *Oracle* provides an upper bound for utility by optimizing based on perfect knowledge of future workload and by ignoring all adaptation costs.

We use the current measured workload at the controller execution point to be the predicted workload for the next control window for the CS and CO strategies. The measurement interval is set to 2 minutes to ensure quick reaction in response to workload changes. The workload monitor gets the workload for each measurement interval by parsing the Apache log file. Finally, we choose a narrow workload band b of 4 req/sec to ensure that even small workload changes will cause the controller to consider taking action.

End-to-End Response Time. First, we compare the mean end-to-end response time for all the strategies as measured at each measurement period. The

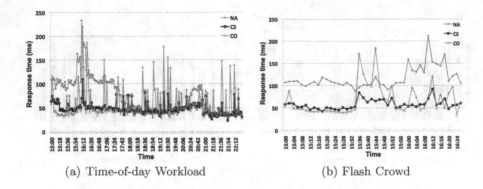

(a) Time-of-day Workload   (b) Flash Crowd

Fig. 12. Response times for RUBiS-1 under different adaptation strategies

results for the RUBiS-1 application are shown for the CS, CO, and NA strategies in Figures 12; the Oracle and 1-Hour plots are omitted for legibility. Figure 12(a) shows the results for the time-of-day workload. Predictably, the NA strategy is very sensitive to workload changes and shows large spikes once the workload intensity reaches the peak in both applications. For the CO and CS strategies, a series of spikes corresponds to when the adaptation engine triggers adaptations. The CS strategy has relatively short spikes and then the response time stabilizes. Meanwhile, the CO strategy has more and larger spikes than the CS strategy. This is because the CO strategy uses more adaptation actions, including relatively expensive ones such as live-migration of MySQL and Tomcat and MySQL replication, while the CS strategy uses fewer and cheaper actions, especially when the estimated stability interval is short.

Although the response time of the CO strategy is usually better than the CS strategy after each adaptation has completed, the overall average response time of CS is 47.99 ms, which is much closer to the Oracle's result of 40.91ms than the CO, 1-Hour, and NA values, which are 58.06 ms, 57.41 ms, and 71.18 ms respectively. Similarly, for the flash crowd scenario, although the ARMA filter over- and under-estimates several stability intervals, the CS strategy's mean response time of 57.68 ms compares favorably with the CO, 1-Hour, and NA values of 67.56 ms, 70.42 ms, and 116.35 ms, respectively, and is closer to the Oracle result of 40.14ms. Not surprisingly, the difference between CS and Oracle is larger for the flash crowd workload than the time-of-day one because the ARMA filter is wrong more often in its stability interval predictions. Also, the 1-Hour strategy does more poorly in the flash crowd case because it is unable to respond to the sudden workload spike in time. The results for RUBiS-2 were similar. Thus, the CS controller is able to outperform the CO strategy over the long run by trading-off short-term optimality for long-term gain.

To appreciate how the different strategies affect adaptation in the flash crowd scenario, consider what happens when the load to RUBiS-2 suddenly increases at 15:30. The CO controller removes a MySQL replica of RUBiS-1 and adds a MySQL replica to RUBiS-2. Meanwhile, the CS strategy also removes a MySQL

Table 4. Total Number of Actions Triggered

Action	CS	CO	Action	CS	CO
CPU Increase/Decrease	14	36	Migrate (Apache replica)	4	10
Add (MySQL replica)	1	4	Migrate (Tomcat replica)	4	10
Remove (MySQL replica)	1	4	Migrate (MySQL replica)	0	2

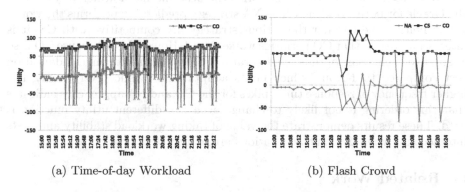

(a) Time-of-day Workload   (b) Flash Crowd

Fig. 13. Measured utility for different adaptation strategies

replica from RUBiS-1, but then it only tunes the CPU allocation of Tomcat servers, which are much cheaper actions than adding a replica to RUBiS-2. Table 4 summarizes the number of actions of each type produced by the CS and CO strategies for the flash crowd scenario.

Utility. Using the monitored request rates and response times, we compute the utility of each strategy at every measurement interval to show the impact of adaptation actions on the overall utility. For the time-of-day workload, Figure 13(a) shows that both the CO and CS strategies have spikes when adaptation actions are triggered. However, the CO strategy has more and much deeper spikes than the CS strategy including some that lead to negative utility by violating SLAs of both applications. Meanwhile, the CS strategy chooses actions that do not violate SLAs. The utility for the flash crowd scenario in Figure 13(b) similarly shows that the CS strategy has a couple of spikes corresponding to the onset and exit of the flash crowd. However, these spikes are less severe than those of the CO strategy. The CS strategy violates the SLA of RUBiS-1 only in the measurement periods where it removes or adds a MySQL replica of RUBiS-1 (when the flash crowd starts and then after it disappears), while the CO strategy violates SLAs of both applications in many periods.

We also computed the total utility accumulated over the entire experiment duration. The values for all the different strategies and workloads are shown in Table 5. Because the absolute value of the utility can differ greatly depending on the exact reward, penalty, and response time threshold values used in the SLA, it is more important to note the relative ordering between the different approaches.

Table 5. Cumulative Utility for all Strategies

Workload	Oracle	CS	1 Hour	CO	NA
Time of day	16535	15785	10645	9280	2285
Flash Crowd	3345	3120	2035	1620	-630

As can be seen, the CS strategy performs the best and has a utility very close to the Oracle for both workloads. The NA strategy predictably performs the worst. While neither the CO nor the 1-Hour strategy are competitive with CS, it is interesting to note that CO performs worse than 1-Hour. This is because CO is so aggressive in choosing optimal configurations that it incurs too much adaptation cost compared to 1-Hour, which limits adaptations to once every hour. The higher frequency of response time spikes for the CO and NA approaches indicates that this ordering is not likely to change even if a different utility function is used. These results demonstrate the value of taking workload stability and costs into account when dynamic adaptations are made.

5   Related Work

The primary contributions of this paper are (a) a model for comparing on a uniform footing dramatically different types of adaptation actions with varying cost and application performance impacts (e.g., CPU tuning vs. VM migration), and (b) considering workload stability to produce adaptations that are not necessarily optimal in the short term, but produce better results over the long run when workload variations are taken into account. We are not aware of any other work that addresses these issues, especially in the context of multitier systems with response time SLAs.

Several papers address the problem of dynamic resource provisioning [20, 21, 4, 5, 6, 7]. The authors in [7] even use queuing models to make decisions that preserve response time SLAs in multitier applications. However, none of these papers consider the performance impact of the adaptations themselves in their decision making process. The approach proposed in [22] learns the relationships between application response time, workload, and adaptation actions using reinforcement learning. It is implicitly able to learn adaptation costs as a side-benefit. However, it cannot handle never-before seen configurations or workloads, and must spend considerable time relearning its policies in case of even workload changes.

Recently, some efforts including [23, 25, 27, 26] address adaptation costs. Only one adaptation action, VM migration, is considered in [23], [25], and [24]. These papers propose controllers based on online vector-packing, utilization to migration cost ratios, and genetic algorithms, respectively, to redeploy components whose resource utilization causes them to fit poorly on their current hosts while minimizing the number or cost of migrations. Migrations are constrained by resource capacity considerations, but once completed, they are assumed not to impact the subsequent performance of the application. Therefore, the approaches cannot be easily extended to incorporate additional action types since they possess no mechanisms to compare different performance levels that could result from actions such as CPU tuning or component addition. pMapper focuses on optimizing power given fixed resource utilization targets produced by an external performance manager [27]. It relies solely on VM migration, and propose a variant of bin-packing that can minimize the migration costs while discarding migrations that have no net benefit. It also does not provide any way to compare the performance of different types of actions that achieve similar goals. Finally, [26] examines an integer linear program formulation in a grid job scheduler setting to dynamically produce adaptation actions of two types — VM migration and application reconfiguration — to which users can assign different costs. However, there is again no mechanism to compare the different performance benefits of the different actions, and the user must resort to providing a manual weight to prioritize each type of action.

In summary, the above "cost aware" approaches only minimize adaptation costs while maintaining fixed resource usage levels. They do not provide a true cost-performance trade-off that compares different levels of performance resulting from different kinds of actions. Furthermore, none of the techniques consider the limited lifetime that reconfiguration is likely to have under rapidly changing workloads and adjusts its decisions to limit adaptation costs accordingly. In that sense, they are more comparable to our "cost oblivious" policy which reconfigures the system whenever it finds a better configuration for the current workload, irrespective of future trends.

The only work we are aware of that explicitly considers future workload variations by using a limited lookahead controller (LLC) is presented in [9]. The algorithm balances application performance with energy consumption by switching physical hosts on and off. However, it only deals with a single type of coarse grain adaptation action, and requires accurate workload predictions over multiple windows into the future, something that is hard to get right. In contrast, our approach does not require any workload predictions, but can benefit from much simpler to obtain estimates of stability windows if they are available. Moreover, it is not clear whether it is practical to extend the LLC approach to allow multiple types of actions with a range of granularities.

Energy saving is considered an explicit optimization goal in [9] and [27] and is realized by shutting down machines when possible. Our current approach does not factor in the cost of energy and therefore does not consider power cycling actions. CPU power states are virtualized in [28] to produce "soft power states" exported by an hypervisor to its VMs. In this approach, each VM implements its own power management policy through the soft-states, and the management framework arbitrates requests from multiple VMs to either perform frequency scaling, or VM capacity scaling along with consolidation. It leaves policy decisions, i.e., (a) how performance goals and workload are mapped to resource targets, and (b) when and which VMs are consolidated to which physical hosts, to the application to decide. Our goal is to automatically produce such policies.

6 Conclusions

In this paper, we have shown that runtime reconfiguration actions such as virtual machine replication and migration can impose significant performance costs in multitier applications running in virtualized data center environments. To address these costs while still retaining the benefits afforded by such reconfigurations, we developed a middleware for generating cost-sensitive adaptation actions using a combination of predictive models and graph search techniques. Through extensive experimental evaluation using real workload traces from Internet applications, we showed that by making smart decisions on when and how to act, the approach can significantly enhance the satisfaction of response time SLAs compared to approaches that do not take adaptation costs into account.

Acknowledgments. Thanks to our shepherd A. Verma for his many helpful suggestions. This research has been funded in part by NSF grants ENG/EEC-0335622, CISE/CNS-0646430, and CISE/CNS-0716484; AFOSR grant FA9550-06-1-0201, NIH grant U54 RR 024380-01, IBM, Hewlett-Packard, Wipro Technologies, and the Georgia Tech Foundation through the John P. Imlay, Jr. Chair endowment. Any opinions, findings, and conclusions or recommendations expressed are those of the authors and do not necessarily reflect the views of NSF or the other funding agencies and companies.

References

[1] Galletta, D., Henry, R., McCoy, S., Polak, P.: Web site delays: How tolerant are users? J. of the Assoc. for Information Sys. 5(1), 1–28 (2004)

[2] Ceaparu, I., Lazar, J., Bessiere, K., Robinson, J., Shneiderman, B.: Determining causes and severity of end-user frustration. Intl. J. of Human-Computer Interaction 17(3), 333–356 (2004)

[3] WebSiteOptimization.com: The psychology of web performance. WWW (May 2008),
http://www.websiteoptimization.com/speed/tweak/
psychology-web-performance/ (accessed, April 2009)

[4] Bennani, M., Manesce, D.: Resource allocation for autonomic data centers using analytic performance models. In: Proc. IEEE ICAC, pp. 217–228 (2005)

[5] Xu, J., Zhao, M., Fortes, J., Carpenter, R., Yousif, M.: On the use of fuzzy modeling in virtualized data center management. In: Proc. IEEE ICAC, pp. 25–34 (2007)

[6] Zhang, Q., Cherkasova, L., Smirni, E.: A regression-based analytic model for dynamic resource provisioning of multi-tier applications. In: Proc. IEEE ICAC, pp. 27–36 (2007)

[7] Urgaonkar, B., Shenoy, P., Chandra, A., Goyal, P., Wood, T.: Agile dynamic provisioning of multi-tier internet applications. ACM Trans. on Autonomous and Adaptive Sys. 3(1), 1–39 (2008)

[8] Jung, G., Joshi, K., Hiltunen, M., Schlichting, R., Pu, C.: Generating adaptation policies for multi-tier applications in consolidated server environments. In: Proc. IEEE ICAC, pp. 23–32 (2008)

[9] Kusic, D., Kephart, J., Hanson, J., Kandasamy, N., Jiang, G.: Power and performance management of virtualized computing environments via lookahead control. In: Proc. IEEE ICAC, pp. 3–12 (2008)

[10] Clark, C., Fraser, K., Hand, S., Hansen, J.G., Jul, E., Limpach, C., Pratt, I., Warfield, A.: Live migration of virtual machines. In: Proc. ACM/Usenix NSDI (2005)

[11] Cecchet, E., Chanda, A., Elnikety, S., Marguerite, J., Zwaenepoel, W.: Performance comparison of middleware architectures for generating dynamic web content. In: Endler, M., Schmidt, D.C. (eds.) Middleware 2003. LNCS, vol. 2672, pp. 242–261. Springer, Heidelberg (2003)

[12] Barham, P., Dragovic, B., Fraser, K., Hand, S., Harris, T., Ho, A., Neugebauer, R., Pratt, I., Wareld, A.: Xen and the art of virtualization. In: Proc. ACM SOSP, pp. 164–177 (2003)

[13] Franks, G., Majumdar, S., Neilson, J., Petriu, D., Rolia, J., Woodside, M.: Performance analysis of distributed server systems. In: Proc. Intl. Conf. on Software Quality, pp. 15–26 (1996)

[14] Govindan, S., Nath, A., Das, A., Urgaonkar, B., Sivasubramaniam, A.: Xen and co.: Communication-aware CPU scheduling for consolidated Xen-based hosting platforms. In: Proc. ACM VEE, pp. 126–136 (2007)

[15] Box, G., Jenkins, G., Reinsel, G.: Time Series Analysis: Forecasting and Control, 3rd edn. Prentice Hall, Englewood Cliffs (1994)

[16] Kim, M., Noble, B.: Mobile network estimation. In: Proc. ACM Conf. Mobile Computing & Networking, pp. 298–309 (2001)

[17] Russell, S.J., Norvig, P.: Artificial Intelligence: A Modern Approach. Prentice Hall, Englewood Cliffs (2003)

[18] Arlitt, M., Jin, T.: Workload characterization of the 1998 World Cup web site. HP Tech. Rep., HPL-99-35 (1999)

[19] Dilley, J.: Web server workload characterization. HP Tech. Rep., HPL-96-160 (1996)

[20] Appleby, K., Fakhouri, S., Fong, L., Goldszmidt, M., Krishnakumar, S., Pazel, D., Pershing, J., Rochwerger, B.: Oceano SLA based management of a computing utility. In: Proc. IFIP/IEEE IM, pp. 855–868 (2001)

[21] Chandra, A., Gong, W., Shenoy, P.: Dynamic resource allocation for shared data centers using online measurements. In: Proc. IEEE IWQoS, pp. 155 (2003)

[22] Tesauro, G., Jong, N., Das, R., Bennani, M.: A hybrid reinforcement learning approach to autonomic resource allocation. In: Proc. IEEE ICAC, pp. 65–73 (2006)

[23] Khanna, G., Beaty, K., Kar, G., Kochut, A.: Application performance management in virtualized server environments. In: Proc. IEEE/IFIP NOMS, pp. 373–381 (2006)

[24] Gmach, D., Rolia, J., Cherkasova, L., Belrose, G., Turicchi, T., Kemper, A.: An integrated approach to resource pool management: Policies, efficiency and quality metrics. In: Proc. IEEE/IFIP DSN, pp. 326–335 (2008)

[25] Wood, T., Shenoy, P., Venkataramani, A.: Black-box and gray-box strategies for virtual machine migration. In: Proc. Usenix NSDI, pp. 229–242 (2007)

[26] Garbacki, P., Naik, V.K.: Efficient resource virtualization and sharing strategies for heterogeneous grid environments. In: Proc. IFIP/IEEE IM, pp. 40–49 (2007)

[27] Verma, A., Ahuja, P., Neogi, A.: pMapper: Power and migration cost aware application placement in virtualized systems. In: Issarny, V., Schantz, R. (eds.) Middleware 2008. LNCS, vol. 5346, pp. 243–264. Springer, Heidelberg (2008)

[28] Nathuji, R., Schwan, K.: Virtualpower: Coordinated power management in virtualized enterprise systems. In: Proc. ACM SOSP, pp. 265–278 (2007)

Rhizoma: A Runtime for Self-deploying, Self-managing Overlays

Qin Yin[1], Adrian Schüpbach[1], Justin Cappos[2],
Andrew Baumann[1], and Timothy Roscoe[1]

[1] Systems Group, Department of Computer Science, ETH Zurich
[2] Department of Computer Science and Engineering, University of Washington

Abstract. The trend towards cloud and utility computing infrastructures raises challenges not only for application development, but also for management: diverse resources, changing resource availability, and differing application requirements create a complex optimization problem. Most existing cloud applications are managed externally, and this separation can lead to increased response time to failures, and slower or less appropriate adaptation to resource availability and pricing changes.

In this paper, we explore a different approach more akin to P2P systems: we closely couple a decentralized management runtime ("Rhizoma") with the application itself. The application expresses its resource requirements to the runtime as a constrained optimization problem. Rhizoma then fuses multiple real-time sources of resource availability data, from which it decides to acquire or release resources (such as virtual machines), redeploying the system to continually maximize its utility.

Using PlanetLab as a challenging "proving ground" for cloud-based services, we present results showing Rhizoma's performance, overhead, and efficiency versus existing approaches, as well the system's ability to react to unexpected large-scale changes in resource availability.

1   Introduction

In this paper, we investigate a new technique for distributed application management over a utility computing infrastructure. Commercial "cloud computing" facilities like Amazon's EC2 [3] provide a managed, low-cost, stable, scalable infrastructure for distributed applications and are increasingly attractive for a variety of systems. However, such services do not remove the burden of application management, but instead modify it: deployment of hardware and upgrades of software are no longer an issue, but new challenges are introduced.

First, such services are not totally reliable, as recent Amazon outages show [4]. Second, changing network conditions external to the cloud provider can significantly affect service performance. Third, pricing models for cloud computing services change over time, and as competition and the pressure to differentiate in the sector intensifies, we can expect this to happen more frequently. Finally, the sheer diversity of pricing models and offerings presents an increasing challenge to application providers who wish to deploy on such infrastructures.

J.M. Bacon and B.F. Cooper (Eds.): Middleware 2009, LNCS 5896, pp. 184–204, 2009.
© IFIP International Federation for Information Processing 2009

These challenges are typically addressed at present by a combination of a separate management machine outside the cloud (possibly replicated for availability or managed by a company like RightScale[1]) and human-in-the-loop monitoring. Such arrangements have obvious deficiencies: slow response time to critical events, and the cost of maintaining an infrastructure (albeit a much smaller one) to manage the virtual infrastructure which the application is using.

This paper evaluates an alternative approach whereby the application manages itself as a continuous process of optimization [23], and makes the following contributions. First, we present Rhizoma, a runtime for distributed applications that obviates the need for a separate management console and removes any such single point of failure by turning the application into a *self-deploying* system reminiscent of early "worm" programs [19]. Second, we show how constraint logic programming provides a natural way to express desired application behavior with regard to resources, and can be applied to simplify the task of acquiring and releasing processing resources autonomously as both external conditions and the needs of the application itself change. Finally, using PlanetLab, we show that in spite of its flexibility, our approach to resource management results in better application performance than a centralized, external management system, and can adapt application deployment in real time to service requirements.

In the next section, we provide background and motivation for our approach, and Section 3 describes how application providers deploy a service using Rhizoma. In Section 4 we detail how Rhizoma operates at runtime to manage the application and optimize its deployment. Section 5 presents our current experimental implementation on PlanetLab, and Section 6 shows results from running Rhizoma in this challenging environment. Finally, Section 7 covers related work, and we discuss future work and conclude in Section 8.

2   Background and Motivation

Deploying and maintaining applications in a utility computing environment involves important decisions about which resources to acquire and how to respond to changes in resource requirements, costs, and availability.

An operator deploying an application must first consider the offerings of assorted providers and their costs, then select a set of nodes on which to deploy the application. Amazon's EC2 service currently offers a choice of node types and locations, and the selection will become increasingly complex as multiple providers emerge with different service offerings and pricing models.

The selected compute resources must then be acquired (typically purchased), and the application deployed on the nodes. Following this, its status must be monitored, as offered load may change or nodes might fail (or an entire service provider may experience an outage [4]). These factors may require redeploying the application on a larger, smaller, or simply different set of nodes. This leads to a control and optimization problem that in many cases is left to a human operator working over timescales of hours or days.

---

[1] http://www.rightscale.com/

Alternatively, a separate management system is deployed (and itself maintained) on dedicated machines to keep the application running and to respond to such events. In autonomic computing this function may be referred to as an "orchestration service", and typically operates without the application itself being aware of such functionality. Such separation and (logical) centralization of management can have benefits at large scales, but introduces additional complexity and failure modes, which are particularly significant to operators deploying smaller services where the cost of an additional dedicate node is hard to justify.

To address these problems, we explore an alternative model for application management and present our experience building a runtime system for distributed applications which are *self-hosting*: the application manages itself by acquiring and releasing resources (in particular, distributed virtual machines) in response to failures, offered load, or changing policy. Our runtime, Rhizoma, runs on the same nodes as the application, performing autonomous resource management that is as flexible and robust to failure as the application itself.

In order to remove a human from direct management decisions, and to decouple Rhizoma's management decisions from the application logic, we need a way to specify the application's resource requirements and performance goals. This specification needs to be extensible in terms of resource types, must be able to express complex relationships between desired resources, and must allow for automatic optimization. These requirements led us to choose *constraint logic programming* (CLP) [21] as the most tractable way to express application demands; we introduce CLP and further motivate its use below.

2.1   Constraint Logic Programming

CLP programs are written as a set of constraints that the program needs to meet and an objective function to optimize within those constraints. This provides a direct mapping between the operator's expression of desired performance and cost, and the application's underlying behavior. Rather than an operator trying to find out how many program instances need to be deployed and where to deploy them, the CLP solver treats the task as an optimization problem and uses application and system characteristics to find an optimal solution.

A constraint satisfaction problem (CSP) consists of a set of variables $V = V_1, \ldots, V_n$. For each V_i, there is a finite set D_i of possible values it can take (its domain). Constraints between the variables can always be expressed as a set of admissible combinations of values. CLP combines logic programming, which is used to specify a set of possibilities explored via a simple inbuilt search method, with constraints, which are used to minimize the reasoning and search by eliminating unwanted alternatives in advance. A solution of a CSP is an assignment of values to each variable such that none of the constraints are violated.

CLP is attractive for application management for another reason: As in the resource description framework (RDF), CLP programs have powerful facilities for handling diversity in resource and information types, since CLP can use logical unification to manage the heterogeneity of resource types, measurement and monitoring data, and application policies. This allows a CLP program to easily add new resources and data sources while continuing to utilize the existing ones. Unlike RDF query languages, however, CLP provides a natural way to express high-level optimization goals.

We are not the first to make this observation. There is an increasing consensus that constraint satisfaction has a powerful role to play in systems management (for example, in configuration management [7]), and indeed the CLP solver we use in Rhizoma was originally written to build network management applications [5]. A novel feature of Rhizoma is embedding such a CLP system within the application, allowing it to manage and deploy itself.

2.2 Network Testbeds

The challenges outlined above will also be familiar to users of networking and distributed systems testbeds such as PlanetLab [15]. A number of systems for externally managing PlanetLab applications have appeared, such as Plush [2] and AppManager [9]. In this paper, we evaluate Rhizoma on PlanetLab, however our target is future cloud computing infrastructure. PlanetLab is a very different environment to cloud providers like EC2 in several important respects.

Firstly, PlanetLab is much *less* stable than services like EC2. This helps us to understand how Rhizoma can deal with server, provider or network outages. PlanetLab is an excellent source of trouble: deploying on PlanetLab is likely to exercise weaknesses in the system design and reveal problems in the approach.

Secondly, PlanetLab nodes are more diverse (in hardware, location, connectivity and monitored status) than current cloud offerings nodes, allowing us to exercise the features of Rhizoma that handle such heterogeneity without waiting for commercial offerings to diversify.

Finally, we can deploy measurement systems on PlanetLab alongside Rhizoma for instrumentation, which is hard with commercial infrastructure services.

3   Using Rhizoma

In this section, we describe how Rhizoma is used as part of a complete application deployment. The Rhizoma runtime executes alongside the application on nodes where the application has been deployed, and handles all deployment issues. Consequently, the only nodes used by Rhizoma are those running the application itself – there are no management nodes *per se* and no separate daemons to install.

We use our current, PlanetLab implementation for concrete details, and use the term "application" to refer to the whole system, and "application instance" or "instance" for that part of the application which runs on a single node.

3.1   Initial Deployment

Rhizoma targets applications that are already capable of handling components which fail independently and organize into some form of overlay. To deploy such an application, a developer packages the application code together with the

Rhizoma runtime, and supplies a constraint program specifying the deployment requirements (described in Section 3.2 below) and short scripts that Rhizoma can call to start and stop the application on a node. These scripts can be extremely short (typically one or two lines) and are the only part where explicit interaction between the application and Rhizoma is required.

Other interaction is optional, albeit desirable, for applications that wish to direct resource allocation based on application metrics. For example, a Rhizoma-aware web cluster can scale up or down in response to workload changes while considering the current system configuration, so that resource consumption can be optimized without sacrificing quality of service. Application developers can also benefit from the underlying Rhizoma facilities, as described in Section 3.4.

A developer can deploy the application by simply running the package on one node (even a desktop or laptop computer). No further action and no specific software is required on any other node – Rhizoma will start up, work out how to further deploy the application on a more appropriate set of nodes, and vacate the initial machine when it has acquired them. Rhizoma can in fact be seen as a "worm", albeit a benign one, in that it moves from host to host under its own control. We discuss the relationship with early worm programs in Section 7.

3.2 The Constraint Program

The constraint program specifies how the application is to be deployed, and can be supplied by the developer or operator of the application. It can also be changed (with or without human intervention) while the application is running, though this capability has not been used to date. The program specifies a *constraint list*, a *utility function*, and a *cost function*.

The constraint list is a set of logical and numeric constraints on the *node set*, i.e. the set of nodes on which the application is to execute. These are conditions which must be satisfied by any solution.

The utility function $U(N)$ for a given node set gives a value in the interval $(0, 1)$ representing the value of a deployment. This function may make use of anything that Rhizoma knows about the nodes, such as their pairwise connectivity (latency, bandwidth), measured CPU load, etc.

The cost function $C(\Delta)$ specifies a cost for deploying or shutting down the application on a node. As with utility, this function may take into account any information available to Rhizoma. Its definition might range from a constant value to a complex calculation involving pricing structures and node locations.

Rhizoma will attempt to find a node set which satisfies the constraints and maximizes the value of the *objective function*, defined as the utility $U(N)$ minus the cost $C(\Delta)$ of moving to the new set from the current one.

3.3 Example: PsEPR

To provide a concrete example of deploying an application with Rhizoma, we take a publish/subscribe application inspired by the (now defunct) PsEPR service on PlanetLab [6]. Informally, PsEPR's requirements were to run on a small set of

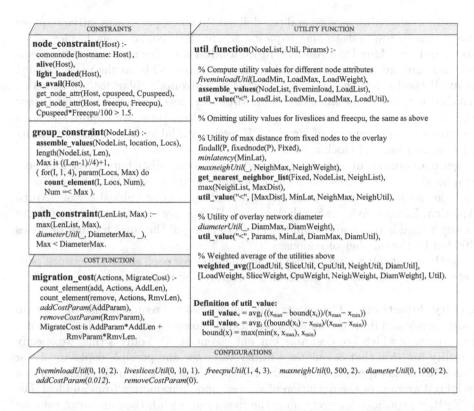

Fig. 1. PsEPR application requirements

well-connected, lightly loaded, and highly available PlanetLab nodes which were sufficiently distributed to be "close" to the majority of other PlanetLab nodes.

Deployment of the original PsEPR system was performed by hand-written parallel SSH scripts. Nodes were selected based on informal knowledge of location properties, together with human examination of data from the CoMon monitoring service [14], which includes status information such as node reachability, load, and hardware specifications. Node failures were noticed by human operators, and new nodes were picked manually. The set of nodes was reviewed irregularly (about once a month) [1].

Constraints: PsEPR is an example of a distributed application with requirements that cannot be expressed simply as number of nodes or minimum per-node resources. Figure 1 shows how PsEPR's requirements can be expressed as a set of Rhizoma constraints. These constraints are applied to data acquired by Rhizoma as described in Section 5.2, and include node constraints (which a node must satisfy for it to be considered), group constraints (defined over any group of nodes), and network constraints (specifying desired network characteristics).

node_constraint uses several pre-defined Rhizoma predicates. **alive** requires that the node responds to ping requests, accepts SSH connections, has low clock skew, and a working DNS resolver. **light_loaded** specifies maxima for the memory pressure, five-minute load, and number of active VMs on the node. Finally, **is_avail** checks that the node is not listed in Rhizoma's "blacklist" of nodes on which it has previously failed to deploy. Moreover, developers can also define new logical and numeric constraints on node properties. Here, we require the node to have a certain amount of "free" CPU cycles available, as calculated from its CPU utilization and clock speed.

group_constraint specifies that nodes are evenly distributed over four geographical regions. Here we use the fact that the data available for every node includes an integer in the range $[1, 4]$ indicating a geographical region (North America, Europe, Asia, or South America). We specify that the number of nodes in any region is no greater than the integer ceiling of the total number of nodes divided by the number of regions.

path_constraint limits a maximum diameter for each shortest network path between any two nodes of the resulting overlay network.

Utility Function: The constraints define "hard" requirements the system must satisfy and limit the allowable solutions. However, a system also has "soft" requirements which are desirable but not essential. To address this, we specify a utility function that calculates a utility value for any possible deployment, for which Rhizoma attempts to optimize. Here, we construct the utility function as a weighted average of the deviation of various node parameters from an ideal. For PsEPR, we consider for every node the five-minute load, the number of running VMs (or *live slices*, in PlanetLab terminology) and available CPU, the network diameter, and the maximum latency to the overlay from each of a set of ten manually chosen, geographically dispersed anchor nodes.

In **utility_function**, **assemble_values** gathers a list of values for a given parameter for every node in the node list. **util_value** is a built-in function that computes the utility for an individual parameter given the list of values for the parameter: $(x_{min}, x_{max}, weight)$. As an example, for the experiments reported in Section 6, the values are configured as shown at the bottom of Figure 1. **util_value** computes utility as an average of the deviations of a parameter x_i from the ideal (x_{max} or x_{min}) as defined in **utility_function** of Figure 1. **get_nearest_neighbor_list** finds for every node in the list of fixed nodes, the nearest neighbor to it in the overlay. **minlatency** is the minimum latency to any node, as determined by Rhizoma at run-time. Finally, **weighted_avg** computes the weighted average of a list of values given a list of weights.

Cost Function: This function incorporates two notions: the cost of a particular deployment, and the cost of migrating to it. The former is relatively straightforward: in PlanetLab it is generally zero, and for commercial cloud computing services can be a direct translation of the pricing structure. Indeed, the ability to optimize for real-world costs is a powerful feature of Rhizoma.

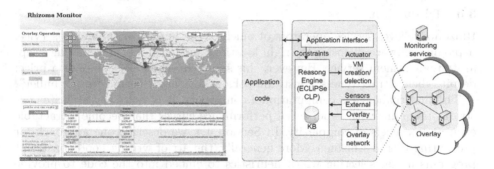

Fig. 2. Visualizing a Rhizoma application   **Fig. 3.** Rhizoma architecture

However, quantifying the cost of migration is much harder, and does not correspond to something a developer is generally thinking of. In Figure 1, we adopt a simple linear model in which the migration cost increases with the number of nodes added and removed. The deployment effect of varying the migration cost by tuning the constant coefficients is investigated in Section 6.5. The migration cost could also consider application details and configuration changes. Ideally, it would be learned online by the system over time.

3.4   Rhizoma-Aware Programs

Although we have presented the minimal interface required for existing applications to be deployed with Rhizoma, the runtime's functionality is also available to applications. Rhizoma maintains an overlay network among all members of the node set, and uses this for message routing. It also maintains up-to-date status information for all nodes in the application, plus considerable external monitoring data gathered for the purpose of managing deployment, along with a reasoning engine that applications can use to execute queries.

This functionality is exposed via a service provider/consumer interface for applications written using Rhizoma's module framework. The framework maintains module dependencies through service interaction, and can be extended by developers with additional application modules.

3.5   Observing the Application

Since the node set on which the application is deployed is determined by Rhizoma as an ongoing process, a human user cannot necessarily know at any moment where the application is running (though it is straightforward to specify some "preferred" nodes in the constraint program). For this and debugging reasons, Rhizoma additionally stores the IP addresses of the node set in a dynamic DNS server, and also exports a management interface, which allows arbitrary querying of its real-time status from any node in the application. It is straightforward to build system visualizations, such as the one in Figure 2, using this data.

3.6   Discussion

Rhizoma relieves service operators of much of the burden of running a service: deploying software, choosing the right locations and machines, and running a separate management service. However, this simplicity naturally comes at a price: despite their attractiveness, constraint solvers have never been a "magic bullet".

The first challenge is computational complexity. It is very easy to write constraint programs with exponential performance curves that become intractable even at low levels of complexity. In Section 4.4, we describe one approach for preventing this in Rhizoma. More generally, the art of writing good constraint programs lies in selecting which heuristics to embed into the code to provide the solver with enough hints to find the optimum (or a solution close enough to it) in reasonable time. This is a hard problem (and a topic of much ongoing research in the constraint community).

Application developers may find it difficult to write constraints in a language such as the Prolog dialect used by our CLP solver. While constraints and optimization provide a remarkably intuitive way to specify requirements at a high level, there is a gap between the apparently simple constraints one can talk about using natural language, and the syntax that must be written to specify them.

We address both of these issues by trading off expressivity for complexity (in both senses of the word). We provide a collection of useful heuristics based on our experience with PlanetLab, embedded in a library that provides high-level, simplified constraints which use the heuristics. This library can also serve as the basis for a future, simplified syntax. In this way, developers are assured of relatively tractable constraint programs if they stick to the high-level constructs we supply (and need only write a few lines of code). However, the full expressive power of CLP is still available if required.

4   Operation

The architecture of a Rhizoma node is shown in Figure 3. As well as the reasoning engine introduced in the previous section, Rhizoma consists of an overlay maintenance component, and resource interfaces to one or more distributed infrastructures (such as PlanetLab). The application interface could be as simple as configuring a constraint file or as complex as using the component services to build an application from scratch.

In this section, which describes the operation of a Rhizoma system in practice, we first introduce the sensors/actuators and knowledge base (KB in the figure), two key components of the Rhizoma architecture, and describe the maintenance of an overlay network. We then give a detailed discussion of the steady-state behavior of Rhizoma, including the components used to construct it, followed by what happens at bootstrap and when a new node is started.

4.1   Sensors and Knowledge Base

Sensors in Rhizoma periodically take a snapshot of resource information about node or network status from external and internal monitoring services. External monitoring services provide coarse-grained information about the whole hosting environment, while internal monitoring services provide fine-grained measurement of more up-to-date resource information on a given overlay.

To maintain and optimize the system, Rhizoma stores data collected by the sensors in the *knowledge base* used by the CLP solver. Every member of the overlay maintains its own knowledge base, though their content and usage differ, as described in the following section. As part of the CLP solver, the knowledge base provides a query interface. High-level knowledge can be derived from low-level facts. For example, based on the overlay status data, we can compute the network diameter in terms of latency.

The knowledge base in the current implementation stores only the latest information retrieved by the sensors, however in the future we intend to time-stamp the available data and maintain historical information such as moving averages, which could be used by constraint programs.

4.2   Coordinator Node

To manage the overlay, Rhizoma elects one node as a coordinator. The coordinator can be any node in the overlay, and any leadership election algorithm may be used. The currently-implemented election algorithm simply chooses the node with the lowest IP, although we intend to explore leadership-election based on node resources as future work. This node remains the coordinator as long as it is alive and in the overlay. A new coordinator is elected if the node crashes, or if the optimization process decides to move to another node.

Only the coordinator node runs the constraint program, storing in its knowledge base the complete data set, which provides it with a global view of the hosting environment. To optimize the use of communication and computation resources within the overlay, other nodes maintain only the overlay status.

4.3   Steady-State Behavior

To respond to changes in resource utilization, Rhizoma performs several periodic operations in its steady state. First, the coordinator collects information from the sensors, and updates the knowledge base periodically. The periods are based on the characteristics of different sensors, such as their update frequency and data size. Real-time overlay information from the resource monitoring service is collected by the coordinator and disseminated to each member in the overlay.

Since every member in the overlay knows the current overlay status, it can take decisions to optimize the resource usage. Rhizoma currently supports shortest-path routing and minimum spanning-tree computation for broadcast communication. In the future, the performance optimization of applications subject to available overlay resources could also be investigated.

To adapt to changes in the host environment, the coordinator periodically solves the developer-provided constraints based on the current resource capacity and utilization. If the current overlay state is not suitable, it yields a list of actions to apply to it. These actions will move the current network configuration towards a new one that meets the application's constraints and has higher utility.

4.4   Optimization Process

The actions derived from periodic solving include acquiring new nodes and releasing existing nodes. In principle, the solver tries to maximize the value of the objective (defined as the utility function minus the cost function) based on the current knowledge base, subject to the constraints.

In practice, this approach would lead to exponential complexity increases, particularly in a PlanetLab-like environment where the number of node options is very large (more than 600 live nodes at any time) – an optimal overlay of c nodes would require examining on the order of $\binom{600}{c}$ possible configurations. Rhizoma's solver instead derives an optimal set of at most n *add(node)* or *remove(node)* actions which will improve the utility of the current deployment subject to the cost of the actions. Here, n is a relatively small horizon (such as two or three), which makes the optimization considerably more tractable. Such incremental optimization also has a damping effect, which prevents Rhizoma from altering its configuration too much during each period.

This technique is a case of the well-known hill-climbing approach, and can lead to the familiar problem of local maxima: it is possible that Rhizoma can become stuck in a sub-optimal configuration because a better deployment is too far away to be reached. In practice, we have not observed serious problems of this sort, but it can be addressed either by increasing the horizon n, or using one of several more sophisticated optimization algorithms from the literature.

4.5   Adding or Removing Nodes

The actions chosen by the solver are executed by an actuator. To remove a node, the actuator calls a short cleanup script on that node, for example, copying back logs and stopping the application. To add a node, the actuator will first test its liveness, and then copy the relevant files (the application and Rhizoma) before starting Rhizoma. If Rhizoma runs successfully on the new node, it connects to other members of the overlay using a seed list passed by the actuator, replicates the overlay status into its knowledge base, and starts the application.

All nodes in Rhizoma's overlay run a failure detector to identify failed nodes. If the coordinator itself fails, a new one is elected and takes over running the constraint program. To handle temporary network partitions and the possible situation of multiple coordinators, each node maintains a "long tail" list of failed nodes that it attempts to re-contact. If a failed node is contacted, the node sets will be merged, a new coordinator elected, and the reasoning process restarted.

5   Implementation

In this section we provide an overview of the current Rhizoma runtime system, as implemented for PlanetLab. Rhizoma is implemented in Python, using the

ECL^{i}PS^e [5] constraint solver (which is written in C). We currently assume the presence of a Python runtime on PlanetLab nodes, although Rhizoma is capable of deploying Python as part of the application, and a port to Windows uses this technique. Rhizoma is built in a framework loosely inspired by the OSGi module system, allowing sensors, actuators, the routing system, CLP engine, and other interfaces to be easily added or removed. The bulk of the runtime is a single-threaded, event-driven process, with the CLP engine (see below) in a separate process that communicates over a local socket.

5.1   Use of ECL^{i}PS^e

Our implementation uses the ECL^{i}PS^e constraint solver, which is based around a Prolog interpreter with extensions for constraint solving, and a plugin architecture for specialized solvers (such as linear or mixed-integer programming). At present, Rhizoma uses only the core CLP functionality of the solver.

We also use ECL^{i}PS^e to hold the knowledge base. Status information about the nodes and the connectivity between them, sensor data and overlay membership are stored in the form of Prolog facts – expressions with constant values that can easily be queried by means of the term and field names. Since ECL^{i}PS^e is based on logic programming, it is easy to unify and fuse data from different sources by specifying inference rules, the equivalent of relational database views. This provides writers of constraint programs with logical data independence from the details of the sensor information and its provenance, and also provides Rhizoma with a fallback path in case of incomplete data.

ECL^{i}PS^e runs on each node in the Rhizoma overlay, but only the coordinator executes the constraint program. This approach is suitable for an environment such as PlanetLab with well-resourced nodes and a uniform runtime environment, and it is useful to have the knowledge base available on each node. We discuss relaxing this condition for heterogeneous overlays in Section 8.

5.2   PlanetLab Sensors and Actuators

Sensors: Our PlanetLab implementation of Rhizoma uses three external information sources: the PlanetLab Central (PLC) database, the S3 monitoring service [22], and CoMon [14]. S3 provides Rhizoma with connectivity data (bandwidth and latency) for any two PlanetLab nodes. The CSV text format of a complete S3 snapshot is about 12MB in size, and is updated every four hours. CoMon provides status information about individual nodes and slices, such as free CPU, CPU speed, one-minute load, DNS failure rates, etc. The text format of a short CoMon node-centric and slice-centric view is about 100kB, and is updated every five minutes. PLC provides information which changes infrequently, such as the list of nodes, slices, and sites.

Rhizoma also measures a subset of the information provided by S3 and CoMon for nodes that are currently in the overlay. This data is more up-to-date, and in many cases more reliable. Inter-node connectivity and latency on Rhizoma's overlay is measured every 30 seconds, and the results are reported back to the coordinator, together with current load on the node as a whole, obtained by querying the local CoTop daemon[2]. Rhizoma's rules privilege more frequently-updated information over older data.

Actuators: Rhizoma uses a single actuator on PlanetLab for acquiring and re-leasing virtual machines. Releasing a VM is straightforward, but adding a new node is a complex process involving acquiring a "ticket" from PLC, contacting the node to create the VM, and using an SSH connection to transfer files and spawn Rhizoma. Failures and timeouts can (and do) occur at any stage, and Rhizoma must deal with these by either giving up on the node and asking the solver to pick another, or retrying. Rhizoma models this process using a state machine, allowing all deployment operations to run concurrently, rather than having to wait for each action to complete or timeout before proceeding.

The actuator is naturally highly platform-specific. An experimental actuator for Windows clusters uses an entirely different mechanism involving the `psexec` remote execution tool, and we expect node deployment on Amazon EC2 to be a more straightforward matter of XML RPC calls.

5.3   Discussion

PlanetLab is, of course, not representative of commercial utility computing, though it shares many common features. PlanetLab is more dynamic (with nodes failing and performance fluctuations), and so has been useful in revealing flaws in earlier versions of Rhizoma. Current and future commercial utility-computing platforms will (one hopes) be more predictable.

Different providers also have different methods of deploying software, some-thing that Rhizoma in the future must handle gracefully. We have started work on a cross-platform Rhizoma, using PlanetLab and clusters, which picks an ap-propriate node deployment mechanism at runtime, but do not present it here.

However, cloud computing is still in its infancy and PlanetLab is perhaps a more interesting case than current providers in aspects other than reliability and deployment. Note that Rhizoma does not need to deal with specific nodes and is just as capable of dealing with generic "classes" of nodes when running. Where PlanetLab offers several hundred distinct, explicitly named nodes, com-mercial providers typically offer a small number of node classes (for example, EC2 currently offers five node types, each available in the US or Europe).

As utility computing evolves, we expect to see many more deployment alter-natives in the commercial space, and increasingly complex pricing models (as we have seen with network connectivity). An open question is whether the external measurement facilities seen in PlanetLab will be duplicated in the commercial space. If not, Rhizoma would have to rely on its own measurements.

---

[2] CoTop is the per-node daemon responsible for collecting information for CoMon.

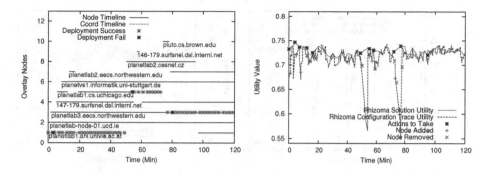

Fig. 4. Short trace deployment timeline and utility

6 Evaluation

Rhizoma is a (rare) example of a system not well served by controlled emulation environments such as FlexLab [18]. Since Rhizoma can potentially choose to deploy on any operational PlanetLab node (there are more than 600), realistic evaluation under FlexLab would require emulating all nodes, a costly operation and not something FlexLab is designed for.

We adopt an approach conceptually similar in some respects. We deploy Rhizoma with PsEPR application requirements (though in this experiment no "real" application) on PlanetLab for about 8 hours to observe its behavior, and log three sources of information:

1. All local measurements taken by Rhizoma, the coordinator's actions, and overlay status. This includes per-node CoTop data, per-link overlay latency, the coordinator's decisions, and successful or failed deployment attempts. This logging is performed by Rhizoma and backhauled to our lab.
2. The results of querying CoMon, S3, and PLC (as Rhizoma does) during the period of the trace. Unlike Rhizoma, we perform this centrally.
3. For this trace, we also run a measurement slice on all usable PlanetLab nodes, which performs fine-grained measurement of inter-node latency. We expect this to resemble the measurements taken by Rhizoma (1), but the extra coverage represents more of a horizon than is available to Rhizoma. This trace is stored on the nodes and transferred to our lab after the experiment.

Unless otherwise stated, our constraints, utility and cost function are as in Figure 1. For space reasons, we focus on one trace; other results are similar.

6.1 Basic Performance Measures

We first consider the initial two hours of the overall trace. Figure 4 shows Rhizoma's behavior during this period. From the timeline in the left graph, we see that Rhizoma ran on a total of ten different nodes, and redeployed 18 times,

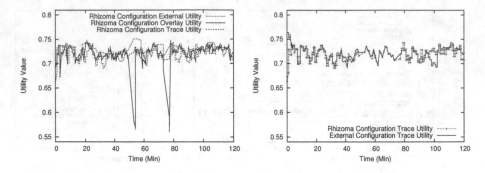

Fig. 5. Measures of utility   **Fig. 6.** Effect of overlay monitoring

with the coordinator changing three times. The right graph explains Rhizoma's behavior; it shows both the utility value and actions taken by Rhizoma to change the overlay. *Configuration utility* depicts the actual performance of the Rhizoma configuration. Whenever Rhizoma detects a significant opportunity to improve the utility, it generates a new deployment plan (shown by points marked *actions to take*) which is then executed as node additions and removals. *Solution utility* shows what the solver expects the utility value to be after taking the actions. As we can see, the configuration follows this expectation but does not exactly meet it due to variance between the sensor data and actual node performance.

The two sharp drops in utility are due to short periods of very high latency (one more than three seconds) observed to the coordinator node. In both cases, Rhizoma responds by redeploying, although the first redeployment attempt fails.

6.2   Different Measures of Utility

Rhizoma attempts to move its configuration to one that maximizes an objective function (utility minus cost), which expresses the cost of deploying on new nodes or vacating old ones. Utility is a measure of the value of a given configuration, but since this is itself a function of machine and network conditions, it can be calculated in different ways.

Figure 5 shows the utility of Rhizoma's actual configuration for the trace duration, as calculated using different information sources. *Overlay utility* uses the information Rhizoma uses for optimization: CoMon and S3 data, plus its own real-time overlay monitoring results – this is Rhizoma's view of itself, and matches the *configuration utility* in Figure 4. *External utility* users only CoMon and S3 data, and excludes Rhizoma's overlay measurements. This is how Rhizoma's performance appears to an observer with access to only the external monitoring information. As CoMon updates every five minutes, and S3 every four hours, the utility value changes less frequently. *Trace utility* is based on CoMon, S3, and our detailed PlanetLab-wide trace data.

As expected, the overlay and trace utilities are almost identical, since Rhizoma is in this case duplicating data collected by the monitoring slice, and both are

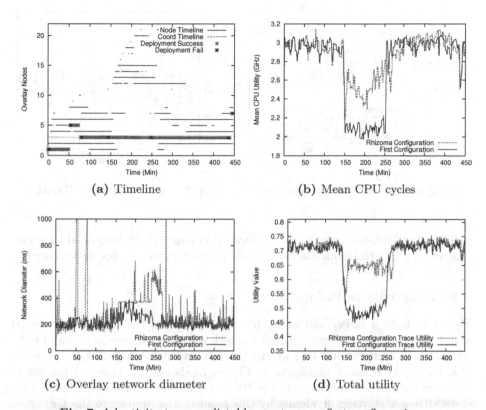

(a) Timeline

(b) Mean CPU cycles

(c) Overlay network diameter

(d) Total utility

Fig. 7. Adaptivity to unpredictable event versus first configuration

reflected by the external utility. However, we also see that the trace utility lags behind the overlay utility, since Rhizoma's monitoring information is updated every 30 seconds, whereas the trace data is updated once per minute (due to the overhead of measuring latency between *all* pairs of PlanetLab nodes).

Furthermore, only Rhizoma observes the sharp spikes in latency to the coordinator. An observer or management system using the external data would not have noticed this problem. Under extreme conditions, this effect may lead to Rhizoma taking actions that would appear detrimental to an external observer.

6.3   Effect of Overlay Monitoring

Rhizoma's resource allocation decision-making is integrated with the application, rather than relegated to a separate management machine. One potential advantage is that Rhizoma can use real-time measurements of application performance in addition to externally-gathered information about PlanetLab.

We use our trace data to simulate Rhizoma without overlay data. Figure 6 shows a somewhat negative result: compared to the full system (*Rhizoma configuration*), the achieved utility of the simulation (*external*) is similar. While we

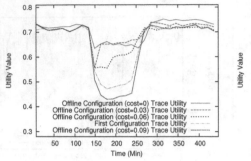 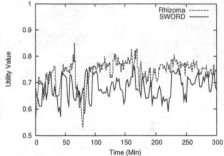

Fig. 8. Sensitivity to cost function   **Fig. 9.** Comparison with SWORD

believe that high-level application information can still be beneficial, it seems that in this case Rhizoma has little to gain from its own overlay measurements.

6.4 Adaptivity to Failure

Figure 7 shows a larger and more dramatic section of the complete trace. At about 150 minutes, a buggy slice on PlanetLab caused a large increase in CPU usage across many nodes. Our utility function in this deployment favors available CPU over network diameter. As Figure 7a shows, this caused Rhizoma to redeploy from nodes in Europe to the US and Asia (the coordinator remains up, since although starting in Vienna by this point it was running in the US).

Figure 7b shows the mean CPU availability on the node set during the event. After an initial drop, Rhizoma's redeployment recovers most CPU capacity in a few minutes, and continues to optimize and adapt as conditions change. By comparison, the mean CPU availability across the nodes in the initial stable configuration has dropped by more than 30%. The tradeoff to enable this is shown in Figure 7c: for the duration of the event, the overlay diameter increases by about 80% as Rhizoma moves out of Europe. After two hours, more CPU capacity becomes available and Rhizoma moves back, reducing the overlay diameter to its former value. The overall effect on utility is shown in Figure 7d.

This reaction to a sudden, transient change in network conditions at these timescales is infeasible with a human in the loop, moreover, it requires no dedicated management infrastructure – indeed, as Figure 7a shows, Rhizoma maintains its service even though *no* node participates in the system for the full duration of the trace. We are unaware of any other system with this property.

6.5 Cost Function Sensitivity

To explore the effect of the cost function on Rhizoma's behavior, we simulated different cost weights (that is, different values of *addCostParam*). Figure 8 plots the simulated utility value (calculated using the trace data), averaged over 30-

minute windows. *First configuration* shows the utility of the first stable configuration achieved by the system, which is equivalent to an infinite cost.

We see that, in general, increasing cost reduces the likelihood that Rhizoma
changes nodes, and thus its ability to adapt to changes in resource availability.
The simulated Rhizoma with cost weight of 0.09 performs worse than the first
configuration because it changed nodes to satisfy the free CPU constraint, but
the nodes that it moved to were also affected, and although the first solution
happens to perform slightly better during the period of 150–250 minutes, the
difference (utility ≈ 0.05) is not great enough to cause it to redeploy. The period
around 200–300 minutes shows a situation where the simulated Rhizoma with
zero cost found a local maximum, as described in Section 4.4.

6.6   Strawman Comparison with SWORD

We next present a comparison with configurations returned by SWORD [12], a
centralized resource discovery tool for PlanetLab. Figure 9 shows a trace of the
utility function for a Rhizoma overlay. During the trace, we also captured the
results of a periodic SWORD query designed to match the Rhizoma constraint
program as closely as possible, and use our PlanetLab-wide measurements to
evaluate the utility function of this hypothetical SWORD-maintained network.

SWORD is not as expressive as Rhizoma, and in particular does not support
network-wide constraints such as diameter, and so we omit these from Rhizoma's constraint program here. Moreover, SWORD cannot consider migration
cost. Rhizoma still performs significantly better, largely due to its optimization
framework. However, the differences in design and goals between the two systems
make this comparison purely illustrative.

6.7   Overhead

Finally, we briefly describe the overhead of using Rhizoma to maintain an application overlay. Rhizoma currently uses link-state routing which, while suitable
for the modest (tens of nodes) overlays we are targeting, would need to be replaced for very large overlays, perhaps with a DHT-like scheme.

In the current implementation, a Rhizoma node in a network of size N must
send about 100 bytes each minute for failure detection, leader election, and local
CoTop information, plus $128 \times N$ bytes for link-state and latency information.
Rhizoma must send this information to all $N - 1$ other nodes. For a 25-node
network, this therefore results in about 1500 bytes/second/node of maintenance
bandwidth, which is roughly comparable with that used in DHTs [17]. Each run
of the ECL^{i}PS^e solver takes around five seconds of CPU time.

7   Related Work

Early examples of autonomous, mobile self-managing distributed systems were
the "worm" programs at Xerox PARC [19], themselves inspired by earlier

Arpanet experiments at BBN. As with Rhizoma, the PARC worms were built on a runtime platform that maintained a dynamic set of machines in the event of failures. Rhizoma adds to this basic idea the use of CLP to express deployment policy, a more sophisticated notion of resource discovery, and an overlay network for routing. We are aware of very little related work in the space of autonomous, self-managing distributed systems since then, outside the malware community. However, the use of knowledge-representation techniques (which arguably includes CLP) in distributed systems is widespread in work on intelligent agents [20], and techniques such as job migration are widely used.

Oppenheimer et al. [13] studied the problem of service placement in Planet-Lab, concluding (among other things) that redeployment over timescales of tens of minutes would benefit such applications. While they target large-scale applications, their findings support our motivation for adaptive small-scale services.

In PlanetLab-like environments, management is generally performed by a separate, central machine, although the management infrastructure itself may be distributed [9,10,11]. The Plush infrastructure [2] is representative of the state-of-the-art in these systems. Plush manages the entire life cycle of a distributed application, provides powerful constructs such as barriers for managing execution phases, performs resource discovery and monitoring, and can react to failures by dynamically acquiring new resources. In addition to its externalized management model and emphasis on application life-cycle, the principal difference between Plush and Rhizoma is that the former's specification of resource requirements is more detailed, precise, and low-level. In contrast, Rhizoma's use of constraints and optimization encourages a higher-level declaration of resource policy.

The resource management approach closest to Rhizoma's use of CLP is Condor's central Matchmaking service [16], widely used in Grid systems. Condor matches exact expressions against specifications in disjunctive normal form, a model similar to the ANSA Trading Service [8]. Rhizoma's specification language is also schema-free, but allows more flexible expression of requirements spanning aggregates of nodes, and objective functions for optimizing configurations.

8   Conclusion and Future Work

We showed that a fully self-managing application can exist on a utility computing infrastructure, dynamically redeploying in response to changes in conditions, according to behavior specified concisely as a constraint optimization program.

A clear area for future work on Rhizoma is in autotuning the cost function based on performance measurements, and feeding application-level metrics back into the optimization process. Also in the near term, we are enhancing Rhizoma to run across multiple clusters and commercial utility computing providers, and to incorporate real pricing information into our cost functions, in addition to continuing to gain experience with using Rhizoma on PlanetLab.

Longer term, the same features of CLP that are well-suited to heterogeneous providers can be used to express additional constraints on which functional components of an application can or should run on which nodes – at present, Rhizoma assumes all nodes in the overlay run the same application software.

The Rhizoma approach is no panacea, and we see a place for both externally and internally managed applications in cloud computing. We have demonstrated the feasibility of the latter approach, and pointed out some of the challenges.

Acknowledgements

We would like to thank the anonymous reviewers for their comments, and Rebecca Isaacs and Simon Peter for many helpful suggestions for how to improve the paper.

References

1. Adams, R.: PsEPR operational notes (May 2008),
   http://www.psepr.org/operational.php
2. Albrecht, J., Braud, R., Dao, D., Topilski, N., Tuttle, C., Snoeren, A.C., Vahdat, A.: Remote control: distributed application configuration, management, and visualization with Plush. In: LISA 2007, pp. 1–19 (2007)
3. Amazon Elastic Compute Cloud, http://aws.amazon.com/ec2
4. Amazon Web Services. Amazon S3 availability event (July 2008),
   http://status.aws.amazon.com/s3-20080720.html
5. Apt, K.R., Wallace, M.G.: Constraint Logic Programming using ECL^{i}PS^e. Cambridge University Press, Cambridge (2007)
6. Brett, P., Knauerhase, R., Bowman, M., Adams, R., Nataraj, A., Sedayao, J., Spindel, M.: A shared global event propagation system to enable next generation distributed services. In: WORLDS 2004 (December 2004)
7. Delaet, T., Anderson, P., Joosen, W.: Managing real-world system configurations with constraints. In: ICN 2008 (April 2008)
8. Deschrevel, J.-P.: The ANSA model for trading and federation. Architecture Report APM.1005.1, Architecture Projects Management Limited (July 1993)
9. Huebsch, R.: PlanetLab application manager (November 2005),
   http://appmanager.berkeley.intel-research.net/
10. Isdal, T., Anderson, T., Krishnamurthy, A., Lazowska, E.: Planetary scale control plane (August 2007),
    http://www.cs.washington.edu/research/networking/cplane/
11. Liang, J., Ko, S.Y., Gupta, I., Nahrstadt, K.: MON: On-demand overlays for distributed system management. In: WORLDS 2005, pp. 13–18 (2005)
12. Oppenheimer, D., Albrecht, J., Patterson, D., Vahdat, A.: Distributed resource discovery on PlanetLab with SWORD. In: WORLDS 2004 (December 2004)
13. Oppenheimer, D., Chun, B., Patterson, D.A., Snoeren, A., Vahdat, A.: Service placement in a shared wide-area platform. In: USENIX 2006 (June 2006)
14. Park, K., Pai, V.S.: CoMon: a mostly-scalable monitoring system for PlanetLab. SIGOPS Oper. Syst. Rev. 40(1) (2006)
15. Peterson, L., Culler, D., Anderson, T., Roscoe, T.: A Blueprint for Introducing Disruptive Technology into the Internet. In: HotNets-I (October 2002)
16. Raman, R., Livny, M., Solomon, M.: Matchmaking: Distributed resource management for high throughput computing. In: HPDC7 (July 1998)
17. Rhea, S., Geels, D., Roscoe, T., Kubiatowicz, J.: Handling Churn in a DHT. In: USENIX 2004 (June 2004)

18. Ricci, R., Duerig, J., Sanaga, P., Gebhardt, D., Hibler, M., Atkinson, K., Zhang, J., Kasera, S., Lepreau, J.: The Flexlab approach to realistic evaluation of networked systems. In: NSDI 2007 (April 2007)
19. Shoch, J.F., Hupp, J.A.: The "worm" programs — early experience with a distributed computation. Commun. ACM 25(3), 172–180 (1982)
20. Sycara, K., Decker, K., Pannu, A., Williamson, M., Zeng, D.: Distributed intelligent agents. IEEE Expert (December 1996)
21. Wallace, M.: Constraint programming. In: Liebowitz, J. (ed.) The Handbook of Applied Expert Systems. CRC Press, Boca Raton (1997)
22. Yalagandula, P., Sharma, P., Banerjee, S., Basu, S., Lee, S.-J.: S3: a scalable sensing service for monitoring large networked systems. In: INM 2006 (2006)
23. Yin, Q., Cappos, J., Baumann, A., Roscoe, T.: Dependable self-hosting distributed systems using constraints. In: HotDep 2008 (December 2008)

How to Keep Your Head above Water While Detecting Errors

Ignacio Laguna, Fahad A. Arshad, David M. Grothe, and Saurabh Bagchi

Dependable Computing Systems Lab (DCSL)
School of Electrical and Computer Engineering, Purdue University
{ilaguna,faarshad,dgrothe,sbagchi}@purdue.edu

Abstract. Today's distributed systems need runtime error detection to catch errors arising from software bugs, hardware errors, or unexpected operating conditions. A prominent class of error detection techniques operates in a stateful manner, i.e., it keeps track of the state of the application being monitored and then matches state-based rules. Large-scale distributed applications generate a high volume of messages that can overwhelm the capacity of a stateful detection system. An existing approach to handle this is to randomly sample the messages and process a subset. However, this approach, leads to non-determinism with respect to the detection system's view of what state the application is in. This in turn leads to degradation in the quality of detection. We present an *intelligent sampling* algorithm and a *Hidden Markov Model (HMM)-based* algorithm to select the messages that the detection system processes and determine the application states such that the non-determinism is minimized. We also present a mechanism for selectively triggering computationally intensive rules based on a light-weight mechanism to determine if the rule is likely to be flagged. We demonstrate the techniques in a detection system called *Monitor* applied to a J2EE multi-tier application. We empirically evaluate the performance of Monitor under different load conditions and error scenarios and compare it to a previous system called Pinpoint.

Keywords: Stateful error detection, High throughput distributed applications, J2EE multi-tier systems, Intelligent sampling, Hidden Markov Model.

1 Introduction

1.1 Motivation

Increased deployment of high-speed computer networks has made distributed applications ubiquitous in today's connected world. Many of these distributed applications provide critical functionality with real-time requirements. These require online error detection functionality at the application level.

Error detection can be classified as *stateless* or *stateful* detection. In the former, detection is done on individual messages by matching certain characteristics of the message, for example, finding specific signatures in the payload of network packets. A more powerful approach is stateful error detection, in which the error detection

J.M. Bacon and B.F. Cooper (Eds.): Middleware 2009, LNCS 5896, pp. 205–225, 2009.

system builds up knowledge of the application state by collecting information from multiple application messages. The stateful error detection system then matches behavior-based rules, based on the application's state rather than on instantaneous information. For simplicity, we refer to stateful error detection as just *detection* in this paper.

Stateful detection is looked upon as a powerful mechanism for building dependable distributed systems [1][10]. However, scaling a stateful detection system with increasing rate of messages is a challenge. The increasing rate may happen due to a greater number of application components or increasing load from existing components. The stress on the detection system is due to the increased processing load of tracking the application state and performing rule matching. The rules can be heavy-duty and can impose large overhead for matching. Thus the stateful detection system has to be designed such that the resource usage, primarily computation and memory, is minimized. Simply throwing more hardware at the problem is not enough because applications also scale up demanding more from the detection system.

In prior work, we have presented *Monitor* [10] which provides stateful detection by observing the messages exchanged between application components. Monitor has a breaking point in terms of the rate of messages it has to process. Beyond this breaking point, there is a sharp drop in accuracy or rise in latency (i.e., the time spent in rule matching) due to an overload caused by the high incoming rate of messages. All detection systems that perform stateful detection are expected to have such a breaking point, though the rate of messages at which each system breaks will be different. For example, the stateful network intrusion detection system (NIDS) Snort running on a general-purpose CPU can process traffic up to 500 Mbps [15]. For Monitor, we have observed that the breaking point on a standard Linux box is around 100 packets/sec [10].

We have shown in previous work [11] that we can reduce the processing load of a stateful detection system by randomly sampling the incoming messages. The load per unit time in a detection system is given by the *incoming message rate × processing overhead per message*. Thus, processing only a subset of messages by sampling them reduces the overall load. However, sampling introduces *non-determinism* in the detection system. In sampling mode, messages are either sampled (and processed) or dropped. When a message is dropped, the detection system loses track of which state the application is in. This causes inaccuracies in selecting the rules to match because the rules are based on the application state (and the observed message). This leads to lower quality of detection, as measured by accuracy (the fraction of actual errors that is detected) and precision (the complement of false alarms).

1.2 Our Contributions

— **Intelligent Sampling:** We propose an intelligent sampling technique to reduce the non-determinism caused by sampling in stateful detection systems. This technique is based on the observation that in an application's Finite State Machine (FSM), a message type can be seen as a state transition in multiple states. If the system selectively samples and processes the messages with a high discriminating property, i.e., ones that can narrow down which state the application is in, this would limit the non-determinism.

— **Probabilistic State Determination:** Even with the proper selection of messages, there is remaining non-determinism about the application state. We propose a Hidden Markov Model (HMM)-based technique to estimate the likelihood of the different application states, given an observed sequence of messages, and perform rule matching for only the more likely states.

— **Efficient Just-in-Time Rule Matching:** We propose a technique for selectively matching computationally expensive rules. These rules are matched only when evidence of an imminent error is observed. Instability in the system, which is detected through a light-weight mechanism, is taken as evidence of such an imminent error.

We show that the three techniques make Monitor scale to an application with a high load, with only a small degradation in detection quality.

For the evaluation, we use a J2EE multi-tier application, the Duke's Bank application [12], running on Glassfish [13]. We inject errors in pairs of the combination (*component, method*), where 'component' can be a Java Server Page (JSP), a servlet, or an Enterprise Java Bean (EJB), and 'method' is a function call in the component. The injected errors can cause failures in the web interaction in which this combination is touched, for example, by delaying the completion of the web interaction or by prematurely terminating a web interaction without the expected response to the user. Our comparison points are Pinpoint [7] for detecting anomalies in the structure of web interactions and Monitor with random sampling [11].

The rest of the paper is organized as follows. In Section 2 we present background material on stateful detection. In Sections 3 and 4, we present the intelligent sampling and HMM-based application state estimation algorithms. In Section 5 and 6 we explain our experimental testbed, experiments and results for the intelligent sampling and HHM-based techniques. In Section 7 we present our efficient rule matching technique. In Section 8 we review related work and in Section 9 we present the conclusions, limitations of this work and future directions.

2 Background

In previous work we developed Monitor, a framework for online error detection in distributed applications [10]. Online implies the detection happens when the application is executing. Monitor observes the messages exchanged between the application components and thereby performs error detection under the principle of *black-box instrumentation*, i.e., the application does not have to be changed to allow Monitor to detect errors.

2.1 Fault Model

Monitor can detect any error that manifests itself as a deviation from the application's model and expected behavior that is given to the Monitor as input—an FSM and a set of application-level behavior-based rules. The FSM can be generated from a human-specified description (e.g., a protocol specification), or from analysis of application observations (e.g., function call traces, as done here). We define a *web interaction* as the set of inter-component messages that are caused by one user request. The end point of the interaction is marked by the response back to the user. In the context of component-based web applications, an FSM is used to pinpoint deviations in the structure of the observed web interactions, while rules are used to determine deviations from the expected normal behavior of application's components.

2.2 Stateful Detection

Monitor architecture consists of three primary components, as shown in **Fig. 1**: the PacketCapturer engine, the StateMaintainer engine, and the Rule-Matching engine. The PacketCapturer engine is in charge of capturing the messages exchanged between the application components, which can be done through middleware forwarding (as done here) or through network assist (such as, port forwarding or using a broadcast medium). When Monitor receives a rate of incoming messages close to the maximum rate that it can handle, the PacketCapturer is responsible for activating a sampling mechanism to reduce the workload for state transition and rule matching [11].

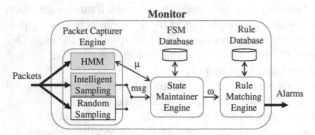

An incoming message into Monitor may be *sampled*, meaning, it will be processed (by performing a state transition and matching rules based on that message), or it may be *dropped*. In random sampling, messages are sampled randomly without looking at the type or content of the message. As shown in [10],

Fig. 1. Monitor architecture. One-sided and two-sided arrows show unidirectional and bidirectional flow of information re-. spectively. Gray boxes indicate new components added to Monitor in this work.

under non-sampling conditions, Monitor's accuracy and precision suffer when the rate of incoming messages goes above a particular point which is denoted as R_{th}. Therefore, random sampling is activated at any rate $R > R_{th}$, in which Monitor drops messages uniformly.

Sampled messages are passed to the StateMaintainer engine to perform state transitions according to the FSM. For each received message, the StateMaintainer engine is in charge of determining which states the application may be in. This is called the *state vector* and represented by ω. Here, the *events* are messages from the application that are observed at Monitor. When Monitor is in non-sampling mode, the state vector typically contains only one state ($|\omega|=1$) since Monitor has an almost-complete view of the events generated in the application—some states that do not involve externally visible messages will not be revealed to Monitor, thus ω will not always reflect the current state of the application. However, when sampling mode is activated, Monitor loses track of the actual state of the application since it is not observing every event generated by the application. Then, ω becomes a set of the possible states in which the application *can* be in. Once a message m is sampled, ω is updated. This is performed by observing (in the FSM) the new state (or states) to where the application could have moved, from each state in ω given m. We define this mechanism as *pruning* the state vector and it is explained in further detail in Section 3.1. Typically, when ω is pruned, its size is reduced. The RuleMatching engine is responsible for matching rules associated with the state(s) in ω. In previous work [10] we developed a syntax for rule specification for message-based applications. We now extend the syntax to be more flexible so that it can be applied more naturally to RPC-style component-based applications. For detecting performance problems in distributed applications, we use a set of *temporal rules* that characterize allowable response time of subcomponents, i.e., the lower bound and upper bound for response time of each subcomponent. We consider that the issue of how to generate appropriate rules is outside the scope of this paper. If RuleMatching engine determines that the application does not satisfy a rule, we say the rule is flagged, implying the error is detected.

A challenge in Monitor, when performing random sampling, is to maintain high levels of accuracy and precision even while dropping messages. Due to the randomness of the sampling approach proposed in [11], we obtained a maximum accuracy of 0.7 when detecting failures in TRAM, a reliable multicast protocol. Systems running critical services often demand higher levels of accuracy while having low detection latency.

2.3 Building FSM from Traces

We build an FSM for the Duke's Bank Application from traces when the application is exercised with a given workload. A state S_i in the FSM is defined as a tuple (*component, method*). In the rest of the paper we use the term *subcomponent* to denote the tuple (*component, method*). This level of granularity allows Monitor to pinpoint performance problems or errors in particular methods, rather than only in components. A state change is caused by a *call* or *return* event between two subcomponents. We create the FSM by imposing a workload on the application which consists of as nearly an exhaustive list of transactions supported in the application as possible. We cannot claim this *is* exhaustive since it is manually done and no rigorous mechanism is used to guarantee completeness. When we generate application traces, no error injection is performed and we assume that design faults in the application, if any, are not activated, an assumption made in many learning-based detection systems [4][7][16]. For large-scale distributed applications, the traces may grow large, but this does not pose a significant problem because the process is offline and traces can be stored on tertiary storage and parts of them can be cached in an as-needed basis.

3   Handling High Streaming Rates: Intelligent Sampling

3.1   Sampling in Monitor

With increasing incoming message rates, Monitor opts for sampling (and dropping) messages to maintain acceptable detection latency. When a message is dropped, Monitor cannot determine the correct application state, resulting in an undesirable condition, which we call *state non-determinism*. As an example, consider an FSM fragment in **Fig. 2**. Suppose that the application is in state S_A at time t_1, and that a message is dropped. From the FSM, Monitor determines that the application can be in state S_B or state S_C, so the state vector $\omega = \{S_B, S_C\}$. If another message is dropped at time t_2, ω grows to $\{S_B, S_D, S_E, S_F\}$.

Monitor's `RuleMatching` engine matches rules for all the states in ω. To avoid matching rules in incorrect states, Monitor prunes invalid states from the state vector once a message is sampled. For example, if the current state vector is $\{S_B, S_C\}$ and message m_2 is sampled, the state vector is reduced to $\{S_B\}$ because this is the only possible transition from any state in the state vector given the event m_2, assuming that the sampled message is not erroneous. The HMM-based algorithm (Section 4) handles the case when the sampled message may be erroneous.

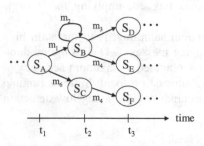

Fig. 2. A fragment of a Finite State Machine (FSM) to demonstrate non-determinism introduced by sampling

A large state vector increases the computational cost since a larger number of potentially expensive rules have to be matched leading to high detection latency. For example, an expensive rule we encounter in practice is checking consistency of multiple database tables. Worse, a large and inaccurate state vector degrades the quality of detection through an increase in false alarms and missed alarms. Our goal is then to keep the state vector size bounded so that the detection latency does not exceed a threshold (L_{th}), and the detection quality stays acceptable.

3.2 Intelligent Sampling Approach

We hypothesize that sampling based on some inherent property of messages from the FSM can lead to a reduction in the state vector size when pruning is performed. We have observed that messages in the application have different properties with respect to the different transitions in the FSM that they appear in. For example, some messages can appear in multiple transitions while others appear in only one. Suppose for example that state vector $\omega = \{S_B, S_C\}$ at time t_2 following **Fig. 2**. If m_3 is sampled, `StateMaintainer` would prune ω to $\{S_D\}$, while if m_4 is sampled, ω would be pruned to $\{S_E, S_F\}$. Thus, the fact that m_3 appears in one transition while m_4 appears in two ones, makes a difference to the resulting state vector. We say therefore that m_3 has a more desirable property than m_4 in terms of sampling.

We use an *intelligent sampling* approach whereby all incoming messages are *observed*, and a subset of messages with a desirable property is *sampled*; the others are *dropped*. A message is observed by determining its type at the application level, which determines the transition in the FSM. For our application, type is given by the combination (component, method, call|return). Let us define *discriminative size* d_m as the number of times a message m appears in a state transition to different states in the FSM. In the intelligent sampling approach, a message with a small d_m is more likely to be sampled. The discriminative sizes of all messages can be determined by considering the message labels on edges that are incoming into the states of the FSM.

3.3 Intelligent Sampling Algorithm

To guarantee that the rate of messages processed by Monitor is less than R_{th}, it samples n messages in a window of m messages, where $n < m$ and the fraction n/m is determined by the incoming message rate. Now, given a window of m messages, which particular messages should Monitor sample? Ideally, Monitor should wait for n messages with a discriminative size less than a particular threshold d_{th}. However, since we do not know in advance what the discriminative sizes of messages in the future will be, Monitor could end up with no sampled messages at all by the end of the window. To address this, Monitor tracks the number of messages seen in the window and the number of messages already sampled in counters *numMsgs* and *num-Sampled* respectively. If Monitor reaches a point where the number of remaining messages in the window ($m - numMsgs$) is equal to the number of messages that it still needs to sample ($n - numSampled$) all the remaining messages ($m - numMsgs$) are sampled without looking at their discriminative sizes. We call this point the *last resort point*. Before reaching the last resort point, Monitor samples only those messages with discriminative sizes less than d_{th}; after that, it samples all remaining messages in the window. Because of lack of space we omit the pseudocode of the intelligent sampling algorithm. The interested reader can find the pseudocode in [22].

4 Reducing Non-determinism: HMM-Based State Vector Reduction

There are two remaining problems when pruning the state vector with the intelligent sampling approach. First, when a message is sampled and the state vector is pruned, the size of the new state vector can still be large making detection costly and inaccurate. This situation arises if the FSM has a large number of states and the FSM is highly connected, or if highly discriminative messages are not seen in a window. The second disadvantage is that if the sampled message is *incorrect*, Monitor can end up with an incorrect state vector—a state vector that does not contain the actual application's state. An incorrect message is one that is valid according to the FSM, but is incorrect given the current state. For example, in **Fig. 2**, if state vector $\omega = \{S_B, S_C\}$, only messages m_2, m_3, and m_4 are correct messages. Incorrect messages can be seen due to a buggy component, e.g., a component that makes an unexpected call in an error condition. To overcome these difficulties, we propose the use of a Hidden Markov Model to determine probabilistically the current application state.

4.1 Hidden Markov Model

A Hidden Markov Model (HMM) is an extension of a Markov Model where the states in the model are not observable. In a particular state, an outcome, which is observable, is generated according to an associated probability distribution.

The main challenge of Monitor, when handling non-determinism, is to determine the correct state of the application when only a subset of messages is sampled. This phenomenon can be modeled with an HMM because the correct state of the application is hidden from Monitor while the messages are observable. Therefore, we use an HMM to determine the probability of the application being in each of its states.

An HMM is characterized by the set of states, a set of observation symbols, the state transition probability distribution A, the observation probability distribution B (given a state i, what is the probability of observation j), and the initial state probability distribution π. We use $\lambda = (A, B, \pi)$ as a compact notation for the HMM.

We used the Baum-Welch algorithm [24] to estimate HMM parameters to model the Duke's Bank application. The HMM is trained with the same set of traces used to build the application FSM. More details about the estimation of the HMM parameters can be found in [22].

4.2 Algorithm for Reducing the State Vector Using HMM

We have implemented the `ReduceStateVector` algorithm (**Fig. 3**) for reducing the state vector using an HMM. When Monitor samples a message, it asks the HMM for the k most probable application states. Monitor then intersects the previous state vector with the set of k most probable states. Then an updated state vector is computed from the FSM using pruning (as defined in Section 2.2), i.e., by asking the FSM that given the set of states from the intersection and the sampled message, what are the possible next states.

The HMM is implemented in Monitor in the frontend thread, the `PacketCapturer`. Thus, the HMM observes all messages since they are needed to build complete sequences of observations.

The `ReduceStateVector` algorithm consists of three steps:

— **Step 1**: Calculate what is the probability that, after seeing a sequence of messages O, the application is in each of the possible states $s_1, \ldots s_N$? This is expressed as $P(q_t = s_i \mid O, \lambda)$. This step produces a vector of probabilities μ_t (lines 1–3).

— **Step 2**: Sort the vector μ_t by the probability values. This produces a new vector of probabilities α_t (line 4).

ReduceStateVector computes a new state vector based on: the HMM, an observation sequence and a previous state vector.

Input: λ: Hidden Markov Model; O: observation sequence $O = \{O_1, O_2, \ldots, O_t\}$; ω_t: application' state vector at time t; k: Filtering criteria for the number of probabilities estimated by the HMM.

Output: ω_{t+1}

Variables: μ_t: probability vector $\mu_t = \{p_1, p_2, \ldots, p_N\}$, where $p_i = P(q_t = s_i \mid O, \lambda)$, for all i in $S = \{s_1, \ldots, s_N\}$ (the states in the FSM) and q_t is the state at time t; α_t: sorted μ_t.

ReduceStateVector (λ, O, ω_t, k):
1. $\mu_t \leftarrow \varnothing$
2. **For** each i in S
3.   **Add** $P(q_t = s_i \mid O, \lambda)$ to μ_t
4. $\alpha_t \leftarrow sort(\mu_t)$ by p_i
5. $I \leftarrow \varnothing$
6. $I \leftarrow \omega_t \cap \alpha_t[1 \ldots k]$
7. **if** ($I = \varnothing$) **then**
8. $\omega_{t+1} \leftarrow \omega_t \cup \alpha_t[1 \ldots k]$
9. **else**
10. $\omega_{t+1} \leftarrow I$
11. **return** ω_{t+1}

Fig. 3. Pseudocode for reducing state vector using HMM's estimate of probability of each application state

— **Step 3**: Compute a new state vector ω_{t+1} as the intersection of the current state vector ω_t and the top k elements in α_t. By using a small k, Monitor is able to reduce the state vector to few states. If the intersection of ω_t and α_t is null, we take the union of the two sets. This is a safe choice because having the intersection of ω_t and α_t equal to null implies that either the HMM or ω_t is incorrect. We acknowledge that if both HMM and state vector are incorrect, this scheme will not work. However, proper training of the HMM makes a concurrent error highly unlikely, and one that never occurred in any of our experiments. This step is executed in lines 5-11.

Fig. 4 shows points in time when the algorithm is invoked in `StateMaintainer`. FSMLookup(ω, n) calculates the new state vector from ω given that n consecutive messages have been dropped (as explained in Section 3.1).

Time	Operations in Monitor
:	(Sampled messages. Last sampled message at time t_{10}.)
t_{11}	Dropped message
	$\omega_{t10} \leftarrow$ ReduceStateVector(λ, O, ω_{t10}, k)
	$\omega_{t11} \leftarrow$ FSMLookup(ω_{t10} , 1 dropped message)
:	(Dropped messages. Last dropped message at time t_{15}.)
t_{16}	m_{16} is sampled
	$\omega_{t15} \leftarrow$ ReduceStateVector(λ, O, ω_{t15}, k)
	ω_{t16} is pruned from ω_{t15} given m_{16}

Fig. 4. Example of points in time when the ReduceStateVector algorithm is invoked

The time complexity of the algorithm is proportional to the time in computing $P(q_t = s_i | O, \lambda)$ for all the states, the time to sort the array μ_t, and the time to compute the intersection of ω_t and the top k elements in α_t. The vector μ_t can be computed in time $O(N^3 T)$, where N is the number of states in the HMM (and the FSM), and T is the length of the observation sequence O. Sorting μ_t can be performed in $O(N \log N)$, and the intersection of ω_t and $\alpha_t[1...k]$ can be performed in O(Nk). Hence, the overall time complexity is $O(N^3 T)$.

5 Experimental Testbed

5.1 J2EE Application and Web Users Emulator

We use the J2EE Duke's Bank Application [12] running on Glassfish v2 [13] as our experimental testbed. Glassfish has a package called `CallFlow` that provides a central function for Monitor—a unique ID is assigned to each web interaction. It also provides caller and called component and methods, without needing any application change.

To evaluate our solutions in diverse scenarios such as high user request rates and multiple types of workload, we developed *WebStressor*, a web interactions emulator. WebStressor takes different traces and replays them by sending each message to the tested detection systems. Each trace contains sequences of web interactions that would be seen in `CallFlow` when a user of Duke's Bank application is executing multiple operations. WebStressor also has error injection capabilities which are explained in Section 6.3.

5.2 Pinpoint Implementation

We implemented Pinpoint [7] that proposes an approach for tracing paths through multiple components, triggered by user requests. A Probabilistic Context Free Grammar (PCFG) is used to model normal path behavior and to detect anomalies whenever a path's structure does not fit the PCFG. A PCFG has productions represented in Chomsky Normal Form (CNF) and each production is assigned a probability after a training phase. Pinpoint-PCFG is trained using the same traces from Duke's Bank that are used to build the FSM and to train the HMM. We call this implementation Pinpoint-PCFG in the paper.

6 Experiments and Results

In this section we report experiments to evaluate the performance of Monitor and compare it with that of the Pinpoint-PCFG algorithm. When we refer to Monitor, we mean baseline Monitor [10], with the addition of two techniques intelligent sampling and HMM. The machines used have 4 processors, each an Intel Xeon 3.4 GHz with 1024 MB of memory and 1024 KB of L1 cache. All experiments are run with exclusive access to the machines. We show 95% confidence intervals for some representative plots, but not all, to keep the graphs readable.

6.1 Benefits of Intelligent Sampling

We run experiments to verify our hypothesis that intelligent sampling helps in reducing the size of the state vector ω. For this, we run WebStressor with a fixed moderate user load (8 concurrent users) and with no error injection. When a message is dropped, ω increases or stays constant. When a message is sampled, ω is pruned and it is passed to the RuleMatching engine.

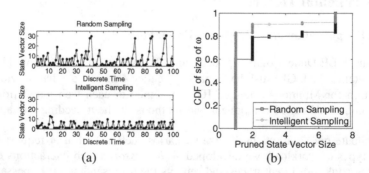

Fig. 5. Performance results when comparing Monitor random sampling and intelligent sampling. (a) Sampled values of state vector ω for Monitor with random and intelligent sampling; (b) CDF for the pruned state vector ω with random and intelligent sampling.

In each mode, we obtained 3337 sample values of ω's size. **Fig. 5**(a) shows 100 snapshots of these values for Random Sampling (RS) and Intelligent Sampling (IS) modes. Here the size of ω is shown for every message arriving at Monitor. The high-peaks pattern that we observe in RS mode is due to the deficiency of random sampling in selecting messages with small discriminative size. In contrast we do not observe this pattern in IS mode, because it preferentially samples the discriminating messages, producing smaller pruned state vectors ω.

Next, we measure ω's size only *after* it is pruned. Recall that the pruned state vector ω is the one used for rule instantiation and matching. Hence, it is at this point that it is critical to have a small ω. **Fig. 5**(b) shows the cumulative distribution function (CDF) for the observed values of ω's size. In IS mode, ω's size of 1 has a higher frequency of occurrence (about 83%) than in RS mode (60%). In contrast, all ω's size values > 1 have higher frequency of occurrence in RS than in IS. After being pruned, ω can have a maximum size of 7. This is due to the nature of Duke's Bank application in which the maximum discriminative size of a message is 7.

6.2 Definition of Performance Metrics

We introduce the metrics that we use to evaluate detection quality. Let W denote the entire set of web interactions generated in the application in one experimental run. For W, we collect the following variables, I: out of W, the web interactions where faults were injected; D: out of W, the web interactions in which Monitor detected a failure; C: out of I, the web interactions in which Monitor detected a failure (these are the correct detections).

Based on these variables, we calculate two metrics:

$$Accuracy = |C| / |I|; \ Precision = |C| / |D|$$

Accuracy expresses how well the detection system is able to identify the web interactions in which problems occurred, while precision is a measure of the inverse of false alarms in the system.

Another performance metric is the latency of detection. Let T_i denote the time when a fault is injected and T_d the time when the failure caused by the injected fault is detected by the detection system. We define *detection latency* as $T_d - T_i$. When a delay δ is injected (emulating a performance problem in a component of the application), δ is subtracted from the total time since it represents only a characteristic of the injected fault and not the quality of the detection system.

6.3 Error Injection Model

Errors are injected by WebStressor at runtime when mimicking concurrent users. This results in errors in the application traces which are fed to the detection systems. We inject four kinds of errors that occur in real operating scenarios:

1. *Response delay*: a delay d is selected randomly between 100 msec and 500 msec, and is injected in a particular subcomponent. This error simulates subcomponent's response delays due to performance problems.

2. *Null Call:* a called subcomponent is never executed. This error terminates the web interaction prematurely and the client receives a generic error report, e.g., HTTP 500 internal server error.
3. *Runtime Exception*: an undeclared exception, or a declared exception that is not masked by the application, is thrown. As in null calls, the web interaction is terminated prematurely and the client receives an error report.
4. *Incorrect Message Sequences:* an error that occurs for which there is an exception handler that invokes an error handling sequence. This sequence changes the normal structure of the web interaction. We emulate this by replacing the calls and returns in N consecutive subcomponents. The value of N is selected randomly between 1 and 5.

Of these, Pinpoint-PCFG cannot detect response delay errors. We perform comparative evaluation of Monitor with Pinpoint-PCFG for the other error types.

6.4 Detecting Performance Problems

We inject delays to simulate performance problems in the set of 5 subcomponents listed in **Table 1**. A category of errors that is difficult to detect is transient errors—those that are caused by unpredictable random events and that are difficult to reproduce and isolate. We want to test Monitor in detecting this category of errors. In order to mimic this scenario in our injection strategy, we inject delays only 20% of the time a subcomponent is touched in a web interaction.

Before running the experiment, we determine the best set of parameter values in Monitor. We generate ROC (Receiver Operating Characteristic) curves by varying their configuration parameters (i.e., number of rules) and the imposed load of users to the application. Then, we select the operational point as the one closest to the ideal point (0, 1); in case of a tie, we use the point with the better precision. Because of lack of space we omit the ROC curves; however, the reader can refer to [22] for these.

Table 1. List of subcomponents (component, method) in which performance delays are injected

Name	Method	Type of Component
AccountControllerBean	createNamedQuery	EJB
TxControllerBean	deposit	EJB
/template/banner.jsp	JspServlet.service	servlet
/bank/accountList.faces	FacesServlet.service	servlet
/logon.jsp	JspServlet.service	servlet

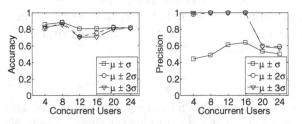

Fig. 6. Accuracy and precision of Monitor in detecting performance delays for three type of rules

For the performance delay rules, first, we measure the average (μ) and standard deviation (σ) of the response time from the components in the application during the training phase. We then create rules with the following thresholds for response times in each component: $\mu \pm \sigma$, $\mu \pm 2\sigma$ and $\mu \pm 3\sigma$.

Fig. 6 shows the results of this experiment. We observe that using $\mu \pm 2\sigma$ provides the best combination of accuracy and precision. For rule types $\mu \pm \sigma$ and $\mu \pm 2\sigma$ we observe a decrease in accuracy of about 10% as concurrent users are increased from 4 to 16, and an increase in the same order of magnitude as users are increased to 24. The reason for the increase in accuracy is due to the precision rate that decreases rapidly after 16 concurrent users. Because of the large rate of false alarms generated after this point, accuracy is increased as a trade-off.

We also evaluate the performance of random and intelligent sampling in detecting performance delays. For this experiment, we use similar definitions for accuracy and precision as in the previous experiments, but we change the granularity of detection from web interactions to individual subcomponents. Detection at the level of a sub-component is helpful in diagnosis—finding the root cause of the problem—since it helps in pinpointing suspect subcomponents. The results are shown in **Fig. 7**(f). We observe that accuracy and precision are higher for IS for most loads (4–16 concurrent users). Although, for high loads (20 and 24 users), random and intelligent sampling exhibit almost the same (poor) performance.

6.5 Detecting Anomalous Web Interactions

We evaluate Monitor's performance in detecting anomalous web interactions by injecting null calls, runtime exceptions and incorrect message sequences. We also evaluate Pinpoint-PCFG's performance here.

Monitor detects anomalous web interactions at the StateMaintainer. If an event is unexpected according to the current state in Monitor's state vector, an error is flagged. This avoids the need for explicit rules for this type of detection. For the Duke's Bank application, if the correct state is S_c and the state vector after a message is sampled and pruning is completed, is ω, then we find empirically that in all cases $S_c \in \omega$. Thus, a detection happens at Monitor only if the message is incorrect, i.e., there is an actual fault. This gives a precision value of 1 for Monitor's detection of anomalous web interactions in Duke's Bank.

We empirically determine the best value of parameter k for the HMM-based state vector reduction algorithm. **Fig. 7**(a) shows Monitor running with different values of k while we inject anomalous web interactions. Parameter $k=0$ represents Monitor running without HMM. We observe that, with no HMM, in both low and high loads, accuracy is very low (about 0.4). Since Monitor with $k > 0$ performs better than with $k = 0$, this validates our design choice of using an HMM. In high load, two conditions cause Monitor to have a decreasing accuracy with increasing k. Monitor samples less often leading to an increase in the size of ω. With large k, few states get pruned and if the observed erroneous message is possible in any of the remaining states of ω, the error is not detected. Second, when the erroneous message may not be sampled, the HMM is particularly important. Increasing k effectively reduces the impact of the HMM, since even states with low probabilities given by the HMM are considered.

For the remaining experiments, we use $k=1$ as it allows Monitor to have the best accuracy in both low and high load. We determine the best configuration parameter setting for Pinpoint-PCFG to get ROC curves under low and high loads. Pinpoint-PCFG's ROC curves can be found in [22].

Fig. 7(b)–(c) show the results for accuracy and precision of Monitor and Pinpoint-PCFG. We observe that on average, Monitor's accuracy is comparable to that of Pinpoint-PCFG. In Monitor, accuracy decreases for higher loads due to dropping more messages in a sampling widow. As the load increases, Pinpoint-PCFG maintains a high accuracy because it is not dropping messages—messages are being enqueued for eventual processing. However its latency of detection suffers significantly in high loads—it is in the order of seconds (**Fig. 7**(e)) while in Monitor it is in the order of milliseconds (**Fig. 7**(d)).

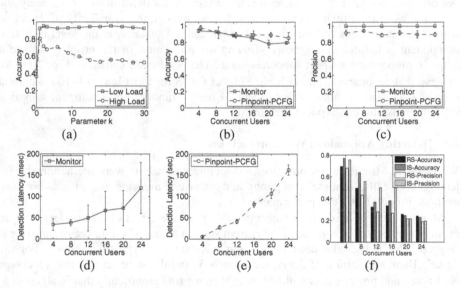

Fig. 7. Performance results for Monitor and Pinpoint when detecting anomalous web interactions. (a) Accuracy in Monitor when varying parameter k in the HMM-based state vector reduction algorithm; (b)–(c) Accuracy and precision for Monitor and Pinpoint-PCFG; (d)–(e)Detection latency for Monitor and Pinpoint-PCFG; (f) Accuracy and Precision for Random Sampling and Intelligent Sampling for performance delay errors.

Table 2. Memory consumption for the compared systems

	Average Memory Usage (MB)	
	Virtual Memory	Memory in RAM
Monitor	282.27	25.53
Pinpoint-PCFG	933.56	696.06

We observe the robustness of Pinpoint-PCFG to false positives as it maintains on average almost the same precision (0.9) with increasing number of users. However, the precision in Pinpoint-PCFG is lower than that in Monitor of 1.0.

The high detection latency in Pinpoint-PCFG is due to the fact that the parsing algorithm in the PCFG has time complexity $O(L^3)$ and space complexity $O(RL^2)$, where R is the number of rules in the grammar and L is the size of a web interaction. In the

Duke's Bank application we observe that the maximum length of a web interaction is 256 messages, and the weighted average size is 70. Previous work [14] has shown that the time to parse sentences of length 40 can be 120 seconds even with optimized parameters. Moreover, in Pinpoint-PCFG, error detection can only be performed after the end of web interactions which also explains longer detection latencies than in Monitor. Another cause of the high latency in Pinpoint-PCFG is the large amount of virtual memory that the process takes (933.56 MB for a load of 24 concurrent users as shown in **Table 2**). This makes the Pinpoint-PCFG process thrash.

To look into the issue of memory consumption further, we measure average memory consumption for Monitor and Pinpoint-PCFG under a load of 24 concurrent users. Physical and virtual memory usage are collected every 5 seconds by reading the /proc file system and averaged over the duration of each experimental run. **Table 2** shows the results of this experiment.

7 Efficient Rule Matching

7.1 Motivation

We present a technique for selectively matching computationally expensive rules in Monitor, thereby allowing it to operate under higher application message loads. The technique is based on the observation that the computationally expensive rules do not have to be matched all the time. Rather they can be matched when there is evidence of system instability. Previous work [21] has shown that errors are more likely when instability in the system is observed. For example, an increasing average response time in a web server may indicate an imminent failure because of resource exhaustion. Therefore, we use a light-weight mechanism of determining system instability to trigger the computationally expensive rules.

Many rules can be computationally expensive both in time and space. For example, a pattern matching rule such as calculating the convolution of two signals, as presented in [8], requires long computations, while matching strings with probabilistic context free grammars, as in Pinpoint [7], demands a large amount of memory space. For other rules, the system requires to re-train its model for detecting anomalies based on newly observed data, as in semi-supervised learning techniques [23]. The re-training is often quite expensive.

7.2 Selective Rule Matching Approach

We propose an approach for matching computationally expensive rules if evidence of instability is observed in the system. Instability can be observed by measuring different metrics in the application or the underlying middleware, for example, response time, memory, or CPU usage. Manifestation of instability can be in the form of abrupt changes in the measurements (either increasing or decreasing), or in fluctuations in the measurements.

Our approach for selectively matching rules is as follows. Let C_t denote the condition of the system at time t. Thus, C_t can take one of two conditions of the set $\{stable, unstable\}$; let $\{c^+, c^-\}$ denote these conditions. Suppose that at time t, a message m_t is observed, a rule R has to be matched, and a sequence of the n previously observed messages $\{m_{t-n}, m_{t-n+1}, \ldots, m_{t-1}\}$ are kept in a buffer B. Then, if $C_t = c^-$, R is matched, otherwise, B becomes $\{m_{t-n+1}, \ldots, m_t\}$ and Monitor waits for the next message to arrive.

The main challenge in this approach is to infer and use an accurate classifier function F mapping the universe of possible messages (i.e., system-level measurements) to the range of system conditions C, so that the probability of catching an error when $C_t = c^-$ and the rule R is matched is maximized. A complete study for addressing this challenge is out of the scope of this paper and will be pursued in future work. However, we present an example in which this technique is used in Monitor for detecting a memory leak in the Apache Tomcat web server [17] by using a simple estimator of instability.

7.3 Memory Leak Injection

We instrumented the Apache Tomcat web server to inject a memory leak dynamically. Upon receiving a request, an unused object is created with probability p_{leak} in the server's thread-pool, and it is kept referenced so that it is not taken by the Java garbage collector. The result is an increase in memory usage that can be observed from the Java process running the server.

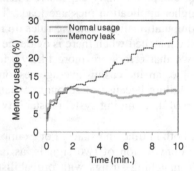

Fig. 8. Percentage of memory usage of the Apache Tomcat web server under normal conditions and with a memory leak fault injection

We perform experiments to observe the pattern of memory consumption of the web server in both normal conditions and when the memory leak is injected. We use a testbed of an e-commerce site that simulates the operation of an online store as specified by the TPC-W benchmark [18]. We use the benchmark WIPSo mixture (50% browsing and 50% ordering) that is intended to simulate a web site with a significant percentage of order requests.

Fig. 8 shows the results of the experiment when the probability p_{leak} of the memory leak injection is set to 0.5, and when a load of 50 concurrent users is imposed. Memory measurements are taken in a fixed interval of 1 second for a window of 10 minutes after the server is started.

7.4 Rule for Detecting Memory Leak Error

Previous work on software rejuvenation [19] has proposed the use of time series analysis to model memory usage patterns in the Apache web server. In this paper, we use time series analysis to build rules that are able to pinpoint a memory leak. In particular, the web server memory consumption is modeled as an autoregressive (AR) moving average (MA) process ARMA(p, q). This process is formally defined as follows [20]:

- A memory usage measurement X_t is an ARMA(p, q) process if for every time t,

$$X_t = C + \sum_{i=1}^{p} \varphi_i X_{t-i} + \varepsilon_t + \sum_{i=1}^{q} \theta_i \varepsilon_{t-i},$$

where ε_t is the error term, C is a constant, and $\{\varphi_1, ..., \varphi_p\}$ and $\{\theta_1, ..., \theta_p\}$ are the parameters of the model.
- The error term ε_t is considered to be white noise, i.e., independently and identically distributed with mean 0 and variance σ^2.

We collect training data in several runs of the Apache Tomcat server for generating two ARMA(p, q) models λ and λ' that represent memory usage under normal conditions and memory leak conditions respectively. The models are inferred by maximum likelihood estimation by using the statistical tool R. To estimate the number of p and q parameters that best fit the models, while keeping the number of parameters small, we vary p and q over 1, 2, and 3. We then select the values of p and q that produce the minimum root-mean-square (RMS) error when comparing test data and new data generated with the models. For this, test data is labeled as being normal or erroneous when selecting the parameters in λ and λ' respectively. For our test-bed, $p=3$ and $q=2$ resulted in the best configuration for the models.

7.5 Rule Matching Latency Reduction

After the two models λ and λ' are trained, we build a rule for detecting the memory leak in the web server by observing to which model the test data fits better. The rule takes as input a sequence A of n old observed messages, and a sequence B of n new observed messages in which it will look for errors. Then, two simulated sequences S and S' are generated by using the two models λ and λ' respectively on observations A. Finally, S and S' are compared to B by measuring the RMS error. If B fits better with S', an error is flagged by the rule indicating a possible memory leak.

We detect instability in the system by measuring the standard deviation σ of the m previous observed memory consumption values and if it is greater than a threshold P_{th} we conclude $C_t = c^-$, the rule is matched.

Table 3 shows the results for 3 different configurations in Monitor when the memory leak is injected in the web server. For the three experiments, $n=10$, $m = 5$, and the same workload that we used for training is imposed on the web server. The initial values of 0.5 and 1.0 for σ are taken from the average standard deviation observed in the training data set for the web server

Table 3. Detection coverage and average rule matching delay for the ARMA-based rule

Rule Matching Criteria	Memory Leak Detected	Average Matching Latency (msec.)
Always matched	yes	19.283
$\sigma \geq 0.5$	yes	7.115
$\sigma \geq 1.0$	no	1.25

running under normal conditions which is around 1.2 % of memory usage. This confirms that, in normal conditions, memory usage variation is much less than in unstable conditions.

We notice that when the rule is always matched, the average latency is the maximum as expected, and as we increase σ, the latency decreases. This is due to an inherent reduction in the chances of matching the ARMA-based rule which is more computationally expensive than evaluating σ. However, if σ is too low, the error may be missed since the ARMA-rule may not be matched at all, as is the case when $\sigma=1.0$.

Detection of the memory leak presented here can be done by many other profiling tools. The point behind this experiment is not to claim any novel detection capability. Rather, it is to show how instability can be used to trigger more computationally expensive rule matching.

8   Related Work

Error Detection in Distributed Systems: Previous approaches of error detection in distributed systems have varied from heartbeats to watchdogs. However, these designs have looked at a restricted set of errors (such as, livelocks) as compared to our work, or depended on alerts from the monitored components.

A recent work closely related to ours is Pinpoint [7]. Authors present an approach for tracing paths from user requests and use a Probabilistic Context Free Grammar (PCFG) to model normal path behavior as seen during a training phase. A path's structure is then considered anomalous if it significantly deviates from a pattern that can be derived from the PCFG. Pinpoint however does not consider the problem of dealing with high rates of requests. We provide a comparative evaluation of Monitor with Pinpoint in Section 6.5. A variant of the Pinpoint work [16] uses a weighting for long web interactions so that they are not mistakenly flagged as erroneous. This weighting seems less useful for Duke's Bank since the probabilities for the less likely transitions differ significantly from the expected probability. This work also uses an additional parameter (α) to pick a particular point in the false alarm-missed alarm spectrum. We believe that an equivalent effect is achieved through our ROC-based characterization.

Performance Modeling and Debugging in Distributed Systems: There is recent activity in providing tools for debugging problems in distributed applications, notably Project5 [8][9] and Magpie[6]. These approaches provide tools for collecting trace information at different levels of granularity which are used for automatic analysis, often offline, to determine the possible root causes of the problem.

Project5's main goal is detecting performance characteristics in black-box distributed systems. In [8] models for performance delays on RPC-style and message-based application for LAN environments are proposed—authors focus on finding causal path patterns with unexpected timing or shape. In [9] authors present an algorithm for performance debugging in wide-area systems. We determined that this work's focus is on determining the performance characteristics of different components in a complete black-box manner. Since Project 5 does not assume a uniform middleware, such as J2EE, it cannot assign a unique identifier to all messages in a causal path as they occur. We use the GlassFish-assigned unique identifier to a path of causal request-responses. In our work, we use both these features. However, Project5's accuracy suffers greatly when detecting anomalous patterns under concurrent load (in fairness, this is not the goal of the work either). Therefore, we did not perform a quantitative comparison with Project5 for detecting performance problems (in Section 6.4).

The Magpie project [6] is complementary to our work—it is a tool that helps in understanding system behavior for the purposes of performance analysis and debugging in distributed applications. Magpie collects CPU usage and disk access for user requests as they travel though the system components. These workload models of request behavior can be used in Monitor to specify performance-based rules.

Stateful Intrusion Detection in High Throughput Streams: In the area of intrusion detection, techniques have been proposed to allow network-based intrusion detection systems (NIDS) to keep up with high network bandwidths by parallelizing the workload [1] and by efficient pattern matching [2]. Although distributing the detection load in multiple machines helps, this does not solve the fundamental problem of how to manage the resource usage in individual machines, which we address.

Sampling Techniques for Anomaly Detection: Recently there is an increased effort in finding network failures, anomalies and attacks through changes in high-speed network links. For example, in [3] authors propose a sketch-based approach, where a sketch is a set of hash tables that models data as a series of (*key*, *value*) pairs; key can be a source/destination IP address, and the value can be the number of bytes or packets. A sketch can provide accurate probabilistic estimates of the changes in values for a key. Sampling has also been used in high-speed links as input for anomaly detection [4], for example, for detecting denial-of-service (DoS) attacks or worm scans. However, some studies show that these sampling techniques introduce fundamental bias that degrades performance when detecting network anomalies [5]. Our work matches rules based on aggregated information at the application level, while this work matches rules based on network level traffic statistics of the traffic.

9 Conclusions and Limitations

This paper presents an intelligent sampling algorithm and an HMM-based technique to enable stateful error detection in high throughput streams. The techniques are applied and tested in the Monitor detection system and provide a high quality of detection (accuracy and precision) for a range of real-world errors in distributed applications with low detection latency. It compares favorably to an existing detection system for distributed component-based systems called Pinpoint. We also present a technique to optimize the cost of matching computationally expensive rules for detecting resource exhaustion. Our technique relies on triggering the expensive rules only on detecting, through lightweight means, evidence of system instability.

The techniques were tested successfully in Dukes's Bank (an online banking application) and in the Apache Tomcat web server, and they can be applied to distributed systems that are composed of multiple interacting components. In general the advantage of Monitor would be the highest when messages are discriminating in terms of state transitions to different extents in the application's FSM.

A disadvantage of our HMM-based technique is that an application with a large number of states can make the HMM processing too expensive. It is a subject of future work to determine what size of the FSM would cause a cross-over beyond which

HMM execution will have to be done with an incomplete sequence of messages, which will call for a novel algorithm itself. Another limitation of Monitor is that in sampling mode some states may not be examined. If such a state happens to contain the error condition, Monitor will miss the error. In future work we will address this problem by developing a sampling scheme that allows Monitor to preferably sample messages (or sequence of messages) that are likely to point to errors in the application. We will also work on automatic generation of rules from traces that can be obtained in previous runs of the applications, and on scaling the matching of different computationally expensive rules.

Acknowledgements

The authors would like to thank Patrick Reynolds for discussions explaining the powers and limits of Project5's algorithms, and Harpreet Singh of Sun Microsystems for his help in understanding and instrumenting CallFlow in the Glassfish server.

References

[1] Kruegel, C., Valeur, F., Vigna, G., Kemmerer, R.: Stateful intrusion detection for high-speed network's. In: IEEE Symp. on Security and Privacy (2002)
[2] Jiang, W., Song, H., Dai, Y.: Real-time Intrusion Detection for High-speed Networks. Computers & Security 24(4), 287–294 (2005)
[3] Krishnamurthy, B., Sen, S., Zhang, Y., Chen, Y.: Sketch-based change detection: Methods, evaluation, and applications. In: IMC 2003 (2003)
[4] Lakhina, A., Crovella, M., Diot, C.: Mining Anomalies Using Traffic Feature Distributions. ACM SIGCOMM Comput. Commun. Rev. 35(4) (October 2005)
[5] Mai, J., Chuah, C., Sridharan, A., Ye, T., Zang, H.: Is Sampled Data Sufficient for Anomaly Detection? In: IMC 2006 (2006)
[6] Barham, P., Donnelly, A., Isaacs, R., Mortier, R.: Using Magpie for Request Extraction and Workload Modeling. In: USENIX OSDI (2004)
[7] Chen, M.Y., Accardi, A., Kiciman, E., Lloyd, J., Patterson, D., Fox, A., Brewer, E.: Path-based failure and evolution management. In: USENIX NSDI (2004)
[8] Aguilera, M.K., Mogul, J.C., Wiener, J.L., Reynolds, P., Muthitacharoen, A.: Performance debugging for distributed systems of black boxes. In: ACM SOSP (2003)
[9] Reynolds, P., Wiener, J.L., Mogul, J.C., Aguilera, M.K., Vahdat, A.: WAP5: black-box performance debugging for wide-area systems. In: WWW 2006 (2006)
[10] Khanna, G., Varadharajan, P., Bagchi, S.: Automated online monitoring of distributed applications through external monitors. IEEE Trans. on Dependable and Secure Computing 3(2), 115–129 (2006)
[11] Khanna, G., Laguna, I., Arshad, F.A., Bagchi, S.: Stateful Detection in High Throughput Distributed Systems. In: SRDS 2007 (2007)
[12] The Java EE 5 Tutorial (September 2007), http://java.sun.com/javaee/5/docs/tutorial/doc/
[13] GlassFish: Open Source Application Server (2008), https://glassfish.dev.java.net/
[14] Klein, D., Manning, C.D.: Parsing with treebank grammars. Assoc. for Computational Linguistics (2001)

[15] Schuff, D.L., Pai, V.S.: Design Alternatives for a High-Performance Self-Securing Ethernet Network Interface. In: IPDPS 2007 (2007)
[16] Kiciman, E., Fox, A.: Detecting application-level failures in component-based Internet services. IEEE Trans. Neural Networks 16(5), 1027–1041 (2005)
[17] Apache Tomcat: An Open Source JSP and Servlet Container, http://tomcat.apache.org/
[18] TPC-W Benchmark, http://www.tpc.org
[19] Grottke, M., Li, L., Vaidyanathan, K., Trivedi, K.S.: Analysis of Software Aging in a Web Server. IEEE Trans. on Reliability 55(3), 411–420 (2006)
[20] Brockwell, P.J., Davis, R.A.: Time Series: Theory and Methods, 2nd edn. (1998)
[21] Williams, A.W., Pertet, S.M., Narasimhan, P.: Tiresias: Black-Box Failure Prediction in Distributed Systems. In: IPDPS (2007)
[22] Laguna, I., Arshad, F.A., Grothe, D.M., Bagchi, S.: How To Keep Your Head Above Water While Detecting Errors. ECE Technical Reports, Purdue University, http://docs.lib.purdue.edu/ecetr/379
[23] Wu, Y.S., Bagchi, S., Singh, N., Wita, R.: Spam Detection in Voice-Over-IP Calls through Semi-Supervised Clustering. In: IEEE/IFIP DSN 2009 (2009)
[24] Rabiner, L.R.: A tutorial on Hidden Markov Models and selected applications in speech recognition. Proceedings of the IEEE 77(2) (February 1989)

PAQ: Persistent Adaptive Query Middleware for Dynamic Environments

Vasanth Rajamani[1], Christine Julien[1], Jamie Payton[2], and Gruia-Catalin Roman[3]

[1] The University of Texas at Austin
{vasanthrajamani,c.julien}@mail.utexas.edu
[2] The University of North Carolina, Charlotte
payton@uncc.edu
[3] Washington University in Saint Louis
roman@wustl.edu

Abstract. Pervasive computing applications often entail continuous monitoring tasks, issuing persistent queries that return continuously updated views of the operational environment. We present PAQ, a middleware that supports applications' needs by approximating a persistent query as a sequence of one-time queries. PAQ introduces an integration strategy abstraction that allows composition of one-time query responses into streams representing sophisticated spatio-temporal phenomena of interest. A distinguishing feature of our middleware is the realization that the suitability of a persistent query's result is a function of the application's tolerance for accuracy weighed against the associated overhead costs. In PAQ, programmers can specify an inquiry strategy that dictates how information is gathered. Since network dynamics impact the suitability of a particular inquiry strategy, PAQ associates an introspection strategy with a persistent query, that evaluates the quality of the query's results. The result of introspection can trigger application-defined adaptation strategies that alter the nature of the query. PAQ's simple API makes developing adaptive querying systems easily realizable. We present the key abstractions, describe their implementations, and demonstrate the middleware's usefulness through application examples and evaluation.

1 Introduction

Computing and communication have undergone a dramatic change with the introduction of mobile devices and sensor networks, enabling new applications characterized by a tight embedding of computation to the environment, dynamic network topologies, and the physical distribution of application components. The ad hoc nature of such networks aligns with fluid applications that must respond to rapid and frequent changes. As such, applications are often designed to monitor changes in information or conditions in the surrounding environment. As examples, an application on a construction site may monitor for the presence of a hazardous materials leak to ensure safety conditions, and a driver's navigation

J.M. Bacon and B.F. Cooper (Eds.): Middleware 2009, LNCS 5896, pp. 226–246, 2009.

system may monitor a network of vehicles to detect traffic conditions that could impact the planned travel route.

Programming applications that monitor information across an open and rapidly changing network can be challenging. A *persistent query* is an abstraction that can simplify the development of applications that require continuous monitoring. A persistent query allows a programmer to describe the data of interest to the application without requiring him to specify network communication details. At the abstract level, a persistent query may be defined as the continuous reporting of relevant state changes in a dynamic network. However, accurate evaluation of a persistent query that continuously reports all state changes is feasible only in relatively static networks; the cost of continuous monitoring is prohibitive in the face of networks that exhibit rapid change.

To support application development using persistent queries, we introduce the Persistent Adaptive Query (PAQ) middleware. PAQ introduces strategies that approximate a persistent query using a sequence of reports generated by successive one-time queries, i.e., queries evaluated once at a given time over some portion of the network. Although query processing systems exist which execute long-lived queries in this manner [1,2,3,4], the results are typically presented to the application in a traditional static database format. In contrast, PAQ presents the results in a way that more closely simulates continuous monitoring, conveying the dynamic and streaming nature of the persistent query. Key to supporting this is a new abstraction called an *integration strategy*, which specifies how the history generated by consecutive one-time queries is transformed into a semantically precise approximation of the corresponding persistent query. Integration strategies go beyond capturing simple aggregation schemes, such as those in [1,3], allowing the programmer to specify compositions of one-time query results that relate to spatial, temporal, and semantic properties of the collected information. For example, a developer can specify an integration strategy in which the result delivered to a construction site supervisor shows materials that were not used throughout the day (i.e., the result includes data items that remained available and unchanged throughout the execution of a persistent query).

A key insight in our work is that the suitability of an *inquiry strategy*, which controls when, how, where, and what type of one-time queries are issued, depends on the application's needs with respect to overhead and the desired degree of accuracy in the approximated persistent query result. For example, an application that requires a high degree of accuracy and can tolerate significant overhead may employ a query that floods the entire network, while an application with stricter overhead constraints may employ an inquiry strategy that randomly samples a set of network nodes. To balance these tradeoffs, PAQ allows an application developer to specify an inquiry strategy that is best suited to serve the application's needs. More important, however, is the realization that the suitability of the inquiry strategy changes as the dynamics of the network change. Therefore, PAQ provides a programming abstraction called an *introspection strategy*, which assesses properties of a persistent query's execution as well as returned results to determine its suitability. For example, an introspection strategy may use the locations of responding hosts to determine if the query adequately covers a desired area. Based on the value of such introspection metrics, an application can use an *adaptation strategy* to dynamically adjust its inquiry strategy.

In this paper, Section 2 reviews related work on query processing and adaptation. Section 3 presents an overview of the PAQ middleware. Details on PAQ's abstractions for query execution and appear in Section 4, while Section 5 describes abstractions related to adapting query execution. Section 6 describes our prototype implementation using two application examples, and Section 7 presents a performance evaluation. Section 8 concludes.

2   Related Work and Motivation

In the sensor networks and database communities, several query processing systems provide some version of persistent queries [1,2,3]. Persistent queries (also called "continuous queries") are typically implemented either as 1) a continuous push of updated data from sensors to a collector with queries executed over the collected data, or 2) as a sequence of one-time queries periodically propagated over the network. The "push" approach requires maintenance of a distributed data structure, which can be costly in dynamic settings. In addition, this method often requires that a query issuer interact with a collector that is known in advance and reachable at any instant, which is often an unreasonable assumption. Therefore, we think of a persistent query as being approximated by a sequence of one-time queries issued with a given frequency from any node.

Researchers have recognized that a query's environment changes over time and that query processing should adapt [5]. The focus is typically to change the order of query operations to optimize for the dynamics. For example, Continuous Queries (CACQ) [6] relies on eddies [7] to determine the order in which tuples are processed by different operators. Similarly, SteamMon [8] adapts the query plan to accommodate arbitrary changes in the data stream. These approaches use system-defined adaptations. Alternate approaches use a model that suppresses the amount of data collected from the network. In model-driven approaches [9], a local model of the environment is constructed and used to answer queries. The model obtains data from the network only when it cannot answer a query. Adaptive filters [10] uses a model of the network to adjust the rate of updates that stream from each node in the network to a collector as part of a persistent query; the adjustment is based on acceptable tradeoffs between an application's tolerance of numerical imprecision and the current cost of sending updates. A centralized coordinator periodically adjusts the bounds of each update filter on each node to suit application needs. Such model-based approaches are not well-suited for dynamic environments because they are computationally expensive. Also, these systems lack non-relational operators for the temporal analysis.

None of the above approaches to adaptive query processing provide general support for dynamically adapting a persistent query based on application-specified strategies. For example, while using numerical precision bounds as a trigger for adaptation is useful, support is still needed for expressing richer types of adaptation triggers, such as "does the query cover an adequate area of the network", that would be useful in applications deployed in dynamic environments. We focus on providing the tools required to expose information about changes taking place in a dynamic environment and the ability to respond to them.

In general, this ability to inspect and act is called *reflection* [11,12], and the PAQ middleware embodies our effort to systematically provide abstractions for reflection on persistent queries in dynamic networks. Consequently, we provide programming abstractions that support the construction of applications that dynamically evaluate the cost of executing a query in the current environment and adjust the query's processing according to the application's needs.

3   A Middleware for Persistent Query Processing

A persistent query should provide a reflection of the "ground truth," the actual state of the world during query execution. This is equivalent to a complete picture of all of the states of the environment that exist during the persistent query's execution. We approximate the results by modeling a persistent query as a sequence of non-overlapping *one-time queries*, or queries that appear to be issued over a single state of the environment. In this section, we introduce foundational concepts to create and control this kind of approximated persistent query. We begin by reviewing a model of one-time query execution [13] and then use the model to precisely define the PAQ perspective and its abstractions.

3.1   A Model of One-Time Query Execution

A mobile ad hoc network is a closed system of hosts, each represented as a triple (ι, ζ, ν), where ι is the host's unique identifier, ζ is its context, and ν is its data value. In a simple model, the context can be simply a host's location, but it can be extended to include a list of neighbors, routing tables, and other information. A snapshot of the global abstract state of a network, a *configuration*, C, is simply a set of these host tuples, one for every host in the network.

We capture network connectivity through a binary logical connectivity relation, $\mathcal{K}$, to express the ability of a host to communicate with a neighbor. Using the values in a host triple, one can derive physical and logical connectivity relations, e.g., if a host's context, ζ, includes the host's location, a connectivity relation can be defined based on communication range.

The environment evolves as the network topology changes, value assignments occur, and hosts exchange messages. Network evolution is modeled as a state transition system where the state space is the set of possible configurations and transitions are *configuration changes*. A single configuration change consists of a: 1) *neighbor change*: the connectivity relation, $\mathcal{K}$ changes; 2) *value change*: a single host changes its stored data value; or 3) *message exchange*: a host sends a message that is received by one or more neighboring nodes.

We assign subscripts to configurations (e.g., C_0, C_1, etc.) and use $\mathcal{K}_i$ to refer to the connectivity relation for configuration i. We define *query reachability* informally, to determine whether it was possible to deliver a one-time query to and receive a response from some host h within the sequence of configurations [13]. A host's response to a one-time query is a copy of its host tuple. A one-time query's result (ρ), then, is a subset of a configuration: it is a collection of host tuples that constitute responses to the query. No host in the network is represented more than once in ρ, though it is possible that a host is not represented at all (e.g., because it was never reachable from the query issuer).

3.2   The PAQ Perspective

Ideally, a persistent query reflects the ground truth. An exact reflection of the ground truth is equivalent to acquiring all of the configurations ($C_0 \ldots C_j$) of the persistent query's execution. Since providing such accuracy is feasible only in relatively static networks, we extend our model to approximate a persistent query as a sequence of non-overlapping one-time queries. Fig. 1 provides an overview of our middleware model, described below.

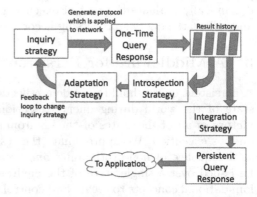

Fig. 1. A Persistent Query Framework

In evaluating a persistent query's component one-time queries, it is important to understand the behavior of an underlying query processing protocol. For example, flooding may be expensive but may achieve strongly consistent results, while randomly sampling a few nodes provides much weaker consistency, but is much less expensive. The manner in which we query the environment, the *inquiry strategy*, includes not only the one-time query protocol (called the *inquiry mode*) but also the frequency of the one-time queries.

A persistent query's result is formed from the component queries using an *integration strategy*, a function f evaluated (and reevaluated) over the sequence of one-time query results. We denote the results of the sequence of one-time queries as $\rho_0 \ldots \rho_i$, and the result of a persistent query after the results of the ith component query have been incorporated as $\pi_i = f(\rho_0 \ldots \rho_i)$. This result is still a set of host tuples, but without the constraint that the set contain only one result from any single host.

As application requirements and conditions change, applications must determine the suitability of their particular inquiry strategy. We define an *introspection strategy* also as a function over host tuples. However, in the introspection strategy, a function, d, generates not a set of host tuples but instead a value for a metric that describes the quality of that history. Based on the value of this metric, an application can specify *adaptation strategies* that govern how the inquiry strategy is changed. In the remainder of this paper, we discuss how inquiry, integration, introspection, and adaptation work together to enable applications to process expressive persistent adaptive queries over dynamic mobile networks.

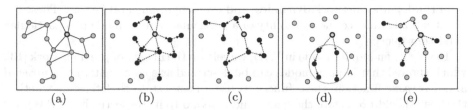

Fig. 2. Query protocols. The query issuer has a dark boundary. (a) Sample network. (b) Flooding. (c) Probabilistic protocol. Every node within the constraint (3 hops) that receives the packet retransmits it to 2 randomly selected neighbors. (d) Location based protocol that queries the nodes in region A. (e) Random protocol that queries 5 nodes.

4   Two Abstractions for Persistent Query Processing

We next present PAQ abstractions that are essential to creating a persistent query result. Using these, applications can specify how to retrieve information from the network and how to combine intermediate results over time.

4.1   Inquiry Strategies

A persistent query's inquiry strategy comprises the *inquiry mode*, or the protocol used to disseminate the one-time queries, and the frequency with which one-time queries are issued, represented as a tuple $\langle \mathcal{I}, freq \rangle$. The PAQ interface is:

Listing 1: InquiryStrategy

```
public class InquiryStrategy{
    public InquiryStrategy(InquiryMode mode, int frequency);
}
```

Defining an inquiry mode effectively entails generating a routing protocol that defines how the query and its replies propagate in the network. Fig. 2 depicts a sample network and example inquiry modes. The most common type of queries in mobile networks are flooding queries and their derivatives that reduce overhead by restricting the query's scope [1,14,15]. Fig. 2(b) depicts a simple scoped flooding query restricted to a two hop radius around the query issuer. Several approaches explore parameterizing flooding protocols using probabilities [16,17,18], as shown in Fig. 2(c). Location information can direct queries to particular regions (Fig. 2(d)). Finally, a random sampling algorithm randomly selects k hosts to send the query, as depicted in Fig. 2(e). The network paths used to communicate in random sampling depend on the network's connectivity. In all these cases, significant differences between successive one-time queries can occur even if they are issued close in time using the same inquiry mode. Variance stems from randomness, network dynamics, and even environmental factors. These aspects can all influence the suitability of a particular inquiry mode to a particular persistent query.

To specify an inquiry mode in PAQ, we rely on the insight of previous work [13], which showed that inquiry modes can be described as a combination of a *forward* and a *respond* function; these functions use a host's state to determine whether the host should propagate the query and respond to it, respectively. In PAQ, we leverage these abstractions to allow developers to create new inquiry modes as a combination of forwards and responds functions.

4.2   Integration Strategies

A PAQ application can define an integration strategy, which dictates how a history of one-time query results are transformed into a persistent query result. An integration strategy's execution is managed by the PAQ middleware. As we will see, since a one-time query's result is a set of host tuples, a natural way to express integration is through the use of set operations.

In the PAQ middleware, an application developer can introduce a new integration strategy by implementing the `IntegrationStrategy` interface:

Listing 2: IntegrationStrategy

```
public interface IntegrationStrategy{
    QueryResult integrate(Vector<QueryResult> history);
}
```

In the above, `history` is the complete set of historical one-time query results. Next, we present a set of integration strategies; this set is not exhaustive, but instead demonstrates PAQ's ability to address the needs of a variety of queries.

The simplest way to get a persistent query result from a sequence of one-time queries' results is to simply return all results to the application. Such cumulative integration is useful when a persistent query is intended to generate a picture of all results available over the query's lifetime. For example, on a construction site, the supervisor may want to monitor the identities of all workers and visitors to the site. In this case, the persistent query result is: $\pi_i = \pi_{i-1} \cup \rho_i$. Cumulative integration is depicted in Fig. 3(a).

A cumulative integration strategy that uses only a specified window of the history of one-time query results to construct a persistent query result can be expressed by providing an implementation for the `IntegrationStrategy` interface, and, most importantly, defining the `integrate` method[1]:

---

[1] We provide only this single example of an integration strategy implementation due to space constraints. Section 6 demonstrates their use, and the complete PAQ implementation can be found at
http://mpc.ece.utexas.edu/AdaptiveFramework/index.html

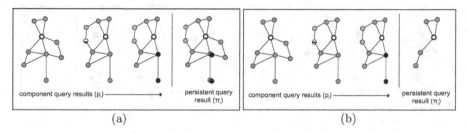

| (a) | (b) |

Fig. 3. Cumulative Integration (a) and Stable Integration (b). The query issuer is white. Other colors indicate data values. Between the first two queries, two nodes were added and two departed. Between the last two queries, two nodes' values changed.

Cumulative integration may result in delivering an overwhelming amount of data to an application, much of which may not be required. More tailored strategies may better serve the needs of specific applications; we give examples below.

Stable Integration (Fig. 3(b)). A *stable integration* gives the results that have not changed during the query. A construction supervisor may want to know which materials are not commonly used and thus available for reallocation. A stable integration's persistent query result is: $\pi_i = \pi_{i-1} \cap \rho_i$. This result depends only on the result at the previous stage and the result of the current query.

Additive and Departure Integration (Fig. 4). Two additional integrations collect results that have added or departed since the start of the query. The former allows the construction supervisor to monitor materials that have been delivered, while the latter allows him to keep track of assets that have been consumed. An *additive* integration is the difference between the current result and the first result: $\pi_i = \rho_i - \rho_0$. A *departure* integration is the difference between the first and current results: $\pi_i = \rho_0 - \rho_i$. These compare results for two instances

---

Listing 3: WindowedCumulativeIntegration

```
public QueryResult integrate(Vector<QueryResult> history){
    //omitted: define top and bottom of history window
    QueryResult temp = new QueryResult();
    for(int i = top; i>=bottom; i--){
        QueryResult nextResult = history.elementAt(i);
        Vector<HostResult> results = nextResult.getResults();
        for(int j = 0; j < results.size(); j++){
            if(!temp.getResults().contains(results.elementAt(j)))
                temp.addResult(results.elementAt(j));
        }
    }
    return temp;
}
}
```

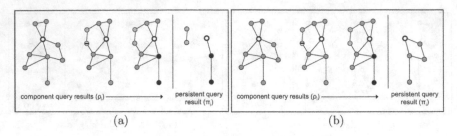

Fig. 4. Additive Integration (a) and Departure Integration (b)

in time; they cannot collect transient changes. More sophisticated (and therefore potentially more expensive) transient integrations can capture these semantics.

Transient Additive and Departure Integration (Fig. 5). *Transient additive* integration provides a complete view of all assets added to the site, even if they were subsequently consumed: $\pi_i = (\pi_{i-1} \cup \rho_i) - \rho_0$. *Transient departure* integration monitors results that departed, even if they returned. For example, a construction supervisor may keep track of tool usage since frequently used equipment may require maintenance. Recursively, this is: $\pi_i = \pi_{i-1} \cup (\rho_0 \cap (\rho_{i-1} - \rho_i))$. A straightforward extension would count the number of times a particular result departed, the result π_i being a set of pairs.

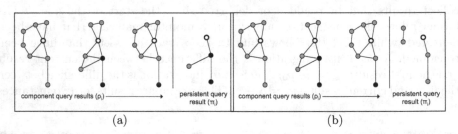

Fig. 5. Transient Additive Integration (a) and Transient Departure Integration (b)

Returns Integration (Fig. 6). A *returns* integration gives exactly those results that departed, but have since returned; this could give a construction site supervisor a picture of all of the tools used today.

The returns integration is more difficult to state in terms of previous persistent query results, but the result is directly

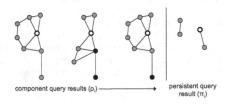

Fig. 6. Returns Integration

related to a transient departure integration. A returns integration simply checks whether a departed result is present in the current query result:

$$\pi_i = \pi_{i-1} \cup \langle \text{set } p : p \in \rho_i \wedge p \in \pi_{i-1}^{t\_\text{departs}} :: p \rangle^2$$

The negation of this could monitor tools that went missing during the query. This example demonstrates the power of integration; by defining fundamental integration strategies, new strategies can be defined.

5   Two Abstractions for Persistent Query Adaptation

Different inquiry and introspection strategies entail different tradeoffs. A programmer must be able to evaluate these tradeoffs in light of his application needs. We describe PAQ's two abstractions for query adaptation: introspection and adaptation. The former specifies *when* to adapt and the latter defines *how*.

5.1   Introspection Strategies

We define an introspection strategy as the use of information about a persistent query's execution to determine how well-suited the associated inquiry strategy is. An introspection strategy examines the persistent query's history and compares it to an idealized result[3]. We model introspection as a function d over the component query results and the ideal result; d maps to a single numeric value that conveys the quality of the result; the range of d must be a partial ordering. The application also defines a threshold δ that is the application's tolerance for the introspection metric. Although introspection strategies may often be similar to integration strategies, the purpose is fundamentally different. While the result of integration answers an application-level question, the result of introspection measures the quality of that answer. In PAQ, an application developer can introduce a new introspection strategy through the following interface:

Listing 4: IntrospectionStrategy Interface

```
public interface IntrospectionStrategy{
   double introspect(Vector<QueryResult> history);
}
```

Environmental Introspection Metrics. Introspection can determine the quality of a persistent query with respect to a desired property of the *execution environment*, as captured by the context (ζ) for each host tuple. In general, this kind

---

[2] In the three-part notation: $\langle$ op *quantified_variables* : *range* :: *expression* $\rangle$, the variables from *quantified_variables* take on all possible values permitted by *range*. Each instantiation of the variables is substituted in *expression*, producing a multiset of values to which op is applied. If no instantiation of the variables satisfies *range*, the value of the three-part expression is the identity element for op, e.g., *true* if op is $\forall$.

[3] In this section, we expand on concepts developed in [13] for persistent queries.

of distance metric can be expressed as $d = (\gamma, \mathcal{P})$, where γ is the ideal property and $\mathcal{P}$ is a function over the history of query results. The context-aware computing community has performed introspection over context data successfully in the past. For example, context-aware tour guides adapt displays according to a tourist's location and interests [19]. Consider the following example of environmental introspection in the PAQ middleware.

Spatial Coverage Introspection. Applications may require queries to provide sensing coverage of a physical area. For example, a persistent query that monitors a chemical's dissipation across a construction site to ensure readings are within safety guidelines will have to acquire readings from across the entire site. We can determine the spatial coverage achieved by the persistent query using the location information included in the context associated with query results. We can then compare this achieved spatial coverage to the desired spatial coverage to determine whether or not the inquiry strategy is appropriate in the current operational environment. The distance metric can be expressed simply as the difference between the achieved spatial coverage region s and the ideal region (i.e., $d = |ideal - s|$).

For example, a construction supervisor may describe the desired coverage area as a circle centered at some point on the site. For each component query, we can find the radius of the region by finding the maximum distance between a pair of points using the location information λ in the context variable ζ:

$$r = \langle \max \zeta.\lambda, \zeta'.\lambda', i : (\iota, \zeta.\lambda, \nu) \in \rho_i \wedge (\iota, \zeta'.\lambda', \nu) \in \rho_i :: |\zeta.\lambda - \zeta'.\lambda'| \rangle$$

We can then find the center of the circle; using the center of the spatial coverage area and the radius, we can plot the actual circular coverage area achieved by the component query. We can then determine the amount of overlap between the circle that represents the achieved spatial coverage region and the circle that represents the ideal spatial coverage region.

Semantic Introspection Metrics. The quality of a query can also be assessed based on data collected; we call this *semantic introspection*. These metrics are computed over the data values (ν) in result's host tuples. We give the implementation of the `introspect` method for a simple semantic discovery metric. Here, the introspection metric evaluates to 1 if a specified value is found in the history of query results and to 0 otherwise. We model the complete history of results as always being provided to an introspection strategy, even if the introspection only uses part of the history (in this case the most recent result). In this strategy, the variable `value` is the target value that triggers adaptation.

This metric could be used in a construction site supervisor's safety monitoring application to trigger adaptation from a low-overhead inquiry strategy like random sampling to a flooding inquiry with higher accuracy when a dangerous chemical reading is discovered. Semantic introspection metrics like this one, however, are not limited to evaluation over data values of direct interest to an application. Instead, these metrics can be evaluated over any data values collected for the purpose of measuring the quality of the query's execution.

Listing 5: SemanticDiscoveryIntrospection

```
double introspect(Vector<QueryResult> history)
  QueryResult newResult = history.elementAt(history.size()-1)
  Vector<HostResult> results = newResult.getResults();
  for(int i = 0; i < results.size(); i++){
   if(results.elementAt(i).getValue().equals(value))
     return 1;
  }
  return 0;
}
```

Each of our integration strategies can be translated into a semantic introspection metric that quantifies the kinds of changes that occur. In general, this is captured by quantifying the difference between the query result at stage k and a windowed history of previous results. For example, we can define an introspection metric based on stable integration. The interesting part of this metric describes an evaluation over the history of results; here, $\mathcal{P}$ is defined as:

$$\mathcal{P} = | \langle \text{set } \nu : (\iota, \zeta, \nu) \in \rho_k :: \nu \rangle - \bigcup_{i=j}^{k-1} \langle \text{set } \nu : (\iota, \zeta, \nu) \in \rho_i :: \nu \rangle |$$

where k is the current stage of the persistent query, and $0 \leq j < k - 1$.

Data Change Rate Introspection. In many cases, the suitability of an inquiry strategy depends on the data dynamics. Our *data change rate* introspection measures the rate at which values change over time. For example, if the data values in the network are relatively stable, an expensive flooding based high frequency strategy may not be necessary. Similarly, we define *additive data change rate* introspection as a running percentage of data values that have been added to the persistent query's result. The introspection metric relates to the use of the history of results to describe the achieved quality in defining $\mathcal{P}$:

$$\frac{\sum_{j=i-k+1}^{i} | \frac{\langle \text{set } \nu : (\iota, \zeta, \nu) \in \rho_j :: \nu \rangle - \langle \text{set } \nu : (\iota, \zeta, \nu) \in \rho_{j-1} :: \nu \rangle}{\langle \text{set } \nu : (\iota, \zeta, \nu) \in \rho_j :: \nu \rangle} |}{k}$$

When $k = i$, this measures the rate since the beginning of the persistent query. This introspection can be specified for departures and changes in a similar fashion. In measuring the rate of change due to newly arriving hosts, we instead sum the number of data values associated with new unique host identifiers.

5.2 Adaptation Strategies

Applications can use introspection to assess the quality of the persistent query's reflection of the environment. If the persistent query's result does not meet the application's requirements, adaptation strategies can be used to change the persistent query to achieve, for example, higher quality results or to process the persistent query at a lower cost. In general, an adaptation strategy is:

$$\langle\langle \mathcal{I}, \textit{freq}\rangle, d, \delta^{+/-}, \langle \mathcal{I}^*, \textit{freq}^*\rangle\rangle,$$

where $\langle \mathcal{I}, \textit{freq}\rangle$ is the persistent query's current inquiry strategy, d is the introspection strategy used when the persistent query uses this particular inquiry strategy, and $\delta^{+/-}$ is a threshold on the value resulting from applying d to the history of one-time query results. If the superscript on δ is $+$, the adaptation is triggered if the value of d exceeds δ; if the superscript is $-$, then the adaptation is triggered if the value of d falls below δ. The persistent query switches to the new inquiry strategy, $\langle \mathcal{I}^*, \textit{freq}^*\rangle$, when the computed value of the introspection strategy, d goes either above or below the threshold δ.

As a simple example of how an adaptation strategy could be employed, consider a persistent query using the basic flooding inquiry mode in which the component one-time queries are issued every 10 seconds. The application may associate with this persistent query an introspection strategy that changes the frequency of the one-time queries if the rate of change between the component queries grows too large. This adaptation policy would be defined as:

$$\langle\langle \mathcal{I}_{flooding}, 10s\rangle, d_{data\_change\_rate}, 0.05^+, \langle \mathcal{I}_{flooding}, 5s\rangle\rangle$$

where the initial inquiry strategy $\langle \mathcal{I}_{flooding}, 10s\rangle$ adapts to be $\langle \mathcal{I}_{flooding}, 5s\rangle$ when the data rate of change introspection strategy indicates a greater than 5% rate of change in the data reported for successive one-time queries.

To define adaptation strategies in the PAQ middleware, an application developer instantiates an `AdaptationStrategy` that comprises a set of `AdaptationPolicy` instances. Specifically, to create an `AdaptationStrategy`, the interface presented to the developer is:

Listing 6: AdaptationStrategy

```
public class AdaptationStrategy{
  public AdaptationStrategy();
  public addAdpatationPolicy(AdaptationPolicy toAdd);
  public removeAdpatationPolicy(AdaptationPolicy toRemove);
}
```

The interface to construct an `AdaptationPolicy` is:

Listing 7: AdaptationPolicy

```
public class AdaptationPolicy{
  public AdaptationPolicy(InquiryStrategy start,
                          IntrospectionStrategy introspect,
                          double threshold, InquiryStrategy end);
}
```

More complex realizations of adaptation policies are also possible; for example, the adaptation may change not only the inquiry but also the integration strategy.

6   The PAQ Middleware: Example Applications

This section describes our Persistent Adaptive Query (PAQ) Middleware and demonstrates its use and performance through a pair of application examples.

6.1   Monitoring Hazardous Conditions

We first explore an application for an instrumented construction site that would allow monitoring recording, and reacting to the presence of a dangerous volatile organic compound (VOC). If a VOC leak occurs, the area of the incident may spread as liquid chemicals spill and as airborne droplets are released. A site supervisor wants emergency response crews to have as much and as accurate information about the incident as possible to facilitate containment and response.

The application issues a persistent query over sensors scattered across the construction site. If there is not a high risk for or evidence of a leak, the application should be conservative in its use of network resources to perform background monitoring of hazardous materials. So the query initially uses random sampling with a low frequency to sample over the entire construction site. If the query detects a dangerous concentration, the supervisor requires additional information to determine if the reading is anomalous or indicative of an actual leak. Therefore, this query will use introspection for detection of a particular value (a high concentration) and will adapt the query to a much more frequent flood of the entire site to attempt to corroborate the initial detection. To summarize:

- **Inquiry strategy:** random sampling with a low probability (e.g., $k = 0.5$), low frequency (e.g., 5 seconds)
- **Integration strategy:** windowed cumulative integration, to acquire all concentrations that were sampled over the last 20 seconds
- **Introspection strategy:** semantic discovery of any dangerous reading
- **Adaptation strategy:** upon detection of a value over the threshold, change the approach to flood the network with high frequency

In the PAQ middleware, defining this persistent query requires instantiating each of the strategies, and creating and starting the persistent query.

Listing 8: Initial Query

```
private void startQuery(){
  myInquiry = new Inquiry(new RandomSampling(0.5), 5000);
  myIntegration = new WindowedCumulativeIntgration(4);
  myIntrospection =
    new SemanticDiscoveryIntrospection(new Integer(thresh));
  PersistentQuery initialQuery =
    new PersistentQuery(myInquiry, myIntegration,
                        myIntrospection, initialAdaptation);
}
```

The initial adaptation (initialAdaptation) takes the persistent query from this query strategy to its second phase. In this second phase, the application is alerted to a potential hazardous leak and begins a more expensive but robust detection to corroborate the initial detection. This new query is:

- **Inquiry strategy:** flooding with a high frequency (e.g., 0.5 seconds)
- **Integration strategy:** cumulative integration, to acquire all concentrations sampled since adapting the persistent query
- **Introspection strategy:** semantic additive change rate to measure the rate of discovery of corroborating detections
- **Adaptation strategy:** if more than 10% of the sensors are newly detecting a leak, localize the persistent query around the area of detection

Listing 9: Flooding Query

```
private void adaptQuery(){
  ...
  myInquiry = new Inquiry(new Flooding(), 500);
  myIntegration = new CumulativeIntegration();
  myIntrospection =
    new SemanticAdditiveIntrospection(new Integer(thresh));
  PersistentQuery initialQuery =
    new PersistentQuery(myInquiry, myIntegration,
                        myIntrospection, leakAdaptation);
}
```

This second adaptation policy (leakAdaptation) changes the query strategy from this second phase to target the persistent query exactly around the area of the detected leak. This allows the network's resources and the application's attention to be focused on exactly the desired sensing area. The persistent query continues to monitor this area, adapting the size and scope of the target area as the detected values change. This phase of the query continues until the danger dissipates, when the query returns to the original random sampling:

- **Inquiry strategy:** location-based flooding, focused around the leak
- **Integration strategy:** windowed cumulative, to acquire the readings over the threshold in the last 60 seconds
- **Introspection strategy:** spatial coverage, to ensure the area around the leak is well-covered
- **Adaptation strategy:** adjust the flooding area if the coverage is poor; return to random sampling if the leak disappears

Here, mid is the location at the center of the detected leak and radius is the sensed spread of the leak. This application and the PAQ middleware are available for download[4]. Fig. 7 shows a sequence of screenshots that demonstrate the three phases described above.

[4] http://mpc.ece.utexas.edu/AdaptiveFramework/index.html

Listing 10: Location Query

```
private void adaptQuery(){
  ...
  myInquiry = new Inquiry(new LocBased(mid.x, mid.y, radius), 500);
  myIntegration = new WindowedCumulativeIntegration(6);
  myIntrospection =
    new SpatialCoverageIntrospection(mid.x, mid.y, radius);
  PersistentQuery initialQuery =
    new PersistentQuery(myInquiry, myIntegration,
                        myIntrospection, locationAdaptation);
}
```

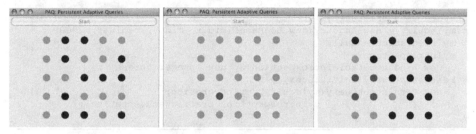

Fig. 7. A sample execution for a network of 25 nodes. The values of black nodes are unknown. The values of green nodes are below the threshold. The values of red nodes are above the threshold. The left shows a snapshot in the middle of the first phase of the persistent query; the middle shows a snapshot in the middle of the second phase; the right shows a snapshot in the middle of the third phase.

6.2   Road Traffic Monitoring

Most cities have troublesome spots that have periodic episodes of jammed traffic. We next use the PAQ middleware to construct an application for intelligent traffic monitoring. The application monitors an area of interest and informs the application if there is a backlog of vehicles. We imagine a scenario where both vehicles and stationary objects are equipped with networked sensors.

The application issues a persistent query over sensors that have been scattered across the an area of interest to monitor location information of the vehicles in the area. Initially, the query probes only the area of interest to conserve the battery of the hosts in the area. If the application detects several stationary vehicles in the monitored area for an extended period of time, it can be deduced that a traffic jam has indeed occurred. Therefore, this query will use an introspection strategy that checks whether a certain number of hosts are present in several continuous query results. Once, the traffic jam has been detected, the application performs a random sample the entire network to detect alternative routes to the application. This phase can be summarized as:

- **Inquiry strategy:** location-based random sampling, focused on a known traffic trouble spot, low frequency query (e.g., 20 seconds)
- **Integration strategy:** None

- **Introspection strategy:** windowed stable integration to measure whether the same cars remain in the query area in multiple consecutive queries
- **Adaptation strategy:** upon detection of a value over the threshold indicating stranded cars, change the approach to random sampling of the entire network with higher frequency

In the PAQ middleware, defining this persistent query requires instantiating each of the strategies, and creating and starting the persistent query:

Listing 11: Initial Query

```
private void startQuery(){
  myInquiry = new Inquiry(new LocBased(mid.x, mid.y, radius), 20000);
  myIntegration = null;
  myIntrospection =
    new WindowedStableIntrospection(3, new Integer(thresh));
  PersistentQuery initialQuery =
    new PersistentQuery(myInquiry, myIntegration,
                        myIntrospection, trafficjamAdaptation);
}
```

This adaptation (`trafficjamAdaptation`) is invoked if the initial query notices an unacceptable number of stranded cars. It takes the persistent query from this query strategy to its second phase in which the application issues randomly distributed queries to find alternate routes to re-route the stalled traffic:

- **Inquiry strategy:** random sampling with a relatively low probability (e.g., $k = 0.5$) but a higher frequency (e.g., 5 seconds)
- **Integration strategy:** cumulative integration, to observe all elements of all of the roadways and get a picture of where to reroute the stranded cars
- **Introspection strategy:** counting introspection, to ensure that this particular component query has been issued a given number of times (e.g., 5)
- **Adaptation strategy:** when the query has sent alternate routes to the jammed cars (not part of the persistent query), return to monitoring the initial area to ensure that the traffic is clearing.

Aside from its use of `CountingIntrospection`, this query is similar to the initial query in the first application; we omit its listing for brevity.

This second query's adaptation policy changes the query strategy to once again target the original location to see if the rerouting instructions are causing it to clear of traffic. This phase continues unless the re-route did not succeed, and cars cleared from this location are returning:

- **Inquiry strategy:** location-based flooding, focused on the original location
- **Integration strategy:** windowed cumulative integration, to acquire the readings over the threshold (i.e., returning a number of cars indicative of a traffic jam) in the last 60 seconds

- **Introspection strategy:** windowed returns introspection, to see if cars that were instructed to reroute are in fact returning to the trouble spot
- **Adaptation strategy:** if the process has failed to clear the traffic, repeat by resampling for rerouting possibilities

Listing 12: Location Based Query

```
private void adaptQuery(){
  ...
  myInquiry = new Inquiry(new LocBased(mid.x, mid.y, radius), 5000);
  myIntegration = new WindowedCumulativeIntegration(10);
  myIntrospection =
    new WindowedReturnsIntrospection(5, new Integer(thresh));
  PersistentQuery locationQuery =
    new PersistentQuery(myInquiry, myIntegration,
                        myIntrospection, trafficjamAdaptation);
}
```

This query employs `WindowedReturnsIntrospection`, which checks for vehicles that return to the trouble spot. If many of the same vehicles return, (`trafficjamAdaptation`) is used again, and the process repeats. An application may also define a more complex persistent query that becomes increasingly aggressive about finding alternate routes as it cycles through the process.

7 Evaluating the PAQ Middleware

In addition to the middleware implementation, we also prototyped PAQ using OMNeT++ [20,21]. We executed the described applications, modeling the network space as a 1000m × 900m rectangular area. We used the 802.11 MAC protocol.[5] The included graphs show 95% confidence intervals.

We used the first example application to explore PAQ's performance in the absence of mobility. We implemented two different types of adaptation: "moderate" and "aggressive." Given a leak detection, the "aggressive" version immediately starts issuing flooding queries at a high frequency. The "moderate" adaptation increases the query rate more slowly (i.e., by increasing the query rate by one every five seconds). We compare the behavior of these two adaptive approaches with two standard query styles: "flooding," a query that floods all of the time, and "sampling," a query that always samples half of the reachable hosts.[6] Fig. 8 highlights the value of employing adaptation to lowering overhead.

---

[5] The source code and settings used are available at
   http://mpc.ece.utexas.edu/AdaptiveFramework/index.html
[6] While we experimented with different values of k for the random sampling approach, $k = 0.5$ provides representative results.

Allowing applications to adapt leads to substantially lower overhead, especially as network density increases. The moderate version has lower overhead than randomly sampling. At first glance, the overhead of the aggressive approach is similar to flooding; however, the aggressive version issues three times as many queries because it adapts the query rate after leak detection based on the application's requirements. Even the moderate version issues 30% more queries in certain time periods but still transmits far fewer messages.

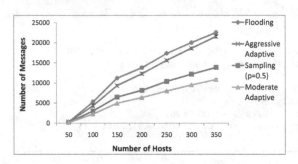

Fig. 8. Number of packets exchanged

These performance benefits may come at a cost to accuracy. Since the nodes are initially randomly sampled, it is possible for the leak to go undetected if relevant sensors are not sampled. Fig. 9 shows the percentage of times the leak is successfully detected for the different versions. In sparse networks, none of the versions are very effective because the leak is often in an unreachable network partition. The moderate approach does not flag a leak unless two values pass the semantic introspection test while the aggressive version requires only one detected leak value before switching to a flooding based inquiry. Consequently, the moderate version misses more leaks. Both the aggressive and flooding approaches produce a highly accurate picture. A similar effect can be observed when the leak detection latency is compared. A flooding strategy detects the leak slightly faster than the aggressive strategy which in turn is slightly faster than the moderate strategy. This graph is omitted for brevity.

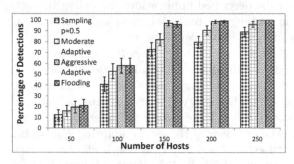

Fig. 9. Percentage of Detections

Using our second application scenario (the traffic monitoring example), we have also evaluated the impact of mobility on PAQ's query processing capabilities. In our experiment, the query is issued from a central station at one end of the 1000m × 900m field. The simulation consists of a well connected network with 150 hosts. One-half of these hosts are on vehicles while the remaining one-half half represent sensors on stationary objects (e.g., traffic signals). A location is deemed to be "jammed" if more than five vehicles are stationary at a region of interest over three consecutive queries. In this experiment, we varied the speed at which hosts are moving from very slow (5mph) to reasonably fast (45 mph).

Fig. 10 shows rates of traffic jam detections. Regardless of the strategy used, some traffic jams go undetected due to the network dynamics. This is corroborated by the consistent downward slope for all of the approaches with increasing mobility. However, in addition to maintaining its lower overhead, the adaptive strategy achieves a slightly *better* traffic jam detection success rate than

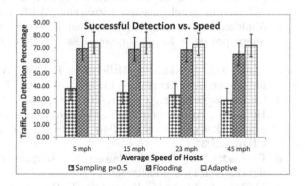

Fig. 10. Percentage of Detections

flooding. This is because the flooding approach generates many more messages in the network, resulting in more messages dropped due to collision. Our adaptive strategy targets only a particular area of the network, thereby reducing the number of messages in the network. Consequently, fewer messages are dropped leading to better detection.

From these results it can be seen that having a flexible mechanism for adaptation is clearly beneficial to application developers. The PAQ middleware provides software developers a flexible and simple API that allows domain experts to specify their design choices in a powerful way, allowing applications to explicitly consider performance tradeoffs in developing their query uses.

8   Conclusions

In this paper, we introduced the PAQ middleware to help programmers quickly construct applications that use adaptive persistent queries in dynamic networks. We highlighted the different abstractions (and class implementations) in PAQ that support simple specification of policies for adaptive applications. Integration allows programmers to create application-specific methods of composing and interpreting approximate one-time query results into a result that resembles streaming data. Inquiry strategies elegantly dictate how data should be gathered from a network. PAQ's introspection strategy abstraction provides programmers with the power to specify arbitrary methods of assessing the quality of achieved results as the persistent query executes; this assessment can be used to trigger adaptation of the query. Our evaluation of PAQ through the implementation of two adaptive applications indicates that our approach is feasible and can support adaptivity, and can potentially reduce persistent query costs.

References

1. Intanagonwiwat, C., Govindan, R., Estrin, D., Heideman, J., Silva, F.: Directed diffusion for wireless sensor networking. IEEE Trans. on Net. 11(1), 2–16 (2003)
2. Madden, S., Franklin, M., Hellerstein, J., Hong, W.: The design of an acquisitional query processor for sensor networks. In: Proc. of ACM SIGMOD, pp. 491–502 (2003)
3. Madden, S., Franklin, M., Hellerstein, J., Hong, W.: Tag: A tiny aggregation service for ad-hoc sensor networks. In: Proc. of OSDI (December 2002)
4. Chandrasekaran, S., Cooper, O., Deshpande, A., Franklin, M., Hellerstein, J., Hong, W., Krishnamurthy, S., Madden, S., Raman, V., Reiss, F., Shah, M.: TelegraphCQ: Continuous dataflow processing for an uncertain world. In: Proc. of CIDR (2003)
5. Deshpande, A., Ives, Z., Raman, V.: Adaptive query processing. Found. Trends databases 1(1), 1–140 (2007)
6. Madden, S., Shah, M., Hellerstein, J., Raman, V.: Continuously adaptive continuous queries over streams. In: Proc. of ACM SIGMOD (2002)
7. Avnur, R., Hellerstein, J.: Eddies: Continuously adaptive query processing. In: Proc. of ACM SIGMOD (2000)
8. Babu, S., Widom, J.: Streamon: an adaptive engine for stream query processing. In: Proc. of ACM SIGMOD, pp. 931–932 (2004)
9. Deshpande, A., Guestrin, C., Madden, S., Hellersetin, J., Hong, W.: Model-driven data acquisition in sensor networks. In: Proc. of VLDB (2004)
10. Olston, C., Jiang, J., Widom, J.: Adaptive filters for continuous queries over distributed data streams. In: Proc. of ACM SIGMOD (2003)
11. Capra, L., Blair, G.S., Mascolo, C., Emmerich, W., Grace, P.: Exploiting reflection in mobile computing middleware. ACM Mobile Comput. and Comm. Review 6(4), 34–44 (2002)
12. Chan, A., Chuang, S.N.: Mobipads: a reflective middleware for context-aware mobile computing. IEEE Trans. Soft. Eng. 29(12), 1072–1085 (2003)
13. Rajamani, V., Julien, C., Payton, J., Roman, G.C.: Inquiry and introspection for non-deterministic queries in mobile networks. In: Proc. of FASE, March 2009, pp. 401–416 (2009)
14. Johnson, D.B., Maltz, D.A., Broch, J.: Dsr: The dynamic source routing protocol for multi-hop wireless ad hoc networks. Ad Hoc Networking 1, 139–172 (2001)
15. Roman, G.C., Julien, C., Huang, Q.: Network abstractions for context-aware mobile computing. In: Proc. of ICSE, pp. 363–373 (2002)
16. Haas, Z., Halpern, J., Li, L.: Gossip-based ad hoc routing. IEEE Trans. on Networking 14(3), 479–491 (2006)
17. Kyasanur, P., Choudhury, R., Gupta, I.: Smart gossip: An adaptive gossip-based broadcasting service for sensor networks. In: Proc. of MASS (October 2006)
18. Ni, S.Y., Tseng, Y.C., Chen, Y.S., Sheu, J.P.: The broadcast storm problem in a mobile ad hoc network. In: Proc. of MobiCom, pp. 151–162 (1999)
19. Cheverst, K., Davies, N., Mitchell, K., Friday, A., Efstratiou, C.: Experiences of developing and deploying a context-aware tourist guide: The GUIDE project. In: Proc. of MobiCom, pp. 20–31. ACM Press, New York (2000)
20. Loebbers, M., Willkomm, D., Koepke, A.: The Mobility Framework for OMNeT++ Web Page, http://mobility-fw.sourceforge.net
21. Vargas, A.: OMNeT++ Web Page, http://www.omnetpp.org

Middleware for Pervasive Spaces: Balancing Privacy and Utility

Daniel Massaguer, Bijit Hore, Mamadou H. Diallo, Sharad Mehrotra, and Nalini Venkatasubramanian

Donald Bren School of Information and Computer Science
University of California, Irvine
{dmassagu,bhore,mamadoud,sharad,nalini}@ics.uci.edu

Abstract. Middleware for pervasive spaces has to meet conflicting requirements. It has to both maximize the utility of the information exposed and ensure that this information does not violate users' privacy. In order to resolve these conflicts, we propose a framework grounded in utility theory where users dynamically control the level of disclosure about their information. We begin by providing appropriate definitions of privacy and utility for the type of applications that would support collaborative work in an office environment—current definitions of privacy and anonymity do not apply in this context. We propose a distributed solution that, given a user's background knowledge, maximizes the utility of the information being disclosed to information recipients while meeting the privacy requirements of users. We implement our solution in the context of a real pervasive space middleware and provide experiments that demonstrate its behaviour.

1 Introduction

Large and dense sensing, communications, and computing infrastructures are enabling the creation of pervasive spaces that offer new possibilities, conveniences and functionalities. Instrumented pervasive spaces that allow observation of entities enable a rich set of applications ranging from surveillance, situational awareness to collaborative applications. Consider for instance, an office environment—here, collaboration can be greatly enhanced if members of a team know where teammates are, what they are doing, and if they are available for discussions. Unfortunately, while a system that provides this information has the potential to improve efficiencies, it can encroach on the privacy of the target individuals (e.g., Peter wants to find Alice who may not wish to be interrupted). A typical technology solution is to provide opt-in/opt-out mechanisms, where targets disable the capture/release of personalizing information either physically (e.g., Alice turns off localization device) or via suitable access control policies.

We argue that such a binary modality is not sufficient to address the privacy needs of future pervasive space applications—individuals are often willing to make personalizing information available based on the needs and context of the request and requestor (e.g Alice is willing to be interrupted if Peter needs an urgent signature). In this paper, we develop a utility-centric formulation of pervasive applications. Observers requesting information specify the utility of the information and targets (about whom information is being requested) express their privacy needs as a negative utility of releasing that information, e.g. Alice's negative utility of being interrupted and Peter's positive utility of finding Alice.

J.M. Bacon and B.F. Cooper (Eds.): Middleware 2009, LNCS 5896, pp. 247–267, 2009.

Fig. 2 illustrates the role of a pervasive system middleware. Given application needs, the system observes the pervasive space by probing sensors and interprets the sensor readings to obtain a useful view of the state of the pervasive space. The role of the pervasive space middleware is to (a) generate a semantically meaningful view of the pervasive space state (e.g., where people are and what they are doing) while hiding the details of how this state is obtained and (b) determine whether (and in what format) to release information to an observer in the pervasive space by realizing the privacy/utility tradeoffs expressed via privacy/utility policies. This paper focuses on the design of the privacy manager, a key component in such a system.

While the basic idea is straightforward, there are a few complications in developing a generalized and flexible system that can address the privacy/utility tradeoff. First, information can be *inferred* in such a system, without explicit requests. For example, knowledge of associations (e.g. Alice and Mary co-program for a project) can inadvertently reveal information. In the above case, knowledge that Alice is in the conference room and that Mary is in a meeting regarding the project reveals Mary's location (i.e., the conference room). This is a problem if Mary perceives this additional knowledge as a violation of her privacy. This leads us to our first challenge: *the system must account for inferred information in determining a tradeoff*. Second, information can be represented at different granularities—information can be characterized in a hierachical manner—from least descriptive to most descriptive. In the above request, the system can preserve Mary's location privacy by (a) generalizing Alice's location or (b) hiding information on the nature of Mary's meeting. The latter solution would provide Alice's location but increment the uncertainty of Mary's inferred location, which might preserve Mary's privacy. The system must be able to capture and exploit the natural generalization hierarchy offered by the information revealed instead of completely denying access to the information. Third, the discussion above implicetly assumes that people can specify their privacy and information needs. What those needs are, however, is often not clear. Typical privacy definitions where privacy is a binary concept on top of which statistical guarantees are formulated (e.g., k-anonymity, l-diversity, and the like [35,29,30], or those based on differential privacy [18,28]) do not suffice in our scenario since privacy is no longer a binary concept. Furthermore, specifying these needs is at best cumbersome, cognitively difficult and even unfeasible if we expect users to continuously specify their needs for all possible values, contexts, and users. Realistic mechanisms must be in place to obtain the utility functions.

The goal of this paper is to develop a principled approach and framework that can address the above challenges and enable the privacy-utility balance in pervasive space applications.

Contributions. The following are the key contributions of this paper.

1) We develop a model of pervasive spaces to represent the various entities (e.g. users, objects), their static properties (e.g. name), and their dynamic properties (e.g. location, activity) the values of which can be represented at different levels of granularity (Section 2).

2) We model the notion of privacy (for targets), not as a binary concept, but as the negative utility associated with each piece of information, and formulate the problem of maximizing the net utility of the information released by the

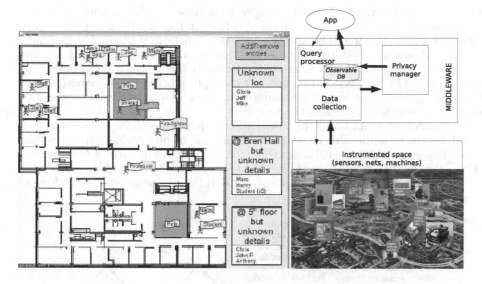

Fig. 1. OfficeMonitor: a sample application   **Fig. 2.** Our pervasive space

pervasive space system (to an observer) while avoiding privacy violations due to inference (Section 3).

3) We propose a solution to address the privacy preservation and utility maximization problem based on a distributed simulated annealing algorithm (Section 4).

4) We extend the existing SATware middleware [21] for pervasive spaces with a privacy manager module (Fig. 2) which incorporates (i) a policy language and mechanisms to express privacy and utility requirements, and (ii) a background knowledge model based on first-order probabilistic datalog clauses and machine learning techniques to populate it, and (iii) the disclosure component that implements the aforementioned simulated annealing-based algorithm (Section 5).

5) We study the performance of our techniques as implemented in a real system (Section 6) by experimenting with scenarios typical from a motivating *Office-Monitor* application. *OfficeMonitor* is a collaborative application that allows a user (observer) to graphically browse through a university campus map and observe locations and tasks of other people. *OfficeMonitor* also allows targets (users being monitored) to specify rules on *whether* and *how* information about them (e.g., current location, activity) should be released. With this improved awareness, office occupants, for example, are able to prompt their co-workers for impromptu meetings in the most appropriate time

2   Pervasive Space Model as Viewed by the Applications

From the point of view of the applications, a pervasive space is a physical space in which activities and objects are embedded. In this space, there are 3 types of objects: (1) spatial objects such as rooms, floors, and buildings, (2) people such as Mary, Peter, and Alice, and (3) inanimate objects such as coffee pots, recycle bins, and refrigerators. Each of these objects have attributes such as name, occupancy level, location, salary, level of coffee, and so on. These attributes are either static or dynamic (i.e., they change as a function of time). For instance, name and salary are static whereas location is static for spatial objects but dynamic for people. We call *observable attributes* the subset of attributes that can be sensed by the pervasives space. For example, a pervasive space with video-based people counters and RFID readers can detect both the level of occupancy of a room as well as recognize the people in it.

Our pervasive space middleware will allow applications to view the space as a database whose main table contains the values of the observable attributes over time. The main table has 4 columns: *ObjectId, AttributeName, AttributeValue,* and *Time.* We call such a database an observable database (*ODB*), and the main table is called the *Base* table. An example of an ODB.Base table is depicted in Fig. 3.

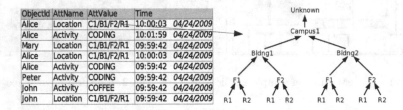

Fig. 3. ODB.Base and generalization hierarchy

OfficeMonitor type of applications pose continuous queries on ODB.Base. The pervasive space middleware continously answers these queries by deciding which sensors need to be queried and how to interpret the data streams generated by the sensors [21]. At any point of time t the query answers are a set of tuples $Y_{req} = \{< id, att, v, t >\}$ where id identifies an object, att identifies an attribute, and v is the observed value. For the *OfficeMonitor*-type of applications we only need simple filter queries that use selections on the observable attributes such as[1]

SELECT AttributeValue FROM ODB.Base WHERE ObjectId=Alice
AND AttributeName=Location AND Time=Now

We refer to the users who pose these queries as *observers.* We refer to the objects of queries as *targets.* Target identities, attribute values, and time are considered to be generalizable—hierarchies exist to capture these concepts.

2.1 Modeling Generalization Hierarchies

People may be organized into a hierarchy according to their occupation, location may be organized according to physical inclusion, and time may be generalized from seconds to minutes, hours, and days. Given the type of pervasive applications we are interested in enabling (e.g., *OfficeMonitor*), in this paper we only

---

[1] More complex queries (e.g., "select the location and picture of whoever is nearest to the exit"), can be modeled as queries on views that are defined on top of ODB.Base and other tables that contain extra information regarding the space objects, the sensing infrastructure, and so on.

focus on generalizing attribute values. Fig. 3 illustrates a generalization hierarchy for the attribute *Location*. A query for Alice's location may now use this hierarchy to return information at the room, floor, building, or campus level.

We denote generalizations with the $\prec$ partial order and use the notation $x \prec_n y$ to indicate that the minimum number of generalizations between x and y is n. For example, $<Mary, Location, Campus1, Now> \prec_1 <Mary, Location, Campus1/Building1, Now>$ and $<Mary, Location, Unknown, Now> \prec_2 <Mary, Location, Campus1/Building1, Now>$. We extend the definition of $\prec$ to sets of tuples; we say that $X \prec_1 Y$, iff $\exists y \in Y, x \in X$ s.t. $x \prec_1 y$ and $X - \{x\} = Y - \{y\}$; we say that $X \prec_n Y$, iff $\exists Z \prec_{n-1} Y$ and $X \prec_1 Z$. We define the partial order $\preceq$ as $x \preceq y$ iff $x = y$ or $x \prec y$, and $X \preceq Y$ iff $X = Y$ or $X \prec Y$. At the top of each attribute generalization hierarchy (i.e., at level 0) there is the null value [35], which we call *Unknown*.

Last, two further assumptions that we make in our model are: (i) we trust the sentient system software and hardware—no privacy leakage is due to them, and (ii) the interest is in the current state: information utility regarding an attribute value decreases exponentially with time.

3   Problem Formulation

The task of pervasive space applications such as the OfficeMonitor is to provide answers to users' queries. While the utility of a query response is maximized for the observer when the data is in "the most precise" form, the utility may be quite the opposite for the target of the query. For instance, if location privacy is a concern then revealing accurate information about location is certainly detrimental for the target. There is often such a conflict between the "positive" and "negative" utilities associated with a piece of information that comprises a query response. Traditional access control mechanisms are geared towards deciding between the binary options of *granting* and *denying* access to a piece of information. In contrast, we consider a much larger set of options where the same information is revealed to the observer at a different granularity, i.e. *level of generalization*. For instance, the system may decide to send the tuple $<Mary, Location, Campus1/Building1, Now>$ instead of the most accurate version $<Mary, Location, Campus1/Building1/Floor1/Room1, Now>$ if it determines (using some criteria which we will describe later) that this is the resolution that achieves the desired degree of tradeoff between privacy of targets and utility of the observer. We claim that our approach allows a greater amount of useful information to be released in general and is acceptable for many pervasive application scenarios where strict access control happens to be too restrictive. Another important feature of our privacy analysis is that we factor in the information disclosed due to inference. The inference problem is especially critical in pervasive spaces where the observer may have substantial amount of background knowledge and historic information (i.e., the contents of ODB.Base over time) using which he can deduce more facts besides what is revealed directly by the response generated by the system. The inference algorithms can lead to substantial increase in load on a real-time system as the knowledge base grows. Therefore, an efficient and scalable implementation is required to deliver a practical solution. In the remainder of this section we describe how we model background knowledge, observer and target utilities, and the information release problem as a constrained optimization problem in an utility theoretic framework. In the next section, we will describe our solution methodology and give efficient algorithms for the optimization problem.

3.1 Background Knowledge Model

We model an observer's background knowledge (BK^{obs}) as a set of probabilistic first-order Datalog (pDatalog) clauses [25]. pDatalog is much more expressive than propositional logic variations usually used in inference control on statistical databases [30] in that it allows us to model relationships among attributes as well as relationships between attributes and time. With the use of variables, rules can be expressed more concisely. Moreover, pDatalog allows us to reason with probabilities. An example of a rule is:

$$Tuple(Alice, Location, l, t) : p * 0.8 \leftarrow Tuple(Mary, Location, l, t) : p \quad (1)$$

A data element is represented as a multi-attribute tuple of the form *Tuple (objectId, attributeName, attributeValue, time):certainty*. The rule above states that if Mary is at location l at time t with probability p, then Alice is also present at the same location (as Mary) with a probability of *0.8*p*. Here *0.8*p* is the *certainty* factor associated with the consequent tuple. The knowledge base consists of rules of the above form along with some other auxiliary information in the form of hierarchies and facts.

The background knowledge base with respect to each observer is the set of rules in the union of a general knowledge base (KB_G) (which is common to all observers) and a knowledge base KB_{Told} consisting of the facts that the system has recently revealed to that observer i.e., $KB^{obs} = KB_G \cup KB_{Told}$. The general knowledge base KB_G, in turn comprises generalization hierarchies (KB_{GH}) as shown in Fig. 3, a knowledge base that expresses the intended usage of the space and its characteristics (KB_S), and a set of rules that expresses the individual usage of the space and further attribute and value relationships (KB_D) (i.e., $KB_G = KB_{GH} \cup KB_S \cup KB_D$). We call BK^{sys} the union of all observer's background knowledge model, a.k.a. the system's background knowledge. In Section 5.2 we give examples of rules in KB_D and KB_S and describe how the knowledge bases are populated.

3.2 Privacy vs Utility

We argue that the potential use (or misuse) of information is what defines the expected utility of information. Given this premise, we derive the definitions of **positive expected utility** of a piece of information for the observer and **negative expected utility** of a piece of information for the target. We formulate our problem as a maximization problem based on these utilities.

Let $Tell(obs, Y_{rel} \subseteq ODB.Base)$ be the action of the system releasing information Y_{rel} to an observer *obs*, where Y_{rel} is a set of tuples of the form $y_r = <id, att, v, t>$ where id identifies an object, att identifies an attribute, and v is the attribute's value at time t. Given that an observer's possible actions are a function of the information he believes in [31,40,39], the possible outcomes of $Tell(obs, Y_{rel})$ is defined by the set of actions that the observer could respond with. For example, if due to $Tell(Peter, Y_{rel})$ Peter believes that Mary is in her office, he might go there, and if she is actually in her office, Mary will get interrupted. Furthermore, we assume that the probability of the observer attempting to perform that action is equal to his belief that the piece of information is true.

The outcome of an observer's action has a utility for both the observer and the target of the information released by the system. Namely, it has an immediate positive utility for the observer (Peter gets help from Mary) and an immediate non-positive utility for the target (Mary gets interrupted). We will classify a tuple as *private information* if it has some associated negative utility. Furthermore, since the observer can potentially infer information about other targets (e.g., Alice's location), the observer's might incur a non-positive utility for other targets[2]. The functions $utilityO(obs, y, ctxt^{obs})$ and $utilityT(obs, y, ctxt^{tgt})$ return a number between $[0.0, 1.0]$ and $[-1.0, 0.0]$ respectively, which represent the utility for the observer and the target of an observer learning a specific piece of information $y \in ODB.Base$ in a given *context*. A user's context is defined as a subset of tuples regarding himself and some "benign" objects whose state does not disclose (directly or via inference) private information[3]:

$$ctxt^u = \{y =< id, att, v, t > \,|id = u \ or \ id = benignObj, y \in ODB.Base\} \quad (2)$$

We define the observer's *expected* utility for a piece of information as the product of "the probability of the user successfully performing an action (which is equivalent to the observer's belief that a piece of information is true *times* the probability that the information is true)" and "the utility of the outcome of such an action". For notational simplicity, we suppress the *obs* and *context* terms from the expression:

$$EU_O(y) \ = \ P(y \mid Y_{rel}, KB_{GH}) * P(y \mid Y_{rel}, BK^{sys}) * utilityO(y) \quad (3)$$

where $P(y \mid Y_{rel}, KB_{GH})$ represents the observer's belief that y is true, and $P(y \mid Y_{rel}, BK^{sys})$ represents the probability that y is true.

We define the target's *expected* utility in a similar manner except for the fact that we have to consider inferences regarding (a) future data and (b) other targets. For example, if Peter knows that Mary joins Alice for dessert, he can infer where Mary might be in the near future if he knows where Alice is having lunch. This way, the target's expected utility can be defined as the product of the probability that the observer will deduce a new piece of information, the information being true, and the (negative) utility for the target[4]:

$$EU_T(y) \ = \ P(y \mid Y_{rel}, BK^{obs}) * P(y \mid Y_{rel}, BK^{sys}) * utilityT(y) \quad (4)$$

Note that for the target's expected utility we consider the entire observer's background knowledge (BK^{obs}) whereas for the observer's expected utility we consider the generalization knowledge base (KB_{GH}). For the targets, we are interested in a worst-case scenario; thus we need to consider any possible leakage of information. For the observer, on the other hand, we are only concerned

---

[2] Utility can also be negative for the observer and positive for the targets [17,11]. In this paper, however, we focus on a simpler model.

[3] In general, there exists no "benign" object since for any given information, theoretically exists some background knowledge that can be applied to obtain some private information [18]. In practice, however, there is information which is more unlikely to allow an observer to infer private information. For example, benign information includes tuples such as $< Campus1/Building1, onFire, true, now >$.

[4] Note how this definition is very similar to the disclosure risk definitions of privacy-preserving data publishing [30]. The main difference is that we multiply the disclosure risk by the utility and the probability of a future action happening.

Table 1. Symbols

Symbol	Description
Y_{req}	tuples before discl. control
Y_{rel}	tuples after discl. control
$Y_{derived}$	info inferrable from Y_{rel}
$GH(Y_{rel})$	info inferrable from y_{rel} based on gen. hierarchies
$Tell(obs, Y_{rel})$	sentient system's action
$\prec, \preceq$	generalization relations
$BK^{obs} = KB_G \cup KB_{Told}$	obs's background knowledge
$KB_G = KB_{GH} \cup KB_S \cup KB_D$	general KB
KB_{GH}	generalization hierarchy KB
KB_S	intended space usage KB
KB_D	domain KB
$utilityO$	obs's utility for a piece of info
$utilityT$	tgt's utility for a piece of info
EU_O	Observer's expected utility
EU_T	Target's expected utility

with the attributes he posed the continuous queries on—i.e., the attributes he is in fact interested in. All the notations are summarized in the Table 1 for easy reference.

Let us denote by $GH(Y_{rel})$ all the information that can be inferred from Y_{rel} given the generalization hierarchy knowledge base KB_{GH}. Denote by $Y_{derived}$ all the information that can be inferred from Y_{rel} given the observer's knowledge base KB^{obs}. Then, we define the expected utility of $Tell(obs, Y_{rel})$ as the sum of the expected utilities of the data the observer receives as long as these data do not violate the privacy constraints:

$$EU_{Tell(obs, Y_{rel})} = \begin{cases} \sum_{y \in GH(Y_{rel})} EU_O(y) & \text{if } Private(Y_{derived}) \\ -\infty & \text{otherwise} \end{cases} \tag{5}$$

where $Private(Y_{derived})$ is a boolean function that decides whether privacy is violated or not. In this paper, we take a simple criteria for checking privacy violation. We say that *privacy is met if there is no data whose negative utility is larger than the observer's utility of either that data or any other piece of data that contributed to its inference*. Let us define a minimal independent partition Y_{rel}^i as a subset of Y_{rel} such that no piece of information in Y_{rel}^i allows one to infer a piece of information in $Y_{derived} - Y_{rel}^i$ and vice versa, then privacy is met if:

$$Private(Y_{rel}^i) = \begin{cases} \text{true if } |EU_T(y_d) * \omega(y_d.t)| \leq EU_O(y_r) \\ \qquad \forall y_r \in GH(Y_{rel^i}), \forall y_d \in Y_{derived}^i \\ \text{false} \qquad \qquad \text{otherwise} \end{cases} \tag{6}$$

where $\omega(t) = 2\frac{1}{1+e^{|now - y_d.t|/\tau}}$, with τ as a small constant (e.g., 1), accounts for information utility decreasing exponentially with time (Section 2).

3.3   The Utility Maximization Problem

We cast the problem as a maximization problem where the objective is to find a generalization $Y_{rel}^i \preceq Y_{req}^i$ for each minimum independent partition Y_{rel}^i that maximizes (5) and meets the privacy requirements (6). Namely, the objective is to maximize the observer aggregated expected utility of the information released while ensuring that the largest negative utility of all the information pieces the observer can infer, given his background knowledge and the information being released, is not greater than the largest positive utility of all the information pieces the observer can infer given the generalization hierarchy and the information being released. Formally it can be stated as:

$$\max_{Y_{rel}^i} EU_O(Y_{rel}^i) \tag{7}$$

such that

$$min\_EU_T(Y_{rel}^i) + max\_EU_O(Y_{rel}^i) \geq 0.0 \tag{8}$$

$$Y_{rel}^i \preceq Y_{req}^i \tag{9}$$

where

$$EU_O(Y_{rel}^i) = \sum_{\forall y_r \in GH(Y_{rel i})} EU_O(y_r)$$

$$min\_EU_T(Y_{rel}^i) = \min_{y_d \in Y_{derived}^i} EU_T(y_d)$$

$$max\_EU_O(Y_{rel}^i) = \max_{y_r \in GH(Y_{rel}^i)} EU_O(y_r) \tag{10}$$

4   Solution

In this section, we describe how the optimization problem is solved in our system. We utilize the generalization hierarchies to compute a suitable generalization of the tuples before releasing them to the observer. If an observer poses N continuous queries, it is possible that on an event N distinct tuples might need to be generalized. The algorithm therefore has to search for a joint generalization scheme for these N tuples. If there are m levels of generalization per attribute (on average) and N tuples, the number of different generalization schemes is $O(m^N)$. Similar to problems of privacy preservation in data publishing applications, it can be easily shown that this problem is in fact NP-hard for most cases and, hence, efficient polynomial time solutions are unlikely. Now, we describe the properties of the objective function and, based on those, propose a stochastic and distributed scalable algorithm based on simulated annealing to look for an optimal generalization.

4.1   Problem Characterization

An important property of the objective function (5) is its parallel nature. That is, minimal independent partitions can be solved independently and in parallel. Another important property, is the fact that the utility of a piece of information is never smaller than its generalization, which allows for prunning of the solution space. Formally:

Property 1. If Y_{rel}^j is a feasible solution, it is better than any $Y_{rel}^q \prec Y_{rel}^j$.

Proof. For any $Y_{rel}^q \prec Y_{rel}^j$, $\sum_{y \in Y_{rel}^j} EU_O(y) = \sum_{y \in Y_{rel}^q} EU_O(y) + \sum_{y \in \{Y_{rel}^j - Y_{rel}^q\}} EU_O(y) \rightarrow \sum_{y \in Y_{rel}^j} EU_O(y) > \sum_{y \in Y_{rel}^q} EU_O(y)$. In other words, the utility of a piece of information is never smaller than its generalization.

Given the exponential size of the feasible region, the need for real-time solutions, the parallel nature of the problem formulation, and the distributed computing affinity of sentient systems, we propose a distributed stochastic solution.

4.2   A Simulated Annealing Based Solution

Our solution is based on distributed simulated annealing [26,32,34,27]. Fig. 4 depicts the algorithm. We use the Rete algorithm [19] (an optimized incremental forward-chaining algorithm [34]) on the union of Y_{rel}^i and BK^{obs} to find the minimal independent partitions (*findMinIndPartitions*). That is, every time a rule fires in Rete, all the involved facts along with the rule are joined with every other set that contains any of the involved facts. The time complexity of this first step is polynomial because we make the following assumptions on the background knowledge model. We assume that uncertainty functions (f) adhere to the "natural restrictions" [25] of monotonicity ($f(x_1, \ldots, x_n) \leq f(y_1, \ldots, y_n) \; \forall_{i \in [1..n]} \; x_i \leq y_i$), boundedness ($f(x_1, \ldots, x_n) \leq x_i \forall_{i \in [1..n]}$), and continuity w.r.t its arguments—that is, the higher the premises the higher the consequent, the new data being inferred is as good as its premises, and the certainty function is continuously defined. Since the background knowledge is used to model *possible* privacy violations, resulting facts that are identical except for their associated uncertainty are combined with the MAX function. In the worst-case, the observer will know the rule that resulted in the highest certainty. With these assumptions, the inference analysis terminates in a finite number of steps [25].

Furthermore, the worst-case time complexity of Rete is still linear w.r.t. the number of rules (r) and polynomial w.r.t. the number of facts (f^c, $c = ruleLength + ruleArity$) as it is for non-probabilistic Datalog clauses [34]. Given that the actions taken for every time a rule is fired have a time complexity of $O(f^3 + 2fr)$, this first part of the algorithm has a worst-case time complexity of $O(rf^c + r(f^3 + 2rf)) = O(rf^c + r^2 f)$.

Every minimal independent partition Y_{rel}^i is optimized by multiple simultaneous instances of the simulated annealing algorithm from Fig. 5. In this algorithm, a state's neighbor is generated by randomly selecting a tuple and then generalizing it. A neighbouring state is accepted according to the typical acceptance function for simulated annealing $accept(s, T) = e^{-\Delta E / T}$. We define a state's energy $E(Y_{rel}^j)$ as:

```
Y_rel =findMinIndPartitions(Y_req,BK^obs)
for each(Y_rel^i ∈ Y_req)
  do n times in parallel
    SimulatedAnnealing(Y_rel^i)
  enddo
endfor
```

Fig. 4. Maximization algorithm

$$E(Y_{rel}^j) = \rho(\frac{\sum_{y_r \in Y_{rel}^j} EU_O(y_r)}{|Y_{rel}^j|}) + \frac{1}{\rho}(Nat(- \max_{y_r \in Y_{rel}^j} (EU_O(y_r)) -$$

$$\min_{y_d \in Y_{derived}^j} (EU_T(y_d) * \omega(y_d.t))) \quad (11)$$

where $Nat(y)$ returns y if $y >= 0.0$ or 0.0 otherwise, and $\rho = 10^{-r}$, with $r \geq 1$, is the *penalty* associated with violating Constraint 8 . Note that if the initial solution Y_{req}^i is feasible, then $\Delta E(Y_{req}^i) \leq \rho$, which is a number close to 0.0.

We choose the initial temperature T_0 to be $\frac{1}{\rho}$ according to the following reasoning. The worst-case ΔE that we consider is when the neighboring state violates Constraint 8 by the approximate same amount but utility drops drastically. An upper bound on ΔE is thus $\Delta E = \rho$. In order to accept this state with a high probability at high temperatures, we set $T_0 = \frac{1}{\rho}$ since $\frac{1}{e^{\rho/T_0}} = 0.99$ for $\rho = 0.1$.

We change the temperature every $\frac{N' * max(m')}{2}$ iterations ($m' < m$ is the maximum number of granularities in Y_{rel}^i) because $\frac{N' * max(m')}{2}$ is the average distance from the initial state to the optimal. The temperature schedule follows the typical geometric rule $T_k = \delta * T_{k-1}$. Normally, with such a temperature schedule, δ is chosen very close to 1.0 such as 0.9 or 0.99 [32]; however,

```
function SimulatedAnnealing(Y_rel^i)
  Y_rel^j = Y_rel^i.neighbor()
  Y_rel^* = max(Y_rel^j, Y_rel^i)
  T = initial Temperature
  while(!terminate)
    if(accept(Y_rel^j, T))
      if(Y_rel^j.energy < Y_rel^*.energy)
        Y_rel^* = Y_rel^j
      endif
    endif
    if(!change temperature)
      Y_rel^j = Y_rel^j.neighbor()
    else
      T.decrease();
      if(!terminate)
        Y_rel^j = Y_rel^j.neighbor()
      endif
    endif
  endwhile
  return Y_rel^*
endfunction
```

Fig. 5. Simulated annealing

and in a manner similar to [27], since we are running multiple instances of the simulated annealing operator in parallel, we choose a small δ (e.g, for $r = 1$, $delta = \rho = 0.1$).

The algorithm terminates when a state with energy 0.0 has been found, the temperature reaches δ, or a feasible solution has been found (Property 1). The time complexity of the distributed simulated annealing becomes $O(\log_\delta(\delta/T_0) * \frac{N' * m'}{2} * (rf^c + N)) = O(\log_\delta(\delta * \rho) * \frac{N' * m'}{2} * (rf^c + N)) = O(\log_\delta(\delta^2) * \frac{N' * m'}{2} * (rf^c + N)) = O(Nrf^c + N^2)$. Consequently, the worst-time complexity of the whole maximization algorithm is $O((rf^c + r^2 f) + (Nrf^c + N^2))$—i.e., polynomial w.r.t. the size of the knowledge base and number of queries.

5   Implementation

We implemented the Privacy Manager in a real pervasive space composed of the Responsphere infrastructure [4] and the SATware middleware [21]. Together,

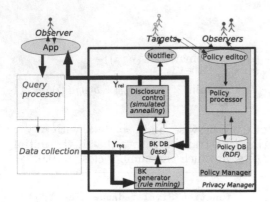

Target	
Labels	Utilities
Extremely Sensitive	−1.00
Very Sensitive	−0.75
Sensitive	−0.50
Somewhat Sensitive	−0.25
Not Sensitive	0.00
Observer	
Labels	Utilities
Don't Care	0.00
Information Curiosity	0.25
Information Useful	0.50
Information Needed	0.75
Always Needed	0.99

Fig. 6. PrivacyManager   **Fig. 7.** Utility Scales

Responsphere and SATware provide a campus-wide pervasive testbed for inter-disciplinary research in situation monitoring and awareness. Responsphere is a pervasive sensing, communications, computing, and storing infrastructure that covers a third of our university campus. It includes more than 200 sensors of different types such as video cameras, RFID readers, networked people counters, and wireless sensor networks (i.e., motes). SATware [21] is a middleware we have developed for executing pervasive applications on top of such an infrastructure. It provides applications with a semantically richer level of abstraction of the physical world compared to raw sensor streams. SATware's processing and pro-gramming model is based on operators, which serve as the transition between raw sensor streams to semantically richer information streams. Operators are Java-based mobile agents that implement a simple and data-centric function. For example, SATware provides operators that given a stream of video frames generates a stream of tuples that indicate whether motion has been detected. The Responsphere-SATware framework has been and is being used to test and develop applications such as privacy-preserving video surveillance [22,7,43], sit-uational awareness for firefighters (SAFIRE) [6], building visitor tracking [5], technology-induced recycling behaviour, fresh coffee alerts, and others.

In order to enable further applications such as the *OfficeMonitor*, we extended SATware with the Privacy Manager. The high-level design for integrating the Privacy Manager into SATware is shown in Fig. 6, which has 3 key components: (1) Policy Manager, (2) Background Knowledge Generator, and (3) Disclosure Control module.

In the Policy Manager, privacy policies and utilities are specified by users through the Policy Editor, validated by the Policy Processor, and stored into the Privacy DB. The knowledge base representing the background knowledge of users is partly populated by system and space administrators and partly learned (on-the-fly) by the system using the BK Generator, and stored into the BK-DB. Continuous queries are posed by an observer through an application, and their results are transmitted to the Disclosure Control module which analyses the possible information (using the proposed distributed simulated annealing tech-nique) that the observer could infer and, with the active policies, decides which information should be generalized and how. We now describe implementation details (and issues) for the 3 modules.

5.1   Policy Manager

We developed the Policy Language for Pervasive Spaces (PLPS) based on the Platform for Privacy Preference (P3P) [16] to assist users (observers and targets) in specifying the privacy policies and utilities (positive for observers and negative for targets). P3P is a W3C standard that enables websites to express their privacy policies in a computer-readable format and provides a protocol to read and process the policies automatically through web browsers. Additionally, it allows web users to express their privacy preferences that can be match with privacy policies specified by the websites. Based on these concepts, PLPS is designed to enable users of pervasive spaces to express their privacy policies to protect their personal information. In PLPS, a policy is defined as a set of statements, where each statement contains: (a) a piece of information; (b) the observer; (c) the retention that defines the length of the observation; (d) the context; and (e) the utility. In addition, each policy is associated with the mandatory elements name of the policy and observer who owns the policy, and the optional elements policy creation date, expiration date, and description. A policy is formally defined as a tuple of the form PP = {PolicyID, Target, CreationDate, ExpirationDate, Statements}, where *Statements* is a set of statements and each statement is formally stated as a tuple of the form Statement = {Observer, Retention, Context, Data, Utility}. The *Retention* element is defined as a tuple of the form {StartDate, EndDate, Frequency}. The *Frequency* element indicates the repetition of the observation defined in the statement and it is drawn from the set {Once, Daily, Weekly, Monthly, Yearly}. An example of a target's privacy policy in the *OfficeMonitor* application could be "Between 01/01/2009 and 03/30/2009, every Monday between 1pm and 4pm, Mary allows the system to tell if she is in her office to her research group members, but not to other users". This example is encoded as follows:

```
{Policy1, Mary, 01/01/2009, 03/30/2009,
{Group1, [01/05/09-1:00, 01/05/09-4:00, Weekly], Location, C1/B1/F2/R1, 0.0},
{Others, [01/05/09-1:00, 01/05/09-4:00, Weekly], Location, C1/B1/F2/R1, -1.0}}.
```

PLPS is not only flexible in terms of representing, managing, and interconnecting various types of policies; it also allows the definition of policies at different granularity levels for data attributes. Furthermore, policies are not static but rather the system dynamically updates them as the users specify new needs or tune old ones. We use the Web Ontology Language (OWL) [2] to represent the privacy policy rules modeled in PLPS in the form of ontology and complement it with the Semantic Web Rule Language (SWRL) [3] to express more complex rules. The advantage of using the Semantic Web to represent the policies, is the ability to perform various operations on the policies, including consistency checking, through ontology reasoners. We used the Jena API to implement the module.

Specifying Utilities: An important factor in defining the privacy policies is how to obtain the utility values. Obtaining the user's utility function is cognitively difficult [14] and specifying the utility of every possible piece of information for every target, observer, and context is an incredibly tedious task, which can hinder the usability of the approach. To address this issue, we propose a model that allows users to dynamically change their utility values for each policy statement based on their experiences and needs using a graphical continuous sliding scale with 5 labels homogeneously distributed[5]. Fig. 7 shows the 5 labels and the utility values associated with them. Recall that the utility for the observer is in the range $[0.0, 1.0)$ and the utility for the target in the range $[0.0, -1.0]$.

We extended the scale approach by adopting the Conditional Outcome Preference Network (COP-network) [12], for eliciting user preferences and estimating utilities. Applied to our policy model, a COP-network is a directed graph that represents the relative user preferences of the different data. Using this network of preferences and a few utilities "anchored" in some of the labels from Fig. 7, one can estimate the remaining utilities. Three techniques for estimating utilities are included with the COP-network approach, and we have selected and implemented the one that is proven to be more effective: the Longest-Path technique. In short, this technique takes as inputs a COP-network and a set of known "anchored" utilities, selects the longest path of private data in the network for which utilities are unknown, and compute utilities for those private data in a way that the preference ordering in the network is preserved. This process continues until all the private data has been considered.

5.2 Background Knowledge Generator

The privacy manager implementation also needs to deal with the issue of populating the knowledge base that represents the background knowledge of the users. In our background knowledge model, we identified three types of background knowledge that we modeled with pDatalog clauses: the generalization hierarchy (KB_{GH}), the space intended usage (KB_S) such as most people check their emails in their office, and the space individual usage (KB_D). We propose populating the knowledge bases as follows. The information in KB_{GH} and KB_S is initially populated by system and space administrators and continuously calibrated by the middleware. Calibration of rules in KB_{GH} and KB_S is done by regularly matching the recent data observed by the system with their rules. Borrowing the terminology from rule-mining algorithms, we call support $s\%$ the number of times a rule's premises appear divided by the number of tuples observed, and we call confidence $c\%$ the percentage of these times that the rule consequent also appears. We update a rule in KB_{GH} or KB_S when $s\%$ is above a threshold and we cannot reject the null hypothesis that the average times the rule holds for all individuals $c\%$ has not changed.

The information in KB_D is not pre-populated; rather, it is learned by the system overtime. Similar to KB_{GH} or KB_S, we create an exception rule in KB_D when $s\%$ is above a threshold and we cannot reject the null hypothesis that the average times the rule holds for some individual i ($c_i\%$) and the average times the rule holds for all individuals ($c\%$) are different (e.g., whereas most people check their emails in their office, Peter does it at the conference room). Furthermore, KB_D contains rules learned by regularly running association-rule mining algorithms, such as [9], on the information observed by the system. Given a set of items $I = \{i_0, \ldots, i_k\}$ and a set of transactions/baskets $T = \{t_0, \ldots, t_n \mid t_i \subseteq I\}$, rule association mining algorithms produce propositional rules of the form $Y \leftarrow X$, with $X \subset I$ and $Y \subset I$, where each rule has an associated confidence $c\%$ and support $s\%$. We propose *basketizing* the data observed by the

---

[5] We used 5 intervals as in the Likert scale, which is a well-accepted psychometric ordinal scale used in questionnaires and survey research [1]. Five levels are the usual choice since 3 do not provide enough variability and 7 offer to many choices.

system into time-based baskets at different time granularities and then mining association rules for each granularity. For instance, we would (i) put all the tuples whose time is within the same second in the same basket and then mine for rules such as "Mary writes emails at her office"; (ii) put all the tuples whose time is between 8 a.m. and noon in the same basket and mine for rules such as "Peter has coffee in the mornings"; (iii) put all the tuples whose time is in a Tuesday and derive that "Alice goes to board meetings on Tuesdays"; and so on up to weekly baskets. Note that we can, this way, derive both rules regarding the space usage (e.g, "Mary writes emails at her office") and inter-object relationships (e.g., "Mary's location is the same as Alice's 4/5 times").

We will then *upgrade* the resulting propositional rules to pDatalog rules by using $c\%$ as the uncertainty associated with the rule and fixing $s\%$ as a system parameter. Moreover, whenever a rule appears consistently among entities it will be generalized and added to KB_S—for example, if most people have coffee in the morning. The implementation details of the background knowledge learning algorithms are out of the scope of this paper. In here, we limit ourselves to show that the knowledge can be obtained and, hence, assumed that it has.

5.3 Disclosure Control

The disclosure control module is the key to the approach. Given a set of base results to an observer's queries, the disclosure control consults the policy database and BK to determine how to release the information without violating the target privacy, while maximizing the observer utility. Fig. 8 depicts the details of the implementation of the disclosure control module. Our solution is implemented as a graph of operators. The B operator outputs a series of sets where each set contains meta-information on an independent component. Namely, each set contains a small knowledge base with the relevant rules for this component and a subset of the tuples in Y_{req}. Similar to [15], we extend the Jess *deffact* template with an extra slot for the associated uncertainty and an extra rule to handle the combination of evidences on the same fact. The output of the B operator is forwarded to the scheduling operator, which forwards each input to a different PSA operator in a round-robin manner. Each PSA operator executes the parallel simulated annealing on the minimum independent components using also the extended Jess. The utility functions come from the $CTXT$ operators which, depending on the current context, query the policy DB for the active policies. The

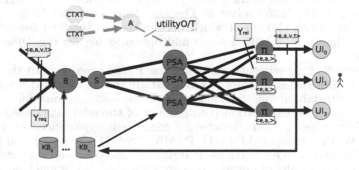

Fig. 8. Disclosure control

results of the *PSA* operators are forwarded to the π operators. The π operators then filter the data so the *UI* operators receive the $< id, att, v, t >$ tuples they expected.

6   Experiments

The main goal of the disclosure control submodule is to be able (i) to produce good results (high utility with adequate privacy) and (ii) to do so in real-time. To test the parallel simulated annealing based approach (PSA), we compared it to two simpler and centralized approaches: a brute force search (BF) and an anonymity-based approach (minGen). The BF approach was implemented as a depth-first search (DFS) with pruning based on Property 1. The minGen approach was an adaptation of the typical privacy definition in data publishing [37], where data is either private or public and the goal is to guarantee that private data attains a certain degree of anonymity while the information lost due to generalization is minimized. We measured the information lost as the average uncertainty introduced. Formally:

$$\max_{Y_{rel}} \sum_{y_q \in Y_{req}} \frac{P(y_q | Y_{rel}, KB_{GH})}{|Y_{req}|}$$

$$s.t. \forall_{(y_d \in Y_{derived}, y_d \in P)} \; P(y_d | Y_{rel}, BK^{obs}) > (1/k) \tag{12}$$

where P is the set of private data. This algorithm was implemented also with DFS with pruning. For comparison purposes, we considered all data with negative utility to be private and we assumed a fixed value of $k = 4$. We implemented 3 versions of the disclosure control submodule, one for each approach.

The experiments setup was as follows. We used scenarios from the *OfficeMonitor* application to create a realistic experimental setup. For the basic case, we instantiated the *OfficeMonitor* queries for a typical project group (7 people). Queries generated tuples of the form $<id, att, v, t>$ which were then routed to the Disclosure Control submodule. The query set generated 9 tuples every second over a period of time (our results are an average of 36 of such runs). The tuples represented 2 different minimal independent partitions. For the first partition, the utility values were set such that the solution was 5 generalizations away from the initial solution (the distance to generalizing everything to unknown was 28 generalizations). For the second partition, the solution was 0 generalizations away from the initial solution. The knowledge base had 12 facts, and 47 rules (similar to rule (1)), 14 of which were related to the 9 tuples being sent. We believe this to be a typical setup and dimensioning for the *OfficeMonitor* application.

Our first set of experiments compared the PSA approach with the BF and the minGen approaches. In order to further study the characteristics of the PSA approach, we instantiated 5 variations of it. These instantiations differed on the degree of concurrent exploration (i.e., number of threads) being used. We call these PSA(x) where x is the number of concurrent explorations on the same partition. We then compared PSA(1), PSA(6), PSA(11), PSA(16), and PSA(21) with the BF and minGen versions in terms of time overhead and utility loss. Fig. 9 shows the results of our experiments with a dual-core machine featuring an AMD Turion 64 X2 at 2.0Ghz, with 3GB of memory, and running Linux.

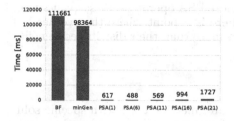
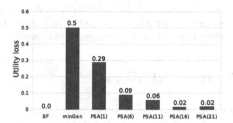

Fig. 9. Comparing average time overhead and utility loss of PSA with different concurrent explorations with BF and minGen

While the BF approach always finds the optimal, it takes far more time than the PSA approaches (minutes *versus* a few hundred milliseconds), which manage to return a solution very close to the optimal when incrementing the amount of concurrent exploration. The greatest utility loss is incurred by minGen, as expected (recall from above that minGen can only differentiate between public and private data and thus, it considers all data with negative utility equally private).

Our second set of experiments studied the scalability properties of the PSA approach. Fig. 10 suggests that, whereas our approach still takes a feasible amount of time for 12, 18, 24, and 30 tuples per second, it does not scale linearly but polynomially (which is expected, recall from Section 4.2 that the time-complexity of the disclosure control algorithm is polynomial w.r.t. the number of queries). PSA might not scale for other applications beyond the *OfficeMonitor* where applications need a large amount of tuples per second. However, the scalability of our approach can be improved by making use of (a) the parallel nature of the problem at hand and (b) the very nature of pervasive spaces which allows for distributed computing. In most cases, query results will have several minimum independent partitions in it. Each of these partitions can be optimized separately. Fig. 11 studies the effect of adding more PSA operators. It shows that, since, we had 2 minimum partitions, there is an important reduction of the time needed to find the solution when we had a number of PSA operators close to the number of independent partitions. With one PSA operator, independent partitions get

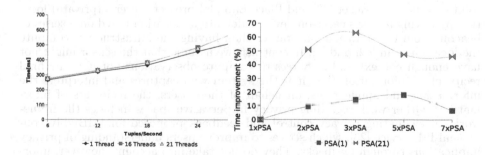

Fig. 10. Behaviour of PSA as the number of tuples/sec increases

Fig. 11. Effect of the increase of number of PSA operators

queued in front of the operator; with 2 or more PSA operators, these queues tend to be small or almost empty; however, there is a point where the overhead of having the extra operators starts weighing more than their distributed benefit.

7 Related Work

Several privacy and anonymity definitions and metrics along with specific solutions have been proposed in the literature. For instance, [35] presents the metric of k-anonymity, which expresses the fact that in the worst-case the value of a user's sensitive attribute can only be narrowed to a set of size k. In [37], the authors present a framework to achieve k-anonymity by generalization and suppression. In [29] the authors extend the k-anonymity metric with l-diversity which guarantees that it takes at least $l-1$ pieces of negative background knowledge (i.e., "Tom does not have arthrities") to sufficiently disclose *the* sensitive value of any individual by assuring that the l most frequent sensitive values are approximatly equi-probable. Positive background knowledge regarding *the* sensitive attribute of the type "If Tom has the flu his wife has it as well" is considered in [30], where its authors show the k worst rules that can be in a users' background knowledge and provide polynomial mechanisms to still be able to guarantee a degree of anonymity. In [18] the author proves the impossibility for absolute privacy in statistical databases and defines the alternative metric of *differential privacy*, which is a metric relative to the risk of a user participating in a statistical database. Nonetheless, none of the previous definitions applies to our scenario: we need a non-binary definition regarding information that is not useful in an anonymous manner—the *OfficeMonitor* is not interested in statistical data.

Our work here is similar to QoS-related work in stream systems. Stream systems such as Aurora [13] use semantic shedding [38] as one of the techniques to decide which tuples to drop when resources run low—that is, the less useful the data is for the recipient, the earlier it gets dropped. Here we take this concept further by deciding to drop (or generalize) tuples when a user's privacy would be violated.

Privacy in pervasive spaces has been researched at multiple levels. At the network layer, [10] combines hop-to-hop routing based on handles with limited public-key cryptography to preserve privacy from eavesdroppers and traffic analyzers. At the architectural level, and in a manner similar to outdoor GPS [24], solutions such as Cricket [33] and Place Lab [36] protect a user's (private) location by having a user's carry-on device calculate its location based on a series of beacons from the infrastructure rather than having the infrastructure compute the location as in [42] and [8]. In contrast, we assume that the sensor might not have enough context and resources to compute observations nor it is the final recipient of information (i.e., it is the system who captures and interprets the information and applications, on behalf of their users, the recipients of information). Other work regarding privacy in pervasive spaces includes the framework for evaluating privacy control and feedback proposed for IMBuddy contextual IM service [23], which strives to improve users understanding of privacy implications through feedbacks. They do not take into account, however, information that can be inferred as a result of the information being disclosed.

Using Semantics Web technologies as means for describing and reasoning about privacy policies in different domains including pervasive environments are becoming common [41,20]. Relevant to our privacy policy language is the semantic context-aware policy model based on Description Logic (DL) ontologies and Logic Programming (LP) rules in [41]. Central to this approach is the specification of policies based on context rather than the usual way of using roles and identities of users. In user-centric pervasive space applications such as OfficeMonitor, however, identity-based policies are still necessary since privacy is an individual-centric concept.

8   Conclusions and Future Work

To build a pervasive space middleware that allows applications to query the state of the objects in a given space is indeed a challenging task. One of the main challenges stems from the fact that some of the objects being monitored are people. The middleware needs to make sure that the query answers it provides to the applications do not violate privacy. In this paper, we proposed a novel approach for modeling privacy in the context of pervasive-space-supported collaborative work. We turned away from a traditional binary definition where information is either public or private and proposed a utility-based definition where information is associated with a positive utility for the querier and a negative utility for the target of the query. Moreover, further information that the querier might be able to infer is also associated with a negative utility. With this definition, we proposed a framework where the system has to decide, at every time instant, which information should be generalized and how much, such that privacy is preserved and utility for the querier is maximized.

Our first approach to solve the maximization problem is based on a distributed simulated annealing algorithm. We implemented our approach in an existing pervasive space middleware. To realistically instantiate such an approach, we also had to address the problem of obtaining and representing the utility functions and obtaining and representing a user's background knowledge. We proposed solutions for both problems.

Future directions opened by this paper include considering other types of applications where aggregated information and other mechanisms beyond generalization of attributes are relevant. We did not deal here with queries such as "Select the room with the maximum number of people in it". Privacy on these type of information is of a different nature and has its own challenges—anonymity-based definitions might be more appropriate. Examples of further mechanisms one might want to explore are generalization of identity and time. Identity generalization is specially interesting and, again, of a different nature: a system can only safely generalize "Alice" to "programmer" if the querier is learning information about other $k - 1$ programmers and he cannot tell who they really are. Last, another mechanism would be to trade delay for privacy to avoid time-and-domain based inferences such as inferring that Alice is still in the building because she was in its top floor two minutes ago—which could be a privacy violation if the context had changed over the last two minutes.

Acknowledgements

The authors would like to thank the SATware team for their dedication to the project and specially to Roberto Gamboni and Jay Lickfett for his help on mantaining and extending the implementation, Francisco Servant for implementing the first version of the policy management system, Haynes Mathew George for implementing the first prototype of the SATware's query processor, and Ronen Vaisenberg for his advise on the early stages of the paper on how to focus it. We would also like to thank the anonymous reviewers for their helpful comments.

This research has been supported by the National Science Foundation under award numbers 0331707, 0403433, and 0331690.

References

1. Likert scale. wikipedia, the free encyclopedia
2. Owl web ontology language guide (February 2004)
3. Swrl: A semantic web rule language combining owl and ruleml (May 2004)
4. Responsphere (2007), http://www.responsphere.org
5. RFID Tag lookup (2009),
   http://www.ics.uci.edu/community/events/openhouse/rfid.php
6. SAFIRE (2009), http://www.ics.uci.edu/%7Eprojects/cert/verticals.html
7. SATrecorder (2009), http://www.ics.uci.edu/%7Eprojects/SATware
8. Addlesee, M., Curwen, R., Hodges, S., Newman, J., Steggles, P., Ward, A., Hopper, A.: Implementing a sentient computing system. Computer 34(8), 50–56 (2001)
9. Agrawal, R., Srikant, R.: Fast algorithms for mining association rules. In: VLDB (1994)
10. Al-Muhtadi, J., Campbell, R., Kapadia, A., Mickunas, M., Yi, S.: Routing through the Mist: Privacy Preserving Communication in Ubiquitous Computing Environments. In: ICDCS, vol. 22, pp. 74–83 (2002)
11. Anderson, K., Dourish, P.: Situated privaces: Do you know where you mother (trucker) is? In: Proc. HCI International (2005)
12. Buffett, S., Fleming, M.: Applying a Preference Modeling Structure to User Privacy. NRC Publication Number: NRC 49372 (2007)
13. Carney, D., Cetintemel, U., Cherniack, M., Convey, C., Lee, S., Seidman, G., Stonebraker, M., Tatbul, N., Zdonik, S.: Monitoring streams–a new class of data management applications. Technical Report CS-02-04, Brown Computer Science (February 2007)
14. Chajewska, U., Koller, D., Parr, R.: Making Rational Decisions Using Adaptive Utility Elicitation. In: AAAI, pp. 363–369 (2000)
15. Corsar, D., Sleeman, D., McKenzie, A., Aberdeen, U.: Extending Jess to Handle Uncertainty. In: AI 2007. Springer, Heidelberg (2007)
16. Cranor, L., Langheinrich, M., Marchiori, M., Presler-Marshall, M., Reagle, J.: The Platform for Privacy Preferences 1.0 (P3P1. 0) Specification. W3C Recommendation, 16 (2002)
17. Dourish, P., Anderson, K.: Collective information practice: Exploring privacy and security as social and cultural phenomena. In: HCI, vol. 21, pp. 319–342 (2006)
18. Dwork, C., et al.: Differential privacy. In: Bugliesi, M., Preneel, B., Sassone, V., Wegener, I. (eds.) ICALP 2006. LNCS, vol. 4052, pp. 1–12. Springer, Heidelberg (2006)
19. Forgy, C.: Rete: a fast algorithm for the many pattern/many object pattern match problem. In: IEEE Computer Society Reprint Collection, pp. 324–341 (1991)
20. Hogben, G.: Describing the p3p base data schema using owl. In: A WWW 2005 Workshop on Policy Management for the Web (2005)
21. Hore, B., Jafarpour, H., Jain, R., Ji, S., Massaguer, D., Mehrotra, S., Venkatasubramanian, N., Westermann, U.: Design and implementation of a middleware for sentient spaces. In: Proceedings of ISI 2007 (2007)
22. Hore, B., Wickramasuriya, J., Mehrotra, S., Venkatasubramanian, N., Massaguer, D.: Privacy-preserving event detection in pervasive spaces. In: PerCom 2009 (2009)

23. Hsieh, G., Tang, K., Low, W., Hong, J.: Field deployment of IMBuddy: A study of privacy control and feedback mechanisms for contextual IM. In: Krumm, J., Abowd, G.D., Seneviratne, A., Strang, T. (eds.) UbiComp 2007. LNCS, vol. 4717, pp. 91–108. Springer, Heidelberg (2007)
24. Ivan, A.: Getting. The global positioning system. IEEE Spectrum 30(12), 36 (1993)
25. Kifer, M., Li, A.: On the semantics of rule-based expert systems with uncertainty. In: Gyssens, M., Van Gucht, D., Paredaens, J. (eds.) ICDT 1988. LNCS, vol. 326, pp. 102–117. Springer, Heidelberg (1988)
26. Kirkpatrick, S., Gelatt, C.D.J., Vecchi, M.P.: Optimization by Simulated Annealing. Science 220(4598), 671–680 (1983)
27. Krishna, K., Ganeshan, K., Ram, D.J.: Distributed simulated annealing algorithms for job shop scheduling. IEEE Transactions on Systems, Man. and Cybernetics 25(7) (July 1995)
28. Machanavajjhala, A., Kifer, D., Abowd, J., Gehrke, J., Vilhuber, L.: Privacy: Theory meets practice on the map. In: ICDE 2008, pp. 277–286 (2008)
29. Machanavajjhala, A., Kifer, D., Gehrke, J., Venkitasubramaniam, M.: l-Diversity: Privacy Beyond k-Anonymity
30. Martin, D., Kifer, D., Machanavajjhala, A., Gehrke, J., Halpern, J.: Worst-Case Background Knowledge for Privacy-Preserving Data Publishing. In: ICDE (2007)
31. Massaguer, D., Balasubramanian, V., Mehrotra, S., Venkatasubramanian, N.: Multi-Agent Simulation of Disaster Response. In: ATDM–AAMAS 2006 (May 2006)
32. Pham, D., Karaboga, D.: Intelligent Optimisation Techniques: Genetic Algorithms, Tabu Search, Simulated Annealing and Neural Networks. Springer-Verlag New York, Inc, Secaucus (1998)
33. Priyantha, N., Chakraborty, A., Balakrishnan, H.: The Cricket location-support system. In: MobiComp, pp. 32–43. ACM Press, New York (2000)
34. Russel, S., Norvig, P.: Artificial Intelligence: a modern approach, 2nd edn. Prentice-Hall, Englewood Cliffs (2003)
35. Samarati, P., Sweeney, L.: Protecting privacy when disclosing information: k-anonymity and its enforcement through generalization and suppression. In: Proceedings of the IEEE Symposium on Research in Security and Privacy (1998) (Technical report)
36. Schilit, B., LaMarca, A., Borriello, G., Griswold, W., McDonald, D., Lazowska, E., Balachandran, A., Hong, J., Iverson, V.: Challenge: ubiquitous location-aware computing and the" place lab" initiative. In: WMASH, pp. 29–35. ACM, New York (2003)
37. Sweeney, L.: Achieving k-Anonymity Privacy Protection Using Generalization and Suppression. Int'l. journal of uncertainty fuzziness and knowledge based systems 10(5), 571–588 (2002)
38. Tatbul, N., Çetintemel, U., Zdonik, S.B., Cherniack, M., Stonebraker, M.: Load shedding in a data stream manager. In: VLDB, pp. 309–320 (2003)
39. Thow-Yick, L.: The basic entity model: A Fundamental Theoretical Model of Information and Information Processing. Information Processing and Management 30(5), 647–661 (1994)
40. Thow-Yick, L.: The basic entity model: A theoretical model of information processing, decision making and information systems. Information Processing and Management 32(4), 477–487 (1996)
41. Toninelli, A., Montanari, R., Kagal, L., Lassila, O.: A semantic context-aware access control framework for secure collaborations in pervasive computing environments. In: Cruz, I., Decker, S., Allemang, D., Preist, C., Schwabe, D., Mika, P., Uschold, M., Aroyo, L.M. (eds.) ISWC 2006. LNCS, vol. 4273, pp. 473–486. Springer, Heidelberg (2006)
42. Want, R., Hopper, A., Gibbons, V.: The Active Badge Location System. ACM Transactions on Information Systems 10(1), 91–102 (1992)
43. Wickramasuriya, J., Datt, M., Mehrotra, S., Venkatasubramanian, N.: Privacy protecting data collection in media spaces. In: ACM Multimedia 2004 (2004)

Achieving Coordination through Dynamic Construction of Open Workflows

Louis Thomas, Justin Wilson, Gruia-Catalin Roman, and Christopher Gill

Department of Computer Science and Engineering
Washington University in St. Louis
{thomasl,wilsonj,roman,cdgill}@cse.wustl.edu

Abstract. Workflow middleware executes tasks orchestrated by rules defined in a carefully handcrafted static graph. Workflow management systems have proved effective for service-oriented business automation in stable, wired infrastructures. We introduce a radically new paradigm for workflow construction and execution called open workflow to support goal-directed coordination among physically mobile people and devices that form a transient community over an ad hoc wireless network. The quintessential feature of the open workflow paradigm is dynamic construction of custom, context-specific workflows in response to unpredictable and evolving circumstances by exploiting the knowledge and services available within a given spatiotemporal context. This paper introduces the open workflow approach, surveys open research challenges in this promising new field, and presents algorithmic, architectural, and evaluation results for the first practical realization of an open workflow management system.

1   Introduction

With the development of small, powerful wireless devices, computing must embrace the frequent, transient, ad hoc interactions of mobile environments. As computing and communication become more and more integrated into the fabric of our society, new kinds of enterprises and new forms of social interactions will continue to emerge. We ask the fundamental question: how can ad hoc communities of people (and their personal devices) coordinate to solve problems? Application domains that motivate or even require this form of interaction include low profile military operations, emergency responses to major natural disasters, scientific expeditions in remote parts of the globe, field hospitals, and large construction sites. These application domains share several key features: ad hoc interactions among people, high levels of mobility, the need to respond to unexpected developments, the use of locally available resources, prescribed rules of operation, and specialized knowhow. For instance, consider a construction worker discovering a mercury spill. While there is a prescribed response, it is his supervisor who has the needed expertise and training. She initiates the response, but access to the spill is made difficult by a support structure whose dismantling requires special intervention which only the chief engineer can manage. The

J.M. Bacon and B.F. Cooper (Eds.): Middleware 2009, LNCS 5896, pp. 268–287, 2009.

result is a series of frantic phone calls and the dispatching of various workers and equipment to execute what might be seen as a *workflow* that is reactive, opportunistic, composite, and constrained by the set of participants present on the site along with their knowledge and resources.

Current workflow middleware allows people to initiate complex goal-oriented activities that leverage services made available by a wide range of service-oriented portals. In the typical scenario, a user employs a web browser to make a request to a workflow engine responsible for executing a predefined workflow that can satisfy the specific user need, e.g., to print photos, reserve tickets, or make a bid in an online auction. The workflow is a directed acyclic graph with vertices denoting tasks and edges defining an execution order along with the flow of data and control. Each task is a specification for a service to be discovered and invoked by the workflow engine. What makes the workflow paradigm successful is the high degree of decoupling that it exhibits at multiple levels: between the user's need and the workflow required to satisfy it, between the task specifications and the services that implement them, and between the workflow engine that invokes a service and the service provider that executes it.

Despite workflow middleware being well established, efforts toward using it in ad hoc wireless environments are relatively new. Our previous research in this area includes the development of workflow execution engines targeted to small portable devices [1], and techniques for executing workflows in mobile wireless networks [2]. These studies reveal the need for a major reevaluation of the way one thinks about workflow middleware: hosts may move, service availability may depend upon which hosts are within communication range, user needs tend to be situational, and one cannot anticipate the range of responses demanded by changing circumstances. These observations suggest that in ad hoc wireless settings it is desirable to tailor or generate workflows dynamically.

Starting with this premise, we pose the question of how workflow middleware might be reshaped for use *in the absence of any wired connectivity*. In this paper, we explore whether workflow middleware can become a coordination mechanism for activities that are carried out in an ad hoc setting.

We use the term *open workflow* to denote a workflow specification, construction, and execution paradigm that is shaped by the dynamics and constraints of an activity whose underlying infrastructure is a mobile ad hoc wireless network. We assume a set of participants (people and the host devices they carry) who share a sense of purpose and who can move about and interact with each other and with the real world. The participants form a transient community that evolves over time. In our approach, one of the members of a community identifies a need for action, which then results in the dynamic construction of a workflow to satisfy the need and the execution of that workflow in a distributed and cooperative manner. The defining feature of the open workflow paradigm is the workflow construction process: workflow fragments encoding individual knowledge distributed across the set of participants are assembled into a custom workflow both automatically and contextually. In doing so, we also consider the available resources (expressed as services offered by the participants) along with the mobility of the participants and their willingness to commit to being present at a specific place and time and to delivering results to any dependent participants. The latter highlights another feature of the open workflow paradigm, its sensitivity to the time and location considerations necessary when performing activities in the real world.

Exploring the challenges of building a workflow on the fly from available contextual knowledge, i.e., the open workflow paradigm, and building a platform for further experimentation with that approach define the core technical contribution of this paper. We present a formalism for describing open workflow construction in Section 2. Section 3 explains our algorithms for the collaborative construction, allocation, and execution of open workflows. In Section 4, we present our open workflow management system and discuss its architecture. In Section 5, we evaluate its performance and discuss directions for future work. Section 6 highlights related research and contrasts it with this work. We provide conclusions in Section 7.

2   Problem Definition

2.1   Motivating Example

To highlight the possibilities and advantages of the open workflow paradigm, consider how a corporate catering facility might use open workflow to organize meals for a meeting of corporate executives. Suppose an executive assistant calls the manager at the catering office and requests breakfast and lunch for the upcoming meeting. The manager adds the request to the open workflow system on her mobile device to schedule the activities necessary to prepare the meals for the meeting. The open workflow engine begins by collecting knowledge contained on other mobile devices owned by the employees in the catering office, which include a master chef, kitchen staff, wait staff, and other personnel. For example, the master chef's PDA contains a workflow fragment consisting of tasks and conditions that describe how to serve omelets for breakfast. Figure 1 shows the collection of workflow fragments obtained from the office community.

Using the available knowledge, the open workflow engine searches for a subgraph that meets the conditions and requirements given by the manager. Assuming breakfast and lunch ingredients are available, we see that setting up an omelet bar and cooking omelets will result in breakfast being served, and preparing a soup and salad and setting them out as a buffet will result in lunch being served. Thus, this sub-graph constitutes a workflow that meets the requirements. The open workflow engine then searches for participants that are able to perform the activities indicated by the sub-graph. The system schedules the kitchen staff to set out the ingredients for breakfast and an appointment is added to the master chef's PDA to cook the omelets. Similarly, the kitchen staff must later cook lunch and set out the buffet. The manager's work is complete, and the members of the staff go about their scheduled activities.

Clearly, changes in the requirements will affect the generated workflow. For example, if lunch was not requested, then no lunch activities will be included

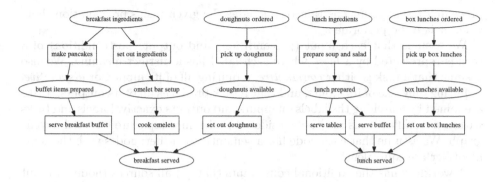

Fig. 1. Available knowledge in a corporate catering facility

in the final workflow. Consider a scenario where the master chef is out of the office. The workflow fragment concerning the preparation of omelets will never be collected and considered by the workflow engine. Consequently, one of the two alternatives (coffee and doughnuts or a breakfast buffet) will be chosen instead. A similar scenario where the wait staff are absent demonstrates how changes in the set of available capabilities can affect the construction of the workflow. The master chef knows that lunch can either be served with buffet service or with table service but the open workflow engine must select buffet service since no one in the available community is capable of serving tables.

Consider the difficulties of using a traditional static workflow to manage the catering facility. To be sensitive to the variety of catering requests and the individual capabilities and dynamic availability of the employees, the workflow would contain a large number of conditional branches which must be carefully crafted and assiduously maintained. Such a static workflow cannot respond rapidly to new resources or changes in the environment. Sensitivity to context, in the form of knowledge, capabilities, and availability, is the driving force behind the creation of our open workflow system.

2.2   Formalization

A *workflow* is defined as a collection of interlinked abstract *tasks*. A task represents a single abstract behavior or accomplishment without completely specifying how it must be performed. A *service* is a concrete implementation of a task and may involve a computation by the device, an activity performed by the user, or some combination of the two. Execution of a task thus consists of the invocation of a service satisfying the respective task specification. Within a workflow, different tasks may be performed in sequence or in parallel by one actor or by multiple actors. Each task has *preconditions* that must be met before the task can be performed, and *postconditions* that describe the results of performing the task. Abstractly, we can enable the performance of a given task by performing one or more preceding tasks whose postconditions taken together ensure the preconditions necessary for the given task. The order, timing, and executors of the preceding tasks are unconstrained so long as the given task's preconditions hold when it is to be performed.

We assume that each input (precondition) and output (postcondition) of a task is represented by a *label*, where each label has a distinct meaning. We also assume that a task is either *conjunctive*, requiring all of its inputs, or *disjunctive*, requiring only one of its inputs, and that a task produces all of its outputs. Tasks are joined by matching the labels on inputs and outputs exactly. Labels and tasks within a workflow thus may be considered nodes in a bipartite directed acyclic graph. We assume that each node has a semantic identifier; nodes with the same identifier are equivalent.

A workflow has the additional constraints that (1) all sources (nodes without any incoming edges) and all sinks (nodes without any outgoing edges) are labels, (2) a label can have at most one incoming edge, and (3) there are no duplicate nodes in the graph. This definition allows us to *compose* two workflows by merging (a) identical sinks from one workflow with the corresponding sources from the other workflow and (b) identical sources in both workflows. Two workflows are *composable* if and only if matching sinks and sources yields a valid workflow. For instance, a workflow W_1 with sources $\{a, b, c\}$ and sinks $\{d, e, f\}$ and a workflow W_2 with sources $\{c, d, e\}$ and sinks $\{g, h\}$ can be composed into a new workflow W with sources $\{a, b, c\}$ and sinks $\{f, g, h\}$. Workflow *fragments* are merely small workflows (possibly even a single task) that are intended to be composed into larger workflows at a later time. In the example graph in Figure 1, the boxes are tasks and the ovals are labels. The graph represents the available knowledge of the catering facility but is *not* a valid workflow because some labels have multiple incoming edges.

A workflow is constructed in response to an expressed need. In general, this need is stated in terms of a *specification* S: a *predicate* that indicates whether or not a workflow is *satisfactory*. The *inset* and the *outset* of a workflow are its sources and sinks respectively. We assume S is of the form

$$S \in \mathcal{P}(Labels) \times \mathcal{P}(Labels) \mapsto Boolean$$

A workflow W with inset $W.in$ and outset $W.out$ then satisfies a specification S if and only if $S(W.in, W.out)$ is true.

Composing workflow fragments may produce a workflow that cannot satisfy a specification S only due to the existence of extra sinks or sources. We can prune a workflow to remove unnecessary data flows, subject to the following constraints which ensure the result remains a valid workflow: (1) task outputs that are sinks can be pruned so long as every task has at least one output, (2) task inputs that are sources can be pruned for disjunctive tasks so long as every task has at least one input, and (3) tasks can be pruned so long as any task inputs that are sources and any task outputs that are sinks are also pruned.

Once a problem has been identified and a specification given, the *knowhow* (in the form of workflow fragments) and *capabilities* (in the form of services) of the local community are synthesized to form a plan by constructing a workflow. The construction problem is defined as follows. Given a workflow specification

S and a set of workflow fragments K, find a set of workflow fragments in K which may be composed (subject to pruning) into a workflow W that satisfies S — we say that W is *feasible* given S and K. It is important to note that the defining features of the open workflow paradigm rest with the fact that the specification S can be generated dynamically in response to a new need, context change, or other event, and that the set K represents the combined knowledge of the community as a whole. K is distributed and dynamic. As participants move around in space, the knowledge available to the community changes with its membership and their experiences. For the same specifications, different communities may respond differently or may be unable to construct an appropriate workflow.

As the plan is formed, tasks must be *allocated* to participants who will eventually *execute* corresponding services. The *availability* of services and resources within the community determines to whom tasks are allocated. Service availability is determined by whether any participant can commit to providing a service: that is, (1) whether the participant is *capable* of performing the service, (2) whether the participant has time available, (3) whether the participant can travel to the necessary location to perform the service, (4) whether the participant can gather the necessary inputs and distribute any outputs in a timely manner, and (5) whether the participant is willing (according to their preferences) to perform the service. If the community is stable and all participants are mutually reachable, it is easy to guarantee that the participants supporting the execution of tasks that depend upon each other are able to communicate the needed results in a timely fashion. More sophisticated routing techniques and analysis [3] may be needed if the movement of participants results in temporary disconnections. Once a participant has made a commitment, it is responsible for ensuring the service is executed as agreed. A participant is thus free to move about and requires no further communication with the community except possibly for previously agreed upon meetings to gather inputs or distribute outputs. As individual participants execute their assigned services from the dynamically constructed workflow, the community as a whole thus performs the activities necessary to satisfy the specification and achieve the original goal.

3   Collaborative Construction, Allocation, and Execution

3.1   Construction

We begin this section by introducing a construction algorithm for open workflows. We assume a participant has identified a need for action and generated a specification S of the form

$$W.in \subseteq \iota \wedge W.out = \omega$$

where ι and ω are sets of labels with ι being the labels that represent the triggering conditions and ω being the labels that represent the goal. The participant is in contact with the other members of a community and can collect from each a set of workflow fragments. For the purposes of illustration, we start with the simplifying assumption that the participant initially collects all the fragments in the community to create the set K. Using the gathered information, the participant runs our algorithm to find a feasible workflow — a workflow composed of fragments from K (subject to pruning) that satisfies S — if one exists. We only consider here the issue of generating one feasible workflow, although there are potentially many ways of combining fragments in K to satisfy S. While our algorithm chooses arbitrarily among equivalent options, any heuristic may be incorporated to direct the search toward more favorable solutions.

Our algorithm is based on graph traversal and graph coloring, and takes its inspiration from spanning tree algorithms and routing algorithms such as AODV [4]. Our strategy is to combine all workflow fragments from K into one large graph, henceforth called the workflow *supergraph* G. The supergraph represents a unified view of all possible actions represented in the set K, however it is not necessarily a valid workflow since it may have cycles, outputs produced by multiple tasks, unavailable inputs, or undesired outputs. We use a node coloring process on the supergraph G to identify one feasible workflow within this graph. We start by coloring the nodes corresponding to set ι of the specification S. Following the data flows, we explore the graph, growing the colored section as we identify which tasks and labels are *reachable* from ι. We call a label reachable when it is in ι or when it denotes the output of a reachable task; a task is reachable when all necessary input labels are available for its execution via some path starting from ι.

Once we have reached all the elements of ω, we prune the reachable set down to a valid workflow. Working backwards with a new color, we identify only those paths which are actually required to reach ω. The pruning phase removes cycles, ensures only one task produces each output, and excludes undesirable outputs. Once the second color has swept all the way back to ι, we have fully identified W, a valid workflow that satisfies specification S and that is composed only of fragments in K that have been pruned of unneeded outputs and paths.

With this general strategy in mind, we present the full pseudo-code in Algorithm 1. For purposes of the algorithm, we annotate every node and edge in G with a *color* (initially *uncolored*) and every node with a *distance* (initially ∞) from a source on the graph. Nodes are marked *green* for reachability during the exploration phase and *blue* for workflow membership during the pruning phase; *purple* identifies nodes on the boundary of the blue region. Label nodes are considered disjunctive. The algorithm selects nodes nondeterministically; any node may be processed next so long as it matches the guard condition.

We offer a proof sketch of the correctness of our algorithm by highlighting several key invariants. First, we claim that every green node is reachable starting from ι, and all of its prerequisites have a smaller distance. A node is reachable when it is in ι, or when its prerequisites are reachable. The invariant holds after every step of the algorithm because we start with the nodes in ι with distance 0 and we work outward one edge at a time, coloring a node n green only when n's

Algorithm 1. Workflow Construction (given ι, ω, and K)

— *Construct Supergraph* —
$G \leftarrow \emptyset$
for all fragments $F \in K$ **do**
    for all nodes $n \in F$ **do**   **if** $n \notin G$ **then** $G \leftarrow G \cup \{n\}$ **end if**   **end for**
    for all edges $e \in F$ **do**   **if** $e \notin G$ **then** $G \leftarrow G \cup \{e\}$ **end if**   **end for**
end for

— *Exploration Phase* —
Track the set of *greenNodes* (initially empty).
for all $n \in \iota$ **do** $(n.color, n.distance) \leftarrow (green, 0)$ **end for**
until $\omega \subseteq greenNodes$ $\vee$ none of the following cases apply, for some $n \in G$ **do**
    if n is disjunctive $\wedge$ <u>any</u> of n's parents are *green* **then**
        $d \leftarrow \min\{p \in n\text{'s parents} \vee p.color = green \,|\, p.distance\}$
        if $(n.color = uncolored \vee (n.color = green \ \wedge \ n.distance > d + 1))$ **then**
            $(n.color, n.distance) \leftarrow (green, d + 1)$
        end if
    else if n is conjunctive $\wedge$ <u>all</u> of n's parents are *green* **then**
        $d \leftarrow \max\{p \in n\text{'s parents} \vee p.color = green \,|\, p.distance\}$
        if $(n.color = uncolored \vee (n.color = green \wedge n.distance > d + 1))$ **then**
            $(n.color, n.distance) \leftarrow (green, d + 1)$
        end if
    end if
end until
if $\neg(\omega \subseteq greenNodes)$ **then** there is no solution — exit.

— *Pruning Phase* —
Track the set of *purpleNodes* (initially empty).
for all $n \in \omega$ **do** $n.color \leftarrow purple$ **end for**
until $purpleNodes = \emptyset$ for some $n \in purpleNodes$ **do**
    if $n.distance = 0$ **then**
        $requiredParents \leftarrow \emptyset$
    else if n is disjunctive **then**
        $requiredParents \leftarrow \{$the parent of n with minimum *distance*$\}$
    else if n is conjunctive **then**
        $requiredParents \leftarrow n$'s parents
    end if
    for all $p \in requiredParents$ **do**
        $edge(p, n).color \leftarrow blue$
        if $p.color = green$ **then** $p.color \leftarrow purple$ **end if**
    end for
    $n.color \leftarrow blue$
end until
The set of nodes and edges colored *blue* is the constructed workflow.

prerequisites are already green (reachable) and assigning n a distance greater than any of its prerequisites.

Second, once ω is colored blue, we claim that after every even number of iterations, the graph of blue nodes and blue edges is a valid workflow. At each step we choose a node n which is in the inset of the blue portion of the supergraph as it has no blue parents. Once we color the prerequisites of n blue, n is no longer a member of the inset but the prerequisite nodes are now members, so n and thus n's dependents are still reachable from the inset. On an odd iteration we color a task, and on the even iteration we color its prerequisite labels. Thus, after each pair of steps, the sinks and sources of the graph will be labels and the graph will be a valid workflow.

Finally, we claim that the coloring of blue nodes will eventually terminate, and upon termination the graph formed by the blue nodes and edges will be a workflow satisfying specification S. From the first invariant, every node n with distance greater than 0 must have prerequisites with distance strictly less than n's distance. Every time a node n in the inset is replaced with its prerequisites, the distance of the nodes added to the inset is strictly less than the distance of the node removed. Eventually the inset will consist solely of nodes with distance 0 (thus nodes in ι) and the algorithm will terminate. As the inset is a subset of ι and the outset is equal to ω, the workflow consisting of the blue nodes and edges satisfies S.

While there are many ways to maintain a community and share knowledge within that community, we chose an approach that places few restrictions on the members. We define a community as the participants who are within communication range of each other and announce their willingness to participate; consequently, the community is dynamic as members join and leave at will.

We observe that the coloring process requires only local knowledge. Thus, we relax the assumption that all of the workflow fragments are collected from the community before the coloring process begins. In our implementation, the member constructing the workflow builds the set of workflow fragments K and thus the supergraph G incrementally by querying other members of the community for workflow fragments that can be used to extend G. Members joining after the algorithm has started can still contribute knowledge, and the departure of a member does not affect the knowledge already collected in the supergraph.

3.2   Allocation and Execution

After a workflow is constructed, it must be allocated to participants in the community. The approach we take here is an auction algorithm similar to prior work done for Collaboration in Ad hoc Networks (CiAN). A more in-depth discussion may be found in [2].

The participant who constructs the workflow assumes the role of *auction manager*. The auction manager begins the allocation phase by computing metadata for each task used in allocating and executing the workflow. Next, the auction manager solicits bids for each task in the workflow from all of the participants in the community. The participants compare the task's required time, location, and service with their own capabilities and availability. If a participant can commit to performing a task, it submits a firm bid on that task to the auction manager. The bid includes ranking information such as the degree to which the participant is specialized for the task in question. The auction manager uses this information to select a best-suited participant to perform the task. A participant which provides fewer services is preferred over a participant with a wider array of services, because scheduling the more capable participant removes a larger number of services from the community's resource pool. Participants also submit a deadline for a response from the auction manager based on their schedule.

The auction manager selects the bid that best matches the selection criterion and makes a tentative task allocation to that participant. As new bids arrive, the tentative allocation is continually re-evaluated. A final decision is made when the deadline given by the participant who has the current tentative allocation has arrived. The auction manager waits as long as possible to assign a task to a participant in order to obtain the best possible bid, but once some participant has been found who can do a task, the task is guaranteed to be allocated. As bids are firm, a participant cannot cancel a bid, but they can update the deadline for a bid and force the auction manager to make a decision.

When a participant is allocated a task, it adds a commitment to its schedule that contains all the necessary information to execute the appropriate service as directed by the auction manger. The participant is free to roam, but is responsible for meeting its commitments. Thus the execution phase of an open workflow proceeds in a fully decentralized, distributed manner. To meet a commitment, the participant must (1) acquire the required inputs for the service from the executor of the preceding tasks, (2) be at the required location for executing the service, and (3) execute the service at the required time. The participant monitors these conditions and, based upon their knowledge of their location and the travel times involved, travels and communicates as necessary to meet the conditions and successfully execute the service. Once the service has been executed, the participant's final responsibility is to communicate the service's outputs to any other participants that require them.

4   System Architecture

4.1   An Open Workflow Management System

We have designed and implemented a complete open workflow management system in Java. Our approach offers an intuitive calendar-like interface, behind which integrated goal specification, communication, and service invocation features combine to enable construction and execution of sophisticated open work-flows. Source code and executables for the application are available at our web site [5].

The basic steps in deploying an application using our open workflow management system are (1) installing the program on the users' devices, (2) adding knowhow in the form of workflow fragments, and (3) adding service descriptions. In our implementation, we use XML configuration files to provide the task and service definitions for each device. Once this initial configuration has been completed, any participant can use their device to create a problem specification. In response, the system will automatically construct, allocate, and (by prompting the users) execute an appropriate workflow.

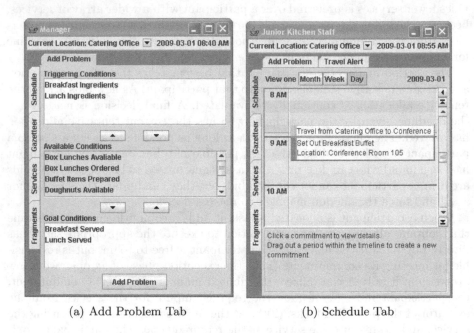

(a) Add Problem Tab   (b) Schedule Tab

Fig. 2. Application Screenshots

Figure 2 shows two screenshots from community members participating in an open workflow. The tabs on the left are for reviewing static knowledge. On the top are tabs for dynamic activities and alerts. Figure 2(a) shows the form that allows the user to create a problem specification by entering information about the triggering conditions and goal. In Figure 2(b), the Schedule tab allows the user to view their schedule of commitments. The necessary travel time is also blocked out in the schedule, and the system has added an alert tab to notify the user that they must soon begin traveling to meet their scheduled commitment. The system supports services that require user action by presenting a form for data entry or just a button to click when the task is complete. The remaining tabs allow the user to configure the list of workflow fragments (knowhow), the list of local services (capabilities), and other system settings.

4.2   Goals, Design Principles, and Architecture

Our goal is a system that will support the coordination and participation of devices with diverse capabilities. Further, we want to build a system robust enough and flexible enough to encourage rather than hinder innovations from future research. Consideration of these goals led us to the following two design principles. First, the architecture should break apart the major responsibilities of the system into independent components, allowing each host to provide only the components that are appropriate to the host's physical capabilities. Second, the architecture should isolate and hide the highly variable details of the transports, protocols, and caching schemes used during communication by providing an abstract communications layer. Furthermore, passing messages through an intermediary ensures that local and remote components are accessed uniformly.

Based upon these design principles, we identified the following major responsibilities for our open workflow management system, as illustrated in Figure 3. We first observe that for a particular open workflow problem, one host acts as the initiator while all hosts (including the initiator) may act as participants. We therefore split the system responsibilities into two corresponding subsystems: the construction subsystem and the execution subsystem. The construction subsystem is responsible for identifying the problem to be solved, issuing queries to discover knowhow and capabilities, formulating the plan of action, and assigning work. The execution subsystem is responsible for replying to knowhow and capability queries, accepting appropriate work assignments, and actually doing the processing or communicating necessary to complete the work.

Construction Subsystem. The Workflow Initiator is responsible for interacting with the user to define the trigger conditions and goal for the new problem. The Workflow Manager is the core component of the construction subsystem. The Workflow Manager creates and maintains a separate workspace for each open

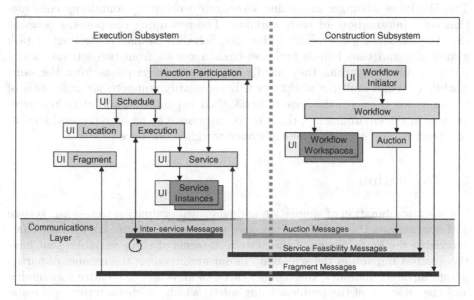

Fig. 3. System Architecture

workflow, allowing it to work simultaneously on multiple isolated and independent problems. The Workflow Manager issues queries to discover knowhow and capabilities, integrates the responses into the graph, and constructs the open workflow. It then delegates to the Auction Manager the job of allocating each task to a suitable host.

Execution Subsystem. The Fragment Manager is responsible for maintaining a host's database of workflow fragments and responding to knowhow queries during workflow construction. The Auction Participation Manager encapsulates the complex interactions and state tracking needed for the host to bid in task auctions during the allocation phase. The Schedule Manager is the keystone component of the execution subsystem. It manages the host's availability by tracking the host's location, schedule, and scheduling preferences. It maintains a database of all commitments, primarily consisting of scheduled service invocations and their associated location and travel time details, which is the key data structure for both allocation and execution of an open workflow. The Execution Manager monitors the input and temporal conditions required for each scheduled service invocation during the execution phase. Once an invocation's necessary conditions are met, it triggers service execution, and publishes any output messages. Finally, the Service Manager maintains the list of services exposed by this host and responds to capability queries from the Workflow Manager. It also provides a uniform service invocation interface to the Execution Manager by handling parameter marshaling and any other mechanics required to actually invoke a local service during the execution phase.

Our architecture permits multiple open workflows to be constructed and executed concurrently within the same community and even within the same host. The Workflow Manager maintains a separate workspace containing construction state information for each workflow. The remaining components (such as the Auction Manager, Fragment Manager, Schedule Manager, etc.) act at task granularity and thus handle two task-based requests from two separate workflows no differently than they handle two task-based requests from the same workflow. While multiple workflows will necessarily compete for utilization of the same resources (in the form of hosts, their capabilities, and other resources present in the environment), there is no impedance at an architectural level to constructing and executing multiple open workflows at once.

5   Evaluation

We use a combination of simulation and empirical evaluation to test our system and demonstrate the viability of the open workflow paradigm. We focus on characterizing the performance of the system in terms of three variables that have the greatest impact on the scalability of our architecture: the number of participants in the community, the number of tasks known to the entire community, and the difficulty of the problem being solved which we characterize by the size of the resulting workflow.

Our experimental set up is as follows. Given the number of hosts, the global number of tasks, and the length of the workflow as parameters for an experiment, we configure the hosts, establish connectivity within the community, and then measure the time taken from when the specification is given to the initiating host to the time when all tasks of the resulting workflow have been successfully allocated to some host.

To configure the hosts, we first construct a workflow supergraph of the chosen size by creating the desired number of nodes and then repeatedly adding edges between disconnected nodes until the graph is strongly connected. From this single supergraph we can then draw a large number of guaranteed-satisfiable specifications by randomly picking any triggering conditions and goal. We use only disjunctive task nodes in order to maintain the guarantee of satisfiability during our automated evaluations. Given a supergraph and a chosen number of hosts, we finish setting up the scenario by distributing the tasks randomly and evenly amongst the hosts, and *independently* distributing corresponding services randomly and evenly amongst the hosts. Each of the n hosts has only $\frac{1}{n}$th of the entire supergraph, so the hosts must cooperate to solve the posed problem. For each test run, the test driver randomly choses a path of the desired length through the supergraph, and the initial and final label nodes of the path are used as the specification for that test run. In all of the figures below, the results for each path length are the average of one thousand runs.

For the simulations, all the hosts were run within in a single JVM and communicate solely through a simulated network. The simulations were run on a Windows XP workstation with a 2.8 GHz Intel Xeon processor and 2.75 GB of memory, running the Java 1.6.0_11 HotSpot Client VM.

In Figure 4, we show the average time for each path length from a supergraph with 100 task nodes as the number of participating hosts varies from 2 to 15. The average time grows roughly linearly with the number of hosts as the initiating host communicates pairwise with every member of the community during the construction and allocation phases. We note that even if we were to broadcast requests rather than using pairwise communication, the processing of responses by the initiating host would still require time linear in the number of hosts in the community.

In Figure 5, we show the average time for each path length for 2 participating hosts as the number of task nodes in the supergraph varies from 25 to 500. The rate of increase grows with the number of task nodes because the Workflow Manager encounters more nodes during its search through the densely connected supergraph as the number of tasks increases. The longest path through the graph also increases as the size of the graph increases, which explains the absence of timings for path lengths greater than 10 in the small 25 task supergraph.

After the simulations, we performed empirical evaluation of our application using four laptops connected by an ad hoc wireless network using 802.llg (54Mbit/s). The first host (which was the initiating host during these tests) was a MacBook Pro running OS X 10.5.5 with a 2.16 GHz Intel Core Duo processor and 1 GB of 667 MHz DDR2 memory. The second host was a MacBook Pro

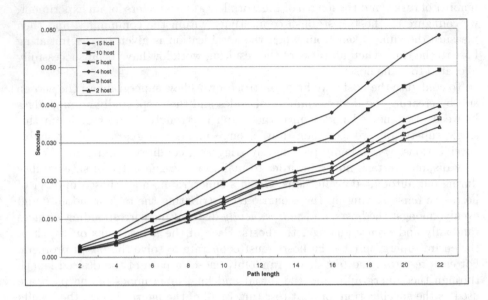

Fig. 4. Simulation of 100 task nodes partitioned across different numbers of hosts

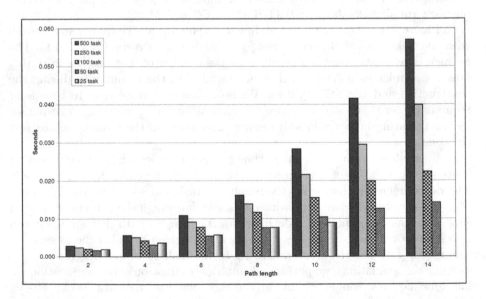

Fig. 5. Simulation of different numbers of task nodes partitioned across 2 hosts

running OS X 10.5.6 with a 2.33 GHz Intel Core 2 Duo processor and 2 GB of 667 MHz DDR2 memory. The third and fourth hosts were MacBook Pros running OS X 10.5.6 with 2.4G Hz Intel Core 2 Duo processors and 4 GB of 1067 MHz DDR3 memory. All hosts were running the Java 1.5.0_16 HotSpot Client VM. Connectivity among the hosts was verified before the measurements were started. The timing results for workflow graphs with 25, 50, and 100 task nodes are shown Figure 6.

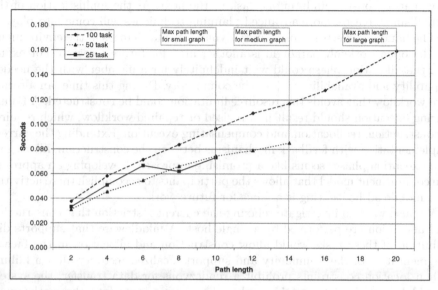

Fig. 6. Empirical performance of ad hoc wireless networking for different numbers of task nodes partitioned across 4 hosts

We can see from this graph that even in a realistic networking environment, our system shows the potential to solve large problems quickly. For example, even with a community knowledge base of one hundred tasks to explore, and a solution path length of twenty, our system finds and allocates a solution in under two tenths of a second on average.

5.1   Directions for Future Work

These encouraging results demonstrate that our system is ready to be evaluated against large-scale real-world problems. In order to accomplish this, we will seek a community to serve as a source of realistic benchmarks. We expect to face new issues when adapting our system to the rigors and challenges posed by our sample community.

One such concern for future research is the representation of tasks and specifications. Weakening our initial assumption that a specification only involves the inset and outset would allow specifications that include constraints on all aspects of the workflow graph, such as path length, task preferences, and external temporal and spatial constraints. Furthermore, the specification can be expanded to influence the allocation and execution phases. A specification, for example, could minimize the set of participants or restrict the locations of certain tasks. In order to realize richer specifications, a more expressive formalism for describing tasks and preconditions and postconditions is necessary. For example, an extended formalism may allow associating variables and constraints with preconditions and postconditions such as type, capacity, and duration, or propagating constraints from one task to the next. As the sophistication of the formalism increases, more advanced planning techniques will come into play.

The handling of errors, community dynamics, and changes in the environment by the open workflow paradigm is another area for future research. For example, the allocation phase could wait indefinitely for a member with the needed capability and availability to join the community. During this time, an alternative workflow that avoids this resource limitation could be constructed. A failure during execution should result in a revised or repaired workflow, which requires reconstruction, reallocation, and compensating execution. Extending the current implementation with feedback mechanisms between the construction, allocation, and execution phases seems like a promising approach. Developing an appropriate commitment model that allows the participants to accomplish these activities in a mobile ad hoc setting is a focus for future work.

We also want to investigate relaxing the current restriction that construction and allocation are performed by a single host. A middleware that supports distribution of these tasks would allow construction and allocation in the face of fragmentation of the community and support localized recovery after a failure. When location constraints prohibit a rendezvous for data transfer, the system should be extended to consider scheduling participants into the workflow as couriers.

Finally, as with any application facing the rigors of the real world, security is critical. In addition to the usual concerns of trust, authorization, and privacy, the open workflow paradigm presents new challenges as it encourages participation across multiple administrative domains and social networks. Recognizing and handling changes in authorization and privacy due to roles and social context and resolving conflicting and competing specification ontologies are topics for future research.

6   Related Work

In this paper, we have focused on overcoming the challenges of bringing workflows to transient communities connected by mobile ad hoc networks. Standard workflow management systems, such as ActiveBPEL [6], Oracle Workflow Engine [7], JBoss [8], and BizTalk [9], are designed to work in fully wired environments, such as corporate LANs or across the Internet. Reliance on centralized control and reliable communication mean such solutions cannot successfully operate under the constraints of dynamic mobile environments.

Several workflow systems have been developed which extend the realms in which workflows may operate. The work on federating separate execution engines running independent workflows by Omicini, et al., [10] removes the requirement of centralized control. Chafle, et al., [11], investigate decentralized orchestration of a single workflow by partitioning the workflow at build time and using message passing at run time. Both approaches still assume reliable communication and a fixed group of participants. MoCA [12] uses proxies for distributed control and has some design features that support mobile environments while Exotica/FDMC [13] describes a scheme to handle disconnected mobile hosts. In AWA/PDA [14], the authors adopt a mobile agent based approach based on the GRASSHOPPER agent system. WORKPAD [15] is designed to meet the challenges of collaboration in a peer-to-peer MANET involving multiple human users, however WORKPAD retains the requirement that at least one member of the MANET be connected with a central coordinating entity that orchestrates the workflow and shoulders any heavy computational loads. Sliver [1] brings a full BPEL execution engine to a single cell phone, however that phone still acts as the sole coordinator. Finally, CiAN [2] presents a workflow management system which eliminates the need for a central arbiter by distributing not only service execution but also the task allocation problem across multiple hosts.

While our system builds upon CiAN's model of distributed workflow allocation and execution, all these systems assume that a thoughtfully designed and fully specified workflow already exists. Open workflow is designed for settings where the availability of resources and the range of responses demanded by changing circumstances cannot be anticipated. The workflow to be executed must be generated on the fly to match the present situation.

The automatic composition of services has been explored using a variety of AI planing engines, including Golog [16], Workflow Prolog [17], and PDDL [18]. A review of further automated service composition methods may be found in [19]. Ponnekanti and Fox create workflows by rule-based chaining in SWORD [20], and discuss situations in which the resulting workflows may not produce the desired results due to the preconditions and postconditions of each task not being sufficiently specified. Fantechi and Najm [21] present an approach for ensuring correct service composition by using a more detailed formal specification of the service behavior. While the initial open workflow construction algorithm we present is a simplified alternative to the powerful techniques presented in these papers, it also addresses a new problem specific in the mobile ad hoc environment. All these systems assume that the knowledge base from which to build the workflow already exists. We have built upon their work by showing how to construct both the knowledge base and the derived workflow on the fly based on the knowhow and capabilities available within the community.

7   Conclusions

In this paper we have introduced the open workflow paradigm and presented the first algorithm for constructing open workflows in ad hoc wireless mobile environments. A system for open workflow creation, allocation, and execution was proposed, implemented, and evaluated.

The open workflow paradigm is novel and enables the development of new classes of applications that are designed to exploit community knowledge in solving real world problems that arise unexpectedly and can be addressed only through the coordinated exploitation of capabilities distributed among the members of the community. The open workflow paradigm presents significant new challenges for the middleware, MANET, workflow, planning, and human-computer interaction research communities. The work presented in this paper is only the first step toward characterizing and addressing these concerns.

In producing the first practical implementation of an open workflow management system, we have affected a major paradigm shift in workflow middleware. Open workflows are much more than sophisticated scripts that enable one to exploit available services — they are a coordination vehicle for social and business activities that allows cooperating participants to construct and execute responses to needs identified by the participants. The open workflow paradigm enables the development of an entirely new class of systems that are nimble, mobile, and supportive of this new style of coordination.

Acknowledgments. This paper is based upon work supported in part by the National Science Foundation (NSF) under grant No. IIS-0534699. Any opinions, findings, and conclusions or recommendations expressed in this paper are those of the authors and do not necessarily reflect the views of NSF.

References

1. Hackmann, G., Haitjema, M., Gill, C., Roman, G.C.: Sliver: A BPEL workflow process execution engine for mobile devices. In: Dan, A., Lamersdorf, W. (eds.) ICSOC 2006. LNCS, vol. 4294, pp. 503–508. Springer, Heidelberg (2006)
2. Sen, R., Roman, G.C., Gill, C.D.: CiAN: A workflow engine for MANETs. In: Lea, D., Zavattaro, G. (eds.) COORDINATION 2008. LNCS, vol. 5052, pp. 280–295. Springer, Heidelberg (2008)
3. Handorean, R., Gill, C.D., Roman, G.C.: Accommodating transient connectivity in ad hoc and mobile settings. In: Ferscha, A., Mattern, F. (eds.) PERVASIVE 2004. LNCS, vol. 3001, pp. 305–322. Springer, Heidelberg (2004)
4. Perkins, C.E., Belding-Royer, E.M.: Ad-hoc on-demand distance vector routing. In: WMCSA, pp. 90–100. IEEE Computer Society, Los Alamitos (1999)
5. Mobilab Group: Open workflow project web site, http://mobilab.wustl.edu/projects/openworkflow/
6. Active-Endpoints: ActiveBPEL engine, http://www.active-endpoints.com/active-bpel-engine-overview.htm
7. Oracle Inc.: Oracle workflow, http://www.oracle.com/technology/products/integration/workflow/workflow_fov.html
8. JBoss Labs: JBoss application server, http://www.jboss.com/docs/index
9. Microsoft Corp.: The BizTalk server, http://www.microsoft.com/biztalk/

10. Omicini, A., Ricci, A., Zaghini, N.: Distributed workflow upon linkable coordination artifacts. In: Ciancarini, P., Wiklicky, H. (eds.) COORDINATION 2006. LNCS, vol. 4038, pp. 228–246. Springer, Heidelberg (2006)
11. Chafle, G., Chandra, S., Mann, V., Nanda, M.G.: Decentralized orchestration of composite web services. In: Proc. of the 13th Intl. WWW Conference, pp. 134–143 (2004)
12. Sacramento, V., Endler, M., Rubinsztejn, H.K., Lima, L.D.S., Gonçalves, K., Bueno, G.A.: An architecture supporting the development of collaborative applications for mobile users. In: Proc. of WETICE 2004, pp. 109–114 (2004)
13. Alonso, G., Gunthor, R., Kamath, M., Agrawal, D., Abbadi, A.E., Mohan, C.: Exotica/FDMC: A workflow management system for mobile and disconnected clients. Parallel and Distributed Databases 4(3) (1996)
14. Stormer, H., Knorr, K.: PDA- and agent-based execution of workflow tasks. In: Proceedings of Informatik 2001, pp. 968–973 (2001)
15. Mecella, M., Angelaccio, M., Krek, A., Catarci, T., Buttarazzi, B., Dustdar, S.: WORKPAD: an adaptive peer-to-peer software infrastructure for supporting collaborative work of human operators in emergency/disaster scenarios. In: International Symposium on Technologies and Systems, pp. 173–180 (2006)
16. McIlraith, S., Son, T.C.: Adapting golog for composition of semantic web services. In: Proceedings of the 8th International Conference on Knowledge Representation and Reasoning (KR 2002), pp. 482–493 (2002)
17. Gregory, S., Paschali, M.: A prolog-based language for workflow programming. In: Murphy, A.L., Vitek, J. (eds.) COORDINATION 2007. LNCS, vol. 4467, pp. 56–75. Springer, Heidelberg (2007)
18. McDermott, D.: Estimated-regression planning for interactions with web services. In: Proceedings of the 6th International Conference on AI Planning and Scheduling, pp. 204–211. AAAI Press, Menlo Park (2002)
19. Rao, J., Su, X.: A survey of automated web service composition methods. In: Cardoso, J., Sheth, A.P. (eds.) SWSWPC 2004. LNCS, vol. 3387, pp. 43–54. Springer, Heidelberg (2005)
20. Ponnekanti, S.R., Fox, A.: SWORD: A developer toolkit for web service composition. In: Proceedings of the 11th World Wide Web Conference, Honolulu, Hawaii, USA (May 2002)
21. Fantechi, A., Najm, E.: Session types for orchestration charts. In: Lea, D., Zavattaro, G. (eds.) COORDINATION 2008. LNCS, vol. 5052, pp. 117–134. Springer, Heidelberg (2008)

Power Aware Management Middleware for Multiple Radio Interfaces

Roy Friedman and Alex Kogan

Department of Computer Science, Technion
{roy,sakogan}@cs.technion.ac.il

Abstract. Modern mobile phones and laptops are equipped with multiple wireless communication interfaces, such as WiFi and Bluetooth (BT), enabling the creation of ad-hoc networks. These interfaces significantly differ from one another in their power requirements, transmission range, bandwidth, etc. For example, BT is an order of magnitude more power efficient than WiFi, but its transmission range is an order of magnitude shorter. This paper introduces a management middleware that establishes a power efficient overlay for such ad-hoc networks, in which most devices can shut down their long range power hungry wireless interface (e.g., WiFi). Yet, the resulting overlay is fully connected, and for capacity and latency needs, no message ever travels more than $2k$ short range (e.g., BT) hops, where k is an arbitrary parameter. The paper describes the architecture of the solution and the management protocol, as well as a detailed simulations based performance study. The simulations largely validate the ability of the management infrastructure to obtain considerable power savings while keeping the network connected and maintaining reasonable latency. The performance study covers both static and mobile networks.

Keywords: Wireless Ad-hoc Networks, Power Aware Overlays, Multiple Radio Interfaces.

1 Introduction

Mobile devices enabled with multiple wireless interfaces are becoming increasingly common. As evidence, most laptops, smartphones and PDAs are equipped with WiFi and BlueTooth (BT) radios. Future devices are expected to include even more interfaces, supporting currently emerging standards, such as WiMax and ZigBee. An important aspect of these technologies is their ability to create mobile ad-hoc networks (MANETs), which enable direct communication between devices in an infrastructure independent manner and offer fast and easy deployment in situations where it is not possible or not cost effective otherwise.

Yet, mobile devices are typically battery operated. Hence, any application or middleware for such ad-hoc networks must be energy efficient. Researchers have found that wireless communication is one of the main sources of power consumption in mobile devices [2,15,7]. Consequently, efficient power utilization by the wireless communication sub-system is crucial for the success of such networks.

J.M. Bacon and B.F. Cooper (Eds.): Middleware 2009, LNCS 5896, pp. 288–307, 2009.

All aforementioned technologies for wireless communication differ dramatically one from another in several parameters, e.g., maximum transmission range, energy requirements and available bandwidth [8, 15]. Hence, the choice of which wireless technology to use has great impact on the power consumption of the devices, but also on the network connectivity and capacity. For example, a simple approach of switching off WiFi and only keeping BT operational may result in a disconnected network. On the other hand, leaving all interfaces up all the time is too wasteful. This is because, especially in WiFi, the power consumed by an idle interface is only slightly lower than the power consumed while transmitting or receiving [3, 4, 7, 15].

Power utilization in mobile ad-hoc networks has received substantial attention in recent years. Most previous works, however, consider devices with a single wireless interface. The proposed solutions range from constructing an energy-efficient overlay of active nodes, e.g., [4, 19, 20], through adjusting transmission range of radios, e.g., [9, 11, 13], to exploiting interface-specific techniques, such as the power-saving mode (PSM) of WiFi, e.g., [1, 2, 12]. All approaches, however, share the problem of potentially lost connectivity and pose non-trivial assumptions on the underlying system, such as the availability of location information, radios with a varying transmission range, synchronized clocks, etc.

In this paper, we take a different, more integrated approach to the problem of power utilization for networks in which the devices own two wireless communication interfaces, e.g., WiFi and BT.[1] Specifically, we develop a middleware service, called *Overlay Construction and Maintenance (OCM)*, that controls which wireless interfaces should be used on each device in the following manner: OCM constructs an overlay of devices such that each device who is a member of the overlay keeps both its interfaces active. All other devices not in the overlay shut down their long range power hungry wireless interfaces (typically WiFi). In order to keep the network latency and capacity reasonable, no device is further than k short range hops from its nearest overlay member, where k is an arbitrary parameter. Moreover, the transitive network formed by the collection of short range radios and active long range radios must be fully connected. Also, devices elected by OCM to the overlay tend to be the ones with highest remaining battery power, and the overlay is constantly maintained in order to reflect both dynamic changes in the network topology as well as remaining battery power.

Each overlay member acts as a *cluster-head* for its non-overlay short-range k-hop neighborhood. OCM interacts with a slightly modified routing infrastructure at the IP layer such that messages are routed using a standard reactive routing protocol, such as DSR [10], to the cluster-head closest to the target node. From the cluster-head, the message is forwarded through table driven routing, also managed and dictated by OCM, along short range hops to the actual destination device.

Although at the abstract level our solution does not assume any specific technology, the most natural scenario for the application of OCM is a network composed from laptops and mobile phones equipped with BT and WiFi radios. Hence, we evaluate the performance of OCM with typical power consumption parameters for BT and WiFi network cards under several network conditions, such as density and mobility of nodes. For the latter, we use several mobility models, e.g., a static model with random

---

[1] Extending our solution to multiple interfaces is straight forward.

placement and random way-point [10]. Yet, one of the possible domains for the application of OCM is a university campus or a school. In these settings, the entire network can consist of hundreds of nodes. However, at any given time, there are sets of dozens of devices that remain in proximity for long periods of time, but may also move from one location to another. In order to capture the specific characteristics of this domain, we introduce and evaluate OCM under a novel mobility model. In this model nodes prefer to stay or move in the vicinity of one of the preselected hot-spots, corresponding to classrooms and gathering places (such as cafeterias, libraries, meeting rooms, etc.). Nodes mostly switch between these places at the same times, corresponding to beginnings and endings of classes and breaks.

Since measuring the performance for a network of a few hundreds of nodes was not feasible, we opted to present simulation results. Yet, the simulations were performed with the complete Java code of the implementation. Through extensive simulations, we show that OCM is able to save significant portions of energy, while keeping the latency under tolerable limits. As could be expected, the energy gain produced by OCM is especially high when the network becomes denser and mobility is low, which matches well campus and school environments.

The rest of the paper describes and evaluates the OCM middleware. The related work is surveyed in Section 2. Section 3 presents the architecture of OCM and Section 4 provides details on its management module. The integration of OCM with routing is discussed in Section 5. Section 6 presents an extensive simulation based evaluation of the performance of OCM. The technical details on extensions implemented in the simulator to enable our evaluation are given in Appendix A. We conclude in Section 7.

2 Related Work

A few recent papers consider wireless networks consisting of devices equipped with multiple radio interfaces. The most related to our work is that of Bahl et al. [3], which outlines the advantages behind systems that use two radios in an integrated manner. They investigate multi-radio solutions to several problems in wireless computing, such as energy management and capacity enhancement, and show significant benefits for such solutions over single-radio ones. Although their work does not rely on any particular radio technology, it requires, however, that all radios of the sender should be able to communicate with all radios of the receiver, meaning effectively that devices should stand close enough or all radios should have the same transmission range.

Pering et al. [15] introduce a system called CoolSpot that enables traditional WiFi hot-spots with BT interfaces and with a policy for multi-radio management. The paper considers single-hop communication between a wireless mobile device and such a hot-spot, where a closely located device is able to switch automatically between two interfaces in order to reduce its power consumption. The authors also provide an empirical evaluation of several policies that effectively manage radio switching.

Energy efficiency in single-radio wireless networks is a well studied problem. Brevity precludes us from mentioning all of the works, so we will refer to exemplary ones, and explain the difference between their approach and ours.

The idea of constructing an overlay of active nodes responsible for routing while other nodes may turn their radios off was examined by several researchers. Xu et al. [20]

propose the GAF algorithm, which partitions a wireless network into small virtual grids. Based on location information provided by a GPS or similar systems, GAF selects one node in each grid to remain active, while the rest of the nodes are put into sleep. Chen et al. [4] present SPAN, a probabilistic power-saving technique where a node decides to join an overlay if it discovers two neighboring nodes that cannot communicate directly or through another node in the overlay. Similar ideas are used by Wu et al. [19] in order to build an overlay consisting of nodes with high remaining energy level. Since these works consider a single wireless interface (SPAN is even designed for WiFi only), when a node turns its radio off, it is unable to receive incoming messages, eventually increasing the number of lost messages, or requiring overlay nodes to store messages for relatively long durations, increasing the latency and buffering requirements. Thus, this approach is inappropriate in systems with heavy communication patterns.

Another extensively studied power-saving technique is to control the topology by varying the transmission range of the radios, e.g., [9, 11, 13]. The main tradeoff in the topology control comes from the following fact: Decreasing the transmission range decreases the power consumption significantly and reduces the interference. On the other hand, it may hurt network connectivity and increase the diameter of the network (in terms of number of hops), which in turn may increase the communication latency and decrease the network capacity. In addition, power consumption in idle state still remains a problem.

The IEEE 802.11 standard defines a power-saving mode (PSM), which allows to switch the wireless card into sleep mode in case of no activity and wake it periodically to probe an access point for pending messages. While PSM can significantly reduce the power consumption during idle periods, it was found that in certain common interactive applications it may cause substantial increase in latency and even in power [1, 12]. In order to cope with the limitations of PSM, several enhancements were proposed, tailored mainly to application specific domains, such as web-browsing [2, 12] and distributed file systems [1]. Besides being developed solely for WiFi, though, PSM is orthogonal to the approach presented in this paper, and thus can be used in addition to it.

In order to evaluate the performance of OCM, we integrate it with an ad-hoc routing protocol in a way that uses a reactive routing on the long range interface between the overlay nodes, while the routing to/from non-overlay nodes is done proactively on the short range interface. The resulting scheme resembles several protocols proposed for hierarchical routing in single-radio networks (e.g., [14, 16]). The main benefit of such protocols is scalability, since only a small fraction of nodes, i.e., those in the overlay, are involved in the route discovery process.

3   Architecture of OCM

The OCM architecture is depicted in Figure 1. Its main part is a *management* module, accompanied by a couple of *heartbeat* modules, all running as independent processes within a MANET device equipped with two radio interfaces. The management module is responsible for the construction of the power aware overlay and its maintenance according to dynamic changes in the topology and remaining battery power of the devices. Based on the internal logic described in the following section, the management

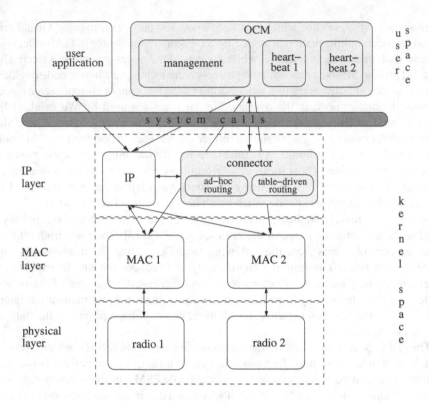

Fig. 1. Architecture overview

module decides to switch radios on and off by executing system calls to corresponding MAC modules of the radios, as shown in Figure 1. By a slight abuse of terminology, in the sequel, when referring to OCM, we actually mean the management module.

The management module is assisted by heartbeat modules that utilize the common technique of periodically broadcasting heartbeat messages for discovery of new neighbors and notification on lost neighbors. When a heartbeat message from a previously unknown node is received, this node is considered as a new neighbor. When no heartbeat message is received from a neighbor during some predefined period of time, the link with this neighbor is considered to be lost. A clear trade-off exists between the accuracy of the information and the frequency of broadcasts.

The OCM middleware interacts with a *connector* module, which is a slightly modified routing infrastructure at the IP layer. The module gets its name from the capability to connect between two independent radio interfaces. It exposes a standard routing API for the IP module and encompasses two routing protocols: a reactive ad-hoc routing intended for the long range interface and a proactive table-driven routing intended for the short range interface. The routing table for the latter is managed by OCM through system calls. When the connector module is given a packet to be routed from the IP module, it passes this packet to one of the two routing protocols depending on source and destination addresses of the packet. The integration of OCM with the connector module is detailed in Section 5.

4   The OCM Management Module

OCM is designed to manage the wireless communication interfaces by clustering the network. This section presents the assumed network model and data structures used by OCM, and gives high-level as well as elaborated details of the clustering process.

4.1   Network Model and Data Structures

The system consists of a set of nodes communicating by exchanging messages over a wireless network. Each node is equipped with two wireless network interfaces A and B, with transmission ranges R and r, respectively, so that $R \gg r$. The nodes have unique identifiers and may move independently. Two nodes may communicate through an interface A (B) when the distance is less than or equal to R $(r$, respectively). Communication links of both types are unreliable, FIFO and mostly bidirectional. To cope with possible omissions, OCM employs local, unsynchronized clocks. Yet, the system as a whole is asynchronous.

We assume that the power consumed by B is lower than the power consumed by A. In other words, it is preferred to use interface B over A for communication whenever possible. Note that we do not make any assumptions on the technology type of A and B: they can be completely different (i.e., A is WiFi, while B is BT or TR100 low-power radio [3]) or can be identical (i.e., both A and B are WiFi's, operating at different predefined transmission ranges). At any given time, each interface may be active or turned off.

Each node p_i maintains up to three data structures, depending on the number of its active interfaces. They are: a list of the long range interface neighbors (for brevity, referred later as *long neighbors*), a list of the short range interface neighbors (referred later as *short neighbors*) and an intra-cluster routing table. As the name of the latter suggests, it is used for routing messages between nodes inside clusters created by OCM, and implemented as an adjacency matrix with a row and a column allocated for each node in the cluster to which the owner of the table belongs. Note that the total space required at each node is proportional to k and the maximal number of neighbors on each interface, but does not depend on the total number of nodes. This makes OCM very scalable for large systems.

4.2   High-Level Overview

The objective of the middleware protocol is to create an overlay consisting of nodes with both interfaces turned on. The overlay is required to be connected at the level of the long interface. Additionally, the protocol strives to minimize the value of the function $\sum_i \frac{1}{el(i)}$, where $el(i)$ is the energy level of a node i belonging to the overlay. The idea is to have an overlay, which is small in the number of nodes, and which consists of nodes that have high remaining energy level. Another requirement from OCM is that all nodes

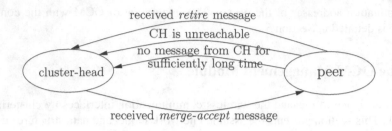

Fig. 2. State transitions in OCM. CH stands for the "cluster-head".

which are not a part of the overlay are associated with some node in the overlay and are within k short range hops from it, where k is an arbitrary parameter of the protocol.

To achieve the above requirements, OCM employs the following scheme. A node p_i with an active long range interface periodically publishes information regarding its cluster to long neighbors. The neighbors check several conditions and decide whether they wish to merge with the cluster of p_i. If they decide positively, they send a corresponding message, and p_i chooses the best candidate p_j from those who agreed for the merge. Then p_i sends a message to that candidate, and if p_j is still ready for the merge, it becomes the head of the united cluster. The details are described below.

4.3 Clusters Merging

During the run of the protocol, each node can be in one of two states: *cluster-head* or *peer*. A cluster-head is the node that has both interfaces enabled; this is the initial state of every node in the network. A node becomes a peer when it decides to turn its power-consuming long range interface off and associate itself with some cluster-head. A state transition diagram is shown in Figure 2.

A cluster-head p_j periodically broadcasts *merge-inquiry* messages (on its long interface), which include information on its energy level, current short and long neighbors and the intra-cluster routing table. When a cluster-head p_i receives such a message from p_j, it decides to respond with *merge-agree* if all four conditions hold: (1) p_i and p_j are connected by a path of short edges; (2) in the united routing table there is no path from any peer to p_i consisting of more than k short links; (3) the set of p_i's long neighbors contains a certain portion, β, of the long neighbors of p_j; (4) p_i's rank is higher than the rank of p_j. In our implementation, the ranking was based solely on the energy level of a node (with IDs used to break ties), although more sophisticated functions are possible (e.g., a ratio between the energy level and the number of nodes in the cluster).

Condition (3) is motivated by the request to create an overlay connected at the level of the long range interface. In order to ensure connectivity, one should set β to 1, i.e., p_i's set of long neighbors should include all long neighbors of p_j. This is a very strong limitation on the ability of clusters to merge, especially in dense networks. On the other hand, setting β close to 0 increases the chances of ending up with a disconnected overlay, especially in sparse networks. Although many heuristic approaches are possible, including the ones that adapt dynamically to the sparsity of the network, in our implementation we simply use the value of 0.25. We show empirically that this value suffices to achieve a connected overlay with relatively large clusters (see Section 6).

After sending the *merge-inquiry* message, node p_j waits T_{mi} seconds (in our implementation, $T_{mi} = 1$) for *merge-agree* messages from its neighbors, which include information on their energy level. Then p_j selects the cluster-head with the highest energy level, p_k, as a candidate for the merge and sends a *merge-request* message to p_k. Node p_k responds with *merge-accept* if it does not wait for such a message from another cluster-head. Finally, if p_j receives the *merge-accept* message within T_{mr} seconds (in our implementation, $T_{mr} = 1$), it broadcasts a *new-cluster-head* message to all peers in its cluster, which notifies them on the change of their cluster-head, and switches the long range interface off to become a peer.

A node in the peer state remains with the long range interface turned off until one of the following three events occurs (cf. Figure 2): (1) it receives a *retire* message from its cluster-head, sent by the cluster-head when its energy level reduces below a predefined threshold (see details below); (2) it does not receive any message from its cluster-head for sufficiently long period of time; (3) it receives a notification on a failure of its adjacent short link, which makes the cluster-head unreachable by a path of short links between nodes in the cluster.

In order to implement the last event, as well as to keep the overlay structure current with the temporal network topology, the OCM protocol utilizes the common heartbeat technique. The technique is implemented in the corresponding heartbeat module discussed in Section 3. Note that OCM employs the heartbeat module on every active interface, i.e., a cluster-head runs two such modules, while a peer only issues heartbeats on a single interface.

To extend the lifetime of the network and distribute the load of the cluster-head duty on all nodes, OCM employs the following simple load balancing approach. The cluster-head p_i records its current energy level at the first time some peer joins the cluster. Node p_i continues to serve as the cluster-head for its peers until its energy level reduces below a predefined threshold compared to the recorded value. When it happens, p_i broadcasts a *retire* message to all its peers, indicating that they need to transit into the cluster-head mode. Hence, they start running the merge procedure. Since p_i wasted much more energy than those in the peer state and since the ranking of nodes relates directly to their remaining energy, p_i is unlikely to serve as a cluster-head for too long.

The detailed pseudo-code for the merge procedure is presented in Algorithm 1. Besides the *el* variable used to specify the energy level of each node, the pseudo-code uses RT, LN and SN variables to specify the intra-cluster routing table and the set of long and short neighbors, respectively.

5   Integration of OCM with Routing

Although routing is purely a networking issue not related to the core operation of the OCM middleware, for the clarity of the whole picture we provide more details on the integration of OCM with the connector module, presented in Section 3. When the connector receives a packet to route, it looks-up the destination of the packet in the routing table provided by OCM. If the destination is in the routing table, the packet is given to

Algorithm 1. Merge procedure, executed periodically by cluster-heads; code for node i

1:      broadcast *merge-inquiry*(el_i, RT_i, LN_i, SN_i) to all long neighbors
2:      wait for *merge-agree*(el_j) messages from all $j \in LN$ for T_{mi} seconds
3:      *chosen* $\leftarrow$ choose j with *merge-agree*(el_j) s.t. el_j is maximal
4:      **if** *chosen* $\neq nil$ **then**   // there was some j that can be joined
5:          send *merge-request*(RT_i) to *chosen*
6:          wait for *merge-accept* from *chosen* for T_{mr} seconds
7:          **if** received *merge-accept* **then**
8:              broadcast *new-cluster-head*(*chosen*) to all peers in the cluster
9:              switch to *peer* state   // and switch long interface off

10: **when** *merge-inquiry*(el_j, RT_j, LN_j, SN_j) is received from j
11:     **if** $\langle el_j, id_j \rangle < \langle el_i, id_i \rangle \wedge$
12:         there is a path of short edges between i and $j \wedge$
13:         max distance between any peer and i in the joined $RT \leq k$ short edges $\wedge$
14:         $|LN_i \cap LN_j|/|LN_j| \geq \beta$ **then**
15:             send *merge-agree*(el_i) to j

16: **when** *merge-request*(RT_j) is received from j
17:     **if** not waiting for *merge-accept* **then**
18:         send *merge-accept* to j
19:         update RT_i with RT_j
20:         **if** inside merge procedure **then**
21:             stop merge procedure

the table-driven routing mechanism to be sent to its destination. If not, but the source of the packet is not a cluster-head, the table-driven routing is used again, this time to route the packet to the cluster-head of the source. Otherwise, the packet is given to the standard, off the shelf, ad-hoc routing mechanism, slightly modified as described below.

Consequently, the routing between nodes inside a cluster is managed solely by OCM, based on the intra-cluster routing table maintained at every node as part of the management module. A reactive ad-hoc routing protocol is not used for intra-cluster routing since the clusters are expected to be relatively small and dynamic, thus the overhead created by routing protocols on routes discovery and/or maintenance would not be cost-effective. A cluster-head is responsible for updating the routing table every time it absorbs another cluster (during the process of clusters merging) or when it gets a notification on failed links inside the cluster. Such a notification may arrive from the heartbeat module after a failure of an adjacent link or from some peer. The routing table is broadcasted periodically to all peers in the cluster. If a peer does not receive the update for sufficiently long time, it assumes that its cluster-head is unreachable and therefore transits into the cluster-head state, switching its long range interface on (cf. Figure 2).

As indicated above, inter-cluster routing is performed through an off the shelf ad-hoc routing protocol, which is run solely by cluster-heads. In principle, the OCM protocol can utilize any ad-hoc routing algorithm. The only required modification is that an instance of the routing protocol running on a cluster-head should act as a proxy for peers in its cluster. In practice, this means that when the ad-hoc routing algorithm running on a cluster-head inspects a message addressed to another node, it should query OCM whether the destination node is a peer in the cluster. If this is the case, the routing protocol should generate a response as expected from the actual destination. In our experiments, we evaluate OCM integrated with the well-known DSR [10] algorithm, modified according to the above.

Note that OCM decides to switch nodes to a peer state independently of the routing protocol. Thus, if a node is actively participating in routing, such transition may cause message losses, especially when the node serves as a cluster-head for a large cluster. In practise, however, the DSR algorithm succeeded to rediscover new routes and adapt to a new topology very fast, keeping the failure rate below 1% in most simulated scenarios. A possible optimization that may further reduce the failure rate is to inform the routing protocol about the planned change in the state of the node. Additionally, a cluster-head that merges its cluster into another cluster may update the new cluster-head regarding active routes.

6 Performance Evaluation

We evaluate the performance of OCM in the Java-based SWANS simulator [6]. We would like to emphasize that the code used in the simulations is the full Java implementation of the protocol, including all modules specified in Section 3. To enable our evaluation, we have made two extensions to the simulator: monitoring the energy level of nodes and supporting two radio interfaces on the same device. The first extension is implemented by collecting information on the times each interface is in sending/receiving/idle/sleeping modes. The second extension required to synchronize the location of two radios and address interference issue. For more technical details, refer to Appendix A.

We assume a simulation area of size $500 \times 500 m^2$ with nodes placed at uniformly random locations. The number of nodes varies from 100 to 500 or from 100 to 1000 in steps of 100. The length of each simulation is 1000 (real time) seconds, where the first 100 seconds are considered as a warmup time and measurements are taken during the last 900 seconds. Each reported data point is produced by taking an average over 10 experiments.

In our experiments, each node is equipped with two types of radios: (1) WiFi with a transmission range of 100m and bandwidth of 11Mbps; (2) BT with a transmission range of 10m and bandwidth of 1Mbps. The numbers are taken according to the nominal transmission ranges and bandwidths of WiFi and BT technologies, as reported in [8]. We assume (and extend the simulator accordingly) that transmissions emitted by these radios do not interfere. This is in accordance with findings of several works that propose techniques to significantly mitigate the interference of BT and WiFi [5, 18].

Due to lack of support for a true BT MAC layer in the simulator, both radios use the same 802.11 MAC layer. We also do not explore the specific limitations existing in BT's network configuration, where the network is composed from *piconet* units, which are built from up to eight devices working together [8]. (Nevertheless, due to the short

Table 1. The summary of simulation parameters. The power consumed by BT in the sleeping mode is not stated since we do not use this mode in our simulations.

Common		
Signal Propagation model (PathLoss)	Free-space model	
Signal Interference model	Independent noise model	
Fading	None	
Radio-specific		
	WiFi	**BT**
Transmission range	100m	10m
Bandwidth	11Mbps	1Mbps
Power consumption:		
Transmitting	1346mW	81mW
Receiving	900mW	81mW
Idle	740mW	5.8mW
Sleeping	47mW	N/A
Simulation Scenarios		
Field size	500x500 m²	
Message length	256 bytes + IP + MAC + PHY headers	
Nodes	100 to 500 or 100 to 1000 in steps of 100	
Mobility	1. Static 2. Random way-point with pause time of 60s 3. Random way-point with pause time of 180s 4. Two-phase with hot-spots, with pivot of 1 5. Two-phase with hot-spots, with pivot of 0.75	
Java pseudo random number generator, initialized with the current time in millis as seed		

range of BT, the simulated networks are not dense enough at the BT level. Hence, this does not pose a real limitation). All these issues are left for the future work. We note that we are not aware of any simulator providing a precise implementation of both BT and WiFi MAC layers.

The performance metrics we consider are the average latency of the sent messages and the average energy consumed by nodes during the simulation. Specifically, the consumed energy reflects the instantaneous consumed power multiplied by the duration of consumption. Simulation traffic was generated by choosing random source and destination nodes every second and sending a packet of 256 bytes. The latency is calculated only for packets received at the selected destinations. Unless otherwise specified, the failure rate of transmissions, i.e., the ratio of packets not received by the selected destination nodes, was below 1%. The simulation parameters are summarized in Table 1.

6.1   Energy Model

The power consumption model of the WiFi interface is based on the measurements reported by Feeney and Nilsson [7] for a 802.11 wireless card operating at 11Mbps. They report costs of 1346mW for transmission, 900mW for receiving, 740mW for idle state and 47mW for sleeping. The numbers are similar to those reported by several other works for similar cards, e.g., [4, 20]. As for the BT interface, we use the measurements reported by Pering et. al. [15] for BlueCore3 BT radio operating at 1Mbps: 81mW for transmission and 5.8mW for idle state. This work does not report on the power consumed during receiving, thus we conservatively assume that receiving requires as much as transmitting, i.e., 81mW.

These values for instantaneous power are summarized in Table 1. Note that in the simulation, we are not really turning off the WiFi radio, but put it into sleep mode. Although it still incurs a small cost in power (which is negligible compared to other WiFi modes), it allows to ignore the time required to switch from sleeping to active mode: as specified in [2], this time is insignificant.

To ensure that our measurements are fair, we conservatively assume that when the OCM middleware is disabled, nodes operate with BT radio turned off. Thus, in the following figures, when OCM is disabled, we report only on energy consumed by WiFi. Hence, the actual benefit from OCM might be even slightly better than reported if this is not the case. Note that our consumed energy measurements account for all messages transmitted, including messages generated by OCM and/or DSR as well as traffic generated for the purpose of the simulation.

6.2 Mobility Models

We evaluate the performance of OCM under several mobility models. The first one is a static setting where nodes remain in their initial random locations during the entire simulation. The second model is the well-known random way-point model [10], where nodes alternate between pausing and moving to a randomly chosen position at a fixed speed. We consider speeds selected randomly from the range between 1 and $2m/s$ (thereby avoiding some of the pitfalls of the random way-point model), corresponding to walking speeds, and two pause times: 60 and 180 seconds. Note that the first (static) model can be considered as a private case of the second model with the pause time set to the length of the simulation.

In order to better capture the environment of a campus or a school, which appears to be an attractive domain for OCM implementation, we propose a new mobility model. In this new model, two sets of special locations, or *hot-spots*, are preselected and nodes alternate between the following two phases: In the first phase, the nodes are static and assigned random locations near one of the hot-spots from the first set, corresponding to classrooms. In the second phase, the nodes move to a new position, which is selected randomly (with low probability) or near one of the hot-spots from the second set (with high probability), corresponding to a gathering place in the campus, such as a cafeteria or a library. When a node reaches a position near the hot-spot, it prefers to remain nearby (i.e., move to a close location) with high probability, move to another hot-spot with lower probability, or choose a completely random location with low probability. The movement is done with speeds selected randomly from the range between 1 and $2m/s$ (walking speed).

We refer to the model presented above as a *two-phase model with hot-spots*. In addition to the already mentioned parameters, such as probabilities and speeds, the model is tuned by the number of iterations during the simulation, where each iteration consists of two phases, and a pivot controlling the ratio between duration of the first phase and duration of the whole iteration. We set the number of iterations to 3: this is a small value, meaning relatively long phases, yet larger than 1, allowing to capture the effect of transitions between phases. We experiment with two pivots: 1, which means that the

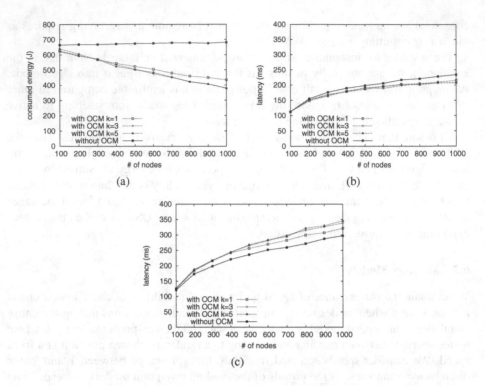

Fig. 3. Comparison of energy consumed by wireless communication (a) and latency ((b) and (c)) vs. the number of nodes in the static system, when OCM is run with various values of k and when OCM is disabled. The traffic in (a) and (b) consists of 256B messages and in (c) of 10KB messages.

second phase is empty, and 0.75, which means the first phase is three times longer than the second, corresponding to an alternation between classes and breaks.

To summarize, we have experimented with five mobility models: static, random way-point with pause time of 60 and 180 seconds and the two-phase model with hot-spots with pivots of 1 and 0.75.

6.3   The Impact of k on the Performance of OCM

The first set of results presents the impact of the value of k, the maximal number of short range hops between a peer and its cluster-head, on the performance of OCM. In order to exploit the potential of larger clusters, nodes should remain close enough (i.e., in the transmission range of BT of up to 10 meters one from another) and stay that way as long as possible. Thus, we first evaluate the impact of k in the static system.

Figure 3(a) presents the measurements of the energy consumed by the wireless communication as a function of the number of nodes in the system. The average energy consumed without OCM is almost stable, increasing only slightly with the number of nodes. The increase in the denser network occurs because of the *overhearing* effect observed in [17], due to which more nodes receive transmissions not intended for them.

On the other hand, the power consumed when OCM is enabled reduces linearly with the number of nodes, since more effective clustering can be created, and thus more nodes may turn their WiFi radios off. The gain in power produced with $k = 1$ is lower than with larger k's, since when OCM is restricted to create small clusters, the result is larger overlays. There is no observable difference, however, between $k = 3$ and $k = 5$. This can be explained by the fact that even with 1000 nodes, the system is not dense enough at the BT level to allow for the creation of very large clusters. Thus, under the densities we experimented with in the static setting, further increase in k does not provide OCM with an opportunity to reduce the size of the overlay and save more energy.

Figure 3(b) compares the latency of transmitted messages. Here, surprisingly, we can see that although OCM uses slower BT hops, it performs better than communication without OCM. In addition, the latency exposed by OCM is insensitive to the value of k, even though larger k means that a message may traverse larger number of BT hops. The explanation to these phenomena is hidden in the relatively small size of generated messages (256 bytes), which cancels the superiority of faster WiFi links and, on the other hand, emphasizes the advantage of the hierarchical routing: the overhead of route discovery is eliminated when both source and destination belong to the same cluster or when the route is already cached by a cluster-head.

In order to validate this claim, we have measured the latency (and consumed energy) with traffic produced by larger messages of 10 kilobytes. The latency results, shown in Figure 3(c), fully comply with our hypothesis (the measurements of consumed energy exhibit similar behavior to the one shown in Figure 3(a) and thus are omitted). With larger messages, the higher bandwidth of WiFi plays a significant role. Thus, the latency produced with OCM is higher, and it increases for $k > 1$. The difference between $k = 3$ and $k = 5$ is almost not observable, due to the reasons explained above in the comparison of consumed energy.

To summarize, it seems that for the densities we experiment with, OCM achieves the best trade-off between consumed energy and latency with $k = 3$. Thus, the rest of the experiments are conducted with this value for k.

6.4   The Effect of Mobility on the Performance of OCM

Figure 4 presents the behavior of the network under the random way-point mobility model with two values for pause times: 60 and 180 seconds. The power savings produced by OCM are expected to be less than in the static setting, since when nodes move, BT links are very unstable due to their relatively short range. As a result, according to Figure 2, peers transit frequently to the cluster-head state. This intuition is confirmed by Figure 4(a), which compares the energy consumed by nodes: OCM succeeds to save less energy than in the static setting and the savings are higher with longer pause time.

Figure 4(b) compares the latencies exhibited by the network. For the longer pause time, the latency does not change much due to the use of OCM; when the pause time is short, however, OCM introduces more considerable increase in latency. This happens, again, due to frequent changes in BT links, which break routes discovered by the DSR routing protocol. As explained in Section 5, a cluster-head responds to route discovery messages intended for its peers. In the time interval until the actual message arrives, its peer may move far enough to break the path of BT links between them, thus the

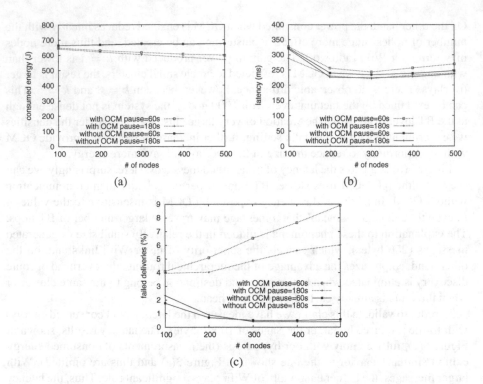

Fig. 4. Comparison of energy consumed by wireless communication (a), latency (b) and percentage of failed deliveries (c) vs. the number of nodes in the system. The nodes move according to the random way-point model with a pause time of $60s$ and $180s$.

cluster-head would not be able to forward the message and would generate a route error. As a result, the sender of the message would retry to discover another route and then resend the message with a new route.

The process of route rediscovery may occur several times, until the routing protocol gives up and drops the message. As Figure 4(c) presents, this happens too often with OCM, especially when the pause time is short. Another source for failed deliveries, originating from the same issue of failing BT links, is intra-cluster routing. When a message is originated at a peer and destined to some node outside the cluster, it is relayed first to the cluster-head of the peer using the intra-cluster routing table (same for a message received by a cluster-head, but intended for its peer). Such relay is done by table-driven routing mechanism using point-to-point transmissions along the shortest path consisting of BT links. A failure of even one link along that path may cause to the omission of the message.

In order to cope with the problem of such intra-cluster omissions, we propose the following recovery mechanism: whenever a notification on a failed point-to-point transmission is received from the BT MAC layer, the connector module notifies OCM that considers the link as lost (which may cause the peer to switch into the cluster-head state) and tries to resend the message. The retransmission may occur on another BT

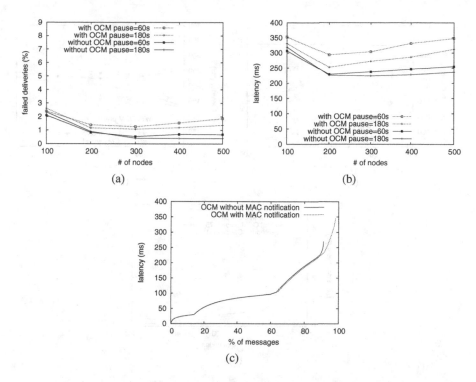

Fig. 5. Comparison of percentage of failed deliveries (a) and latency (b) when the MAC notification mechanism is enabled. Figure (c) compares average latency vs. the percentage of delivered messages sorted by latency (i.e., data point (x, y) shows the average latency (y) for $x\%$ of the fastest messages) in the system of 500 nodes with and without the MAC notification mechanism. The nodes move according to the random way-point model with a pause time of $60s$ and $180s$ in (a) and (b), and $60s$ in (c).

link or on a WiFi link, enabling the DSR routing with its own retrying mechanism mentioned above. Note that such a notification can be generated by any implementation of the MAC layer which provides reliable point-to-point transmissions and, in particular, by 802.11 MAC.

Figure 5 studies the impact of the recovery mechanism on the performance of OCM. As can be seen in Figure 5(a), the reliability of the protocol increases sharply: for example, for the short pause time and 500 nodes, the percentage of failed deliveries drops from 9% to less than 2%. The average latency, on the other hand, increases from 269 to 347 milliseconds (Figure 5(b)). This increase is introduced by messages that now succeed to reach their target using the recovery mechanism, but suffer from a delay caused by the first unsuccessful transmission on the BT link.

In order to validate that only recovered messages are delayed by the introduction of the recovery mechanism, we compile a graph showing the average latency of $x\%$ shortest deliveries in the setting of 500 nodes and the pause time of 60 seconds vs. x (Figure 5(c)). Here we can see that in both scenarios, i.e., with and without the

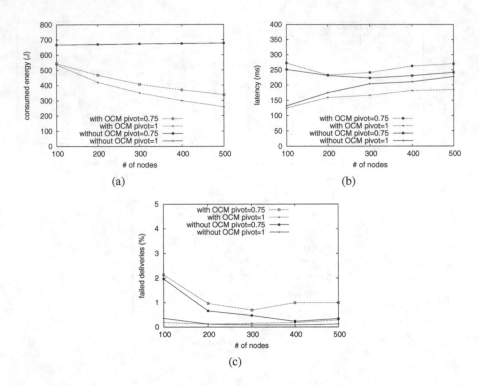

Fig. 6. Comparison of energy consumed by wireless communication (a), latency (b) and percentage of failed deliveries (c) vs. the number of nodes in the system. The nodes move according to the two-phase mobility model with hot-spots, with pivots of 0.75 and 1.

recovery mechanism, approximately 90% of messages experience the similar average delay, confirming that the increase in the total latency occurs due to recovered messages. As a conclusion, the recovery mechanism appears to be a successful tool in coping with the reliability issue of OCM in mobile setting, while the latency of messages not requiring this tool remains unchanged.

6.5   The Performance of OCM under Two-Phase Mobility with Hot-Spots

The performance of OCM under the two-phase mobility model with hot-spots is shown in Figure 6. Due to similarity of phenomena to the ones discussed in the previous section, we present only the measurements performed with the recovery mechanism detailed above. The energy savings produced by OCM are impressive: in the static setting, i.e., when the pivot is set to 1, only 38.2% of the energy is consumed when OCM is enabled in the system of 500 nodes compared to the system without OCM (Figure 6(a)). When nodes move, i.e., when the pivot is set to 0.75, less than half of the energy is consumed. Such encouraging results are explained by the characteristics of the mobility model, where nodes concentrate around hot-spots, providing OCM with a potential to create smaller overlays.

The latency exhibits similar behavior to the ones measured under the static and random way-point models (Figure 6(b)). With the pivot set to 1, OCM achieves much better latency due to the hierarchical routing employed, while with the pivot set to 0.75, the latency of OCM is higher due to the recovery mechanism used (without it, OCM performs better even though nodes move). The percentage of failed messages is slightly higher for OCM, but still kept under 1% in most scenarios (Figure 6(c)).

7 Conclusions

This paper presents OCM, an efficient middleware that reduces power consumption in mobile ad-hoc networks composed of devices with multiple communication interfaces. OCM does not assume any specific communication technology; it requires only one interface with a larger transmission range and power consumption than the other. Moreover, it way be applied in addition to other power-saving techniques, such as PSM of WiFi [2].

OCM constructs an overlay of nodes connected at the level of long range interface, having the rest of nodes with their long range interface turned off and connected to some node in the overlay through an adjustably short path of short range links. The nodes are selected into the overlay based on their remaining energy level and the number of neighbors they can communicate with on both interfaces. OCM adapts quickly to topology changes by using local timers and turning long range interfaces on when a node suspects that it has lost a connection with its associative node in the overlay. Thus, wrong detection of link failures may hurt only the performance, but not the correctness of the protocol.

We evaluate the performance of OCM with typical parameters of BT and WiFi cards and show that the power savings produced by OCM are significant, while the latency and message loss are almost the same as with the standard ad-hoc routing algorithm. It is notable that in the static setting, OCM even achieves considerably better latency. In addition, OCM adapts well to the density of the network, exhibiting the behavior of "add more to improve service", similar to [20] and opposite to [4]. This feature is particularly important as the number of devices equipped with several communication interfaces continuously increases.

A possible direction for future research would be to evaluate the middleware with other technologies for wireless communication, e.g., WiMax and ZigBee, in addition to WiFi and BT or instead of them. The middleware can be easily extended to manage more than two wireless interfaces. For example, given a network consisting of devices that have also WiMax radio, OCM would construct an overlay with nodes having all radios active; this overlay would be connected at the level of WiMax. Another sub-overlay would be created out of nodes having WiMax turned off; every node in the sub-overlay would have a path of up to k WiFi links to some node in the overlay. Finally, the rest of nodes in the network would have both WiMax and WiFi turned off and have a path of up to k BT links to some node in the sub-overlay.

Another issue that warrants investigation is dealing with capacity enhancement. Although OCM keeps the number of short links in each path below the predefined threshold and thus preserves a significant portion of the original capacity, it may not be enough for certain applications. A possible direction is to adapt the middleware to local communication requirements on each node. That is, switch a peer into the cluster-head state when it generates or receives traffic above some threshold.

References

1. Anand, M., Nightingale, E.B., Flinn, J.: Self-tuning wireless network power management. Wireless Networking 11(4), 451–469 (2005)
2. Anastasi, G., Conti, M., Gregori, E., Passarella, A.: 802.11 power-saving mode for mobile computing in Wi-Fi hotspots: limitations, enhancements and open issues. Wireless Networks 14(6), 745–768 (2008)
3. Bahl, P., Adya, A., Padhye, J., Walman, A.: Reconsidering wireless systems with multiple radios. ACM SIGCOMM Comput. Commun. Rev. 34(5), 39–46 (2004)
4. Chen, B., Jamieson, K., Balakrishnan, H., Morris, R.: Span: An energy-efficient coordination algorithm for topology maintenance in ad hoc wireless networks. ACM Wireless Networks Journal, 85–96 (2001)
5. Chiasserini, C.F., Rao, R.R.: Coexistence mechanisms for interference mitigation between IEEE 802.11 WLANs and Bluetooth. In: Proc. IEEE INFOCOM, vol. 2, pp. 590–598 (2002)
6. Cornell University. JiST/SWANS – Java in Simulation Time / Scalable Wireless Ad Hoc Network Simulator, http://jist.ece.cornell.edu
7. Feeney, L.M., Nilsson, M.: Investigating the energy consumption of a wireless network interface in an ad hoc networking environment. In: Proc. IEEE INFOCOM, pp. 1548–1557 (2001)
8. Ferro, E., Potorti, F.: Bluetooth and Wi-Fi wireless protocols: a survey and a comparison. IEEE Wireless Communications 12(1), 12–26 (2005)
9. Gomez, J., Campbell, A.: Variable-range transmission power control in wireless ad hoc networks. IEEE Transactions on Mobile Computing 6(1), 87–99 (2007)
10. Johnson, D.B., Maltz, D.A.: Dynamic source routing in ad hoc wireless networks. In: Mobile Computing, pp. 153–181. Kluwer Academic Publishers, Dordrecht (1996)
11. Kirousis, L.M., Kranakis, E., Krizanc, D., Pelc, A.: Power consumption in packet radio networks. Theoretical Computer Science 243(1-2), 289–305 (2000)
12. Krashinsky, R., Balakrishnan, H.: Minimizing energy for wireless web access with bounded slowdown. Wireless Networking 11(1-2), 135–148 (2005)
13. Li, L., Halpern, J.Y., Bahl, P., Wang, Y.-M., Wattenhofer, R.: Analysis of a cone-based distributed topology control algorithm for wireless multi-hop networks. In: Proc. 20th ACM Symposium on Principles of Distributed Computing (PODC), pp. 264–273 (2001)
14. Pei, G., Gerla, M., Hong, X.: LANMAR: Landmark routing for large scale wireless ad hoc networks with group mobility. In: Proc. IEEE/ACM MobiHOC, pp. 11–18 (2000)
15. Pering, T., Agarwal, Y., Gupta, R., Power, C.: Coolspots: Reducing the power consumption of wireless mobile devices with multiple radio interfaces. In: Proc. ACM MOBISYS, pp. 220–232 (2006)
16. Rieck, M.Q., Dhar, S.: Hierarchical routing in ad hoc networks using k-dominating sets. SIGMOBILE Mob. Comput. Commun. Rev. 12(3), 45–57 (2008)
17. Singh, S., Raghavendra, C.S.: PAMAS: Power aware multi-access protocol with signalling for ad hoc networks. ACM Computer Communication Review 28, 5–26 (1998)
18. Song, M., Shetty, S., Gopalpet, D.: Coexistence of IEEE 802.11b and Bluetooth: An integrated performance analysis. Mobile Networks and Applications 12(5), 450–459 (2007)

19. Wu, J., Dai, F., Gao, M., Stojmenovic, I.: On calculating power-aware connected dominating sets for efficient routing in ad hoc wireless networks. J. Communications and Networks, 59–70 (2002)
20. Xu, Y., Heidemann, J., Estrin, D.: Geography-informed energy conservation for ad hoc routing. In: Proc. 7th Int. Conf. on Mobile Computing and Networking (MOBICOM), pp. 70–84 (2001)

A   Extensions to SWANS

This section provides technical details on the extensions introduced into the SWANS simulator [6] in order to enable the experiments with OCM. The sources can be downloaded from http://www.cs.technion.ac.il/~sakogan/SWANS.

Consumed energy measurements: Our energy model implies that a radio may be in one of the four following states: sleeping, idle, receiving or transmitting. These are also the modes used by SWANS for its radios. Thus, we intercept an event of the mode change in a radio, recording the time of the change and the new mode. At the subsequent mode change, we calculate the length of the interval for the current mode and, again, record the time of the change and the new mode. Thus, we accumulate the times during which the radio was in each of the four modes. During the simulation and at its end, we multiply these values by the power consumed at each mode (cf. Section 6.1) to receive the amount of energy consumed by wireless communication sub-system at each node up to that point.

Supporting multi-radio devices: The SWANS simulator features a limited support for nodes with multiple radios, which is summarized by an ability to add more than one radio and MAC module to the same node. These radios, however, operate independently from one another, which means that a movement of one does not imply the movement of another. In our extension, we eliminated this shortcoming by synchronizing the location of both radios, i.e., under any mobility model, both radios are always moved to a new location simultaneously.

Another issue we addressed in our support for multiple radios is interference. As opposite to the previous point, the handling of the interference depends tightly on the types of radios as well as on the system model assumptions. As mentioned above, in the base version of SWANS radios behave independently, which results in interference of a transmission by one radio with any other transmission in the range, no matter what the types of transmitting radios are and even if both transmissions are emitted from the same device. Moreover, the transmissions on one interface can be received by the other interface (in fact, two interfaces on the same device always receive transmissions one of the other). Choosing to experiment with common wireless technologies, namely BT and WIFI, and following the findings of several papers [5, 18], we assumed that transmissions by different types of radios do not interfere. Thus, we extended the way a packet is transmitted on a simulation field by filtering packets sent by one radio type from being received by another radio type.

COLA: Optimizing Stream Processing Applications via Graph Partitioning

Rohit Khandekar, Kirsten Hildrum, Sujay Parekh, Deepak Rajan, Joel Wolf,
Kun-Lung Wu, Henrique Andrade, and Buğra Gedik

IBM T.J. Watson Research Center, Hawthorne, NY 10532, USA
{rohitk,hildrum,sujay,drajan,jlwolf,klwu,hcma,bgedik}@us.ibm.com

Abstract. In this paper, we describe an optimization scheme for fusing compile-time operators into reasonably-sized run-time software units called processing elements (PEs). Such PEs are the basic deployable units in SYSTEM S, a highly scalable distributed stream processing middleware system. Finding a high quality fusion significantly benefits the performance of streaming jobs. In order to maximize throughput, our solution approach attempts to minimize the processing cost associated with inter-PE stream traffic while simultaneously balancing load across the processing hosts. Our algorithm computes a hierarchical partitioning of the operator graph based on a *minimum-ratio cut* subroutine. We also incorporate several fusion constraints in order to support real-world SYSTEM S jobs. We experimentally compare our algorithm with several other reasonable alternative schemes, highlighting the effectiveness of our approach.

Keywords: stream processing, operator fusion, graph partitioning, optimization, scheduling.

1 Introduction

We live in an increasingly data-intensive age. By some estimates [1], roughly 15 petabytes of new data are generated every day. It is becoming an ever more mission critical goal for corporations and other organizations to process, analyze and make real-time operational decisions based on immense quantities of data being dynamically generated at high rates. Distributed systems built to handle such requirements, called stream processing systems, are now becoming extremely important. Such systems have been extensively studied in academic settings [2, 3, 4, 5, 6, 7, 8], and are also being implemented in industrial environments [9, 10]. The authors of this paper are involved in one such stream processing project, known as SYSTEM S [11,12,13,14,15,16,17,18,19,20], which is highly scalable distributed computer system middleware designed to support complex analytical processing. It has been evolving for the past six years.

1.1 Operator Graphs and the Fusion Problem

Application development in SYSTEM S is facilitated by the SPADE development environment. Among other things, SPADE defines a programming model based on

J.M. Bacon and B.F. Cooper (Eds.): Middleware 2009, LNCS 5896, pp. 308–327, 2009.

type-generic streaming *operators*, as well as a stream-centric language to compose these operators into parameterizable, distributed stream processing applications. In this model, depicted in Figure 1(a), an application is organized as a *data flow graph* consisting of operators at the nodes connected by directed edges called *streams* which carry data from the source to destination operators. Examples of streaming operators include functors (such as projections, windowed aggregators, filters), stream punctuation markers, and windowed joins. SPADE also allows flexible integration of complex user-defined constructs into the application.

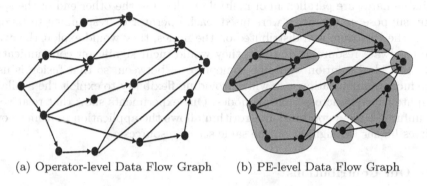

(a) Operator-level Data Flow Graph   (b) PE-level Data Flow Graph

Fig. 1. Operators, PEs and Data Flow Graphs

The operator-level graph of Figure 1(a) represents a *logical* view of the application. When the application is executed on a SYSTEM S cluster, these operators must be distributed onto the compute nodes for execution. From the point of view of the Operating System (OS) on a node, the unit of execution is a process. One of the main tasks of the SPADE compiler is to convert the logical operator-level data flow graph into a set of executables that can be run on the cluster nodes. A SYSTEM S application executable is called a *processing element* (PE), which serves as a container for one or more operators, and maps to a process at the OS level. Coalescing several operators into a single PE is called *fusion* (described in detail in [13]). A compiled SPADE-generated application becomes a *physical* data flow graph consisting of PEs with data streams flowing between them. This is depicted in Figure 1(b), with the shaded regions representing PEs. One can think of the PEs as essentially *supernodes* in the original operator data flow graph.

When data is sent on a stream between two operators in the same PE, the SPADE compiler converts it into a function call invocation of the "downstream" operator by the "upstream" operator. Sending data on streams between PEs is performed by inter-process communication, such as TCP sockets. Thus, only the inter-PE (physical) streams remain as edges in the PE-level graph. As a result of this transformation, passing data on an intra-PE stream has almost no processing cost compared to an inter-PE stream, which requires inter-process communication.

The goal of this paper is to tackle the *fusion problem*: how to map a logical operator-level graph into an optimal physical PE-level graph. A good fusion algorithm is critical to enable high-performance distributed stream processing applications that can be flexibly deployed on heterogenous hardware. But there are tradeoffs involved. To see this, consider the two extreme solutions to the operator fusion problem. On one end of the spectrum, suppose all operators were fused into a *single* PE. This solution eliminates all communication cost because all downstream operators are invoked via function calls. However, the resulting PE is a single process which is limited to one node, and does not exploit the available hardware parallelism of multiple nodes. On the other end of the spectrum, suppose *no* operators were fused, each operator corresponding to its own PE. If the PEs were well distributed on the nodes, they would exploit the available hardware resources. However, they would incur significant communication cost. The ideal solution would be someplace in between, so that fusion is used to reduce communication cost while providing flexibility to exploit the available compute capacity across multiple nodes. Our experiments show that relative to the unfused case, a good fusion algorithm allows the application to achieve over 3 times higher throughput on the same set of resources.

1.2   Our Contributions

In this paper, we describe COLA, a profile-driven fusion optimizer, which operates as part of the SPADE compilation process. COLA supports an environment with heterogeneous hosts, while allowing the user to specify a variety of important real-world constraints about the fusion. Its input is information about an application being compiled by SPADE, along with some attributes of a set of representative SYSTEM S hosts. We say COLA is profile-driven since it relies on application information in the form of performance metrics indicating the CPU demands of the operators and data rates of each stream.

Although we use the phrase *fusion*, COLA works from the top down rather than from the bottom up. Starting with all operators fused together into a single PE, the COLA algorithm iteratively splits "large" PEs into two separate "smaller" PEs by solving a specially formulated *graph partitioning* scheme. Then a *PE*

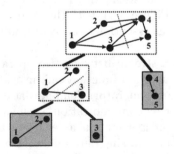

Fig. 2. Iterative graph partitioning in COLA

scheduler, serving as a compile time surrogate for the run time scheduler, hypothetically assigns the resulting PEs to potential hosts in an attempt to balance the load. If the combined solution to the graph partitiong and PE scheduling problems is not satisfactory, an *oracle* chooses one of the current PEs to split next, and the process iterates. Finally, the best solution found is chosen as COLA output, and the fused PEs are compiled. Several sample COLA iterations are shown in the format of a binary tree in Figure 2. At the root of the tree all operators are in one PE. The PEs created by solving the first graph partitioning problem are shown at depth 2. The oracle then picks one of these PEs to partition further (in this example, the first), and these PEs are shown at depth 3. And so the process continues. At the end of the last iteration the leaf nodes of the binary tree (shown shaded) represent the output COLA PEs.

In this paper, we describe two variants of COLA. The first version, called Basic COLA, generates a set of partitions that minimizes the communication cost, while ensuring that the fused PEs will still "fit" within the CPU capacities of the available nodes. While this basic version is not as sophisticated as the second version, it does illuminate several key ideas and components of the overall design. It also suffices for many applications. The second version is called Advanced COLA. In addition to the goals of Basic COLA, it (a) attempts to balance the load across the nodes, and (b) enables the user to restrict the fusion via a set of real-world constraints on the operators and PEs. We support six different types of constraints, three of which are *resource matching* (an operator requires a host with specific attributes such as CPU type), *PE exlocation* (operators cannot be fused together), and *host colocation* (operators must go on the same host). We retain and enhance the graph partitioning scheme used for Basic COLA, and introduce an integer programming formulation and solver to handle the PE scheduling problem in a more precise manner. The basic operator fusion problem has been tackled [13] using a greedy heuristic. We will show in this paper that COLA can provide a significant improvement over this heuristic. No other work to our knowledge has attempted to address the full version of the fusion problem with additional constraints.

Note that although COLA does consider the actual target system during its operation, it is not the same as the SYSTEM S runtime scheduler called SODA [18]. When an application (job) is actually executed on the system, it is SODA that manages the job. In particular, SODA provides functionality such as admission control (based on available resources), as well as load-balancing the cluster among multiple jobs and dynamically adapting to changing load conditions. For its evaluation purposes, COLA, which is invoked only at compile time, includes a simpler PE placement mechanism that mimics the full SODA algorithm.

Our contributions in this paper include the following.

- A new scheme for fusing SPADE operators into nearly optimal PEs in SYSTEM S, appropriate for general, heterogeneous processing host environments, and working synergistically with the scheduler.
- Support within the scheme for a wide variety of additional real-world constraints.

- A new and practical generalization of a classic graph partitioning problem, and a novel solution scheme.
- An effective compile-time PE scheduler which mimics the SODA SYSTEM S run-time scheduler.
- Experimental evidence suggesting that the COLA scheme has a major impact on the performance of SYSTEM S.

The remainder of this paper is organized as follows. Section 2 describes the Basic COLA problem formulation and the solution approach. In Section 3, we describe the formulation and solution strategy for Advanced COLA. Experiments showing the performance of the Basic COLA variant are described in Section 4. (The infrastructure to support the constraints is not yet available in SYSTEM S, so we defer experiments involving the Advanced COLA scheme for now.) Finally, in Section 5 we give conclusions and list future work.

2   Basic COLA

2.1   Problem Formulation

Consider a directed graph $G = (V, E)$ in which the vertices V represent the SPADE operators and the directed edges E represent the streams flowing between the operators. Assume that we are given *operator costs* $w_v \geq 0$ for $v \in V$ that represent the CPU costs of the corresponding operators, and *communication costs* $w_e \geq 0$ for $e \in E$ that represent the CPU costs due to sending and receiving tuples associated with the corresponding streams. (We will measure all CPU costs in terms of *millions of instructions per second*, or *mips*.) This input data is computed in SPADE via the use of efficient profiling methodology [13]. For a subset $S \subseteq V$, let $\delta(S)$ denote the set of edges with exactly one end-point in S. Let the *size* of a subset $S \subseteq V$ be defined as

$$\text{SIZE}(S) = \sum_{v \in S} w_v + \sum_{e \in \delta(S)} w_e. \tag{1}$$

Intuitively speaking, $\text{SIZE}(S)$ denotes the total CPU utilization that a PE consisting of the subset of operators S would incur. Recall that the streams contained completely inside a PE are converted into function calls during compilation and incur negligible CPU cost. For two sets S and T, we denote the set difference (set of elements of S that are not elements of T) by $S \ominus T$. To simplify the notation, we denote $w(S) = \sum_{v \in S} w_v$ and $w(\delta(S)) = \sum_{e \in \delta(S)} w_e$. Thus, $\text{SIZE}(S) = w(S) + w(\delta(S))$.

Assume that we are also given a list of *hosts* $\mathcal{H} = \{h_1, \ldots, h_k\}$ with their CPU speed *capacities* $B_1, \ldots, B_k$, also in *mips*. The COLA fusion optimization problem can be stated as follows: find a fusion of the operators into PEs and an assignment of the PEs to hosts such that the total CPU cost of a host is at most its capacity and the total communication cost across the PEs is minimized. More formally, the problem is to partition V into PEs $\mathcal{S} = \{S_1, \ldots, S_t\}$ and compute an assignment function $\pi : \mathcal{S} \to \mathcal{H}$ such that (i). for any $h_i \in \mathcal{H}$, we have $\sum_{S \in \mathcal{S}: \pi(S) = h_i} \text{SIZE}(S) \leq B_i$, and

(ii). $\sum_{S \in \mathcal{S}} w(\delta(S))$ is minimized.

Expression (i) describes scheduling feasibility: The assigned operators must fit on the hosts. Recall that in this Basic COLA variant we do not require that the load be balanced *well*, just acceptably. The expression (ii) measures the total communication cost across the PEs. Technically, it is twice the total communication cost across the PEs, since each edge going between different PEs is counted coming and going. This multiplicative factor does not, of course, affect the graph partitioning optimization in any way. This problem can be shown to be NP-hard by a reduction from the balanced cut problem [21].

As an application developer, one is primarily interested in maximizing the amount of data that is processed by the job. This can be measured as the aggregate data rate at the source (input) operators of the job, and is commonly referred to as *ingest rate* or *throughput*. Since this metric is hard to model as a function of the operator fusion, COLA attempts to minimize the total inter-PE communication as a surrogate.

2.2 Solution Approach

1. Run **Pre-processor**
2. Use **PE scheduler** to compute an LPT schedule
3. Repeat until the schedule is feasible:
   (a) Use **Oracle** to identify PE p to split next
   (b) Use **Graph Partitioner** to split p into two PEs
   (c) Use **PE scheduler** to compute an LPT schedule
4. Run **Post-processor**

The pseudocode of the Basic COLA algorithm is given above. We will go into the key components in more detail below, but we first describe a high-level view of the scheme. To begin with, a *pre-processor* is used to "glue" certain adjacent operators together provided doing so would not affect the optimality of the final PE solution. Once these operators are identified we will simply revise the problem definition and treat the glued operators from then on as *super operators*. Then the main body of the scheme begins. At any point, the COLA algorithm maintains a current partitioning $\mathcal{S} = \{S_1, \ldots, S_t\}$ of the given graph into PEs. Initially, it places all the operators into a single PE, so that $t = 1$ and $S_1 = V$. The *PE scheduler* then finds an assignment π of PEs to hosts. Next, COLA checks to see if expression (i) is satisfied. If not, the oracle picks the next PE to split, the *graph partitioner* performs the split, attempting to minimize expression (ii), and the process iterates. At some point the PE assignments should become feasible. (For ease of exposition we will not discuss the handling of pathological cases, for example, one in which a single operator is too large to schedule.) Finally, a post-processor is employed in an effort to improve the solution slightly before the PEs are output.

Pre-processor. The pre-processor performs certain immediate fusions of adjacent operators into super operators, motivated by the following lemma. Essentially, the lemma proves that if, for any vertex v, the communication cost of one its edges (say, $e = (u, v)$) is larger than the sum of the operator cost of the vertex and the communication costs of all its other incident edges, then the edge e can be collapsed by fusing vertices u and v. Thus, the pre-processor fuses adjacent operators by collapsing edges with sufficiently large communication costs.

Lemma 1. *Consider a directed edge $e = (u, v) \in E$ from operator u to v and suppose $w_e \geq \min\{w_u + w(\delta(\{u\}) \ominus \{e\}), w_v + w(\delta(\{v\}) \ominus \{e\})\}$ holds. There exists an optimum solution in which u and v belong to the same PE. Here, for two sets X and Y, $X \ominus Y$ denotes the set with the elements from X that are not in Y.*

Proof. Consider any feasible solution in which u and v belong to distinct PEs S_1 and S_2 respectively. It is enough to show how to modify this solution so that u and v belong to the same PE without increasing its cost or violating its feasibility. Assume without loss of generality that $w_e \geq w_u + w(\delta(\{u\}) \ominus \{e\})$. In this case, we move u from S_1 to S_2. That is, we let $S_1' \leftarrow S_1 \ominus \{u\}$ and $S_2' \leftarrow S_2 \cup \{u\}$. It is easy to see that $\text{SIZE}(S_1') \leq \text{SIZE}(S_1) - w_u + w(\delta(\{u\}) \ominus \{e\}) - w_e \leq \text{SIZE}(S_1)$ and $\text{SIZE}(S_2') \leq \text{SIZE}(S_2) + w_u + w(\delta(\{u\}) \ominus \{e\}) - w_e \leq \text{SIZE}(S_2)$. Furthermore, the new objective value is at most the old objective value plus $w(\delta(\{u\}) \ominus \{e\}) - w_e \leq 0$. Thus the proof is complete.

The pre-processor iteratively fuses pairs of operators $\{u, v\}$ for which the condition in the above lemma holds. Once we fuse $\{u, v\}$ into a super operator U, we update its weight as $w_U = w_u + w_v$ and the weight of the edges incident to U as $w_{Ux} = \sum_{x \in V \ominus \{u,v\}} (w_{ux} + w_{vx})$ and $w_{xU} = \sum_{x \in V \ominus \{u,v\}} (w_{xu} + w_{xv})$. The super operators are simply treated operators in the following iterations. Our experiments show that this pre-processing step, while employed rather rarely, helps improve the quality of the final solution.

The resulting graph with all (super and other) operators placed in a single PE is then employed in the first iteration of the main body of the scheme.

PE Scheduler. Given a current set of PEs $\mathcal{S} = \{S_1, \ldots, S_t\}$, the role of the scheduler in the Basic COLA scheme is to determine if these PEs can be feasibly scheduled on the given hosts $\mathcal{H}$. That is, it tries to find an assignment function $\pi : \mathcal{S} \to \mathcal{H}$ such that expression (i) is satisfied. To find a relatively good assignment quickly we borrow and modify for our needs the well-known *Longest Processing Time first (LPT)* scheduling scheme [22]. The LPT scheme enjoys several near-optimality properties [22] and is simple to implement. As its name hints, *LPT* processes the PEs in order of decreasing size. The intuition is that by doing so this greedy scheme will dispense with the largest PEs in the beginning, and then "recover" the load balance by dealing with the smallest PEs in the end. So we order the PEs by size, and reindex so that $\text{SIZE}(S_1) \geq \cdots \geq \text{SIZE}(S_t)$. *LPT* initializes the "current used capacity" B_i' of each host h_i to be $B_i' \leftarrow 0$. At any point, it processes the next PE, say S_i, and assigns it to a host, say h_j, that would have the minimum resulting utilization if assigned there. More formally, it assigns S_i to a host $\pi(S_i) = h_j$ such that

$$h_j = \mathrm{argmin}_{h_k \in \mathcal{H}} \frac{B'_k + \mathrm{SIZE}(S_i)}{B_k}.$$

It then updates the current used capacity of host h_j by setting $B'_j \leftarrow B'_j + \mathrm{SIZE}(S_i)$. So at each stage the current used capacity is simply the sum of the sizes of the PEs assigned to it. The tentative assignment is feasible if, after the last iteration, $\sum_{S \in \mathcal{S}: \pi(S)=h_j} \mathrm{SIZE}(S) = B'_j \leq B_j$ holds for all $h_j \in \mathcal{H}$. If the assignment is feasible, COLA outputs that the current PEs and passes the control to the post-processor. Otherwise, COLA must split another PE. This involves the oracle and the graph partitioner.

Oracle. The oracle decides the next PE to split, and it is very simple. It simply returns that PE with more than one operator which has the largest size. A reasonable alternative would be to split the largest size multi-operator PE assigned to the most over-utilized host. Splitting large PEs is obviously an intuitively good strategy. As a side benefit it will tend to minimize the number of calls to the graph partitioner, helpful because each such call adds to the overall communication cost.

Graph Partitioner. The graph partitioner is the central component of the COLA algorithm. Given a PE S, its role is to determine how to split it into two non-empty PEs, say S_1 and S_2. It bases its decision on two objectives:

1. to minimize the communication cost between the resulting PEs S_1 and S_2, and
2. to avoid highly unbalanced splits such that $\mathrm{SIZE}(S_1)$ is either very large or very small as compared to $\mathrm{SIZE}(S_2)$.

To achieve this, we use the following well-studied problem, called the *minimum-ratio cut* or *sparsest cut* problem. Given a graph $H = (V_H, E_H)$ with vertex-weights $w_v \geq 0$ and edge-weights $w_e \geq 0$, find a cut (S_1, S_2) where $S_2 = V_H \ominus S_1$ such that the following ratio, also called the *sparsity*, is minimized:

$$\frac{w(\delta(S_1))}{\min\{w(S_1), w(S_2)\}}. \tag{2}$$

This objective minimizes the weight of the cut $w(\delta(S_1))$ while favoring the "balanced" cuts for which $\min\{w(S_1), w(S_2)\}$ is large.

Since the sparsest cut problem is NP-hard [23], we use an algorithm of Leighton and Rao [24] to find an approximate solution. We choose their algorithm since it is efficient to implement and provably finds a cut with sparsity within a factor that is logarithmic in the number of operators of the optimum sparsity. We outline their approach here. They first set up a linear programming (LP) formulation of the sparsest cut problem as follows. One can think of the graph H as a flow network where vertices are sources and sinks and the edges $e \in E_H$ are "pipes" that have flow capacity w_e. The LP encodes the following flow problem. Route a demand of $w_u \cdot w_v$ between each pair of vertices $u, v \in V_H$, possibly split along several paths, and minimize the maximum "congestion" on any edge. In other words, minimize $\max_{e \in E_H} f_e / w_e$, where f_e denotes the flow sent on edge $e \in E$. Intuitively, a cut (S_1, S_2) with a small ratio (2) will have edges with high congestion, since the capacity $w(\delta(S_1))$ of the cut is small compared to the total demand $w(S_1) \cdot w(S_2)$ that needs to be routed across the cut. The cut is then identified from the fractional solution of the LP using the above intuition. We omit the details from here and refer the reader to Leighton and Rao [24].

Because finding the solution to the LP can be slow even with the best linear solver packages, we implement this step with a well-known combinatorial algorithm [25] that approximates the solution to the multicommodity flow LP.

Post-processor. The post-processor performs certain "greedy" PE merges in order to improve the solution quality without violating the property that the partitioning has a feasible assignment to hosts. The idea is to partly correct for the possibly less than perfect ordering of the graph partitioning iterations. It first determines if a pair of PEs, say S_i and S_j, *can* be merged, as follows. It tentatively merges S_i and S_j into a single PE $S_i \cup S_j$. If the resulting partitioning has a feasible host-assignment using the *LPT* scheme, it marks this pair of PEs as "mergeable". It then greedily merges that pair of mergeable PEs which gives the maximum reduction in the total communication cost. This process is repeated until there are no pairs that can be merged, and the resulting PEs are the output of the Basic COLA scheme.

3   Advanced COLA

In order to make COLA useful for a wide variety of scenarios, it should allow the user to guide or constrain the fusion process. This version supports six such types of constraints, and it also considers a more complex objective function.

3.1   User-Defined Fusion Constraints

We have incorporated the following six types of constraints, and for each we offer motivating examples.

1. *Resource matching*: An operator may be allowed to be assigned to only a subset of the hosts. The rationale here is that some operators may need a resource or a performance capability not present on all hosts.
2. *PE colocation*: Two operators may be required to be fused into the same PE. Motivation includes the sharing of some per-process resource, such as a JVM instance or some other language-binding runtime.
3. *Host colocation*: Two operators may be required to be assigned to the same host. Clearly, PE colocation implies host colocation, but the reverse need not be true. As motivation, two operators may wish to share a host license, local files, or have shared memory segments.

4. *PE exlocation*: Two operators may be required to be fused into separate PEs. This may allow some work to continue if a PE crashes.
5. *Host exlocation*: Two operators may be required to be assigned to separate hosts. In this case, host exlocation implies PE exlocation, but not the reverse. Motivation for host exlocation includes a common per-process resource requirement for which a single host would be insufficient.
6. *High availability*: In order to support the notion of hot standbys a subgraph of the overall operator data flow graph may be identically replicated several times. See Figure 3(a), where there are three subgraph replicas. The constraint requires that the fused PEs respect this subgraph in the sense that they are either entirely contained within a single replica or do not intersect with any replicas. Figures 3(b) and 3(c) present two feasible PE fusion solutions; each shaded subsection corresponds to a PE. High availability constraints must also ensure that any PE contained within one replica will not be assigned to the same host as a PE contained within another replica. Additionally, one may optionally insist that the PEs within one replica have the identical structures as those within the other replicas. An example of PEs chosen with this *isomorphic* condition turned on is shown in Figure 3(b). An example of PEs chosen with the isomorphic condition switched off is shown in Figure 3(c). In either case, there are implied host exlocation constraints for all pairs of differently shaded PEs. The motivation for all of this is, as the name implies, high availability: If the work in one replica cannot be done, perhaps because of a host failure, there will likely be immediate backups available on disjoint hosts.

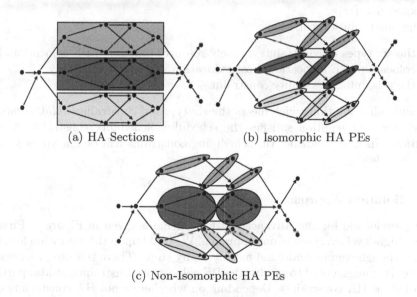

(a) HA Sections   (b) Isomorphic HA PEs

(c) Non-Isomorphic HA PEs

Fig. 3. High Availability

One could also think of two additional constraints, called *PE dedication* and *host dedication*. PE dedication would mean that an operator must be its own PE. Host dedication would mean that an operator must be its own PE *and* assigned alone on a host. Thus, host dedication implies PE dedication. Both these constraints can be easily incorporated via a small change to the COLA pre-processor and the addition of PE exlocation and host exlocation constraints. As a result, we do not treat these as separate constraints in COLA, even though we could expose them as constraints to the user.

3.2 Problem Formulation

The two somewhat competing goals are to ensure that

(iii). the maximum utilization $U = \max_{h_i \in \mathcal{H}} \sum_{S \in \mathcal{S}: \pi(S) = h_i} \text{SIZE}(S)/B_i$ is minimized, and

(iv). the overall communication cost $C = \sum_{S \in \mathcal{S}} w(\delta(S))$ is minimized.

Assuming the maximum utilization in expression (iii) is less than or equal to 1, which we will require, this expression is simply a more quantifiable version of the scheduling feasibility condition employed in the Basic COLA scheme. As before we will omit a discussion of how we handle pathological cases in which this scheduling feasibility is not possible.

We will handle both goals simultaneously by minimizing an arbitrary user-defined function $f(U, C)$ of U and C. This function can (and typically will) be as simple as a weighted average of the two metrics. It represents the tradeoff of the scheduling flexibility measured in expression (iii) with the efficiency measure in expression (iv).

Our final solution will obey:

- the six types of constraints, namely resource matching, PE colocation, host colocation, PE exlocation, host exlocation and high availability.
- the scheduling feasibility constraint.

We will call a solution which meets the six types of constraints *valid*, regardless of whether the solution satisfies the scheduling feasibility constraint. A valid solution which also satisfies the scheduling constraint will be known as *feasible*, as is standard.

3.3 Solution Approach

The pseudocode for the Advanced COLA scheme is given in Figure 4. First we give a high-level overview of our approach. We build upon the algorithm for Basic COLA, though we must add and modify many steps. There is a pre-processor, as before. It is augmented to resolve the PE colocation constraints. It also partially handles the HA constraints. Depending on whether or not HA constraints exist there may be multiple PEs rather than a single PE by the end of the pre-processing stage.

- Run **Pre-processor**
- **Phase 1.** Repeat
  - Compute the communication cost c of the current partitioning
  - If PE exlocation constraints are satisfied, go to Phase 2
  - Use **Oracle** for phase 1 to find a PE p to split next
  - Use **Graph Partitioner** for phase 1 to split p into two PEs
- **Phase 2.** Repeat
  - Use **PE scheduler** to compute a schedule with utilization u
  - If the schedule is *valid*, go to Phase 3
  - Use **Oracle** for phase 2 to find a PE p to split next
  - Use **Graph Partitioner** for phase 2 to split p into two PEs
  - Compute the communication cost c of the current partitioning
- **Phase 3.** Repeat
  - Let $s \leftarrow f(u, c)$
  - If the schedule is *feasible*, go to Phase 4
  - Use **Oracle** for phase 3 to find a PE p to split next
  - Use **Graph Partitioner** for phase 3 to split p into two PEs
  - Compute the communication cost c of the current partitioning
  - Use **PE scheduler** to compute a schedule with utilization u
- **Phase 4.** Repeat
  - Use **Oracle** for phase 4 to find a PE p to split next
  - Use **Graph Partitioner** for phase 4 to split p into two PEs
  - Compute the communication cost C of the current partitioning
  - If $C > (1 + T)c$, go to Post-processor
  - Use **PE scheduler** to compute a schedule with utilization U
  - Let $S \leftarrow f(U, C)$
  - $s \leftarrow \min\{s, S\}$
- Run **Post-processor**

Fig. 4. Advanced COLA Pseudocode

In the main body of our algorithm we solve the problem iteratively, as we did in the basic scheme. In each iteration we employ, as needed, a PE scheduler, an oracle to determine which PE to split next, and a graph partitioner to split that PE. However, the main body of the Advanced COLA scheme is composed of four successive phases of the iterative process. These phases are similar to each other, but not quite identical. During phase 1 the PE exlocation constraints are resolved. During phase 2 the host colocation, host exlocation and high availability constraints are resolved, which means that the solution at this point will be valid. Alternatively, COLA will have shown that there is no valid solution, because the graph partitioner will have split the operator flow graph all the way down into singleton operators without reaching validity. The user will be notified of this, and COLA will terminate. An important property of validity is that it will *persist* as we continue the graph partitioning process. (To see this, consider a single split of a PE in a valid solution, and consider the scheduling assignment in which the two new PEs are assigned to their previous host, and all other PEs are assigned to their previous hosts as well. This assignment also satisfies the six types of

constraints. A corollary of this persistence property is that the existence of a valid
solution can be determined by employing our iterative partitioning scheme.) In
the normal case that a valid solution exists, the scheme continues. During phase
3 the scheduling feasibility constraints will be resolved. This means that we do
have a feasible solution to the COLA problem. Denote the utilization at the end
of phase 3 by u, and the overall communication cost by c. We can compute
the objective function as $s = f(u, c)$. Note that the overall communication cost
is monotonic: It increases with every new graph partitioning. We continue the
iterative process *past* this point, into phase 4, and at each stage we will compute
a new utilization U and a new overall communication cost C. Now scheduling
feasibility does *not* necessarily persist as we split PEs, because the sizes of the
PEs increase. The new solution is *likely* to be scheduling feasible, because of the
the increased sizes should be counterbalanced by increased scheduling flexibilty.
If the solution is scheduling feasible, that is, if $U \leq 1$, we check to see if $S =
f(U, C) < s$. If so, we replace s by S, and we have found an improved solution.
When do we stop the iterative process? The answer is that we will constrain the
overall communication cost to be within a multiplicative user-input threshold
T of the cost c of our first feasible solution: $C \leq (1 + T)c$. We stop when this
condition fails, or when we have reached the bottom of the binary tree, so that
all PEs are single operators. The value of T determines how much the algorithm
is willing to compromise on overall communication cost in an attempt to find
more scheduling flexible solutions. For instance, if $T = 1$, then the algorithm will
continue to find more scheduling flexible solutions until the communication cost
of the current solution (C) is *twice* the cost of the first feasible solution (c). On
the other hand, if $T = 0$, then the algorithm skips phase 4 completely. Finally
there is a post-processor to greedily improve the solution.

Figure 5 shows the four iterative phases of the Advanced COLA scheme. At
the end of each phase we are further down the binary tree. The final solution,
denoted in the figure with stars, occurs at some point in the tree between the
end of phases 3 and 4.

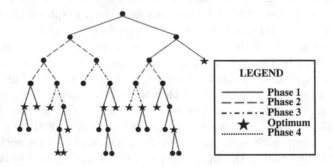

Fig. 5. Iterative Algorithmic Phases

Pre-processor. The pre-processor fuses unconstrained adjacent operators according to the conditions of Lemma 1. It also fuses PE colocated operators. And it separates HA replicas into separate PEs. So there will be one PE for each HA replica, plus potentially a catchall PE for all operators not part of any HA replicas. Recall Figure 3(a). If the isomorphic condition is turned on we will also replace each relevant operator cost with the average values of the corresponding operators across all the replicas. Similarly, we will replace each relevant communication cost with the average values of the corresponding streams across all the replicas. These values will probably be close in any case, but the reason for doing this is overall robustness, as will become clear below in the description of the graph partitioner. Finally, we will mark each relevant pair of PE replicas as host-exlocated, and continue to the main body of the scheme.

PE Scheduler. The component of the Basic COLA scheme that changes most relative to that of the basic algorithm is the PE scheduler. It is not needed in phase 1, but is used in phases 2 through 4. The LPT algorithm of the Basic COLA scheme is very fast, the complexity typically being dominated by the reordering of the PEs. It is an effective and robust scheme in the absense of additional constraints. LPT can certainly be adapted easily to handle resource matching, host colocation and host exlocation. But it will produce far lower quality solutions in a scenario with many such constraints, because it is a one-pass greedy scheme. We therefore formulate and solve the problem as a more computationally expensive integer program (IP). Specifically we define decision variable $x_{p,h}$ to be 1 if PE p is assigned to host h, and 0 otherwise. Let R_p denote the set of resource matched hosts for PE p. Host colocation defines an equivalence relation which we denote by $\equiv_{HC}$. Host exlocation does *not* determine an equivalence relation, but we define the set HE to be the set of pairs (p_1, p_2) of exlocated PEs. We then solve the following:

$$\text{Minimize} \quad \max_h \sum_p \text{SIZE}(S_p) \cdot x_{p,h}/B_h \tag{3}$$

$$\text{subject to} \quad x_{p,h} = 0 \qquad \text{if } h \notin R_p, \tag{4}$$

$$x_{p_1,h} = x_{p_2,h} \qquad \forall\, h, \text{ if } p_1 \equiv_{HC} p_2, \tag{5}$$

$$x_{p_1,h} + x_{p_2,h} \leq 1 \qquad \forall\, h, \text{ if } (p_1, p_2) \in HE, \tag{6}$$

$$\sum_h x_{p,h} = 1 \qquad \forall\, p, \tag{7}$$

$$x_{p,h} \in \{0, 1\} \qquad \forall\, p, h. \tag{8}$$

The objective function 3 measures the maximum utilization of any host. Constraint 4 enforces the resource matching constraints. Constraint 5 enforces the host colocation constraints. Constraint 6 enforces the host exlocation constraints. Constraint 7 ensures that each PE is assigned to one host. Finally, constraint 8 ensures that the decision variables are binary.

Oracle. In phase 1 the oracle will return any PE which fails to meet a PE exlocation constraint. This means there are at least two operators in the PE which are supposed to be PE exlocated. The choice is otherwise irrelevant, since all such constraints will need to be satisfied by the end of the phase. In phases 2 through 4 the oracle is identical to that of the Basic COLA scheme.

Graph Partitioner. Here there are two differences from Basic COLA. One is specific to all four phases, and relates to the HA constraints with isomorphic condition on. The other is relevant, as before, only to phase 1.

- If the isomorphic condition is on and the graph partitioner splits a PE that is part of one replica the scheme will force this solution immediately on all the other replicas. Since we have chosen averages it does not matter which replica is chosen to be split first. Furthermore, the graph partitioning solution should be relatively close to optimal for all replicas. If the isomorphic condition is off each replica can be split independently.
- The graph partitioner approach in phase 1 is again slightly modified. We wish to encourage the PE exlocated operators to be split by the graph partitioning process. So we add additional demand between all such operator pairs, which makes them more likely to be split, and solve the revised graph partitioning problem as before.

Post-Processor. The postprocessor in the Advanced COLA scheme is identical to that of the basic scheme.

4   COLA Experiments

To evaluate how COLA performs in practice, we use a job called VWAP that runs on SYSTEM S. The job VWAP [26] represents a financial markets scenario in which a stream of real-time quotes is processed to detect bargains and trading opportunities. Figure 6 shows the directed graph G corresponding to this job, as well as a typical operator fusion computed by COLA. The boxes correspond to PEs and the numbers in the boxes correspond to the sizes of PEs in terms of CPU fractions. (Figure 6(b) is an enlarged view of a portion of Figure 6(a).) This job consists of 200 operators and 283 arcs.

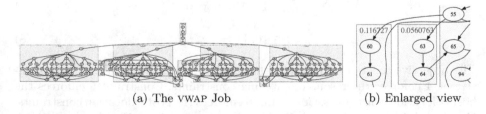

(a) The VWAP Job   (b) Enlarged view

Fig. 6. COLA Operator Fusion

The experiments discussed in this paper were performed using a SYSTEM S deployment on a cluster consisting of IBM BladeCenters running Linux 2.6.9. We employed between 4 and 7 blades, each having dual-CPU, dual-core 3.2GHz Intel Xeon processors with 4GB of RAM. The blades are in the same rack, and are inter-connected using a high-speed 20GB/s backplane. These homogeneous blades were reserved for these experiments. Thus, no other processes were allowed to use the blade resources.

The COLA fusion strategy was compared against two alternative fusion strategies:

- NONE: No fusion. Thus each operator lies in a distinct PE.
- FINT: This FINT fusion strategy, proposed in [13], also takes the operator and communication costs as input. It employs a *bottom-up* rather than a top-down approach to compute a fusion. It initially places all operators into distinct PEs and iteratively fuses them into larger PEs till some criteria is met.

Another natural fusion strategy is to fuse all operators into a single PE. However this typically results in a highly computationally intensive PE yielding very low throughput values. It is therefore not evaluated further in our experiments.

We evaluate a given fusion alternative by job *throughput*. This is a measure of how much data (in Mbps) is processed by the job. It is intended to be a measure of the job's "effective capacity". Each VWAP experiment is characterized by the fusion strategy employed and the number of blades used.

Both the COLA or FINT fusion strategies require operator and communications costs as input. The good news is that SYSTEM S incorporates efficient *profiling* methodology [13]. But there is bad news as well. Specifically, to use the profiling mode in an application run, we need to choose an operator fusion. To create an operator fusion, on the other hand, we need the profiling data. This is a chicken and egg problem. Since the NONE fusion strategy does not require operator or communication costs as input, we first run this fusion in the profiling mode. However, the NONE fusion is observed to yield low throughput values and hence only moderately useful profiling data. So we employ an iterative approach, as follows: Using the NONE profiling data, we compute the fusion, referred to as iteration 1, again in profiling mode. Then, using the new profiling data, we compute the fusion again, this time using the *new* profiling data. This becomes iteration 2, and we continue in this manner. This iterative approach is used for both FINT and COLA fusions.

Furthermore, we adopt one additional heuristic in the iterative process. Since the early fusions yield lower throughputs, we compensate for this in COLA as follows. In iteration 1, we scale the CPU capacities R_i of the hosts by a factor $\gamma < 1$. In the experiments described below, we set $\gamma = 0.5$ in iteration 1. Then we gradually increase γ from 0.5 to 1.0 by 0.1 through 6 subsequent iterations, since we expect to obtain more and more accurate estimates on the operator and communication costs.

Figure 7 demonstrates the benefit of multiple iterations, particularly for COLA. Fortunately, only a few seem to be required. The COLA fusion strategy shows

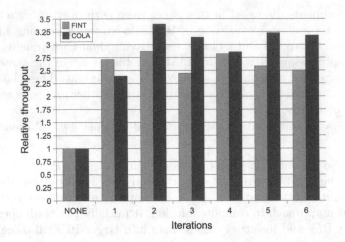

Fig. 7. Profiling iterations for FINT and COLA on 5 blades. The y-axis represents the relative throughput of the runs, scaled so that the throughput of NONE run is 1.

Table 1. Theoretical Comparison of FINT and COLA

VWAP1	NONE		FINT		COLA	
Blades	Cut size	PE size	Cut size	PE size	Cut size	PE size
4	0.3792	0.3218	0.0661	0.5353	0.0332	0.4990
5	0.3703	0.2980	0.0441	0.5476	0.0587	0.4676
6	0.7236	0.8169	0.2698	0.8169	0.1998	0.7560
7	0.6833	0.6697	0.2492	0.6697	0.1860	0.6666

VWAP2	NONE		FINT		COLA	
Blades	Cut size	PE size	Cut size	PE size	Cut size	PE size
4	0.3544	0.3677	0.0618	0.4185	0.0618	0.4185
5	0.5740	0.6030	0.2577	0.6030	0.1530	0.5547
6	0.5571	0.5764	0.3367	0.5764	0.1552	0.5294
7	0.5888	0.5813	0.2600	0.5813	0.1587	0.5813

a significant increase in the throughput in the first two iterations. We typically see that COLA reaches its maximum throughput value quickly.

In Table 1, we show how COLA compares to FINT and NONE in terms of both cut size and maximum PE size. We study two versions of the VWAP job: VWAP1 consists of 200 operators and 283 arcs, while VWAP2 consists of 217 operators and 315 arcs. The cut size is the measure of the total cost of sending traffic between PEs. The larger the cut size, the more CPU cycles are being devoted to sending data. The intuition is that a high quality fusion has a low cut size without making any PEs too big to fit on a processor. We can see that the cut sizes for COLA are signifcantly lower than the cut sizes for FINT, and COLA often maintains a maximum PE size which is smaller than that of FINT.

Table 2. Throughput Values for VWAP Runs with FINT and COLA

VWAP1 blades	NONE	FINT			COLA		
		1st	1st-local	Max	1st	1st-local	Max
4	99.4 (1)	273 (2.75)	295 (2.96)	295 (2.96)	284 (2.86)	286 (2.88)	303 (3.05)
5	97.2 (1)	263 (2.71)	279 (2.87)	279 (2.87)	232 (2.39)	330 (3.40)	330 (3.40)
6	189 (1)	286 (1.51)	286 (1.51)	293 (1.55)	280 (1.48)	379 (2.00)	391 (2.06)
7	179 (1)	268 (1.50)	322 (1.80)	336 (1.88)	267 (1.50)	349 (1.95)	363 (2.03)

VWAP2 blades	NONE	FINT			COLA		
		1st	1st-local	Max	1st	1st-local	Max
4	92.6 (1)	212 (2.29)	212 (2.29)	212 (2.29)	187 (2.02)	237 (2.56)	249 (2.69)
5	150 (1)	219 (1.47)	219 (1.47)	258 (1.73)	229 (1.53)	332 (2.22)	332 (2.22)
6	146 (1)	227 (1.55)	260 (1.78)	260 (1.78)	238 (1.63)	346 (2.37)	346 (2.37)
7	154 (1)	226 (1.46)	369 (2.39)	369 (2.39)	253 (1.64)	362 (2.35)	362 (2.35)

Next we discuss throughput, our prime practical metric. Table 2 presents the throughput values for NONE and various iterations of FINT, and COLA. Since the throughput values from different iterations can be quite different, a natural question to ask is which iteration one should finally chose. To this end, we evaluate several different choices: the first iteration (1st); the first iteration that achieves a local maximum throughput (1st-local); and the iteration (among the first few) that achieves the overall maximum throughput (Max).

We again study two versions, VWAP1 and VWAP2, as described above. The rows represent distinct sets of experiments run on different number of reserved blades given in the first column. For each such set of experiments, 6 iterations were used for each of FINT and COLA. The throughput values are truncated to three significant digits. The numbers in parentheses represent the relative gain over the NONE fusion, i.e., throughput values scaled so that the throughput of the NONE fusion is 1.

The throughput values of both FINT and COLA are significantly higher than those of NONE, while the throughput values of COLA for 1st-local and Max are usually higher than those of FINT.

5   Conclusions and Future Work

In this paper we have described and solved an important operator fusion problem which arises naturally in SYSTEM S. Our scheme works in heterogeneous processor environments, and supports a wide variety of real-world constraints. We believe that the COLA scheme is mathematically novel and interesting. Initial experiments support the value of our approach to the SPADE operator fusion problem. We list some future enhancements.

- As may be seen in Table 2, for example, adding more hosts to the COLA problem does not necessarily improve performance. We are thinking about approaches in which COLA might automatically choose fewer hosts than those offered to it. This issue is easier in the case of the basic scheme with homogeneous hosts.

- The function $f(U, C)$ used by the Advanced COLA scheme could be a weighted average of U and C. But we have not described how to pick these weights. We believe the appropriate weights could be learned by examining the effects of alternative choices on throughput.
- It appears to be useful to have the Advanced COLA scheme quickly decide if the six types of real-world constraints allow a feasible solution or not. (This would allow a user to modify inconsistent constraints and resubmit.) Our current scheme provides an answer this feasibility question, but not necessarily in the fastest timeframe. We plan to modify our approach to better handle this issue.
- We currently consider processing hosts as single units. But in today's environment they are often composed of several multi-core processors. Our LPT and IP PE scheduling scheme does not consider this processor hierarchy at present. We believe both schemes can be enhanced to do so, and we will be experimenting to see if such an approach is valuable.

References

1. ThomsonReuters, http://ar.thomsonreuters.com
2. Abadi, D.J., Ahmad, Y., Balazinska, M., Cetintemel, U., Cherniack, M., Hwang, J.H., Lindner, W., Maskey, A.S., Rasin, A., Ryvkina, E., Tatbul, N., Xing, Y., Zdonik, S.: The design of the Borealis stream processing engine. In: Proceedings of Conference on Innovative Data Systems Research (2005)
3. Balakrishnan, H., Balazinska, M., Carney, D., Cetintemel, U., Cherniack, M., Convey, C., Galvez, E., Salz, J., Stonebraker, M., Tatbul, N., Tibbetts, R., Zdonik, S.: Retrospective on Aurora. VLDB Journal (2004)
4. Chandrasekaran, S., Cooper, O., Deshpande, A., Franklin, M.J., Hellerstein, J.M., Hong, W., Krishnamurthy, S., Madden, S.R., Raman, V., Reiss, F., Shah, M.A.: TelegraphCQ: Continuous dataflow processing for an uncertain world. In: Proceedings of Conference on Innovative Data Systems Research (2003)
5. Girod, L., Mei, Y., Newton, R., Rost, S., Thiagarajan, A., Balakrishnan, H., Madden, S.: XStream: A signal-oriented data stream management system. In: Proceedings of the International Conference on Data Engineering (2008)
6. Arasu, A., Babcock, B., Babu, S., Datar, M., Ito, K., Motwani, R., Nishizawa, I., Srivastava, U., Thomas, D., Varma, R., Widom, J.: STREAM: The Stanford stream data manager. IEEE Data Engineering Bulletin 26 (2003)
7. Thies, W., Karczmarek, M., Amarasinghe, S.: StreamIt: A language for streaming applications. In: Horspool, R.N. (ed.) CC 2002. LNCS, vol. 2304, p. 179. Springer, Heidelberg (2002)
8. Zdonik, S., Stonebraker, M., Cherniack, M., Cetintemel, U., Balazinska, M., Balakrishnan, H.: The Aurora and Medusa projects. IEEE Data Engineering Bulletin 26 (2003)
9. Coral8 (2007), http://www.coral8.com
10. StreamBaseSystems (2007), http://www.streambase.com/

11. Amini, L., Andrade, H., Bhagwan, R., Eskesen, F., King, R., Selo, P., Park, Y., Venkatramani, C.: SPC: A distributed, scalable platform for data mining. In: Proceedings of the Workshop on Data Mining Standards, Services and Platforms (2006)
12. Douglis, F., Palmer, J., Richards, E., Tao, D., Tetzlaff, W., Tracey, J., Yin, J.: Position: Short object lifetimes require a delete-optimized storage system. In: ACM SIGOPS European Workshop (2004)
13. Gedik, B., Andrade, H., Wu, K.L.: A code generation approach to optimizing high-performance distributed data stream processing. In: Proceedings of the ACM International Conference on Information and Knowledge Management (2009)
14. Gedik, B., Andrade, H., Wu, K.L., Yu, P.S., Doo, M.: SPADE: The System S declarative stream processing engine. In: Proceedings of the ACM International Conference on Management of Data (2008)
15. Hildrum, K., Douglis, F., Wolf, J., Yu, P.S., Fleischer, L., Katta, A.: Storage optimization for large-scale stream processing systems. ACM Transactions on Storage 3 (2008)
16. Jain, N., Amini, L., Andrade, H., King, R., Park, Y., Selo, P., Venkatramani, C.: Design, implementation and evaluation of the linear road benchmark on the stream processing core. In: Proceedings of the ACM International Conference on Management of Data (2006)
17. Jacques-Silva, G., Challenger, J., Degenaro, L., Giles, J., Wagle, R.: Towards autonomic fault recovery in System-S. In: Proceedings of Conference on Autonomic Computing (2007)
18. Wolf, J., Bansal, N., Hildrum, K., Parekh, S., Rajan, D., Wagle, R., Wu, K.L., Fleischer, L.: SODA: An optimizing scheduler for large-scale stream-based distributed computer systems. In: Issarny, V., Schantz, R. (eds.) Middleware 2008. LNCS, vol. 5346, pp. 306–325. Springer, Heidelberg (2008)
19. Wu, K.L., Yu, P.S., Gedik, B., Hildrum, K.W., Aggarwal, C.C., Bouillet, E., Fan, W., George, D.A., Gu, X., Luo, G., Wang, H.: Challenges and experience in prototyping a multi-modal stream analytic and monitoring application on System S. In: Proceedings of the International Conference on Very Large Data Bases Conference (2007)
20. Wolf, J., Bansal, N., Hildrum, K., Parekh, S., Rajan, D., Wagle, R., Wu, K.L.: Job admission and resource allocation in distributed streaming systems. In: Workshop on Job Scheduling Strategies for Parallel Processing, IPDPS (2009)
21. Garey, M., Johnson, D.: Computers and Intractability. W.H. Freeman and Company, New York (1979)
22. Pinedo, M.: Scheduling: Theory, Algorithms and Systems. Prentice Hall, Englewood Cliffs (1995)
23. Síma, J., Schaeffer, S.E.: On the NP-completeness of some graph cluster measures. In: Wiedermann, J., Tel, G., Pokorný, J., Bieliková, M., Štuller, J. (eds.) SOFSEM 2006. LNCS, vol. 3831, pp. 530–537. Springer, Heidelberg (2006)
24. Leighton, F.T., Rao, S.: Multicommodity max-flow min-cut theorems and their use in designing approximation algorithms. J. ACM 46, 787–832 (1999)
25. Garg, N., Könemann, J.: Faster and simpler algorithms for multicommodity flow and other fractional packing problems. SIAM J. Comput. 37, 630–652 (2007)
26. Andrade, H., Gedik, B., Wu, K.L., Yu, P.S.: Scale-up strategies for processing high-rate data streams in System S. In: Proceedings of the International Conference on Data Engineering (2009)

Persistent Temporal Streams

David Hilley and Umakishore Ramachandran

College of Computing
Georgia Institute of Technology
davidhi@cc.gatech.edu
rama@cc.gatech.edu

Abstract. Distributed continuous live stream analysis applications are increasingly common. Video-based surveillance, emergency response, disaster recovery, and critical infrastructure protection are all examples of such applications. They are characterized by a variety of high- and low-bandwidth streams as well as a need for analyzing both live and archived streams. We present a system called *Persistent Temporal Streams (PTS)* that supports a higher-level, domain-targeted programming abstraction for such applications. PTS provides a simple but expressive stream abstraction encompassing transport, manipulation and storage of streaming data. In this paper, we present a system architecture for implementing PTS. We provide an experimental evaluation which shows the system-level primitives can be implemented in a lightweight and high-performance manner, and an application-based evaluation designed to show that a representative high-bandwidth stream analysis application can be implemented relatively simply and with good performance.

1   Introduction

Continuous live data streams are ubiquitous and their analysis is a central component of many applications. Network monitoring, surveillance, robotics, inventory tracking, traffic or weather analysis, disaster response and many other application domains fall under this umbrella. All of these applications have one common trait: live streaming data is analyzed continuously, and the results are used in some sort of feedback loop to direct further analysis and perform external side-effects such as triggering alerts, producing continuous data summaries for human monitoring or manipulating the environment. We call this class of applications *live stream analysis applications*, because streams are analyzed and consumed "live," as the data is produced. Many such applications also require access to historical data – data that was streamed in the past and is now archived.

While such applications are becoming ubiquitous, programming support is relatively immature. Our broad goal is the development of a unified distributed programming abstraction for accessing live and historical stream data, suitable in scenarios requiring significant signal processing on heavyweight streams such as audio and video. Existing solutions for constructing such applications tend to fit into two broad categories: 1) "stream database" or "stream processing engine"-style systems or 2) general-purpose distributed programming systems.

J.M. Bacon and B.F. Cooper (Eds.): Middleware 2009, LNCS 5896, pp. 328–348, 2009.

The former category has centrally managed and controlled execution, while the latter does not impose a particular computational model on applications, only modeling data interactions. The latter support loosely coupled systems of independent communicating components with no centralized control. To the best of our knowledge, no prior system has provided a unified abstraction for both transport and storage of live streams as a simple distributed programming primitive. In this paper we propose Persistent Temporal Streams (PTS), a novel distributed system that provides simple and efficient programming idioms for dealing with distributed stream data. At the heart of PTS is the *temporal stream* abstraction, providing a uniform interface for both time-based retrieval of current streaming data and data persistence.

PTS fits between very high-level and heavyweight solutions like full databases with query languages and lower-level non-stream oriented distributed communications facilities typically used for distributed applications (MPI, RMI, etc.) plus separate storage facilities. Our approach represents a middle-ground in a vast design space. At one extreme are high-level heavy-weight solutions that incorporate full databases with query processing capabilities. At the other extreme are lower-level non-stream oriented distributed communication facilities for constructing distributed applications that require a separate treatment of persistent data. This middle-ground for continuous streaming data is roughly analogous to solutions such as Distributed Data Structures [1], BerkeleyDB [2] and Boxwood [3] for non-streaming data. The *temporal stream* provides first-class recognition of time, which is a critical distinguishing aspect of continuous live streams over other types of data; the tailoring of the abstraction to the problem domain makes live stream analysis applications more straightforward to build, as does eliminating a programmer-visible artificial distinction between past streamed data and current "live" data.

This paper's contributions are the following:

- A persistent *temporal stream* abstraction targeted for live stream analysis applications (Section 2)
- An architecture for stream persistence and an analysis of the potential design space of persistent temporal streams (Sections 2.1 & 2.2)
- A system design and implementation of PTS, a distributed runtime realizing the persistent temporal stream abstraction (Section 3)
- A system-level experimental evaluation of PTS and an application-based evaluation using a video-based surveillance system [4] (Section 4)

We conclude with related work (Section 5) and a summation (Section 6).

2 Persistent Temporal Streams

Temporal streams are a key feature of live stream analysis applications – as a concrete example, think of a video feed: the stream is unbounded and produced at a finite rate, and the video frames are temporally ordered. Each frame represents some sampled interval of time based on the frame rate. Event streams and other aperiodic streams may not have fixed output rates, but trigger based on certain environmental conditions, like a temperature sensor sending an alert when a threshold is reached. In both cases, data items are associated with specific time information. All "live" streams have a natural relationship with time (wall-clock time). Broadly, our model of temporal streams is a time-indexed sequence of discrete data items; each item has a timestamp and spans a time interval ending with the timestamp of the next item.

In PTS, a temporal stream is represented by a *channel*, which is a distributed data structure encompassing an interface for both transport and manipulation of streaming data; each channel holds a time-indexed sequence of discrete data items (such as video frames) and analysis code retrieves data items by specifying time intervals of interest. Applications interact with channels by means of "get" and "put" operations. The basic stream operations are 1) $put(i, t)$ – put data item i on the stream with timestamp t (typically the current time); and 2) $get(l, h)$ – get all items falling within the interval $[l, h)$. A variety of expressive *time variables* [5] (such as *now*) are also provided to formulate intervals such as "the most recent 10 seconds of video data", and a wide range producer/consumer patterns can be expressed using these time variables. The system maintains a window of current stream data, automatically garbage collecting older items – for example, an application could specify that channel c_1 should keep 30 seconds worth of data, and items older than that may be reclaimed.

The benefit of this model is that it provides a higher-level stream abstraction, which fits at the intersection of an application's manipulation of data and stream transport. Since the stream abstraction has a familiar get/put-based interface as a data structure, it is simple to use. Finally, by providing first-class recognition of time, it provides a more natural way to write analysis code that deals with continuous streams – similar to tuple models in streaming database work, and higher level than general-purpose distributed programming mechanisms appropriate for high-volume data transfer. Rather than managing and buffering an ephemeral, linear flow of data, the application can access stream data in terms of higher-level time information. Since many live stream analysis applications also need to store and retrieve historical data for trend analysis, a persistence mechanism that fits within the temporal stream model is a useful feature. For instance, a surveillance system might store historical video streams for some predetermined archival period in a degraded form (e.g. lower resolution).

Integrating persistence into the temporal stream abstraction avoids an artificial distinction between data that is currently available in streams (a window of recent data) and data that was streamed in the past but is now archived. This change elevates the temporal stream abstraction from a communication abstraction to a general-purpose *data* abstraction, uniformly modeling stream data interactions. Although the same abstraction is used for live and stored data, information about the source of data should still be made available to the programmer since the difference in access time and data quality or representation can be significant. From a programming perspective, eliminating unnecessary non-uniformity is desirable as it can make applications simpler to construct and less brittle in the face of change.

The issues surrounding the incorporation of persistence into the stream programming model are the core of this paper. In the following subsections, we present an architecture for accomplishing this goal. The architecture explores and answers several important questions related to incorporating persistence in a seamless manner into a distributed programming model for a wide range of streaming applications:

- How is persistence integrated into the programming model API?
- How are data items mapped to persistent forms?
- What factors affect the choice of storage backends for persistent stream data?
- How do we account for information lifecycle management (ILM) issues (e.g. redundancy, free space management, hierarchical secondary storage)?

2.1 An Integrated Architecture for Live and Archived Streams

Our high-level persistence interface is directly enabled by extending the time-oriented channel interface – a channel can now be marked by an application as persistent (at creation time or later). Persistent channels empower the application programmer in the following ways: 1) items are automatically committed to persistent storage with related time-stamp information, and 2) time intervals for retrieval of items may now reference both live and persistent items. Figure 1 depicts a get operation with an interval spanning live and stored data. Other high level interface decisions are described below.

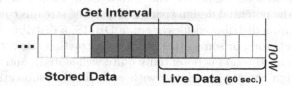

Fig. 1. Get operation spanning stored and live data

Get interface: The application may optionally constrain a retrieval operation to adjust for the difference in latency of access and potential data format differences of stored versus live items. The options are as follows: 1) ANY – any items, live or stored; 2) LIVE – only live items, 3) STORED – only stored items; 4) ANYSPLIT – return live items and load stored items from disk in the background, caching them in a temporary in-memory cache for a subsequent get.

Per-stream data representation: An application can also control how items are mapped to a persistent form. Some may wish to degrade the quality of items, reduce the number of items or otherwise change their format. An application can provide a *pickling handler*, which is responsible for mapping items to their persistent representation (defaulting to the identity function). For example, a video channel's handler may JPEG compress video frames or reduce the image resolution. In addition to one-to-one item mappings, the pickling handler can take N items and produce a single item to store: for example, an event channel's handler may transform thirty small events into some sort of digest. When N items are mapped to one item, the original timestamp information is retained, so the same get request will operate similarly on live and stored data. That is to say, if two items are mapped to a single stored item, it will span the combined time interval of the original items. As a direct extension of this functionality, an application may provide multiple handlers with varying levels of disk usage versus processing time and the runtime can automatically switch based on system-level cues.

Per-item persistence control: In addition to per-stream control via pickling handlers, per-item control is possible: a data producer may mark an item placed into a channel with the NOPERSIST flag. This will cause the persistence mechanism to ignore it, so the item will disappear for good when it is garbage collected from the live stream.

All-in-all, the programmer visible interface to a channel is essentially unchanged – $put(i, t)$ and $get(l, h)$ still operate as before, but the potential span of items available in a channel now includes historical data rather than just a window of current live data. Put takes an optional NOPERSIST flag and get takes an optional ANY, LIVE, STORED or ANYSPLIT modifier (ANY is the default).

2.2   Storage Requirements and Design Choices

At the high level, the stream persistence interface is natural and intuitive; all an application needs to know is that data items are mapped to persistent forms using a known transformation and stored along with timestamp information. Underneath this abstraction, however, the data must be stored to "stable" storage somehow, and the potential design space is large. The streams could be stored to a local filesystem, a distributed filesystem, a DBMS, a distributed virtual block device, an object store, or some other storage abstraction (Boxwood [3]'s persistent B-link tree abstraction is potentially quite well-suited), and there are many orthogonal design choices associated with each. In this subsection, we discuss several PTS design properties.

Redundancy/Availability: Some properties of the underlying storage mechanism manifest themselves as higher-level concerns. For example, an application may desire some form of redundancy so a stored stream does not become inaccessible due to disk or host failure. This could be accomplished in a variety of ways such as using a redundant, distributed storage mechanism as a backend, using primary copy replication, or making use of shared disks (e.g. via a SAN).

Free space management: Another storage-level property exposed at a higher-level is the management of free space. For high-bandwidth data streams, like video, an application will often want to use local storage as a ring-buffer so the oldest stored data will be overwritten when storage is full. Support for some policies may already be provided by a storage backend, however. For example, the GPFS [6] distributed filesystem provides internal support for rich information lifecycle policies based on filesystem metadata – a policy could specify that old data can be reclaimed or moved to lower performance storage.

External applications: One may also want a persistent stream stored in a particular backend for reasons external to the application: for example, a user may want sensor readings inserted into a table in a relational database for offline analysis by another application or a third party.

Suitability for workload: The access patterns created by storing streaming data are atypical workloads for some potential backends. Stored items are never updated and are read rarely (relative to the number stored). From a storage perspective, the data is essentially append-only, which affords simple and efficient consistency management strategies. Ideally, the backend should not block concurrent reads of older data while appending newer data. The system must also support ranged queries since data is accessed by specifying intervals. When multiple streams are involved, the typical access patterns of storing many append-only streams simultaneously do not interact well with most general-purpose filesystem layouts [7]. Hyperion [7] addresses the problem of writing and querying multiple streams of captured high-data rate network traffic with a custom filesystem called StreamFS. The authors also present a "log file rotation" strategy for improving stream data layout on typical Unix filesystems.

To deal with diversity in requirements, we provide pluggable storage backends. Given the design tradeoffs discussed above, our initial prototype supports three backends: 1) a local filesystem backend (called `fs1`), 2) a distributed filesystem backend using GPFS (called `gpfs1`), and 3) a MySQL backend. Since we want to be able to handle multiple high bandwidth streams, we think Hyperion's StreamFS [7] (or a slightly modified version) is best-suited to our target domain when using local disks. StreamFS is not publicly available, so we implemented our own filesystem-based backend called `fs1` as a first-order approximation using the "log file rotation" approach presented in the Hyperion paper. We would also like to provide a distributed storage solution with advanced ILM functionality, so we leverage the distributed filesystem GPFS for this purpose. A MySQL backend is provided for scenarios where streams need to be stored in a relational database (e.g. for analysis by other applications). In general, we do not believe MySQL is a good general backend choice because it imposes a relatively large overhead on the storage process and was not designed for this particular workload.

3   System Design and Implementation

In this section we describe the concrete system architecture of PTS and salient implementation details. First, we provide general high-level system details (Section 3.1), followed by channel implementation details independent of whether a channel is persistent or not (Section 3.2). Section 3.3 summarizes the implementation of the stream persistence architecture. Figure 2 shows the structure of the PTS system software stack.

3.1 System Structure

The system is structured as a distributed runtime and the core of the system is a set of cooperating *peers* using the PTS library – peers are data consumers or producers and host resources. In typical usage, a peer can be thought of as a multi-threaded process with a distinguished identity in PTS. We also have a distributed, replicated directory storing system metadata (for instance, naming information or mappings between opaque PTS endpoints and network endpoints) which is accessed by peers via an RPC-like protocol. Understanding the persistent stream architecture does not require knowledge of the metadata directory design; for the purposes of this discussion, one can simply imagine naming/location metadata is available in some centralized directory.

Channels are PTS's distributed and time-indexed representation of temporal streams and the fundamental mechanism for data transport, manipulation and storage. Almost all of the implementation complexity of peers revolves around hosting or accessing channels. Peers place timestamped items into channels ("put" operations) and retrieve items based on time intervals ("get" operations). Channels are hosted at a single peer, but they may be read-only replicated (primary copy replication) for capacity or availability; a channel may also migrate dynamically to another peer if necessary. Architecturally, every peer is a first class entity that may host channels or interact with existing channels.

The system assumes data producers will have synchronized clocks, which is not an unreasonable burden. NTP [8] is widely deployed and can keep hosts over the Internet synchronized with high precision. For extremely limited devices, more lightweight techniques or producer proxies can be used.

The implementation described here is written in ANSI/ISO C89 with pthreads.

3.2 Channels without Data Persistence

A channel stores current live stream items ordered by timestamp; items older than a given "currency" bound (e.g. 30s) are automatically reclaimed. Conceptually, a channel may be viewed as an ordered list of data items and associated metadata (e.g. timestamps) located at the peer hosting a channel. Each peer has a single *gatekeeper* TCP/IP endpoint where other peers can either interact

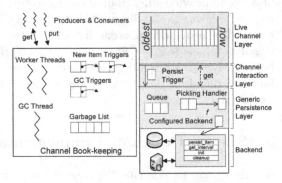

Fig. 2. PTS Architecture

with channels hosted locally or negotiate a separate dedicated connection to a particular channel for bulk data transfer. The transport protocol of dedicated connections can be negotiated on a per-connection basis (e.g. shared memory for colocated processes, RDMA or SCTP within a cluster, etc.). A pool of worker threads is used to handle remote get/put requests on dedicated connections.

When performing get or put operations, a channel is identified by a *channel descriptor*, which is an opaque reference to a particular channel data connection. Each peer has a table mapping channel descriptors to concrete connection endpoint information, which acts like a cache: normally, channel operations use the cached information and no metadata lookup or binding is necessary. When a channel moves or a new connection to a channel is needed, the runtime contacts the system metadata directory to find out which peer is hosting a channel and then contacts the peer's gatekeeper endpoint to negotiate a data connection.

A channel also has an integral *trigger* mechanism with two different types of triggers: 1) garbage collection triggers and 2) new item triggers. Both types of triggers are functions which apply to a single item at a time. Garbage collection triggers are invoked when an item is about to be removed from the channel's "live" data and either freed or placed on a garbage list; new item triggers are invoked when a new item is added to a channel. While this is a very simple concept, it is also remarkably flexible. Triggers are used to implement a variety of functionality – new item triggers are the basis for replication of channels, multicasting channel data, an optional push-style programming interface, and a virtual synchronization mechanism [5]. For example, to set up a copy of channel A replicated at host B, the system creates a new locally hosted channel at host B, and sets up a new item trigger on channel A to send each item to the replica. Any host can now use the copy by updating its channel descriptor table to point to the replicated channel.

To execute triggers, each channel maintains a list of functions to call for each trigger type and invokes them sequentially and in the execution context of the thread that added an item or caused an old item to be prepared for garbage collection. Consequently, trigger functions are expected to have short, bounded execution times. When a trigger is added, an initialization function is run which can set up an event queue and a dedicated listening thread or bind to a shared thread/thread pool for asynchronously servicing longer triggers (analogous to "bottom half" processing for interrupt handlers). Triggers can be loaded by name statically or dynamically (via `dlopen`).

The C-based runtime uses reference counting for internal storage management of channel data. Without persistence, channel garbage collection is easy: since a *put* call places a single timestamped item into a channel, we just check to see if we can reclaim the oldest item in the channel after a put call. If the span between the newest and oldest items is greater than the channel's specified currency bound, the item is removed from the live channel and the system invokes the GC trigger functions. The last trigger will either place the item on a garbage list if its refcount is non-zero or immediately free it otherwise. If the item isn't immediately freed, we walk through a small fixed number of items on the garbage list and free those with refcounts of zero. There is no need for a background GC thread because new garbage is only generated when old items are displaced by newly arriving data, so the system can maintain stasis by doing a small amount of GC work cooperatively during each put call.

3.3 Persistence

The persistence mechanism implements the high-level channel persistence semantics and is separated into three general layers: 1) the channel interaction
layer, 2) the generic persistence layer and 3) specific persistence backends. The
persistence backends are loaded dynamically and handle interfacing with a particular storage mechanism (e.g. a filesystem). Both the generic persistence layer
and concrete persistence backends provide a simple API with four basic calls:
`persist_item` and `get_interval` as well as `init` and `cleanup`. `persist_item`
and `get_interval` directly correspond to the live channel get/put operations.

Channel interaction layer: The channel interaction layer is the small set of
hooks in the channel implementation (described in Section 3.2) which interfaces
with the generic persistence layer. For channel get operations, this consists of the
logic to interpret get types (`ANY`, `LIVE`, etc.) and to call down to the persistence
layer if stored items will be needed. If a get operation is performed on interval
$[l, h]$ and some live item has a timestamp $\leq l$, then no call to the persistence
layer is needed. After a `get_interval` call to the persistence layer is made, this
layer also handles placing temporary items retrieved from the storage backend
on the garbage list.

Triggers are used to send items to the lower levels of the storage stack by calling `persist_item` in the generic persistence layer. The channel interaction layer
also contains routines to initialize the persistence interface. When a channel is
initially marked as persistent, a background garbage collection thread is spawned
since get operations spanning persisted items may create significant additional
garbage and our previous strategy may not be able to keep up (particularly if
put calls are rare).

Generic Persistence Layer: This layer sits between the channel implementation and a particular concrete storage backend. It maintains a small queue of
items to be persisted in batches, and is responsible for calling pickling handlers
to map items into their persistent representation. The `persist_item` call just in-
crements an item's refcount and enqueues it on a processing work queue handled
by a worker thread. This structure has several key properties: 1) it prevents the
`persist_item` call from blocking a long time (since it is called from a trigger),
2) queueing is necessary for pickling handlers that transform N items to 1 item,
3) if items are eagerly pushed to storage on a channel with multiple producers,
some queueing is necessary to ensure items are written out in temporal order,
and 4) it allows the generic persistence layer to serialize writes to the backend.

Several of these properties simplify the assumptions a storage backend must
deal with. For example, serializing writes to the backend by the persistence layer
simplifies backend implementation – it may assume there are no concurrent writers, although a single writer may overlap with item reads. Another feature of
this layer is that it guarantees that items will be presented in temporal order to
the storage backend, which again can simplify the backend's implementation.

To process a `get_inverval` request, the generic persistence layer must search
its work queue for items that are waiting to be persisted as well as call down into

the concrete storage backend layer to retrieve items that have reached "stable" storage. Finally, the generic persistence layer is also responsible for dynamically loading storage backends and pickling functions (via `dlopen`) when a channel is first marked as persistent. The generic persistence layer can also monitor and react to different kinds of resource contention: by measuring the latency of backend `persist_item` calls, it can determine if storage contention is too high. Similarly, by timing pickling handler execution, it can estimate CPU load. The generic persistence layer can adjust to these conditions by switching between pickling handlers or disabling pickling. The persistence layer primarily affects CPU and storage contention; network and memory usage can be monitored and controlled by the live channel implementation (Section 3.2).

Storage backends: As mentioned earlier, the storage backends are responsible for implementing `persist_item` and `get_interval` calls.

MySQL backend: The MySQL backend is not designed for streams with high data rates, but it is certainly appropriate for low bandwidth sensors. `persist_item` simply puts a tuple with (timestamp, data) into a specified table and `get_interval` performs a `SELECT` of items with timestamps in the interval [low, high). Given the `SELECT` query, the timestamp column should also have an index suitable for range queries (e.g. B-trees). Currently the backend simply stores item data as BLOBs, which is not very flexible. We are looking into providing a richer interface by allowing user-defined functions to map binary item data into some number of separate data items matching the desired schema.

Filesystem backend: The `fs1` filesystem backend is implemented as a lightweight overlay on top of a filesystem (SGI's XFS [9] generally has the best overall performance for these workloads [7]), but could also be implemented directly on a block device. The data layout is quite simple and uses the properties provided by the generic storage layer to avoid unnecessary complexity and synchronization. We use the log file rotation approach from the Hyperion paper [7].

A backend needs to store timestamped data items in order and retrieve them by bounded time intervals. To accomplish this, `fs1` uses a two-level indexing scheme. A given channel has a single top-level index file and many individual data files, each with a second-level index; a data file's size is roughly bounded by a *chunk size* parameter (default 16MB per file) and the small, fixed index is stored at the beginning. The overall organization is similar to ISAM.

Since the generic persistence layer guarantees that items arrive in order and there is only a single writer, the data files are append-only, which leads to simple logic for `put_item`. Items are added by first writing file data, adding the offset and length to the index and finally by writing the timestamp into the index. This allows readers to co-exist with writers without much synchronization – a memory fence may be needed to ensure that item data appears before the timestamp in the index, depending on underlying hardware write ordering semantics.

Distributed filesystem backend: This backend is a variant of the `fs1` filesystem backend. It stores streams as whole files with a separate multi-level index directly on GPFS [6], which is already relatively well-tuned for streaming workloads. This backend also takes into account desired replication/failure semantics in placing data into proper filesets/storage pools with GPFS tools.

4   Evaluation

Here we present two sets of PTS evaluations. The first consists of system-level benchmarks testing the performance of pieces of our persistence architecture. The second is an application-based evaluation using a video-based surveillance application. We believe it is representative of a variety of live stream analysis applications in its basic structure and requirements.

4.1   System/Architectural Benchmarks

In order to measure the architectural overhead of our design, we perform several sets of targeted experiments. We start with a relative comparison of the storage backends, the lowest layer. After that we use our most lightweight backend and target the higher layers, showing the overhead for get operations, performing storage scaling tests with pickling handlers and adaptive load shedding, and finally showing the relative performance between live and stored gets in both pathological situations with no locality and locality-friendly scenarios.

The experiment in this section are performed on an x86_64 Linux 2.6.24 host with an Intel Core 2 Duo E6750 (2.66Ghz) processor and 4GB of DDR667 RAM. For storage results, we use the fs1 backend (on a dedicated 300GB Seagate 7200.8 drive with XFS) since it has the lowest overhead and is self-contained.

Single Producer Storage Backend Overhead: As a baseline, we compare the relative overhead of the different storage backends using OProfile [10], a low-overhead, sampling-based system-wide profiling tool integrated with the Linux kernel capable of profiling un-instrumented binaries. Although the results are elided for space, we found that the overheads associated with an RDBMS like MySQL are very high for such workloads (e.g. 2-3x the user+kernel cycles compared to *fs1 backends). These trends validate our decision (and intuition) to build lighter-weight, task-specific storage backends – fs1 is only about 600 lines of C code and gpfs1 is similar.

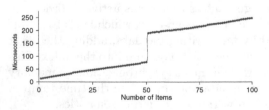

Fig. 3. Cost of gets with an increasing number of items: 50 live items, 100 stored items

Single Consumer Get Overhead: This experiment demonstrates baseline retrieval overheads of the storage layer with fs1. In Figure 3, we measure the cost of a get interval operation as we increase the maximum number of items in the interval to include stored items. We place 100 items in an persistent channel (using the fs1 backend) which will hold up to 50 live items. Each item is 1024 bytes and the gets are performed over loop-back TCP/IP networking. Each get is performed 10,000 times and we report the per-get averages (i.e. measured time / 10,000); the values are averaged over five runs (the standard deviations are less than 1% and thus not drawn on the graph). In the figure, get operations scale roughly linearly with the number of items requested until items must be fetched from the storage backend. At that point, each operation incurs a fixed cost of approximately 118 microseconds, and the roughly linear trend continues – obviously the additional cost of accessing stored items will vary widely depending on the storage backend and underlying storage media, but these figures show baseline overheads for fs1 (when all data is in buffer cache).

Multiple Stream Scaling: This experiment shows how the fs1 backend and our persistence architecture scale with increasing I/O rates by scaling the number of concurrent streams committed to the same disk. Figure 4(a) shows the results of multiple persistent channels simultaneously saving data to the same local XFS partition using the fs1 backend with a chunk-size of 144MB. Each channel is filled by a producer putting 300KB RGB video frames at 30 frames per second, and the experiment runs for 36,000 items in each channel (20 minutes at 9MB/sec per stream). We scale the number of concurrent producers and show results for the normal configuration as well as results where data writes simply go to a file descriptor which throws away the data (/dev/null) – since the local disk will bottleneck long before other components, "no op" disk writes let us isolate the overhead of other pieces of our architecture. We modified the backend to get the current time after an item's data is written out and modify the item's stored timestamp to provide an estimate of the total latency from the time it arrives in the channel to the time it is written out. We also set the level of queuing in the generic persistence layer to one, so each item is sent to the backend as soon as it arrives to the generic persistence layer. We present the results of item latencies in the form of several statistical percentiles (50%, 90%, 99%, 100%) because the general distribution is hard to characterize with a single number. For each percentile, we present the maximum among all producers. The vast majority of items have small latencies and then median times are quite low, but heavy I/O tends to induce a small tail of extreme outliers, particularly when the data rate streaming to disk is high (note the graphs' log scale and broken axes). The 99th percentile latencies seem to be primarily influenced by the amount of filesystem traffic and contention between multiple producers writing to a common disk. The absolute worst case measures (100%) have a high variance and are less meaningful across tests, because they are determined by a single high reading.

Multiple Stream Scaling with Pickling Handlers: The next experiment shows how applying pickling handlers to producers effectively reduces the data rate of streams committed to disk, enabling us to scale up the number of streams. We cannot reliably commit five concurrent 9MB/s streams using fs1 with our particular hard disk and XFS, so we configure a pickling handler to compress each 300KB RGB video frame into a JPEG image. The average JPEG size is 20K, a fifteen-fold reduction in data committed to disk. Figure 4(b) shows the results for runs with 6, 8 or 12 producers all doing JPEG compression, and a mix of RGB and JPEG producers. The item latency now includes a JPEG compression step, performed by `libjpeg6b`, so the median item latencies are ~4.5ms versus

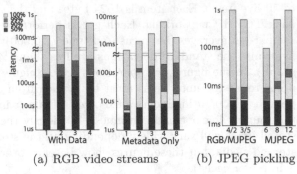

(a) RGB video streams   (b) JPEG pickling

Fig. 4. Item latencies by statistical percentile

~210μs without the added compression and creation of temporary items. The raw measured cost of the JPEG compression by itself (without dynamic allocation of items or buffers) is ~3.7ms per frame on average. Although the data rate of 12 MJPEG streams is still less than a single RGB stream, each producer requires at least 270MB of memory to hold 30 seconds of RGB data in the live channel (plus some extra memory for temporary JPEG items), and we run into some physical memory pressure around 14-15 streams. We could reduce the number of seconds of live data that each channel holds to add more producers, but we eventually hit a CPU bottleneck for JPEG compression before the disk bottlenecks. If we look at the all JPEG producer runs versus the mixed runs, we see that the 99th percentile latencies are now more indicative of CPU contention versus disk contention; since we present the maximum value over all producers for each percentile and compression adds significant latency in the critical path for all JPEG streams, the storage latency for uncompressed items will generally be overshadowed by JPEG items. Again, the 100th percentile measures are less meaningful.

Dynamic Load Adjustment with Pickling Handlers: This experiment shows how PTS can dynamically adjust to overload conditions. By measuring operation latencies in the generic persistence layer,

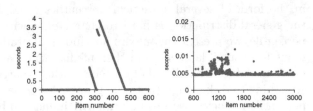

Fig. 5. 8 producers: latency before/after adjustment

the system can react by adding pickling handlers if the disk is overloaded or removing/changing them if the CPU is overloaded. The user could also provide several pickling handlers to compromise between stored item size and computational cost. In our current prototype we've implemented a simple proof-of-concept to illustrate the possibility of dynamic load adjustment: currently we only consider disk load and a single pickling handler, but if the item latency starts to increase heavily, some number of consumers automatically switch to using their pickling handlers until the overload is resolved. We ran successful tests starting with 6, 8 and 12 RGB video producers with JPEG pickling handlers; in all initial configurations (6, 8 and 12 uncompressed video streams), the load is too great for the local disk and the system would normally fall behind and never recover without removing producers. Figure 5 shows the item latencies for a single producer of the 8 producer run before and after it switches to JPEG frames.

Mixed Stored/Live Reader Workload: In order to demonstrate the performance impact of accessing stored versus live items, we vary the percentage of get operations requesting live versus stored items and measure the time to perform 10,000 get operations. Again we use 300KB RGB frames and perform get operations which request 50 items from a point in the channel determined by a probability distribution. 72,000 items are placed into the channel with a storage backend of fs1, and the last 200 items will stay in the live channel. Since the size of all of the items is ~20.6GB, it is much larger than can fit in memory. We measure the cost of gets of exactly 50 items from some random point in the channel (containing all stored or all live items), and we limit the transferred data of each item to 100 bytes to eliminate the network transfer overhead and emphasize the overhead of stored data retrieval (all data is still read from disk when stored items are fetched). We vary the percentage of requests for live items from 0 to 100 and measure the total time to complete 10,000 requests with three different distributions – a uniform random distribution, a Zipf distribution ($s = 2.0$) and a binomial distribution ($p = 0.5$). The uniform random distribution exhibits no locality and rapidly bottlenecks by the raw speed of the disk. Both the Zipf and binomial distributions exhibit a lot of locality and thus benefit from caching, scaling much better (in fact, their differences are too small to see on the graph scale). Figure 6 shows the average per-get time for the distributions (each point is also averaged over five runs). Although none of these test configurations are realistic models of an actual application, which might have many different clusters of "popular" historical data based on detected events, it does show the gamut of scaling behavior between pathologically bad and more locality-friendly workloads. Real workloads should fall in-between these extremes.

These system experiments show that the persistence architecture and primitives can be implemented in a lightweight manner, scaling to store relatively high data rate streams.

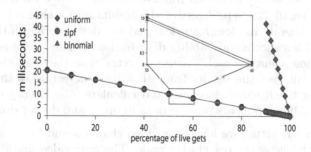

Fig. 6. Per-get time with historical query distribution

4.2 Application-Based Evaluation

For an application-based evaluation, we use a representative kernel of a video surveillance application implemented on PTS. Although live stream analysis applications vary greatly, we believe that the core of a video analytics system can potentially represent a wide range of applications because the general structure of such applications is usually similar. Each application has some set of potentially high bandwidth streams (like video), a set of feature detectors running on these baseline streams to produce more structured high-level data, and a hierarchy of higher-level analysis modules which analyze and aggregate multiple potential feature streams and produce alerts/adjust future analysis/perform actions/etc. Some higher-level analysis will require historical data from archived streams.

Since distributed stream processing is at the heart of these applications, they require efficient low overhead stream transport with persistence management. Using a system like PTS simplifies the application logic significantly and provides greater functionality than non-stream oriented primitives, supporting richer domain-specific communication features, and transparent persistence of data streams. The video surveillance kernel implemented using PTS is only 670 lines of C code, not including command-line argument parsing or interfaces to OpenCV / `libjpeg`. Although it is subjective, the logic is very straightforward with PTS handling stream operations.

Components: Our PTS application consists of six parts: 1) the agents hosting video and sensor channels, 2) video data producers, 3) sensor data producers, 4) video feature detectors – face detection and optical flow, 5) random query agents, and 6) feature aggregation agents. Figure 7 depicts the dataflow between components. Each agent hosts some number of persistent video and sensor channels. The video data is 225KB RGB video frames at ∼29fps, transformed to JPEG format using a pickling handler. The sensor data is random 1024 byte samples produced at ∼15fps. Video producers generate the RGB video frames by decoding MJPEG 3-4 minute compressed video files captured from TV and playing them back on a loop. The feature detectors get video frames one at a time from the channels and run either face detection or optical flow analysis on each frame. The optical flow process first converts each video frame to grayscale but only performs the subsequent optical flow computation on every other frame (the CPUs limited our ability to do full frame-rate optical flow). Each feature detector outputs a small 128-byte digest of the results into a channel. The random query agents generate random historical and live data queries on the video and sensor data with a specific probability distribution. Finally, there is a single feature aggregation agent for each feature detector type (face detector or optical flow); each agent gets the results from all feature detectors of the given type (corresponding to all video channels) and calculates the latency of processing video frames. All components process data in order and do not drop frames.

Topology: In our setup, we host four video channels and two sensor channels per agent, with one agent per cluster node. The four video producers and two sensor data producers corresponding to an agent are also colocated on the same

node, although they are logically separate processes. This node will be decoding 4
MJPEG video streams to produce RGB video frames, encoding 4 MJPEG video
streams from the same RGB frames for pickling handlers and committing all six
data streams to disk. It is also responsible for serving video content to eight feature detectors (four of each type) and handling live and historical queries from
the random query agents. The rest of the pieces run on independent nodes in
different groupings. The feature detectors run two per node and host their own
output channels locally. The random query agents run six per node (four video,
two sensor) and both measurement agents run on separate nodes. For our experiments, we use two agents and eight video streams total. Table 1 summarizes
this setup.

Table 1. Video surveillance experiment

Component	Configuration	Total
Agent	1 per node, hosts 4 vid. / 2 sensor	2
Producers	6 per agent node, one per stream	12
Historical Query	6 per dedicated node	12
Face Detection / Optical Flow	2 per dedicated node	8 / 8
Feature Aggregators	1 per dedicated node	2

Experimental Setup: Our experiments are run on 14 nodes from a cluster of
dual-processor 64-bit Linux nodes. Each node has two Pentium 4-based Xeon
3.2Ghz processors with 1MB of L2 cache, 800Mhz FSB, 6GB of RAM, and IP
over Infiniband networking (4x SDR). The nodes run RHEL 4u6, kernel 2.6.9-
67.0.1.ELsmp (64-bit). The feature detector functionality is from OpenCV 1.0
and libjpeg6b is again used for JPEG operations. All binaries are built with gcc
4.1.2 with -O2 and -g. Persistent channels use fs1, writing to an ext3 filesystem
on a Seagate ST373207LC 10k SCSI drive.

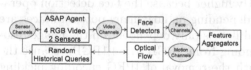

Fig. 7. Video surveillance components

Workload Characteristics: We
perform five runs of each experiment, each normal run lasting
six minutes and involving about
10,500 frames of video for each
channel. Each query agent makes
a video query every 100ms requesting a live or historical frame with equal probability. The historical frames' timestamps are chosen based on a probability distribution that is roughly Zipfian(we use a power-law distribution to approximate
a situation where most video captured will be uninteresting with a few periodic
events of high interest). The standard configuration has all streams converted
to MJPEG before being stored to disk. The 1RGB configuration has one stream
per agent (two total streams) stored to disk without compression to increase the
size of the historical data-set. Similarly, the 2RGB configuration has two streams
per agent stored without compression. Due to the large amount of RAM on each
node, the set of files comprising all historical streams can fit in buffer cache
easily on the shorter runs. Consequently, we also run some significantly longer

experiments to ensure that the historical data set size is large enough to ensure that all requests cannot be serviced from RAM. All of the longer experiments have one RGB stream per agent.

Feature Detector Results: Figure 8 shows the feature detector latencies (in milliseconds) of several different configurations: the first two columns are the processing latency measurements at the face detector and optical flow feature detectors. The Agg columns show the measured latency at the aggregation agents.

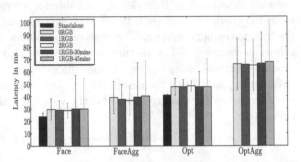

Fig. 8. Component latency in ms

In both cases, the latency is calculated using the timestamp of the original video frame. The aggregation agents include another network hop since they consume the feature detection output data stream; in addition, the aggregation agents get the newest item from all feature detectors of a given type in sequence rather than concurrently, and each get call can potentially block. Consequently, the feature aggregation agents' latencies (and standard deviation) increase with the number of streams they are consuming. Having a separate thread handle each feature stream independently would alleviate this, but the most straightforward implementation (sequential) is entirely adequate for our target application and the performance is still quite good.

Face detection is less expensive than the optical flow calculation, so the latencies are as expected. The baseline costs for the stand-alone feature detectors run on the same datasets on an unloaded node are shown as "Standalone." The face detection standard deviation is slightly higher because the face detection operation takes a varying amount of time depending on how many potential faces are present in an image, while the optical flow is only dependent on the image resolution. The deviation drops slightly going from nRGB to $n+1$RGB because the processing load decreases slightly with the removal of JPEG encoding pickling handlers. The variance on all components increases on the longer runs because of the effect of historical queries that cannot fit into RAM.

Historical Query Results: Figure 9 shows the average time to make a random historical query (in milliseconds) for video streams. We separate the RGB and the compressed streams to show the effect of larger historical data sets. We can see that the average query time and variance grows as the amount of historical data grows – since the RAM size is constant, our locality gets worse as the total dataset grows. The compressed streams' latencies are affected too (but not as severely) because the same node and disk are used to host both types of streams.

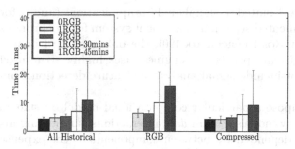

Fig. 9. Query time in ms

To provide a frame of reference for our numbers, ASAP [4] is a video surveillance system implemented in Java; its published end-to-end latency results for live queries are between 135-175 ms, which in practice are perfectly adequate for the application domain. In our PTS-based evaluation, the highest latency we have measured for historical queries is 18ms (+/-16ms). Although the PTS-based implementation and functionality are not directly comparable to the ASAP system, the structure of our application components is derived from the ASAP design and both evaluations were run on the same hardware using the same OpenCV library primitives for analytics. This does show that the results are promising and potentially provide headroom for higher fidelity. These preliminary results also show that the PTS runtime adds minimal overhead to the baseline stream processing operations which are at the core of such applications.

5   Related Work

As mentioned earlier, most work in alleviating higher-level concerns for live stream analysis applications comes in the form of stream processing engines or stream databases. These systems manage execution of stream analysis functionality and often use *continuous queries* in declarative query languages. There are a variety of relevant research systems like domain-specific Gigascope [11] and Hyperion [7] (for network monitoring) as well as more general-purpose systems like TelegraphCQ [12], Borealis [13] (and its predecessor Aurora [14]), and Stanford's STREAM Data Manager [15]. IBM's Stream Processing Core [16] (part of System S) is another research system using a continuous query approach for "stream mining" (data mining on streaming data). General-purpose commercial systems include StreamBase and Coral8. Various extended SQLs and non-SQL based temporal query languages have been proposed over the last twenty years: CQL [17] and GSQL [11] are recent examples.

While these systems are impressive, they represent a different architectural approach than *temporal streams*. These systems provide centrally managed and controlled execution (often with high level query languages), while our system is a glue for loosely coupled systems of independent communicating components with no centralized control. Our system is also targeted at scenarios involving significant feature detection/analysis on streams such as audio and video, in contrast to SQL-like declarative query languages often more suited to domains with highly structured data like network monitoring or stock trading. The authors of the WaveScript language [18]/XStream engine [19] note that traditional stream database approaches are not well suited to signal analysis applications (audio, for example) and provide an augmented stream management system for isochronous signal processing. The Linear Road benchmark [20], the only standard benchmark for stream databases/stream processing engines, uses highly structured data for analysis and does not include signal analysis or feature detection from data sources like video.

Our approach does not impose a particular computational model on stream analysis applications; PTS only models stream *data* interactions, supporting arbitrary communication/data dependencies between components at the expense of being less declarative. In the end, we believe this tradeoff is acceptable given the added flexibility of general distributed applications (e.g. components can be developed independently/in different languages, hold internal state, utilize external resources, be integrated into existing systems, etc.). Our approach also provides a substrate for higher-level domain-specific solutions which raise the level of abstraction for a set of applications.

Ultimately, our approach represents another point in the design space balancing tradeoffs between flexibility/generality as well as performance and the level of abstraction. Our choices are similar to Distributed Data Structures [1] and BerkeleyDB [2], where some higher-level and heavyweight features of a full DBMS are traded off for a simpler, more procedural programmatic interface. In some ways our approach is similar to Boxwood [3], which provides distributed, managed data structures as a fundamental storage abstraction; in our case, the stream abstraction also serves as the storage interface.

PTS builds on the earlier work in Stampede^{RT} [5], which defines a programming model for live stream analysis applications. The Stampede^{RT} paper [5] surveys relevant work related to data-flow programming models like StreamIt [21] or TStreams [22] and the communications aspects of temporal stream abstractions: distributed programming systems/programming models, such as message-passing systems, distributed shared memory, RPC/RMI, group communication, tuple spaces, or publish/subscribe systems. The workload of live stream analysis applications is unique and lends itself well to distributed programming, because stream processing has natural and explicit communication boundaries.

The general concept of processing streamed data as it is made available is fundamental – for example, the Unix pipe [23] is a ubiquitous streaming data flow abstraction, as are lazily-evaluated infinite lists in functional programming languages [24] or various reactive programming constructs. Hundreds of other abstractions in many diverse areas also model streams as a sequence of bytes or messages; this view is significantly different from the data-parallel array model typical in *stream programming*/GPGPU workand much closer to our preferred model for live stream analysis applications. Unlike most previous work, our abstract model of streams used in live stream analysis applications also includes a notion of time and random access.

Distributed programming models and runtime systems designed for processing/mining large amounts of data, such as MapReduce [25] and Dryad [26], often have similar concerns as live analysis applications, which makes many related ideas relevant to our domain. For example, Sawzall [27] provides a small domain-specific language for item-at-a-time processing of stored data sets within MapReduce, but it could also apply to streaming data. The key difference is that live stream analysis is continuous and data is explicitly time-related, while these aforementioned systems operate on stored data for batch processing. Although stored data is often streamed for processing, the time at which a streamed data item becomes available for processing is unrelated to the data itself. In live stream analysis, time is semantically significant. Also, systems such as MapReduce are generally optimized for throughput over latency, are not limited to one-pass processing, and often have foreknowledge of the size of a dataset to partition processing.

6 Conclusion

Many critical applications involve continuous and computationally intensive analysis on live streaming data and also require access to historical data. While distributed programming support for traditional high-performance computing applications is fairly mature, existing solutions for live stream analysis applications are still in their early stages and, in our view, inadequate. We have described *Persistent Temporal Streams* (PTS), which are specifically designed to address the needs of these distributed applications by providing a higher-level unified abstraction for dealing with live and archived streams. The *channel* primitive of our PTS system unifies transport, manipulation and storage of streams. We have presented a detailed description of the PTS system architecture and elements of its implementation. Finally, we have presented a set of system-level benchmarks looking at pieces of the system in isolation as well as a whole-system, application-based evaluation. Although preliminary, these results show that the PTS architecture can be implemented in a lightweight manner and provide good performance in a video-surveillance application scenario based.

References

1. Gribble, S.D., Brewer, E.A., Hellerstein, J.M., Culler, D.: Scalable, Distributed Data Structures for Internet Service Construction. In: Proceedings of OSDI 2000, p. 22 (2000)
2. Olson, M.A., Bostic, K., Seltzer, M.: Berkeley DB. In: Proceedings of USENIX ATC 1999, p. 43 (1999)
3. MacCormick, J., et al.: Boxwood: Abstractions as the Foundation for Storage Infrastructure. In: Proceedings of OSDI 2004, p. 8 (2004)
4. Shin, J., et al.: ASAP: A Camera Sensor Network for Situation Awareness. In: Tovar, E., Tsigas, P., Fouchal, H. (eds.) OPODIS 2007. LNCS, vol. 4878, pp. 31–47. Springer, Heidelberg (2007)
5. Hilley, D., Ramachandran, U.: Stampede^{RT}: Programming abstractions for live streaming applications. In: Proceedings of ICDCS 2007, June 2007, p. 65 (2007)
6. Schmuck, F., Haskin, R.: GPFS: A Shared-Disk File System for Large Computing Clusters. In: Proceedings of FAST 2002, Berkeley, CA, USA, p. 19 (2002)

7. Desnoyers, P., Shenoy, P.: Hyperion: High Volume Stream Archival for Retrospective Querying. In: Proceedings of USENIX ATC 2007, June 2007, pp. 45–58 (2007)
8. Mills, D.L., Thyagarajan, A.: Network Time Protocol Version 4 Proposed Changes. EE Deptartment Report 94-10-2, University of Delaware (October 1994)
9. Sweeney, A., et al.: Scalability in the XFS File System. In: Proceedings of USENIX ATC 1996, pp. 1–14 (1996)
10. Levon, J., Elie, P.: OProfile: A System Profiler for Linux, http://oprofile.sf.net
11. Cranor, C., et al.: Gigascope: A Stream Database for Network Applications. In: Proceedings of SIGMOD 2003, pp. 647–651. ACM Press, New York (2003)
12. Chandrasekaran, S., et al.: TelegraphCQ: Continuous Dataflow Processing for an Uncertain World. In: Proceedings of CIDR 2003 (January 2003)
13. Abadi, D.J., et al.: The Design of the Borealis Stream Processing Engine. In: Proceedings of CIDR 2005, Asilomar, CA (January 2005)
14. Balakrishnan, H., et al.: Retrospective on Aurora. The VLDB Journal 13(4), 370–383 (2004)
15. Arasu, A., et al.: STREAM: The Stanford Data Stream Management System. In: Garofalakis, M., Gehrke, J., Rastogi, R. (eds.) Data Stream Management: Processing High-Speed Data Streams. Springer, Heidelberg (2008) (in press)
16. Amini, L., et al.: SPC: A Distributed, Scalable Platform for Data Mining. In: Proceedings of DMSSP 2006, pp. 27–37. ACM, New York (2006)
17. Arasu, A., Babu, S., Widom, J.: The CQL Continuous Query Language: Semantic Foundations & Query Execution. The VLDB Journal 15(2), 121–142 (2006)
18. Girod, L., et al.: The Case for a Signal-Oriented Data Stream Management System. In: Proceedings of CIDR 2007, Monterey, CA (January 2007)
19. Girod, L., et al.: XStream: A Signal-Oriented Data Stream Management System. In: Proceedings of ICDE 2008, Canc'un, M'exico (April 2008)
20. Arasu, A., Cherniack, M., Galvez, E., Maier, D., Maskey, A.S., Ryvkina, E., Stonebraker, M., Tibbetts, R.: Linear Road: A Stream Data Management Benchmark. In: Proceedings of VLDB 2004, VLDB Endowment, pp. 480–491 (2004)
21. Thies, W., Karczmarek, M., Amarasinghe, S.P.: StreamIt: A Language for Streaming Applications. In: Horspool, R.N. (ed.) CC 2002. LNCS, vol. 2304, pp. 179–196. Springer, Heidelberg (2002)
22. Knobe, K., Offner, C.D.: TStreams: How to Write a Parallel Program. Technical Report HPL-2004-193, HP Laboratories Cambridge (October 2004)
23. Ritchie, D.M., Thompson, K.: The UNIX time-sharing system. Communications of the ACM 17(7), 365–375 (1974)
24. Jones, S.P. (ed.): Haskell 98 Language and Libraries: The Revised Report. Cambridge University Press, Cambridge (2003)
25. Dean, J., Ghemawat, S.: MapReduce: Simplified Data Processing on Large Clusters. In: Proceedings of OSDI 2004, p. 10 (2004)
26. Isard, M., et al.: Dryad: Distributed Data-Parallel Programs from Sequential Building Blocks. In: Proceedings of EuroSys 2007, pp. 59–72. ACM, New York (2007)
27. Pike, R., Dorward, S., Griesemer, R., Quinlan, S.: Interpreting the Data: Parallel Analysis with Sawzall. Scientific Programming 13(4), 277–298 (2005)

Why Do Upgrades Fail and What Can We Do about It?

Toward Dependable, Online Upgrades in Enterprise System

Tudor Dumitraş and Priya Narasimhan

Carnegie Mellon University, Pittsburgh PA 15213, USA
tudor@cmu.edu, priya@cs.cmu.edu

Abstract. Enterprise-system upgrades are unreliable and often produce downtime or data-loss. Errors in the upgrade procedure, such as broken dependencies, constitute the leading cause of upgrade failures. We propose a novel upgrade-centric fault model, based on data from three independent sources, which focuses on the impact of procedural errors rather than software defects. We show that current approaches for upgrading enterprise systems, such as rolling upgrades, are vulnerable to these faults because the upgrade is not an atomic operation and it risks breaking hidden dependencies among the distributed system-components. We also present a mechanism for tolerating complex procedural errors during an upgrade. Our system, called Imago, improves availability in the fault-free case, by performing an online upgrade, and in the faulty case, by reducing the risk of failure due to breaking hidden dependencies. Imago performs an end-to-end upgrade atomically and dependably by dedicating separate resources to the new version and by isolating the old version from the upgrade procedure. Through fault injection, we show that Imago is more reliable than online-upgrade approaches that rely on dependency-tracking and that create system states with mixed versions.

1 Introduction

Software upgrades are unavoidable in enterprise systems. For example, business reasons sometimes mandate switching vendors; responding to customer expectations and conforming with government regulations can require new functionality. Moreover, many enterprises can no longer afford to incur the high cost of downtime and must perform such upgrades online, without stopping their systems. While fault-tolerance mechanisms focus almost entirely on responding to, avoiding, or tolerating unexpected faults or security violations, system unavailability is usually the result of planned events, such as upgrades. A 2007 survey of 50 system administrators from multiple countries (82% of whom had more than five years of experience) concluded that, on average, 8.6% of upgrades fail, with some administrators reporting failure rates up to 50% [1]. The survey identified broken dependencies and altered system-behavior as the leading causes of upgrade failure, followed by bugs in the new version and incompatibility with legacy configurations. This suggests that most upgrade failures are not due to software defects, but to *faults that affect the upgrade procedure*.

For instance, in August 1996, an upgrade in the main data center of AOL—the world's largest Internet Service Provider at the time—was followed by a 19-hour outage. The

J.M. Bacon and B.F. Cooper (Eds.): Middleware 2009, LNCS 5896, pp. 349–372, 2009.
© IFIP International Federation for Information Processing 2009

system behavior did not improve even after the upgrade was rolled back, because the routing tables had been corrupted during the upgrade [2]. In November 2003, the upgrade of a customer relationship management (CRM) system at AT&T Wireless created a ripple effect that disabled several key systems, affecting 50,000 customers per week. The complexity of dependencies on 15 legacy back-end systems was unmanageable, the integration could not be tested in advance in a realistic environment, and rollback became impossible because enough of the old version had not been preserved. The negative effects lasted for 3 months with a loss of $100 M in revenue, which had dire consequences for the future of the company [3]. In 2006, in the emergency room of a major hospital, an automated drug dispenser went offline, after the upgrade of a separate system, preventing a patient in critical condition from receiving the appropriate medication [4].

Existing upgrade techniques rely on tracking the complex dependencies among the distributed system components. When the old and new versions of the system-under-upgrade share dependencies (e.g., they rely on the same third-party component but require different versions of its API), the upgrade procedure must avoid breaking these dependencies in order to prevent unavailability or data-loss. Because dependencies cannot always be inferred automatically, upgrade techniques rely on metadata that is partially maintained by teams of developers and quality-assurance engineers through a time-intensive and error-prone manual process. Moreover, the problem of resolving the dependencies of a component is NP-complete [5], which suggests that the size of dependency-repositories will determine the point at which ensuring the correctness of upgrades by tracking dependencies becomes computationally infeasible.

Because the benefits of dependency-tracking are reaching their limit, industry best-practices recommend "rolling upgrades," which upgrade-and-reboot one node at a time, in a wave rolling through the cluster. Rolling upgrades cannot perform incompatible upgrades (e.g., changing a component's API). However, this approach is believed to reduce the risks of upgrading because failures are localized and might not affect the entire distributed system [6, 7].

In this paper, we challenge this conventional wisdom by showing that atomic, end-to-end upgrades provide more dependability and flexibility. Piecewise, gradual upgrades can cause global system failures by breaking *hidden dependencies*—dependencies that cannot be detected automatically or that are overlooked because of their complexity. Moreover, completely eliminating software defects would not guarantee the reliability of enterprise upgrades because faults in the upgrade procedure can lead to broken dependencies. We make three contributions:

- We establish a rigorous, upgrade-centric fault model, with four distinct categories: (1) simple configuration errors (e.g., typos); (2) semantic configuration errors (e.g., misunderstood effects of parameters); (3) broken environmental dependencies (e.g., library or port conflicts); and (4) data-access errors, which render the persistent data partially-unavailable.   §2
- We present Imago[1] (Fig. 1), a system aiming to reduce the planned downtime, by *performing an online upgrade*, and to remove the leading cause of upgrade failures—broken dependencies [1]—by presenting an alternative to tracking depen-

---

[1] The *imago* is the final stage of an insect or animal that undergoes a metamorphosis, e.g., a butterfly after emerging from the chrysalis [8].

dencies. While relying on the knowledge of the planned changes in data-formats in the new version, Imago treats the system-under-upgrade as a black box. We avoid breaking dependencies by installing the new version in a parallel universe—a logically distinct collection of resources, realized either using different hardware or through virtualization—and by transferring the persistent data, opportunistically, into the new version. Imago accesses the universe of the old version in a read-only manner, *isolating the production system from the upgrade operations*. When the data transfer is complete, Imago performs the switchover to the new version, *completing the end-to-end upgrade as an atomic operation*. Imago also enables the integration of long-running data conversions in an online upgrade and the live testing of the new version.   §3

– We evaluate the benefits of Imago's mechanisms (*e.g.*, atomic upgrades, dependency isolation) through a systematic fault-injection approach, using our upgrade-centric fault model. Imago provides a better availability in the presence of upgrade faults than two alternative approaches, rolling upgrade and big flip [9] (result significant at the $p = 0.01$ level).   §4

Compared with the existing strategies for online upgrades, Imago trades off the need for additional resources for an improved dependability of the online upgrade. While it cannot prevent latent configuration errors, Imago eliminates the internal single-points-of-failure for upgrade faults and the risk of breaking hidden dependencies by overwriting an existing system. Additionally, Imago avoids creating system states with mixed versions, which are difficult to

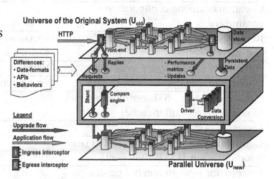

Fig. 1. Dependable upgrades with Imago

test and to validate. Our results suggest that an *atomic, dependency-agnostic* approach, such as Imago, can improve the dependability of online software-upgrades despite hidden dependencies.

2   Fault Model for Enterprise Upgrades

Several classifications of upgrade faults have been proposed [10,11,12,13], but the fault categories are not disjoint, the criteria for establishing these categories remain unclear, or the classifications are relevant only for subsets of the upgrade faults. Moreover, data on upgrade-faults in the industry is scarce and hard to obtain due to the sensitivity of this subject. We analyze 55 upgrade faults from the best available sources, and, through statistical cluster-analysis, we establish four categories of upgrade faults.[2]

We combine data from three independent sources, which use different methodologies: a 2004 *user study* of system-administration tasks in an e-commerce system [12], a

---

[2] We discuss the statistical techniques in more detail in [14]. This technical report and the annotated fault data are available at http://www.ece.cmu.edu/~tdumitra/upgrade_faults.

Table 1. Examples of hidden dependencies (sorted by frequency)

Hidden dependency	Procedure violation	Impact
Service location: – File path – Network address	 Omission	Components unavailable, latent errors
Dynamic linking: – Library conflicts – Defective 3rd party components		Components unavailable
Database schema: – Application/database mismatch – Missing indexes	 Omission Omission	 Data unavailable Performance degradation
Access privileges to file system, database objects, or URLs: – Excessive – Insufficient – Unavailable (from directory service)	 Wrong action Omission Omission	 Vulnerability Components/data unavailable
Constraints among configuration parameters		Outage, degraded performance, vulnerability
Replication degree (*e.g.*, number of front-end servers online)	Omission, inversion, spurious action	Outage, degraded performance
Amount of storage space available	Omission	Transactions aborted
Client access to system-under-upgrade	Wrong action	Incorrect functionality
Cached data (*e.g.*, SSL certificates, DNS lookups, kernel buffer-cache)		Incorrect functionality
Listening ports	Omission	Components unavailable
Communication-protocol mismatch (*e.g.*, middle-tier not HTTP-compliant)		Components unavailable
Entropy for random-number generation		Deadlock
Request scheduling		Access denied unexpectedly
Disk speed	Wrong action	Performance degradation

2006 *survey* of database administrators [13], and a previously unpublished *field study* of bug reports filed in 2007 for the Apache web server [14]. While the administrators targeted by these studies focus on different problems and handle different workloads, we start from the premise that they use similar mental models during change-management tasks, which yield comparable faults. This hypothesis is supported by the observation that several faults have been reported in more than one study. Furthermore, as each of the three methodologies is likely to emphasize certain kinds of faults over others, combining these dissimilar data sets allows us to provide a better coverage of upgrade faults than previous studies.

2.1 The Four Types of Upgrade Faults

We conduct a *post-mortem* analysis of each fault from the three studies in order to determine its root cause [10]—*configuration* error, *procedural* error, *software* defect, *hardware* defect—and whether the fault has broken a hidden dependency, with repercussions for several components of the system-under-upgrade. Errors introduced while editing configuration files can can be further subdivided in three categories [11]: *typographical errors* (typos), *structural errors* (*e.g.* misplacing configuration directives), and *semantic errors* (*e.g.* ignoring constraints among configuration parameters). Additionally, a small number of configuration errors do not occur while editing configuration files (*e.g.*, setting incorrect access privileges). Operators can make procedural errors by performing an *incorrect action* or by violating the sequence of actions in the procedure through an *omission*, an *order inversion*, or the addition of a *spurious action*.

Most configuration and procedural errors break hidden dependencies (see Table 1). Incorrect or omitted actions sometimes occur because the operators ignore, or are not aware of, certain dependencies among the system components (*e.g.*, the database schema queried by the application servers and the schema materialized in the production database). In 56% of cases, however, the operators break hidden dependencies (*e.g.*, by introducing shared-library conflicts) despite correctly following the mandated procedure. This illustrates the fact that even well-planned upgrades can fail because the complete set of dependencies is not always known in advance. We emphasize that the list of hidden dependencies from Table 1, obtained through a *post-mortem* analysis of upgrade faults, is not exhaustive and that other hidden dependencies might exist in distributed systems, posing a significant risk of failure for enterprise-system upgrades.

We perform statistical cluster-analysis, with five classification variables:[3] (i) the root cause of each fault; (ii) the hidden dependency that the fault breaks (where applicable); (iii) the fault location—*front-end*, *middle-tier*, or *back-end*—; (iv) the original classification, from the three studies; and (v) the cognitive level involved in the reported operator error. There are three cognitive levels at which humans solve problems and make mistakes [11]: the *skill-based* level, used for simple, repetitive tasks, the *rule-based* level, where problems are solved by pattern-matching, and the *knowledge-based* level, where tasks are approached by reasoning from first principles. The high-level fault descriptions from the three studies are sufficient for determining the values of the five classification variables. We include all the faults reported in the three studies, except for software defects, faults that did not occur during upgrades and client-side faults. If a fault is reported in several sources, we include only one of its instances in the cluster analysis. We exclude software defects[4] from our taxonomy because they have been rigorously classified before [16] and because they are orthogonal to the upgrading concerns and might be exposed in other situations as well. Moreover, the survey from [1] suggests that most upgrade failures are not due to software defects.

This analysis suggests that there are four natural types of faults (Fig. 2):

- **Type 1** corresponds to simple configuration errors (typos or structural) and to procedural errors that occur on the skill-based cognitive level. These faults break dependencies on network addresses, file paths, or the replication degree.
- **Type 2** corresponds to semantic configuration errors, which occur on the knowledge-based cognitive level and which indicate a misunderstanding of the configuration

---

[3] We compare faults using the *Gower distance*, based on the categorical values of the classification variables. We perform agglomerative, hierarchical clustering with *average linkage* [15].

[4] The fault descriptions provided in the three studies allow us to distinguish the operator errors from the manifestations of software defects.

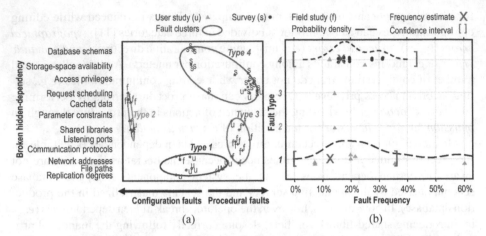

Fig. 2. Upgrade-centric fault model. Principal-component analysis (a) creates a two-dimensional shadow of the five classification variables, The survey and the user study also provide information about the distribution of fault-occurrence rates (b).

directives used. These faults break dependencies on the request scheduling, cached data, or parameter constraints.

– **Type 3** corresponds to broken environmental dependencies, which are procedural errors that occur on the rule-based cognitive level. These faults break dependencies on shared libraries, listening ports, communication protocols, or access privileges.
– **Type 4** corresponds to data-access errors, which are complex procedural or configuration errors that occur mostly on the rule- and knowledge-based cognitive levels. These faults prevent the access to the system's persistent data, breaking dependencies on database schemas, access privileges, the replication degree, or the storage availability.

Faults that occur while editing configuration files are of type 1 or 2. Types 1–3 are located in the front-end and in the middle tier, and, except for a few faults due to omitted actions, they usually do not involve violating the mandated sequence of actions. Type 4 faults occur in the back-end, and they typically consist of wrong or out-of-sequence actions (except order inversions). Principal-component analysis (Fig. 2(a)) suggests that the four types of faults correspond to disjoint and compact clusters. Positive values on the x-axis indicate procedural faults, while negative values indicate faults that occur while editing configuration files. The y-axis corresponds, approximately, to the hidden dependencies broken by the upgrade faults.

We also estimate how frequently these fault types occur during an upgrade (Fig. 2(b)), by considering the percentage of operators who induced the fault (during the user study) or the percentage of DBAs who consider the specific fault among the three most frequent problems that they have to address in their respective organizations (in the survey). We cannot derive frequency information from the field-study data. The individual estimations are imprecise, because the rate of upgrades is likely to vary among organizations and administrators, and because of the small sample sizes (5–51 subjects) used in these studies. We improve the precision of our estimations by combining the individual estimations for each fault type.[5] We estimate that Type 1 faults occur in 14.6% of upgrades (with a confidence interval of $[0\%, 38.0\%]$). Most Type 1 faults (recorded in the user study) occur in less than 21% of upgrades. Similarly, we estimate that Type 4 faults occur in 18.7% of upgrades (with a confidence interval of $[0\%, 45.1\%]$). Because faults of types 2 and 4 are predominantly reported in the field-study, we lack sufficient information to compute a statistically-significant fault frequency for these clusters.

Threats to validity. Each of the three studies has certain characteristics that might skew the results of the cluster analysis. Because the user study is concerned with the behavior of the operators, it does not report any software defects or hardware failures. Configuration errors submitted as bugs tend to be due to significant misunderstandings of the program semantics, and, as a result, our field study contains an unusually-high number of faults occurring on the knowledge cognitive level. Moreover, the results of bug searches are not repeatable because the status of bugs changes over time; in particular, more open bugs are likely to be marked as invalid or not fixed in the future. Finally, Crameri et al. [1], who identify broken dependencies as the leading cause of upgrade failures, caution that their survey is not statistically rigorous.

2.2 Tolerating Upgrade Faults

Several automated dependency-mining techniques have been proposed such as static and semantic analysis [18], but these approaches cannot provide a complete coverage of dependencies that only manifest dynamically, at runtime. Our upgrade-centric fault model emphasizes the fact that different techniques are required for tolerating each of the four types of faults. Modern software components check the syntax of their configuration files, and they are able to detect many Type 1 faults at startup (e.g., syntax checkers catch 38%–83% of typos [11]). Type 2 faults are harder to detect automatically; Keller et al. [11] argue that checking the constraints among parameter values can improve the robustness against such semantic faults. To prevent faults that fall under Type 3, modern operating systems provide package managers that make a best-effort attempt to upgrade a software component along with all of its dependencies [19, 20]. Oliveira et al. propose validating the actions of database administrators using real workloads, which prevents some Type 4 faults but is difficult to implement when the administrator's goal is to change the database schema or the system's observable behavior.

Industry best-practices recommend carefully planning the upgrades and minimizing their risks by deploying the new version gradually, in successive stages [6]. For instance, two widely-used upgrading approaches are the *rolling upgrades* and the *big-flip* [9]. The first approach upgrades and then reboots each node, in a wave rolling through the cluster. The second approach upgrades half of the nodes while the other half continues to

---

[5] The *precision* of a measurement indicates if the results are repeatable, with small variations, and the *accuracy* indicates if the measurement is free of bias. While in general it is not possible to improve the accuracy of the estimation without knowing the systematic bias introduced in an experiment, minimizing the sum of squared errors from dissimilar measurements improves the precision of the estimation [17].

process requests, and then the two halves are switched. Both these approaches attempt to minimize the downtime by performing an *online upgrade*. A big flip has 50% capacity loss, but it enables the deployment of an incompatible system. Instead, a rolling upgrade imposes very little capacity loss, but it requires the old and new versions to interact with the data store and with each other in a compatible manner.

Commercial products for rolling upgrades provide no way of determining if the interactions between mixed versions are safe and leave these concerns to the application developers [7]. However, 47 of the 55 upgrade faults analyzed break dependencies that remain hidden from the developers or the operators performing the upgrade (see Table 1), and some procedural or configuration errors occur despite correctly following the upgrading procedure. This suggests that a novel approach is needed for improving the dependability of enterprise-system upgrades.

3   Design and Implementation of Imago

To provide dependable, online upgrades, we built Imago with three design goals:

- **Isolation:** The dependencies within the old system must be isolated from the upgrade operations.
- **Atomicity:** At any time, the clients of the system-under-upgrade must access the full functionality of either the old or the new systems, but not both. The end-to-end upgrade must be an atomic operation.
- **Fidelity:** The testing environment must reproduce realistically the conditions of the production environment.

Distributed enterprise-systems typically have one or more *ingress points* ($\mathbf{I}$), where clients direct their requests, and one or more *egress points* ($\mathbf{E}$), where the persistent data is stored (see Fig. 1). The remainder of the infrastructure (*i.e.*, the request paths between $\mathbf{I}$ and $\mathbf{E}$) implements the business-logic and maintains only volatile data, such as user-sessions or cached data-items. We install the new system in a *parallel universe*—a logically distinct collection of resources, including CPUs, disks, network links, *etc.*—that is isolated from the universe where the old system continues to operate. The new system may be a more recent version of the old system, or it may be a completely different system that provides similar or equivalent functionality. Imago updates the persistent data of the new system through an opportunistic data-transfer mechanism. The logical isolation between the universe of the old system, $\mathbf{U_{old}}$, and the universe of the new system, $\mathbf{U_{new}}$, ensures that the two parallel universes do not share resources and that the upgrade process, operating on $\mathbf{U_{new}}$, has no impact on the dependencies encapsulated in $\mathbf{U_{old}}$. Our proof-of-concept implementation provides isolation by using separate hardware resources, but similar isolation properties could be achieved through virtualization. Because Imago always performs read-only accesses on $\mathbf{U_{old}}$, the dependencies of the old system cannot be broken and need not be known in advance.

Assumptions. We make three assumptions. We assume that (1) the system-under-upgrade has well-defined, static ingress and egress points; this assumption simplifies the task of monitoring the request-flow through U_{old} and the switchover to U_{new}. We further assume that (2) the workload is dominated by read-only requests; this assumption is needed for guaranteeing the eventual termination of the opportunistic data-transfer. Finally, we assume that the system-under-upgrade provides hooks for: (3a) flushing in-progress updates (needed before switchover); and (3b) reading from U_{old}'s data-store without locking objects or obstructing the live requests in any other way (to avoid interfering with the live workload). We do not assume any knowledge of the internal communication paths between the ingress and egress points.

These assumptions define the class of distributed systems that can be upgraded using Imago. For example, enterprise systems with three-tier architectures—composed of a front-end tier that manages client connections, a middle tier that implements the business logic of the application, and a back-end tier where the persistent data is stored—satisfy these assumptions. An ingress point typically corresponds to a front-end proxy or a load-balancer, and an egress point corresponds to a master database in the back-end. E-commerce web sites usually have read-mostly workloads [21], satisfying the second assumption. The two U_{old} hooks required in the third assumption are also common in enterprise systems; for instance, most application servers will flush the in-progress updates to their associated persistent storage before shutdown, and most modern databases support snapshot isolation[6] as an alternative to locking.

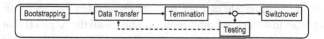

Upgrade Procedure. Imago uses a procedure with five phases: bootstrapping, data-transfer, termination, testing, and switchover. Imago lazily transfers the persistent data from the system in U_{old} to the system in U_{new}, converts it into the new format, monitors the data-updates reaching U_{old}'s egress points and identifies the data objects that need to be re-transferred in order to prevent data-staleness. The live workload of the system-under-upgrade, which accesses U_{old}'s data store concurrently with the data-transfer process, can continue to update the persistent data. The egress interceptor, E, monitors U_{old}'s data-store activity to ensure that all of the updated or new data objects are eventually (re)-transferred to U_{new}. Because Imago always performs read-only accesses on U_{old}, the dependencies of the old system cannot be broken and need not be known in advance. Moreover, E monitors the load and the performance of U_{old}'s data store, allowing Imago to regulate its data-transfer rate in order to avoid interfering with the live workload and satisfying our isolation design-goal. This upgrade procedure is described in detail in [22].

The most challenging aspect of an online upgrade is the switchover to the new version. The data transfer will eventually terminate if the transfer rate exceeds the rate at which U_{old}'s data is updated (this is easily achieved for read-mostly workloads). To complete the transfer of the remaining in-progress updates, we must enforce a brief period of quiescence for U_{old}. Imago can enforce quiescence using the E interceptor, by marking all the database tables read-only, or using the I interceptors, by blocking

---

[6] This mechanism relies on the multi-versioning of database tables to query a snapshot of the database that only reflects committed transactions and is not involved in subsequent updates.

```
The driver executes:                                    Each ingress interceptor I executes:
        ▷ Join the group of ingress interceptors              ▷ Join the group of ingress interceptors
   1    JOIN (IGrp)                                      1    JOIN (IGrp)
   2    Wait until the data-transfer is nearly completed 2    DELIVER (msg)
   3    BCAST (flush)                                    3    if msg = flush
   4    while ∃I ∈ IGrp : I has not delivered flush-done 4       then Block incoming write requests
   5       do DELIVER (msg)                              5          for ∀host ∈ {middle-tier connections}
   6          if msg = self-disconnect                   6          do
   7             then JOIN (IGrp)                                      ▷ Flush in-progress requests
   8          elseif msg ∈ {self-join, interceptor-join} 7             FLUSH (host)
   9             then BCAST (flush)                       8       BCAST (flush-done)
        ▷ Received flush-done from all live interceptors 9    while (TRUE)
  10    Complete data-transfer                          10       do DELIVER (msg)
  11    Send all requests to U_new                      11          if msg = self-disconnect
  12    BCAST (shutdown)                                12             then JOIN (IGrp)
                                                        13          elseif msg ∈ {flush, driver-join}
                                                        14             then BCAST (flush-done)
                                                        15          elseif msg = shutdown
                                                        16             then Shut down I
```

Fig. 3. Pseudocode of the switchover protocol

all the incoming write requests. The first option is straightforward: the database prevents the system in U_{old} from updating the persistent state, allowing the data-transfer to terminate. This approach is commonly used in the industry due to its simplicity [7].

If the system-under-upgrade can not tolerate the sudden loss of write-access to the database, Imago can instruct the I interceptors to block all the requests that might update U_{old}'s persistent data (read-only requests are allowed to proceed). In this case, Imago must flush the in-progress requests to U_{old}'s data store in order to complete the transfer to U_{new}. Imago does not monitor the business logic of U_{old}, but the I interceptors record the active connections of the corresponding ingress servers to application servers in the middle tier and invoke the flush-hooks of these application servers. When all the interceptors report the completion of the flush operations, the states of the old and new systems are synchronized, and Imago can complete the switchover by redirecting all the traffic to U_{new} (this protocol is described in Fig. 3). The volatile data (e.g., the user sessions) is not transferred to U_{new} and is reinitialized after switching to the new system. Until this phase the progress of the ongoing upgrade is transparent to the clients, but after the switchover only the new version will be available.

Imago also supports a series of iterative testing phases before the switchover. Imago checkpoints the state of the system in U_{new} and then performs *offline testing*—using pre-recorded or synthetically-generated traces that check the coverage of all of the expected features and behaviors—and *online testing*—using the live requests recorded at I. In the second case, the testing environment is nearly identical to the production environment, which satisfies our fidelity design-goal. Quiescence is not enforced during the testing phase, and the system in U_{old} resumes normal operation while E continues to monitor the persistent-state updates. At the end of this phase, Imago rolls the state of the system in U_{new} back to the previous checkpoint, and the data transfer resumes in order to account for any updates that might have been missed while testing. A detailed discussion of the testing phase is beyond the scope of this paper.

After adequate testing, the upgrade can be rolled back, by simply discarding the U_{new} universe, or committed, by making U_{new} the production system, satisfying our atomicity design-goal. Imago treats the system-under-upgrade as a black box. Because we do not rely on any knowledge of the internal communication paths between the ingress and egress points of U_{old} and because all of the changes required by the upgrade are made into U_{new}, Imago does not break any hidden dependencies in U_{old}.

Implementation. Imago has four components (see Fig. 1): the *upgrade driver*, which transfers data items from the data store of U_{old} to that of U_{new} and coordinates the upgrade protocol, the *compare-engine*, which checks the outputs of U_{old} and U_{new} during the testing phase, and the **I** and **E** interceptors. The upgrade driver is a process that executes on hardware located outside of the U_{old} and U_{new} universes, while **I** and **E** are associated with the ingress and egress points of U_{old}. We implement the **E** interceptor by monitoring the query log of the database. The **I** interceptor uses library interposition to redefine five system calls used by the front-end web servers: `accept()` and `close()`, which mark the life span of a client connection, `connect()`, which opens a connection to the middle tier, and `read()` and `writev()`, which reveal the content of the requests and replies, respectively. These five system calls are sufficient for implementing the functionality of the **I** interceptor. We maintain a memory pool inside the interceptor, and the redefined `read()` and `writev()` system-calls copy the content of the requests and replies into buffers from this memory pool. The buffers are subsequently processed by separate threads in order to minimize the performance overhead.

In order to complete the data transfer, the upgrade driver invokes the switchover protocol from Fig. 3. We use reliable group-communication primitives to determine when all the interceptors are ready to switch: JOIN allows a process to join the group of interceptors and to receive notifications when processes join or disconnect from the group; BCAST reliably sends a message to the entire group; and DELIVER delivers messages in the same order at all the processes in the group. These primitives are provided by the Spread package [23]. The switchover protocol also relies on a FLUSH operation, which flushes the in-progress requests from a middle-tier server. Each **I** interceptor invokes the FLUSH operation on the application servers that it has communicated with.

We have implemented the FLUSH operation for the Apache and JBoss servers. For Apache, we restart the server with the `graceful swirch`, allowing the current connections to complete. For JBoss, we change the timestamp of the web-application archive (the `application.war` file), which triggers a redeployment of the application. Both these mechanisms cause the application servers to evict all the relevant data from their caches and to send the in-progress requests to the back-end. This switchover protocol provides

Table 2. Structure of Imago's code

	Lines of code	Size in memory
Upgrade driver	2,038 ⎱	216 kB
Egress interceptor	290 ⎰	
Ingress interceptor	2,056 ⎱	228 kB
Switchover library	1,464 ⎰	
Compare engine	571	48 kB
Common libraries	591	44 kB
Application bindings	1,113	108 kB
Total	8,123	—

strong consistency, and it tolerates crashes and restarts of the driver or the interceptors. All the modules of Imago are implemented in C++ (see Table 2). The application
bindings contain all the application-specific routines (*e.g.*, data conversion) and constitute 14% of the code. Most of this application-specific code would also be necessary to
implement and offline upgrade.

4 Experimental Evaluation

We evaluate the dependability of enterprise-system upgrades performed using Imago.
Specifically, we seek answers to the following questions:

- What overhead does Imago impose during a successful upgrade?   §4.1
- Does Imago improve the availability in the presence of upgrade faults? §4.2
- How do types 1–4 of upgrade faults affect the reliability of the upgrade? §4.3

Upgrade Scenario. We use Imago to perform an upgrade of RUBiS (the Rice University Bidding System) [24], an open-source online bidding system, modeled after eBay.
RUBiS has been studied extensively, and several of its misconfiguration- and failure-
modes have been previously reported [12, 13]. RUBiS has multiple implementations
(*e.g.*, using PHP, EJB, Java Servlets) that provide the same functionality and that use
the same data schema. We study an upgrade scenario whose goal is to upgrade RUBiS
from the version using Enterprise Java Beans (EJB) to the version implemented in PHP.
The system-under-upgrade is a three-tier infrastructure, comprising a front-end with two
Apache web servers, a middle tier with four Apache servers that execute the business
logic of RUBiS, and a MySQL database in the back-end. More specifically, the upgrade
aims to replace the JBoss servers in the middle tier with four Apache servers where we
deploy the PHP scripts that implement RUBiS's functionality. The RUBiS database contains 8.5 million data objects, including 1 million items for sale and 5 million bids. We
use two standard workloads, based on the TPC-W specification [21], which are typical
for e-commerce web sites. The performance bottleneck in this system is the amount of
physical memory in the front-end web servers, which limits the system's capacity to
100 simultaneous clients. We conduct our experiments in a cluster with 10 machines
(Pentium 4 at 2.4 GHz, 512 MB RAM), connected by a 100 Mbps LAN.

We compare Imago with two alternative approaches, rolling upgrades and big flip
(see Section 2.2). These procedures are illustrated in Fig. 4. In both cases, the front-end
and back-end remain shared between the old and new versions. Rolling upgrades run
for a while in a mode with mixed versions, with a combination of PHP (Apache) and
EJB (JBoss) nodes in the middle tier, while the big flip avoids this situation but uses
only half of the middle-tier servers. With the former approach an upgraded node is tested
online (Fig. 4(a)), while the latter approach performs offline tests on the upgraded nodes
and re-integrates them in the online system only after the flip has occurred (Fig. 4(b)).
In contrast, Imago duplicates the entire architecture, transferring all of the 8.5 million
RUBiS data-items to U_{new}, in order to avoid breaking dependencies during the upgrade.

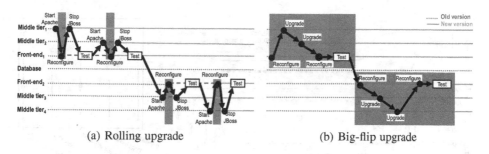

(a) Rolling upgrade   (b) Big-flip upgrade

Fig. 4. Current approaches for online upgrades in RUBiS

Methodology. We estimate Imago's effectiveness in performing an online upgrade, in the absence of upgrade-faults, by comparing the client-side latency of RUBiS before, and during, the upgrade. We assess the impact of broken dependencies by injecting upgrade faults, according to the fault model presented in Section 2, and by measuring the effect of these faults on the system's expected availability. Specifically, we estimate the system's *yield* [9], which is a fine-grained measure of availability with a consistent significance for windows of peak and off-peak load:

$$\text{Yield}(fault) = \frac{\text{Requests}_{completed}(fault)}{\text{Requests}_{issued}}$$

We select 12 faults (three for each fault type) from the data analyzed in Section 2, prioritizing faults that have been confirmed independently, in different sources or in separate experiments from the same source. We repeat each fault-injection procedure three times and we report the average impact, in terms of response time and yield-loss, on the system. Because this manual procedure limits us to injecting a small number of faults, we validate the results using statistical-significance tests, and we complement these experiments with an automated injection of Type 1 faults.

From a client's perspective, the upgrade faults might cause a full outage, a partial outage (characterized by a higher response time or a reduced throughput), a delayed outage (due to latent errors) or they might have no effect at all. A full outage (*Yield* = 0) is recorded when the upgrade-fault immediately causes the throughput of RUBiS to drop to zero. Latent errors remain undetected until they are eventually exposed by external factors (*e.g.*, a peak load) or by system-configuration changes. To be conservative in our evaluation, we consider that (i) the effect of a latent error is the same as the effect of a full outage (*Yield* = 0); (ii) an upgrade can be stopped as soon as a problem is identified; and (iii) all errors (*e.g.*, HTTP-level or application-level errors) are detected. An upgrading mechanism is able to mask a dependency-fault when the fault is detected before reintegrating the affected node in the online system. To avoid additional approximations, we do not attempt to estimate the durations of outages caused by the broken dependencies. As the yield calculations do not include the time needed to mitigate the failures, the values reported estimate the initial impact of a fault but not the effects of extended outages. While the result that Imago provides better availability under upgrade faults is statistically significant, the *quantitative* improvements depend on the system

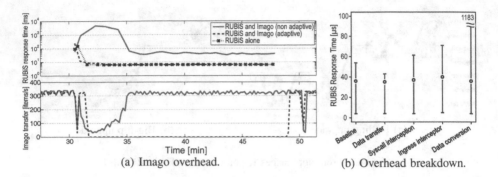

(a) Imago overhead.   (b) Overhead breakdown.

Fig. 5. Upgrade overhead on a live RUBiS system

architecture and on the specific faults injected, and they might not be reproducible for a different system-under-upgrade. The goal of our fault-injection experiments is to determine the *qualitative* reasons for unavailability during online upgrades, and to emphasize the opportunities for improving the current state-of-the-art.

4.1 Performance Overhead without Faults

The latency of querying the content of a data item from U_{old} and inserting it in U_{new} dominates the performance of the data-transfer; less than 0.4% out of the 5 ms needed, on average, to transfer one item are spent executing Imago's code. Fig. 5(a) shows the impact of the data transfer on RUBiS's end-to-end latency (measured at the client-side). If requests arrive while a data-transfer is in progress, the response times increase by three orders of magnitude (note the log scale in the top panel of Fig. 5(a)). These high latencies correspond to a sharp drop in the transfer rate as the U_{old} database tries to adjust to the new load. However, Imago can use the information collected by the E interceptor to self-regulate in order to avoid overloading the production system. We have found that the incoming query rate for U_{old}'s database provides sufficient warning: if Imago uses a simple adaptation policy, which pauses the data transfer when the RUBiS clients issue more than 5 queries/s, the end-to-end latency is indistinguishable from the case when clients do not compete with Imago for U_{old}'s resources (Fig. 5(a)). After resuming the data transfer, Imago must take into account the data items added by RU-BiS's workload. These new items will be transferred during subsequent periods of client inactivity. Under a scenario with 1000 concurrent clients, when the site is severely overloaded, Imago must make progress, opportunistically, for 2 minutes per hour in order to catch up eventually and complete the data transfer.

Fig. 5(b) compares the overheads introduced by different Imago components (the error bars indicate the 90% confidence intervals for the RUBiS response time). The **I** interceptors impose a fixed overhead of 4 ms per request; this additional processing time does not depend on the requests received by the RUBiS front-ends. When Imago performs a data conversion (implemented by modifying the RUBiS code, in order to perform a database-schema change during the upgrade), the median RUBiS latency is not affected but the maximum latency increases significantly. This is due to the fact that the simple adaptation policy described above is not tuned for the data-conversion scenario.

The rolling upgrade does not impose any overhead, because sequentially rebooting all the middle-tier nodes does not affect the system's latency or throughput. The big flip imposes a similar run-time overhead as Imago because half of the system is unavailable during the upgrade. With Imago, the upgrade completes after $\approx$13h, which is the time needed for transferring all the persistent data plus the time when access to U_{old} was yielded to the live workload. This duration is comparable to the time required to perform an offline upgrade: in practice, typical Oracle and SAP migrations require planned downtimes of tens of hours to several days [25].

Before switching to U_{new}, Imago enforces quiescence by either marking the database tables read-only, or by rejecting write requests at the I interceptors and flushing the in-progress updates to the persistent storage. When the middle-tier nodes are running Apache/PHP servers, the flush operation takes 39 s on average, including the synchronization required by the protocol from Fig. 3. In contrast, flushing JBoss application servers requires only 4.4 s on average, because in this case we do not need to restart the entire server. The switchover mechanism does not cause a full outage, as the clients can invoke the read-only functionality of RUBiS (e.g., searching for items on sale) while Imago is flushing the in-progress requests. Moreover, assuming that the inter-arrival times follow an exponential distribution and the workload mix includes 15% write requests (as specified by TPC-W [21]), we can estimate the maximum request rate that the clients may issue without being denied access. If the switchover is performed during a time window when the live request rate does not exceed 0.5 requests/min, the clients are unlikely ($p=0.05$) to be affected by the flush operations.

4.2 Availability under Upgrade-Faults

Table 3 describes the upgrade-faults injected and their immediate, local manifestation. We were unable to replicate the effects of one fault (apache_largefile, which was reported as bugs 42751 and 43232 in the field study) in our experimental test-bed. We inject the remaining 11 faults in the front-end (5 faults), middle tier (4 faults) and back-end (3 faults) during the online upgrade of RUBiS. In a rolling upgrade, a node is reintegrated after the local upgrade, and resulting errors might be propagated to the client. The big flip can mask the upgrade-faults in the offline half but not in the shared database. Imago masks all the faults that can be detected (i.e., those that do not cause latent errors).

Fig.6 shows the impacts that Types 1–4 of upgrade faults have on the system-under-upgrade. Certain dependency-faults lead to an increase in the system's response time. For instance, the apache_port_f fault doubles the connection load on the remaining front-end server, which leads to an increased queuing time for the client requests and a 8.3% increase in response-time when the fault occurs. This outcome is expected during a big-flip, but not during a rolling upgrade (see Fig. 4). This fault does not affect the system's throughput or yield because all of the requests are eventually processed and no errors are reported to the clients.

Table 3. Description of upgrade-faults injected

Name / Instances [source]	Location	Fault-Injection Procedure	Local Manifestation
wrong_apache 2 [12]	Front-end	Restarted wrong version of Apache on one front-end.	Server does not forward requests to the middle tier.
config_nochange 1 [12]	Front-end	Did not reconfigure front-end after middle-tier upgrade.	Server does not forward requests to the middle tier.
config_staticpath 2 [12, 14]	Front-end	Mis-configured path to static web pages on one front-end.	Server does not forward requests to the middle tier.
config_samename 1 [12]	Front-end	Configured identical names for the application servers.	Server communicates with a single middle-tier node.
apache_satisfy 1 [14]	Middle tier	Used satisfy directive incorrectly.	Clients gain access to restricted location.
apache_largefile 2 [14]	Middle tier	Used mmap() and sendfile() with network file-system.	No negative effect (could not replicate the bug).
apache_lib 1 [14]	Middle tier	Shared-library conflict.	Cannot start application server.
apache_port_f 1 [14]	Front-end	Listening port already in use by another application.	Cannot start front-end web server.
apache_port_m 1 [14]	Middle tier	Listening port already in use by another application.	Cannot start application sever.
wrong_privileges 2 [12, 13]	Back-end	Wrong privileges for RUBiS database user.	Database inaccessible to the application servers.
wrong_shutdown 2 [12, 13]	Back-end	Unnecessarily shut down the database.	Database inaccessible to the application servers.
db_schema 4 [13]	Back-end	Changed DB schema (renamed bids table).	Database partially inaccessible to application servers.

The config_nochange and wrong_apache faults prevent one front-end server from connecting to the new application servers in the middle tier. The front-end server affected continues to run and to receive half of the client requests, but it generates HTTP errors ($Yield = 0.5$). Application errors do not manifest themselves as noticeable degradations of the throughput, in terms of the rate of valid HTTP replies, measured at either the client-side or the server-side. These application errors can be detected only by examining the actual payload of the front-end's replies to the client's requests. For instance, db_schema causes intermittent application errors that come from all four middle-tier nodes. As this fault occurs in the back-end, both the rolling upgrade and the big flip are affected. Imago masks this fault because it does not perform any configuration actions on U_{old}. Similarly, Imago is the only mechanism that masks the remaining Type 4, wrong_privileges and wrong_shutdown. The apache_satisfy fault leads to a potential security vulnerability, but does not affect the yield or the response time. This fault can be detected, by issuing requests for the restricted location, unlike the config_staticpath fault, which causes the front-end to serve static web pages from a location that might be removed in the future. Because this fault does not have any observable impact during the rolling upgrade or the big flip, we consider that it produces a latent error. Imago masks config_staticpath because the obsolete location does not exist in U_{new}, and the fault becomes detectable. The config_samename fault

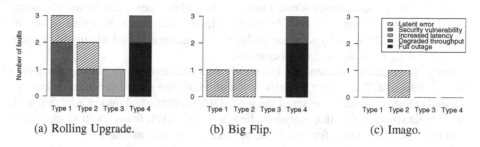

(a) Rolling Upgrade.   (b) Big Flip.   (c) Imago.

Fig. 6. Impact of upgrade faults

prevents one front-end server from forwarding requests to one middle-tier node, but the three application servers remaining can successfully handle the RUBiS workload, which is not computationally-intensive. This fault produces a latent error that might be exposed by future changes in the workload or the system architecture and is the only fault that Imago is not able to mask.

The rolling upgrade masks 2 faults, which occur in the middle tier and do not degrade the response time or the yield, but have a visible manifestation (the application server fails to start). The big flip masks 6 faults that are detected before the switch of the halves. Imago masks 10 out of the 11 injected faults, including the ones masked by the big flip, and excluding the latent error. A paired, one-tailed t-test[7] indicates that, under upgrade faults, Imago provides a better yield than the rolling upgrade (significant at the $p = 0.01$ level) and than the big flip (significant at the $p = 0.05$ level).

4.3   Upgrade Reliability

We observe in Fig. 6 that broken environmental dependencies (Type 3) have only a small impact on enterprise-system upgrades, because their manifestations (*e.g.*, a server's failure to start) are easy to detect and compensate for in any upgrading mechanism. Rolling upgrades create system states with mixed versions, where hidden dependencies can be broken. Contrary to the conventional wisdom, these faults can have a global impact on the system-under-upgrade, inducing outages, throughput- or latency-degradations, security vulnerabilities or latent errors.

Compared with a big flip, Imago improves the availability because (i) it removes the *single points of failure* for upgrade faults and (ii) it performs a clean installation of the new system. For instance, the `config_staticpath` fault induces a latent error during the big flip because the upgrade overwrites an existing system. The database represents a single point of failure for the big flip, and any Type 4 fault leads to an upgrade failure for this approach. Such faults do not always cause a full outage; for instance, the `db_schema` fault introduces a throughput degradation (with application errors). However, although in this case the application error-rate is relatively low (9%

---

[7] The t-test takes into account the pairwise differences between the yield of two upgrading approaches and computes the probability p that the *null hypothesis*—that Imago doesn't improve the yield—is true [17].

of all replies), the real impact is much more severe: while clients can browse the entire site, they cannot bid on any items. In contrast, Imago eliminates the single-points-of-failure for upgrade faults by avoiding an in-place upgrade and by isolating the system version in U_{old} from the upgrade operations.

Imago is vulnerable to latent configuration errors such as config_samename, which escapes detection. This failure is not the result of breaking a shared dependency, but corresponds to an incorrect invariant of the new system, established during a fresh install. This emphasizes the fact that any upgrading approach, even Imago, will succeed only if an effective mechanism for testing the upgraded system is available.

Because our qualitative evaluation does not suggest how often the upgrade faults produce latent errors, we inject Type 1 faults automatically, using ConfErr [11]. ConfErr explores the space of likely configuration errors by injecting one-letter omissions, insertions, substitutions, case alterations and transpositions that can be created by an operator who mistakenly presses keys in close proximity to the mutated character. We randomly inject 10 typographical and structural faults into the configuration files of Apache web servers from the front-end and the middle tier, focusing on faults that are likely to occur during the upgrade (*i.e.*, faults affecting the configuration directives of mod_proxy and mod_proxy_balancer on the front-end and of mod_php on the middle tier). Apache's syntactic analyzer prevents the server from starting for 5 front-end and 9 middle-tier faults. Apache starts with a corrupted address or port of the application server after 2 front-end faults and with mis-configured access privileges to the RUBiS URLs after 1 middle-tier fault. The remaining three faults, injected in the front-end, are benign because they change a parameter (the route from a BalancerMember directive) that must be unique but that has no constraints on other configuration settings. These faults might have introduced latent errors if the random mutation had produced identical routes for two application servers; however, the automated fault-injection did not produce any latent errors. This suggests that latent errors are uncommon and that broken dependencies, which are tolerated by Imago, represent the predominant impact of Type 1 faults.

5 Lessons Learned

Offline upgrades of critical enterprise-systems (*e.g.*, banking infrastructures) provide the opportunity for performing extensive tests for accepting or rejecting the outcome of the upgrade. Online upgrades do not have this opportunity; when there are mixed versions, system states are often short-lived and cannot be tested adequately, while the system-under-upgrade must recover quickly from any upgrade faults. Unlike the existing strategies for online upgrade, which rely on tracking dependencies, Imago trades off spatial overhead (*i.e.*, additional hardware and storage space) for an increased dependability of the online upgrade. Imago was designed for upgrading enterprise systems with traditional three-tier architectures. The current implementation cannot be readily applied to certain kinds of distributed systems, such as peer-to-peer systems, which violate the first assumption by accommodating large numbers of dynamically added ingress-points, or data-intensive computing (*e.g.*, MapReduce), which distribute their persistent data throughout the infrastructure and do not have a well-defined egress point. However, the

Table 4. Design choices for online upgrades in enterprise systems

	In-Place	Out-of-Place

Mixed Versions	– Risk propagating corrupted data
	– Need indirection layer, with:
	  – Potential run-time overhead
	  – Installation downtime
	– Incur run-time overhead for data conversions
	– Risk breaking hidden dependencies
		– Risk propagating corrupted data
		– Need indirection layer, with:
		  – Potential run-time overhead
		  – Installation downtime
		– Incur spatial overhead

Atomic	– Incur run-time overhead for data conversions – Risk breaking hidden dependencies – Incur spatial overhead	– Incur spatial overhead

availability improvements derive from the three properties (isolation, atomicity and fidelity) that Imago provides. Specifically, the isolation between the old and new versions reduces the risk of breaking hidden dependencies, which is the leading cause of upgrade failure [1], while performing the end-to-end upgrade as an atomic operation increases the upgrade reliability by avoiding system states with mixed versions. Imago improves the upgrade dependability because it implements *dependency-agnostic upgrades*. In the future, we plan to investigate mechanisms for implementing the isolation, atomicity and fidelity properties in other distributed-system architectures, and for reducing Imago's spatial overhead through virtualization.

Moreover, upgrades that aim to integrate several enterprise systems (*e.g.*, following commercial mergers and acquisitions) require complex data conversions for changing the data schema or the data store, and such data conversions are often tested and deployed in different environments [13], which increases the risk of upgrade failure. Imago is able to integrate complex data-conversions in an online upgrade and to test the new version online, in an environment nearly identical to the deployment system. While an in-depth discussion of these topics is outside the scope of this paper, we note that there are two major design choices for software-upgrade mechanisms: (i) whether the upgrade will be performed *in-place*, replacing the existing system, and (ii) whether the upgrade mechanisms will allow *mixed versions*, which interact and synchronize their states until the old version is retired. Table 4 compares these choices. Mixed versions save storage space because the upgrade is concerned with only the parts of the data schema that change between versions. However, mixed versions present the risk of breaking hidden dependencies; *e.g.*, if the new version includes a software defect that corrupts the persistent data, this corruption will be propagated back into the old version, replacing the master copy. Mixed, interacting versions also require an indirection layer, for dispatching requests to the appropriate version [26], which might introduce run-time overhead and will likely impose downtime when it is first installed. A system without mixed versions performs the upgrade in a single direction, from the old version to the new one. However, for in-place upgrades, the overhead due to data conversions can have a negative impact on the live workload. When, instead, an upgrade uses separate resources for the new version, the computationally-intensive processing can be performed downstream, on the target nodes (as in the case of Imago). As we have shown in Section 4, in-place upgrades introduce a high risk of breaking hidden dependencies, which degrades the expected availability.

The most significant disadvantage of out-of-place upgrades is the spatial overhead imposed. However, the cost of new hardware decreases while unavailability becomes more expensive [9], and enterprises sometimes take advantage of a software upgrade to renew their hardware as well [25, 27]. Moreover, Imago requires additional resources only for implementing and testing the online upgrade, and storage and compute cycles could be leased, for the duration of the upgrade, from existing cloud-computing infrastructures (*e.g.*, the Amazon Web Services). This suggests that Imago is the first step toward an *upgrades-as-a-service* model, making complex upgrades practical for a wide range of enterprise systems.

6   Related Work

In our previous work [22], we have outlined the upgrade procedure on which Imago is based. Here, we review the research related to our contributions in this paper.

6.1   Upgrade Fault-Models

Oppenheimer *et al.* [10] study 100+ *post-mortem* reports of user-visible failures from three large-scale Internet services. They classify failures by location[8] (front-end, back-end and network) and by the root cause of the failure[8] (operator error, software fault, hardware fault). Most failures reported occurred during change-management tasks, such as scaling or replacing nodes and deploying or upgrading software. Nagaraja *et al.* [12] report the results of a user study[9] with 21 operators and observe seven classes of faults:[8] global misconfiguration, local misconfiguration, start of wrong software version, unnecessary restart of software component, incorrect restart, unnecessary hardware replacement, wrong choice of hardware component. Oliveira *et al.* [13] present a survey of 51 database administrators,[9] who report eight classes of faults:[8] deployment, performance, general-structure, DBMS, access-privilege, space, general-maintenance, and hardware. Keller *et al.* [11] study configuration errors and classify them according to their relationship with the format of the configuration file[8] (typographical, structural or semantic) and to the cognitive level where they occur[8] (skill, rule or knowledge). These models do not constitute a rigorous taxonomy of upgrade faults. Some classifications are too coarse-grained [10] or relevant for only a subset of the upgrade faults [11]. In many cases, the fault categories are not disjoint and the criteria for establishing these categories are not clearly stated.

6.2   Online Upgrades

The problem of dynamic software update (DSU), *i.e.*, modifying a running program on-the-fly, has been studied for over 30 years. Perhaps the most advanced DSU techniques are implemented in the Ginseng system, of Neamtiu *et al.* [28], which uses static analysis to ensure the safety and timeliness of updates (*e.g.*, establishing constraints to

---

[8] We use this subdivision as a classification variable in our upgrade fault-model (Section 2).

[9] We use this data to develop our upgrade fault-model (Section 2).

prevent old code from accessing new data) and supports all the changes required for up-dating several practical systems. When upgrading distributed systems with replicated components (*e.g.*, multiple application servers in the middle tier), practitioners often prefer rolling upgrades [9], because of their simplicity. DSU techniques are difficult to use in practicebecause they require programmers to annotate (*e.g.*, indicating suit-able locations for performing the update) or to modify the source code of the old and new versions. Moreover, active code (*i.e.*, functions on the call stack of the running pro-gram) cannot be replaced, and updating multi-threaded programs remains a challenging task [29]. Like Imago, DSU techniques require state conversion between program ver-sions [28], but Imago never produces mixed versions and does not have to establish correctness conditions for the interactions among these versions. Imago performs the entire end-to-end upgrade as one atomic action.

6.3   Dependable Upgrades

To improve the dependability of single-node upgrades, modern operating systems in-clude package-management tools, which track the dependencies among system com-ponents in depth, to prevent broken dependencies. Instead of tracking the dependen-cies of each package, Crameri *et al.* [1] suggest that the risk of upgrade failure can be reduced by testing new or updated packages in a wide variety of user environments and by staging the deployment of upgrades to increasingly dissimilar environments. Imago is closest in spirit to the previous upgrading approaches that avoid dependency tracking by isolating the new version from the old one. Lowell *et al.* [30] propose up-grading operating systems in a separate, lightweight virtual-machine and describe the Microvisor virtual-machine monitor, which allows a full, "devirtualized" access to the physical hardware during normal operation. The online applications are migrated to a separate virtual machine during the upgrade. To facilitate this application-migration process, Potter *et al.* [31] propose AutoPod, which virtualizes the OS's system calls, al-lowing applications to migrate among location-independent "pods". These approaches do not provide support for application upgrades. While providing better isolation prop-erties than other in-place upgrades, the approaches based on virtual machines induce run-time overhead, which might break dependencies on performance levels (*e.g.*, appli-cations that disable write-access when the response time increases).

Multi-node upgrades are vulnerable to Types 1–4 of upgrade faults. Nagaraja *et al.* [12] propose a technique for detecting operator errors by performing upgrades or configura-tion changes in a "validation slice," isolated from the production system. The upgraded components are tested using the live workload or pre-recorded traces. This approach re-quires component-specific inbound- and outbound-proxies for recording and replaying the requests and replies received by each component-under-upgrade. If changes span more than one node, multiple components (excluding the database) can be validated at the same time. Oliveira *et al.* [13] extend this approach by performing change oper-ations on an up-to-date replica of the production database. Because these approaches operate at component granularity, they require knowledge of the system's architecture and queuing paths, and some errors remain latent if the components are tested in iso-lation [12]. Moreover, implementing the inbound- and outbound-proxies requires an understanding of each component's behavior, *e.g.*, the communication protocols used and its non-determinism. For instance, routing requests to a different application server in the validation slice would produce equivalent results, but processing database transactions in a different order would compromise the replication. To enforce a common order of execution, database requests must be serialized in order to prevent transaction concurrency, for both the production database and the validation slice [13]. Aside from inducing a performance penalty during the upgrade, this intrusive technique prevents testing the upgrade's impact on the concurrency-control mechanisms of the database, which limits the usefulness of the validation results. Compared with these approaches, Imago does not change the way requests are processed in the production system and only requires knowledge of the ingress and egress points. The other components of the system-under-upgrade and the internal queuing paths are treated as a black box. Unlike the previous approaches, Imago targets end-to-end upgrades of distributed systems, and it addresses the problem of coordinating the switchover to the new version. Moreover, Imago's design facilitates upgrades that require long-running, computationally-intensive conversions to a new data format.

6.4   Dependability Benchmarking for Upgrade Mechanisms

Evaluations of most of the previous upgrade mechanisms focus on the types of changes supported and on the overhead imposed, rather than on the upgrade dependability. Because of this reason, while the costs of upgrading techniques (*e.g.*, atomic upgrades, isolation between the old and new versions) can be assessed in a straightforward manner, their benefits are not well understood. User studies [12], fault injection [12, 13] and simulation [1] have been used to assess the effectiveness of previous approaches in reducing the number of upgrade failures. We rely on our upgrade-centric fault model to perform systematic fault-injection experiments, with an improved coverage of upgrade faults. We inject faults manually, in order to determine the impact of each fault type on the three upgrading approaches compared, and we also use an existing fault-injection tool for automatically injecting Type 1 faults. Similar fault-injection tools can be developed for upgrade faults of Types 2–4, in order to evaluate the dependability of future upgrade mechanisms.

7   Conclusions

We propose a new fault model for upgrades in enterprise systems, with four types of faults. The impact of Type 3 faults (broken environmental dependencies) seems to be easy to detect using existing techniques. Faults of Type 1, 2, and 4 frequently break hidden dependencies in the system-under-upgrade. Existing mechanisms for online upgrade are vulnerable to these faults because even localized failures might have a global impact on the system. We present the design and implementation of Imago, a system for upgrading three-tier, enterprise systems online, despite hidden dependencies. Imago performs the end-to-end upgrade as an atomic operation and does not rely on dependency-tracking, but it requires additional hardware and storage space. The upgrade duration is comparable to that of an offline upgrade, and Imago can switch over to the new version without data loss and, during off-peak windows, without disallowing any client requests. Manual and automated fault-injection experiments suggest that

Imago improves the dependability of the system-under-upgrade by eliminating the single points of failure for upgrade faults.

Acknowledgements. We thank Dan Siewiorek, Greg Ganger, Bruce Maggs, and Asit Dan for their feedback during the early stages of this research. We also thank Lorenzo Keller for providing assistance with the use of ConfErr.

References

1. Crameri, O., Knežević, N., Kostić, D., Bianchini, R., Zwaenepoel, W.: Staged deployment in Mirage, an integrated software upgrade testing and distribution system. In: Symposium on Operating Systems Principles, Stevenson, WA, October 2007, pp. 221–236 (2007)
2. Neumann, P., et al.: America Offline. The Risks Digest 18(30-31) (August 8-9, 1996), http://catless.ncl.ac.uk/Risks/18.30.html
3. Koch, C.: AT&T Wireless self-destructs. CIO Magazine (April 2004), http://www.cio.com/archive/041504/wireless.html
4. Wears, R.L., Cook, R.I., Perry, S.J.: Automation, interaction, complexity, and failure: A case study. Reliability Engineering and System Safety 91(12), 1494–1501 (2006)
5. Di Cosmo, R.: Report on formal management of software dependencies. Technical report, INRIA (EDOS Project Deliverable WP2-D2.1) (September 2005)
6. Office of Government Commerce: Service Transition. Information Technology Infrastructure Library, ITIL (2007)
7. Oracle Corporation: Database rolling upgrade using Data Guard SQL Apply. Maximum Availability Architecture White Paper (December 2008)
8. Oxford English Dictionary, 2nd edn. Oxford University Press, Oxford (1989), http://www.oed.com
9. Brewer, E.A.: Lessons from giant-scale services. IEEE Internet Computing 5(4), 46–55 (2001)
10. Oppenheimer, D., Ganapathi, A., Patterson, D.A.: Why do Internet services fail, and what can be done about it? In: USENIX Symposium on Internet Technologies and Systems, Seattle, WA (March 2003)
11. Keller, L., Upadhyaya, P., Candea, G.: ConfErr: A tool for assessing resilience to human configuration errors. In: International Conference on Dependable Systems and Networks, Anchorage, AK (June 2008)
12. Nagaraja, K., Oliveira, F., Bianchini, R., Martin, R.P., Nguyen, T.D.: Understanding and dealing with operator mistakes in Internet services. In: USENIX Symposium on Operating Systems Design and Implementation, San Francisco, CA, December 2004, pp. 61–76 (2004)
13. Oliveira, F., Nagaraja, K., Bachwani, R., Bianchini, R., Martin, R.P., Nguyen, T.D.: Understanding and validating database system administration. In: USENIX Annual Technical Conference (June 2006)
14. Dumitraş, T., Kavulya, S., Narasimhan, P.: A fault model for upgrades in distributed systems. Technical Report CMU-PDL-08-115, Carnegie Mellon University (2008)
15. Kaufman, L., Rousseeuw, P.J.: Finding Groups in Data: an Introduction to Cluster Analysis. Wiley Series in Probability and Mathematical Statistics. Wiley, Chichester (1990)
16. Sullivan, M., Chillarege, R.: Software defects and their impact on system availability-a study of field failures in operating systems. In: Fault-Tolerant Computing Symposium, pp. 2–9 (1991)
17. Chatfield, C.: Statistics for Technology: A Course in Applied Statistics, 3rd edn. Chapman & Hall/CRC (1983)

18. Dig, D., Comertoglu, C., Marinov, D., Johnson, R.: Automated detection of refactorings in evolving components. In: Thomas, D. (ed.) ECOOP 2006. LNCS, vol. 4067, pp. 404–428. Springer, Heidelberg (2006)
19. Anderson, R.: The end of DLL Hell. MSDN Magazine (January 2000)
20. Di Cosmo, R., Zacchiroli, S., Trezentos, P.: Package upgrades in FOSS distributions: details and challenges. In: Workshop on Hot Topics in Software Upgrades (October 2008)
21. Menascé, D.: TPC-W: A benchmark for e-commerce. IEEE Internet Computing 6(3), 83–87 (2002)
22. Dumitraş, T., Tan, J., Gho, Z., Narasimhan, P.: No more HotDependencies: Toward dependency-agnostic upgrades in distributed systems. In: Workshop on Hot Topics in System Dependability, Edinburgh, Scotland (June 2007)
23. Amir, Y., Danilov, C., Stanton, J.: A low latency, loss tolerant architecture and protocol for wide area group communication. In: International Conference on Dependable Systems and Networks, New York, NY, June 2000, pp. 327–336 (2000)
24. Amza, C., Cecchet, E., Chanda, A., Cox, A., Elnikety, S., Gil, R., Marguerite, J., Rajamani, K., Zwaenepoel, W.: Specification and implementation of dynamic web site benchmarks. In: IEEE Workshop on Workload Characterization, Austin, TX, November 2002, pp. 3–13 (2002), http://rubis.objectweb.org/
25. Downing, A.: Oracle Corporation. Personal communication (2008)
26. Boyapati, C., Liskov, B., Shrira, L., Moh, C.H., Richman, S.: Lazy modular upgrades in persistent object stores. In: Object-Oriented Programing, Systems, Languages and Applications, Anaheim, CA, pp. 403–417 (2003)
27. Zolti, I.: Accenture. Personal communication (2006)
28. Neamtiu, I., Hicks, M., Stoyle, G., Oriol, M.: Practical dynamic software updating for C. In: ACM Conference on Programming Language Design and Implementation, Ottawa, Canada, June 2006, pp. 72–83 (2006)
29. Neamtiu, I., Hicks, M.: Safe and timely dynamic updates for multi-threaded programs. In: ACM Conference on Programming Language Design and Implementation, Dublin, Ireland (June 2009)
30. Lowell, D., Saito, Y., Samberg, E.: Devirtualizable virtual machines enabling general, single-node, online maintenance. In: International Conference on Architectural Support for Programming Languages and Operating Systems, Boston, MA, October 2004, pp. 211–223 (2004)
31. Potter, S., Nieh, J.: Reducing downtime due to system maintenance and upgrades. In: Large Installation System Administration Conference, San Diego, CA, December 2005, pp. 47–62 (2005)

DR-OSGi: Hardening Distributed Components with Network Volatility Resiliency

Young-Woo Kwon[1], Eli Tilevich[1], and Taweesup Apiwattanapong[2]

[1] Department of Computer Science, Virginia Tech
{ywkwon,tilevich}@cs.vt.edu
[2] National Electronics and Computer Technology Center
taweesup.apiwattanapong@nectec.or.th

Abstract. Because middleware abstractions remove the need for low-level network programming, modern distributed component systems expose *network volatility* (i.e., frequent but intermittent outages) as application-level exceptions, requiring custom manual handling. Unfortunately, handling network volatility effectively is nontrivial—the programmer must consider not only the specifics of the application, but also of its target deployment environment. As a result, to make a distributed component application resilient against network volatility, programmers commonly create custom solutions that are ad-hoc, tedious, and error-prone. In addition, these solutions are difficult to customize for different networks and to reuse across different applications.

To address these challenges, this paper presents a systematic approach to hardening distributed components to become resilient against network volatility. Specifically, we present an extensible framework for enhancing a distributed component application with the ability to continue executing in the presence of network volatility. To accommodate the diverse hardening needs of various combinations of networks and applications, our framework not only provides a collection of hardening strategies, but also simplifies the creation of new strategies. Our reference implementation, built on top of the R-OSGi infrastructure, is called DR-OSGi[1]. DR-OSGi imposes a very low overhead on the hardened applications, requires no changes to their source code, and is plug-in extensible. Applying DR-OSGi to several realistic distributed applications has hardened them with resiliency to effectively withstand network volatility.

Keywords: Distributed Component Architectures, Network Volatility, Aspect Oriented Programming, OSGi, R-OSGi.

1 Introduction

As the world is becoming more interconnected, our daily existence depends on a variety of network-enabled gadgets. Smart phones, PDAs, GPSs, netbook computers, all run network applications. Many of these gadgets are connected to

---

[1] Pronounced as "Doctor OSGi" (**D**isconnected **R**emote **O**pen **S**ervice **G**ateway Initiative).

J.M. Bacon and B.F. Cooper (Eds.): Middleware 2009, LNCS 5896, pp. 373–392, 2009.
© IFIP International Federation for Information Processing 2009

a wireless network such as Wi-Fi. Despite the significant progress made in improving the reliability of wireless networks in recent years, real-world wireless environments are still subject to *network volatility*—a condition arising when a network becomes temporarily unavailable or suffers an outage. Usually the network becomes operational again within minutes of becoming unavailable.

Volatility is a permanent presence of many network environments for several reasons. For one, Wi-Fi networks transmit radio signals, which are volatile, often making it impossible to reach a 100% reliability. Another condition causing network volatility is congestion, which occurs when radio channels interfere with each other or multiple data is transmitted concurrently over the same radio link [9]. Furthermore, wireless networks are rapidly becoming available in emerging markets (e.g., such as in rural or remote areas), which cannot always rely on the existence of an advanced networking infrastructure [30].

Despite its temporary nature, network volatility can prove extremely disruptive for those distributed applications that are built under the assumption that the underlying network is highly-reliable, and network outages are a rare exception rather than a permanent presence. This could happen, for example, when a distributed application, built for a LAN, is later executed in a wireless environment.

Distribution middleware provides a set of abstractions through a standardized API that hide away various complexities of building distributed systems, including the need for low-level network programming. Distributed component systems such as DCOM [15], CORBA CC [19], and R-OSGi [23] expose network volatility as system-level exceptions that are handled by the programmer in an application-specific fashion. Thus, the programmer writes custom exception-handling code that is difficult to keep consistent, maintain, and reuse.

If the underlying network is expected to be volatile during the execution of a distributed system, a consistent strategy can be beneficial for handling the cases of network outages. Manually written outage handling code makes it difficult to ensure that a consistent strategy be applied throughout the application. Since the outage handling code is also scattered throughout the application, it can create a serious maintenance burden. Finally, the expertise developed in handling outages in one distributed application becomes difficult to apply to another application, with a copy-and-paste approach being the only option.

This paper argues that it is both possible and useful to handle network outages systematically, in a consistent and reusable way. Although software architecture researchers have outlined approaches to continue distributed application execution in the presence of network outages, these approaches are difficult to implement, apply, and reuse.

This work builds upon these approaches to define *hardening strategies*, which are exposed as reusable components that can be seamlessly integrated with an extant distributed component infrastructure. These reusable and customizable components can be added to an existing distributed component application, thereby hardening it against network volatility.

As our experimental platform, we use R-OSGi—a state-of-the-art distributed computing infrastructure that enables service-oriented computing in Java. We have created an extensible framework—DR-OSGi—which can harden any R-OSGi application, enabling it to cope with network volatility. DR-OSGi provides programming abstractions for expressing hardening strategies, which can also be reused across applications. The programmer selects a hardening strategy that is most appropriate for a given R-OSGi application and its deployment environment. DR-OSGi then handles all the underlying machinery required to harden the R-OSGi application with the selected strategy.

In our experiments, we have executed several realistic R-OSGi applications in a simulated networking environment to which we injected periodic network outages. By comparing the execution of the original and hardened versions of each application, we have assessed their respective ability to complete the execution, the total time taken to arrive to a result, and the overhead of the hardening functionality. Our results indicate that it is feasible and useful to systematically harden existing distributed component applications with the ability to cope with network volatility. Based on our results, the technical contributions of this paper are as follows:

- A clear exposition of the challenges of treating the ability to cope with network volatility as a separate concern that can be expressed modularly.
- An approach for hardening distributed component applications with resiliency against network volatility.
- A proof of concept infrastructure implementation—DR-OSGi—which demonstrates how existing distributed component applications can be hardened against network volatility.

The rest of this paper is structured as follows. Section 2 introduces the concepts and technologies used in this work. Section 3 describes our approach and reference implementation. Section 4 evaluates the utility and efficiency of DR-OSGi through performance benchmarks and a case study. Section 5 compares our approach to the existing state of the art. Finally, Section 6 presents future research directions and concluding remarks.

2 Background

In the following discussion, we first look at network volatility from the networking perspective. Then we outline the concepts and technologies used in implementing our framework.

2.1 Network Volatility

Modern computing networks are sophisticated multi-component systems whose reliability can be affected by hardware and software failure. These failure conditions include random channel errors, node mobility, and congestion. The reliability of a wireless network can be additionally afflicted by the contention from hidden stations and frequency interference [7,10].

To improve the performance and reliability of modern networks, researchers have investigated various solutions, including congestion control, error control, and mobile IP. Most of these solutions improve various parts of the actual networking infrastructure. This work, by contrast, is concerned with solutions that treat network volatility as an unavoidable presence to be accommodated in software at the application level.

2.2   Software Components

A software component is an abstraction that improves encapsulation and reusability, thus reducing software construction costs. Typically a component encapsulates some unit of functionality that is accessed by outside clients through the component's interface. Component interfaces tend to remain stable, evolving infrequently and systematically. This reduced coupling between a component and its clients makes it possible to change the component's underlying implementation without having to change its clients. Examples of software component architectures include COM [15], CORBA CC [19], CCA [1], and OSGi [20].

OSGi. For our reference implementation, we have chosen a mature software component platform for implementing service oriented applications called OSGi [20]. Among the reasons for choosing OSGi is its wide adoption by multiple industry and research stakeholders, organized into the OSGi Alliance [20]. OSGi is used in large commercial projects such as the Spring framework and Eclipse, which uses this platform to update and manage plug-ins. The OSGi standard is currently implemented by several open-source projects, including Apache Felix, Knopflerfish, Eclipse Equinox, and Concierge[22].

OSGi provides a platform for implementing services. It allows any Java class to be used as a service by publishing it as *a service bundle*. OSGi manages published bundles, allowing them to use each other's services. OSGi manages the lifecycle of a bundle (i.e., moving between install, start, stop, update, and delete stages) and allows it to be added and removed at runtime.

R-OSGi. Despite its versatility, OSGi only allows inter-bundle communication within a single host. To support distributed services via OSGi, the R-OSGi distributed component infrastructure was introduced [23]. R-OSGi enables proxy-based distribution for services, providing proxies also as standard OSGi bundles. An R-OSGi distribution proxy redirects method calls to a remote bundle via a TCP channel, supporting both synchronous and asynchronous remote invocations. R-OSGi also provides a distributed service registry, thus enabling the treatment of remote services uniformly with local services.

Thus, R-OSGi introduces distribution transparently, without modifying the core OSGi implementation. It can even enable remote access to an existing regular OSGi bundle, transforming the bundle into a remote service. The transformation employs the concept of *the surrogation bundle*, which registers the service and redirects remote calls to the original bundle.

With respect to network volatility, R-OSGi treats it similarly to other distributed component infrastructures. Specifically, in response to a network disconnection, a client accessing a remote R-OSGi service will receive an exception. The programmer can then write custom code to handle the exception.

2.3   Hardening Strategies to Cope with Network Volatility

When the underlying network fails, a distributed application will typically signal an error to the end user, who can then decide on how to proceed. The user, for example, could choose to check the network connection and restart the application. The purpose of hardening strategies is to enable a distributed application to continue executing when the underlying network becomes unavailable. In a recent publication, Mikic-Rakic and Medvidovic classify disconnected operation techniques as well as how they can be applied to improve the overall system dependability [16]. Next we outline these techniques and discuss how they can be applied to harden a distributed component application to cope with network volatility.

Caching—This strategy employs caching techniques to store a subset of remote data locally, so that it could be retrieved and used by remote service requests when the network becomes unavailable. The effectiveness of this strategy depends strongly on the hit rate of the caching scheme in place. That is, since the size of any cache is always limited, the main challenge becomes to cache the remote data that is most likely to be needed by a service invocation when the network is unavailable. This strategy can in effect fail completely if there is a cache miss.

Hoarding—This strategy prefetches all the remote data needed for successfully completing any remote service invocation. It assumes, however, that data alone is sufficient for invoking a remote service. Unfortunately, this assumption fails for any resource-driven distribution—collocating hardware resources with the code and data they use. For example, a remote sensor has to operate at a remote location from which it is collecting data; hoarding any amount of the sensor's output data will fail to provide up-to-date sensor information upon disconnection. Thus, a hoarding-based strategy can be effective only when computation is distributed for performance reasons, and computation with a given data input yields the same results on any network node. These execution properties are often exhibited by high-performance cluster environments that use distribution to improve performance.

Queuing—This strategy intercepts and records remote requests made to an unreachable remote service. The recorded requests are then replayed when the service becomes available. This technique can only work if the results of a remote call are not immediately needed by the client code (e.g., to be used in an **if** statement). Otherwise, the client code will block, not being able to benefit from this strategy. Queuing is also poorly applicable for realtime applications.

Replication—This strategy maintains a local copy of a remote component. When the remote component becomes unreachable, the local copy is used. If the replicated component is stateful, then the states of the local and remote copies have to be kept consistent. When the network is available, client requests can be multiplexed to both local and remote copies. Alternatively, a consistency protocol can be used. Upon reconnection, the remote copy has to be synchronized with the local copy. This strategy has the same applicability preconditions as hoarding.

Multi-modal components—This strategy employs several of the strategies above and can apply them either individually, based on some runtime condition, or together, combining some features of individual strategies. For example, both caching and queuing can be used, depending on which remote service method is invoked. Similarly, replication can be applied to remote components while hoarding the data used by the replicated components.

2.4   Aspect-Oriented Programming and JBoss AOP

This work aims at treating network volatility resiliency as a distributed cross-cutting concern. A powerful methodology for modularizing cross-cutting concerns is aspect oriented programming (AOP)[13]. We believe that network volatility resiliency is similar to other cross-cutting concerns such as logging, persistence, and authentication—essential functionality, but not directly related to the business logic.

AOP modularizes cross-cutting concerns and weaves them into the application at compile-time, load-time, or runtime. Major AOP infrastructures include AspectJ[4], Spring AOP[26], and JBoss AOP[11]. Some AOP technologies have even been applied to OSGi, including the Eclipse Foundation's AspectJ plug-in and Equinox. For our purposes, we needed to weave in the outage handling functionality at runtime, which typically requires modifying the JVM or rewriting the bytecode. We also needed the ability to modify the parameters of a remote service method. Among the major AOP systems, only JBoss AOP provides all the required capabilities. Another draw of JBoss AOP is that it does not either introduce a new language, thus flattening the learning curve, or changes the JVM, thus ensuring portability.

3   DR-OSGi: Treating Symptoms of Network Volatility

Our reasoning behind the name DR-OSGi—our reference implementation of an infrastructure for systematic handling of network volatility—is our skeptical view of the power of modern medicine. Despite all its impressive accomplishments, modern medicine can only treat some of the symptoms of the majority of known diseases—it cannot eliminate the disease itself. Take common cold as an example. They say that "If you treat a cold, it takes seven days to recover from it, but if you do not, it takes a week." When a cold is concerned, modern medicine can only help eliminate its symptoms, such as fever, sneezing, and coughing, thereby improving the patient's quality of life.

By analogy, we treat network volatility as a disease—an annoying but unavoidable condition that cannot be eliminated. All we want to do is to treat the symptoms of this disease systematically. By helping the patient (a distributed system) to effectively cope with the symptoms of network volatility (an inability to make remote service calls), we improve the patient's quality of life (QoS).

We next demonstrate our approach by showing how our approach can systematically harden distributed component applications against network volatility. In the following discussion, we first state our design goals, before presenting the architecture of our reference implementation and its individual components.

3.1   Design Objectives

Can any distributed component architecture be effectively hardened against network volatility? In other words, are there any special capabilities a distributed component architecture must provide to make itself amenable to hardening? For our approach to work, we assume that a distributed component architecture can detect and convey to the distributed application the following two scenarios:

1. **A remote service becomes unavailable**—this scenario should be effectively detected by the underlying distributed component architecture, so that an appropriate exception could be raised.
2. **A temporarily unavailable remote service becomes available again**—this scenario assumes that the component architecture does not "give up" trying to reach a remote service, periodically attempting to access it.

To the best of our knowledge, most distributed component architectures can effectively handle the first scenario. However, only advanced distributed component architectures can handle the second one. As a concrete example, R-OSGi employs the Service Discovery Protocol, which periodically attempts to reconnect to a remote service, if the service were to become unavailable. If, for example, a remote service becomes unreachable due to a network outage, the R-OSGi Service Discovery Protocol will keep trying to reach the service until the network connection is restored. It is these advanced capabilities of R-OSGi that convinced us to use this distributed component architecture as our experimentation platform.

Our system, called DR-OSGi, can harden existing R-OSGi applications to become resilient against network volatility. In designing DR-OSGi, we pursued the following goals:

1. **Transparency**—any hardening strategy should not affect the core functionality of the underlying R-OSGi application.
2. **Flexibility**—DR-OSGi should be capable of adding or removing the hardening strategies at any time without having to stop the application.
3. **Extensibility**—DR-OSGi should provide flexible abstractions, enabling expert programmers to easily implement and apply custom hardening strategies.

3.2   Design Overview

The purpose of DR-OSGi is to harden an R-OSGi application with resiliency to cope with network volatility. Thus, to explain the general architecture of DR-OSGi, we start by outlining the fundamental building blocks of R-OSGi. Figure 1 shows that R-OSGi integrates a remoting proxy that redirects service calls to a remote OSGi bundle and also transfers the results of the calls back to the client.

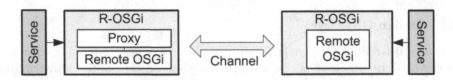

Fig. 1. Initial architecture of R-OSGi

Since the channels to a remote OSGi bundle use TCP, which provides reliable data transport, packet loss is handled at the transport layer. TCP, however, provides no assistance to deal with network volatility conditions arising as a result of link failure, node mobility, or high congestion. Therefore, to detect network instability or disconnection, an R-OSGi channel uses a timer to block the caller until the service has returned or the timeout has been exceeded. In the case of exceeding the timeout, an exception is thrown. R-OSGi handles such exceptions by having a remote OSGi bundle dispose of the channel and remove all proxies, preventing remote service calls while the network in unavailable. R-OSGi periodically checks whether the network has become available again and, if so, recreates the remoting proxies and channels.

DR-OSGi intercepts the handling of R-OSGi network-related exceptions and the successful completions of its reconnection attempts. Specifically, DR-OSGi handles R-OSGi network-related exceptions by triggering a hardening strategy. The type of the triggered strategy is determined by a programmer-specified configuration. The hardening strategy stops being applied when DR-OSGi intercepts a successful R-OSGi reconnection attempt.

Figure 2 shows how DR-OSGi is integrated into a typical R-OSGi application. DR-OSGi augments an R-OSGi application with a hardening manager and a collection of hardening strategies. The manager and each strategy are encapsulated in separate OSGi bundles.

The hardening manager plugs into an R-OSGi application to intercept the handling of network exceptions and of the successful completions of reconnection attempts. In response to these events, the manager starts and stops the hardening strategies as configured by the programmer.

To integrate the hardening manager with an R-OSGi application without changing the application's source code, we employ Dynamic Aspect Oriented Programming. Because OSGi bundles are deployed at runtime, DR-OSGi has to be able to interpose the hardening logic dynamically. The dynamic AOP technology that fits our design objectives is JBoss AOP.

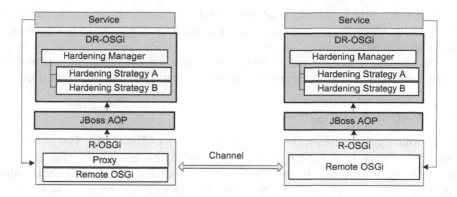

Fig. 2. Hardened architecture

3.3   Programming Model

Next we detail the DR-OSGi programming model and demonstrate how it simplifies the creation and deployment of custom hardening strategies. To harden an R-OSGi application, the programmer has to provide a configuration file that specifies which hardening strategy should be applied to which application bundle. The following configuration file specifies that the application bundle "MyBundle" is to be hardened by the strategy implemented in the DR-OSGi-conformant bundle "CachingHardening":

```
RemoteServiceName=org.mypackage.MyBundle
HardeningServiceName=org.otherpackage.CachingHardening
```

The simple syntax of the DR-OSGi configuration files is sufficiently expressive and supports wildcards which can be used to specify that a hardening strategy be applied to multiple bundles. Several hardening strategies can be applied to the same application bundle simultaneously. For example, remote invocations can be both cached and queued when the network is available. The programmer can specify in the configuration file which strategy bundle should be primary (i.e., to be applied first). If, when the network becomes unavailable, the first strategy succeeds, DR-OSGi does not apply the second one.

To implement a hardening strategy, the programmer needs only to implement interface DisconnectionListener , which is defined as follows:

```
public interface DisconnectionListener {
  public Object disconnectedInvoke(RemoteCallMessage invokeMessage);
  public Object reconnected(String uri );
  public void remoteInvoke(RemoteCallMessage invokeMessage, Object result);
  public void serviceAdded(String uri );
  public void serviceRemoved(String uri );
}
```

Method disconnectedInvoke is called by DR-OSGi, when R-OSGi detects that the network connection has been lost. Method reconnected is called by DR-OSGi, when R-OSGi manages to successfully reestablish a connection to a remote bundle. Finally, remoteInvoke is called when a remote service method has been successfully invoked.

The implemented class has to be deployed as a regular OSGi bundle, and an entry describing the implementation must be added to the configuration file.

3.4   System Architecture

In the following we discuss the system architecture of DR-OSGi. The key objective of this work is to explore how network volatility hardening strategies can be implemented modularly and applied to an existing distributed component application that may have been written without fault-tolerance capabilities in mind. In other words, we argue that it is possible to treat hardening strategies as reusable software components, which can be developed by third-party programmers and reused across multiple applications.

Figure 3 shows how we have designed DR-OSGi, so that it could naturally integrate with the existing OSGi and R-OSGi infrastructures. DR-OSGi makes use of existing OSGi services such as **Service Registration** and **Service Tracker**. Every DR-OSGi component, including the hardening manager and all

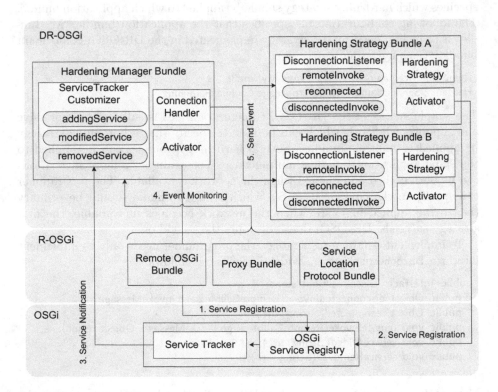

Fig. 3. DR-OSGi Design

hardening strategies, register themselves with OSGi, which manages them as standard registered services. This arrangement makes it possible to locate DR-OSGi components using the OSGi Service Tracker and load them on demand.

To receive service change events from OSGi, the hardening manager implements the ServiceTrackerCustomizer interface, which is discussed below. In turn, to make it possible for the manager to send the relevant events to hardening strategy bundles, each bundle implements the DisconnectionListener interface. All the lifecycle events in DR-OSGi are triggered by sending and receiving events, with Service Tracker and Service Registration enabling the hardening manager and hardening bundles to be loosely coupled.

When a new hardening strategy is deployed, OSGi sends an event—addingService —to Service Tracker, which then forwards the event to the hardening manager by calling the corresponding ServiceTrackerCustomizer interface method.

```
public interface ServiceTrackerCustomizer {
    public Object addingService( ServiceReference  reference );
    public void modifiedService( ServiceReference  reference , Object service );
    public void removedService( ServiceReference  reference , Object service );
}
```

The hardening manager keeps track of which hardening strategies have been registered and maintains a searchable repository of all the registered strategy bundles.

Weaving in Resiliency Strategies with Aspects. To intercept the disconnection/reconnection procedures of R-OSGi, without changing its source code, we use dynamic Aspect Oriented Programming technology, JBoss AOP. The ability to apply aspects dynamically is required due to OSGi loading bundles dynamically at runtime. JBoss AOP makes use of XML configuration files that specify at which points aspects should be weaved. Using AOP enables DR-OSGi to keep its implementation modular and avoid having to modify the source code of R-OSGi.

3.5 Discussion

The hardening approach of DR-OSGi is quite general and can be applied to a variety of distributed components. Although our reference implementation is dependent on R-OSGi and JBoss AOP, DR-OSGi relies only on their core features, which are common in other related technologies. Specifically, we leverage the ability of R-OSGi to convey network failure as application-level exceptions and to reestablish connections once the network becomes available. JBoss AOP effectively modularizes hardening strategies. Although our approach delivers tangible benefits to the distributed component programmers, it also has some inherent limitations.

Advantages. DR-OSGi makes it possible to handle network volatility consistently throughout a distributed component application. This means that the most appropriate hardening strategy can be applied to any subset of application components, and the strategies can be switched through a simple change in the configuration file. Furthermore, each strategy is modularized inside a separate OSGi bundle, thus streamlining maintenance and evolution. Finally, modularized strategies can be easily reused across different distributed component applications.

Limitations. Creating a pragmatic solution that can be implemented straightforwardly required constraining our design in several respects. For example, we chose to maintain a one-to-one correspondence between application bundles and their hardening strategy bundles. That is, a hardening strategy for all the services in a bundle must be implemented in a single DR-OSGi strategy bundle. Strategy bundle implementations, of course, can combine any hardening strategies. We have made this design choice to simplify the deployment and configuration of strategy bundles. Another limitation is inherited from JBoss AOP, which is loaded by the infrastructure irrespective of whether a hardening strategy will be applied, thus possibly consuming system resources needlessly. This may present an issue in a resource-scarce environment such as an embedded system. A possible solution to this inefficiency would be to extend OSGi with a meta-model that would allow the programmer to systematically extend services.

4   Evaluation

To evaluate the effectiveness and performance properties of DR-OSGi, we have conducted three benchmark experiments and a larger case study.

4.1   Benchmarks

Since R-OSGi can easily distribute any existing OSGi application, our benchmarks use third-party OSGi components accessed remotely across the network.

As our benchmark applications, we have used a remote log service, a remote user administration service, and a distributed search engine.

To create a controlled networking environment with predictable network outage rates, we have used a network emulator—`netem` [2]—to introduce network volatility conditions, including transmission delay, packet loss, packet duplication, and packet re-ordering.

In our experimental setup, we have emulated a network with the round trip time (RTT) metrics equal to 14ms, which is typical for a modern wireless network. To emulate network outages, we used `netem` to generate packets losses at the server. Lossy network conditions were emulated by losing a high number of random packets (i.e., over 30% loss); totally disconnected networks were emulated by losing all the transmitted packets.

The experimental environment has comprised a Fujitsu S7111 laptop (1.8 GHz Intel Dual-Core CPU, 2.5 GB RAM) communicating with a Dell XPS M1330 laptop (2.0 GHz Intel Dual-Core CPU, 3 GB RAM) via a IEEE 802.11g wireless LAN, with both laptops running the Sun's client JVM, JDK J2SE 1.6.0_13.

Log Service. For this experiment, we used a log service defined by the OSGi specification [20]. The OSGi log service records standard output and error messages printed during a bundle's execution. The service can be configured to log different amounts of messages by calling its setLevel methods (the higher the level, the more messages are logged).

Imagine needing to log messages generated by a remote service locally. In this experiment, we have used R-OSGi to access the existing log service of Knopflerfish, a popular, open-source implementation of OSGi. To enable remote access, we have used the surrogation bundle approach to register the existing log service.

Network volatility should not cause a remote log service to stop functioning. Logs are typically examined for a postmortem analysis, for which the actual time when the messages are written to a log file is not important, as long as the messages' timestamps reflect their actual origination time.

In our experiment, we used the log service to record 10 text messages generated consecutively without any delay. The network is available during the remote logging of the first 3 messages. Immediately after logging the third message, the network becomes totally disconnected. Then after the fifth message, the network connection is restored.

We have executed this scenario under two setups: plain R-OSGi and DR-OSGi with a queuing strategy. Recall that queuing works by recording remote service calls when the network is unavailable and replays the recorded calls once the connection is restored. Under the original setup, the remote log service recorded only 8 messages (3 before the disconnection and 5 after). Two messages were lost irretrievably. The hardened version recorded all 10 messages.

Table 1 shows the delay for each message delivery. For the queued messages (columns 4 and 5), the delays is significantly higher than for the other messages. Despite the delay of the queued messages, all the messages are delivered in the order in which they are sent. Since real-time guarantees are not required, we can conclude that the hardening strategy has provided the requisite QoS for the remote log service, allowing it to cope with network volatility.

Table 1. Message delivery delay under a queuing hardening strategy

Network condition	connection			disconnection		connection				
Message number	1	2	3	4	5	6	7	8	9	10
Sent log time(min:sec)	0:00	1:12	1:21	1:51	2:51	3:19	4:01	4:03	4:42	4:46
Received log time(min:sec)	0:00	1:15	1:21	3:20	3:20	3:20	4:02	4:05	4:42	4:46

User Admin Service. For this experiment, we used the *User Admin Service*, which comes as a part of the core OSGi system services. The service authenticates and authorizes users by running their credentials against a database. Oftentimes, this service may need to be accessed remotely. To introduce distribution, we have registered the standard User Admin Service bundle using a surrogate bundle, similar to the approach we took in distributing the log service.

A network outage should not prevent a client from using the User Admin Service, if the client has used the service in the past, and the security policy specifies that user credentials change infrequently and can be cached safely. In other words, the caching hardening strategy must be coordinated with the security policy in place, lest the system's security can be compromised. One way to accomplish this is to avoid caching the authentication data that may change while the network is temporarily unavailable.

We have emulated a scenario in which 100 remote authentication attempts have been made across the network, which randomly suffers disconnections with the rate equal to 1 disconnection per 20 authentication attempts. Disconnections always cause the R-OSGi version of the application to fail. The ability of the DR-OSGi hardened version to continue executing depends on the number of clients. In this simulation, we assume that all the clients use the service equally. Thus, if for example, there were n authentication requests made from m users, then the expected number of authentications performed by a single user is n/m. Since the cache size is set to 5, the hit rate is negatively correlated with the number of users, standing at 100% for 2 and 4, and going down to 90%, 85%, and 78% for 6, 8, and 10 users, respectively.

Distributed Lucene. For this experiment, we have used Lucene, a widely-used Java search engine library. Among the capabilities provided by Lucene are indexing files and finding indexes of a given search word. Because searching is computationally intensive, there is great potential benefit in distributing the searching tasks across multiple machines, so that they could be performed in parallel.

Despite several known RMI-based Lucene distributions, for our experiments we have created an R-OSGi distribution, which turned out to be quite straightforward. We have followed a simple Master Worker model, with the Master assigning search tasks to individual Workers as well as collecting and filtering search results. This distribution strategy, depicted in Figure 4, requires that only the Master node be hardened against network volatility. This embarrassingly parallel data distribution arrangement imposes a strict one way communication protocol with the Master always calling Workers but never vice versa.

Once again, a caching hardening strategy has turned out to be most appropriate for hardening the distributed Lucene R-OSGi application. Specifically, every work assignment for individual nodes is used as a key mapped to the returned result. The intuition behind this caching scheme is that files are read-only and searching a file for the same string multiple times must return identical results. For writable files, the caching scheme would have to be modified to invalidate all the cached results for the changed files. As it turns out, the absolute majority of environments that use Lucene feature read-only files only, including digital books, scientific articles, and news archives.

Since distributed Lucene is representative of a large class of realistic applications, we have used it to assess the performance overhead imposed by DR-OSGi. The first benchmark has measured the binding time, which is defined as the total time expended on establishing a remote connection, requesting the service,

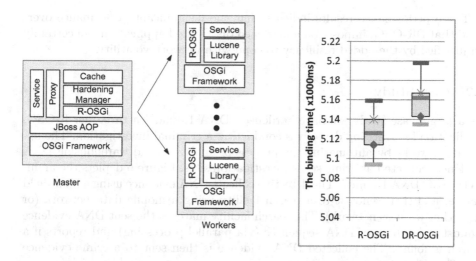

Fig. 4. Distributed Lucene   **Fig. 5.** The Binding Time

receiving the interface, and building the remoting proxy. R-OSGi is quite efficient, with R-OSGi application consistently outperforming their RMI versions [23]. The purpose of our benchmark was to ensure that DR-OSGi does not impose an unreasonable performance overhead on top of R-OSGi. As it turns out, there is not a pronounced difference between the binding time of a plain R-OSGi version of Lucene and its hardened with DR-OSGi version, as shown in Figure 5. One could argue that binding is a one-time expense incurred at the very start of a service and as such is not critical.

To distill the pure overhead of DR-OSGi, we have measured the total time it took to synchronously invoke a remote service under three scenarios:

1. running the original R-RSGi version with no network volatility present
2. running the hardened with DR-OSGi version with no network volatility present
3. running the hardened with DR-OSGi version with a randomly introduced complete network disconnection

The measurements are the result of averaging the total time taken by $1 * 10^3$ remote service invocations. To emulate a complete network disconnection, we have generated a 100% packet loss. While the original R-OSGi version takes 9043.5 ms to execute, the hardened one takes 9321.9 ms, thus incurring only 3% overhead when no volatility is present. When the network becomes unavailable, the DR-OSGi caching strategy improves the performance quite significantly, as it eliminates the need for any computation to be done by the worker node. While, somewhat unrealistically, we used the 100% hit rate to isolate the overhead of DR-OSGi, the actual performance is likely to vary widely depending on the applicaion-specific caching scheme in place.

These performance results indicate that the insignificant performance over-head that DR-OSGi imposes on a hardened distributed application can certainly be justified by the added resiliency to cope with network volatility.

4.2   Case Study

As a larger case study, we have hardened "DNA Hound," a three-tier R-OSGi application for assisting detectives conducting a criminal investigation. The application works by automating the process of analyzing and warehousing DNA evidence, collected at crime scene investigation sites. Figure 6 depicts the architecture of "DNA Hound." The detective collects DNA evidence using a hand-held device, and then sends it to a search facility using a mobile data network (or any other wireless network). The search facility matches the sent DNA evidence against a database of DNA sequences (via parallel processing) and reports if a match is found. The collected DNA evidence is then sent to a crime evidence warehouse for storage.

We have implemented a complete working prototype of "DNA Hound," but in lieu of DNA extracting hardware, we simulated the found DNA evidence by randomly selecting DNA sequences from a GenBank NCBI database [5]. The search is performed using a parallelization of the Smith-Waterman algorithm [25] on a compute cluster.

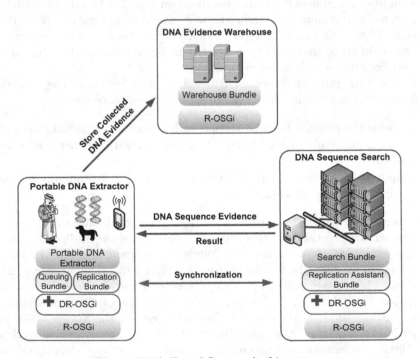

Fig. 6. *DNA Hound* System Architecture

Hardening "DNA Hound". Because "DNA Hound" is used in the field, it relies on a wireless network that can be unreliable. Therefore, to ensure that the application continues to provide service, we have used DR-OSGi to harden it against network volatility. We have used two hardening strategies implemented as regular OSGi bundles.

Replication. To harden the application for the network volatility that can occur between the hand-held DNA extractor and the analyzer, we have used a replication strategy. Although DNA sequence search is very computationally-intensive, usually requiring parallel processing to shorten the search time, it can also be done sequentially, albeit much slower. With the advance in data storage technologies, even a hand-held device can comfortably store a substantial database of DNA sequences. The DNA search bundle is replicated at the hand-held device. We have used the native OSGi replication facilities to install the search bundle at both sites. When the network is up, the search is performed using a compute cluster at the search site, and the index of the most recently searched database sequence is periodically sent to the search bundle at the hand-held site. Once the network becomes unavailable, the search bundle at the hand-held site continues the search locally, using an inefficient sequential algorithm; the search is continued from the index of the last searched sequence at the cluster. If the index is not up-to-date, then some overlap in the search will occur. Once the connection goes back up, the cluster could then report any matches found while the network was not available.

Queuing. To harden the application for the network volatility that can occur between the hand-held DNA extractor and the criminal evidence warehouse, we have used a queuing strategy. The calls to store a new piece of DNA evidence are queued up at the hand-held site once the network becomes unavailable. Then the queued calls are resent to the warehouse once the network connection is restored.

Discussion. The original R-OSGi version of the application was written without any functionality enabling it to cope with network volatility–it thus fails immediately once either network link is lost. DR-OSGi made it possible to harden this unaware application, so that it can meaningfully continue its operation in the presence of network volatility, thus improving the application's utility and safety. This demonstrates how DR-OSGi makes it possible to treat network volatility resiliency as a separate concern that can be implemented separately and added to an existing application. Furthermore, the queuing bundle came from the library of standard hardening strategy bundles that are part of our DR-OSGi distribution, thus requiring no programmer effort. The replication bundle was custom tailored for this application, but we are currently working on generalizing the implementation, so that only the synchronization functionality would require custom coding.

5   Related Work

DR-OSGi derives its hardening strategies from a recent survey of disconnected operation techniques by Mikic-Rakic and Medvidovic [16]. These techniques are used by several systems, including the Rover toolkit [12], Mobile Extension [6], Odyssey [17], and FarGo-DA [28]. Unlike these systems, DR-OSGi enables the programmer to harden distributed applications without having to modify their source code explicitly. By avoiding ad-hoc modification that can be tedious and error-prone, DR-OSGi not only hardens applications more systematically, but also enables greater reuse of the hardening strategies across different applications.

Aldrich et al.'s ArchJava [3] extends Java to integrate architectural specifications with the implementation by providing language support for user-defined connectors. Their techniques bears similarity to DR-OSGi in separating reusable connection logic from the application logic and integrating them together systematically. ArchJava, however, operates at the source code level, using its language extension to express different connectors. DR-OSGi is a middleware solution that does not need to modify the source code.

Sadjadi and McKinley's adaptive CORBA template (ACT) enables CORBA applications to adapt to unanticipated changes [24]. To do so, ACT employs a generic interceptor, a type of CORBA portable request interceptor [18] that works around the constraints of replying to intercepted requests or modifying the invoked method's parameters. Specifically, a generic interceptor forwards requests to a proxy, a CORBA object that can reply and modify the requests. Similarly to DR-OSGi, ACT introduces additional functionality to a distributed application without modifying its code explicitly. Using ACT to harden against network volatility, however, would require that portable interceptors be available, which may not be the case for many distributed component infrastructures including R-OSGi.

A number of techniques for making existing systems fault tolerant [8,21,27] are related to our approach. GRAFT [27] automatically specializes middleware for fault-tolerance. It employs the Component Availability Modeling Language (CAML) to annotate a distributed application's model, and then automatically specializes the application's middleware for domain-specific fault-tolerant requirements. While GRAFT requires that the programmer express the requested fault-tolerance functionality at the model level using a domain-specific language, DR-OSGi provides a simple Java API for implementing hardening strategies as OSGi bundles, which it then manages at runtime.

Our idea of hardening against network volatility was inspired by *security hardening*, a systematic approach to making a pre-existing program artifact more secure such as Wuyts et al's recent work [29]. Our approach hardens distributed components to become more resilient against network volatility.

6   Future Work and Conclusions

One future work direction will assess the generality of our approach by applying it to other distributed component infrastructures. Another direction will focus on identifying suitable hardening strategies through the program analysis of distributed components.

We have presented DR-OSGi, a promising approach for systematically hardening distributed components to cope with network volatility. The reference implementation features an extensible framework for deploying hardening strategies, with caching, queuing, and replication used to demonstrate the effectiveness of our approach. As we rely on greater numbers of network-enabled devices with network volatility remaining a permanent presence, the importance of hardening distributed components will only increase, motivating the creation of systematic and flexible hardening approaches as showcased by DR-OSGi.

Availability: DR-OSGi and all the applications described in the paper can be downloaded from `http://research.cs.vt.edu/vtspaces/drosgi`.

References

1. CCA-Forum, `http://www.cca-forum.org/`
2. Net:Netem, `http://www.linuxfoundation.org/en/Net:Netem/`
3. Aldrich, J., Sazawal, V., Chambers, C., Notkin, D.: Language support for connector abstractions. In: Cardelli, L. (ed.) ECOOP 2003. LNCS, vol. 2743. Springer, Heidelberg (2003)
4. The AspectJ project, `http://www.eclipse.org/aspectj/`
5. Benson, D.A., Karsch-Mizrachi, I., Lipman, D.J., Ostell, J., Rapp, B.A., Wheeler, D.L.: Genbank. Nucleic Acids Res. 30, 17–20 (2002)
6. Dahlin, M., Chandra, B., Gao, L., Khoja, A., Nayate, A., Razzaq, A., Sewani, A.: Using mobile extensions to support disconnected services. Technical Report CS-TR-00-20, University of Texas at Austin (2000)
7. Fullmer, C.L., Garcia-Luna-Aceves, J.: Solutions to hidden terminal problems in wireless networks. In: Proceedings ACM SIGCOMM, pp. 39–49 (1997)
8. Herrero, J.L., Sanchez, F., Sanchez, O., Toro, M.: Fault tolerance AOP approach. In: Workshop on AOP and Separation of Concerns, pp. 44–52 (2001)
9. Hull, B., Jamieson, K., Balakrishnan, H.: Mitigating congestion in wireless sensor networks. In: ACM SenSys 2004, Baltimore, MD (November 2004)
10. Jain, K., Padhye, J., Padmanabhan, V.N., Qiu, L.: Impact of interference on multi-hop wireless network performance. In: MobiCom 2003: Proceedings of the 9th annual international conference on Mobile computing and networking, pp. 66–80. ACM, New York (2003)
11. JBoss AOP, `http://www.jboss.org/jbossaop`
12. Joseph, A.D., de Lespinasse, A.F., Tauber, J.A., Gifford, D., Kaashoek, M.F.: Rover: A toolkit for mobile information access. In: Proceedings of the Fifteenth Symposium on Operating Systems Principles (December 1995)
13. Kiczales, G., Lamping, J., Mendhekar, A., Maeda, C., Lopes, C.V., Loingtier, J.-M., Irwin, J.: Aspect-oriented programming. In: Aksit, M., Matsuoka, S. (eds.) ECOOP 1997. LNCS, vol. 1241, pp. 220–242. Springer, Heidelberg (1997)
14. Knopflerfish - open source OSGi, `http://www.knopflerfish.org`
15. Microsoft. Component Object Model (COM)
16. Mikic-Rakic, M., Medvidovic, N.: A classification of disconnected operation techniques. In: Proceedings of the 32nd EUROMICRO Conference on Software engineering and Advanced Applications (EUROMICRO-SEAA 2006) (2006)

17. Noble, B.D., Sayanarayanan, M., Narayanan, D., Tilton, J.E., Flinn, J., Walker, K.R.: Agile application-aware adaptation for mobility. In: Proceedings of the 16th ACM Symposium on Operating Systems Principles (October 1997)
18. Object Management Group. The common object request broker: Architecture and specification version 3.0 (July 2003), http://doc.ece.uci.edu/CORBA/formal/02-06-33.pdf
19. Object Management Group. The CORBA component model specification. Specification, Object Management Group (2006)
20. OSGi Alliance. OSGi release 4.1 specification. Specification (2007)
21. Polze, A., Schwarz, J., Malek, M.: Automatic generation of fault-tolerant CORBA-services. In: Haverkort, B.R., Bohnenkamp, H.C., Smith, C.U. (eds.) TOOLS 2000. LNCS, vol. 1786. Springer, Heidelberg (2000)
22. Rellermeyer, J.S., Alonso, G.: Concierge: a service platform for resource-constrained devices. In: The 2nd ACM SIGOPS/EuroSys European Conference on Computer Systems 2007, pp. 245–258 (2007)
23. Rellermeyer, J.S., Alonso, G., Roscoe, T.: R-OSGi: Distributed applications through software modularization. In: Cerqueira, R., Campbell, R.H. (eds.) Middleware 2007. LNCS, vol. 4834, pp. 1–20. Springer, Heidelberg (2007)
24. Sadjadi, S.M., McKinley, P.K.: ACT: An adaptive CORBA template to support unanticipated adaptation. In: Proceedings of the 24th International Conference on Distributed Computing Systems (ICDCS 2004), pp. 74–83 (2004)
25. Smith, T., Waterman, M.: Identification of common molecular subsequences. J. Mol. Biol. 147, 195–197 (1981)
26. Spring Framework, http://www.springsource.org/
27. Tambe, S., Dabholkar, A., Balasubramanian, J., Gokhale, A.: Automating middleware specializations for fault tolerance. In: Proceedings of the International Symposium on Object/component/service-oriented Real-time distributed Computing, ISORC 2009 (March 2009)
28. Weinsberg, Y., Ben-Shaul, I.: A programming model and system support for disconnected-aware applications on resource-constrained devices. In: Proceedings of the 24th International Conference on Software Engineering, Orlando, Florida, May 2002, pp. 374–384 (2002)
29. Wuyts, K., Scandariato, R., Claeys, G., Joosen, W.: Hardening XDS-based architectures. In: ARES 2008: Proceedings of the 2008 Third International Conference on Availability, Reliability and Security, Washington, DC, USA, pp. 18–25. IEEE Computer Society, Los Alamitos (2008)
30. Zhang, M., Wolff, R.: Crossing the digital divide: cost-effective broadband wireless access for rural and remote areas. IEEE Communications Magazine 42(2), 99–105 (2004)

Automatic Stress Testing of Multi-tier Systems by Dynamic Bottleneck Switch Generation

Giuliano Casale[1], Amir Kalbasi[2], Diwakar Krishnamurthy[2], and Jerry Rolia[3]

[1] SAP Research, CEC Belfast, UK
giuliano.casale@sap.com
[2] University of Calgary, Calgary, AB, Canada
{akalbasi,dkrishna}@ucalgary.ca
[3] Automated Infrastructure Lab, HP Labs, Bristol, UK
jerry.rolia@hp.com

Abstract. The performance of multi-tier systems is known to be significantly degraded by workloads that place bursty service demands on system resources. Burstiness can cause queueing delays, oversubscribe limited threading resources, and even cause dynamic bottleneck switches between resources. Thus, there is need for a methodology to create benchmarks with controlled burstiness and bottleneck switches to evaluate their impact on system performance. We tackle this problem using a model-based technique for the automatic and controlled generation of bursty benchmarks. Markov models are constructed in an automated manner to model the distribution of service demands placed by sessions of a given system on various system resources. The models are then used to derive session submission policies that result in user-specified levels of service demand burstiness for resources at the different tiers in a system. Our approach can also predict under what conditions these policies can create dynamic bottleneck switching among resources. A case study using a three-tier TPC-W testbed shows that our method is able to control and predict burstiness for session service demands. Further, results from the study demonstrate that our approach was able to inject controlled bottleneck switches. Experiments show that these bottleneck switches cause dramatic latency and throughput degradations that are not shown by the same session mix with non-bursty conditions.

Keywords: Benchmarking, performance, burstiness, bottleneck switch.

1 Introduction

Burstiness refers to temporally dependent workload request patterns that cause serial correlations in service demands at various system resources. Recent work has suggested that burstiness is prevalent in multi-tier systems [17]. Furthermore, bursty workloads are known to stress such systems more than workloads with random patterns. For example, burstiness can trigger frequent bottleneck switches between system resources that limit scalability and make performance

J.M. Bacon and B.F. Cooper (Eds.): Middleware 2009, LNCS 5896, pp. 393–413, 2009.

prediction a challenging task [15]. Consequently, techniques are needed to incorporate burstiness in a controlled manner within the synthetic workloads used for stress testing and system sizing exercises. Unfortunately, due to the session-oriented nature of workloads, this is a non-trivial task for multi-tier systems. A synthetic workload for such systems must simultaneously match many different characteristics such as request mix and session inter-arrival time distribution while using only semantically correct request sequences. Furthermore, the creation of controlled burstiness requires a detailed understanding of hard-to-estimate characteristics of the service demand (e.g., variance, distribution) placed by requests on each performance attribute (e.g., a CPU resource, an IO resource) at each tier of the architecture. In this paper, we propose an automated approach to generate controlled burstiness in benchmarks.

The problem under study can be formulated as follows. Consider a multi-tier system with a pre-existing set of G test suites $g = 1, \ldots G$. Each test suite g is a *group* of sessions chosen from S available session types for a system. Each *session type* is a semantically correct fixed sequence of requests. Requests in a system are assumed to belong to one of R available request types. Requests in sessions are submitted serially; think time between each request is assumed to be zero. Our goal is to automatically create a benchmark B that submits a sequence of sessions to the system by drawing using a uniform distribution sessions from the G groups so that a user-specified request type mix $\boldsymbol{\rho} = (\rho_1, \ldots, \rho_R)$, $\sum_r \rho_r = 1$, where $\rho_r \in [0, 1]$ describes the percentage of type-r requests submitted, is matched while simultaneously causing a user-specified level of burstiness in resource consumption at the different tiers.

The proposed methodology has three steps: *demand characterization, composition,* and *search*. The demand characterization step involves a method that automatically deduces for each test suite g a service demand distribution model for a session drawn using a uniform distribution from that test suite. It relies on commonly available coarse grained resource usage measurements for sessions in the test suites. The composition step describes the service consumption of the benchmark B as a function of the service demand distribution models of the G test suites B is based on. The composition step also allows to define a test suite group mix $\boldsymbol{\gamma} \equiv (\gamma_1, \ldots, \gamma_G)$, $\sum_g \gamma_g = 1$, where $\gamma_g \in [0, 1]$ describes the percentage of sessions drawn from group g used, that generates the desired request mix $\boldsymbol{\rho}$. Finally, the search step combines the results of the composition and demand characterization steps within an optimization program that searches for a policy that governs the sequence of groups from which sessions are randomly selected to cause the desired burstiness.

Our approach can be used to support performance sizing, controller tuning, and system debugging exercises. Sizing requires representative burstiness in synthetic test workloads to ensure a system can handle its load with appropriate response times. In shared virtualized environments, application resource allocations may be governed dynamically by automated controllers. Our approach can be helpful in ensuring that these controllers are tuned appropriately to react effectively to bursts in application workloads and any corresponding bottleneck switches. System debugging also benefits from fine control over burstiness, e.g., it can help determine the impact of burstiness on cache misses and virtual memory swapping effects that may not be present with arbitrary workloads.

Summarizing, the proposed methodology has the following main advantages: (i) it causes a controlled level of burstiness in service demands. We are not aware of any other benchmarking approach that supports the ability to explicitly control the level of burstiness in service demands. Most existing methods focus on burstiness with respect to the arrival of sessions or requests, see [16] and references therein; (ii) it is automated, combining pre-existing non-bursty, semantically correct sessions for the definition of a benchmark with burstiness based on the solution of an optimization program; (iii) it has wide applicability since it only requires information about mean service demands of the pre-existing sessions. Such demands can be deduced directly via system performance measurements or by using techniques such as linear regression [3], operational analysis [3], or LSA [19].

The remainder of the paper is organized as follows. Section 2 describes related work. The demand characterization step is described in Section 3, the composition and search steps are described in Section 4. A case study is offered in Section 5, followed by summary and concluding remarks in Section 6.

We point out that a short version of this paper has been presented in the HotMetrics workshop 2009 [5]. The present paper significantly improves [5] with new or extended discussion in Sections 2, 3, 4.1, 4.4, 5.2, and with new experimental data in Figures 4, 5, and 6. We also point out that a technical report for this work is available at [4]. The report has a summary table of our notation and adds appendices on phase-type distributions and semi-Markov models.

2   Related Work

Benchmarking is a well accepted method for evaluating the behavior of software and hardware platforms [9]. In general, the purpose of benchmarking is to rank the relative capacity, scalability, and cost/performance trade-offs of alternative combinations of software and hardware. Historically, benchmarking does not attempt to directly predict performance behavior for any customized use of a platform. However, recent advances in virtualized and programmable infrastructure are enabling the cost-effective use of benchmarking-like exercises in support of system sizing and highly controlled performance testing.

Dujmovic describes benchmark design theory that models benchmarks using an algebraic space and minimizes the number of benchmark tests needed to provide maximum information [8]. Dujmovic's seminal work informally describes the concept of interpreting the results of a mix of different benchmarks to better predict the behavior of a customized system, but no formal method is given to compute the mix. Krishnaswamy and Scherson [13] also model benchmarks as an algebraic space but also do not consider the problem of finding a mix.

The approach presented in this paper is motivated by the previous work of Krishnamurthy et al. on synthetic workload generation for session-based systems [12]. The work has developed the Session-Based Web Application Tester

(SWAT) tool. The tool includes a method that exploits an algebraic space to automatically select a subset of pre-existing semantically correct user sessions from a session-based system and computes a mix of session types $\sigma_j = (\sigma_{j,1}, \ldots, \sigma_{j,s}, \ldots, \sigma_{j,S})$ to achieve specific workload characteristics, where $\sigma_{j,s} \in [0, 1]$ is the percentage of type-s sessions used in the submitted workload. For example, the technique can reuse the existing sessions to simultaneously match by the session type mix σ a user specified request type mix ρ and a particular session length distribution. It can also prepare a corresponding synthetic workload to be submitted to the system. Our current work exploits and extends these concepts. SWAT can be used to find a mix of session types σ that matches a request type mix ρ and other session properties. The approach presented in this paper then decides the order in which sessions are executed to match a desired level of burstiness for resource demands.

Burstiness in service demands has recently emerged as an important feature of multi-tier systems which has been shown to be responsible of major performance degradation [17]. Service demand burstiness differs substantially from the well-understood burstiness in the arrival of requests to a system. Arrival burstiness has been systematically examined in networking [14] and there are many benchmarking tools that can shape correlations between arrivals [2,11,16,12]. In contrast, service demand burstiness can be seen as the result of serially correlated service demands placed by consecutive requests on a hardware or software system [18,17,15], rather than a feature of the inter-arrival times between requests. For instance, the use of caches at the disk drive, memory, database, and application layers inevitably involves temporal and spatial locality effects which introduce correlation and burstiness in the service demands [18]. It is much harder to model and predict system performance for workloads with service demand burstiness than for traditional workloads [6]. This stresses the need for benchmarking tools that support analytic and simulation techniques to study the performance impact of service demand burstiness. To the best of our knowledge, we are not aware of any benchmarking tools specifically focused on generating service demand burstiness. We believe this to be a significant lack since service burstiness, in contrast to burstiness in arrivals, describes intrinsic properties of the system related to the way requests are served and is thus crucial for outlining insights on the best system configuration decisions.

3   Demand Characterization

The goal of the demand characterization step is to model the service demand distribution of groups. Demand distributions are characterized for the performance attributes of interest belonging to all server tiers. Demand characterization is fundamental for understanding how a given workload consumes individual resources throughout the multi-tier architecture. Specifically, our goal is to infer the service demand distribution of each group from limited or coarse-grained system measurements and fit a set of Markov models, known as phase-type distributions [10], to summarize the observed resource consumption. The phase-type distributions

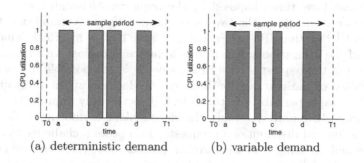

(a) deterministic demand   (b) variable demand

Fig. 1. Utilization sampling for a set of four requests served by a resource

obtained in this step, called *group service demand models*, are fundamental inputs for the burstiness generation methodology presented in Section 4.

The next subsections consider three different abstractions for modeling service demand distributions. Section 3.1 and Section 3.2 discuss request-level and session-level characterizations, respectively. Section 3.3 describes how a session group level abstraction can improve characterization. Section 3.4 introduces group service demand models based on phase-type distributions.

3.1 Request Characterization

To begin, consider CPU usage for a single server of a multi-tier architecture ignoring its dependence with other system components. Figure 1 illustrates two possible examples of CPU utilization measurements within a sample period of duration $T_1 - T_0$. In both examples, four requests of the same type are served within the time period at instants a, b, c, and d. The grey boxes illustrate the demands caused by each request and ther busy time within the sample period. Busy time divided by the duration of the sample period is defined as utilization.

Consider the general case of R request types, it is routine to estimate the mean service demand $E[D_{req,r}]$ of type-r requests using the count of the number of type-r requests served in the jth sample period, $n_r^{(j)}$, and the sampled utilization $U^{(j)}$ in that period. Assume that all sample periods have identical length $T_1 - T_0$, then utilization and number of completed requests are related in the sample period by the utilization law [3]

$$E[U^{(j)}] = \sum_{r=1}^{R} E[D_{req,r}] \left(\frac{n_r^{(j)}}{T_1 - T_0} \right), \tag{1}$$

where $E[U^{(j)}]$ is computed over all available samples $j = 1, \ldots, J$ and $E[D_{req,r}]$ are to be estimated. Estimates for $E[D_{req,r}]$ can be readily obtained from (1) using multivariate linear regression [3].

Figure 1 also illustrates the fundamental difficulty of estimating the request service demand distribution from utilization measurements. The two diagrams show different busy times imposed by the requests. Although the distribution of the service demands in the two cases shows different variabilities, the *total* utilization $U^{(j)}$ of the CPU in Figure 1(a) and 1(b) is identical. That is, the sampling of the utilization values results in information loss with respect to the distribution of the request service times, since it is not possible to discriminate the variability of the two distributions by only looking at the total utilization $U^{(j)}$ in the sample period. Unfortunately, $U^{(j)}$ is the only information returned by standard CPU monitoring tools, therefore making it difficult to characterize the service demand distribution of requests. This poses a challenge to modeling burstiness and injecting it in a controlled manner into synthetic workloads.

Consider the following scheme for estimating the service demand variance that generalizes (1). We observe that $U^{(j)}(T_1 - T_0)$ is the total busy time of the CPU during the jth sample period and therefore is a summation of the service demands of the requests completed in that interval[1]. Assuming request service demands are independent of each other, it follows from the expression for the variance of the sum of independent random variables that

$$Var[U^{(j)}(T_1 - T_0)] = \sum_{r=1}^{R} n_r^{(j)} Var[D_{req,r}], \qquad (2)$$

However, CPU monitors do not provide direct estimates of the left-hand side variance of (2) thus complicating the estimation of the $Var[D_{req,r}]$ values. The variance of total busy times can be calculated by measuring the busy times at J different samples. However, this approach requires that the numbers of requests belonging to each of the R request types be the same for the J different samples (i.e., $n_r^{(j)} = n_r^{(j')}$ for all samples j and j'). Since enforcing this is unrealistic in practice, the expression given in (2) must be approximated by replacing $n_r^{(j)}$ with $E[n_r^{(j)}]$. However, this returns very inaccurate results unless there is very low variability in the $n_r^{(j)}$ values. Summarizing, this discussion highlights a fundamental problem of service variance estimation at the request-level. CPU monitors are unable to provide direct estimates of $Var[U^{(j)}(T_1 - T_0)]$, thus we need to compute this variance from different sample intervals and this cannot be done accurately by (2).

3.2   Session Characterization

In what follows, we show that changing the level of abstraction in the analysis can significantly help in addressing the limitations of the variance estimation at the request level. Suppose we have S session types, the previous observations generalize directly to the estimation of the service demand $D_{sess,s}$ of a session of type s instead of a single request. A generalization of the above analysis

---

[1] Henceforth, we ignore the contribution to the busy period of requests that start in a sample period j and conclude execution in a different sample period $j' > j$. In fact, it is always possible to consider a sampling granularity sufficiently large to make these effects negligible with respect to the total busy time in the sample period j.

leads to formulas almost identical to (1)-(2), but where $n_r^{(j)}$ is replaced by $n_s^{(j)}$ which is the number of sessions of type s completed in the jth sample period. While $E[D_{sess,s}]$ can be estimated reliably, identical difficulties of the request consumption analysis apply to the estimation of $Var[D_{sess,s}]$ for sessions. To the best of our knowledge, the estimation problem of higher-order characteristics of the resource consumption has been never addressed in the literature. In the next subsection, we propose the first available general purpose approximation based on a concept of demand characterization for session groups.

3.3   Session Group Characterization Approach

To overcome the difficulties of variance estimation described above, we propose to evaluate the service demand distribution of a *group* of sessions, instead of each individual session type or request type. These groups can be either suites of pre-existing micro-benchmarks that are already implemented for the multi-tier system (e.g., the TPC-W workload mixes) or user-defined collections of sessions which perform semantically-homogeneous business operations (e.g., sales sessions, financial and business operations sessions). We assume in the rest of the paper that all groups are already defined by the user according to his knowledge of the multi-tier application characteristics or based on an pre-existing test suite.

The fundamental idea behind the group characterization approach is to assume that the variability of resource consumption within a group is mostly due to the heterogeneity of the sessions the group is made of, rather than due to the individual demand variability of each of them. Suppose that a characterization of the mean session service demand $E[D_{sess,s}]$ has been obtained, as discussed in the previous subsection, for each type of session s. Let $D_{grp,g}$ be the service demand of a random session drawn from the group g. Then the mean service demand of a random session in the group g is $E[D_{grp,g}] = \sum_{s \in g} \pi_{s,g} E[D_{sess,s}]$, where $\pi_{s,g}$ is the probability of drawing a session of type s from group g. Given the assumption of ignoring the complete distribution of the session service demand, we approximate higher-order moments of $D_{grp,g}$ with those of a Markov process jumping randomly between values in the set $E[D_{sess,1}], \ldots, E[D_{sess,S}]$. That is, we completely characterization session service demands by their means. The properties of this special class of Markov processes are overviewed in Appendix B of [4] and provide the following estimator for the variance of $D_{grp,g}$:

$$Var[D_{grp,g}] \approx \sum_{s=1}^{S} \pi_{s,g} (E[D_{sess,s}])^2 - E[D_{grp,g}]^2. \tag{3}$$

The last formula translates the concept that a random sampling from a group g imposes a service demand variability that is mostly dominated by the variance in the mean request consumption of the different sessions in the group, rather than by each session type variance.

Based on $E[D_{grp,g}]$ and $Var[D_{grp,g}]$ one can immediately fit, according to the procedure discussed in the next subsection, a service demand model that describes the resource consumption the group g. The above approximation (3) generalizes immediately to higher-order moments k according to the relation $E[D_{grp,g}^k] = \sum_{s=1}^{S} \pi_{s,g}(E[D_{sess,s}])^k$ which provides additional information to fit group service demand models. Finally, this same technique can be applied to different performance attributes at different servers in the multi-tier architecture.

3.4   Group Service Demand Model

Starting from the $E[D_{grp,g}]$ and $Var[D_{grp,g}]$ values obtained in the previous subsection, we specify *group service demand models* using phase-type distributions [10], which are a special family of continuous-time Markov chains such that the execution of a job is modeled as a passage through a number of stages with exponentially-distributed service times. Henceforth, we represent phase-type distributions using the $(\mathbf{D}_0, \mathbf{D}_1)$ matrix notation [10]. The transitions in $\mathbf{D}_1$ are conventionally associated with the completion of service for the job currently in service, while all the remaining transitions describe the accumulation of busy time and are placed in $\mathbf{D}_0$. As an example of the $(\mathbf{D}_0, \mathbf{D}_1)$ notation, a two-stage Erlang distribution is obtained by summing the samples of two exponential distributions with same mean, which can be expressed as

$$\mathbf{D}_0 = \begin{bmatrix} -\lambda & \lambda \\ 0 & -\lambda \end{bmatrix}, \quad \mathbf{D}_1 = \begin{bmatrix} 0 & 0 \\ \lambda & 0 \end{bmatrix} \tag{4}$$

where $\mathbf{D}_0$ describes that a job starting in state 1 (first row) first accumulates exponentially-distributed service time with rate λ as specified by the element $(-\mathbf{D}_0)_{1,1}$, then it jumps with probability $-(\mathbf{D}_0)_{1,2}/(\mathbf{D}_0)_{1,1} = 1$ to state 2 where it receives a new exponential service with rate $(-\mathbf{D}_0)_{2,2} = \lambda$. Finally, $(\mathbf{D}_1)_{2,1}$ implies that after receiving the second exponential service the job is completed and the following job starts service again from state 1.

Details regarding the general fitting of phase-type distributions to match $E[D_{grp,g}]$ and $Var[D_{grp,g}]$ are given in [4]. By applying the fitting techniques proposed in the appendix to all $E[D_{grp,g}]$ and $Var[D_{grp,g}]$ pairs generated in the session group characterization we obtain a set of $(\mathbf{D}_0, \mathbf{D}_1)$ matrices, henceforth denoted by $\mathbf{D}^{i,g} = (\mathbf{D}_0^{i,g}, \mathbf{D}_1^{i,g})$, that describe the service demand distribution of sessions in group g for each performance attribute i.

4   Benchmark Generation Methodology

This section presents the methodology for automatic generation of bursty benchmarks proposed in this paper. Throughout the following sections, we denote by B the benchmark produced as an output by our methodology. As described in Section 2, our approach exploits the SWAT workload generator [12]. SWAT can be easily adapted to compute a group mix vector $\gamma = (\gamma_1, \ldots, \gamma_G)$ defined over the space of the G session groups that matches a desired request mix ρ and other properties such as a desired session length distribution. For the purpose of this paper, we assume that γ has already been computed using SWAT. Therefore, we focus in this section on how to define workload generation mechanisms that

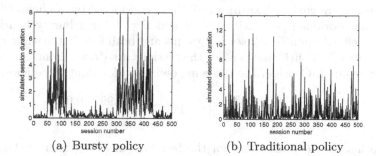

(a) Bursty policy   (b) Traditional policy

Fig. 2. Generation of burstiness using the session submission policy **P**. Engineered definition of the state transition probabilities in the Markov chain **P** enables burstiness properties in the session demand.

insert tunable burstiness in the session service demands. Specifically, we control the sequence in which sessions selected from the G session groups are submitted through a *session submission policy* **P**. The policy **P** is specified as a discrete-time Markov chain responsible for selecting the session type for the next session to be submitted in a benchmark B. Controlling the sequence through **P** allows us to inject a user-specified level of burstiness in B while fixing γ.

4.1   Session Submission Policy

The *session submission policy* **P** determines the sequence of sessions submitted to the system, both in terms of their type and relative ordering. The policy works as follows. **P** is a discrete-time Markov chain

$$\mathbf{P} = \begin{bmatrix} p_{1,1} & p_{1,2} & \cdots & p_{1,G} \\ p_{2,1} & p_{2,2} & \cdots & p_{2,G} \\ \vdots & \vdots & \ddots & \vdots \\ p_{G,1} & p_{G,2} & \cdots & p_{G,G} \end{bmatrix}$$

such that after generating a session from group g there is probability $p_{g,g'}$ that the following one will be sampled from group g'. The challenge is how to define these probabilities to match the desired group mix vector γ and burstiness levels. It is simple to show using standard results for discrete-time Markov chains [3], that if the policy satisfies

$$\gamma = \gamma \mathbf{P}, \tag{5}$$

then **P** generates exactly the desired session group mix γ. Our observation is that (5) leaves considerable flexibility in the definition of **P**, which we can use to controlled generate burstiness in the demands. An illustrative example of this concept is proposed below.

Burstiness Generation Example. We have considered two policies $\mathbf{P}^{trad}$ for a traditional workload generation model and $\mathbf{P}^{burst}$ for a bursty benchmark. These are defined upon $G = 2$ session groups and both satisfy the same requirement $\gamma = (0.5, 0.5)$ such that 50% of the sessions are drawn from group 1 and 50% from group 2. Consider the following definition for the two policies:

$$\mathbf{P}^{trad} = \begin{bmatrix} 0.50 & 0.50 \\ 0.50 & 0.50 \end{bmatrix}, \quad \mathbf{P}^{burst} = \begin{bmatrix} 0.99 & 0.01 \\ 0.01 & 0.99 \end{bmatrix}$$

which both satisfy (5) and differ for the fact that in $\mathbf{P}^{burst}$ there is large 0.99 probability of consecutively sampling sessions from the same group g. This is a critical difference because the high probability of sampling sessions from the same state in $\mathbf{P}^{burst}$ implies formation of bursts, as shown by the simulation in Figure 2(a) that are absent in the traditional workload generation model results shown in Figure 2(b). Therefore, by carefully selecting the transition probability in the submission policies we can create radically different behaviors in terms of burstiness. In the next subsection, we explain how the policy $\mathbf{P}$ creates service demand burstiness on a per-resource level.

4.2 Composition Step and Benchmark Burstiness Model

This subsection describes the composition step of the proposed methodology. We define Markovian arrival processes (MAPs) [10] to predict the service demand burstiness created at the different system tiers by a benchmark B that submits sessions as per a policy $\mathbf{P}$. These models are useful for assessing if $\mathbf{P}$ is a good candidate for generating the requested level of burstiness in the system. We remark that MAPs are similar to phase-type distributions, share the same notation, but they are more general as they can also model burstiness; we point to [10] for technical details.

Given a policy $\mathbf{P}$ and the group demand characterization obtained in Section 3, a burstiness model for a benchmark B for performance attribute i (e.g., front server CPU, DB CPU, ...) is

$$\mathbf{D}^i = f^i(\mathbf{D}^{i,g}, \mathbf{P})$$

where the function $f^i(\mathbf{D}^{i,g}, \mathbf{P})$ specifies how the burstiness model $\mathbf{D}^i$ is constructed from the input parameters. In our methodology, $f^i(\mathbf{D}^{i,g}, \mathbf{P})$ is defined as

$$\mathbf{D}_0^i = \begin{bmatrix} \mathbf{D}_0^{i,1} & \mathbf{0} & \cdots & \mathbf{0} \\ \mathbf{0} & \mathbf{D}_0^{i,2} & \cdots & \mathbf{0} \\ \vdots & \vdots & \ddots & \vdots \\ \mathbf{0} & \mathbf{0} & \cdots & \mathbf{D}_0^{i,G} \end{bmatrix}, \quad \mathbf{D}_1^i = \begin{bmatrix} p_{1,1}\mathbf{D}_1^{i,1} & p_{1,2}\mathbf{D}_1^{i,1} & \cdots & p_{1,G}\mathbf{D}_1^{i,1} \\ p_{2,1}\mathbf{D}_1^{i,2} & p_{2,2}\mathbf{D}_1^{i,2} & \cdots & p_{2,G}\mathbf{D}_1^{i,2} \\ \vdots & \vdots & \ddots & \vdots \\ p_{G,1}\mathbf{D}_1^{i,G} & p_{G,2}\mathbf{D}_1^{i,G} & \cdots & p_{G,G}\mathbf{D}_1^{i,G} \end{bmatrix}. \quad (6)$$

The $\mathbf{D}_0^i$ matrix specifies that the service demands of a session generated by a group g follow its service demand distribution model $\mathbf{D}^{i,g}$; the $\mathbf{D}_1^i$ matrix describes the modulation due to the session submission policy $\mathbf{P}$.

The fundamental result achieved by the composition step described above is that the benchmark burstiness model $\mathbf{D}^i$ defined for a performance attribute i lets us evaluate by closed-form analytical expressions the burstiness in the service demands for performance attribute i due to the benchmark B. Under positive autocorrelations, burstiness levels for a performance attribute can be evaluated and specified by the *index of dispersion* [10]

$$ I = CV^2 (1 + 2 \sum_{k=1}^{\infty} \rho(k)), $$

where CV is the coefficient of variation of the service demands, $\rho(k)$ is the lag-k autocorrelation coefficient of the service demands, see [10,15] for further information. The autocorrelation function $\rho(k)$ is often used as a more accurate burstiness descriptor than the index of dispersion I, therefore we consider both in the rest of the paper. For the model $(\mathbf{D}_0^i, \mathbf{D}_1^i)$, the service demand of performance attribute i has moments

$$ E[D_i^k] = k! \pi_e (-\mathbf{D}_0^i)^{-k} \mathbf{e}, \tag{7} $$

where $E[D_i^k]$ is kth moment of the service demand of the benchmark B on performance attribute i, and $\pi_e = \pi_e(-\mathbf{D}_0^i)^{-1}\mathbf{D}_1^i$ describes the equilibrium state of the MAP. The index of dispersion of performance attribute i which quantifies its burstiness levels is given by

$$ I(i) = 1 + 2 \left(E[D_i] - \frac{\pi_e}{E[D_i]} \mathbf{D}_1^i (\mathbf{D}_0^i + \mathbf{D}_1^i + \mathbf{e}\pi_e)\mathbf{D}_1^i \mathbf{e} \right). \tag{8} $$

Equation (8) shows the full potential of our model-based methodology: starting from the characterization of the session groups and of the submission policy, we are able to evaluate the burstiness of the service demands for all performance attributes of all servers before running the benchmark. This fundamental result is exploited below to search for a submission policy $\mathbf{P}$ that introduces the desired burstiness in the system.

4.3   Searching for a Submission Policy to Match Burstiness

Finally, we use a nonlinear optimization program to search for policy $\mathbf{P}$ that provides the desired levels of burstiness in the service demands. Our approach is to evaluate iteratively the burstiness generated by several policies $\mathbf{P}$ and choose the one that is closest to the target burstiness specified by the user. Additionally, the optimization is constrained on the benchmark B generating the predefined session group mix $\boldsymbol{\gamma}$. Due to limited space, we exemplify the generation of burstiness for a performance attribute i to match a given index of dispersion value $I_{target}(i)$. This is achieved by the following nonlinear optimization program

$$\min_{\mathbf{P}} z = |I(i) - I_{target}(i)| \quad s.t. \tag{9}$$

$$(\mathbf{D}_0^i, \mathbf{D}_1^i) = f^i(\mathbf{D}^{i,j}, \mathbf{P}); \tag{10}$$

$$I(i) = 1 + 2 \left(E[D_i] - E[D_i]^{-1} \boldsymbol{\pi}_e \mathbf{D}_1^i (\mathbf{D}_0^i + \mathbf{D}_1^i + \mathbf{e}\boldsymbol{\pi}_e) \mathbf{D}_1^i \mathbf{e} \right); \tag{11}$$

$$E[D_i] = \boldsymbol{\pi}_e(-\mathbf{D}_0^i)^{-1}\mathbf{e}; \tag{12}$$

$$\boldsymbol{\pi}_e = \boldsymbol{\pi}_e(-\mathbf{D}_0^i)^{-1}\mathbf{D}_1^i; \tag{13}$$

$$\mathbf{P}\mathbf{e} = \mathbf{e}; \tag{14}$$

$$\mathbf{P} \geq \mathbf{0}; \tag{15}$$

$$\boldsymbol{\gamma}\mathbf{P} = \boldsymbol{\gamma}; \tag{16}$$

where $\mathbf{e}$ is a column vector of size G composed of all ones. The search is on the entries of the policy $\mathbf{P}$ which minimize the difference between the target index of dispersion and the one estimated for the service demands of performance attribute i based on the $f^i(\mathbf{D}^{i,j}, \mathbf{P})$ mapping. The constraints are of three types: (11)-(13) are the formulas for computing the index of dispersion I applied to the burstiness model $(\mathbf{D}_0^i, \mathbf{D}_1^i)$; (14)-(15) impose that $\mathbf{P}$ is a stochastic matrix; finally, (16) imposes the session group mix $\boldsymbol{\gamma}$.

The nonlinear program (9)-(16) returns a session submission policy $\mathbf{P}$ that achieves the stated goal of this paper of creating a benchmark B with the desired burstiness I_{target} in a performance attribute i. Theoretically, there are no limits to the maximum achievable index of dispersion in a server, yet very large values create long-range dependence that requires very long executions of the benchmark in order to realize the desired level of burstiness [7]. Although the optimization program is nonlinear, we have found it in practice easy to solve. In the experiments reported in Section 5, we always obtained good solutions in less than one minute.

If one is interested in generating controlled burstiness in several performance attributes simultaneously, it is possible either to consider multiple objective functions, one for each performance attribute of interest, or to inject burstiness into the aggregate service demand of the sessions, i.e., the round-trip time of a session when executed in isolation on the system. For instance, for a system with a front server and a database server, the aggregate service demand is $A = D^{front} + D^{db}$, where D^{front} and D^{db} are service demands at the two servers. We illustrate the effectiveness of this approach in the first case study proposed in the next section.

4.4   Generating Dynamic Bottleneck Switches

Finally, we discuss the relation between generation of burstiness and dynamic bottleneck switches. As observed in [15], significant performance degradation due to burstiness is observed mainly if there are dynamic bottleneck switches between the resources that create adverse queueing conditions. For instance, in the TPC-W benchmark it is observed that the *Best Seller* transaction places a very high demand at the database server CPU while in execution. Due to burstiness, several *Best Seller* transactions may be scheduled for execution consecutively, this results in the front server CPU and the database server CPU cyclically alternating the role of bottleneck in the system.

From the above discussion, it follows naturally that the basic requirement for the benchmark B to create dynamic bottleneck switches between M performance attributes is that there exist for each attribute $m = 1, \ldots, M$ at least a group g that places an average service demand $E[D_{grp,g}]$ on m that is bigger than the average demand placed on any other performance attribute in the system. This implies that when the policy $\mathbf{P}$ starts to draw consecutively from the group g as in the example of Section 4.1, then resource m would become the system bottleneck until $\mathbf{P}$ chooses another group to sample from. Our technique exploits the service demand models to construct benchmarks that will cause a bottleneck switch. One such benchmark is discussed in detail in Section 5.

5 Validation Experiments

To show that our benchmark generation approach is effective in creating controlled burstiness, we present a case study that considers a particular combination of the browsing, ordering, and shopping mix benchmarks of TPC-W. The resulting benchmark B is run on a real testbed; we consider CPU usage at the different computing nodes as performance attributes. The testbed consists of a front server node, a database node, and a client node connected by a non-blocking Ethernet switch that provides a dedicated 1 Gbps connectivity between any two machines in the setup. The front server and database nodes are used to execute the TPC-W bookstore application implemented at Rice University [1]. The client node is dedicated for running the httperf Web request generator. This was configured to emulate multiple concurrent sessions in our experiments. The httperf generator has features such as non-blocking socket calls that allow it to stress servers and sustain overloads without the need for multiple client nodes. All nodes in the setup contain an Intel 2.66 GHZ Core 2 CPU and 2 GB of RAM. The Windows perfmon utility is used to gather CPU, disk, memory, and network usage at the server nodes; httperf provides detailed logs of end user response times. In all our experiments we noticed very little disk, paging, and network activity.

Throughout the experiments, we have used pre-existing test suites created to follow the shopping, browsing, and ordering mixes specified by TPC-W. The matrix $\mathbf{P}$ that results from the benchmark generation step is used to construct a trace of 10,000 sessions with desired mix and burstiness and that combines the three test suites. Finally, httperf is used to submit the session trace to the system. Due to limited space, we report below only two case studies, but we remark that we have considered several other experiments resulting in qualitatively similar results to those reported below.

5.1   Validation of Service Demand and Burstiness Models

We first consider a benchmark B defined only by a mix of sessions of shopping (shp) and ordering (ord) type. The mix is balanced with group request mix $\gamma_{shp} = \gamma_{ord} = 0.50$, and we assume the session submission policy $\mathbf{P}$ is assigned such that shopping (resp. ordering) sessions have a probability $p_{shp,shp} = 0.995$ (resp. $p_{ord,ord} = 0.995$) that the next session generated after them will be again of shopping (resp. ordering) type, i.e.,

$$\mathbf{P} = \begin{bmatrix} 0.995 & 0.005 \\ 0.005 & 0.995 \end{bmatrix}$$

The aim of this case study is to validate the prediction accuracy of the models proposed in Sections 3 and 4. Since it is hard to obtain direct measurement of the service demands, we focus on prediction of utilization and aggregate service demand measurements for the sessions executed in isolation on the system.

For the group service demand model definition, we have run in isolation the shopping and ordering benchmarks and estimated the mean session demands for each of the session types used in the these mixes. Table 1 presents results. The table shows the estimated moments for the different CPU service demands and the respective moments of the phase-type distributions we have fitted; the number of states we have used in the phase-type models is always less than 7. The results indicate that the phase-type distributions match very well mean and CV of the measured group service demands, while they slightly underestimate the value of the skewness probably due to the difficulty in modeling in a Markovian setting the nearly-deterministic demand of individual session types. Using the phase-type distributions $\mathbf{D}^{i,g}$ and the policy $\mathbf{P}$, we have then defined the MAPs that describe the CPU service demands at the front server $\mathbf{D}^{fs}$ and at the database server $\mathbf{D}^{db}$. We have also defined a MAP to describe the aggregate service demand of the sessions generated by B: assuming that each session visits the front server and database server once before completing execution, the MAP that captures the aggregate service demands has $(\mathbf{D}_0, \mathbf{D}_1)$ representation, denoted by $(\mathbf{A}_0, \mathbf{A}_1)$, which is a simple combination of $\mathbf{D}^{fs,shp}$, $\mathbf{D}^{db,shp}$, $\mathbf{D}^{fs,ord}$, $\mathbf{D}^{db,ord}$ weighted by the probabilities $p_{ord,ord}$ and $p_{shp,shp}$ similarly to (6).

Figure 3(a) compares the cumulative distribution function (CDF) for the aggregate service demand of the benchmark B sessions with the ones predicted

Table 1. Group service demand models for CPU. Means are expressed in seconds

	front server demand			DB server demand		
shopping	_mean_	_CV_	_skew_	_mean_	_CV_	_skew_
measured	0.290	0.575	2.671	0.097	7.590	4.509
phase-type	0.290	0.575	1.665	0.097	7.591	3.161
ordering	_mean_	_CV_	_skew_	_mean_	_CV_	_skew_
measured	0.131	0.805	1.797	0.623	1.761	2.530
phase-type	0.131	0.805	1.328	0.623	1.340	2.002

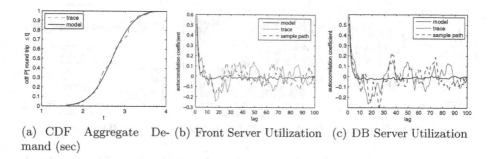

(a) CDF Aggregate Demand (sec)   (b) Front Server Utilization   (c) DB Server Utilization

Fig. 3. Experimental results for the mix of shopping and ordering sessions

by the $(\mathbf{A}_0, \mathbf{A}_1)$ model. The distribution of the MAP matches the empirical distribution of the aggregate service demand very well, thus suggesting the effectiveness of our demand models in capturing the distribution of the service demands. Using $(\mathbf{A}_0, \mathbf{A}_1)$, we have also compared the burstiness of the aggregate service demands predicted by the model with the one measured on the real system using the autocorrelation function as a descriptor of burstiness [17]. The result (not shown graphically due to limited space) indicates good prediction accuracy, with the aggregate service demand autocorrelation coefficients quickly decaying to zero for both the model and the measurements, and with the lag-1 coefficient being $\rho(1) = 0.028$ for the measured aggregate service demands and $\rho(1) = 0.039$ for the $(\mathbf{A}_0, \mathbf{A}_1)$ model.

The results of the aggregate service demand analysis suggest that the models developed in Sections 3 and 4 capture service demands very well, otherwise it would be hard to predict accurately aggregate service demands distribution and burstiness for sessions of the benchmark B. To further validate accuracy, we have also performed a trace-driven analysis of the system to compare the properties of the measured utilizations with those predicted by the MAP models. Figure 3(b)-(c) show the autocorrelation function of the measured and modeled CPU utilizations for the front server and database server, respectively. The autocorrelations of the model are estimated by averaging the autocorrelations over 100 random experiments; conversely, the sample path curve shows a representative example of autocorrelation estimate for one of these random experiments. The results are qualitatively similar for both servers suggesting that the session generation policy impacts equally on the two tiers. For low lags, model and sample path autocorrelations are in very good agreement with the TPC-W trace. Low lags are the most significant for burstiness, as they measure the similarities of consecutive sessions that pack into bursts, while high lags are mostly related to the length of these bursts. The autocorrelation coefficient values for lags greater than 10 seem instead to suffer significant noise due to limited size of the measurement due to the utilization sampling; the presence of noise is proved by the difference between the sample path curve and the model results averaged over 100 experiments. Yet, the good agreement of the sample path with the

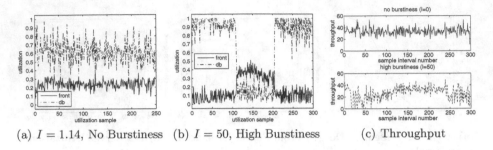

(a) $I = 1.14$, No Burstiness   (b) $I = 50$, High Burstiness   (c) Throughput

Fig. 4. CPU utilization and session throughput for the bursty and the non-bursty benchmarks

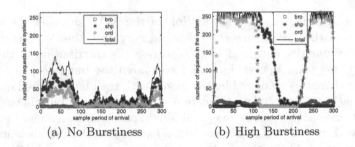

(a) No Burstiness   (b) High Burstiness

Fig. 5. Time series showing the number of requests that are concurrently served by the multi-tier application during each experiment. Measurements are taken at the instant of arrival of a new request.

trace proves that sample paths of the MAP model are representative of system behavior observed in real experiments.

Summarizing, the experiments in this section suggest that the proposed phase-type and MAP models can summarize and predict effectively the properties of the demands in both the pre-existing benchmark suites and in the composed benchmark B. The next case study focuses instead on the quality and practical impact of the burstiness generation methodology.

5.2   Generation of Burstiness and Its Impact

We consider a mix of ordering, browsing and shopping sessions, but we now focus on generating benchmarks to evaluate the performance of the TPC-W system under burstiness conditions. The results presented in this section prove that this can be done successfully with the proposed methodology and prove the existence of scalability problems for systems that are not revealed by executions of traditional benchmarks without burstiness.

Solving the nonlinear optimization program defined in Section 4.3 with the fmincon function of MATLAB 7.6.0, we have created two session submission

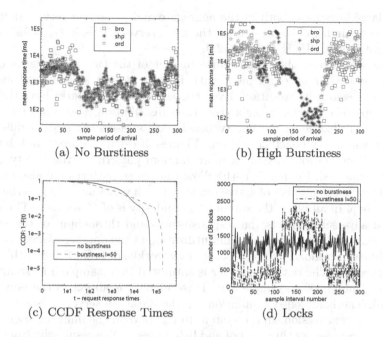

(a) No Burstiness

(b) High Burstiness

(c) CCDF Response Times

(d) Locks

Fig. 6. Performance effects of the dynamic bottleneck switch

policies $\mathbf{P}_{non-burst}$ and $\mathbf{P}_{high-burst}$ that both combine browsing (*bro*), shopping (*shp*) and ordering (*ord*) sessions with group mix $\gamma_{bro} = 0.014$ and $\gamma_{shp} = \gamma_{ord} = 0.493$. The group mix is essentially the same as in Section 5.1, but there is in our workload also a component of about $100 - 200$ browsing sessions which shows that our methodology can apply also to combination of more than two test suites. Only a limited fraction of browsing sessions is used to avoid having a bottleneck switch due to this test suite and not to the policy P that we want to validate. In fact, the browsing mix is known to impose fluctuations between front server and database server CPU utilizations [15]. The two policies differ only with respect to the index of dispersion values in the aggregate demand. The *non-bursty benchmark* defined by $\mathbf{P}_{non-burst}$ has index of dispersion in the aggregate demand $I = 1.14$, which is a case corresponding to the removal of burstiness by imposing a zero value for all the autocorrelation coefficients[2]. This also results in negligible burstiness in the service demands at the server CPUs: the expected index of dispersions at the front server CPUs and at the database server CPUs are $I_{fs} = 0.82$ and $I_{db} = 2.11$, respectively. The scale of the index of dispersion is comparable to the scale of the squared coefficient of variation CV^2, thus $I < 1$ indicates low or no burstiness, whereas I of the order of tens or more generally stands for high burstiness. The *high-burstiness benchmark* defined by $\mathbf{P}_{high-burst}$ has index of dispersion $I = 50$ in the aggregate demand, which

---

[2] In fact, in this workload $CV^2 = 1.14$, thus $I = CV^2$ implies from the definition of the index of dispersion that $\sum_{k=1}^{\infty} \rho(k) = 0$.

creates large burstiness both in the aggregate and per-server service demands. The expected index of dispersion for the front server CPUs is $I_{fs} = 597.34$ and for the database CPUs is $I_{db} = 2242.9$.

Figure 4 compares the performance impact of the two benchmarks on the TPC-W system for an experiment with Poisson session arrivals and multiple concurrent sessions in execution. Even though both benchmarks have the same session type mix, session inter-arrival time distribution, and almost identical server CPU utilizations, the bursty benchmark stresses the system differently than the non-bursty benchmark. From Figures 4(a)-(b), the front and database server CPU utilizations display a more random pattern for the bursty benchmark. As expected, Figures 5(a)-(b) show that these patterns are also reflected immediately in the number of active requests which varies according to the active session group. In all plots, the sampling granularity is of 15 seconds. The bursty workload adversely impacts the responsiveness and throughput of the system. From Figures 4(a)-(b), the maximum utilization of the database server is higher for the bursty workload than the non-bursty workload. From Figure 4(b), it can be observed that the database server is saturated from sample 0 to sample 100 and from sample 200 to sample 300. This behavior is absent in the non-bursty workload. The heightened contention for the database server causes the number of concurrent sessions in the system to rise beyond the limit imposed by the sizes of the front server thread pool and listen queue. As a result, the front server drops several connections leading to a 25% drop in request throughput relative to the non-bursty case. This is evident also in Figure 4(c) which illustrates the number of successfully completed sessions over time. The figure clearly indicates that for the bursty workload the throughput of successfully completed sessions drops below acceptable levels frequently when the database is saturated, whereas throughput is steady in the non-bursty case.

The experiments also reveal that burstiness can cause bottleneck switches that can introduce unpredictable transient behavior into the system. From Figure 4(b), the system bottleneck switches from the database server to the front server near the 100th sample. In contrast, from Figure 4(a), there is no bottleneck switch with the non-bursty workload. The bottleneck switch is caused due to a transition from the database intensive browsing and ordering sessions to the front server intensive shopping sessions in the bursty workload. It can be observed from Figure 5(b) that there is a significant accumulation of shopping sessions in the system exactly at the time of the bottleneck switch, as visible around sample 110 by the number of ordering sessions decreasing while shopping sessions accumulate at a fast rate. This large accumulation of shopping sessions is caused because of these sessions being delayed by the last of the bro wsing and ordering sessions at the database server. As a result of this dynamic, it takes the system around 12 minutes spanning the period from sample 110 to sample 160 to significantly reduce the backlog of shopping sessions. This type of unstable transient behavior was not observed with the non-bursty workload and represents a unique feature of burstiness that cannot be exposed with non-bursty submission policies or by running the two benchmarks in isolation. Specifically, such techniques would result in no backlog for the shopping sessions and therefore would never exhibit the properties highlighted in Figure 5(b).

Furthermore, the accumulation of the backlog due to bottleneck switch dominates the response time results presented in Figure 6. Figure 6(a)-(b) show the mean response times of requests over time. Specifically, Figure 6(b) shows many important points for our analysis. First, ordering and browsing sessions have considerably larger response times when executed on the system from sample 0 to sample 110 and from sample 210 to 300 than in the corresponding periods of the non-bursty benchmark in Figure 6(a). This suggests that burstiness is more critical for the response times of browsing and ordering sessions which are both database intensive and hence place a strongest congestion level if they are executed in the system without shopping sessions interleaved between them that can alleviate the bottleneck by shifting more load on the front server. The second fundamental observation is that, from sample 110 to 130, the first shopping sessions entering into the system receive dramatically large response times due to the bottleneck switch phenomena. Progressively, as the backlog is flushed response times display a reducing trend. From sample 160 the response times of shopping sessions is lower than in the no-burstiness case, suggesting that the front server can cope well with this level of parallelism for shopping sessions. Finally, it is important to observe that the introduction of burstiness has eventually resulted into a generalized spread of delays, with the exception of the small range from sample 160 to 200. Figure 6(c) compares request response times under the bursty and non-bursty benchmarks: most of the requests without burstiness are served in less than 10 seconds, however more than 20% of the requests in the bursty benchmark require at least 100 seconds to be completed, thus making the point that our approach is better suited than other approaches for stress testing.

Finally, Figure 6(d) plots for both the bursty and non-bursty benchmark the number of database queries that are waiting to acquire locks for rows in the database. From the figure the bursty workload causes heightened contention for locks after the first bottleneck switch. Recall that the bottleneck switch was caused by the arrival of a burst of shopping sessions. Furthermore, shopping sessions rely on a common set of data. Consequently, the burst of shopping sessions causes increased locking activity in the system while accessing this common data set. In contrast, the non-bursty workload does not contain significant bursts of sessions of similar type and as a result does not expose heightened lock contention and the associated performance implications.

6 Conclusion

We have proposed a model-based methodology for the automatic generation of benchmarks with customizable levels of burstiness in the service demands. Our methodology extends existing approaches for automatic synthesis of benchmarks such as SWAT [12]. Experiments on a real TPC-W testbed have shown that the proposed models are very accurate in predicting the service demands and their burstiness at the different tiers of the architecture. We have shown a case where the ordering and shopping mixes of TPC-W have been combined to inject controlled burstiness in the demands resulting in critical stress conditions for performance that are not shown by non-bursty combinations of the two mixes.

We plan to further develop and validate this new approach within a framework that aims to characterize, synthesize, and predict the impact of burstiness on multi-tier systems. We want to further investigate in detail the various kinds of system level degradations that can be caused by burstiness and study how to specify groups given different alternatives. Finally, a point that needs to be investigated in future work is to assess the validity of the proposed techniques in presence of long lived sessions, such as those performing long database queries that may take several minutes to execute and may suffer considerable variability in running times. Under these conditions, it may be needed to define ad-hoc estimators for the demand variance of such transactions. Given such variance estimates, a possible approach to extend our methodology could be to isolate these sessions into separate groups and have a phase-type distribution of their demand, however further work is needed to assess the feasibility of this approach.

Acknowledgements

This research was partially funded by the InvestNI/SAP project MORE and by grants from the Natural Sciences and Engineering Research Council of Canada (NSERC). We thank Stephen Dawson for helpful feedback during the preparation of this work.

References

1. Amza, C., Ch, A., Cox, A.L., Elnikety, S., Gil, R., Rajamani, K., Cecchet, E., Marguerite, J.: Specification and implementation of dynamic web site benchmarks. In: Proc. of WWC workshop, Austin, TX (November 2002)
2. Barford, P., Crovella, M.: Generating Representative Web Workloads for Network and Server Performance Evaluation. ACM PER 26(1), 151–160 (1998)
3. Bolch, G., Greiner, S., de Meer, H., Trivedi, K.S.: Queueing Networks and Markov Chains. Wiley, Chichester (2006)
4. Casale, G., Kalbasi, A., Krishnamurthy, D., Rolia, J.: Automated Stress Testing of Multi-Tier Systems by Dynamic Bottleneck Switch Generation. University of Calgary Technical Report SERG-2009-02 (April 2009), http://people.ucalgary.ca/~dkrishna/SERG-2009-02.pdf
5. Casale, G., Kalbasi, A., Krishnamurthy, D., Rolia, J.: Automatically Generating Bursty Benchmarks for Multi-Tier Systems. Presented at the 2nd Workshop on Hot Topics in Measurement and Modeling of Computer Systems (HotMetrics) (June 2009), http://www.sigmetrics.org/conferences/sigmetrics/2009/workshops/papers_hotmetrics/session2_1.pdf
6. Casale, G., Mi, N., Smirni, E.: Bound analysis of closed queueing networks with workload burstiness. In: Proc. of ACM SIGMETRICS, pp. 13–24 (2008)
7. Crovella, M., Lipsky, L.: Long-Lasting Transient Conditions in Simulations with Heavy-Tailed Workloads. In: Winter Simulation Conference, pp. 1005–1012 (1997)

8. Dujmovic, J.J.: Universal benchmark suites. In: Proc. of MASCOTS, pp. 197–205 (1999)
9. Grace, R.: The benchmark book. Prentice Hall, Englewood Cliffs (1996)
10. Heindl, A.: Traffic-Based Decomposition of General Queueing Networks with Correlated Input Processes. Ph.D. Thesis. Shaker Verlag, Aachen (2001)
11. Kant, K., Tewary, V., Iyer, R.: An Internet Traffic Generator for Server Architecture Evaluation. In: Proc. CAECW (January 2001)
12. Krishnamurthy, D., Rolia, J.A., Majumdar, S.: A synthetic workload generation technique for stress testing session-based systems. IEEE Trans. Soft. Eng. 32(11), 868–882 (2006)
13. Krishnaswamy, U., Scherson, D.: A framework for computer performance evaluation using benchmark sets. IEEE Trans. on Computers 49(12), 1325–1338 (2000)
14. Leland, W.E., Taqqu, M.S., Willinger, W., Wilson, D.V.: On the self-similar nature of ethernet traffic. IEEE/ACM Trans. on Networking 2(1), 1–15 (1994)
15. Mi, N., Casale, G., Cherkasova, L., Smirni, E.: Burstiness in multi-tier applications: Symptoms, causes, and new models. In: Issarny, V., Schantz, R. (eds.) Middleware 2008. LNCS, vol. 5346, pp. 265–286. Springer, Heidelberg (2008)
16. Mi, N., Casale, G., Cherkasova, L., Smirni, E.: Injecting Realistic Burstiness to a Traditional Client-Server Benchmark. In: Proc. of ICAC, June 2009, pp. 149–158 (2009)
17. Mi, N., Zhang, Q., Riska, A., Smirni, E., Riedel, E.: Performance impacts of auto-correlated flows in multi-tiered systems. Perf. Eval. 64(9-12), 1082–1101 (2007)
18. Riska, A., Riedel, E.: Long-range dependence at the disk drive level. In: Proc. of QEST, pp. 41–50 (2006)
19. Rolia, J., Krishnamurthy, D., Kalbasi, A., Dawson, S.: Resource demand modeling for complex services (under submission)

DSF: A Common Platform for Distributed Systems Research and Development

Chunqiang Tang

IBM T.J. Watson Research Center
ctang@us.ibm.com

Abstract. This paper presents Distributed Systems Foundation (DSF), a common platform for distributed systems research and development. It can run a distributed algorithm written in Java under multiple execution modes—simulation, massive multi-tenancy, and real deployment. DSF provides a set of novel features to facilitate testing and debugging, including chaotic timing test and time travel debugging with mutable replay. Unlike existing research prototypes that offer advanced debugging features by hacking programming tools, DSF is written entirely in Java, without modifications to any external tools such as JVM, Java runtime library, compiler, linker, system library, OS, or hypervisor. This simplicity stems from our goal of making DSF not only a research prototype but more importantly a production tool. Experiments show that DSF is efficient and easy to use. DSF's massive multi-tenancy mode can run 4,000 OS-level threads in a single JVM to concurrently execute (as opposed to simulate) 1,000 DHT nodes in real-time.

Keywords: distributed systems, simulation, debugging, mutable replay, massive multi-tenancy, chaotic timing test.

1 Introduction

Nowadays, almost every application becomes distributed for one reason or another. Their functions are diverse and their working environments are heterogeneous, ranging from small embedded devices for home healthcare monitoring, to large mainframe servers for extremely reliable transaction processing. Despite their prevalence, it still remains challenging to build robust and high-performance distributed systems, simply because of their very nature: concurrent and asynchronous execution in potentially volatile and failure-prone environments. For example, the "simple" Paxos algorithm was invented in 1990, while its robust implementation remained a challenging problem that was worth publishing in a top research conference in 2007 [1].

In the past, several complimentary methods have been proposed to facilitate the development of distributed systems:

- **Simulation** [6,10,12]: Provide a framework that can execute the same code of a distributed algorithm in both simulation and real deployment. The simulation mode eases the tasks of testing and debugging.

J.M. Bacon and B.F. Cooper (Eds.): Middleware 2009, LNCS 5896, pp. 414–436, 2009.
© IFIP International Federation for Information Processing 2009

- **Deterministic replay** [3,7,8,15,17]: Log application activities during normal execution and, if a bug shows up, replay the execution flow to precisely repeat the bug. This helps capture elusive, unreproducible bugs.

- **Fault injection** [16]: Provide a framework that automatically exercises a distributed application with various failure scenarios, which helps trigger bugs that do not show up under normal operations.

- **Model checking** [11,13,20]: Write assertions that an application's distributed states must satisfy, and then use a runtime or offline tool to discover violations of the assertions. This helps find a bug soon after its inception.

- **Code generation** [14]: Describe a distributed algorithm in a high-level specification language, and then use a tool to translate the specification into a real implementation. This method may help reduce both the development effort and the chance of introducing bugs.

These ideas have been well known for some time, and each of them provides certain benefits in lowering the difficulty of developing distributed systems. However, these ideas mostly still stay in research labs and their wide adoption in mainstream software development (either open-source or proprietary) is yet to be reported. One main reason of their limited adoption is that they often deviate from the mainstream programming environments and rely on customized programming tools that are not familiar to layman programmers, e.g., an "extended" programming language or a hacked hypervisor, OS, runtime, compiler, linker, etc. Moreover, customized tools also limit the lifetime of a research prototype, due to the lack of long-term support and inability to keep up with the evolution of mainstream programming tools.

1.1   Distributed Systems Foundation (DSF)

The authors develop both research prototypes and commercial software products at IBM. Like many past efforts, we build our own framework, called *Distributed Systems Foundation (DSF)*, to ease the task of developing distributed systems. For practical reasons, the design of DSF strictly follows one rule: *no hacking programming tools*. DSF is written entirely in Java, without hacking any external tools such as JVM, Java runtime library, compiler, linker, system library, OS, or hypervisor. We strongly believe that this simplicity is key to ensuring that DSF has a long life as programming tools evolve, and this simplicity is also crucial to the success of DSF not only as a research prototype but more importantly as a production tool.

Like previous work, DSF provides some well-known features to facilitate testing and debugging, including simulation, deterministic replay, fault injection, and model checking. In addition, DSF offers several novel features not available in previous work:

- **Mutable replay:** After observing an elusive bug, the most popular debugging technique perhaps is to add code to do detailed logging for activities related to the bug, re-compile the program, and then run it again, hoping that the bug will show up again but with detailed information logged this time. All existing deterministic replay methods [3,7,8,15,17], however, do not support this popular debugging practice, because they cannot replay a modified program even if the modification has no side effects on the application logic, e.g., simple read-only statements for logging or assertion. Moreover, even if the executable of the program does not change, those methods cannot replay the program with a changed configuration, e.g., changing the logging level of *log4j* from "INFO" to "DEBUG" in order to log detailed debug information. By contrast, DSF supports *mutable replay*. For the example above, DSF guarantees that the bug precisely repeats itself in the replay run as in the original run, while the added (or newly enabled) debugging code logs more information to help pinpoint the root cause of the bug. Moreover, after the code is changed to fix the bug (which is almost certain to have side effects on the application logic), DSF can deterministically replay the original execution flow until right before the new code, and then start to execute the new code and test whether the bug still shows up.

- **Chaotic timing test:** Because of the concurrent and asynchronous nature of distributed systems, many elusive, unreproducible bugs are caused by unexpected interaction sequences between distributed components or unexpected timing of these events. In addition to fault injection [16], DSF introduces randomized, chaotic timing to all event executions in order to systematically exercise a distributed system under diverse timing, by drastically varying delays in thread scheduling, timer wake-up, message propagation, and message processing. Because of this feature, DSF's simulation mode overcomes many limitations of existing systems' simulation modes [10,12], and (in terms of finding bugs) is actually as powerful as a combination of their real deployment mode and simulation mode (see Section 6).

- **Massive multi-tenancy:** In addition to the simulation mode and the real deployment mode, DSF also provides the *massive multi-tenancy mode* that is not available in previous work. With a careful design and implementation, this extremely efficient mode can run thousands of OS-level threads inside a single JVM (i.e., one OS process) to concurrently execute (as opposed to simulate) thousands of instances of a distributed algorithm (e.g., thousands of DHT nodes) in real-time. This not only simplifies testing and debugging, but also makes elusive race condition bugs and subtle performance bugs more evident, due to the severe contention among thousands of threads.

Setting up large-scale distributed testing on many servers is hard, due to both hardware resource constraints and human resource constraints (time and efforts). Moreover, chasing an elusive bug in such a setting can be time consuming, because pieces of the program states related to the bug may be scattered on different servers. One focus in DSF is to test and debug a large-scale setup of a distributed algorithm inside *a single JVM*. The massive multi-tenancy mode and the simulation mode with chaotic timing test are motivated by this need, which allow DSF to trigger most bugs (even those elusive race condition bugs) in a single JVM. Moreover, with all the states of a distributed algorithm readily available in one JVM, these two execution modes allow the user to easily write model checking code to catch violations of global invariants, or to use an interactive debugger to inspect all data structures related to a bug, even if they logically belong to different "distributed" components.

1.2 Contributions

As veteran developers of both research and commercial distributed systems, we constantly feel the pain of low productivity, and DSF grew out of our own needs. DSF takes a pragmatic approach while offering many advanced features. Specifically, we make the following contributions in this paper:

- **Simplicity:** Unlike previous work, DSF offers many advanced features (including simulation, deterministic replay, fault injection, and model checking) without hacking any programming tools. We believe that this simplicity is crucial to the success of DSF not only as a research prototype but more importantly as a production tool.

- **Novel features:** DSF provides several novel features not available in previous work, including mutable replay, chaotic timing test, and massive multi-tenancy. These features help significantly improve development productivity.

- **Implementation:** We build a solid implementation of DSF, demonstrating that our ideas are not only feasible but can also be implemented efficiently. For example, DSF's massive multi-tenancy mode is capable of running 4,000 OS-level threads in a single JVM to concurrently execute 1,000 DHT nodes in real-time.

2   Overview of DSF

This section presents an overview of DSF. We first describe how DSF's API virtualization approach helps improve application portability. We then discuss the challenges in testing and debugging, and how DSF's different execution modes (simulation, massive multi-tenancy, and real deployment) help address these challenges.

2.1   Portability through API Virtualization

Since DSF is written in Java, portability might seem trivial but it is actually not. DSF's implementations of distributed algorithms are intended for broad code reuse across many applications, from small embedded systems to large mainframe servers. Even for tasks as simple as sending a network message, the network APIs vary in different environments.

For servers that can run Java 2 Standard Edition (J2SE), it is natural to implement network communication using the high-performance non-blocking *java.nio* package. For embedded systems that can only run Java 2 Micro Edition (J2ME), *java.nio* is not available and network communication has to use the less efficient *java.net* package. This was exactly the problem faced by people who tried to port FreePastry to J2ME (see https://mailman.rice.edu/pipermail/freepastry-discussion-l/2005-April/000030.html).

Moreover, sophisticated commercial products and open source projects may even mandate the use of certain powerful network packages so that all components handle issues such as security and firewall tunneling in a uniform manner. Examples include Apache FtpServer built atop the Apache MINA network framework, and IBM WebSphere [9] built atop the WebSphere Channel Framework.

Our solution to the portability problem is API virtualization. Figure 1 shows the architecture of DSF, where the DSF APIs provide a programming environment that isolates platform-dependent details. For example, distributed algorithms simply use *TCP.send(Message)* for network communication, and then can run on different platforms, by plugging in different implementations of *TCP.send()*.

2.2   Challenges in Testing and Debugging

Distributed systems are notoriously hard to test and debug, which often consume the biggest fraction of the development time, due to the very nature of distributed systems.

- **Hard to set up large-scale testing:** In most organizations, a developer has only a handful of development machines, and can do large-scale testing only for limited time, by carefully coordinating machine usage with many other developers. This inconvenience results in not only low productivity for developers, but also insufficient testing of code.

- **Unexpected failures:** During design and implementation, it is hard to fully anticipate all possible failure scenarios of distributed components, while a single unexpected failure can move the system into an incorrect state.

- **Unexpected event timing:** During design and implementation, it is hard to fully anticipate all possible interaction sequences and event timing among

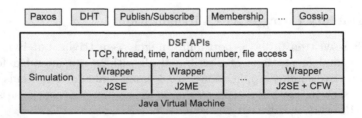

Fig. 1. Architecture of DSF. The DSF APIs are shown in Figure 3.

distributed components, while just one delayed thread activity or one message arriving at an unexpected time can move the system into an incorrect state.

- **Hard-to-repeat bugs:** Sometimes, automated testing may take days or even weeks to experience a rare race condition that triggers a bug. Because the race condition is unexpected, it is not uncommon that the log does not contain sufficient information to help pinpoint the root cause of the bug. After the developer adds more debugging code and then restarts the test, it may take a long time for the bug to show up again, or the bug may simply become dormant due to changes of non-deterministic factors in the execution environment.

- **Lack of a global view for checking global consistency:** Often, testing and debugging involves comparing the internal states of distributed components to catch inconsistency. For example, in an overlay network, if node X considers node Y as its neighbor, after some reasonable delay, Y should also consider X as its neighbor. Otherwise, it is a bug of inconsistency. Automated global consistency checking is difficult for a large-scale distributed system, because the states of its components scatter on different servers.

In addition to improving portability, DSF's API virtualization approach (see Figure 1) provides the opportunity of building a powerful testing and debugging framework to address the challenges described above. A distributed algorithm implemented on top of the DSF APIs can run in different execution modes (simulation, massive multi-tenancy, and real deployment), each of which offers certain advantages in testing and debugging. The DSF APIs are minimal and straightforward. They are listed in Figure 3 and will be discussed in Section 3. Below, we start our discussion with the simulation mode.

2.3 Simulation Mode

The simulation mode allows a developer to write the code of a distributed algorithm on a laptop, and then locally simulate its behavior of running on thousands of servers. During simulation, DSF can conduct large-scale failure tests by continuously failing servers and adding new servers. In the simulation mode, the states of all distributed components (e.g., thousands of DHT nodes) are available in a single JVM, which allows the developer to easily write a debug subroutine to check the global consistency of all nodes. Instead of defining a new scripting language (e.g., as in [12]) for checking consistency, we opt for having the developer write the checking subroutine in Java, because it is simple and flexible, and the developer perhaps has been familiar with doing that for local components since the very beginning of programming.

The timing of every event in DSF (e.g., thread delay, network delay, server failure time, and timer wake-up) is randomized, in order to fully exercise the code under diverse timing. The randomization, however, is controlled by a pseudo random number generator and hence the events are precisely repeatable if the generator is initialized with the same seed. After the developer encounters a bug, she can re-run the test in an interactive debugger and step through the code. The bug is repeatable, because all events are deterministically repeatable.

If the bug is triggered by a rare race condition, the simulation may take days or even weeks before the bug shows up. After observing the bug, what the developer wants is time travel back to, e.g., just five minutes before the bug happens, and then start to debug from there. DSF supports this by periodically checkpointing the simulation state into a file. After a bug happens, the developer can add debugging code to log more information, re-compile the program, and then instantly resume the simulation from a recent checkpoint. This saves weeks of time to re-run the simulation from the very beginning.

If the bug is in a colleague's code, the developer can send the checkpoint file to the colleague, who then can deterministically replay and reproduce the bug, even if the checkpoint was taken on one platform (e.g., Windows) while the colleague's re-run is on another platform (e.g., Linux). The checkpoint file contains the execution environment that triggers the bug. No additional efforts are needed to replicate the environment, which sometimes is hard to do.

DSF's implementation of checkpoint is a pure Java solution. It saves in a file the serialized representations of objects in the JVM. By contrast, traditional OS-level solutions checkpoint the process image of JVM, while traditional hypervisor-level solutions checkpoint the image of the entire OS. They are less flexible as they do not support the most popular practice of debugging—adding debugging code to check conditions or log more information. A replay run from an OS image or a JVM process image always executes exactly the same old code, and does not allow changing the Java program's source code or configurations such as logging level.

If the program reads or writes certain files, DSF saves those files' contents and states (e.g., a random access file's current file pointer position) along with the checkpoint, so that a later run resumed from the checkpoint sees exactly the same file contents and states as the original run does, even if those files have been modified since the checkpoint time.

2.4   Massive Multi-tenancy Mode

The simulation mode is helpful in finding and fixing bugs but it cannot discover all bugs. This is because the simulated implementation of the DSF APIs differs from the real implementation of the DSF APIs that is used in production environments. For example, because the two implementations handle DSF's thread pool APIs differently, the simulation mode may not discover certain synchronization bugs.

We address this problem by providing the massive multi-tenancy mode. It uses exactly the same implementation of the DSF APIs as that in the real deployment mode. Inside one JVM, it creates thousands of OS-level threads to do real-time execution (as opposed to simulation) of thousands of distributed components, e.g., thousands of DHT nodes. Each DHT node has its own thread pool and listens on a different TCP port. Although the nodes are in the same JVM, they still communicate through real TCP connections and the traffic goes through

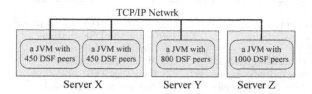

Fig. 2. Distributed multi-tenancy mode

the OS kernel, because the multi-tenancy mode uses the real implementation of the DSF APIs.

The massive multi-tenancy mode allows the developer to easily conduct large-scale testing of thousands of nodes on one powerful server. Because the states of all nodes are in one JVM, the multi-tenancy mode and the simulation mode can use the same debug subroutine to check the global consistency of all nodes. Moreover, synchronization bugs, timing bugs, and performance bugs all become more evident in the massive multi-tenancy mode, as thousands of threads compete for CPUs and their execution orders change constantly.

The scalability of the multi-tenancy mode is limited by the physical resources of one server. The distributed multi-tenancy mode in Figure 2 address this problem by connecting multiple servers running the multi-tenancy mode into one large distributed system. This mode differs from distributed simulation, because it uses the real implementation of the DSF APIs. In Figure 2, server X runs two JVMs instead of one JVM because sometimes one JVM may not be able to fully utilize the resources of a powerful server, due to JVM's internal bottlenecks.

2.5 Real Deployment Mode

Once the implementation of a distributed algorithm passes the rigorous tests in DSF and reaches a stable stage, it can be packaged into a library (i.e., one JAR file) together with an appropriate real implementation of the DSF APIs, and then widely reused by many different distributed applications. Those applications can simply use the high-level APIs provided by the distributed algorithm (e.g., the DHT APIs for routing and storage), and do not even need to know the existence of DSF or its APIs. That is, a distributed application as a whole need not conform to the DSF APIs.

3 The DSF APIs

This section presents the DSF APIs, which provide accesses to TCP, thread, time, random number, and file in a platform-independent manner. Distributed algorithms implemented on top of the DSF APIs are portable and can run in multiple execution modes, each of which offers certain advantages in testing and debugging. We use the term, *DSF runtime*, to refer to an implementation of the DSF APIs.

```
class Peer {
    Peer (Config config);              // Configure the DSF runtime.
    void start ();                     // Boot the DSF runtime.
    void stop ();                      // Emulate a failure.
    Endpoint getLocalEndpoint();       // IP and listening port.
    TCP tcpConnect (Endpoint server);  // Outgoing TCP.
    void submitJob (Runnable job);     // Submit to thread pool.
    void submitFifoJob (String fifoJobQueue, Runnable job);
    TimerHandle submitTimer (long delay, Timer timer); //Timer fires after "delay" ms.
    long localTime ();                 // Like System.currentTimeMillis()
    static Random random ();           // Deterministic in simulation.
    void registerService (String name, Object service);
    boolean deregisterService (String name, Object service);
    Object lookupService (String name);
    RandomAccessFileIfc getRandomAccessFile (String file, String mode);
}

class TCP {
    void send (Message msg);
    void close ();
    boolean registerTCPClosedCallback (TCPClosedCallback callback);
    boolean deregisterTCPClosedCallback (TCPClosedCallback callback);
}

class Message implements java.io.Serializable {
    Message (String fifoMsgQueue);
    void procMessage (Peer peer, TCP tcp);
}
```

Fig. 3. Summary of the DSF APIs

In Figure 3, the *Peer* class represents the execution environment seen by the distributed algorithm. This section uses a DHT algorithm as an example, for which one *Peer* object represents one DHT node. The program can create multiple *Peer* objects in one JVM in order to run multiple DHT nodes.

Node Start and Stop. Suppose the *DHTImpl* class contains the implementation of the DHT protocol. To start a new DHT node, the code creates a *Peer* object and a *DHTImpl* object, invokes *Peer.registerService("DHT", dhtImpl)* to register the *DHTImpl* object, and finally invokes *Peer.start()* to boot the DSF runtime. The code of *DHTImpl* invokes the methods of the *Peer* object to interact with the DSF runtime, e.g., sending messages or executing timers to do periodical DHT maintenance. DSF supports code componentization. Another module can invoke *Peer.lookupService("DHT")* to discover the registered DHT service, without being hard-wired with any particular DHT implementation. The class *Config* used in the constructor *Peer(Config)* specifies configurations such as the node's TCP listening port. The node's local IP address and TCP listening port can be obtained from *Peer.getLocalEndpoint()*, where *Endpoint* is a more efficient representation of *java.net.InetSocketAddress*. To emulate the failure of a DHT node, the testing code can invoke *Peer.stop()* to terminate the node.

TCP and Message. An outgoing TCP connection is created by invoking *Peer.tcpConnect(Endpoint server)*, which returns a *TCP* object. *TCP.send (Message)* sends an outgoing message. When the message arrives at the destination, *Message.procMessage(Peer, TCP)* is automatically invoked by the DSF runtime, where the argument *Peer* is the destination's execution environment, and the argument *TCP* is the connection over which the message arrived. Inside *Message.procMessage()*, the code can invoke *Peer.lookupService("DHT")* to retrieve the registered *DHTImpl* object to assist processing. The code can also use *TCP.registerTCPClosedCallback()* to register a callback, which will be invoked by the DSF runtime when the TCP connection breaks. In DSF, there is no *TCP.receive()*, because message processing is automatically invoked by the DSF runtime when a message arrives.

DSF is designed for developing high-performance implementations of distributed algorithms that can be directly used in production systems. Because massive multi-core processors will become prevalent in the near future, DSF strives to minimize synchronization and maximize concurrency. Following this principle, unless specifically required, the DSF runtime does not promise that it will invoke *Message.procMessage()* in sequential order for messages coming from the same TCP connection, because that would preclude concurrent message processing. For example, in a DHT implementation, a node X may send to another node Y multiple DHT lookup messages through one TCP connection. Unless there are specific semantic restrictions, it would be more efficient for Y to concurrently process these DHT lookup messages on multiple processors, instead of processing them in sequential order on one processor.

The argument of the constructor *Message(String fifoMsgQueue)* controls the order of message processing. Only messages from the same TCP connection and tagged with the same *fifoMsgQueue* are processed in sequential order. In addition to the message ordering specified by *fifoMsgQueue*, the "user code" can freely employ any synchronization mechanisms inside *Message.procMessage()* to protect critical regions. (*Note that, in the rest of this paper, we use the term, "user code", to refer to the code of a distributed algorithm written on top of the DSF APIs.*)

Currently, DSF provides no APIs for UDP communication. They can be added easily, but we explicitly discourage the use of UDP in production systems, because of the complications in security and firewall tunneling. This is a hard lesson we learned from our experience of productizing our research prototypes into WebSphere [9].

Timer and Thread Related Jobs. *Peer.submitTimer(long delay, Timer job)* submits a timer to be executed by the DSF runtime after "*delay*" milliseconds. DSF makes best efforts but does not guarantee the accuracy of the timer delay. Expired timers can run concurrently or in any order. DSF does not guarantee that a timer with expiration time x always executes before a timer with expiration time $x+1$.

Peer.submitJob(Runnable job) submits a job to be executed by the DSF runtime "immediately", which is semantically equivalent to (*new*

Thread(job)).start(). Submitted jobs can be executed concurrently or in any order. By contrast, *Peer.submitFifoJob(String fifoJobQueue, Runnable job)* provides the ordering guarantee. Jobs tagged with the same *fifoJobQueue* are executed in sequential order.

To maximize concurrency and to avoid potential deadlocks, the DSF runtime always invokes the user callback code (e.g., timers, jobs, and *Message.procMessage()*) without holding any locks. It is the developer's responsibility to implement proper synchronization, e.g., by using Java's *synchronized* language construct.

If the developer wants to run a distributed algorithm in the simulation mode and benefit from its testing and debugging capabilities, then the user code is not allowed to directly create its own threads or put threads into sleep by invoking *Thread.sleep(long delay)* or *Object.wait()*. Instead, it should use DSF's jobs or timers to implement the same function. Otherwise, the simulation mode cannot provide the feature of "precise replay of buggy runs," because the execution order of threads not under DSF's control is non-deterministic.

This restriction only applies to the part of the code that the developer wants to run in the simulation mode. If the developer merely uses libraries (e.g., DHT) developed in DSF to build an application and has no intention to run the entire application in the simulation mode, then the application need not follow this restriction and can use threads freely. See the related discussion in Section 2.5.

File Access. In the simulation mode, the DSF runtime periodically serializes and checkpoints the entire state of the program in order to support time travel debugging. Files accessed by the program are part of the state that should be saved in the checkpoint. However, Java's file utilities (e.g., *java.io.RandomAccessFile*) are not serializable and hence cannot be checkpointed. To work around this problem, the program should access files through objects returned by *Peer.getRandomAccessFile(String file, String mode)*. Those objects are serializable and provide functions identical to *java.io.RandomAccessFile*. The DSF APIs also provide the equivalences of other file utilities, including *java.io.FileReader*, *java.io.FileWriter*, *java.io.FileInputStream*, and *java.io.FileOutputStream*.

Random Number. Random numbers are widely used in distributed algorithms. For example, introducing randomness into timer delays helps avoid pathological synchronized behaviors of distributed nodes. To provide the feature of "precise replay of buggy runs," all random numbers used by the code must be pseudo random but actually deterministic in the simulation mode. One simple way to achieve this is to replace the statement *"new Random()"* with *"new Random(Peer.random().nextInt())"*, i.e., using a controlled pseudo random seed to initialize the random number generator. In the real deployment mode, *Peer.random()* is truly random. In the simulation mode, *Peer.random()* is deterministically controlled by *Config.randomSeed*.

System Time. To run properly in the simulation mode, the code should use *Peer.localTime()* to read system time. In the real deployment mode,

Peer.localTime() and *System.currentTimeMillis()* are identical. In the simulation mode, *Peer.localTime()* returns the time in the simulated world.

Optional Testing Framework. Using the DSF APIs in Figure 3, the developer can implement a distributed algorithm as well as its testing environment. Optionally, the developer can also use DSF's built-in testing framework to save efforts. The developer only needs to write a global consistency checking subroutine, which takes as inputs a set of *Peer* objects and reports whether their internal states are consistent. Controlled by a configuration file, DSF starts a certain number of *Peers* with the user's algorithm code registered as a plug-in service of each *Peer*. DSF automatically alternates between churn periods and stable periods. During a churn period, DSF randomly fails existing *Peers* and starts new *Peers*. In the simulation mode and the massive multi-tenancy mode, DSF periodically invokes the user's consistency checking subroutine to detect state inconsistency among *Peers*.

4   Implementations of the DSF APIs

This section describes the simulated and real implementations of the DSF APIs.

4.1   Simulated Implementation of the DSF APIs

In the simulation mode, DSF simulates TCP, thread, and time, but provides real file access. The DSF APIs interact with a discrete-event simulation engine that uses one thread to execute events ordered in time. Timers and jobs submitted by *Peer.submitTimer()*, *Peer.submitJob()*, and *Peer.submitFifoJob()* are treated as future events to be executed. DSF also generates events internally, e.g., for the arrival of TCP messages.

Simulated TCP. DSF simulates the high-level semantics of the TCP protocol, including connection establishment, in-order and reliable data transfer, and connection termination. Currently, DSF does not simulate low-level details such as TCP congestion control, but can simulate volatile network delay and varying available bandwidth. A developer can either use DSF's built-in network model, or link her own network model with DSF through a well defined interface.

DSF simulates a TCP port manager that recycles ports as *Peers* start and stop. It allows the use of much more than 65,536 ports in order to simulate a large system. DSF can be configured to pass messages between *Peers* using either *serialization* or *cloning*. Serialization allows DSF to accurately measure network traffic, but is about 7 times slower than cloning.

Peer.stop() simulates a fail-stop failure, which can be either *apparent* or *silent*. To illustrate the difference, consider a distributed system with two processes X and Y, and a TCP connection between them. The failure of X is apparent to Y, if Y's read operation from the TCP connection returns immediately with an error. For example, if process X crashes but the OS that hosts X still functions, then the OS will close all X's TCP connections and Y will immediately notice the

TCP read error. The failure of X is silent to Y, if Y's TCP read operation returns no errors. This happens, for example, if the machine that hosts X suddenly lost power, or if X encounters an uncaught exception and hangs. Silent failures are usually more subtle to handle and more difficult to test in deployed systems. Simulating silent failure helps test whether the user code handles them properly through mechanisms such as heartbeat timeout.

Chaotic timing test. To discover race condition bugs that depend on event timing, DSF purposely introduces randomized delays into simulated thread scheduling, timers, message propagation, and message processing. Recall that *Peer.submitJob(job)* is semantically equivalent to *(new Thread(job)).start()*. To simulate the delay before the thread is scheduled to run on a CPU and the time it takes to finish the job, DSF adds a randomized delay to the simulated event that represents the execution of this job. As a result, it is possible that a job submitted later actually gets executed before a job submitted earlier. DSF's built-in thread delay model uses a long tailed distribution, and a user can also link her own thread delay model with DSF through a well defined interface. Randomized delays are added to all other types of events as well. DSF's randomized event timing respects event causality as well as event ordering required by semantics, e.g., message processing order mandated by *fifoMsgQueue*.

Checkpoint and rollback. During simulation, DSF periodically checkpoints the states of all distributed components in order to support time travel debugging. We do not use traditional OS or hypervisor level checkpoint methods [3,17], because they rely on customized programming tools and do not support the most popular practice of debugging—adding debugging code to check assertions or log more information. Unlike DSF's mutable replay method, the OS or hypervisor level methods cannot resume from a checkpoint to run a modified version of the program that has added or newly enabled debugging code, even if the modification has no side effects on the application logic.

DSF implements checkpointing by serializing Java objects in the program and saving them in a file. A checkpoint is always taken between the executions of two events, so that we need not worry about local variables in the user code. DSF does not serialize all objects in the JVM, e.g., the objects that represent loaded Java classes. Instead, DSF only serializes the *Peer* objects and the object that represents the simulation engine. Due to the deep-copy semantics of Java serialization, all other objects recursively reachable through those objects are also serialized. For the DHT example in Section 3, the *DHTImpl* object that implements the DHT protocol is serialized along with the *Peer* object, because the *Peer* object adds a reference to the *DHTImpl* object when *Peer.registerService("DHT", dhtImpl)* was invoked in the initialization phase.

DSF also checkpoints files accessed by the user code. Because Java's file utilities are not serializable, the DSF APIs provide our own serializable file utilities. A file "/dirX/dirY/fileZ" accessed through our utilities is saved on the real file system as file "/tmp/dsf/$peer\_id$/dirX/dirY/fileZ", where $peer\_id$ differentiates peers. During a checkpointing operation, DSF flushes all file buffers to ensure that the files on disk are up to date. It then makes a copy of the entire directory "/tmp/dsf" and saves it along with the checkpoint file. DSF also saves in the checkpoint file the states of the files accessed by the user code, e.g., a random access file's current file pointer position.

Suppose the developer encounters a bug, adds some debugging code, re-compiles the program, and resumes the execution from a checkpoint. During the checkpoint recovery, DSF restores the *Peer* objects and the simulation engine object. It copies the saved files back to the directory "/tmp/dsf", re-opens those files, and sets the file pointers to the exact positions before the checkpoint. DSF then continues to execute the next event in the recovered event queue, guaranteeing the bug precisely repeats itself in the resumed run as in the original run, while the added debugging code logs more information to help pinpoint the root cause of the bug. After the developer fixes the bug, she can re-compile the program and resume the execution from the checkpoint again. This time, the resumed run executes the new code and tests whether the bug still shows up. That is, DSF's mutable replay not only helps understand the root cause of the bug, but can also test whether the bug fix actually works.

4.2   Real Implementation of the DSF APIs

This section presents a real implementation of the DSF APIs based on J2SE. In the real implementation, each *Peer* has its own pool of worker threads that execute jobs submitted by *Peer.submitJob()* or *Peer.submitFifoJob()*. Proper synchronization ensures that FIFO jobs are executed in sequential order. The size of the worker thread pool is configurable. Each *Peer* has a dedicated "timer thread" to keep track of all timers submitted by *Peer.submitTimer()*. Inside a loop, this thread sleeps until the first timer expires, and then transfers the expired timer to the worker thread pool for execution.

DSF uses the non-blocking, high-performance *java.nio* package for network communication. A *Message* is serialized before being sent over the network and then deserialized at the destination. Each *Peer* has a dedicated "network thread" that accepts incoming TCP connections on the *Peer's* TCP listening port. This thread also reads data for all established TCP connections. Once a complete *Message* is read in, a job is submitted to the worker thread pool to execute *Message.procMessage()*. Proper synchronization ensures that the ordering requirements of message processing are enforced. If the "network thread" notices that a TCP connection is broken, it submits a job to invoke the user callback code previously registered through *TCP.registerTCPClosedCallback()*.

For an outgoing message, the thread invoking *TCP.send()* serializes the message and then performs a non-blocking network write operation. Unless the message is large, this write typically can send out the entire message. Otherwise, the "network thread" will be responsible for sending out the rest of the message later when this TCP connection is ready for write again. All operations performed by the "network thread" are non-blocking so that a single thread can handle all network I/O operations.

The implementation of other DSF APIs is straightforward. All threads used by the DSF runtime are created inside the constructor *Peer(Config)*, and activated to run by *Peer.start()*. *Peer.localTime()* is mapped to *System.currentTimeMillis()*. *RandomAccessFileIfc* is mapped to *java.io.RandomAccessFile*. *Peer.random()* returns a true random number generator.

5   Experiments and Experience

This section evaluates the efficiency, scalability, and usability of DSF, and reports our experience of using DSF to find bugs.

5.1   Scalability of the Multi-tenancy Mode

We first demonstrate that both the real implementation and the simulated implementation of the DSF APIs are scalable. All experiments are conducted on an IBM System x3850 server with 16GB memory and four dual-core 3GHz Intel Xeon processors, running Linux 2.6.9. To demonstrate that DSF does not make any changes to the programming tools, we use both IBM JDK 1.5.0 and Sun JDK 1.6.0 in our experiments.

We have implemented multiple distributed algorithms in DSF. This experiment uses a DHT implementation called *BlueDHT*, which adopts the ring topology as that in Chord [18], but uses our own algorithms for maintenance and routing. BlueDHT uses a hard-state, rate-limited, reactive maintenance protocol, as opposed to Chord's soft-state, periodical recovery protocol. BlueDHT has low maintenance overhead and is robust under churn, but its implementation is challenging because of its hard-state protocol. The testing and debugging features of DSF provided great help in developing BlueDHT. The details of BlueDHT are beyond the scope of this paper. Below, we use BlueDHT to evaluate the scalability of DSF.

Figure 4 shows the CPU utilization of the x3850 server during one run of BlueDHT in the massive multi-tenancy mode. This experiment runs 4,000 OS-level threads in a single IBM JVM to concurrently execute (as opposed to simulate) 1,000 DHT nodes in real-time. The lifetime of a node is only about 120 seconds (with randomization to avoid synchronized behaviors of nodes). After a node dies, a new node is booted as a replacement. During its lifetime, every node issues a new request roughly every 5 seconds to route a message to the node that is responsible for a random DHT key. The destination node then sends back a confirmation message to the request node.

During the starting phase, a new node is booted roughly every 25 milliseconds. By time 25 seconds, 1,000 nodes have fully booted. The CPU utilization remains high until time 50 seconds, as all nodes are busy with building up their routing tables. DSF's massive multi-tenancy mode is efficient in doing large-scale experiments. With 4,0000 threads running 1,000 DHT nodes in a single JVM, the CPU utilization stays below 30% even under high churn and high traffic, where

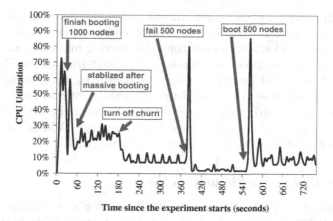

Fig. 4. The massive multi-tenancy mode runs 4,000 threads in a single JVM to concurrently execute (as opposed to simulate) 1,000 DHT nodes in real-time. This experiment was conducted on an IBM System x3850 server with four dual-core 3GHz Intel Xeon processors.

the node lifetime is only 120 seconds and every node initiates a new DHT lookup every 5 seconds. This excellent performance is due to DSF's scalable runtime as well as BlueDHT's efficient hard-state maintenance protocol.

In addition to automated fault injection, DSF provides an interactive debugging console that allows the developer to manually turn on/off churn and boot/fail nodes. At time 178 seconds, churn is turned off so that nodes do not fail anymore unless triggered manually. At time 376 seconds, a command is issued to fail 500 nodes concurrently, which causes a spike in the CPU utilization. Within 15 seconds from the time the command was issued, BlueDHT fully recovers from the massive failure. With 2,0000 threads running the remaining 500 DHT nodes in a steady state, the CPU utilization is only about 3%. BlueDHT uses a hard-state, rate-limited, reactive protocol. The "hard-state" aspect of BlueDHT (as opposed to Chord's soft-state protocol) is the source of the efficiency in the steady state. The "reactive" aspect of BlueDHT (as opposed to Chord's periodical recovery) is the reason behind the fast recovery. The reactive maintenance operations are "rate limited" so that, even under high churn or massive concurrent failures, the maintenance operations do not generate so much traffic as to cause system collapse.

At time 551 seconds, a command is issued to instantly boot 500 nodes, which causes another spike in the CPU utilization. Within 20 seconds, BlueDHT quickly re-stabilizes from this flash crowd join, and the CPU utilization goes back to a low level. Again, BlueDHT's hard-state, rate-limited, reactive protocol is the reason for the fast stabilization and the low CPU utilization.

This experiment shows that the massive multi-tenancy mode is efficient and scalable even with thousands of threads running inside one JVM. Because the multi-tenancy mode and the real deployment mode use exactly the same real implementation of the DSF APIs, this implies that the real deployment mode also has high performance. This experiment also shows that it is easy to conduct sophisticated large-scale tests in the massive multi-tenancy mode. This 1,000-node experiment (which comprises constant churns, massive concurrent node failures, and flash crowd node joins) takes only about 10 minutes. The developer simply starts one JVM and then issues commands on the debugging console. In the background, the global consistency checking subroutine automatically checks system states and catches bugs. Our experience indicates that the ability to easily test and debug a large-scale setup in a single JVM is the single most important factor that boots development productivity.

5.2   Scalability of the Simulation Mode

The experiment in Figure 5 runs BlueDHT in DSF's simulation mode. The lifetime of DHT nodes is only 120 seconds and every node initiates a new DHT lookup every 5 seconds. Figure 5 reports the "relative simulation time" of BlueDHT of different sizes. Suppose a BlueDHT with n nodes has "relative simulation time" t. It means that DSF takes t seconds wall clock time to simulate all the activities conducted in the simulated world by the n nodes during one second simulated time. The 1,000-node system has $t=0.138$, which means that the simulation is $1/t=7.2$ times faster than execution in the real world. In other words, it takes only about 8 minutes wall clock time to simulate one-hour activities (in the simulated world) of the 1,000-node system. This efficiency improves the developer's productivity by reducing the time spent on testing and debugging. This figure also shows that the simulation mode scales well as the system size increases, which is due to the good scalability of both the DSF runtime and the BlueDHT algorithm.

Figure 6 shows the time needed to create a checkpoint and the size of the checkpoint file. The checkpoint size scales well. As the system size increases from 1,000 nodes to 10,000 nodes, the checkpoint size only increases by a factor of 12. The checkpoint size is small because DSF saves only the algorithm states (e.g., the DHT routing tables) as opposed to the memory image of the JVM process. The time to create a checkpoint is also scalable. As the system size grows from 1,000 to 10,000 nodes, the checkpoint time increases from 1.3 seconds to 16.8 seconds, i.e., a 13 fold increase. This experiment uses the Sun JVM.

5.3   Bugs Found in the Simulation Mode

Next, we report our experience of using DSF to find bugs. Because DSF's simulation mode proactively conducts chaotic event timing tests, it is more powerful than the simulation modes of other tools in terms of triggering bugs (see Section 6 for a comparison). Our experience indicates that, equipped with features such as long-running automated tests, randomized fault injection, chaotic event timing, and global consistency checking, the simulation mode often helps discover more than 95% of the total bugs. The tricky bugs are often related to race conditions caused by unexpected event timing. We give a concrete example below.

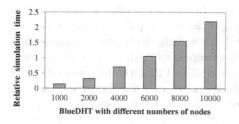

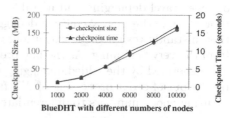

Fig. 5. Relative simulation time of BlueDHT with different numbers of nodes

Fig. 6. Time needed to create a checkpoint for BlueDHT and the size of the checkpoint file

One race condition bug in BlueDHT happens when a node Y reacts to the failure event and the reboot event of another node X out of order. Suppose X and Y are overlay neighbors, and X fails and then immediately reboots with the same IP and TCP listening port. When X fails, Y's DSF runtime detects that the TCP connection to X is broken, and (without holding any locks) invokes Y's callback function $nbrClosed()$ previously registered through $TCP.registerTCPClosedCallback()$. Suppose the actual execution of $nbrClosed()$ is delayed due to thread scheduling. In the meanwhile, X finishes rebooting and becomes a new neighbor of Y. During the neighbor-establishment process, Y uses the new instance of X to replace the old instance of X in its local data structure, which is a correct behavior.

When Y finally executes $nbrClosed()$ after a long delay, it tries to find and remove an existing neighbor with the same IP and port as the failed neighbor X. Y finds the new instance of X, mistakenly considers it as the failed old instance of X, and drops it from the neighbor set without closing the TCP connection to X (because Y considers this connection already closed). The final states are inconsistent: X considers Y as a neighbor, but Y does not considers X as a neighbor.

This bug is a rare race condition in real deployments, because typically X's reboot is slow so that Y processes the failure event of X before processing the reboot event of X. A combination of DSF's testing features helped find the bug. (1) Randomized fault injection triggers one condition of the bug. (2) Randomized network delay triggers one condition of the bug. (3) Randomized thread scheduling delay triggers one condition of the bug. (4) Long-running, automated testing triggers even rare event timing. (5) Finally, global consistency checking automatically catches the bug.

A colleague reported this bug to us and sent us the related checkpoint file. The colleague took the checkpoint on an AIX/Power server, but we were able to resume the execution in our Linux/x86 environment, because the checkpoint file contains serialized Java objects in an platform-independent format. Moreover, there was no need for us to figure out or manually replicate the colleague's setup that triggered the bug. All that information was in the checkpoint file and was taken care of by DSF's replay component automatically. The combined powers of time travel debugging and mutable replay helped us quickly understand the root cause of the bug. We added debugging code, re-compiled the program, and then instantly resumed the execution, without waiting to re-run the simulation from the very beginning. As the bug precisely repeated itself in the resumed run, logs generated by the added debugging code revealed that the bug was triggered by the out-of-order processing of X's failure and rejoin. We then fixed the bug by using epoch numbers to differentiate multiple incarnations of the same node.

5.4   Bugs Found in the Multi-tenancy Mode

The simulation mode randomizes event timing at the event boundary. It cannot trigger race conditions that exist below the event granularity, i.e., inside the subroutine for processing an event. Most of these low-level race condition bugs are caused by incorrect uses of locks. For example, a *ConcurrentModificationException* bug happened in BlueDHT when it processed an incoming message and read a *java.util.collection* data structure without holding a lock.

Synchronization and timing bugs become more evident in the massive multi-tenancy mode, as thousands of threads compete for CPUs and their execution orders change constantly. On the other hand, even under the extreme competition of thousands of threads, it still took about 24 hours of automated testing to trigger the *ConcurrentModificationException* bug described above. This is because the code that accesses the *java.util.collection* data structure without properly holding a lock is very short and hence the probability of concurrent accesses is very low. This indicates that detecting synchronization bugs without the massive multi-tenancy mode would be even more difficult.

Running thousands of threads in one JVM also makes performance bugs (e.g., over synchronization and code inefficiency) more evident, because any performance problems are drastically magnified. For example, an early version of DSF locks the *TCP* object before deserializing an incoming message. This lock unnecessarily prevents other threads of the same *Peer* from using this *TCP* object to send outgoing messages. Because Java deserialization is relatively slow, the locking duration sometimes can be long. DSF has a built-in utility that periodically logs snapshots of all thread stacks. With thousands of threads in one JVM, their blocking patterns easily pop up. We identified this over-synchronization problem and moved the deserialization code outside the lock.

5.5   Bugs Found in Real Deployments

To understand the limitations of testing tools (including DSF), it is interesting to report some bug that slipped through our hands and got into deployed systems. We implemented a distributed performance monitoring algorithm, which collects real-time performance data (e.g., CPU utilization and transaction response time) from a large number of servers to guide resource allocation [9,19]. This algorithm builds a distributed tree out of an overlay network to collect the data. To ensure the responsiveness of data gathering, a parent node in the tree may bypass a child node to directly collect data from the grandchildren nodes if the child node is temporarily slow, e.g., due to Java garbage collection. Our responsiveness goal is to gather data from most servers in a 1,000-server system within one second most of the time. The algorithm worked well in our environment, but the responsiveness goal was violated from time to time in a deployment environment. By activating DSF's utility that logs the processing time of every event, we first located events that introduced long delays, and then found that the problem was caused by slow DNS lookups—a piece of obsolete debugging code that nobody cared anymore was "accidentally" activated to resolve IP addresses to host names, solely for the purpose of printing user-friendly debugging information. DNS lookups were fast in our development environment but sometimes were slow in the deployment environment. We subsequently disabled all code on the critical path that does DNS lookups. This example shows the difficulty of capturing all bugs in the development environment.

6   Related Work

We first discuss in detail the work that is closest to DSF, and then summarize other related work.

WiDS [12,13]. The closest work to DSF is WiDS, which provides a set of powerful tools for debugging, e.g., replay-based predicate checking. Like DSF, WiDS also defines a set of APIs, under which different implementations can support simulation and real deployment. DSF and WiDS, however, differ significantly in many aspects. Compared with our three contributions listed in Section 1.2, WiDS (1) is significantly more complicated as it hacks many programming tools, including compiler and linker; (2) does not have DSF's novel features such as mutable replay, chaotic timing test, and massive multi-tenancy; and (3) cannot be used to build high-performance production systems running on multi-core processors, because it uses only a single OS kernel thread to execute all events (i.e., all messages, timers, and user-level thread jobs). The WiDS APIs allows the creation of multiple user-level threads. However, in order to guarantee deterministic replay, all the user-level threads are multiplexed onto a single OS kernel thread.

In its simulation mode, WiDS does not introduce random delays into timers, user-level thread jobs, or message processing. It strictly executes all events in sequential order and always processes an event in "one (simulated) clock tick" [12]. Because "event handling (in the real deployment) can take arbitrarily long," the authors of WiDS [12] noted that "the sequence of events (in the real deployment mode) can differ in unexpected ways (from that in the simulation mode), making it difficult to discover those (race condition) bugs in the simulation environment." Because of this limitation, WiDS Checker [13] has to collect event traces from a system running in the real deployment mode, and then feeds the traces into simulation in order to find race condition bugs.

By contrast, DSF's simulation mode purposely introduces random delays into event timing in order to proactively trigger race condition bugs. One limitation of DSF's simulation mode is that it randomizes event timing at the event boundary, and hence cannot trigger race conditions that exist below the event granularity, i.e., inside the subroutine for processing an event. However, even WiDS' real deployment mode cannot trigger race condition below the event granularity, because it uses a single OS kernel thread to process all events. Therefore, in terms of finding bugs, DSF's simulation mode alone is as powerful as the combination of WiDS' real deployment mode and simulation mode. (This observation is not unique to WiDS. It applies to other previous work [10] as well.) Moreover, all the bugs found by WiDS' real deployment mode can actually be found more easily by DSF's simulation mode, because DSF's chaotic timing tests proactively trigger (as opposed to just passively observe) race condition bugs. Specifically, it would be difficult for WiDS' real deployment mode or simulation mode to trigger the race condition bug described in Section 5.3, because the failure event and the rejoin event are rarely processed out of order.

Other related work. There is an enormous body of work related to development framework for distributed systems, including simulation [6,10,12], deterministic replay [3,7,8,15,17], fault injection [16], model checking [11], and code generation [14]. Below, we only review some representative ones.

Jones and Dunagan [10] developed peer-to-peer systems that use the same code base for simulation and real deployment. Like WiDS, their systems use a single-threaded event-processing model. PlanetSim [6] also supports both simulation and real deployment. These systems, however, do not provide advanced debugging features such as deterministic replay.

Checkpoint and rollback is a well studied topic [5]. Our serialization-based checkpoint method is novel in that it supports mutable replay, i.e., the resumed run can execute a modified program with added debugging code while still getting deterministic replay. ReVirt [3] logs all non-deterministic events in hypervisor to help replay the execution of a guest OS. Flashback [17] modifies the OS kernel to support rollback.

MACEDON [14] allows the user to specify overlay network algorithms in a domain-specific language, and then automatically generates the corresponding C++ code. TLA [11] is a formal specification language for concurrent systems, and the correctness of an algorithm described in TLA can be verified mechanically.

DejaVu [2] modifies JVM to support deterministic replay of multi-threaded Java programs. ConTest [4] uses source code instrumentation to introduce chaotic timing into every shared memory accesses and synchronization operation. Because of its heavy instrumentation, our evaluation shows that ConTest can cause application slowdown by a factor of 100 or more. DSF introduces chaotic timing only at event boundary, which is more efficient but may miss some bugs. ConTest is not designed for testing distributed systems and does not handle bugs caused by concurrent and asynchronous interactions between distributed components.

7   Conclusions

We have presented DSF, a common platform for distributed systems research and development. It can run a distributed algorithm written in Java under multiple execution modes—simulation, massive multi-tenancy, and real deployment. DSF grew out of our own needs in developing research prototypes and commercial software products. It takes a pragmatic approach while offering many advanced features.

Compared with a large body of related work, we made several contributions in this paper. First, we presented a simple yet powerful design that does not hack any programming tools. This simplicity stems from our goal of making DSF not only a research prototype but more importantly a production tool. Second, DSF provides a set of novel testing and debugging features that are not available in previous work, including mutable replay, chaotic timing test, and massive multi-tenancy mode. Finally, we demonstrate through a robust and efficient implementation that our ideas are practical. For example, DSF's massive multi-tenancy mode can run 4,000 OS-level threads in a single JVM to concurrently execute 1,000 DHT nodes in real-time.

The design of DSF takes a pragmatic approach, which naturally has many limitations and leaves room for future improvements. So far, our focus is to provide rich features in the simulation mode and the massive multi-tenancy mode, which allow the developer to easily test and debug a large-scale setup of a distributed algorithm inside a single JVM. This perhaps is the single most important factor that boosts development productivity. Next, we may move on to focus on the real deployment mode. For example, currently DSF's real deployment mode provides no global consistency checking. We may follow the approach in Stardust [20] to store events in a database, and then use SQL to check global consistency.

Acknowledgements

We thank the anonymous reviewers and our shepherd Antony Rowstron for their valuable feedback.

References

1. Chandra, T., Griesemer, R., Redstone, J.: Paxos Made Live—An Engineering Perspective. In: PODC (2007)
2. Choi, J.-D., Srinivasan, H.: Deterministic replay of Java multithreaded applications. In: Proceedings of the SIGMETRICS symposium on Parallel and distributed tools (1998)
3. Dunlap, G.W., King, S.T., Cinar, S., Basrai, M.A., Chen, P.M.: ReVirt: Enabling Intrusion Analysis through Virtual-Machine Logging and Replay. In: OSDI (2002)
4. Edelstein, O., Farchi, E., Nir, Y., Ratsaby, G., Ur, S.: Multithreaded Java program test generation. IBM Systems Journal 41(1), 111–125 (2002)

5. Elnozahy, E., Alvisi, L., Wang, Y., Johnson, D.: A survey of rollback-recovery protocols in message-passing systems. ACM Computing Surveys (CSUR) 34(3), 375–408
   (2002)
6. García, P., Pairot, C., Mondéjar, R., Pujol, J., Tejedor, H., Rallo, R.: Planetsim:
   A new overlay network simulation framework. In: Gschwind, T., Mascolo, C. (eds.)
   SEM 2004. LNCS, vol. 3437, pp. 123–136. Springer, Heidelberg (2005)
7. Geels, D., Altekar, G., Shenker, S., Stoica, I.: Replay Debugging for Distributed Applications. In: USENIX (2006)
8. Guo, Z., Wang, X., Tang, J., Liu, X., Xu, Z., Wu, M., Kaashoek, F., Zhang, Z.: R2:
   An Application-Level Kernel for Record and Replay. In: OSDI (2008)
9. IBM WebSphere Extended Deployment,
   http://www-306.ibm.com/software/webservers/appserv/extend/
10. Jones, M., Dunagan, J.: Engineering Realities of Building a Working Peer-to-Peer
    System. Technical report, MSR Technical Report MSR-TR-2004-54 (2004)
11. Lamport, L.: Specifying Systems: The TLA+ Language and Tools for Hardware
    and Software Engineers. Addison-Wesley Longman Publishing Co., Inc., Amster-
    dam (2002)
12. Lin, S., Pan, A., Zhang, Z., Guo, R., Guo, Z.: WiDS: an Integrated Toolkit for Dis-
    tributed System Development. In: HotOS (2005)
13. Liu, X., Lin, W., Pan, A., Zhang, Z.: WiDS Checker: Combating Bugs in Distributed
    Systems. In: NSDI (2007)
14. Rodriguez, A., Killian, C., Bhat, S., Kostic, D., Vahdat, A.: MACEDON: Method-
    ology for Automatically Creating, Evaluating, and Designing Overlay Networks. In:
    NSDI (2004)
15. Saito, Y.: Jockey: a user-space library for record-replay debugging. In: Proceedings of
    the sixth international symposium on Automated analysis-driven debugging (2005)
16. Segall, Z., Vrsalovic, D., Siewiorek, D., Yaskin, D., Kownacki, J., Varton, J., Dancey,
    R., Robinson, A., Lin, T.: FIAT–Fault injection based automated testing environ-
    ment. In: Proc. 18th Int. Symp. Fault-Tolerant Comput., pp. 102–107 (1988)
17. Srinivasan, S.M., Kandula, S., Andrews, C.R., Zhou, Y.: Flashback: A lightweight
    extension for rollback and deterministic replay for software debugging. In: USENIX
    (2004)
18. Stoica, I., Morris, R., Karger, D., Kaashoek, M.F., Balakrishnan, H.: Chord: A scal-
    able peer-to-peer lookup service for internet applications. In: SIGCOMM (2001)
19. Tang, C., Steinder, M., Spreitzer, M., Pacifici, G.: A Scalable Application Placement
    Algorithm for Enterprise Data Centers. In: WWW (2007)
20. Thereska, E., Salmon, B., Strunk, J., Wachs, M., Abd-El-Malek, M., Lopez, J.,
    Ganger, G.R.: Stardust: tracking activity in a distributed storage system. In: SIG-
    METRICS (2006)

Author Index